AFRICAN SYSTEMS
OF KINSHIP
AND MARRIAGE

NOTE

In July 1948, in response to an invitation from the United Nations Educational, Scientific, and Cultural Organization, the International African Institute submitted a memorandum setting forth particulars of a number of research projects which the Institute was prepared to undertake in collaboration with U.N.E.S.C.O.

One of these projects related to the publication of a volume devoted to studies of kinship and marriage in a number of representative African societies. It was proposed that the volume should be published in English and French.

In fulfilment of a resolution adopted by the General Conference of the United Nations Educational, Scientific, and Cultural Organization at its third Session, and in accordance with the decisions taken by the Executive Board of U.N.E.S.C.O. at its sixteenth Session, a grant was allocated towards the cost of preparation and publication of this volume.

The English version of the volume, in which a number of distinguished British and South African anthropologists have collaborated under the joint editorship of Professor A. R. Radcliffe-Brown and Professor Daryll Forde, is now presented; the French version is in preparation and will be available shortly.

AFRICAN SYSTEMS
OF KINSHIP
AND MARRIAGE

Edited by

A. R. RADCLIFFE-BROWN

and

DARYLL FORDE

Published for the
INTERNATIONAL AFRICAN INSTITUTE
by the
OXFORD UNIVERSITY PRESS
LONDON NEW YORK TORONTO

Oxford University Press, Ely House, London W. 1

GLASGOW NEW YORK TORONTO MELBOURNE WELLINGTON
CAPE TOWN SALISBURY IBADAN NAIROBI DAR ES SALAAM LUSAKA ADDIS ABABA
BOMBAY CALCUTTA MADRAS KARACHI LAHORE DACCA
KUALA LUMPUR SINGAPORE HONG KONG TOKYO

SBN 19 724147 6

FIRST EDITION 1950
TENTH IMPRESSION 1970

PRINTED IN GREAT BRITAIN

PREFACE

KINSHIP looms large among peoples who obtain their livelihood in small groups with simple tools. Among such peoples differences of aptitude and special training and duties do not, as in more complex societies, overwhelm the bonds between those who are born together and intermarry. The local groups within which personal relations are developed in work, rite, and recreation are at the same time bodies of relatives who have ancestors in common and among whom a complex web of ties links every person with others throughout the community. The way in which comprehensive obligations of kinship direct the activities and relations which, in our society, are segregated out as more specifically political, economic, and religious is a commonplace of social anthropology. But the detailed operation of particular factors, their relative weight in different circumstances, the principles under which these can be subsumed, and the real character and role of the many patterns of kinship organization that result are less clearly grasped. These are, however, fundamental questions in a scientific sociology. They are also of immediate practical urgency when peoples who have lived in a largely kinbound society are reacting to pressures and incentives from another social world. For those attempting to achieve a smooth transition, and to elicit the energies and loyalties of such peoples, the reason for many intangible obstacles and discords lies in unintended and often avoidable disharmony between the indigenous and the invading social values.

The concomitant of culture contact is social strain. The International African Institute has sought to promote research in the social anthropology of Africa in the belief that more adequate resources, intellectual and financial, should be devoted to such studies if scientific knowledge is to advance on a scale commensurate with the social problems to which it should be applied. In an earlier volume on African Political Systems some of the results of researches into the political systems of African peoples by Fellows and others associated with the Institute were brought together. The wide and continuing demand for this study, which has afforded insight into the situations with which every student, educator, and administrator has to deal, has encouraged an attempt to provide a similar conspectus on an equally fundamental aspect of the indigenous social life of African peoples. The present volume consists of an Introduction, in which the general principles underlying African systems of kinship and marriage are reviewed in the light of our present knowledge, and a series of detailed studies by authors who have made intensive field investigations of the particular social systems they analyse. Each presents the essential characteristics of one or more varieties of African patterns of kinship.

The purpose of the volume is to present a general view of the nature and implications of kinship in Africa. It cannot claim to be formally comprehensive, for our knowledge is patchy and there are many studies —one on the Galla-speaking peoples of north-east Africa might be instanced—that remain to be carried out. But much valuable work in this field has appeared and is appearing elsewhere and it will become easier to remedy the more serious omissions from other sources in the future. Meanwhile, save for the peoples of the smallest scale of social organization, the Bushmen and Negritos, and the kinship pattern among the Amhara of the Ethiopian Kingdom, for none of which studies were available, the chief varieties of kinship organization occurring in trans-Saharan Africa are illustrated and considered. Their significance is discussed by the several authors to whom we express our thanks for their ready co-operation in the preparation of this volume.

January 1950   A. R. RADCLIFFE-BROWN
                                        DARYLL FORDE

CONTENTS

PREFACE v

LIST OF ILLUSTRATIONS ix

INTRODUCTION. *By* A. R. RADCLIFFE-BROWN, *Professor Emeritus of Social Anthropology, Oxford University* . . 1

Importance of scientific study of kinship—An analytical as opposed to an historical approach—Definition of kinship—Kinship relations exhibited in social behaviour—Structural principles of kinship systems illustrated in the Teutonic and the Masai systems—The unilineal principle—Classificatory terminology—The generation principle—Rank in social relations—Omaha classificatory terminology—Principle of lineage unity expressed in terminology—Privileged behaviour—Clans and lineages—Marriage customs—Early English marriage—Modern English and American conceptions of marriage—African marriage: marriage payments, marriage as a developing process—Modification of kinship relations by marriage—Rights of husband over wife and children—Marriage as an alliance between two groups—'Mother-in-law avoidance'—'Joking relationships'—Regulations concerning marriage between relatives—Prohibited and preferential marriages—Exogamy—Relation between rules of marriage and kinship structure—Incest, parricide, and witchcraft—Mother-right and father-right—The social functions of kinship systems.

KINSHIP AMONG THE SWAZI. *By* HILDA KUPER, *Lecturer in Social Anthropology in the University of the Witwatersrand* . 86

The clan—The family unit—The homestead—Basic behaviour patterns: husband and wife; parent and child; siblings—Maternal and paternal kin: paternal aunt and maternal uncle; cousins; grandparents—Affines: parents-in-law; sisters- and brothers-in-law; the groups—Rank and kinship.

NYAKYUSA KINSHIP. *By* MONICA WILSON, *Professor of Anthropology, Rhodes College, Grahamstown* 111

Introductory—Kinship groups—Kinship and locality—Bonds of kinship and affinity—Cattle and kinship relations—Cattle and marriage—Dissolution of marriage—Permanence of tie created by marriage—Religious interdependence of relatives—Father-in-law avoidance—Extensions of kinship behaviour—Kinship and political organization—General principles—Maintenance of kinship and marriage relationships—Relationship terms.

KINSHIP AND MARRIAGE AMONG THE TSWANA. *By* I. SCHAPERA, *Professor of Social Anthropology, University of Cape Town* 140

The social setting—The kinship system—Kinship terminology—Prohibited and preferential mating—Marriage regulations—Secondary unions—Frequency of kinship marriages—Conclusions.

KINSHIP AND MARRIAGE AMONG THE LOZI OF NORTHERN RHODESIA AND THE ZULU OF NATAL. *By* MAX GLUCKMAN, *Professor of Social Anthropology, Victoria University, Manchester, formerly Director of the Rhodes–Livingstone Institute* 166

Introduction—Kinship structure and the affiliation of children—Forms, conditions, and personal consequences of marriage—Property consequences of marriage—Marriage payment and the social structure.

SOME TYPES OF FAMILY STRUCTURE AMONGST THE
CENTRAL BANTU. *By* A. I. RICHARDS, *Director of the East
African Institute of Social Science, Makerere, formerly Reader in
Social Anthropology, London School of Economics* . . . 207

Characteristics of matrilineal kinship organizations in Central Africa—
Varieties of family structure: *a*. Mayombe-Kongo: Economic determinants; ideology and principles of descent and succession; the marriage contract; authority; residential units—*b*. i. Bemba-Bisa-Lamba
group: economic determinants; ideology and principles of descent;
the marriage contract; domestic authority; residential units—*b*. ii.
Yao-Cewa group—*c*. Ila type: principles of descent and succession;
the marriage contract; domestic authority; residential unit—Variations in lineage structure—Conclusions.

KINSHIP AND MARRIAGE AMONG THE ASHANTI. *By*
M. FORTES, *Professor of Social Anthropology, Cambridge University* . 252

Introduction—Matrilineal descent: political aspect; domestic
aspect; mother and child—Paternity: concept of Ntoro; father
and child—Relations between other kin: mother's brother; siblings;
grandparents; father's sister—Marriage—Conclusion.

DOUBLE DESCENT AMONG THE YAKÖ. *By* DARYLL FORDE,
*Professor of Anthropology, University of London, Director, Inter-
national African Institute* 285

Introduction—Household and family—Patrilineage and clan—Leadership in patriclan and lineage—Adoption into a patrilineage—Matrikin
and matriclan—Matrilineal rights and obligations—Ritual and political authority of matriclan priests—Yakpan—Terminology of kinship
—Marriage and affinal relations—Conclusion: Dual sentiments of
kinship.

DUAL DESCENT IN THE NUBA HILLS. *By* S. F. NADEL,
Reader in Anthropology, King's College, Durham University . 333

Nyaro society: settlement; descent, patrilineal and matrilineal; clan
rights and obligations; gens rights and obligations; family and
kindred; political and religious institutions; dual principle—Tullishi
society: settlement; descent, patrilineal and matrilineal; myth of
origin; sex antagonism—Conclusions.

KINSHIP AND THE LOCAL COMMUNITY AMONG THE
NUER. *By* E. E. EVANS-PRITCHARD, *Professor of Social Anthropology,
Oxford University* 360

Introduction—Villages and camps—Lineage and kinship—Village
of Konye—Village of Nyueny—Cattle camp at Yakwac—Village of
Yakwac—Village of Mancom—Village of Kurmayom—Conclusions.

INDEX 393

LIST OF ILLUSTRATIONS

1. Paternal and Maternal Kin (Swazi) . . . *page* 101
2. Affinal Kin (Swazi) . . . . . ,, 101
3. Zulu Man's Terms for Cognates . . . *facing p.* 170
4. Zulu Man's Terms for Affines . . . ,, 172
5. Zulu Woman's Terms for Affines . . . ,, 172
6. Lozi Man's Terms for Cognates . . . ,, 170
7. Lozi Man's Terms for Affines . . . ,, 174
8. Lozi Woman's Terms for Affines . . . ,, 174
9. Sketch Map of the Territory and Settlements of the Yakö and their Neighbours . . . *page* 287
10. Woman's House; Man's House . . . ,, 292
11. Composition and Affiliation of Compounds . . ,, 295
12. The Village of Umor . . . . ,, 297
13. Diagram to Show the Location and Relations of Patri-clans in Umor . . . . . ,, 300
14. Diagram of Matriclan Links in Umor . . ,, 308
15. Yakö Terms for Kin . . . . ,, 318
16. Konye Village . . . . . ,, 369
17. Konye Village—genealogy . . . . *facing p.* 370
18. Nyueny Village—genealogy . . . . ,, 370
19. Nyueny Village . . . . . *page* 372
20. Yakwac Cattle Camp . . . . ,, 376
21. Yakwac Cattle Camp—genealogy . . . *facing p.* 376
22. Yakwac Village . . . . . *page* 381
23. Mancom Village . . . . . ,, 381

INTRODUCTION

By A. R. RADCLIFFE-BROWN

'Avoir affaire aux nations sans les connaître, sans les comprendre, c'est bon pour les conquérants; moins bon pour des alliés et même pour les protecteurs; et rien n'est plus détestable et plus insensé pour des civilisateurs, ce que nous avons la prétention d'être.' GOBINEAU.

I

FOR the understanding of any aspect of the social life of an African people—economic, political, or religious—it is essential to have a thorough knowledge of their system of kinship and marriage. This is so obvious to any field anthropologist that it hardly needs to be stated. But it is often ignored by those who concern themselves with problems relating to economics, health, nutrition, law, or administration amongst the peoples of Africa, and it is hoped that this book will be read not only by anthropologists but by some of those who are responsible for formulating or carrying out policies of colonial government in the African continent.

A book that would deal thoroughly and systematically with kinship organization throughout Africa cannot yet be written. This volume of essays is intended only to illustrate by a few samples the results that have been reached by social anthropologists at the present time in this branch of their studies. It has been thought desirable to add the present essay, which offers an introduction to the general comparative and theoretical study of kinship organization.

The literature dealing with kinship is loaded with theories that can only be described as pseudo-historical. There are many varieties of such theories, but they all have one thing in common. Starting from some known condition in the present or in the historically recorded past, an 'explanation' of it is invented by imagining some condition or event in the unrecorded past and arguing on *a priori* grounds that the known condition might or must have had its origin in this way. The devotion to pseudo-history has had unfortunate results. It has led to the adoption of false ideas about the facts as they are, and has often influenced or vitiated observation and description. This legacy of erroneous ideas is only gradually being got rid of by field studies aiming at the analysis of social systems as they are without reference to their origin, where that origin is not known from history and can only be conjectured by *a priori* reasoning.

History, the authentic record of events and conditions of the past, is entirely different from pseudo-history. If we ask how it is that a society has the social institutions that it does have at a particular time the answer can only be supplied by history. Where we have records we can trace in

B

greater or less detail the way in which the institutions have come to be
what they are. For European countries we can thus trace the development of social institutions over several centuries. For most African
societies the records from which we can obtain authentic history are
extremely scanty or in some instances entirely lacking except for a very
short period of the immediate past. We cannot have a history of African
institutions.

The method adopted here is neither that of history nor of pseudo-
history but one combining comparison and analysis. Social systems are
compared so that their differences may be defined and beneath their
differences more fundamental and general resemblances may be discovered. One aim of comparison is to provide us with schemes of classification. Without classification there can be no science.

Analysis, as the term is here being used, is a procedure that can only
be applied to something that is in itself a whole or synthesis. By it we
separate out, in reality or in thought, the components of a complex whole
and thereby discover the relation of these components to one another
within the whole. To arrive at an understanding of kinship systems we
must use comparison and analysis in combination by comparing many
different systems with one another and by subjecting single systems to
systematic analysis.

A study of kinship systems all over the world by this method reveals
that while there is a very wide range of variation in their superficial
features there can be discovered a certain small number of general
structural principles which are applied and combined in various ways.
It is one of the first tasks of a theoretical study of kinship to discover
these principles by a process of abstractive generalization based on
analysis and comparison.

There are two sides to science and to the activities of scientists. On the
one side there is the task of creating and establishing a general theory of
a certain class of phenomena. For the scientist engaged in this task, or
while he is so engaged, any particular instance of the phenomena in
question is only of interest as part of the material that he can use to
formulate or test his hypotheses. This kind of scientific activity is frequently referred to as 'pure' or theoretical science. On the other side
there is the task of applying whatever theoretical knowledge has been
established to the explanation or understanding of particular phenomena.
Such activities are often referred to as applied science, and in this sense
medicine is an applied science based on such theoretical sciences as
physiology and pathology. For the scientist engaged in a task of this
kind the aim is not so much to make an addition to general theoretical
conclusions as to arrive at an interpretation of a particular instance of the
phenomena with which the science is concerned. The doctor uses his
theoretical knowledge in order to understand a particular instance of
disease, to interpret the symptoms, and make a diagnosis and prognosis.

The two kinds of scientific activity are in close interdependence and may on occasion be carried on together. To understand their relation to one another, however, it is necessary to distinguish them. In any study it is a good thing to know what you are trying to do.

In the study of social institutions such as the study of kinship, the theoretical social anthropologist regards any particular social system as supplying him with a body of factual material which he can use for formulating or testing theory. But on the other side theoretical knowledge can be used to give an understanding of the features of some particular system. In the light of the general theoretical knowledge that has resulted from the comparative study of societies of diverse types the scientist may undertake the analysis of a particular system so that any single feature is seen in its relation to other features of that system and in its place in the system as a whole. The value and validity of any such study of a particular system will obviously depend on the extent and soundness of the general theoretical concepts by which it is directed.

A system of kinship and marriage can be looked at as an arrangement which enables persons to live together and co-operate with one another in an orderly social life. For any particular system as it exists at a certain time we can make a study of how it works. To do this we have to consider how it links persons together by convergence of interest and sentiment and how it controls and limits those conflicts that are always possible as the result of divergence of sentiment or interest. In reference to any feature of a system we can ask how it contributes to the working of the system. This is what is meant by speaking of its social function. When we succeed in discovering the function of a particular custom, i.e. the part it plays in the working of the system to which it belongs, we reach an understanding or explanation of it which is different from and independent of any historical explanation of how it came into existence. This kind of understanding of a kinship system as a working system linking human beings together in an orderly arrangement of interactions, by which particular customs are seen as functioning parts of the social machinery, is what is aimed at in a synchronic analytic study. In such an analysis we are dealing with a system as it exists at a certain time, abstracting as far as possible from any changes that it may be undergoing. To understand a process of change we must make a diachronic study. But to do this we must first learn all that we possibly can about how the system functioned before the changes that we are investigating occurred. Only then can we learn something of their possible causes and see something of their actual or probable effects. It is only when changes are seen as changes in or of a functioning system that they can be understood.

II

We have first of all to try to get a clear idea of what is a kinship system or system of kinship and marriage. Two persons are kin when one is descended from the other, as, for example, a grandchild is descended from a grandparent, or when they are both descended from a common ancestor. Persons are cognatic kin or cognates when they are descended from a common ancestor or ancestress counting descent through males and females.

The term 'consanguinity' is sometimes used as an equivalent of 'kinship' as above defined, but the word has certain dangerous implications which must be avoided. Consanguinity refers properly to a physical relationship, but in kinship we have to deal with a specifically social relationship. The difference is clear if we consider an illegitimate child in our own society. Such a child has a 'genitor' (physical father) but has no 'pater' (social father). Our own word 'father' is ambiguous because it is assumed that normally the social relationship and the physical relationship will coincide. But it is not essential that they should. Social fatherhood is usually determined by marriage. The dictum of Roman law was *pater est quem nuptiae demonstrant*. There is an Arab proverb, 'Children belong to the man to whom the bed belongs'. There was a crude early English saying, 'Whoso boleth my kyne, ewere calf is mine'. Social fatherhood as distinct from physical fatherhood is emphasized in the Corsican proverb, *Chiamu babba a chi mi da pane*.

The complete social relationship between parent and child may be established not by birth but by adoption as it was practised in ancient Rome and is practised in many parts of the world to-day.

In several regions of Africa there is a custom whereby a woman may go through a rite of marriage with another woman and thereby she stands in the place of a father (pater) to the offspring of the wife, whose physical father (genitor) is an assigned lover.

Kinship therefore results from the recognition of a social relationship between parents and children, which is not the same thing as the physical relation, and may or may not coincide with it. Where the term 'descent' is used in this essay it will refer not to biological but to social relations. Thus the son of an adopted person will be said to trace descent from the adopting grandparents.

The closest of all cognatic relationships is that between children of the same father and mother. Anthropologists have adopted the term 'sibling' to refer to this relationship; a male sibling is a brother, a female sibling is a sister.[1] The group consisting of a father and a mother and their children is an important one for which it is desirable to have a name. The term 'elementary family' will be used in this sense in this essay. (The term 'biological family' refers to something different,

---

[1] In Anglo-Saxon 'sibling' meant 'kinsman'.

namely, to genetic relationship such as that of a mated sire and dam and their offspring, and is the concern of the biologist making a study of heredity. But it seems inappropriate to use the word 'family' in this connexion.) We may regard the elementary family as the basic unit of kinship structure. What is meant by this is that the relationships, of kinship or affinity, of any person are all connexions that are traced through his parents, his siblings, his spouse, or his children.

We must also recognize what may conveniently be called 'compound families'. Such a family results in our own society when a widower or widow with children by a first marriage enters into a second marriage into which children are born. This gives such relationships as those of half-siblings and of step-parent and stepchild. In societies in which polygynous marriages are permitted a compound family is formed when a man has two or more wives who bear him children. Families of this kind are, of course, common in Africa, and the difference between full siblings (children of the same father and mother) and half-siblings (children of one father by different mothers) is generally socially important.

Where there are truly polyandrous marriages, as among the Todas of south India, a family may consist of a woman with two or more husbands and her children.[1] But we should distinguish from this an arrangement by which the oldest of two or more brothers takes a wife, of whose children he will be the father (pater), and access to the wife for sexual congress is permitted to the man's younger brother until such time as he in turn is married. For it is not sexual intercourse that constitutes marriage either in Europe or amongst savage peoples. Marriage is a social arrangement by which a child is given a legitimate position in the society, determined by parenthood in the social sense.

The elementary family usually provides the basis for the formation of domestic groups of persons living together in intimate daily life. Of such groups there is a great variety. One common type is what may be called the 'parental' family in which the 'household' consists of the parents and their young or unmarried children. We are familiar with this type of family amongst ourselves, but it is also a characteristic feature of many primitive peoples. The group comes into existence with the birth of a first child in marriage; it continues to grow by the birth of other children; it undergoes partial dissolution as the children leave it, and comes to an end with the death of the parents. In a polygynous parental family there are two or more mothers but only one father, and a mother with her children constitute a separate unit of the group.

What is sometimes called a patrilineal extended family is formed by a custom whereby sons remain in their father's family group, bringing their wives to live with them, so that their children also belong to the group. Among the Bemba of Northern Rhodesia there is found a matrilineal

[1] Rivers, *The Todas*, 1906, p. 515.

extended family, a domestic group consisting of a man and his wife with their daughters and the husbands and children of the latter. The group breaks up, and new groups of the same kind are formed, when a man obtains permission to leave his parents-in-law, taking his wife and children with him.

Most men who live to maturity belong to two elementary families, to one as son and brother, and to the other as husband and father. It is this simple fact that gives rise to a network of relations connecting any single person with many others. We can get a good idea of this by considering what may be called orders of relationship by kinship and marriage. Relationships of the first order are those within the elementary family, viz. the relation of parent and child, that of husband and wife, and that between siblings. Relationships of the second order are those traced through one connecting person such as those with father's father, mother's brother, stepmother (father's wife), sister's husband, brother's son, wife's father, &c. Those of the third order have two connecting links, as mother's brother's son, father's sister's husband, and so on. So we can go on to the fourth, fifth, or nth order. In each order the number of relationships is greater than that in the preceding order. This network of relationships includes both cognatic relationships and relationships resulting from marriage, a person's own marriage, and the marriages of his cognates.

The first determining factor of a kinship system is provided by the range over which these relationships are effectively recognized for social purposes of all kinds. The differences between wide-range and narrow-range systems are so important that it would be well to take this matter of range as the basis for any attempt at a systematic classification of kinship systems. The English system of the present day is a narrow-range system, though a wider range of relationship, to second, third, or more distant cousins, is recognized in rural districts than in towns. China, on the contrary, has a wide-range system. Some primitive societies have narrow-range systems, others have wide-range. In some of the latter a man may have several hundred recognized relatives by kinship and by marriage whom he must treat as relatives in his behaviour. In societies of a kind of which the Australian aborigines afford examples every person with whom a man has any social contact during the course of his life is a relative and is treated in the way appropriate to the relationship in which he or she stands.

Within the recognized range there is some method of ordering the relationships, and it is the method adopted for this purpose that gives the system its character. Later in this essay we shall consider some of the principles which appear in the ordering of relatives in different systems.

A part of any kinship system is some system of terms by which relatives of different kinds are spoken of or by which they are addressed as relatives. The first step in the study of a kinship system is to discover what terms are used and how they are used. But this is only a first step. The terminology has to be considered in relation to the whole system of which it is part.

There is one type of terminology that is usually referred to as 'descriptive'. In systems of this type there are a few specific terms for relatives of the first or second order and other relatives are indicated by compounds of these specific terms in such a way as to show the intermediate steps in the relation. It is necessary in any scientific discussion of kinship to use a system of this kind. Instead of ambiguous terms such as 'uncle' or 'cousin' we have to use more exact compound terms such as 'mother's brother', 'father's sister's son', and so on. When we have to deal with a relationship of the fifth order, such as 'mother's mother's brother's daughter's daughter', and still more in dealing with more distant relations, the system presents difficulties to those who are not accustomed to it. I have found it useful to invent a system of symbols to use instead of words.[1] Descriptive terminologies in this sense, i.e. those using specific terms and compounding them, are to be found in some African peoples, and illustrations are given in the section on the Yakö in this volume.[2]

In many systems of kinship terminology a single term is used for two or more kinds of relatives, who are thus included in a single terminological category. This may be illustrated by the English system of the present day. The word 'uncle' is used for both the father's brother and the mother's brother and also by extension for the husband of an 'aunt' (father's sister or mother's sister). Similarly with such terms as 'nephew', 'niece', 'cousin', 'grandfather', &c.

The categories used in the terminology often, indeed usually, have some social significance. In English we do something which is unusual in kinship systems when we apply the term uncle (from Latin *avunculus*, mother's brother, literally 'little grandfather') to both the mother's brother and the father's brother. But this corresponds with the fact that in our social life we do not make any distinction between these two kinds of relatives. The legal relationship in English law, except for entailed estates and titles of nobility, is the same for a nephew and either of his uncles; for example, the nephew has the same claim to inheritance in case of intestacy over the estate of either. In what may be called the socially standardized behaviour of England it is not possible to observe any regular distinction made between the paternal and the maternal uncle. Reciprocally the behaviour of a man to his different kinds of nephews is in general the same. By extension, no significant difference

[1] 'A System of Notation for Relationships', *Man*, xxx, 1930, p. 93.

[2] See Herskovits, *Dahomey*, 1938, i, pp. 145 et seq.; Northcote W. Thomas, *Anthropological Report on the Edo-speaking Peoples of Nigeria*, 1910, Part I, pp. 112 et seq. and *Anthropological Report on the Ibo-speaking Peoples of Nigeria*, 1913, Part I, p. 72.

is made between the son of one's mother's brother and the son of one's father's brother. In Montenegro, on the contrary, to take another European language, there is a different system. The father's brother is called *stric* and his wife is *strina*, while the mother's brother is *ujak* and his wife is *ujna*, and the social relations in which a man stands to his two kinds of uncles show marked differences.

In the eighteenth century Lafitau[1] reported the existence amongst American Indians of a system of terminology very unlike our own.

'Among the Iroquois and Hurons all the children of a cabin regard all their mother's sisters as their mothers, and all their mother's brothers as their uncles, and for the same reason they give the name of fathers to all their father's brothers, and aunts to all their father's sisters. All the children on the side of the mother and her sisters, and of the father and his brothers, regard each other mutually as brothers and sisters, but as regards the children of their uncles and aunts, that is, of their mother's brothers and father's sisters, they only treat them on the footing of cousins.'

In the nineteenth century Lewis Morgan, while living with the Iroquois, was impressed by this method of referring to kin and set to work to collect kinship terminologies from all over the world. These he published in 1871 in his *Systems of Consanguinity and Affinity*. He found systems of terminology similar to that of the Iroquois in many parts of the world, and such systems he called 'classificatory'.

The distinguishing feature of a classificatory system of kinship terminology in Morgan's usage is that terms which apply to lineal relatives are also applied to certain collateral relatives. Thus a father's brother is 'father' and mother's sister is 'mother', while, as in the type described by Lafitau, there are separate terms for mother's brother and father's sister. Consequently in the next generation the children of father's brothers and mother's sisters are called 'brother' and 'sister' and there are separate terms for the children of mother's brothers and father's sisters. A distinction is thus made between two kinds of cousins, 'parallel cousins' (children of father's brothers and mother's sisters), who although 'collateral' in our sense are classified as 'brothers' and 'sisters', and 'cross-cousins' (children of mother's brothers and father's sisters). There is a similar distinction amongst nephews and nieces. A man classifies the children of his brothers with his own children, but uses a separate term for the children of his sisters. Inversely a woman classifies with her own children the children of her sisters but not those of her brothers. Classificatory terminologies of this kind are found in a great many African peoples.

There are other types of classificatory system, found less frequently, in which the term 'father' is applied to the brothers of the mother as well as to those of the father, and both mother's sister and father's sister

---

[1] Lafitau, *Mœurs des Sauvages Ameriquains*, Paris, 1724, vol. i, p. 552.

are called 'mother'; or cousins, both parallel and cross-cousins, may all be treated as 'brothers' and 'sisters'.

In classificatory systems the principle of classification may be applied over a wide range of relationship. Thus a first cousin of the father, being his father's brother's son, whom he therefore calls 'brother', is classified with the father and the same term 'father' is applied to him. His son in turn, a second cousin, is called 'brother'. By this process of extension of the principle of classification nearer and more distant collateral relatives are arranged into a few categories and a person has many relatives to whom he applies the term 'father' or 'mother' or 'brother' or 'sister'.

The most important feature of these classificatory terminologies was pointed out long ago by Sir Henry Maine. 'The effect of the system', he wrote, 'is in general to bring within your mental grasp a much greater number of your kindred than is possible under the system to which we are accustomed.'[1] In other words, the classificatory terminology is primarily a mechanism which facilitates the establishment of wide-range systems of kinship.

There is more to it than this, however. Research in many parts of the world has shown that the classificatory terminology, like our own and other non-classificatory systems, is used as a method of dividing relatives into categories which determine or influence social relations as exhibited in conduct. The general rule is that the inclusion of two relatives in the same terminological category implies that there is some significant similarity in the customary behaviour due to both of them, or in the social relation in which one stands to each of them, while inversely the placing of two relatives in different categories implies some significant difference in customary behaviour or social relations. Some anthropologists make a great point of real or supposed exceptions to this rule, but they seem to forget that there can only be an exception when there is a general rule to which it is an exception.

There is a complication resulting from the fact that in classificatory systems there are necessarily distinctions between near and distant relatives included in the same category. Thus amongst the men referred to as 'father' the nearest relative is, of course, the actual 'own' father. After him come his brothers and after them his parallel first cousins and perhaps in some systems the husbands of the mother's sisters. So on to more and more distant relatives of the same terminological category. The attitude and behaviour of a person towards a particular relative is affected not only by the category to which he belongs but also by the degree of nearness or distance of the relationship. In classificatory systems there are many women whom a particular man calls 'sister'. In some systems he will be prohibited from marrying any of these women. In some others he may not marry any 'near' 'sister', i.e. any one of these

[1] *The Early History of Institutions*, 1874, p. 214.

women who is related to him within a certain degree of cognatic relationship, but may marry a more distant 'sister'.

Morgan tried to classify all terminological systems into two classes
as being either classificatory or descriptive. But the ordinary English
system should not be called descriptive and there are many other non-
classificatory systems that are also not descriptive.[1] A people using a
classificatory terminology may also make use of the descriptive principle
or method in order to refer to the exact genealogical relation between
two persons.[2] The study of kinship terminologies is valuable because
they frequently, or indeed usually, reveal the method of ordering
relationships.

The reality of a kinship system as a part of a social structure consists
of the actual social relations of person to person as exhibited in their
interactions and their behaviour in respect of one another. But the actual
behaviour of two persons in a certain relationship (father and son,
husband and wife, or mother's brother and sister's son) varies from one
particular instance to another. What we have to seek in the study of a
kinship system are the norms. From members of the society we can
obtain statements as to how two persons in a certain relationship ought
to behave towards one another. A sufficient number of such statements
will enable us to define the ideal or expected conduct. Actual observations of the way persons do behave will enable us to discover the extent
to which they conform to the rules and the kinds and amount of devia-
tion. Further, we can and should observe the reactions of other persons
to the conduct of a particular person or their expressions of approval or
disapproval. The reaction or judgement may be that of a person who is
directly or personally affected by the conduct in question or it may be
the reaction or judgement of what may be called public opinion or public
sentiment. The members of a community are all concerned with the
observance of social usage or rules of conduct and judge with approval
or disapproval the behaviour of a fellow member even when it does not
affect them personally.

A kinship system thus presents to us a complex set of norms, of usages,
of patterns of behaviour between kindred. Deviations from the norm
have their importance. For one thing they provide a rough measure of
the relative condition of equilibrium or disequilibrium in the system.
Where there is a marked divergence between ideal or expected behaviour
and the actual conduct of many individuals this is an indication of
disequilibrium; for example, when the rule is that a son should obey his

---

[1] For an example of a terminology that is neither descriptive nor classificatory
see N. W. Thomas, *Anthropological Report on Sierra Leone*, 1916, Part I, 'Law
and Custom of the Timne'.

[2] For a kinship terminology making use of both the descriptive and the
classificatory principles see 'Double Descent among the Yakö', by Daryll Forde,
in this volume.

father but there are notably frequent instances of disobedience. But there may also be a lack of equilibrium when there is marked disagreement amongst members of the society in formulating the rules of conduct or in judgements passed on the behaviour of particular persons.

In attempting to define the norms of behaviour for a particular kind of relation in a given system it is necessary to distinguish different elements or aspects. As one element in a relation we may recognize the existence of a personal sentiment, what may be called the affective element. Thus we may say that in most human societies a strong mutual affection is a normal feature of the relation of mother and child, or there may be in a particular society a typical or normal emotional attitude of a son to his father. It is very important to remember that this affective element in the relation between relatives by kinship or marriage is different in different societies.

We may distinguish also an element that it is convenient to refer to by the term 'etiquette', if we may be permitted to give a wide extension of meaning to that word. It refers to conventional rules as to outward behaviour. What these rules do is to define certain symbolic actions or avoidances which express some important aspect of the relation between two persons. Differences of rank are given recognition in this way. In some tribes of South Africa it would be an extreme, and in fact unheard of, breach of the rules of propriety for a woman to utter the name of her husband's father.

An important element in the relations of kin is what will here be called the jural element, meaning by that relationships that can be defined in terms of rights and duties. Where there is a duty there is a rule that a person should behave in a certain way. A duty may be positive, prescribing actions to be performed, or negative, imposing the avoidance of certain acts. We may speak of the 'performance' of a positive duty and the 'observance' of a negative duty. The duties of *A* to *B* are frequently spoken of in terms of the 'rights' of *B*. Reference to duties or rights are simply different ways of referring to a social relation and the rules of behaviour connected therewith.

In speaking of the jural element in social relations we are referring to customary rights and duties. Some of these in some societies are subject to legal sanctions, that is, an infraction can be dealt with by a court of law. But for the most part the sanctions for these customary rules are what may be called moral sanctions sometimes supplemented by religious sanctions.

There are, first, what we may call personal rights and duties, rights *in personam* in legal terminology. *A* has a right *in personam* in relation to *B* when *A* can claim from *B* the performance of a certain duty. The right and the duty are both determinate. Thus, in the relation between an African husband and his wife each of the partners has personal rights imposing duties upon the other. Those personal rights and duties that form a most important part of relations by kinship and marriage are different from those established by contract or in a contractual relationship. In such a relationship a person accepts a certain definite obligation or certain obligations towards another. When the specific obligations on both sides have been fulfilled the contractual relation is terminated. But relations of kinship are not of this kind. They are not entered into voluntarily and they normally continue throughout life. It is true that a marital relationship is entered into; but it is not a contractual relationship between husband and wife; it is best described as a union.[1] It may be terminated by death, but in some societies not even then (witness the custom of the levirate by which a woman continues to bear children for her husband after he is dead); where divorce is recognized it may be terminated by that means. But the rights and duties of husband and wife are not like the obligations defined in a contract; they are incident to the relationship in the same sort of way as the rights and duties of parents and children.

We must distinguish from personal rights (*jus in personam*) what are designated rights *in rem*. Such a right is not a claim in relation to a certain particular person but a right 'against all the world'. The most characteristic form of such rights is in relation to things. The right which I have over something which I possess is infringed if someone steals it or destroys it or damages it. The use of the legal term *jus in rem* implies that in certain circumstances a person may be treated as a thing (*res*).

'Thus when a father or master brings an action for the detention of, or for injuries inflicted upon, his child or apprentice, or when a husband sues for injuries inflicted upon his wife, the child, apprentice, and wife are in fact held to be *things*. The action is not brought in pursuance of the legal rights of the child, apprentice, or wife.'[2]

I shall refer to these rights (*in rem*) over persons as 'possessive rights', but it must be remembered that the term is used in this special sense.

In the formation of systems of kinship and marriage these possessive rights over persons are of great importance. Thus in most African systems a husband has possessive rights in relation to his wife. His rights are infringed, i.e. he suffers a wrong, if a man commits adultery with her or if someone kills her or abducts her. Later in this essay we shall have to consider the subject of possessive rights over children. It should be noted that possessive rights over persons can be shared by a

---

[1] An agreement between two families, whereby one promises to give a daughter in marriage and the other undertakes to see that the marriage payments are made, is a contract in the proper sense of the term. This is a preliminary to the marriage, just as the Roman *sponsalia* or betrothal was a preliminary promise or contract which was fulfilled in the *nuptiae*.

[2] Sheldon Amos, *The Science of Law*, 1888, p. 87. See also Sir Frederick Pollock, *First Book of Jurisprudence*, chap. iv.

number of persons or may be held collectively by a definite group of persons, just as may possessive rights over land or other property.

A kinship system is therefore a network of social relations which constitutes part of that total network of social relations which is the social structure. The rights and duties of relatives to one another are part of the system and so are the terms used in addressing or referring to relatives.

By using the word 'system' we make an assumption, for the word implies that whatever it is applied to is a complex unity, an organized whole. This hypothesis has already received a considerable measure of verification by anthropological studies. But we must distinguish between a stable system which has persisted with relatively little change for some period of time and the unstable condition of a society which is undergoing rapid change. It is in the former, not in the latter, that we may expect to find some fair degree of consistency and congruence amongst the items that make up the whole.

III

In this and following sections the more important structural principles which are found in kinship systems will be briefly indicated.

Two persons who are kin are related in one or other of two ways: either one is descended from the other, or they are both descended from a common ancestor. It is to be remembered that 'descent' here refers to the social relationship of parents and children, not to the physical relation. Kinship is thus based on descent, and what first determines the character of a kinship system is the way in which descent is recognized and reckoned.

One principle that may be adopted is the simple cognatic principle. To define the kin of a given person his descent is traced back a certain number of generations, to his four grandparents, his eight great-grandparents, or still farther, and all descendants of his recognized ancestors, through both females and males, are his cognates. At each generation that we go backwards the number of ancestors is double that of the preceding generation, so that in the eighth generation a person will have sixty-four pairs of ancestors (the great-grandparents of his great-great-grandparents). It is therefore obvious that there must be some limit to tracing kinship in this way. The limit may simply be a practical one depending on the inability to trace the genealogical connexions, or there may be a theoretically fixed limit beyond which the genealogical connexion does not count for social purposes.

Another way of ordering the kindred may be illustrated by the system of ancient Rome. Within the body of a person's recognized cognates certain are distinguished as agnates. Cognates are agnates if they are descendants by male links from the same male ancestor.[1] In the Roman

---

[1] 'Sunt autem agnati per virilis sexus personas cognatione juncti' (Gaius); 'Agnati sunt a patre cognati' (Ulpian).

system there was the strongest possible emphasis on agnatic kinship, i.e. on unilineal descent through males.

In some other societies there is a similar emphasis on unilineal descent through females. With such a system a person distinguishes from the rest of his cognates those persons who are descended by female links only from the same female ancestress as himself. We can speak of these as his matrilineal kin.

There are few, if any, societies in which there is not some recognition of unilineal descent, either patrilineal (agnatic) or matrilineal or both. Thus in the modern English system surnames descend in the male line. In many countries, in a mixed marriage, children acquire by birth the nationality of the father, not that of the mother. But what matters in the study of any society is the degree of emphasis on the unilineal principle and how it is used.

One important way in which the unilineal principle may be used is in the formation of recognized lineage groups as part of the social structure. An agnatic lineage consists of an original male ancestor and all his descendants through males of three, four, five, or n generations. The lineage group consists of all the members of a lineage alive at a given time. A woman belongs to the lineage of her father, but her children do not. With matrilineal reckoning the lineage consists of a progenetrix and all her descendants through females. A man belongs to his mother's lineage, but his children do not. Lineage groups, agnatic or matrilineal, are of great importance in the social organization of many African peoples.

A lineage of several generations in depth, i.e. back to the founding ancestor or ancestress, will normally be divided into branches. In an agnatic lineage of which the founding ancestor has two sons each of them may become the founder of a branch consisting of his descendants in the male line. The two branches are united by the fact that their founders were brothers. As a lineage continues and increases the branching process continues, resulting in a large and complex organization. In some parts of China we find in one village a body of persons all having the same name and tracing their descent in the male line to a single ancestor who may have lived eight or nine hundred years ago. This is therefore a very large lineage which may number several hundred living persons. Genealogical records of the whole lineage are usually preserved and are sometimes printed for the use of the families of the lineage. There is a complex ramification of branches. An important feature of the Chinese system is the maintaining of the distinction of generations. A common method of giving names is one by which a man has three names; the first is the lineage or family name; the second indicates the generation to which he belongs; the third is his distinctive personal name. From the second part of the name any member of the lineage can tell to which generation any particular individual belongs.

What is here called a branch of a lineage is, of course, itself a lineage. A lineage of ten generations may include two or more branches of nine generations and one of these may contain two or more of eight, and so on. A lineage of several generations includes dead as well as living. We may conveniently use the term 'lineage group' to refer to a group formed of the members of a lineage who are alive at a particular time. Lineage groups as thus defined are important as components of the social structure in many African societies. A lineage group that is socially important may itself consist of smaller groups (branch lineages) and it may itself be part of a more extended and recognized group formed of related lineages.

It is desirable to illustrate by examples the differences in the ordering of kindred as the result of relative emphasis on the cognatic principle or on the unilineal principle. As an example of a cognatic system we may take the kinship system of the Teutonic peoples as it was at the beginning of history. This was based on a widely extended recognition of kinship traced through females as well as males. The Anglo-Saxon word for kinsfolk was *maeg* (*magas*). A man owed loyalty to his 'kith and kin'. Kith were one's friends by vicinage, one's neighbours; kin were persons descended from a common ancestor. So, for 'kith and kin' Anglo-Saxon could say 'his magas and his frŷnd', which is translated in Latin as *cognati atque amici*.

The arrangement of kin by degrees of nearness or distance was based on sib-ship (English *sib*, German *Sippe*). A man's sib were all his cognates within a certain degree. One method of arranging the sib was by reference to the human body and its 'joints' (*glied*). The father and mother stand in the head, full brothers and sisters in the neck, first cousins at the shoulders, second cousins at the elbow, third cousins at the wrists, fourth, fifth, and sixth cousins at the joints of the fingers. Finally come the nails, at which would stand the seventh cousins. On one scheme these nail kinsmen (*nagel magas*) were not included in the sib, though they were recognized as kinsmen (*magas*) if known to be such. The sib therefore included all kinsfolk up to and including sixth cousins. They were the *sibgemagas*, the sib kinsfolk.[1]

It is evident that no two persons can have the same sib, though for two unmarried full brothers, A and B, every person who was sib to A was sib to B, and A and B were sib-kinsmen of one another. A person cannot be said to 'belong' to a sib or be a member of a sib in the sense

[1] This account of the 'joints' of the sib is the one given in article 3 of the first book of the *Sachsenspiegel*. I have used the Leipzig edition of 1545. The statement about the 'nail kinsmen' is as follows: 'in dem siebenden steht ein nagel und nicht ein glied darumb endet sich da die sip und heisst ein nagel freund. Die sip endet sich in dem siebenden glied erbe zu nemen'. This is explained in a Latin *nota*: 'gradus cognationis finitur in septimo gradu, necesse est ergo in petitione haereditatis, q. haeres et petitor articulet eum, vel se defuncto infra septem gradus attigisse'.

in which he can be said to belong to a lineage or a clan or a village community.

The innermost circle of the sib of an individual included his father and mother, his brother and sister, and his son and daughter—the 'six hands of the sib'. Another circle that was recognized was that of relatives 'within the knee'. This word (*cneow*) seems to have referred to the elbow, so that kinsfolk 'within the knee' would include all the descendants of the eight great-grandparents.

The sib was thus an arrangement of kindred as it were in a series of concentric circles, with the person whose sib it was at the centre. One circle included all those kin with whom marriage was forbidden. It is difficult to discover exactly where this was. In some Teutonic systems and in ancient Wales it is said that the prohibition against marriage extended to 'the fifth degree'. This would seem to include all third cousins, but the matter is not quite clear.

Another way of reckoning degrees of kinship was by 'stocks'. There were first the four 'quarters' of the sib (*klüfte*, in Frisian), the four stocks of the grandparents, each consisting of the descendants of one of the four pairs of great-grandparents. The wider sib included the eight stocks (*fechten* or *fange*) of the great-grandparents, each consisting of the descendants of one of the eight pairs of great-great-grandparents. The eight stocks (Old High German *ahta*, Old Norse *oett*) therefore included all kinsfolk as far as third cousins.

In the Middle Ages another method of reckoning was adopted, the parentelic system (Latin *parentela*). A person's sib was arranged in five parenteles: (1) his own descendants; (2) all descendants of his parents (excluding 1); (3) all descendants of his two pairs of grandparents (excluding 1 and 2); (4) all descendants of his four pairs of great-grandparents (excluding 1, 2, and 3); (5) all descendants of his eight pairs of great-great-grandparents (excluding 1, 2, 3, and 4). This system seems to have been used principally for regulating inheritance. Within a parentele the degree of relationship was fixed by the greater or smaller distance from the common ancestor. Thus the uncle is more nearly related than his son, the cousin. But nephews (in the second parentele) are more nearly related than uncles (in the third). Both the 'stock' and the parentelic method of reckoning seem to go only as far as the wrist 'joint', i.e. as far as third cousins on both sides. They include, therefore, only part of the total sib.

In more recent times the present method of reckoning by cousinage was introduced. It has been suggested that the system of reckoning by first, second, third cousins originated in Spain and Portugal as a result of Teutonic invasions. In England this reckoning by cousins has replaced the older system of the sib.

'Sib' may be defined as meaning computable cognatic relationship for definite social purposes. We have seen that it was used for fixing the degrees within which marriage was forbidden. After the introduction of Christianity the relation between godparents and godchildren was included under sib. The godfather and godmother were 'god-sib' (modern 'gossip') to their godchildren and marriage between them was forbidden. Sib-ship also regulated the inheritance of property. Persons who were not related to a deceased person within a certain degree had no claim to inherit.

Where the functioning of the Teutonic sib can be best studied is in the customs relating to wergild, which was the indemnity that was required when one person killed another. It was paid by the person who had killed and his sib, and was received by the sib of the deceased. When the system was in full force the number of kinsmen who might be called on to contribute to the payment or who might receive a share of it was considerable. Theoretically it seems to have extended in some communities as far as sixth cousins on both sides, i.e. to all the 'joints' but not to the nail. But practically, and in some instances in theory, duties and claims seem to have been effective only as far as fourth cousins. There were laws or rules fixing the total amount of the wergild and the amounts or shares to be contributed or shared by each class of kinsfolk. The nearest kin paid and received most, the most distant paid and received least.[1]

The payment of wergild was an indemnity for homicide paid to those persons who had possessive rights (rights *in rem*) over the person who was killed. In the Teutonic system these rights were held by the cognatic relatives of the slain man by what was essentially a system similar to partnership. Each relative held as it were a share in the possession, and the consequent claim for indemnity and the share of any relative depended on the nearness of the relation so that, for example, the share claimed by the second cousins was twice that belonging to third cousins.

We have now to ask what use was made of the unilineal principle in the Teutonic systems. A man's kin were divided into those of the spear side (his paternal kin) and those of the spindle side (his maternal kin). In some of the Teutonic systems relatives on the father's side paid or received twice as much as those on the mother's side in a wergild transaction. This was so in the England of King Alfred. Similarly in ancient Welsh (British) law the *galanas* (the Celtic term for wergild) was paid two-thirds by paternal kinsmen and one-third by maternal, up to the fifth cousin, but not including the son of the fifth cousin or the sixth cousin. So far as the Teutonic peoples are concerned this may have been a late development. But in any case this did not mean the recognition of unilineal descent, but only that a father's sister's son was a nearer relative than a mother's sister's son.

Amongst some at least of the Teutonic peoples there existed large

[1] The most readily accessible account in English of wergild payments is Bertha S. Phillpotts, *Kindred and Clan*, Cambridge, 1913.

C

house-communities under the control of a house-father or house-lord, of the type of what it is usual to call the patriarchal family. Sons continued to live with their father under his rule and daughters usually joined their husbands elsewhere. But although the patrilineal principle was general or usual, it was not always strictly adhered to. Thus in the Icelandic *Nyal's Saga* the house-community of old Nyal included not only his wife Bergthora and his three married sons but also a daughter's husband, and, with children, men-servants, and others, the household numbered some fifty persons.

The patrilineal principle also appears in the preference given to sons over daughters in the inheritance of land. But in default of sons, daughters might inherit land in some Teutonic societies. It appears that the principle of unilineal descent was only used to a limited extent in the Teutonic system.

About the Teutonic system two pseudo-historical theories have been advanced. One is that these peoples in prehistoric times had a system of matriarchy, which, whatever else it may or may not mean, implies an emphasis on unilineal descent through females. As evidence is quoted the statement of Tacitus that amongst the Germans the mother's brother was an important relative.[1]

The other theory is that in prehistoric times the Teutonic peoples had a system of patriarchy emphasizing agnatic descent. This is a deduction from the general theory that originally all the Indo-European peoples had a patriarchal system. For neither theory is there any historical evidence.

An example of an arrangement of relations of kinship on the basis of unilineal descent may be taken from the Masai of East Africa. Though the kinship system of the Masai has not been adequately studied, the arrangement of the various kin can be seen in the terminology which has been recorded by Hollis.[2]

The terminology is classificatory. The father, the father's brother, and the father's father's brother's son are called by the same term, *menye*. The sons and daughters of these men are called 'brother' and 'sister' (*ol-alashe* and *eng-anashe*). To all the children of men he calls 'brother' a man applies the same terms as to his own son and daughter (*ol-ayoni* and *en-dito*). All these persons belong to a man's own agnatic lineage (descendants of the father's father's father). We do not know how far the recognition of the lineage connexion is extended, but for our present purpose this does not matter.[3]

---

[1] Tacitus, *Germania*, c. 20. 4: 'Sororum filius idem apud avunculum qui ad patrem honor.'

[2] A. C. Hollis, 'A Note on the Masai System of Relationship and other Matters connected therewith', *J. Roy. Anthrop. Inst.* xl, 1910, pp. 473–82. There are two misprints in the table facing p. 482. The terms *e-sindani e-anyit* (wife's sister) and *ol-le-'sotwa* (her husband) have been transposed.

[3] The Masai are divided into five clans and each clan is subdivided into

MASAI KINSHIP TERMINOLOGY

Own lineage

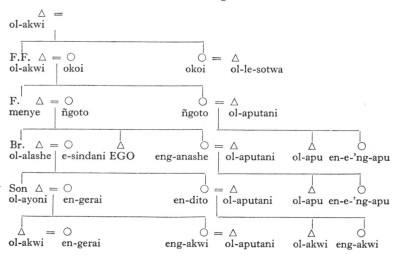

Mother's lineage

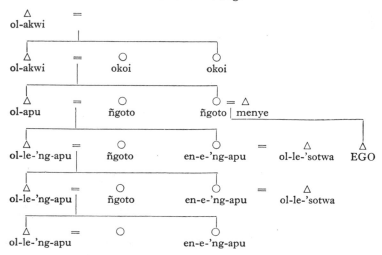

A feature of the Masai system is that these terms for 'father', 'brother', 'sister', 'son', 'daughter', though used as classificatory terms, are not applied except to a man's agnatic kindred. Thus while in some societies with a classificatory terminology[1] the mother's sister's husband is called 'father' and her children are 'brother' and 'sister', this is not so in Masai. Thus the Masai terminology emphasizes the distinction between agnatic and other kindred.

It is of some significance that the distinction between agnatic and other kin is not carried back into the generations of the grandparents and great-grandparents. Male relatives of the second and third ascending generations on both the father's and the mother's side are *ol-akwi* and their wives and sisters are *okoi*. Similarly, and reciprocally, the terms *ol-akwi* (grandson) and *eng-akwi* (granddaughter) are applied to daughters' children as well as sons' children and to the grandchildren, through sons or daughters, of any 'brother' of the lineage.

The emphasis on the agnatic lineage also appears in the fact that there are certain terms which apply only to women who have come into the lineage by marriage: *e-sindani* for the wife of any 'brother', and *en-gerai* for the wife of any 'son' or 'grandson' of the lineage.

Let us consider the women of a man's own lineage of his own and the preceding generation. The sisters of the men he calls 'father' are referred to descriptively (*eng-anashe-menye*) or the term for 'mother' (*ñgoto*) is applied to them. The husband of a 'father's sister' or a 'sister' is called *ol-aputani*, which simply means 'relative by marriage', but their children are called *ol-apu* and *en-e-'ng-apu*. A man's *ol-apu* is his 'sister's son' or 'father's sister's son' and is connected with the man's own lineage through the mother. The children of his *ol-apu* are again his kin, *ol-le-'ng-apu* and *en-e-'ng-apu*, and the son of *ol-le-'ng-apu* is again *ol-le-'ng-apu*. The cognatic relationship is continued from father to son in the male line. But the offspring of an *en-e-'ng-apu* (sister's daughter, father's sister's daughter, sister's son's daughter, &c.) are *ol-le-'sotwa* and *en-e-sotwa*. It is evident from the account given by Hollis that these two terms do not refer to any definite relation of kinship but simply mean

sub-clans. The sub-clan is the exogamous group, i.e. marriage is permitted within the clan but not within the sub-clan. A similar organization is found in tribes related to the Masai. The Kipsigis, for example, are divided into clans (*oret*) and the clan is subdivided into segments which Peristiany refers to by the native term *kot op chi* and calls a subdivision of the clan (Peristiany, *The Social Institutions of the Kipsigis*, 1939). For the Nandi, Hollis tells us that 'second cousins, like cousins, are called brothers; more distant cousins are called *piek-ap-oret* (people of the family)'. This presumably refers to agnatic cousins only, and it would mean that the lineage proper (within which cousins are 'brothers') consists of the descendants of father's father's father. The Masai system may have been similar.

[1] In the Kipsigis, for example, who belong to the same general area as the Masai and have a somewhat similar social organization. See Peristiany, op. cit.

'relative'. The husband of an *en-e-'ng-apu* is not *ol-aputani* (relative by marriage) but simply *ol-le-'sotwa*.

A man is connected through his mother with her agnatic lineage. He calls his mother's brother *ol-apu*. This is therefore a self-reciprocal term used between mother's brother and sister's son. The relationship, according to Hollis, is an important one. The mother's brother's son and daughter, the cross-cousins, are *ol-le-'ng-apu* and *en-e-'ng-apu*. Once again the relationship is continued within the lineage, i.e. through males but not through females. The son and daughter of the mother's brother's son are *ol-le-'ng-apu* and *en-e-'ng-apu*, but the children of the mother's brother's daughter are simply *sotwa* relatives. Specific kinship is also not continued through the mother's sisters, whose children are *sotwa* relatives.

A man also recognizes the mother's brother of his father as a kinsman and calls him *ol-apu*, as he does his own mother's brother. This man would call him *ol-le-'ng-apu* since he is his sister's son's son. Hollis does not inform us what a man calls his father's mother's brother's son, but it seems likely that he would be *ol-le-'ng-apu*.

The emphasis on agnatic descent is also observable in the relation of man to his wife's lineage. All the male members of the lineage, including the wife's father's father and the wife's father's father's brother and all their male descendants in the male line, are *ol-aputani*. On the other hand, while the wife's father's sister is *eng-aputani*, the relationship does not continue and her children are only *sotwa*. In the wife's mother's lineage she is *eng-aputani* and her brothers and sisters are *ol-aputani* and *eng-aputani*, but the relationship continues no farther and the wife's mother's brother's children become *sotwa*.

The Masai kinship terminology thus presents an interesting and illuminating example of a system in which the emphasis is placed on agnatic lineage. The most important kinship relations of a man are evidently those with the members of his own agnatic lineage. But the children of his sister and father's sister (female members of his lineage) are persons with whom his kinship is important. The kinship connexion is maintained in the male line but not in the female line. The other side of this relationship is that of a man with his mother's lineage. Here again he is related to the members of the lineage, his mother's sister and his mother's brother, but the relationship only continues in the male line to the children and the son's children of his mother's brother, and not to the children of his mother's sister or to the children of his mother's brother's daughter. By marriage he is related to his wife's agnatic lineage, to female members as well as male, and again the relationship is only continued in the male line. His relationship to his wife's mother is continued to her brothers and sisters but not to the rest of her lineage.

The emphasis on the agnatic line is shown clearly in the fact that the husband of the father's sister is *ol-aputani*, a relative by marriage, and her children are kinsfolk, while the husband of a mother's sister, far from being a 'father', as he is in some systems, is merely a relative (*sotwa*), as also are her children. The general principle is that relationships, including those established through females or by marriage, continue in the male line only.

An interesting and distinctive feature of the Masai system is the use of the terms *ol-le-'sotwa* and *en-e-sotwa*. Hollis tells us that *sotwa* means 'peace' or 'relative'. It does not connote any definite kind or degree of relationship either by kinship or by marriage. Thus *sotwa* relatives may marry. Hollis states that the restrictions on marriage are two: (1) a man may not marry a woman of his own sub-clan, which is a patrilineal group; (2) 'No man may marry a nearer relation than a third cousin, and then only if the terms of address used are *ol-le-sotwa* and *en-e-sotwa*.' This statement as it stands implies that there are certain *sotwa* relatives who may not be married, for example, the mother's sister's daughter and the mother's mother's sister's daughter's daughter. On such a point as this it would be better if we had more precise information. The fact is clear, however, that the *sotwa* relationship is not itself a bar to marriage while other kinship relations are.

The Masai system arranges a man's kin into a few large categories. (1) His agnatic relatives belonging to his own lineage (or sub-clan); (2) his *apu* kin, if we may call them so, the descendants of those women of his lineage who are his father's sisters or his sisters, and on the other hand, the members of the mother's lineage: the relationship is established through a female and is then continued in the male line only; (3) his *aputani* relatives, i.e. relatives by marriage, either the kin of his wife or persons who have married one of his kinswomen; (4) those relatives to whom he applies the classificatory terms 'grandfather', 'grandmother', 'grandson', 'granddaughter', some of whom belong to his lineage while others do not; (5) his *sotwa* relatives, a sort of fringe of persons not belonging to the first four classes, with each of whom some indirect connexion can be traced: they are vaguely his 'relatives', persons with whom he should be at peace.

The structural difference between organization by sib and by lineage can be readily seen by comparing a 'stock' with a 'lineage'. A 'stock' includes all the descendants of a man and his wife counting descent through females as well as males. In the sib system a man belongs to each of the eight stocks of his eight pairs of great-great-grandparents and all descendants of these ancestors are his kin. With a patrilineal lineage system he belongs to a lineage which includes the descendants of a male ancestor counting through males only. The persons of his mother's lineage are his kin, but he does not belong to the lineage.

We are here concerned with the ways in which different societies provide an ordering of the kin of an individual within a certain range, wide or narrow. One way is by tracing kinship equally and similarly through males and through females. There is a close approximation to this in modern European societies and in some primitive societies. In various societies we find some greater or less emphasis placed on unilineal descent, but there are many different ways in which this principle can be applied. In the Masai system there is marked emphasis on the male line, so that the most important of a man's social connexions are with the members of his own agnatic lineage and with those of his mother's agnatic lineage and those of the agnatic lineage of his wife. In other societies there may be a similar emphasis on the female line, so that a man's chief relations through his father are with the latter's matrilineal lineage. There are also systems in Africa and elsewhere in which unilineal descent through males is given recognition and also unilineal descent through females.

There are a great variety of ways in which the unilineal principle may be used. It is therefore only misleading to talk about matrilineal and patrilineal societies as was formerly the custom of anthropologists. Some more complex and systematic classification is needed to represent the facts as they are.

IV

Reference has already been made to the classificatory systems of kinship terminology which are found in very many African peoples. The theory of pseudo-history is that this method of referring to kin is a 'survival' from a time in the past when the family as it now exists had not made its appearance. In those remote days it is imagined that there existed a system of 'group-marriage' in which a group of men cohabited with a group of women and when a child was born all the men were equally its fathers and all the women equally its mothers. This fantastic example of pseudo-history was put forward by Lewis Morgan in his *Ancient Society* (1878).

The theory here proposed is not in any way concerned with the origins of classificatory terminologies, which are found widely distributed in Asia, Africa, America, and Australasia, but with their social functions. It starts from the simple and obvious postulate that in order to have a system of kinship it is necessary to have some way of distinguishing and classifying a person's kin, and that one very obvious and natural means of doing this is through the kinship nomenclature. We give the same name to a number of things when we think that in some important respect they are similar. We use in English the same name—uncle—for the mother's brother and the father's brother because we think of them as similar, as relatives of the same kind. In a classificatory system a man uses the same term for his father and his father's brother because he thinks of them as relatives of one general kind.

The principle on which the classificatory terminology is based may be called the principle of the unity of the sibling group. This refers not to

the internal unity of the group as shown in the relations of its members
to one another but to the fact that the group may constitute a unity for
a person outside it and connected with it by a specific relation to one of
its members. Thus a son may, in a particular system, be taught to regard
his father's sibling group as a united body with whom he is related as
their 'son'.

The sibling group, i.e. the body of brothers and sisters of common
parentage, has its own internal structure. In the first place there are the
very important social distinctions between the sexes, which divide the
brothers from the sisters. These distinctions are differently exhibited in
usages in different societies, and the relation between brother and sister
is therefore an important feature of any particular kinship system.
Secondly there is the order of birth, which is translated into social terms
in the distinction of senior and junior. The importance of this distinction in African tribes is shown by the existence of separate terms for
'senior brother' and 'junior brother'. In a polygynous family there is the
further difference between full siblings and half-siblings, and in African
peoples this is usually, if not always, important.

Within an elementary family, i.e. amongst full brothers, the dis-
crimination between older and younger siblings is made on the basis of
order of birth. But in a polygynous compound family the wives may be
unequal in rank, the great wife, or the first wife, having a higher rank
than others. In the Kaffir tribes of the Transkei a son of a wife of
inferior rank will apply to all the sons of the great wife (his half-brothers)
the term used for 'elder brother' even when they are younger than
himself. The two words are therefore better translated as 'senior brother'
and 'junior brother'.

In these same tribes (which have a classificatory terminology) the
sons of an older brother of the father must be called 'senior brother'
irrespective of actual age, and those of the father's younger brother will
be called 'junior brother'. Amongst the Yao, who have matrilineal
descent, not only the sons of the older brother of the father, but also
those of the older sister of the mother, must be called 'senior brother'
(Sanderson).

The main principle of the classificatory terminology is a simple one.
If A and B are two brothers and X stands in a certain relation to A, then
he is regarded as standing in a somewhat similar relation to B. Similarly
if A and B are two sisters. In any particular system the principle is
applied over a certain range. The similarity of the relation is indicated
by applying a single term of relationship to A and B. The father's brother
is called 'father' and the mother's sister is called 'mother'. The father's
father's brother is regarded as similar to the father's father and therefore
his son is also called 'father'. Once the principle is adopted it can be
applied and extended in different ways. However the principle is used,
it makes possible the recognition of a large number of relatives and their

classification into a relatively few categories. Within a single category relatives are distinguished as nearer or more distant.

As a general rule, to which, of course, there may be exceptions, towards all persons to whom a given term of relationship is applied there is some element of attitude or behaviour by which the relationship is given recognition, even if it is only some feature of etiquette or an obligation to exhibit friendliness or respect. Rules of behaviour are more definite and more important for near relatives than for more distant ones.

It is a general characteristic of classificatory terminologies that the father's brother is called 'father' and the mother's sister 'mother'. When we come to the mother's brother and the father's sister, for these relatives there is a possible choice between two different structural principles. One may be called the 'generation' principle. There are a few examples in Africa of peoples with classificatory systems who call the father's sister and the mother's brother's wife 'mother'. The Masai provide one example, and there are others. This means that female cognates of the first ascending generation are placed in a single category. It is only rarely, and not, so far as I am aware, anywhere in Africa, that the mother's brother is called 'father'. Where this principle is used the emphasis is on generation and sex.

The other principle is that of the unity of the sibling group. The father's sister belongs to the father's sibling group and therefore she is a relative of the same general kind as the father and the father's brother, and similarly the mother's brother is a relative of the same kind as the mother and her sister. This way of thinking about uncles and aunts is shown in the kinship terminology of many African societies. Writing about the Kongo, Father van Wing says: 'All the sisters and brothers of the mother are considered as the mothers (*ngudi*) of the Mukongo (*ngudi nsakela* or *ngudi nkasi*) while all the brothers and sisters of the father (*se*) are considered by the Mukongo as fathers (*mase*).'[1] The term for 'mother's brother' in many Bantu tribes is *umalume*, which is literally 'male mother', *uma* being the term for 'mother' and *lume* meaning 'male'. Similarly, in a number of African peoples the father's sister is referred to by the term for 'father' or is called 'female father'. Examples are the Kitara, the Ndau, the Yao, the Huana, and there are others.

To some Europeans this use of the terms 'female father', 'male mother' may seem the height of absurdity. The reason for this is simply a confusion of thought resulting from the ambiguity of our own words for father and mother. There is the purely physical relation between a child and a woman who gives birth to it or the man who begets it. The same relation exists between a colt and its dam and sire. But the colt does not have a father and a mother. For there is the social (and legal) relation between parents and children which is something other than the physical relation. In this sense an illegitimate child in England is a child without

[1] *J. Roy. Anthrop. Inst.* lxxi, 1942, p. 96.

a father. In the African tribes with which we are dealing it is the social and legal relationship that is connoted by the words which we have to translate 'father' and 'mother'. To call the father's sister 'female father' indicates that a woman stands in a social relation to her brother's son that is similar in some significant way to that of a father with his son. It is more exact, however, to say that a father's sister is regarded as a relative of the same kind as a father's brother, with such necessary qualifications as result from the difference of sex.

The principle of social structure with which we are here concerned is therefore one by which the solidarity and unity of the family (elementary or compound) is utilized to order and define a more extended system of relationships. A relationship to a particular person becomes a relation to that person's sibling group as a social unit. This shows itself in two ways. First, in some similarity in behaviour, as when the kind of behaviour that is required towards a father's brother is in some respects similar to that towards a father. Second, in the provision that in certain circumstances one relative may take the place of another, the two being siblings. Thus in some African societies the place of a father, a husband, or a grandfather may be taken by his brother. In the custom known as the sororate the place of a deceased wife is taken by her sister. In one form of the levirate the brother of a deceased man becomes the husband of the widow and the father of her children. Amongst the Hehe the grandmother plays an important part in the life of a child. This should be the child's own grandmother, but if she is dead her sister can take her place.[1]

Miss Earthy[2] says that amongst the Lenge the father's sister (*hahane*, female father) 'ranks as a feminine counterpart of the father, and sometimes acts as such, in conjunction with or in the absence of the father's brothers'. She may offer a sacrifice on behalf of her brother's child, in case of illness, in order that the child may recover. Such sacrifice would, of course, normally be made by the father or his elder brother.

The purpose of this section has only been to indicate the existence of a structural principle which is of great importance in a very large number of kinship systems not only in Africa but also in many other parts of the world. Where the principle influences the terminology of kinship it may appear in the form of a classificatory terminology. But the absence of such a terminology does not mean that the principle of the unity of the sibling group is not effectively present in the social structure and in the organization of norms of behaviour. The classificatory terminology in its most characteristic form is the utilization of the

[1] Elizabeth Fisher Brown, 'Hehe Grandmothers', *J. Roy. Anthrop. Inst.* lxv, 1935, pp. 83–96.
[2] E. Dora Earthy, 'The Role of the Father's Sister among the Valenge of Gazaland', *South African Journal of Science*, xxii, 1925, pp. 526–9. Also in *Valenge Women*, 1933, pp. 14 et seq.

principle of the unity of the sibling group to provide a means for ordering relatives in a system of wide-range recognition of relationships.

V

Within·the elementary family there is a division of generations; the parents form one generation, the children another. As a result, all the kin of a given person fall into generations in relation to him, and there are certain general principles that can be discovered in his different behaviour towards persons of different generations.

The normal relation between parents and children can be described as one of superordination and subordination. This results from the fact that children, at least during the early part of life, are dependent on their parents, who provide and care for them and exercise control and authority over them. Any relationship of subordination, if it is to work, requires that the person in the subordinate position should maintain an attitude of respect towards the other. The rule that children should not only love but should honour and obey their parents is, if not universal, at least very general in human societies.

There is therefore a relation of social inequality between proximate generations, and this is commonly generalized so that a person is subordinate and owes respect to his relatives of the first ascending generation —that of his parents. To this rule there may be specific exceptions, for the mother's brother in some African societies, for example, or for the father's sister's husband in some societies in other parts of the world, whereby these relatives may be treated disrespectfully or with privileged familiarity. Such exceptions call for explanation.

The relation between the two generations is usually generalized to extend beyond the range of kinship. Some measure of respect for persons of the generation or age of one's parents is required in most if not all societies. In some East African societies this relation is part of the organization of the society into age-sets. Thus among the Masai sexual intercourse with the wife of a man belonging to one's father's age-set is regarded as a very serious offence amounting to something resembling incest. Inversely, so is sexual connexion with the daughter of a man of one's own age-set.

The social function of this relation between persons of two proximate generations is easily seen. An essential of an orderly social life is some considerable measure of conformity to established usage, and conformity can only be maintained if the rules have some sort and measure of authority behind them. The continuity of the social order depends upon the passing on of tradition, of knowledge and skill, of manners and morals, religion and taste, from one generation to the next. In simple societies the largest share in the control and education of the young falls to the parents and other relatives of the parents' generation. It is their authority that is or ought to be effective. All this is obvious, and it is unnecessary to dwell upon it.

But the further effects of this in the organization of the relations of generations are not always so immediately obvious. We shall be concerned in what follows with the relations between persons and their relatives of the second ascending generation, that of their grandparents.

If the exercise of authority on the one side and respect and obedience on the other were simply, or even primarily, a matter of relative age, we should expect to find these features markedly characteristic of the relations between grandparents and grandchildren. Actually we find most commonly something almost the opposite of this, a relation of friendly familiarity and almost of social equality.

In Africa generally there is a marked condition of restraint on the behaviour of children in the presence of their parents. They must not indulge in levity or speak of matters connected with sex. There is very much less restraint on the behaviour of grandchildren in the presence of their grandparents. In general also, in Africa as elsewhere, grandparents are much more indulgent towards their grandchildren than are parents to their children. A child who feels that he is being treated with severity by his father may appeal to his father's father. The grandparents are the persons above all others who can interfere in the relations between parents and children. The possibility of this interference has important social functions. Elizabeth Brown remarks that 'in Hehe society the presence of the grandmother minimizes possible friction between mother and daughter'.[1] In any relation of subordination and superordination conflict is always possible. This is true of the relation of fathers and sons and of mothers and daughters in a great many societies. The son is subordinate to his father, but the latter is subordinate to his father in turn, and similarly with a mother and mother's mother. Control of the behaviour of parents towards their children therefore falls in the first place to their parents. In South Africa a man who is appealing to his ancestors for help, as when he is offering them a sacrifice, frequently, perhaps usually, makes his first appeal to his deceased father's father, and asks him to pass on the request to the spirit of his father and to the other ancestors.

In the passage of persons through the social structure which they enter by birth and leave by death, and in which they occupy successive positions, it is not, properly speaking, children who replace their parents, but those of the grandparents' generation are replaced by those of the grandchildren's generation. As those of the younger generation are moving into their positions of social maturity those of the older generation are passing out of the most active social life. This relation of the two generations is recognized in some African peoples. In East Africa, where age-sets are arranged in cycles, the cycles are such that a son's son may

_____
[1] Elizabeth Fisher Brown, op. cit.

frequently belong to the same one as his father's father. This explains also some of the African customs as to the relation of a child to its great-grandparent. Rattray reports for the Ashanti that a great-grandchild is called 'grandchild don't touch my ear', and the touch on the ear of such a relative is said to cause speedy death. Remembering the way in which small infants frequently reach for the ear of anyone close to them, this is a way of indicating the existence of a social distance between men and the children of their grandchildren. In the normal organization of generations there is no place for any close definite relation between these two relatives. For any man the birth of children to his grandchildren is the sign that he is approaching the end of his life.

The relation between grandparents and grandchildren that has here been briefly indicated is institutionalized in various ways in African and other societies. There is a widespread custom of privileged familiarity between grandchildren and grandparents. The grandchild may tease his relative and joke at his expense. This custom of permitted disrespect to grandparents is found in tribes of Australia and North America as well as in many African peoples. A good example is one from the Oraons of India reported by Sarat Chandra Roy.[1]

The replacement of grandparents by their grandchildren is in a way recognized in the widespread custom of giving a child the name of a grandparent. Amongst the Henga, when a child is born the husband is greeted with the words 'A father has been born to you to-day', having reference to the fact that the child will be given the name of its grandfather. A further step is taken in some peoples by the formation of a belief that in some sense the grandparent is 'reincarnated' in a grandchild.

One aspect of the structural principle with which we are here concerned is that one generation is replaced in course of time by the generation of their grandchildren. Another aspect of the same principle is that the two generations are regarded as being in a relation, not of superordination and subordination, but of simple friendliness and solidarity and something approaching social equality. This may sometimes result in what may be called the merging of alternate generations, a structural principle of fundamental importance in the native tribes of Australia and in some Melanesian peoples. A man with his 'father's fathers', his 'son's sons', and his 'brothers' in the classificatory sense form a social division over against his 'fathers' and 'sons', who constitute another division.

Where the principle makes itself apparent in some African peoples is in a peculiar feature of the kinship terminology, whereby the term that primarily means 'wife' is applied by a man to his granddaughters or his grandmothers, and a woman applies to her grandson the term meaning 'husband'. The custom has been reported for the Ganda, the

[1] Sarat Chandra Roy, *The Oraons of Chota Nagpur*, Ranchi, 1915, pp. 352-5.

Pende, the Ila, the Yao, the Ngonde, and the Henga. Thus amongst the Ngonde the term *nkasi* which is applied to the wife and to the brother's wife is also applied to all a man's 'granddaughters' in the classificatory sense (but not to the 'granddaughters' of his wife) and to the wives of his 'grandsons', own and classificatory. Inversely it is applied to the wives of the men who are called 'grandfather'. The real significance of this is that these women are thus merged with those of his own generation. That this is the real meaning of the custom may be seen by reference to the term *mwinangu* which Sanderson translates 'compeer' and which is applied primarily to persons of one's own generation and implies equality. 'For a grandson *mwisukulu-mwinangu* is always used in preference to *mwisukulu* by itself, and indicates that a grandson is treated as a "brother", a younger "brother" but an equal.' Similarly the term *wamyitu*, meaning 'kinsman', is used for relatives of one's own generation, and may also be used for any relative or connexion except the generation immediately above or below that of the speaker (e.g. father or son) as it implies a degree of intimacy not permitted with those degrees.[1]

The use of a term meaning 'wife' for a granddaughter must not be assumed to imply the existence of a custom of marriage with a granddaughter either in the present or in the past. Amongst the Ngonde and Henga such marriages are not permitted. But once the granddaughters and grandmothers have been included in one's own generation by this merging of alternate generations, the possibility of marriage suggests itself. There are therefore African tribes in which such marriages are regarded as permissible. It is said to be legal, though rare, amongst the Yao for a man to marry the daughter of his own child (Sanderson). Amongst the Kaonde a man may marry the daughter of his brother's son or of his brother's daughter, but may not marry the daughter of his sister's daughter (Melland). In the reverse direction, in the Ngonde tribe a man may be required to marry a 'grandmother' on the death of his 'grandfather', apparently in order to provide for her if she would otherwise be destitute.

There is therefore discoverable in African societies, as in many other societies in various parts of the world, a social structure based on relations of generation. Between two proximate generations the relation is normally one of essential inequality, authority, and protective care on the one side, respect and dependence on the other. But between the two generations of grandparents and grandchildren the relation is a contrasting one of friendly familiarity and near equality. The contrast between the two kinds of relation is itself an important part of the structural system and is emphasized in some of the accompanying institutions; for example, the contrast between restraint in the presence

[1] Meredith Sanderson, 'The Relationship Systems of the Wangonde and Wahenga Tribes, Nyasaland', *J. Roy. Anthrop. Inst.* liii, 1923, pp. 448–59.

of a father or his brother and the freedom of joking with a grandfather. The way in which this structural principle provides for a condition of equilibrium in social relations is one deserving of careful investigation. There is not room to deal with it here.

In most African kinship terminologies no distinction is made between grandparents on the father's side and those on the mother's side. We have seen that even in a system such as that of the Masai, where there is great emphasis on the distinction between agnatic and other cognatic relatives, this distinction is not made in the second ascending generation. This seems to be associated with a single general pattern of behaviour towards all those one calls 'grandfather' or 'grandmother', which does not, of course, exclude the existence of certain special relations, such as that of a man with his own father's father.

VI

In what might perhaps be called the normal use of the generation principle in kinship structure, the generations provide basic categories. Any category of relatives can be placed in one particular generation: uncles in the first ascending, nephews in the first descending, and so on. But in some terminologies a single term may be used for relatives of two or more generations. A study of instances of this serves to throw light on the principles involved in the various methods of ordering relationships.

In order to deal with this subject we have to consider the question of interpersonal rank or status in relationships. In a social relation two persons may meet as equal or approximately equal in rank, or one may be of superior rank to the other. Differences in rank may show themselves in many different forms. They are perhaps most easily seen in the rules of etiquette, or in an attitude of deference that the inferior is expected to show to his superior.

There may be inequality of rank within one generation. There are systems in Oceania and Africa in which a father's sister's son is superior in rank to his mother's brother's son. In a great number of systems an older brother, or a classificatory 'senior brother', is superior in rank to his junior. The difference in rank may be more emphasized in some systems than in others.

There seems to be universally some more or less marked inequality of rank between certain relatives belonging to two proximal generations, as between father and son, and there is some evidence of the existence of a tendency to extend this to all relationships between two such generations, the person who is senior by generation being superior to the one who is junior. But, as we shall see, this general tendency is sometimes overborne. We have already seen that between the alternate generations (of grandparents and grandchildren) there is a widespread tendency to make the relationship one of approximate equality.

A relationship of unequal rank is necessarily asymmetrical. A symmetrical relationship is one in which each of the two persons observes the same, or approximately the same, pattern of behaviour towards the other. In an asymmetrical relationship there is one way of behaviour for one of the persons and a different, complementary behaviour for the other; as when a father exercises authority over a son, and the son is deferential and obedient. Terminology can also be symmetrical or asymmetrical. In the former case each applies the same term of relationship to the other; in the latter there are two different, reciprocal terms, as uncle—nephew. Where terminology in a relationship is symmetrical it is frequently an indication that the relationship is thought of as being approximately symmetrical in respect of behaviour.

We sometimes find terms of relationship that have no generation reference. An example is provided by the Masai term *sotwa*, which may be applied to relatives of any generation. It refers to persons who are 'relatives' in a general sense but do not belong to any one of the specific categories into which nearer relatives are divided. It corresponds to some extent to the Old English term 'sib', and it is interesting that both these terms have reference to 'peace'; sib or *sotwa* are those with whom one should live at peace.

The English 'cousin' can be used for kin of different generations, and generation position has to be indicated by terms such as 'once removed'. The word is derived from the Latin *consobrinus* (mother's sister's son), and therefore originally had a generation reference to one's own generation, but in the Middle Ages it seems to have been regarded as equivalent to the Latin *consanguineus*.

The frequently observed absence of marked inequality between grandparents and grandchildren may be occasionally reflected in the terminology, either by the use of a single self-reciprocal term between these relatives or by applying to grandparents and to grandchildren a term that is normally used for relatives of one's own generation. This has been noted in the last section.

An interesting example of a system in which terms having a primary reference to one generation are applied to relatives of other generations is provided by the Nandi of East Africa. The term *kamet* refers in the first instance to the mother and her sisters (first ascending generation). But the mother's brother's daughter is also called *kamet* and is addressed by the same term of address as the mother. Correspondingly the term *imamet* refers primarily to the mother's brother, but is also applied to the mother's brother's son. Further, the children of the mother's brother's son, who belong to the first descending generation, are also called 'mother's brother' and 'mother'.

The same feature appears amongst the Bari and the Kitara. In the former a single term (*mananye*) is used for the mother's brother, his children, and his son's children, and we may note that the wife of any male *mananye* is called 'grandmother' (*yakanye*). Amongst the Kitara the mother's brother and his son are both called 'male mother' (*nyina rumi*) and the mother's brother's daughter is called 'little mother' (*nyina ento*) like the mother's sister. Reciprocally a man calls both his sister's son and his father's sister's son by the same term *mwhiwha*. There is a partial application of the same principle amongst the Masai, where the mother's brother is *ol-apu* and his children and his son's children are *ol-le-'ng-apu* and *en-e-'ng-apu*.

This peculiar type of terminology has been found in a number of societies in different parts of the world, and is called by anthropologists the Omaha type. Its widespread occurrence shows that it cannot be regarded as the product of some accident of history; we should seek some theoretical explanation. It can be regarded as a method of expressing and emphasizing the unity and solidarity of the patrilineal lineage group. A man belongs to a patrilineal lineage. He is closely connected with his mother's lineage, which plays an important part in his life, second only to that of his own. His connexion with that lineage, being through his own mother, is with the first ascending generation. By the terminology he treats all the members of that group, through three (or more) generations, beginning with that of his mother, as belonging to a single category; the females are 'mothers' to him and the males are 'mother's brothers'. For all these persons, and for the group as a whole, he is a 'sister's son'. Thus in its relation to this person the lineage of three generations is a unity; we can therefore speak of the structural principle that is applied in these systems as the principle of the unity of the lineage.

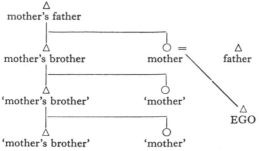

In systems of the Omaha type the principle is applied not only to the mother's lineage but also to other lineages with which a person is closely connected by some individual relationship. Amongst the Masai, for example, all the members of the lineage of a man's wife, beginning with his wife's father's father, are his *aputani*.

In a previous section the classificatory terminology in general was interpreted as a way of recognizing the principle of the unity of the sibling group. The special Omaha form of the classificatory system is

D

here interpreted as a way of recognizing the unity of the lineage group. Thus a single method of interpretation is applied throughout, and this gives a simplification or economy of theory. If the whole question were merely one of the use of terms of relationship the subject would not be of any importance; but it is here held that the terminology is used as a means of ordering relationships for social purposes, and of this there is already abundant evidence.[1]

For the purpose of the analysis that is to follow we must note here that in some of the tribes of this region of Africa there is a single self-reciprocal term for mother's brother and sister's son. In Masai this term is *ol-apu*. In Nandi the two relatives may each address the other as *mama*. This symmetrical terminology suggests that the social relation may also by symmetrical, i.e. that there is a single pattern of behaviour towards an *ol-apu* or a male *mama* whether he is a mother's brother or a sister's son. The accounts we have of these tribes do not permit the assertion that this is really so, though there is some slight indication in Hollis that it may be so for the Nandi.

The use of a symmetrical (self-reciprocal) terminology between mother's brother and sister's son is also found in some of the tribes of the Nuba Hills in Kordofan, namely, Heiban, Otoro, Tira, Mesakin, Koalib, and Nyima. All these tribes also use a self-reciprocal terminology for the relationship of wife's father and daughter's son, as do the Masai. Also, the first four of the Nuba tribes mentioned above use a self-reciprocal terminology between grandparent and grandchild. The use of self-reciprocal terms for these relationships puts relatives of different generations into one terminological category.

There is a special variety of the Omaha type of terminology found in the Shona, Ndau, and Shangana-Tonga peoples of Southern Rhodesia and Portuguese East Africa.[2] The most southerly tribe of the Shangana-Tonga group is the Ronga; according to Junod this tribe uses the common Southern Bantu term *malume* (literally 'male mother') for the mother's brother and his son, the reciprocal being *mupsyana*, which thus applies to the sister's child and the father's sister's child; the mother's brother's daughter is called *mamana* ('mother'). Thus the Ronga terminology is similar to that of the Kitara.

The other tribes of this cluster have a different system involving an extended use of the term for grandfather. The mother's brother is called

---

[1] For an exposition of the theory see A. R. Radcliffe-Brown, 'The Study of Kinship Systems', *J. Roy. Anthrop. Inst.* lxxi, 1941, pp. 1–18.

[2] For the Shangana-Tonga tribes see Henri Junod, *The Life of a South African Tribe*, 1913, and E. Dora Earthy, *Valenge Women*, 1935. For the Ndau, Franz Boas, 'Das Verwandtschaftsystem der Vandau', *Zeitschrift für Ethnologie*, 1923, pp. 41–51. For the Shona, B. H. Barnes, 'Relationships in Mashonaland', *Man*, xxi, 1931, p. 210. Mr. J. F. Holleman has kindly permitted me to see the manuscript of his very thorough analysis of the system of the Hera tribe of Mashonaland.

'grandfather'—*sekuru* in Shona, *tetekulu* in Ndau, *kokwana* in Lenge and other tribes of the Shangana-Tonga group; both the Shona and the Ndau terms are derived from a stem meaning 'father' and *kulu* or *kuru* meaning 'great'. The sons and son's sons of the mother's brother are also called 'grandfather'. The reciprocal of 'grandfather' is, of course, 'grandchild'—*muzukuru* in Shona, *muzukulu* in Ndau, *ntukulu* in Shangana-Tonga. This term, which is used by a man for the children of his son or daughter, is thus also applied to his father's sister's child and his sister's child, both of whom call him 'grandfather'. A man thus may have 'grandchildren' who are older than himself and 'grandfathers' who are younger.

In these tribes, as in the Ronga, the daughter and the son's daughter of the mother's brother are called 'mother'—*mayi* or *mayi nini* (little mother) in Shona, *mai* in Ndau, *manana* in Shangana-Tonga. The children of these women are therefore called 'siblings' (*makwabu* or *makweru* in Shangana-Tonga).

This terminology expresses the unity of the mother's lineage. All the female members of a man's mother's lineage in her own and succeeding generations are his 'mothers'. All the men of the lineage through several generations fall into a single category, but instead of being called 'mother's brother' they are called 'grandfather'. The male members of the lineage are placed in a category that refers primarily to the second ascending generation, while the females are placed in one that refers primarily to the first ascending generation.

The principle of lineage unity is recognized in these tribes in other features of the terminology. Thus in the Shona tribes a man calls all the men and women of all generations of the lineages of his father's mother and his mother's mother 'grandfather' and 'grandmother', and they all call him 'grandchild'. In each of these lineages his individual genealogical relation is with a grandmother, so the whole lineage as a unity becomes a collection of 'grandfathers' and 'grandmothers'. When a man marries, all the women of his wife's lineage are his 'wife's sisters'; the term in the Hera tribe is *muramu*, and Holleman translates this as 'potential or even preferential wife or husband', the term being a self-reciprocal one. The term for wife's father is *mukarabghwa* or *mukarahwe*, reciprocal *mukwasha*; all the male members of the wife's lineage through all generations are called 'father-in-law'. There is inequality of rank between father-in-law and son-in-law, the former having the position of superiority, and this applies apparently to all relationships in which these terms are used. These systems of terminology are clearly based on the principle of the unity of the lineage. But that does not explain why the mother's brother is called 'grandfather'. To understand that we must refer to certain features of the social relationship between mother's brother and sister's son in these tribes.

In the type of kinship system with which we are now dealing a person is under the authority and control of his agnatic kin, his father and father's brothers and the male, and sometimes the female, members of his own agnatic lineage. It is with this group and its members that a person has his most important jural relationships, i.e. relationships defined by duties and rights. The mother does not belong to this group, though she is attached to it by marriage and is to some extent herself under its control, particularly under the control of her husband. A father, however affectionate he may be to his son, is a person to be respected and obeyed, and so are his brothers and, in most of the systems of this type, his sisters. The mother, though she must, of course, exercise some discipline over her young children, is primarily the person who gives affectionate care. Just as the relation to the father is extended to his sibling group, so the relation to the mother is extended to hers. The mother's sisters are also 'mothers' and the mother's brothers are 'male mothers'. The mother's brother is not a person to exercise authority over his sister's son; that right is reserved to his 'fathers'. It is the mother's brother's part to show affectionate interest in his nephew and give him aid when he needs it. In the family of his mother's brother a man is a specially privileged person.

To establish and maintain a fixed pattern of behaviour for a particular type of relationship it is useful, and in some instances necessary, to adopt some conventionalized symbolic mode of behaviour which expresses in some way the character of the relationship. In the type of kinship system we are here considering the kind of relationship that is appropriate for a sister's son is symbolically expressed in certain definite customs of privileged familiarity exercised by the nephew. He may, for example, be permitted, or indeed expected, to joke at his uncle's expense, as in the Winnebago and other tribes of North America. He may be permitted to take his uncle's property, as in the *vasu* custom of Fiji and Tonga and as described for South Africa by Junod.[1]

This relation of privileged behaviour may be extended from the mother's brothers to the whole of her lineage, though it will be primarily exercised towards the own mother's brother. The extension sometimes takes in the dead members of the lineage, the ancestral spirits. In South-east Africa a man's own ancestors of his own lineage are believed to watch his conduct and punish him for any breach of duty. His mother's ancestors have no business to exercise authority over him in this way; on the contrary he may go to them for help, not approaching them directly, but through his mother's brother or mother's brother's son, who can sacrifice to his own ancestors to obtain their help for his nephew or cousin. Junod gives an account of how the sister's sons and daughter's sons of a dead man symbolically express their relation at the final funeral

[1] See A. R. Radcliffe-Brown, 'The Mother's Brother in South Africa', *South African Journal of Science*, xxi, 1924, pp. 542–55, in which this analysis was first offered.

ceremony, interrupting the prayers and grabbing and running away with the sacrificial offering, which they then eat.

There is an East African custom which has, I think, been misinterpreted. This is the custom of the mother's brother's curse. It is said that a man fears the curse of his mother's brother more than that of any other relative. This is sometimes interpreted as though it means that the mother's brother regularly exercises authority over his nephew and that his authority is greater than that even of a father. I suggest that the proper interpretation is that the mother's brother will be the last person to use his power of cursing and will only do so in exceptional and serious situations, and that it is for this reason that it is feared more than the curse of the father. A matter that ought to be inquired into is whether, where the relationship appears to be symmetrical, as in the Nandi, the uncle may also be cursed by his sister's son.

In these systems the behaviour towards a mother's brother is in marked contrast to that towards a father. A man's relation to his mother's relatives is as important as that to his father's kin, but of a different and contrasting kind. In the matter of interpersonal rank the father is very definitely superior to his son. But the mother's brother is not, or not markedly, superior to his nephew. The relationship may be treated as one of approximate equality, or the nephew may even be treated as superior. Thus in Tonga and Fiji the sister's son is quite definitely superior in rank to his mother's brother and to his mother's brother's son. In Tonga the term *eiki* (chief) is used to indicate a person of superior rank, and a sister's son is said to be *eiki* to his mother's brother. Similarly, Junod reports from the Ronga that a nephew is described as being a 'chief' to his mother's brother.

If there is, indeed, as there seems to be, a general tendency to attribute superior rank in interpersonal relations to relatives of the parents' generation, the special relation to the mother's brother that exists in these societies is directly contrary to it. The 'normal' rank relation of proximal generations, if we may venture to call it so, is destroyed in the relation to a mother's brother. There are two ways in which this may be reflected in the terminology. One is the use of a self-reciprocal term between mother's brother and sister's son, as in the Masai and Nandi and some Nuba tribes, whereby the relationship is treated as one that is symmetrical and therefore of approximate equality. Another is to place the mother's brother in the second ascending generation (by a sort of fiction) and call him 'grandfather'. We have already seen that there is a widespread tendency to make the relation between the grandparent generation and the grandchild generation one in which there is an absence of marked inequality of rank and one in which the junior generation is privileged in its behaviour towards the senior. This does not prevent the recognition of some measure of superiority for some relatives of the second ascending generation, for example, the father's father and his sister in some patrilineal systems. The inclusion of the mother's brother in the category of 'grandfathers' removes him from that generation-category to which there is a tendency to attach superiority of interpersonal rank and places him, by a fiction, in one towards which the relation is one of easy familiarity, approximate equality, or privilege.

In the system of the Shona–Ndau–Tonga cluster of tribes, therefore, we have first of all the application of the principle of unity of the lineage. For any person his mother's lineage is a single united group. The women of the lineage, who are mostly dispersed amongst the families into which they have married, are all relatives of one kind, his 'mothers'. Amongst the men of the group his closest connexion is with his mother's father and brother and his mother's brother's son. With them he stands in a specially privileged position; they are expected to show him affectionate indulgence. They and all the other males of the lineage constitute a single unity of which the representative individual is the mother's father; they are all 'grandfathers' and he is for them a 'grandchild'. For the lineage as a unity the women born into it are its children, but their children are not. In Africa the term 'child of our child' is sometimes used for the child of a woman of the family, a sister's or daughter's child. So for the lineage treated as a unity the children borne by its female members into other lineages are 'children of our children'—grandchildren.

It may be noted, for the purpose of comparison, that our English word 'uncle' is derived from the Latin *avunculus*, which was the term for mother's brother but not for father's brother, and which is literally 'little grandfather', from *avus*. Moreover, the philologists believe that the Old English term for mother's brother, *eme* or *eam*, was originally a modification of the word for grandfather.

One purpose of this section has been to show how the division of kin into generations can be used as a means of formalizing relations of interpersonal rank. One further example may be added by referring to the arrangement of nominal generations in the Nkundo of the Belgian Congo. Although Father Hulstaert's statements are not very clear, it would seem that the important social group, which he speaks of as a clan or exogamous group, is a patrilineal lineage of seven generations or so. The brothers and sisters of the father and members of the lineage of that generation are all 'fathers' (*baise*). The children of a female 'father' (father's sister) are also 'fathers' male and female, and therefore the children of a mother's brother (male mother—*nyangompane*) are 'children' (*bana*). There is thus established a difference of rank between cross-cousins, the father's sister's children ranking above their mother's brother's children in a way similar to that in which a father ranks above his child. That this is a matter not merely of terminology but also of behaviour is evident from Father Hulstaert's account. Consistently with this a man treats the children of his father's sister's son (who is 'father'

to him) as 'brothers' and 'sisters'. A diagram may help to make the
matter clear.

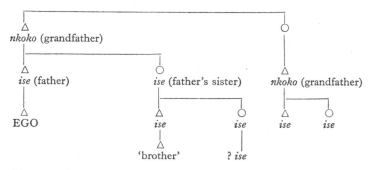

Since my father calls his father's sister's children 'fathers' I call them
'grandparents', and I call the children of my father's father's sister's
son 'fathers' male and female. Father Hulstaert does not tell us the relation of a man to the children of his father's sister's daughter (who is
his female 'father'). It seems very probable that they also are male
and female 'fathers'. If this be so, then for any person there is a series
of female lines each stemming from his own lineage; the descendants
through females of a father's sister or a father's father's sister are
'fathers' to him and rank above him, he being 'child' to them. For our
present purpose the Nkundo system affords another example of the use
of terms having a generation reference to establish relations of rank,
together with the use of such terms to establish categories containing
relatives of different real generations. Relatives of one's own generation
are given superior rank by being called 'father'.

VII

Every kinship system provides each person in a society with a set of
dyadic (person to person) relationships, so that he stands, as it were, at
the centre of a narrower or wider circle of relatives. During his life the
body of his relatives is constantly changing by deaths and births and by
marriages—his own marriage and the marriages of his relatives.

In many societies the kinship system also includes a different kind of
structure by which the whole society is divided into a number of separate
groups, each consisting of a body of persons who are or who regard themselves as being a unilineal body of kindred. Such kinship groups are
moieties, clans, and lineages. Moieties, by which the society is bisected,
do not exist in Africa except amongst the Galla, though they are important in some parts of the world. The distinction between clan and lineage
is that in a lineage group each member can actually, or at least theoretically, trace his genealogical connexion with any other member by
descent from a known common ancestor, whereas in a clan, which is

usually a larger body, this is not possible. A moiety may be divided into clans and usually is so. Clans may be divided into sub-clans, and clans or sub-clans may be divided into lineages. A lineage of any considerable size is usually divided into branches, which are themselves smaller lineages, and these again may be subdivided. For structures having successive segmentations the term 'polysegmentary' has been suggested. Such systems have been excellently described by Evans-Pritchard for the Nuer, and by Fortes for the Tallensi.

It is usual to apply the term 'clan' to both patrilineal and matrilineal groups, but some American ethnographers use the term 'clan' only for matrilineal groups and 'gens' for patrilineal, and Dr. Nadel has adopted this usage in describing in this volume the two sets of groups of the Nyaro. Some writers in the volume have made use of compounds— patri-clan, matri-clan, patri-lineage, and matri-lineage. If these seem to some readers somewhat barbarous it must be remembered that some technical terms are needed for concise description, and have to be invented.

The term 'clan' has often been used without any clear definition. There are, of course, many different kinds of clan systems, but the term should be used only for a group having unilineal descent in which all the members regard one another as in some specific sense kinsfolk. One way of giving recognition to the kinship is by the extensive use of the classificatory terminology, so that in a system of patrilineal clans a man regards all the men of his clan as being his classificatory 'fathers', 'brothers', 'sons', 'grandfathers', or 'grandsons'. Frequently, but not universally, the recognition of the kinship bond uniting the members of the clan takes the form of a rule of exogamy which forbids marriage between two members of the same clan. Where clans are divided into sub-clans it may be only to the smaller group that the rule of exogamy applies.

Membership of a clan is normally determined by birth: where clans are matrilineal the children of a woman belong to her clan; where they are patrilineal the children belong to the father's clan. But in some tribes there is a custom of adoption. Where a man is adopted into a patrilineal clan, thereby abandoning his membership of the clan into which he was born, his children belong to the clan of his adoption, not that of his birth. In some African tribes the position of a child in the social structure depends on the source of the marriage payment for his mother. Thus, among the Lango children belong to the clan that has provided the cattle for the marriage payment for their mother. The father might not be a clansman, but might be a war captive or the sister's son of a clansman who was provided with a wife through cattle belonging to the clan, or the children might have been born outside marriage and the mother later married into the clan.[1]

[1] T. T. S. Hayley, *The Anatomy of Lango Religion and Groups*, 1947, p. 40.

If we look at a structure of clans or lineages from the point of view of an individual it appears as a grouping of his relatives. In a patrilineal system the members of his own clan are his agnatic kinsfolk, and the nearest of these to him are the members of his own lineage. The members of his mother's clan or lineage are also his kin, through his mother. He may apply to them the appropriate classificatory terms, and in some systems he may be forbidden to marry any woman of his mother's patrilineal clan. The members of his father's mother's clan and his mother's mother's clan may also be recognized as relatives, and those of his wife's clan or lineage may all have to be treated as relatives by marriage.

A clan system, however, also provides a division of the tribe into a number of distinct separate groups, each having its own identity. The clans may then, as groups, play an important part in the social, political, or religious life of the tribe. The extent to which they do this depends on the degree to which they are corporate groups. A group may be spoken of as 'corporate' when it possesses any one of a certain number of characters: if its members, or its adult male members, or a considerable proportion of them, come together occasionally to carry out some collective action—for example, the performance of rites; if it has a chief or council who are regarded as acting as the representatives of the group as a whole; if it possesses or controls property which is collective, as when a clan or lineage is a land-owning group. In parts of Africa it is very common to find that land is held or owned by lineage groups, which are thus corporate groups.

An example of a society in which there are both patrilineal and matrilineal corporate kin groups is provided by the Yakö, described in this volume by Professor Daryll Forde. There are corporate patrilineal lineages (*yeponema*) each having a leader and collectively owning landed property. There are also corporate patrilineal clans (*yepun*), each containing several lineages, and the ideal arrangement is one by which the clan has a ritual head, a shrine for clan rites, and a meeting-house for the men. The Yakö have, in addition, a system of matrilineal clans (*yejima*) divided into lineages, and these also are corporate groups uniting for clan rituals. The patrilineal clans are 'compact', i.e. the male members with their families live together in one delimited area; whereas the matrilineal clans are 'dispersed', the various members being scattered through the village settlement and living in the different areas of the patrilineal clans.

It should be noted that as a rule it is the adult men who really constitute the corporate kin group, and this is so for those systems that have descent through females. A good example is provided by the tribes of the lower Congo, described by Dr. Richards in this volume. Villages or hamlets are formed of matrilineal lineages; all the men of a single lineage live together with their wives and young children, boys when they reach a certain age leaving their parents to join their mother's brother and his village. It is therefore the men of the lineage who form the corporate group, holding rights over land and acting collectively in various ways.

Professor Gluckman regards the absence of corporate kin groups (clans or lineages) as an important distinguishing characteristic of a number of tribes of Central Africa. The typical corporate group in that region is a village constituted by the persons who attach themselves to a headman. This group is an open, not a closed group; that is, individuals or families may join or leave it, moving from one village to another. It is usual that a number of the inhabitants of a village at any time should be related, either by cognatic ties or through marriage with the headman or with one another, but they do not form a unilineal kin group, which is by its constitution a 'closed' group.

Some of these tribes have clans, patrilineal in some instances, matrilineal in others, but the clans are dispersed and not corporate. Thus the Ila and Bemba and other tribes have dispersed matrilineal clans. The members of one clan are scattered through the tribe; they do not ever come together to take any kind of collective action, and have no single authority (headman or clan council). They have no positive clan rites; the identity of the clan, and its unity as a separate group of kindred, is maintained by negative ritual observances common to all the members, such as refraining from killing or eating a certain animal (the 'totem' of the clan). A member of the clan does not know all the other members, but if two persons meet who know or discover that they belong to the same clan they are expected to behave towards one another as kinsfolk, and since all members are kin they may not intermarry. It does not seem that in these tribes matrilineal lineages are given social recognition except in royal families.

One of these Central African tribes, the Lozi, described in this volume,[1] does not recognize either clans or lineages. The system, though it shows a slight preference in some respects for kinship in the male line, is characteristically one of cognatic kinship, tracing relationship through males and females. Theoretically the range of recognized kinship extends to the descendants of a common great-great-grandparent, i.e. to third cousins.

The unilineal principle of reckoning relationship in one line (male or female) is utilized in a great variety of ways in different kinship systems. Where it is used to create a system of clans it facilitates that wide-range recognition of relations of kinship to which there is a tendency in many societies. A person will thereby find himself connected by specific social ties, subject to established institutional modes of behaviour, with a large number of other persons. In the absence or weak development of political structure this gives an effective system of social integration. It is not

[1] See below, pp. 166 ff.

possible to provide such very wide range in a system based on cognation, since that implies the tracing of genealogical relationships through all lines. But even more important is that unilineal reckoning makes it possible to create corporate kin groups having continuity in time extending beyond the life of an individual or a family. There are innumerable social activities that can only be efficiently carried out by means of corporate groups, so that where, as in so many non-literate societies, the chief source of social cohesion is the recognition of kinship, corporate kin groups tend to become the most important feature of social structure.

Thus it is the corporate kin group, whether clan, sub-clan, or lineage, that controls the use of land, whether for hunting, for pastoral life, or for cultivation; that exacts vengeance for the killing of a member, or demands and receives an indemnity. In the sphere of religion the kin group usually has its own cult, whether of its ancestors or connected with some sacred shrine. A continuing social structure requires the aggregation of individuals into distinct separated groups, each with its own solidarity, every person belonging to one group of any set. The obvious instance is the present division of the world into nations. In kinship systems cognatic kinship cannot provide this; it is only made possible by the use of the principle of unilineal descent. This is, indeed, obvious, but there have been writers who have used much misplaced ingenuity in trying to conjecture the origin of clans.

VIII

In order to understand the African customs relating to marriage we have to bear in mind that a marriage is essentially a rearrangement of social structure. What is meant by social structure is any arrangement of persons in institutionalized relationships. By a marriage certain existing relationships, particularly, in most societies, those of the bride to her family, are changed. New social relations are created, not only between the husband and the wife, and between the husband and the wife's relatives on the one side and between the wife and the husband's relatives on the other, but also, in a great many societies, between the relatives of the husband and those of the wife, who, on the two sides, are interested in the marriage and in the children that are expected to result from it. Marriages, like births, deaths, or initiations at puberty, are rearrangements of structure that are constantly recurring in any society; they are moments of the continuing social process regulated by custom; there are institutionalized ways of dealing with such events.

We tend, unless we are anthropologists, to judge other people's customs by reference to our own. To understand African marriage we must remember that the modern English idea of marriage is recent and decidedly unusual, the product of a particular social development. We think of a marriage as an event that concerns primarily the man and woman who are forming a union and the State, which gives that union

its legality and alone can dissolve it by divorce. The consent of parents
is, strictly, only required for minors. Religion still plays some part, but
a religious ceremony is not essential.

We may compare English marriage with the following account of
a 'wedding' in early England.[1]

'If people want to wed a maid or a wife and this is agreeable to her and
to her kinsmen, then it is right that the bridegroom should first swear
according to God's right and secular law and should wage (pledge himself)
to those who are her forspeakers, that he wishes to have her in such a way
as he should hold her by God's right as his wife—and his kinsmen will
stand pledge for him.

'Then it is to be settled to whom the price for upfostering her belongs,
and for this the kinsmen should pledge themselves.

'Then let the bridegroom declare what present he will make her for
granting his desire, and what he will give if she lives longer than he does.

'If it is settled in this way, then it is right that she should enjoy half the
property, and all if they have a child, unless she marries another man.

'All this the bridegroom must corroborate by giving a gage, and his
kinsmen stand to pledge for him.

'If they are agreed in all this, then let the kinsmen of the bride accept
and wed their kinswoman to wife and to right life to him who desires her,
and let him take the pledge who rules over the wedding.

'If she is taken out of the land into another lord's land, then it is advis-
able that her kinsmen get a promise that no violence will be done to her
and that if she has to pay a fine they ought to be next to help her to pay,
if she has not enough to pay herself.'

The marriage here is not any concern of the State or political authorities; it is a compact between two bodies of persons, the kin of the woman
who agree to wed their daughter to the man, and his kinsmen who
pledge themselves that the terms of the agreement will be carried out.
The bridegroom and his kinsmen must promise to make a payment (the
'marriage payment') to her father or other legal guardian. He must also
state what present he will give to his bride for permitting the physical
consummation of the marriage; this was the so-called 'morning-gift' to
be paid after the bridal night. There was further an agreement as to the
amount of the dowry, the portion of the husband's wealth of which the
wife should have the use during her lifetime if her husband died before
her. The agreement is concluded by the giving of the *wed*, the symbolic
payment made by the bridegroom and his kin to the woman's kinsmen.

In modern England the pledge or gage, in the form of a 'wedding'
ring, is given, not to the bride's kinsmen when the marriage arrange-

---

[1] Quoted by Vinogradoff, *Outlines of Historical Jurisprudence*, i, p. 252, from
Liebermann, *Gesetze der Angelsachsen*, i, p. 442. The 'wedding' was the agreement or contract entered into by the kinsfolk of bride and bridegroom, equivalent
to the Roman *sponsalia*, not the ceremony of handing over the bride (the Roman
traditio puellae).

ment is made, but to the bride herself at the wedding ceremony. The change in custom is highly significant. The 'giving away' of the bride is a survival of something which at one time was the most important feature of the ceremonial of marriage.

Thus in Anglo-Saxon England a marriage, the legal union of man and wife, was a compact entered into by two bodies of kin. As the Church steadily increased in power and in control of social life, marriage became the concern of the Church and was regulated by canon law. There was a new conception that in marriage the man and woman entered into a compact with God (or with His Church) that they would remain united till parted by death. The marriage was under the control of the Church; matrimonial cases were dealt with in the ecclesiastical courts.

At the end of the Middle Ages there came the struggle for power between Church and State in which the State was, in Protestant countries, victorious. Marriage then came under State control. At the present day to legalize a union of man and wife the marriage, whether there is or is not a religious ceremony, must be registered by someone licensed by the State and a fee must be paid. It is the State that decides on what conditions the marriage may be brought to an end by a divorce granted by a court which is an organ of the State.

A most important factor in the development of the modern English (and American) conception of marriage was the idea of romantic love, a theme that was elaborated in the nineteenth century in novel and drama and has now become the mainstay of the cinema industry. In its early development romantic love was conceived as not within but outside marriage, witness the troubadours and their courts of love and Dante and Petrarch. In the eighteenth century Adam Smith could write: 'Love, which was formerly a ridiculous passion, became more grave and respectable. As a proof of this it is worth our observation that no ancient tragedy turned on love, whereas it is now more respectable and influences all the public entertainments.' The idea that marriage should be a union based on romantic love leads logically to the view that if the husband and wife find they do not love one another they should be permitted to dissolve the marriage. This is the Hollywood practice, but conflicts with the control of marriage by the Church or by the State.

Another very important factor has been the change in the social and economic position of women during the nineteenth and twentieth centuries. A married woman may now hold property in her own right; she may take employment that has no connexion with her family life but takes her away from it. In the marriage ceremony many women now refuse to promise that they will obey their husbands.

Not only are marriage and ideas about marriage in England and America the product of a recent, special, and complex development, but there is good evidence that they are still changing. The demand for greater freedom of divorce is one indication of this. Yet it is clear that despite all this some people take twentieth-century English marriage as a standard of 'civilized' marriage with which to compare African marriage.

The African does not think of marriage as a union based on romantic love although beauty as well as character and health are sought in the choice of a wife. The strong affection that normally exists after some years of successful marriage is the product of the marriage itself conceived as a process, resulting from living together and co-operating in many activities and particularly in the rearing of children.

An African marriage is in certain respects similar to the early English marriage described above. The dowry or dower does not exist in Africa, though writers who do not know, or do not care about, the meanings of words use the term 'dowry' quite inappropriately to refer to the 'marriage payment'.[1] There is also in Africa nothing exactly corresponding to the English 'morning-gift' regarded as a payment for accepting sexual embraces, though it is usual for the bridegroom to give gifts to his bride. The two other features of the early English marriage are normally found in African marriages. Firstly, the marriage is not the concern of the political authorities but is established by a compact between two bodies of persons, the kin of the man and the kin of the woman. The marriage is an alliance between the two bodies of kin based on their common interest in the marriage itself and its continuance, and in the offspring of the union, who will be, of course, kin of both the two kin-groups. The understanding of the nature of this alliance is essential to any understanding of African kinship systems. Secondly, in Africa generally, as in early England, and in a great number of societies in ancient and modern times in all parts of the world, a marriage involves the making of a payment by the bridegroom or his kin to the father or guardian of the bride. Africans distinguish, as we do, between a 'legal' marriage and an irregular union. In modern England a marriage is legal if it is registered by a person licensed by the State. Only children born of such a union are legitimate. But in Africa the State or political authority is not concerned with a marriage. How, then, are we to distinguish a legal marriage? The answer is that a legal marriage, by which the children who will be born are given definite 'legitimate' status in the society, requires a series of transactions and formalities in which the two bodies of kin, those of the husband and those of the wife, are involved. In most African marriages, as in the early English marriage, the making of a payment of goods or services by the bridegroom to the bride's kin is an essential part of the establishment of 'legality'.

Some people regard payments of this kind as being a 'purchase' of a wife in the sense in which in England to-day a man may purchase

---

[1] Belgian and some French writers make a similar misuse of the term 'dot', which is a woman's marriage portion of which the annual income is under her husband's control.

a horse or a motor-car. In South Africa it was at one time held officially that a marriage by native custom with the payment of cattle (*lobola*) was 'an immoral transaction' and not a valid marriage. The Supreme Court of Kenya in 1917 decided that 'a so-called marriage by the native custom of wife-purchase is not a marriage'. The idea that an African buys a wife in the way that an English farmer buys cattle is the result of ignorance, which may once have been excusable but is so no longer, or of blind prejudice, which is never excusable in those responsible for governing an African people.

A marriage in many, perhaps most, African societies involves a whole series of prestations[1] (payments, gifts, or services), and while the most important of these are from the husband and his kin to the wife's kin, there are frequently, one might say usually, some in the other direction. One of the best accounts of the whole procedure is that given by Father Hulstaert for the Nkundo of the Belgian Congo.[2] The procedure begins with the presentation, on the part of the future husband, of the *ikula*, at one time an arrow, now two copper rings. The acceptance of this by the woman and her kin constitutes a formal betrothal. The marriage, i.e. the 'tradition' of the bride, may take place before any further payment. At the marriage, gifts are made to the bride by the parents of the bridegroom, by other of his relatives, and by the bridegroom himself. The next step is the formal prestation of the *ndanga*, formerly a knife, to the bride's father. It signifies that the husband thereafter becomes responsible for accidents that might befall his wife. In return there is a prestation from the bride's family to the husband and his family. This is part of the *nkomi*, the payment that is made to the bridegroom by the wife's family. The marriage is not fully established until the husband pays his father-in-law the *walo*, a substantial payment consisting chiefly of objects of metal. After this the woman becomes fully the man's wife. When the *walo* is handed over the woman's family make a return payment (*nkomi*) and give a present of food to the husband's family. The husband must also make a special payment to his wife's mother and must give a considerable number of presents to the father, mother, brothers, and other relatives of the bride. The relatives of the husband then demand and receive presents from the wife's family. The final payment to be made by the husband is the *bosongo*, formerly a slave, now a quantity of copper rings.

There is, of course, an immense diversity in the particulars of prestations connected with betrothal and marriage in different societies and in

[1] 'Prestation' is defined in the *Oxford Dictionary* as 'the act of paying, in money or service, what is due by law or custom'. The prestations with which we are here concerned are all those gifts and payments of goods or services which are required by custom in the process of establishing a valid marriage.

[2] R. P. G. Hulstaert, *Le Mariage des Nkundo*, Inst. roy. colon. belge, Mémoires, tome viii, 1938, chap. ii.

each case they have to be studied, with regard to their meanings and functions, in relation to the society in which they are found. For general theory, however, we have to look for general similarities. In the first place it is necessary to recognize that whatever economic importance some of these transactions may have, it is their symbolic aspect that we chiefly have to consider. This may be made clear by the English customs of the engagement ring, the wedding ring, and the wedding presents. Though an engagement ring may have considerable value (more than many Africans 'pay' for their wives), the giving of it is not regarded as an economic or at least not as a business transaction. It is symbolic.

In what follows the term 'marriage payment' will be used for the major payment or payments made by the bridegroom to the wife's kin. Where there is a payment from the wife's kin to the husband (as in the Nkundo) this will be called the 'counter-payment'. The rule in many African societies is that if there is a divorce the marriage payment and the counter-payment must be returned. There are qualifications of this; for example, in some tribes where on divorce there are children and they belong to the father the marriage payment may be not returnable, or returnable only in part. Also, there are tribes in Africa in which, instead of a payment in goods, the bridegroom must serve for his wife by working for her kin, just as Jacob served his mother's brother Laban seven years for each of the two sisters, Leah and Rachel, his cousins, whom he married (Genesis xxix). This service, the equivalent of the marriage payment or of part thereof, is of course not returnable if there is divorce.

Let us return to the early English marriage. In the formulary quoted above the marriage payment was called 'the price of upfostering' and was thus interpreted as a return to the father or guardian of the expense of rearing a daughter. But in somewhat earlier times the payment was differently interpreted. It was a payment for the transfer of the woman's *mund* from the father or guardian to the husband, whereby the latter gained and the former lost certain rights. The term for a legitimately married wife in Old Norse law was *mundi kjöbt*, meaning one whose *mund* has been purchased. In Sweden the transfer of *mund* was not by purchase but by gift, and the expression for marriage was *giftarmal*. In Roman law the marriage by *coemptio*, sometimes called 'marriage by purchase', was not the sale of a woman but the legal transfer of *manus* to her husband, and *mund* and *manus* are roughly equivalent terms. In these Roman and Teutonic marriages the important point is that to legalize the union of a man and a woman, so that it is really a marriage, legal power over his daughter must be surrendered by the father and acquired by the husband, whether the transfer be by gift or by payment. The early English marriage was of this type.

In Africa an unmarried woman is in a position of dependence. She lives under the control and authority of her kin, and it is they who afford her protection. Commonly, if she is killed or injured her guardian or her kinsfolk can claim an indemnity. At marriage she passes to a greater or less extent, which is often very considerable, under the control of her husband (and his kin), and it is he (and they) who undertake to afford her protection. (Note the *ndanga* payment amongst the Nkundo, by which the bridegroom accepts responsibility for accidents that may befall the bride.) The woman's kin, however, retain the right to protect her against ill treatment by her husband. If she is killed or injured by third parties it is now the husband and his kin who can claim an indemnity. It is this transfer of *mund*, to use the Old English term, that is the central feature of the marriage transaction.

To understand African marriage we must think of it not as an event or a condition but as a developing process. The first step is usually a formal betrothal, though this may have been preceded by a period of courtship or, in some instances in some regions, by an elopement. The betrothal is the contract or agreement between the two families. The marriage may proceed by stages, as in the instance of the Nkundo mentioned above. A most important stage in the development of the marriage is the birth of the first child. It is through the children that the husband and wife are united and the two families are also united by having descendants in common.

We may consider African marriage in three of its most important aspects. First, the marriage involves some modification or partial rupture of the relations between the bride and her immediate kin. This is least marked when the future husband comes to live with and work for his future parents-in-law while his betrothed is still a girl not old enough for marriage. It is most marked when, as in most African societies, the woman when she marries leaves her family and goes to live with her husband and his family. Her own family suffers a loss. It would be a gross error to think of this as an economic loss.[1] It is the loss of a person who has been a member of a group, a breach of the family solidarity. This aspect of marriage is very frequently given symbolic expression in the simulated hostility between the two bodies of kin at the marriage ceremony, or by the pretence of taking the bride by force (the so-called 'capture' of the bride). Either the bride herself or her kin, or both, are expected to make a show of resistance at her removal.

Customs of this kind are extremely widespread not only in Africa but all over the world, and the only explanation that fits the various instances is that they are the ritual or symbolic expression of the recognition that marriage entails the breaking of the solidarity that unites a woman to the family in which she has been born and grown up. Ethnographical literature affords innumerable instances. One example may be given

---

[1] This is the view of modern English law. If an unmarried woman is seduced her father can recover damages for the loss of her 'services'; as though the only value attached to a daughter is as a servant.

here. In Basutoland, or at least in some parts of it, on the day fixed for the marriage the young men of the bridegroom's group drive the cattle that are to constitute the marriage payment to the home of the bride. When they draw near, the women of the bride's party gather in front of the entrance to the cattle kraal. As the bridegroom's party try to drive the cattle into the kraal the women, with sticks and shouts, drive them away so that they scatter over the veld and have to be collected together again and a new attempt made to drive them into the kraal. This goes on for some time until at last the cattle are successfully driven into the kraal. The women of the group make a show of resistance at the delivery of the cattle which will have as its consequence the loss of the bride. The proper interpretation of these customs is that they are symbolic expressions of the recognition of the structural change that is brought about by the marriage.

When this aspect of marriage is considered the marriage payment can be regarded as an indemnity or compensation given by the bridegroom to the bride's kin for the loss of their daughter. This is, however, only one side of a many sided institution and in some kinship systems is of minor importance. In societies in which the marriage payment is of considerable value it is commonly used to replace the daughter by obtaining a wife for some other member of the family, usually a brother of the woman who has been lost. A daughter is replaced by a daughter-in-law, a sister by a wife or sister-in-law. The family is compensated for its loss.

A second important aspect of legal marriage is that it gives the husband and his kin certain rights in relation to his wife and the children she bears. The rights so acquired are different in different systems. Some of these are rights of the husband to the performance of duties by the wife (rights *in personam*) and he accepts corresponding duties towards her. He has, for example, rights to the services of his wife in his household. But the husband usually also acquires rights *in rem* over his wife. If anyone kills or injures her, or commits adultery with her, he may claim to be indemnified for the injury to his rights.

The husband acquires his rights through an action by the wife's kin in which they surrender certain of the rights they have previously had. The marriage payment may be regarded in this aspect as a kind of 'consideration' by means of which the transfer is formally and 'legally' made. It is the objective instrument of the 'legal' transaction of the transfer of rights. Once the payment, or some specific portion of it, has been made the bride's family have no right to fetch their daughter back, and in most tribes, if the union is broken by divorce at the instance of the husband, the payment has to be returned and the woman's family recover the rights they surrendered.

The rights obtained by a husband and his kin are different in some respects in different systems. The most important difference is in the matter of rights over the children the wife bears. An African marries because he wants children—*liberorum quaerendorum gratia*. The most important part of the 'value' of a woman is her child-bearing capacity. Therefore, if the woman proves to be barren, in many tribes her kin either return the marriage payment or provide another woman to bear children.

In a system of father-right, such as the Roman *patria potestas*, the rights of the father and his kin over the children of a marriage are so preponderant as to be nearly absolute and exclude any rights on the part of the mother's kin. On the other hand, in a system of mother-right such as that formerly existing amongst the 'Nayars of southern India, the father has no legal rights at all: the children belong to the mother and her kin. This does not, of course, exclude a relationship of affection between father and child. Both father-right and mother-right are exceptional conditions; most societies have systems which come between these extremes and might be called systems of joint right or divided right. The system of division varies and there may be an approximation either to father-right or to mother-right.

Some societies in Sumatra and other parts of the Malay Archipelago have two kinds of marriage. If a full marriage payment is made the children belong to the father; we may call this a father-right marriage. But if no payment is made the children belong to the mother and her kin, the marriage being one of mother-right.

The same sort of thing is reported from some parts of Africa, for example from Brass in Southern Nigeria.[1] The father-right marriage, with a substantial marriage payment, is the usual form, but if only a small payment is made the children belong to the mother's kin. The most definite example is from the Nyamwezi. In the *kukwa* form of marriage there is a payment (*nsabo*) made by the bridegroom to the father or guardian of the bride; children of such a marriage fall into the possession of the husband and his agnatic kin. In the *butende* form of marriage there is no payment and the children belong to the mother and her kin.

There is another aspect of marriage that must be taken into account. In Africa a marriage is not simply a union of a man and a woman; it is an alliance between two families or bodies of kin. We must consider the marriage payments in this connexion also.

In so-called primitive societies the exchange of valuables is a common method of establishing or maintaining a friendly relation between separate groups or between individuals belonging to separate groups. Where material goods are exchanged it is common to speak of gift-exchange. But the exchange may be of services, particularly those of a ritual character. There are societies in which there is an exchange of women, each group (family, lineage, or clan) providing a wife for a man of the

[1] P. Amaury Talbot, *Southern Nigeria*, 1926, vol. iii, pp. 437-40.

other. The rule governing transactions of this kind is that for whatever is received a return must be made. By such exchanges, even by a single act of exchange, two persons or two groups are linked together in a more or less lasting relation of alliance.[1]

There are societies in some parts of the world in which the marriage payment and the counter-payment are equal or approximately equal in value. We may regard this as an exchange of gifts to establish friendship between two families, of which the son of one is to marry a daughter of the other. The kind, and to some extent the amount of the gifts is fixed by custom. But where the marriage payment is considerable in amount and there is a much smaller counter-payment, or none at all, we must interpret this as meaning that the bride's family is conferring a specific benefit on the bridegroom by giving him their daughter in marriage, a benefit that is shared by his kin, and that the marriage payment is a return for this. The transaction can still be regarded as a form of 'gift-exchange' and as such establishes a relation (of alliance) between the parties.

It is characteristic of a transaction of purchase and sale that once it has been completed it leaves behind no obligations on either the buyer or the seller. (This does not, of course, exclude claims based on warranty.) In an African marriage the position is very different. For one thing the marriage payment may in certain circumstances have to be repaid. In some tribes where the payment consists of cattle it is the same cattle with all their increase that should be returned. Further, in some African societies the family that has made the marriage payment continues to have an interest in the cattle or other goods of which it consists. The payment received for a woman's marriage may be used to obtain a wife for a member of her family, usually her brother. This sets up a number of important relations between the persons involved.

$$A = b \qquad B = c \qquad C = d$$

B and b are brother and sister, and so are C and c. A marries b and makes a marriage payment which is used to obtain a wife (c) for B. In various tribes the marriage payment establishes a series of special personal relations between b and B, between A and B, between b and c, and between A and c. These are defined differently in different tribes. We may briefly consider three varieties.

It is usual to speak of B and b as 'linked' brother and sister, and B is the 'linked' mother's brother of the children of A and b, while b is the 'linked' father's sister of B's children. In the Shangana-Tonga tribes there is a very special relation between A and his 'great *mukonwana*' c, the wife that B married with the payment provided by A. A can claim

_____
[1] See Marcel Mauss, *Essai sur le Don.*

in marriage a daughter of *c*, particularly if his wife *b* dies and there is no younger sister to take her place.[1]

In the Lovedu the relations between the families of *A*, *B*, and *C* ought to be continued in the next and succeeding generations. A son of *A* should marry a daughter of *B* and a son of *B* should marry a daughter of *C*. There is thus established a chain of connected families. The *B* family (or lineage) gives brides to and receives cattle from the *A* family and gives cattle to and receives brides from *C*. The linked sister *b* is said to have 'built the house for her brother' *B*, and she 'has a gate' by which she may enter the house. She has the right to demand a daughter of the house to come as her daughter-in-law, to marry her son and be her helper. Thus, in this tribe, cross-cousin marriage is systematized in terms of marriage payments, and a complex set of relations between persons and between families is created.[2] In the Shangana-Tonga tribes *b* can demand a daughter of *c* as her co-wife or 'helper', the wife of her husband, not as her daughter-in-law.[3]

Amongst the Nkundo the relationships are given a different form. There is a special relation of *b* to *c*, the wife of her linked brother whose marriage was provided for by her marriage payment. The sister *b* is the *nkolo* of *c*, who is her *nkita*. The *nkolo* (*b*) stands in a position of superiority to the *nkita* (*c*). This relation is continued in the succeeding generations; the children of *b* (the *nkolo*) are in a position of superiority to the children of *c*. This is connected with a peculiar ordering of relations amongst the Nkundo by which the relation between cross-cousins is an asymmetrical one in which they are treated as if they belonged to different generations. The children of the father's sister are 'fathers', male and female (*baise*), to their cousins, the children of the mother's brother who are their 'children' (*bana*). The 'children' must show respect to their 'fathers' and help them. As a consequence a man regards the son of his father's sister's son as his 'brother' and uses that term for him.[4]

It should now be evident that the marriage payment is a complex institution having many varieties in form and function. In any given society it has to be interpreted by reference to the whole system of which it is a part. Nevertheless, there are certain general statements that seem to be well grounded. In Africa the marriage payment, whether it be small or large, is the objective instrument by which a 'legal' marriage is established. In some instances it is a compensation or indemnity to the woman's family for the loss of a member. This is particularly so where the marriage payment is considerable and is used to obtain a wife for the

[1] H. Junod, op. cit., pp. 231 et seq.
[2] E. J. and J. D. Krige, *The Realm of a Rain Queen*, 1943; J. D. Krige, 'The Significance of Cattle Exchanges in Lovedu Social Structure', *Africa*, xii. 4 Oct. 1939, pp. 393–424.
[3] E. Dora Earthy, *Valenge Women*.
[4] Hulstaert, *Le Mariage des Nkundo*, p. 164 et seq.

woman's brother. The payment may in some instances be regarded as part of an exchange of a kind that is used in many parts of the world to establish a friendly alliance between two groups. In some societies of South Africa and the Nilotic region it is the derivation of the cattle used in the marriage payment that fixes the social position of the children born of the union. Where the same cattle or other goods are used in two or more successive marriages this is in some tribes held to establish a special relation between the families thus formed. Where cattle are sacred in the sense that the cattle of a lineage are the material link between the living and their ancestors (having been received from those ancestors and being used for sacrifices to them), the use of cattle in marriage payments has a significance which a transfer of other goods would not have. This is not intended as a complete survey, which would be impossible within the limits of this essay. It is only an indication of how this institution, which is the procedure by which a husband acquires those rights which characterize a legal marriage (rights that vary in different societies), may be elaborated in different ways.

IX

It has been said above that an African marriage has to be regarded as a developing process. One aspect of this is the development of the relation between the two allied families as children are born and grow up. We think of kinship only as a relation between two persons who have a common ancestor. But there is a kind of reverse kinship between persons who have a common descendant, and it is relationships of this kind that are created by the marriage conceived as a process. When a child is born the father-in-law of the child's father becomes the grandfather (mother's father) of the child, and the man's brother-in-law becomes his child's uncle. It is usual to speak of the relation of a man to his brother-in-law as an affinal relation and to trace it through the wife. But the real relation that is established as the marriage proceeds is between the father and the mother's brother of a child or children. This is an elementary observation to make, but the failure to recognize clearly this simple fact is an obstacle to the understanding of a number of features of kinship systems.

African systems differ as to the rules concerning marriage between kin. In many the general rule is that a man and woman who are kin, or at any rate closely related, may not marry, and thus no bonds of kinship unite the two families before the marriage. On the other hand, there are many African societies in which it is thought very appropriate that a man should marry his cross-cousin, most usually the daughter of his mother's brother, more rarely the daughter of his father's sister. In such marriages the two families are already related before the marriage occurs. In marriage with the mother's brother's daughter a connexion between the families or lineages that has been formed in one generation is repeated in the next. There is also the very exceptional case of the Tswana, where a man may marry not only a mother's brother's daughter but such a near relative as the father's brother's daughter. We may expect that the social relations that result from a marriage alliance will differ in these different kinds of marriage, and a comparative study of the difference is desirable. It cannot be undertaken here. This section will deal only with certain features that characterize the relations of a man to his wife's relatives in a great number of African peoples and are also found among many other peoples in many parts of the world.

For seventy years anthropologists have paid a good deal of attention to a custom found in many parts of the world and commonly referred to as 'mother-in-law avoidance'. This is a custom by which social contact between a husband and his wife's mother is limited in significant ways or in extreme cases entirely prohibited.

A theory favoured by a number of anthropologists is that the purpose of this custom is to prevent incestuous intercourse with the wife's mother. It is not explained why such special and in some instances drastic measures are necessary, when incest with the mother or sister and other relatives is avoided without them. It would seem to be assumed that in some societies every man has a strong desire to have connexion with his wife's mother. It is an example of the kind of speculative theory that has been all too frequent in anthropology, made, in defiance of scientific method, without consideration of the relevant facts.

What is really the same custom varies from complete or nearly complete avoidance to the maintenance of social distance by a reciprocal attitude of reserve and respect. Amongst the Ganda 'no man might see his mother-in-law or speak face to face with her'.[1] Amongst the Galla a man must not mention the name of his mother-in-law (actual or prospective), but he does not appear to be prohibited from speaking to her. But he may not drink milk from a cup she has used nor eat food of her cooking.[2] Thus the custom has many varied forms.

It is not confined to a man's own mother-in-law. In some societies a man must practise the same sort of avoidance towards the mother-in-law of his brother. In many there is a similar avoidance of the sisters of the mother-in-law, and occasionally of the wife's grandmother. But a man must also avoid, or maintain a respectful distance from, some of his wife's male relatives, particularly her father, sometimes her father's brothers, and in some societies her mother's brothers. It is said that amongst the Toro of Albert Nyanza the avoidance between son- and father-in-law is even more rigid than that between son- and mother-in-law; and amongst the Lendu, another tribe in Uganda, the father-in-law can never visit his son-in-law except in the event of the serious illness of

[1] Roscoe, *The Baganda*, 1911, p. 129.
[2] Werner, in *J. Afr. Soc.* xiii, 1914, p. 139.

his daughter, whereas the mother-in-law may visit her son-in-law and his wife when two months have passed since the marriage.[1]

With this custom of maintaining a respectful distance between a man and his wife's parents and other relatives of the same generation there is frequently associated a directly contrary relation between a man and his wife's brothers and sisters. This is the kind of relationship that is usually called the 'joking relationship'. It is fundamentally a relation expressed in disrespectful behaviour. Persons between whom such a relationship exists are not merely permitted but are expected to speak and behave to one another in ways that would be insulting and offensive between persons not so related.[2]

These customs of 'avoidance' and 'joking' are too frequently found together for us to treat the association as accidental, particularly as in them we find two directly contrary modes of behaviour used in a single social context, that created by a marriage. We cannot regard as worthy of serious consideration any theory or explanation that does not deal with both of them.

As a first step towards the formation of a theory we must bear in mind that in these relationships (both of 'avoidance' and of 'joking') behaviour is highly conventionalized. In any society the kinds of abusive speech or behaviour that joking relatives may use are defined by custom. The rules that must be observed towards the wife's parents are similarly defined in detail, such as the Galla rule that a man must not drink milk from a cup that his wife's mother has used, while this does not apply to *dadi*, the intoxicating drink made from honey or from the fruit of the Borassus palm, because this drink is 'a thing of great kindness'. A very widespread rule is that forbidding the uttering of the personal name of an avoidance relative. Thus much of the behaviour imposed in these relationships must be described as symbolic behaviour and the rules are essentially similar to rules of etiquette. The acts and abstentions imposed by such rules are the conventionalized symbolic expression of the relative position of persons in a particular social relation or situation.

The view taken here is that the customs of 'avoidance' and 'joking' have the same general social function. The differentiating principle between them is that by which, as a general rule (to which, as we have seen, there are exceptions which require special explanation), behaviour towards relatives of the parents' generation should be respectful while towards relatives of one's own generation there is a nearer approach to equality and familiarity. But within one's own generation there is often a differentiation of senior and junior with a rule that the junior person must show respect to the senior. So in some societies the rules of avoidance are applied to the wife's elder sister as well as to the wife's

---

[1] J. F. Cunningham, *Uganda and Its Peoples*, 1905, pp. 54, 331.

[2] A. R. Radcliffe-Brown, 'On Joking Relationships', *Africa*, xiii. 3, July 1940, pp. 195–210.

INTRODUCTION 57

mother, even where there is a joking relationship with the wife's younger sister.

In the building of social structures means must be provided for avoiding, limiting, controlling, or settling conflicts. In the new structural situation resulting from marriage there are possibilities of conflict. While there is a union of the husband and wife the two families (in the sense of bodies of kin) remain separated, only linked together by their separate connexion with the new family that is coming into existence. It is the separateness of the two groups, together with the need of maintaining friendly relations between them, that has to provide the basis for their personal relations.

The 'joking' relationship in its reciprocal form can be regarded as a kind of friendliness expressed by a show of hostility. The mutual abusive behaviour would be simple hostility in other connexions, but the joking relatives are required not to take offence but to respond in the same way. The social separation of the man and his wife's relatives is symbolically represented in the sham hostility, ruled by convention, and the friendliness is exhibited in the readiness not to take offence. This interpretation applies to other instances of the reciprocal joking relationship that have nothing to do with marriage.[1]

The joking relationship is clearly only appropriate between persons who in the general social structure can treat each other as equals, and this generally means persons of the same generation or those related as 'grandparent' and 'grandchild'. For the wife's parents and other relatives of that generation, and sometimes for the wife's elder sister, an attitude of respect is required. But it must be a different kind of respect from that which a man shows in some African tribes to his father and in others to his mother's brother as the person who is entitled to exercise authority over him. This respect is totally incompatible with any open show of hostility. In a man's relations with his wife's parents the social separation is symbolically expressed in conventional rules such as the avoidance of the utterance of their personal names or the Galla prohibition against eating food cooked by the wife's mother. In the most extreme form of the custom there is complete avoidance of social contact with the wife's mother, to whom a man may never speak and whom he may never meet face to face, and there is sometimes a similar complete avoidance of the wife's father.

There might be a temptation to regard this avoidance as a form of hostility, since we tend to avoid persons with whom we do not get on well. This would be a mistake. Amongst the Australian aborigines there is complete avoidance of the wife's mother. When I asked a blackfellow why he had to avoid his mother-in-law his reply was: 'She is my best

[1] A. R. Radcliffe-Brown, op. cit.; R. E. Moreau, 'The Joking Relationship (*Utani*) in Tanganyika', *Tanganyika Notes and Records*, xii, 1941, pp. 1–10, and 'Joking Relationships in Tanganyika', *Africa*, xiv. 3, July 1944, pp. 386–400.

friend in the world: she has given me my wife.' Though this may seem strange to our way of thinking, I think his answer was logical and adequate. What disturbs or breaks a friendship is a quarrel. You cannot quarrel with a person with whom you have no social contact, or with whom your contacts are strictly limited and regulated by convention.

A marriage produces a temporary disequilibrium situation. In the small and close-knit groups with which we are here concerned any removal of a member results in disequilibrium. The event that most markedly produces this result is a death. But on a smaller scale the removal of a daughter by marriage is also a disturbance of equilibrium in her family. Moreover, the intrusion of a stranger into a group of kin is similarly a disturbance. Among the Nguni of South Africa the bride during the early period of her marriage has to give presents to and perform services for the women of her husband's group and only after a lapse of time is she accepted as one of themselves. Any reconstruction of a disturbed equilibrium inevitably takes time—longer or shorter as the case may be.

The establishment of a new equilibrium after a marriage requires that in certain types of kinship or family structure there is a need felt for emphasizing the separateness of the two connected families. There are many customs in which this is shown, but a single example must suffice. In the Nguni tribes the personal name that a woman has in her own family, as a daughter, may not be used by her husband's family, who have to provide her with a new name, which again will not be used by her own relatives. She is a different person in the two groups.

The principal points of tension in the situation created by a marriage are between the wife and the husband's parents and between the husband and his wife's parents. In order to condense and simplify the argument we are considering only the latter, but we must remember that the former is equally important. The point of maximum tension seems to be between the wife's mother, who is the person most closely and intimately connected with the wife before the marriage, and the son-in-law to whom have been transferred control and sexual rights over her daughter. This is, of course, what lies behind the vulgar English jokes about the mother-in-law.[1] The conventionally maintained 'distance' between son-in-law and wife's mother does have the effect of avoiding conflict between them.

In Bantu languages the customs of avoidance are referred to by a word of which some of the various forms are *ntloni*, *nthoni*, *hloni*. Some writers translate this as 'shame'. Thus Torday and Joyce report that

[1] After a lecture given more than thirty years ago in which this theory was explained, a member of the audience asked: 'Would it not be a good thing to introduce this custom (the avoidance of the wife's mother) amongst ourselves?' His question aroused a roar of laughter from the audience, which, I imagine, was what he aimed at.

amongst the Huana a man may never enter the house of his parents-in-law, and if he meets them on a road he must turn aside into the bush to avoid them. 'Repeated inquiries as to the reason of this avoidance on the part of a man of his parents-in-law elicited the invariable reply "that he was ashamed"; to a further inquiry of what he was ashamed, the answer would be "of marrying their daughter". No other reason could be obtained.'[1]

This 'shame' has been interpreted by Westermarck and other writers as being specifically sexual shame, but it is something much more fundamental and general than that, and indeed the English word 'shame' is not adequate as a description. What is really referred to is a felt constraint of one person in the presence of another, which limits his behaviour and keeps him at a distance from that other. Shyness is a similar phenomenon, and both shyness and shame are commonly associated with blushing. But it is to be noted that this constraint on a person in his relations with his wife's parents is not the spontaneous product of his own feelings, but is imposed upon him by social custom and the rules of etiquette that give expression to it, just as is the relative absence of constraint that is exhibited in the joking relationship with a wife's brothers or sisters.

Westermarck makes much of the fact that in Morocco all indecent talk is particularly prohibited in the presence of a man and his parent-in-law. But in a great many African tribes it is not only the father-in-law but also the father in whose presence one may not utter or listen to such talk. Obscene expressions are used in many societies as expressions of hostility, as in swearing. Their use is therefore often considered appropriate in joking relationships, and since these are the polar contrary of the relationship to parents-in-law, it is easy to see the meaning of avoiding obscenity in the presence of these relatives. Freedom to refer to sexual topics is in general characteristic of a certain kind of social intimacy, and is directly contrary to the distant reserve that has to be observed towards the wife's parents.

The argument could be supported by the examination of other features of the etiquette relating to parents-in-law, but only one can be mentioned here. It has been noted above that amongst the Galla a man may not eat food cooked by his wife's mother nor drink from a cup that she has used. In many other African tribes a man may not eat food from his wife's family, and where there is not complete avoidance of all contact a man may not eat food in the presence of his parent-in-law. Dr. Nadel, in his book on the tribes of the Nuba Hills, suggests that such customs also express, symbolically, sexual shame; though he has himself indicated their true significance by referring to rules that forbid members of different clans to eat meat or drink milk together, stating that these

[1] E. Torday and T. Joyce, 'Notes on the Ethnography of the BaHuana', *J. Roy. Anthrop. Inst.* xxxvi, 1906, p. 285.

eating avoidances are the medium 'through which these tribes express social proximity and distance'. The sharing of food, and still more, eating and drinking together (commensality), are all over the world expressions of social solidarity. The symbolism of customs of etiquette in the matter of eating is obvious in the customs themselves, and there is no need to search for obscure Freudian symbols by which eating is a sexual activity. Amongst the Nguni of South Africa a bride may not drink the milk of her husband's kraal until after a lapse of time, usually not till after she has borne a child, and after a ceremony has been performed. This is the symbolic expression of the fact that she is no longer a stranger or outsider but a member of the group.

Customs about the avoidance of names can be interpreted in the same way as customs about eating, and it has not yet been suggested that they have sexual significance. All these various rules, it is here held, are conventional rules by which a man is obliged to maintain social distance between himself and his wife's parents. By maintaining this kind of relationship any tensions that exist or may arise are prevented from breaking, by open conflict, what should be a friendly relation.

In some societies in Africa and elsewhere, the rules of avoidance are somewhat relaxed in the course of time, i.e. as the marriage develops through the birth of children. This is, for example, reported of the Kamba.[1] It is probably true of many other societies from which it has not been reported. This is easy to understand if we think of the marriage as a developing process. Whatever tensions or dangers of conflict there may be between the son-in-law and his wife's parents are at a maximum in the early period of the marriage. The imposed 'shyness' between them is functionally most significant immediately after the marriage.

X

A part of every kinship system is a set of regulations concerning marriage between persons related by kinship or through marriage. There are, in the first place, rules which prohibit marriage between persons who stand in certain relationships. An example is afforded by the list of prohibited degrees in the English Book of Common Prayer. The rules vary greatly from one system to another, and in a given society may vary from one period of its history to another. In many societies there is what is called a rule of exogamy, by which a man is forbidden to take a wife from amongst the women of his own group (lineage, sub-clan, clan, or moiety). On the other hand, in some systems there are certain relatives between whom marriage is not merely permitted but is regarded as desirable. The term 'preferential marriage' is commonly applied to customs of this kind. The commonest examples are cross-cousin marriage (marriage with the daughter of the mother's brother or of the father's

[1] Lindblom, *The Akamba*, which gives a good account of the relations between *athoni* (avoidance relatives).

sister) and marriage with the wife's sister or the wife's brother's daughter.

There are also rules relating to sexual intercourse outside marriage. Incest is the sin or crime of sexual intercourse between persons related either by kinship or through marriage within degrees defined by law or religion. Marriage and sexual intercourse outside marriage are not the same thing, and the rules relating to them must be separately considered. Most of the discussions about these rules have been vitiated by the failure to distinguish two distinct, though obviously related, problems. Here we are concerned primarily with the problem of the rules relating to marriage.

There is, in most societies, a tendency to condemn sexual intercourse between persons who are forbidden to marry. But there are many instances in which a man and woman who may not marry may carry on a temporary affair without this being considered the grave offence to which we give the name of incest, and without being subjected to any legal or religious sanction. Amongst the Tallensi of West Africa there are women whom a man is prohibited from marrying but with whom intercourse is not regarded as incestuous; the Tallensi themselves say 'copulation and marriage are not the same thing'. Similarly, amongst the Nkundo of the Belgian Congo there is a special term (*lonkana*) for sexual intercourse with women whom a man may not marry but with whom such connexion does not constitute incest; they are women of a clan (or lineage?) which is related to his own and into which he may not marry for this reason.[1]

Confining our attention to the regulation of marriage, we can see that there are certain requirements that must be met by a theory if it is to be worthy of any consideration. It must offer a general theory of the variations in these rules in different societies, and it must therefore deal not only with prohibited but also with preferred marriages. It must give some significant clue towards an understanding of why any given society has the rules it does. The test of a scientific theory is in its application to the explanation of particular instances. By this criterion many of the speculative hypotheses that have been put forward are entirely useless and it would be a waste of time to discuss them. To anyone propounding a theory we might put the following question: How does the theory give us a clue to the understanding of why, amongst the Nkundo, a woman is forbidden to marry (in a second marriage) the husband's father's brother's son of her first husband's mother's brother's daughter; or why, amongst the Hera of Mashonaland, a man may not marry a woman of the lineage of his wife's brother's wife, although he may marry his wife's sister or a woman of the lineage of his mother's brother's wife?

[1] M. Fortes, 'Kinship, Incest and Exogamy of the Northern Territories of the Gold Coast', in *Custom is King*, ed. Dudley Buxton, 1936; Hulstaert, op. cit.

The theory here proposed is simply a special application of the general theory that the *raison d'être* of an institution or custom is to be found in its social function. The theory is, therefore, that the rules or customs relating to prohibited or preferred marriages have for their social function to preserve, maintain, or continue an existing kinship structure as a system of institutional relations. Where a marriage between relatives would threaten to disrupt or throw into disorder the established system it tends to be disapproved or forbidden, and the greater and more widespread the disturbance that would be caused by a marriage, the stronger tends to be the disapproval which it meets with. Inversely, preferential marriages are those which have for their effect to renew or reinforce the existing system.

What is here called a tendency is something that can be discovered by observation. In some instances the objection to a certain type of marriage takes a quite definite form, as in a system of law. But in other instances there may be, in a given society at a particular time, a disagreement between individuals as to the desirability of encouraging, permitting, or prohibiting a certain type of marriage. This can be illustrated from English history. Until the Reformation marriage with a deceased wife's sister was forbidden by the canon law of the Roman Church. But persons of influence who could pay for the privilege could obtain a special dispensation permitting the marriage to take place. By an Act of King Henry VIII dispensations were abolished and marriage with a deceased wife's sister or with a deceased husband's brother was made illegal. An Act of Queen Mary legalized marriage with a deceased husband's brother but not with a deceased wife's sister. In 1835 Lord Lyndhurst brought forward in the House of Lords a Bill to legalize marriage with the deceased wife's sister; from that date till 1907, when an Act was finally passed permitting such marriages, there was a continued and passionate controversy. This can be studied in the debates on the subject that occurred at intervals in the Lords and Commons and were reported in Hansard. An association called the Marriage Law Defence Union was formed to prevent the passing into law of the proposal. Articles and pamphlets were printed on both sides of the controversy and of these a bibliography by Huth has 257 entries between the years 1840 and 1887. After the law permitting such marriages was passed some clergymen refused to solemnize them in church; though permitted by the law of the State they were judged by some to be contrary to religion.

This episode from the history of the English kinship system has been mentioned for several reasons. It illustrates the fact that while in a particular society there may sometimes be unanimity of opinion as to the desirability or otherwise of a particular kind of marriage, there may sometimes exist a marked divergence of opinion. In England there was, and still perhaps is among some people, a very strong sentiment against marriage with the sister of a deceased wife, while others feel that such marriage is permissible or even desirable. Similar divergence of opinion can sometimes be noted in primitive societies and its existence calls for theoretical explanation and affords a good means of testing any general theory.

An examination of the documents of the controversy that lasted in England for seventy years shows that the objection to this kind of marriage is based on sentiment rather than on any sort of reason. It is just felt to be wrong.

Nevertheless, it is possible, by analysis of the English kinship system, to see how this divergence of opinion and sentiment was possible. The decline in the social importance of kinship which has been taking place in England for several centuries, and is still continuing, resulted in a situation in which there was no clearly defined and generally accepted pattern of behaviour as between a man and the brothers and sisters of his wife. In the absence of any institutional norm this kind of relationship could be, and inevitably was, differently treated by different persons. Since thought and sentiment may be very strongly influenced by words, the English term 'sister-in-law', understood as 'sister' by marriage, served to provide some persons with a pattern for the relationship; the sister-in-law is a sort of sister. Marriage with any sort of 'sister', implying sexual intimacy, was emotionally felt to be a sort of symbolic incest. Other persons felt that sister-in-law and brother-in-law are not really relatives at all. If any man, on the death of his wife, wishes to enter another marriage, the wife's sister should be just as eligible as any unrelated person. There was a third view: the relation between two sisters is, or should be, one of affection and intimacy; for a widower with young children there is no one who could so suitably replace his wife as her unmarried sister; on this view marriage with the wife's sister was viewed as a marriage to be preferred.

From this well-documented historical instance, and from the parallel instance of the discussions in South Africa over the proposal to legalize marriage with a deceased husband's brother, which had previously been forbidden by Roman–Dutch law, we can draw a generalization. Where the kinship system is one that has a structure with a set of clearly defined institutional relationships there is likely to be complete agreement as to whether a particular kind of marriage should be prohibited, permitted, or preferred. Divergence of opinion or sentiment indicates an absence of rigidity, and that, of course, is not a bad thing in itself. A political system, such as that of England, may depend essentially on the differences of opinion and sentiment of political parties. But in a system of law some rigidity is necessary, even though from time to time the law may be modified. A law works best when it is backed by a nearly unanimous public opinion.

There are significant differences in human societies in this matter of prohibiting, permitting, or preferring marriage of a woman with her husband's brother, or of a man with his wife's sister. Polyandry, the marriage of a woman to two or more husbands, is an institution that is only rarely found, but its most usual form is adelphic polyandry, in which the woman marries two or more brothers. Corresponding to this there is the much more widespread institution of sororal polygyny, in which a man marries two or more sisters. Amongst the Australian aborigines this is regarded as the ideal form of marriage, and still more ideal is the arrangement by which an elder brother marries the two eldest sisters of a family and his younger brother marries one or two of the younger sisters.

There are very widespread marriage customs that are commonly referred to by the terms 'levirate' and 'sororate', but we have to distinguish different institutions to which these terms are applied. In the true levirate, exemplified by the customs of the Hebrews, and in Africa by the Nuer and Zulu and many other peoples, when a man dies and his wife has not passed the age of child-bearing it is the duty of the man's brother to cohabit with the widow in order to raise children, which will be counted, not as his, but as children of the deceased. The widow remains the wife of the dead man, for whom the brother is a surrogate and thus not strictly speaking her husband. A different institution is widow inheritance, in which a brother takes over the position of husband and father to the widow and her children.

There is a similar distinction with regard to the sororate. In some tribes of South Africa, such as the Zulu, if a woman proves to be barren her kin will provide a sister to bear children who will be counted as children of the barren wife. This is parallel to the true levirate. A different custom is that by which when a wife dies her kin may supply a sister to replace her. In sororal polygyny a man, having married an older sister, also marries her younger sister.

All these customs of preferential marriage can be seen to be continuations or renewals of the existing structure of social relations. All of them are also examples of the principle of the unity of the sibling group, since brother replaces brother and sister replaces or supplements sister.

Professor Gluckman's paper in this volume gives an illuminating comparison between the Lozi and the Zulu in this matter of the sororate and sororal polygyny. The Zulu have both; they approve of marriage with the wife's younger sister which reinforces the relationships established by the first marriage, and which, if sisters behave in a 'sisterly' way, increases the solidarity of the family group. The Lozi object to marriage with even a classificatory 'sister' of the wife, and say that the competition and rivalry between co-wives is likely to destroy the relationship that ought to exist between sisters. But there is really more in the matter than this, and it may be held that the basis of this difference between the Zulu and the Lozi lies in certain very important differences of social structure. The unity of the sibling group, with its implication of

substitution of brother for brother and sister for sister, is a major principle of the Zulu system and a relatively minor feature in that of the
Lozi. Following this the Zulu system emphasizes the solidarity of the
lineage group, and this can hardly be said to exist in Lozi. In sororal
polygyny one woman of a sibling group as part of a lineage supplements
another; in the sororate she replaces her. Her duties are imposed on her
by her lineage affiliation. To quarrel with her sister or neglect her sister's
children is not simply a neglect of her marital duties; it is contrary to her
obligations to her own closest kin. In the Zulu system a marriage establishes a relation between a man and his brothers and the family of his
wife, which should be permanent. Divorce is objected to because it is
destructive of this permanence. If the man dies his wife passes to a
brother. If the woman dies the relation can only be fully continued if she
is replaced by a sister, unless she has borne children or is beyond the
child-bearing age. In the very different Lozi system the levirate and
sororate could not possibly have the functions they have in the Zulu
system.

Marriage with the wife's sister is, on the whole, more frequently found
in association with the patrilineal lineage and what may be called father-
right marriage, and it is precisely in such circumstances that it functions
most effectively to maintain or strengthen the relationships set up by
a marriage. In societies with matrilineal institutions there are variations.
Thus the Ashanti do not permit marriages of this kind, and the paper by
Dr. Fortes enables us to see why. On the contrary, amongst the Bemba
such marriages are approved, and the reason again lies in the social
structure. By his first marriage a man becomes attached to the family of
his wife, with whom, for at least some time, he must take up residence.
Marriage with the wife's sister would strengthen this bond and introduce
no new factor; whereas if, in a second marriage he unites himself with
a different family this must complicate and is likely to disturb the existing system of relations. Theoretically one would expect that the Bemba
should have given, at any rate in former times, a definite preference to
marriage with the wife's sister.

In a number of African tribes there is a custom by which a man is
given his wife's brother's daughter as a wife. This is in a sense a variant
of marriage with the younger sister of the wife. It exists in tribes in which
the patrilineal lineage is a predominant feature of the social structure,
and in such tribes a marriage of this sort renews by repetition the
relationship set up by a first marriage between a man and the patrilineal
lineage of his wife; he takes a second wife from the same lineage group,
just as in the sororate he receives a second wife from the sibling group
of the first wife. The second wife supplements or replaces, not her elder
sister, but her father's sister. The structural principle involved is that of
the unity of the lineage group.   .

In some African societies a man is not permitted to marry the daughter

F

of his mother's brother, and this rule is extended to the whole lineage to which she belongs, and sometimes to the clan. Other societies permit such marriages of cross-cousins, and in some they are given preference. (It must be noted that in a system of lineages or clans, whether patrilineal or matrilineal, cross-cousins belong to different groups.) There is no space available here for a general discussion of the reasons for this variation, as the subject is complex. Where the institutionalized relations of a man to his mother's brother (and his wife) are in important respects incompatible with his relations to his wife's father and mother, marriage with the mother's brother's daughter tends to be forbidden. Where there is no reason of this kind, then marriage of this sort renews in one generation a relation between families that was established in the preceding generation, and thus tends to be approved or preferred. A man takes a wife from a certain family or lineage and establishes a relation with her kinsfolk. His wife's brother becomes the mother's brother of his children; if his son marries the daughter of this man there is a repetition of the previous connexion.

The Hehe of East Africa do not forbid marriages of this kind. Gordon Brown has reported the existence of a difference of opinion in this tribe. Some people think that marriage with the mother's brother's daughter is desirable because it renews the already established relation between the families, but others think that the tensions that are likely to arise between the kin of a man and those of his wife may disrupt the existing friendly relations that have resulted from a former successful marriage, and therefore think it better to avoid a marriage of this kind. By way of contrast it is apparently the unanimous opinion of the Lobedu of the Transvaal that a relationship established in one generation by a marriage should if possible be renewed or repeated in the next generation through marriage with the mother's brother's daughter.

The paper on the Ashanti by Professor Fortes gives us further insight. The Ashanti formerly gave definite preference to marriage with the mother's brother's daughter, and had their own particular rationalizations for the custom. This kind of marriage is becoming less frequent as a result of social changes, and there is now a divergence of opinion as to the desirability of what was apparently formerly accepted as an established custom. Recognizing the existence of a number of factors in the minds of the people themselves, Professor Fortes sees the change as one involved in the gradual transformation that is taking place in the social structure of the Ashanti people.

There is a very important general difference in the regulation of marriage between societies that build their kinship system on cognatic relations traced equally through males and through females and those that adopt the unilineal principle. In a purely cognatic system, such as that of Anglo-Saxon England or ancient Wales, the prohibition against marriage applies to all cognates within a certain degree of kinship;

marriage is forbidden between persons who have a common ancestor or ancestress within a certain number of generations. For example, two persons who have a common great-great-grandparent may be forbidden to marry. In a unilineal system the primary rule is that two persons may not marry if they both belong to a socially recognized unilineal descent group. This may be a lineage, or it may be a clan. A rule of this kind is called 'exogamy'. Perhaps the most extreme example is the Chinese rule, not always, I believe, observed in these days, that two persons having the same surname may not marry, since such names are patrilineally inherited and therefore the two persons of one name may be supposed to have had an ancestor in common, though it may be three thousand years ago. There is no special problem about exogamy. The exogamy of a clan is the same thing as the exogamy of a lineage, with a wider recognition of kinship. The essence of the system of clans is that a man is required to recognize all the members of his own clan as his kin and to behave to them accordingly. The rule of exogamy, where it exists, is a way of giving institutional recognition to this bond of kinship. Like the classificatory system of terminology, which is frequently found associated with clans, exogamy is part of the machinery for establishing and maintaining a wide-range kinship system.

In unilineal systems cognatic kinship outside the unilineal group may also be recognized. Thus in ancient Indian law a man might not marry a *sapinda*, a person descended patrilineally from one of his patrilineal ancestors within seven generations. He might also not marry certain cognatic kin, but the connexion had to be a nearer one, within five, or in another system of law within three generations. There is also such a thing as lineal-cognatic kinship. In a system of patrilineal lineages or clans the rule of exogamy forbids marriage within the group; but there may also be a prohibition against marriage with a person of the mother's group. Inversely, in a system of matrilineal groups a man may be forbidden to marry a woman of his father's group; the relationship is what is here called lineal-cognatic.

It is evident from these remarks that in societies that make use of the unilineal principle there is an immense variety in the rules relating to marriage. The contrast between a cognatic system and a unilineal system is brought out in the comparison of the Lozi with the Zulu. Amongst the Lozi, with a cognatic kinship system, the regulation of marriage takes the form that marriage is forbidden between any two persons who are cognatically related within a certain degree; for this purpose genealogical relationships are not traced farther back than the fourth generation, and in fact marriages do take place within these limits. The rule, therefore, even if it is not always observed, is that third cousins, descendants of one great-great-grandparent, should not marry. This seems to have been the rule at one time in England and Wales.

The Zulu have a system of agnatic lineages, as did the ancient Romans, and marriage between agnates recognized as such within a certain range is forbidden. The Zulu also recognize lineal-cognatic kinship and forbid the marriage of a man with a woman of his mother's lineage. The regulation of marriage is very different in the Lozi and the Zulu, and the difference corresponds to a fundamental difference in social structure.

In the construction of a kinship system it is necessary to fix in some way the range over which relationships are to be institutionally recognized. In this the rules relating to marriage may have great importance. The system of the Australian aborigines is one in which every person in the society is related to every other person with whom he has any social contact whatever. The regulation of marriage therefore takes the form of a rule that a man may only take a wife from some one category, or some categories, of kin. Endogamy is a rule one of the functions of which, at any rate in some parts of India, is to circumscribe the range of relationships, since a member of an endogamous group cannot possible be related, by kinship or through marriage, with any person outside the group. In a cognatic system the range of relationships depends on how far any person traces his genealogical connexions. In the Teutonic system of the sib, theoretically, any descendant of any of the sixty-four pairs of the grandparents of one's great-great-grandparents was a sib-kinsman, thus including all cousins up to sixth cousins. It would seem quite impossible that anyone would recognize as kinsmen all of these; it was a theoretical construction of the lawyers, not something used in daily practice. It illustrates the fact that a wide-range cognatic system is not very practicable. In setting up rules for marriage, therefore, a cognatic system, such as the Lozi, rarely, if ever, goes beyond third cousins, descendants of a common great-great-grandparent.

Unilineal systems have to work in quite a different way. Unilineal kin groups normally tend to increase in size in successive generations. A clan may grow into a group numbering many hundreds; but membership of the same clan in the case of dispersed clans may only be of significance amongst persons in regular and frequent social contact. Lineages also tend to expand in volume, and in lineage systems we find some procedure by which a lineage that has grown to a size in which the institutions that maintain its unity do not function well can be divided into two or more separate but still connected lineages. A method by which this is sometimes brought about in the Nguni tribes of South Africa is interesting as illustrating the thesis of this section. It may happen that when a lineage group has grown to a considerable size a young man may decide that he wants to marry a girl of the lineage who is not closely related to him. The natives themselves say that a marriage within the lineage is disruptive of its unity, since it would create within the group relationships by marriage which are entirely incompatible with the established lineage relations. There will therefore be resistance to the proposed marriage. But if there is sufficient opinion in favour of it the lineage can be divided into two separate connected lineages between which marriage becomes possible. Even when a lineage has become too large to be functionally fully effective the Nguni are inclined to try to maintain its unity, and therefore tend to wait for such an occasion as the one here described. Marriage within the lineage group would be thoroughly disruptive of its structure, and therefore cannot be permitted; but if the structure is changed by fission of the group the marriage is permissible between the two newly created groups. This illustrates the relation between rules as to marriage and the kinship structure.

A brief reference must be made to the Tswana, whose system is described in this volume by Professor Schapera. The Tswana are decidedly exceptional in Africa, and might almost be regarded as an anomaly; but in the comparative study of social systems exceptions and apparent anomalies are of great theoretical importance. There is a strong contrast between the Tswana and the Nguni tribes. The Tswana recognize patrilineal lineage; they seem to have had a preference for marriage with mother's brother's daughter, which is characteristic of a number of tribes with whom they are ethnically related. But they also permit marriage within the lineage to the daughter of a father's brother. This would be impossible amongst the Nguni, who indeed refer to the Sotho, related to the Tswana, with expressions of disgust as 'those people who wear breeches and marry their sisters.' How the Tswana arrived at their present system is an historical question about which we can unfortunately only speculate. But the way the system works can be studied. Amongst the Nguni the way a man is required to behave towards the relatives of his wife is entirely incompatible with the way in which he behaves to persons of his own patrilineal lineage, his father's brother, with the wife and children of the latter. The absence of such incompatibility amongst the Tswana, while it makes possible the marriage with father's brother's daughter, also marks their system as being of an unusual type amongst indigenous African peoples. The Arabic peoples also practise marriage with the father's brother's daughter, but their kinship system is in many respects very different from that of the Tswana or those of African peoples in general.

It is only possible here to deal very briefly with the subject of incest in its relation to the regulation of the marriage of kin. Incest is properly speaking the sin or crime of sexual intimacy between immediate relatives within the family, father and daughter, mother and son, brother and sister. In human societies generally such conduct is regarded as unthinkable, something that could not possibly occur, and the idea of it arouses a strong emotional reaction of repugnance, disgust, or horror. It is characteristically conceived as an 'unnatural' action, contrary not so much to law and morals as to human nature itself. It is this emotional reaction that we have to explain if we are to have a theory of incest. Another example of a kind of action frequently regarded as 'unnatural' is parricide, the killing of a father or mother. The parallel between incest and parricide is illustrated in Greek drama.

Almost everywhere in human societies as we know them the first experience that any person has of society is in the parental family, the intimate domestic group of father, mother, and children. Certain emotional attitudes are developed in such a group with sufficient force to come to be thought of as 'natural' in the sense of being part of human nature itself. The kind of emotional attitude existing in sexual intimacy, and the kinds of emotional attitude developed in the family towards the nearest kin, are felt to be violently contrary, incapable of being combined or reconciled. This is a matter of the logic of sentiments, not the logic of reason, and this is what is really meant when writers say that the repugnance to incest is instinctive, for there is a certain logic of the emotions which is the same in all human beings and is therefore inborn, not acquired. Individuals who behave contrary to this logic of sentiment, as by the murder of a mother, are behaving 'unnaturally'.

The study of what are regarded as 'unnatural' offences, incest, bestiality, in some societies homosexuality, patricide, and matricide, is a special branch of the comparative study of morals. One offence that is frequently thought of as 'unnatural' is witchcraft in the sense of working evil on members of one's own social group. (Black magic used against one's enemies in other groups, as amongst the Australian aborigines, is an altogether different matter.) In Africa incest and witchcraft are often thought of as connected. A South African native with whom I was discussing the subject remarked about sexual intimacy with a sister, with horror in his voice, 'That would be witchcraft.' There is a widespread belief in Africa that a man can obtain the greatest possible power as a sorcerer by incestuous intercourse with his mother or sister. Intercourse with a more distant relative would be quite ineffective.

In Europe in Christian times incest, bestiality, homosexuality, witchcraft, as 'unnatural' offences were quite logically regarded as offences against the Creator, and therefore the concern of the Church. In England it is only recently that incest has been treated as a crime to be dealt with by the secular courts. In many primitive societies it is thought that incest will be punished by supernatural sanctions. These points are all significant for an understanding of the attitude towards incest. The family is normally regarded as something sacred; incest, like patricide or matricide, is sacrilege.

The attitude towards incest, in the narrow sense, may be extended to sexual intimacy between other relatives, but in different ways in different societies. In some primitive societies sexual intimacy with the wife's mother is felt to be not less evil than with one's own mother. But there are other societies in which a man may be married at one time to a woman and to her daughter by another husband. Sexual intercourse between husband and wife is an element in the institutional complex of marriage.

Every society therefore makes a distinction between this and sexual intimacy outside marriage. There is a tendency to make a distinction between persons between whom marriage is prohibited and other persons, a tendency that is much more powerful in some societies or in some instances than in others. There is very great variation in such matters.

The categories of relationship recognized in classificatory terminologies undoubtedly have considerable effect. If a woman is to be called 'mother' or 'sister' or 'daughter' the relationship with her is thought of as being similar to that with one's own mother or sister or daughter, and it is obvious that this will very frequently be felt to forbid any sexual intimacy. It would be a sort of 'symbolic' incest and as such objectionable; to have a sexual relation with a classificatory 'mother' is a symbolic offence against one's own mother. Such symbolic incest, except ritually on specific occasions, is strongly reprobated amongst the Australian aborigines.

Some writers assume, or seem to assume, that prohibitions against marriage are the result of feelings that sexual intercourse between the persons concerned would be wrong. The truth, in the majority of instances, is the reverse of this; sexual intercourse is felt to be wrong between two persons if by the rules of society they may not marry. It is extremely rarely, however, that the reaction to such conduct, or to the idea of it, is of the same kind and intensity as reaction to the idea of real incest with immediate relatives. This is exemplified in the laws of modern states where sexual intimacy between relatives who are by law forbidden to marry is not in all cases punishable as a crime.

Theoretical discussions on the subject of incest and the regulation of marriage are often, one might even say usually, full of confusions. The theory outlined here attempts to get rid of these. (1) Incest is the sin or crime of sexual intercourse between members of a parental family. It is not a question of prohibition of marriage. There are societies in which intercourse between brother and sister is incestuous, but kings or chiefs may marry, or may even be expected to marry, their own sisters. The condemnation of incest is based on the emotionally or 'instinctively' felt violent incompatibility between sexual intimacy and family relations of affection and respect. This may be rationalized in different ways. (2) The rules relating to marriages between related persons in any society are an intrinsic part of the complex of institutions that make up a kinship system. In each instance the rules can only be understood by reference to the system to which they belong and the social structures that constitute the basis of the system. The general law which each instance exemplifies is that the rules have for their function to maintain the continuity of the general system of institutional relationships, either by preventing marriages which would be disruptive or by encouraging marriages which reinforce the existing arrangement of persons. (3) The strong feelings about incest, by a readily recognizable psychological process, tend to spread, so that sexual intimacy between persons who may not marry tends to be regarded as being somewhat of the same kind as incest, though differing in the degree with which it meets with condemnation or reprobation.

The whole theory is therefore one of social structure and of the necessary conditions of its stability and continuity. Incest, as here defined, is not merely disruptive of the social life of a single family, it is disruptive of the whole system of moral and religious sentiments on which the social order rests. Prohibited marriages are for the most part simply those which would prevent the continuance of normal relations between the few persons who would be immediately affected. There are, however, instances in which a marriage between kin, not necessarily closely related, is felt to be an attack on the whole social order; this is so in the kinship systems of Australian aborigines. Such a marriage, if attempted, is a sort of crime against society and is likely to be treated as such.

XI

One of the most famous pseudo-historical speculations of the anthropology of the last century was the idea that the earliest form of society was one based on 'matriarchy' or 'mother-right'. One definition of this, given in the *Encyclopaedia Britannica* of 1910, is 'a term used to express a supposed earliest and lowest form of family life, typical of primitive societies, in which the promiscuous relations of the sexes result in the child's father being unknown'. An alternative definition, frequently used, was a social condition in which kinship is reckoned through females only, and in which there would be no recognition of any social relationship of fatherhood. We have no knowledge of any societies of this kind in the present or in the past; it is, as Robertson remarked in his *History of America* in the eighteenth century, a pure product of imagination.

But early anthropologists also applied the term 'mother-right' to certain existing societies, McLennan to the Nayars of southern India, and Tylor to the Menangkabau Malays. We may take these two societies as providing us with a special type of system to which we may continue to apply the term 'mother-right', and we may add to them the Khasi of Assam. It is to be noted that the Nayars and the Malays, so far from being 'primitive', are advanced, literate, and cultivated peoples. The Nayars are a military, ruling, and land-owning aristocracy in a civilized community; they esteem learning and the arts and have produced an extensive, and according to accounts, admirable, literature in their own language, Malayalam. The Malays similarly have an extensive literature which is admired by those who know it. Though the Khasi are less advanced they are very far from being savages. Thus the typical instances of mother-right are found, not amongst the more primitive peoples, but in advanced or relatively advanced societies.

The Nayars are sometimes referred to as a caste, but they are a numerous people divided into a number of subdivisions, 130 such being enumerated in the census of 1901. There are undoubtedly differences of custom in different sections of this large community. Their system of marriage and kinship has been undergoing change during the past seventy years, and with regard to some of its features there is a lack of agreement in different accounts. I believe that what follows is a substantially accurate generalized account of the system as it formerly existed. It is put in the past tense because it is not an accurate description of the conditions of the present day.[1]

The important unit of structure in the Nayar kinship system was a matrilineal lineage group called *taravad*. It consisted of all the descendants through females of a single known ancestress, and might number more than a hundred persons. It is spoken of in Indian law as a 'joint family', since the property is jointly owned by the group as a corporate unity; but this is not a family in the ordinary sense, since it includes women and their daughters and sons and brothers, but not their husbands. All sons of the *taravad* inherited from their mothers the right to share during their lives in the produce of the land or other property, but could transmit no rights to their children. The control of the property was in the hands of the *karanavan* (known in legal terminology as the 'manager'), who was normally the oldest male member. If a *taravad* became too large, or for other reasons, it might be divided. If the first ancestress had three daughters, all of whom had left descendants, three new lineage groups would be formed, the property being divided into three equal portions. The partition of property did not destroy the relationship, and kinship therefore extended beyond the *taravad*. A number of related *taravad* formed a group for which the name in north Malabar is *kulam*; we may call this a clan, though it may have been a very large lineage. The clan was exogamous, and the various lineages of one clan shared pollution, a birth or death in one lineage group causing pollution in the other groups of the clan. A number of clans constituted a sub-caste, and in south India the sub-caste is normally the endogamous group. Within the sub-caste it would seem that a *taravad* had a special relationship with one or more other lineages, not belonging to the same clan, whose members were their *enangar* (allies). This was an important feature of the kinship system. The Nayars had a cult of the

---

[1] There have been many accounts of the Nayars from the early fifteenth century to the present day. The *Report of the Malabar Marriage Commission* of 1894 is important in relation to Nayar marriage. More easily accessible is the article 'Nayars' in Hastings's *Encyclopaedia of Religion and Ethics* and an article by K. M. Panikkar on 'Some Aspects of Nayar Life' in *J. Roy. Anthrop. Inst.* xlviii, 1918, pp. 254–93.

ancestors or deceased members of the lineage; once a year an offering of
food and drink was made to the ancestral spirits, including the mother's
brothers and mother's mother's brothers of the living members.[1]

Before a Nayar girl reached puberty she had to undergo a ceremony of
which the essential feature was the tying on of an ornament, usually of
gold, called a *tali*. A number of girls of one *taravad* might pass through
the ceremony together provided that they were all of the same generation. The *tali* was tied by a man invited for the purpose, called the
manavalan, selected from the *enangar* of the *taravad*. There is some
evidence that, at least in former times, the ceremony included the ritual
defloration of the girl. There are two interpretations of the ceremony.
One is that it is a sort of religious marriage which was dissolved at the
end of the ceremony. The rite of tying the *tali* is a marriage or betrothal
rite amongst some of the peoples of south India. At the end of the Nayar
ceremony, which lasted four days, a cloth was severed in two parts and
one part given to the *manavalan* and the other to the girl; this is a rite
commonly used in south India as a rite of divorce. When the *manavalan*
died the girl or woman on whom he had tied the *tali* had to observe formalities of mourning. Dr. Aiyappan, on the other hand, holds that
amongst the Nayars the tying of the *tali* is nothing more than a rite of
initiation into womanhood.[2] For present purposes it does not matter
which view we accept, and indeed it is largely a matter of the choice of
words. The *manavalan* does not become the real effective husband of the
girl on whom he ties the *tali*.

When a Nayar young woman reached a suitable age she formed a
union which will here be called a marriage. The most usual union was
with a man of her own sub-caste, who must be of the same generation
as the woman and must be older. It seems that marriage with an
enangan was regarded as specially suitable. While the evidence is imper-
fect, what there is points to the members of the allied *taravad* of the
girl's own generation being all her cross-cousins; so that the Nayar
system, like so many others in Dravidian India, would be based on
cross-cousin marriage; the woman would take a husband preferably
from the *taravad* of her father's sister. These marriages were referred
to by the Sanskrit term *sambandham*, and the Nayars did not apply to
them the usual Malayalam term for marriage. The Sanskrit *bandhu*
refers to friendship, and may sometimes be used for the relation between
a woman and her lover. The rite of marriage was of a simple kind, the
essential feature being a gift of clothing (*pudaka*) from the man to the
woman, which is a rite of marriage observed in some other castes of
south India.

[1] See V. K. Raman Manon, 'Ancestor Worship among the Nayars', *Man*,
xx, 1920, p. 25.
[2] Dr. A. Aiyappan, 'The Meaning of the Tali Rite', *Bulletin of the Rama
Varna Research Institute*, ix, part ii, July 1941, pp. 68–83.

An important feature of the Nayar system was that a woman might form a *sambandham* union with a man of the caste of Nambutiri Brahmans. That caste had a patrilineal system in which only the oldest son of a family might marry a woman of his own caste and bring her home with him to raise up children. The children born of a union of a Nambutiri man and a Nayar woman would have no legal position in the family of the father.

The *sambandham* husband did not take his wife to live with him, but visited her in her own home. He did not have any legal rights over her or her property or over any children that resulted from the union. It seems that the wife could divorce her husband by asking him to discontinue his visits. It would appear that he was expected to offer her gifts from time to time. The Nayars have been often quoted as a people practising polyandry, but on this subject there is a difference of opinion amongst recent writers.[1] It seems clear from the historical evidence that in former times, at any rate amongst some of the Nayars, a woman might form a union with two or more men who might be simultaneously her *sambandham*; the Nayar marriage did not give a man exclusive right to sexual relations with the woman.

There has been discussion whether the Nayar *sambandham* union is or is not marriage; this obviously depends on how the word is, defined. The Malabar Marriage Commission of 1894 decided that it did not constitute a legal marriage according to systems of law accepted in India. We may say that it was a marriage in the sense of a socially recognized union which always had some permanence and might continue through a lifetime. It was, however, a union based not on legal bonds but on ties of personal affection.

We can use the Nayars to define a certain type of kinship organization to which the term 'mother-right' may be suitably applied. The system of the Menangkabau Malays was similar in essentials, and so was that of one section of the Khasis. The domestic group (the joint family of Indian legal terminology) is a matrilineal lineage of fewer or more generations. The parental family, the domestic group of man and wife with their young children living together as a household, does not exist. Jural relationships are practically confined to persons connected in the female line; so also are those religious relationships that are constituted by ancestor worship. All important property passes down in the matrilineal lineage, and only members of the lineage have claims over it; inversely the most important duties of a person are towards his or her lineage group and its members.

In the purest form of the system a man does not acquire by marriage any rights of possession over his wife and her children. His relationship with them contains no jural element, but is one of mutual affection. He

[1] See, for example, the correspondence in *Man*, March, April, October, November, and December 1932 and August 1934.

gives his wife gifts, but cannot transfer to her or to his children property which belongs to his lineage or over which the lineage members have a claim. There are some variations. Amongst the Khasi a man did have certain rights over his wife since adultery was severely punished, and in this system there was an elaborate religious ceremony for marriage. The Khasi father occupies a position of respect and is revered by his children after his death. A widow may keep her deceased husband's bones for a time (thus keeping his spirit with her), but sooner or later the bones must go back to the man's lineage and clan. But yet divorce is common and may occur for a variety of reasons.

Mother-right is contrasted with 'father-right' and the people chosen by anthropologists as affording a typical example of the latter were the ancient Romans, or rather one form of family that existed in Rome, characterized by *manus mariti* and *patria potestas*. There was a structure of patrilineal clans (*gentes*) and lineages. The father-right type of marriage must be distinguished from what is sometimes called 'free marriage' or marriage *sine manu*, which also existed in Rome, and in which a woman retained her connexion with her own family. In the father-right marriage possessive rights over a woman were ceremonially transferred from her father or guardian to her husband, and in the *coemptio* marriage a payment was made to the woman's family in consideration of this transfer of rights. The wife thus passed under the power and authority of her husband; she transferred her allegiance from her own household deities and ancestral spirits to those of her husband. The father, the *paterfamilias*, had exclusive possessive rights over his children; they were under his power, the *patria potestas*. Over his sons he had the power of life and death, and might sell a son—the *jus vitae et necis et vendendi*. With this right the law or the mother's relatives could not interfere, but in his exercise of his power the father had to observe the duties of religion, and for an abuse of power might receive censure from the members of his gens, or at one period perhaps from the Censors.

While in one sense mother-right and father-right are opposite types of system, there is another sense in which they are only contrasting varieties of a single type. What they have in common is the extreme emphasis on the lineage, matrilineal or patrilineal, and they both contrast strongly with systems based mainly on cognatic kinship; in both, the jural relations in kinship are rigidly confined to one lineage and clan. Possessive rights over the children belong entirely to the lineage, and inversely it is within the lineage that the individual has his most important duties and also his most significant rights, such as the right of support and rights of inheritance over property. In religion also (remembering that the Romans had patrilineal ancestor worship) it is the lineage or clan ancestors to whom one owes religious duties, and from whom one may ask for succour. The institutional complex of which mother-right and father-right are contrasting forms is thus one that can hardly make its appearance except at a relatively high stage of social development, where property and its transmission have become important, and where social continuity has come to be based on lineage.

We have to ask, therefore, what is the differentiating principle between the two contrasting forms of the complex. It has sometimes been supposed that mother-right is the result of emphasis on the social bond between mother and child, but an examination of evidence gives no support whatever to this view. In primitive societies, whether they have matrilineal or patrilineal institutions, it is normally recognized that the closest of all kinship bonds is that between mother and child. Even in societies that incline to father-right it is felt that a child is of the same flesh and blood as its mother. So children born from one womb have the same flesh and blood, and in the patrilineal tribes of Africa children of the same mother are much more closely connected than children of the same father by different mothers. As Gluckman, following Evans-Pritchard, points out, in strongly patrilineal societies such as the Nuer and Zulu it is through the mother that the social position of a child is determined.[1] We have only to consider the position of the *materfamilias* in the Roman family to realize that under father-right the most intimate personal bond is with the mother.

The contrast between father-right and mother-right is one of two types of marriage. A woman is by birth a member of a sibling group; strong social bonds unite her to her brothers and sisters. By marriage she enters into some sort of relation with her husband. To provide a stable structure there has to be some sort of institutional accommodation of the possibly conflicting claims and loyalties, as between a woman's husband and her brothers and sisters. There are possible two extreme and opposite solutions, those of father-right and mother-right, and an indefinite number of compromises.

In the solution provided by mother-right the sibling group is taken as the most important and permanent unit in social structure. Brothers and sisters remain united, sharing their property, and living together in one domestic group. In marriage the group retains complete possession of a woman; her husband acquires no legal rights at all or a bare minimum; but at the same time he has few duties towards her or her group. Rights of possession over children therefore rest with the mother and her brothers and sisters. It is these persons to whom the child must go for every kind of aid and comfort, and it is they who are entitled to exercise control or discipline over the child.

It must be emphasized that this is a matter of jural (including legal) relations only, and these do not constitute the whole of social life. We may revert to the theory of Aristotle that the two chief factors on which social harmony depends are justice and *philotes*. Justice corresponds to what are here being called jural elements in social relationships. We may

[1] See p. 185.

take the other term as applying to all personal relationships of attachment and affection. A system of mother-right, in which a father has no, or almost no, legal rights over or legal duties towards his children, does not debar, but possibly encourages, mutual affection; for affectionate attachment can perhaps flourish best where there is a minimum of the kind of constraint that may result from the obligations of a jural relationship. Certainly there is evidence of frequent instances of strong and lasting affection between a man and his wife and children under a system of mother-right. The system simply separates out the jural relations, which are confined within the lineage, and the personal relations of affection, esteem, and attachment.

The solution offered by father-right is opposite. Possession of a woman, and therefore of the children of her body, are surrendered by marriage to her husband and his kin. The Roman husband acquires *manus* over his wife and her children fall under his *potestas*. The mother's kin, her brothers and sisters, in this kind of marriage, have no rights over the children, who, in turn, have no rights over them. The jural bonds between a woman and her siblings are severed by her marriage. But this leaves open the possibility of relations of personal affection. It is characteristic of systems that approximate to father-right that the mother's brothers and sisters are expected to extend to her children affectionate care and friendly indulgence, and that the sister's child is expected to exhibit affection towards the maternal uncles and aunts. Once again there is a separation made between jural relations and relations of personal attachment.

Mother-right as represented by the Nayars, and father-right as represented by one form of marriage in Rome, give us useful points of reference for an attempt to establish a systematic typology of kinship systems. In both these types the structure is one in which legal and jural relationships are as nearly as may be possible limited to the lineage and its connexions. The contrary of this is to be found in what are here called cognatic systems, in which jural relations are based on cognatic kinship traced equally through males and females. Such systems, or close approximations, are found in some primitive societies such as the Andaman Islands, and in advanced societies such as Anglo-Saxon and modern England.

In Africa a system that approximates fairly closely to the ideal type of a cognatic system is that of the Lozi, in which there is a minimal emphasis on unilineal kinship, so that lineages can hardly be said to exist as features of social structure. Professor Gluckman has brought out the marked contrast there is between the Lozi system and that of the Zulus which is a very close approximation to father-right.[1] The Lozi system also contrasts with one of mother-right.

Relations of kinship involving rights and duties may also be traced

[1] See below, pp. 166 ff.

through both male and female lines in a double lineage system in which the structure includes both patrilineal and matrilineal lineages or clans. An example of this type of system is provided in this volume by the paper on the Yakö by Professor Daryll Forde. Every individual has a well-defined set of relationships within his patrilineal lineage and clan, and another within his matrilineal lineage and clan.

Thus we have four types of systems (ideal types based on empirical examples) to give us a framework within which to construct a typology: father-right, mother-right, purely cognatic systems, and double lineage systems.

In Africa the nearest approach to pure mother-right is the system of Ashanti, of which an analytical description is given in this volume by Professor Fortes.[1] The system is undergoing modification under European influences of various kinds, but still retains some of its former features. What has in this discussion been held to be the basic structural feature of mother-right, the close and continued solidarity of the sibling group of brothers and sisters of one flesh and blood, is illustrated in Professor Fortes's paper. It is true that the parental family exists, but it is not the standardized form of the domestic group. The importance of lineage transmission of property is well illustrated, and also the religious bonds that unite persons of common descent in the female line.

What can be called 'qualified' systems approximating not very closely to mother-right are characteristic of some parts of central Africa and have been compared in the paper by Dr. Audrey Richards. In the system of the lower Congo, the type A of Dr. Richards, there is an interesting compromise in the form of a division of rights. The male members of a matrilineal lineage continue to live together in a corporate group owning property and having their own religious cult. But the group surrenders certain rights over its female members to her husband when she marries. She retains a significant connexion with the group of her brothers, but does not live with them. The domestic unit is the parental family, man, wife, and young children. Boys, when they reach a certain age, leave the parental family to join the group which consists of the male members of the lineage. The system is one of a division of rights; the father has rights over his wife and his young children within the parental family, and of course corresponding duties. But his sons ultimately fall under the power and authority of the brothers of their mother.

The system of certain tribes of Rhodesia and Nyasaland is a compromise formation in which the division of rights does not seem to be clearly defined, so that there are variations in practice not only from one tribe to another, but also within a tribe. This is connected with the local structure of this region, with its marked mobility by which persons move from one village to another, or establish new villages, so that the personnel

[1] See below, pp. 252 ff.

of a particular village varies from time to time. The structural principle of mother-right appears in a contrary form to that of the Congo tribes, in the tendency for the group of sisters to continue living together, at any rate for some time. This is illustrated by the enlarged domestic group of the Bemba, consisting of a man and his wife and their married daughters with their husbands and children; the group breaks up when a man with his daughters forms a new domestic group of the same kind.

Both Professor Fortes and Dr. Richards draw attention to the existence of tensions and strains in the kinship systems of the Ashanti and the Bemba. But tensions and strains and possibilities of conflict exist in any system of rights and duties. The constraint of social obligations may often be felt as irksome. There is an unfortunate tendency for human beings in some circumstances to insist on their rights rather than to be punctilious in performance of duty. But it is obvious that a system based on compromise or on successive compromises is more likely to reveal tensions or conflicts than one in which jural relations are clearly defined and socially accepted. There is no reason why a system of mother-right should present more difficulties for individual adjustment than a system of father-right. But a system like the Bemba, with its division of rights and its occasions of rearrangement of structure, must obviously depend on the way in which individuals make personal adjustments with each other.

The Ila appear to have a mixed system which is farther removed from mother-right than it is from father-right, in spite of the existence of matrilineal clans and some other matrilineal features.

The Nguni peoples of South Africa, represented in this volume by the Swazi and the Zulu, may be described as having father-right. Possession of children is determined by the marriage payment. 'Cattle beget children' and 'The children are where the cattle are not' is the way the people themselves express this. But during their infancy the children belong to their mother. This is symbolically expressed in the custom by which she may protect them from sickness by making for them necklaces of hairs from the tail of her *ubulunga* cow, which belongs to the ancestral herd of her own lineage, and which she takes with her on marriage, so that during the first period of her marriage she can drink the milk of her own lineage cattle. The *ubulunga* beast, cow for a woman and bull for a man, is a link between the individual and the *sacra* of his or her lineage, the cattle, the kraal, and the ancestral spirits. A woman after her marriage is entitled to the protection of the gods of her own family, and so also are her infant children who are attached to her more than to their father. It is at adolescence that a boy or girl becomes fully incorporated in the father's lineage. There is something similar in the Ashanti system, and still more definitely in the Congo systems, in the way in which a boy's relation with his mother's brothers becomes the preponderant fact in his life after adolescence.

This section illustrates the method of typological analysis applied to institutions of kinship. The procedure is to select certain types which can be used as standards with which to compare others. For the type of mother-right it was necessary to go outside Africa, since even the Ashanti have only a qualified system of mother-right and, moreover, the Nayar and Menangkabau systems had been selected by anthropologists of the last century as best representing actual mother-right or matriarchy. It has also long been customary to take the ancient Romans as an example of father-right or patriarchy, though if we want an African example it might be possible to take the Zulu. It has been argued that the major structural principle of both father-right and mother-right is the maximum emphasis on the lineage as the source of jural and legal relations. The opposite type is therefore that of cognatic systems in which lineage has very little or no recognition. This gives three fixed points on what can be pictured as a chart on which systems could be given position by reference to these points.

To understand certain features of kinship we have to recognize that in many systems the structural unit consists of a woman and her children. This is very clearly seen in the patrilineal tribes of South Africa in which a polygynous family consists of two or more such units, each with its separate dwelling and food-supply, united by the relation to the man who is husband and father. It is by the position of this structural unit in the total kinship structure that we can define the contrast between mother-right and father-right. In true mother-right the unit group of mother and children is completely incorporated, jurally or legally, in the group of the woman's brothers and sisters. In true father-right the unit group is incorporated for jural purposes in a group consisting of brothers with their wives and children.

In trying to classify kinship systems a most important feature to consider is the way in which the relationship of a person to his mother's siblings and to his father's siblings is institutionally defined. In any system that approximates to the cognatic type there is a tendency to treat the father's brother and the mother's brother as relatives of the same kind, and similarly with father's sister and mother's sister; but the assimilation may be less complete where there is some recognition, even though it be slight, of unilineal relationships. The degree of assimilation may sometimes be indicated in the terminology, as in the English use of 'uncle' and 'aunt'. In classificatory terminologies it may appear in the inclusion of the mother's brother under the term for 'father' and of father's sister under the term for 'mother'. In the Lozi system a man calls all the cognatic relatives of his mother in her generation (the children of her father's and mother's brothers and sisters) 'mothers', male and female, and classifies as 'fathers' all the cognatic relatives of his father. It is therefore not patrilineal or matrilineal lineage that is recognized in this terminology, but the Old English distinction amongst the cognates

G

of a person between those on the 'spear' side (through the father) and those on the 'spindle' side (through the mother). It contrasts with the common Bantu custom of using 'father' for the father's brothers and sisters and other persons of the father's lineage and generation, which is an application of the unilineal principle.

Cognatic systems are rare, not only in Africa but in the world at large. The reasons have already been indicated: it is difficult to establish and maintain a wide-range system on a purely cognatic basis; it is only a unilineal system that will permit the division of a society into separate organized kin-groups.

In a typological classification of unilineal systems an important place must be given to those systems, of which the Yakö are a good example, which recognize and attach importance to both matrilineal and patrilineal lineage relationships. This provides a special way of organizing a system of divided right by a cross-segmentation of the society.

XII

The view advanced in this Introduction is that to understand any kinship system it is necessary to carry out an analysis in terms of social structure and social function. The components of social structures are human beings, and a structure is an arrangement of persons in relationships institutionally defined and regulated. The social function of any feature of a system is its relation to the structure and its continuance and stability, not its relation to the biological needs of individuals. The analysis of any particular system cannot be effectively carried out except in the light of the knowledge that we obtain by the systematic comparison of diverse systems.

All the kinship systems of the world are the product of social evolution. An essential feature of evolution is diversification by divergent development, and therefore there is great diversity in the forms of kinship systems. Some idea of the diversity of African systems can be obtained from the sections of this volume. Comparison of diverse systems enables us to discover certain resemblances. Some of these are features which are confined to one ethnic region. An example in Africa is the important part played by cattle and their transfer in the system of marriage and kinship. This is a feature of the patrilineal cattle-keeping peoples of East and South Africa from the Sudan to the Transkei. It is illustrated in this volume in Professor Wilson's paper on the Nyakyusa. It would be valuable if some student could give us a systematic comparative study of the various customs of this kind. As an example of the kind of thing that is meant may be mentioned the custom in some parts of the Transkei that if a man drinks milk from the cattle of a lineage other than his own he may not thereafter marry a woman of that lineage; he is their kinsman through milk and cattle. In the same region the ceremony that completes a marriage is that in which the wife, who has usually borne at least one child, drinks for the first time the milk of her husband's herd.

There are other similarities of custom which, so far from being limited to one ethnic region, are widely distributed in parts of the world distant from one another. Customs of avoidance and joking between relatives by marriage are found in regions scattered all over the world. The custom of privileged familiarity of a sister's son towards his mother's brother is found in some peoples of Africa, Oceania, and North America. Then again the Swazi in South Africa and the Cherokee in North America both apply the term 'grandmother' (*ugogo* in Swazi) to all the women of the lineage or clan of certain grandparents (father's father and mother's father in the matrilineal Cherokee, father's mother and mother's mother in the patrilineal Swazi) and give some measure of preference to marriage with such a 'grandmother'. A general theory of kinship must be tested by the help it gives us in understanding or explaining these resemblances.

For a kinship system to exist, or to continue in existence, it must 'work' with at least some measure of effectiveness. It must provide an integration of persons in a set of relationships within which they can interact and co-operate without too many serious conflicts. Tensions and possibilities of conflict exist in all systems. Professor Fortes and Dr. Richards have pointed out the tensions that exist in societies that approximate to mother-right. In systems approximating to father-right the tensions are different but exist none the less, as may be seen in the account of the Swazi. For a system to work efficiently it must provide methods of limiting, controlling, or resolving such conflicts or tensions. Dr. Nadel, in his paper on the Nuba, contrasts the Nyaro system, which he regards as providing an effective social integration, with the Tullishi system, which functions less efficiently. The Tullishi, he thinks, have been less successful than the Nyaro in constructing a well-ordered system of social relations, and he looks for the reason.

Whether a kinship system functions well or not so well as a mode of social integration depends on the way it is constructed. Just as an architect in designing a building has to make a choice of structural principles which he will use, so, though in less deliberate fashion, in the construction of a kinship system there are a certain limited number of structural principles which can be used and combined in various ways. It is on the selection, method of use, and combination of these principles that the character of the structure depends. A structural analysis of a kinship system must therefore be in terms of structural principles and their application.

The unit of structure everywhere seems to be the group of full siblings —brothers and sisters. The group has its own internal structure by virtue of the distinction between the sexes and the order of birth. Its members, however, are of 'one flesh and blood', and every system makes some use of this solidarity between siblings. This means that everywhere it is felt that brothers and sisters ought to exhibit affection and ought to co-operate and interact without serious conflict. Some of the ways in which the solidarity and unity of the sibling group is utilized in building wider structures have been illustrated in this Introduction.

Since in all societies the closest parental bond is that of children with their mother, the group of brothers and sisters with their mother constitutes a more extended unit of structure. This can be best seen in the polygynous families of patrilineal societies, and is illustrated in the accounts of the Zulu and Swazi. There the compound parental family consists of mother-children groups, each forming a separate 'hut' or 'house' (*indlu*), united to the man who is the father and husband.

In this Introduction it has been suggested that one of the most important questions to ask about a system is, in what way, if at all, it makes use of unilineal kinship as distinct from cognatic kinship. Unilineal kinship receives only a minimum of recognition, if even that, in the Lozi; matrilineal kinship is emphasized in the Ashanti, and patrilineal kinship in the Zulu and Nuer: both matrilineal and patrilineal kinship are made use of in the construction of the system of the Yakö. Between these four selected types there are many intermediate forms.

A further important feature of the social structure of any people is the way in which the kinship system is connected with the territorial arrangement of persons. In the past this has been often overlooked. Careful studies of this are now being made in Central Africa by the Rhodes-Livingstone Institute and the paper in this volume by Professor Evans-Pritchard is directed to a study of this aspect of the social structure of the Nuer. It is in the contact and co-operation of neighbours in a territorial group such as a village, or what Professor Schapera calls a ward, that relations of kinship have their most continuous influence on the social life. Professor Evans-Pritchard draws attention to the difference between the dyadic, person to person, relationships that every kinship system includes, and the group relationships that are established by a system of lineages or clans. They are, of course, both included in what has been called here a kinship system, but the difference between them needs to be recognized.

In this volume it has not been possible to deal systematically with the relation of kinship systems to other parts of the social system, to religion, to political organization, and to economic life. This can, however, be studied in monographic studies of particular peoples. Professor Evans-Pritchard in his book on the Nuer, for example, has dealt with the part played by the system of lineages in the political organization of that people, and Dr. Kuper in *An African Aristocracy* has shown how the kinship system is connected with the political organization of the Swazi.

African societies are undergoing revolutionary changes, as the result of European administrations, missions, and economic factors. In the past the stability of social order in African societies has depended much more on the kinship system than on anything else. In the new conditions kinship systems cannot remain unaffected. The first changes are inevitably destructive of the existing system of obligations. The anthropological observer is able to discover new strains and tensions, new kinds of conflict, as Professor Fortes has done for the Ashanti and Professor Daryll Forde shows for the Yakö. How far the disruption of the existing social order will go, and in what direction reconstruction will be attempted or possible, it is at present impossible to judge. The sanctions provided by the kinship systems for the control of conduct are being weakened. For example, some of those sanctions were religious and cannot persist where missionary enterprise is successful. Judging by what is happening in some parts of Africa the new sanctions, of which the agents are the policeman and the priest or minister of the church, are proving much less effective than those of which the agents were kinsmen speaking with the authority of the ancestors behind them.

The process of change is inevitable. To a very limited extent it can be controlled by the colonial administration, and it is obvious that the effectiveness of any action taken by an administration is dependent on the knowledge they have at their disposal about the native society, its structure and institutions, and what is happening to it at the present time. A wise anthropologist will not try to tell an administrator what he ought to do; it is his special task to provide the scientifically collected and analysed knowledge that the administrator can use if he likes.

KINSHIP AMONG THE SWAZI

By HILDA KUPER

THE Swazi of south-eastern Africa are an amalgamation of Nguni and Sotho clans, welded into a political unit in the late eighteenth century by a conquering Nguni aristocracy. By this military conquest, allegiance to the king overrode clan loyalty and gave rise to a system of government in which the clans—the farthest unilateral extension of a kinship group—were subordinated to a centralized military and political organization. Kinship patterns of the Sotho were blended, as we shall see, with those of the dominant Nguni.

Fictional kinship extending throughout the nation was created through the royal family, with the king and his mother as symbolic parents of the people, and much of their authority is expressed in kinship terms and the associated rights and obligations. Thus in the field of religion the rulers appeal to their royal ancestors on behalf of the entire nation, on the same principle by which the head of each homestead appeals to his own ancestors on behalf of his related dependants. Swazi kinship operates on both the domestic and national level, but the latter is a derivative and I will concentrate in this essay on the domestic aspects.[1]

The Swazi word for kinship—*ubunini*—defines relationship in the general as well as the specific sense. The term *isinini* (kinsman or kinswoman) is extended to non-relatives as a title of affection and gratitude.

THE CLAN

Every Swazi belongs to a patrilineal clan, each of which has a distinctive *isibongo* or clan name. The clan names (of which I counted over seventy) are either eponymous or refer to episodes in the history of the founders. A number of clans which are now separate were once one, and this appears from the *isinanatelo* (from *ukwenana*, to borrow with the intention of returning). The *isinanatelo* is really an extended clan name providing useful historical clues to clan movements and affiliations. If the same name appears in more than one *isinanatelo*, the groups can be regarded as related sub-clans and intermarriage between members is taboo for them as well as for clansmen. Only in the case of the royal clan—the Nkosi—is intermarriage between sub-clans permitted.

Clan subdivision continued at the same time as the centralized political authority developed, and fission was most frequent in the ruling (Nkosi) clan. The Nkosi Ginindza, Mamba, Dvu, Ngwenya, and others are all offshoots of the original Nkosi Dlamini. When the tie with the royal parent became so distant that it carried no privileges,

---

[1] I have described the national aspect of kinship in *An African Aristocracy*, 1947, pp. 54 ff.

the clan name Nkosi was itself occasionally dropped. Clans subdivided through the rivalry of brothers for leadership; or to reward a clan member for services, thereby bestowing on him a following and an area; or (in the Nkosi clan) to sanction intermarriage. Subdivision is now only continued in the royal clan enabling the king to marry women otherwise prohibited by the law of exogamy. Indirectly this keeps the Dlamini nobility a numerical minority and at the same time allows the king to reaffirm his hold on all sections of the people through the ties of polygynous marriage.

At one period of Swazi history every clan had a territorial centre, but at present only a limited number have a clearly defined locality. Evidence of the local base is provided by the changing meaning of the word *isifunza*: in reply to the question, what is your *isifunza*, informants usually give their *isibongo*, but when asked 'Who is the chief of the *isifunza*?' some give the name of the political head of the district though his clan name is different from their own, and others give the name of the man they consider the direct heir of the founder of their clan though he does not live in the same locality. A distinction has thus emerged between the *isibongo*, which may be scattered over a number of political units, and the *isifunza*, which is a local political unit with or without a kinship nucleus.

Segmentation of the Swazi clans has not given rise to any distinctive interlinked lineage structure, that is, to a structure in which the links are remembered. The senior lineage is not even always known, except in clans which have specific tasks in the national organization. As a rule the lineages are parallel, unable to trace exact genealogical connexion. There is no specific word for a lineage: the closest approximation is the word *lusendvo*, which was originally applied to the entire clan but is now restricted to the effective family council which coincides roughly with a lineage. The lineage depth of a commoner is rarely more than five generations; for the aristocrats it increases to eight or ten.

Clan members follow similar taboos and rituals, but only a few clans still practise rituals involving the clan as such. There is a grading of clans into a rough hierarchy according to their position in the tribal structure: at the apex is the conquering Nkosi Dlamini in which the lineage of the king is pre-eminent. This is followed by clans that have provided queen mothers, then by clans with their own ritual of chief-tainship, then by clans holding positions of national importance, and finally by clans with no co-ordinating clan ceremonies, no national officials, and no local centre. The grading of clans does not depend on the customs, all of which are regarded as having equal merit for their members. Moreover, the grading is flexible, some clans having risen through diplomacy or loyalty and others having been demoted through conquest or treachery. The position of the royal clan sets the limit of promotion.

It is clear that the effectiveness of clan membership depends on the national standing of the clan. To men and women of the more important clans clanship involves political and social privileges, but to isolated members of scattered, defeated, or immigrant clans, the clan is simply an exogamous group with a common name and a few common customs; it has no defined organization or claim on active loyalties.

Swazi exogamy extends beyond the sub-clan to the clan, but, as has been mentioned, this is not enforced in the case of the king. Moreover, in contrast with other Nguni a man may, as will be shown, marry into the clans of his mother, paternal grandmother, and maternal grandmother, although certain relatives in each of these clans are forbidden him. The principles affecting the kinship side of the clan activities are developed from behaviour in the family.

THE FAMILY UNIT

The starting-point of the Swazi kinship system—the 'elementary family' of father, mother, and child—depends as in all societies on a recognition of a social relationship which may or may not coincide with a physical tie. The Swazi say 'A child is one blood with its father and its mother', but if a man has refused to perform the recognized marriage ceremony the children will belong to the mother's kin. The indisputable, but by no means sole, evidence of legal marriage is the acceptance by the bride's people of a number of cattle known as *emabeka* under the custom of *ukulobola*.[1] *Ukulobola* is specifically connected with the woman's fertility and with rights over children. In cases where the woman is sterile and cattle have already been paid, a substitute must be sent 'to bear for her'. The rights conferred over the children appear when a subject obtains marriage-cattle from his chief; the first daughter of the union is then spoken of as the chief's child, and cattle received on her marriage go to his heir. If the king contributes even one beast, he receives the full *emabeka* of the first daughter. In both cases the woman is recognized as the legal wife of the subject and the payment of the cattle gives the other men no sexual rights. All children other than the first daughter are regarded as the husband's, even though he may not be the genitor. A man may *lobola* a woman long after she has borne him children, and thereby establish them as his legitimate offspring, but— and in this the Swazi differ markedly from neighbouring Bantu tribes— he may simply *lobola* the children, leaving the woman to marry elsewhere.

The sociological relationship of father and child may conflict with the physiological bond, for while the genitor may be denied the right of social paternity, a child is said to be impelled by the 'call of blood' to seek him out in later life. Here we have one of the many instances in which a social norm is challenged by individual emotions; viewed from

---

[1] Only the king need not give *emabeka* for his queens.

the other angle, the emotional interests of a man and woman for legitimate 'blood' offspring is a major sanction behind family stability. The importance which children attach to the respectability of their mother, and to their own rights in the paternal family, appears from the cases where sons, after the death of the father and sometimes even after the death of the mother, give *emabeka* for her to her people.

Swazi consider the production of legitimate children a social obligation of adult men and women. For a few years after puberty, boys and girls are expected to have *tingani* (sweethearts), but the girls may not fall pregnant without losing value on the marriage market and the boys are fined anything up to ten head of cattle depending on the rank of the girl and the ruling of the court. After marriage the emphasis is on childbearing. 'The marriage-cattle are closed by the carrying sling' (in which the baby is tied on the mother's back) is a common saying. Should a grown man die without children, but leaving behind a lover, it is the duty of his father or his father's heir to give cattle for her and provide a 'thigh' from the kinship group to raise children for the deceased. This is an instance of what Evans-Pritchard has styled 'ghost marriage'. Should a woman be childless, her husband is entitled to a co-wife from her family to produce children, and they are spoken of as the children of the older woman as well as of the younger. The extension of maternity through kinship of co-wives is described as 'to put into the womb of another'. A husband may even take the child of any junior wife and 'put it into the womb' of a senior unrelated co-wife as heir. This type of adoption is most frequently practised in the case of main wives who have no sons, and it is then always best to choose boys whose own mothers are dead or whose mothers are deeply attached to the senior woman. Adoption of non-related children is unknown, the nearest thing to this being the ancient custom of taking over orphans whose parents had been killed in war or for witchcraft. In many respects these children were identified with those of the family head, but they were described—in their absence—as *tigcili* (domestic serfs), and were not included in the full kinship circle.

Wives and children are regarded as a man's greatest assets and polygyny is the ambition of the tribesmen, an ambition most frequently achieved by aristocrats and wealthy elderly commoners. The king is expected to take more wives than any of his subjects, and the present king, who was born in 1902, has more than forty wives. Not only do the queens enhance his prestige and provide him with labour, but they are diplomatically selected from a wide range of clans which are thereby drawn into in-law relationship with the royal family. Swazi say, 'polygamy (*isithembu*) is the nature of man, while the nature of woman is satisfied through children'.

THE HOMESTEAD

On marriage a Swazi girl leaves her family and goes to live in her husband's homestead (*umuti*). If his parents are alive he may attach his huts to the paternal circle or build in the vicinity. Should a patriarch have a number of wives, there is a strong tendency, especially when the sons marry, for his homestead to subdivide into smaller units of mothers and sons. Women always move with their own sons, but as long as the patriarch is alive he is the main authority in all legal and economic issues. Full brothers are more likely to continue to share a homestead after marriage than sons by different mothers, but when they have many wives, full brothers often build separately, the mother staying with the older son and visiting the younger. The section of the homestead in which the mother lives is known as the capital (*umpakatsi*), and in relation to it any other section is merely the barracks (*lilau*).

The homesteads, scattered irregularly over the country-side, vary considerably in size, with the wealth and status of the headman. In a sample area of 66 homesteads, the average number of occupants was 7·2 for commoners' families and 22·5 in the homesteads of aristocrats. The largest *umuti* in the whole county is owned by the ruling family; the smallest that I came across belonged to a Christian widow living with two unmarried sons several miles from their nearest kin. The small isolated group without even a single complete family unit is a modern development and is still most unusual, though for various reasons— economic, religious, and political—homesteads are undoubtedly dwindling in size. The diminishing of the local kinship group is an indication of certain changes taking place in the traditional structure, but space does not permit an analysis of these changes.

A conservative homestead is shaped in a semicircle facing a central circular cattle byre. Each married woman has her own quarters consisting of living- and store-huts and kitchen enclosed by a high reed fence. An enclosure is spoken of as 'the hut of so-and-so' and relationship is counted through the different 'huts'. There is no rigid placing of 'huts' in order of rank as amongst some southern Bantu, but the 'great hut' (*indlunkulu*) is usually in the middle of the semicircle. It is occupied by the mother of the headman, or, if she is dead, by a classificatory mother or a special wife raised to the status of 'mother'. The *indlunkulu*, associated with the elders of the headman's lineage, is the shrine of the homestead. Wives are grouped on either side of it in an order largely determined by the wishes of the headman, though he frequently places the enclosure of the first wife on the right of the 'mother' and the second on her left, the third on the right, and so on. Subdivision of a homestead does not, however, follow any defined grouping of huts, and it breaks up the original order. In the harem of the king and leading princes the arrangement of the wives is somewhat different: there are a number of 'big queens', each with a number of 'little queens' attached to their huts.

In every homestead the headman's line is dominant. All his children have the paternal *isibongo*, which is the same as that of his brothers and their children and any sisters living in his home. Wives always keep their own clan names and this distinguishes them as the 'strangers', the out-group. Unrelated people may attach themselves to the headman and live in his *umuti*, but a sharp distinction following the difference in *isibongo* is drawn between 'our folk' and 'cold people'.

Like all southern Bantu, the Swazi live by cultivating crops and by animal husbandry, and the homestead is the main unit of tribal economy, with the division of labour regulated by sex and age. The women are primarily responsible for the routine work, which carries lower prestige value than the activities monopolized by men.

In the homestead Swazi religion, like Swazi economics, gives greater power to the males than to the females. While both men and women become ancestral spirits after death, it is the men who officiate as family priests for the entire homestead.

The group living in the homestead is always impermanent and fluctuating, affected by marriages, births, deaths, migration, and immigration. At the same time, initial behaviour is shaped in the elementary family with its local basis in the homestead. Here the individual acquires the stereotyped norms reflecting the economic, legal, and religious values of the society, essential for the stability and perpetuation of the total social structure.

BASIC BEHAVIOUR PATTERNS

In the following section I will outline the three basic sets of behaviour patterns in the immediate family—between the spouses, parents and children, and siblings. Since the ideal family is polygynous, the position of co-wives will also be discussed. The behaviour patterns fit into a legal framework which curtails individual preferences and aversions. Inevitably the norms of kinship formulated by the people give little idea of the degree of latitude, or of flagrant violation, or of counter interests, which emerge from observed behaviour, and this can be but touched upon in this article.

(a) Husband and wife

The formally expressed relationship between husband and wife emphasizes the husband's legal rights and makes little mention of the wife's emotional influence. Marriages based on affection are common, but in polygynous homes bestow lower status on the wife and her offspring than marriages arranged by parents or than preferential marriages. A husband is described as the owner (*umnikati*) of his wife;

he cannot, however, do with her as he wishes without being called to account not only by his kinsmen but by her own family. While he is the legal head of the home, she is entitled to definite considerations. She has the right of *ubufati* (wifehood) to demand land to support herself and her children, cattle to provide the children with milk and an inheritance, help in various economic and social ventures, protection against insults and attacks from outsiders. While she may not dispose of her crops without her husband's consent, he may not use any of the property of her hut—even the animals he has allocated to her children—without her consent. Only over the property of the main hut has he, together with his 'mother', undisputed control. By payment of a beast to her parents he acquires rights to his wife's independent earnings as a herbalist or diviner, though he must consult with her as to their distribution. Swazi say, 'A wife is bound to her husband with a law case'; at the same time a husband knows that if he wishes to have a harmonious home, he must temper mastery with consideration. Should a wife be lazy, neglect her children, refuse to cook for the man and his kin, or in other ways break her side of the marriage bargain, he is entitled to beat her, albeit not to excess—he must not 'break the skin'—and if he should, she returns home and her people will exact a fine before allowing her to return. Adultery by the wife is spoken of as 'stealing' from the husband, and in former times the wife was sorely beaten and the lover, if caught in the act, could be killed. To-day the lover is fined in the court, and the woman may be beaten—though if the husband has been away for some years her action is often condoned and she is said 'to hit birds' for her husband who has the right to the adulterine children. This recent tolerance of adultery under present conditions, when large numbers of men are away from their homes for long periods working for Europeans, appears to be a defence technique of the husband and his group anxious to benefit by the fertility of the woman for whom they gave the marriage-cattle.

Divorce is practised by the Swazi, but is extremely rare. A husband can 'return his wife' if she continually misbehaves, and he will receive back his cattle minus two for a daughter and one for a son. It is very much more difficult for a woman to refuse to return to her husband if he asks her people to send her back and is prepared to pay a fine for any wrong he admits to having committed. In the only case that I came across of a woman succeeding in her divorce, her husband had beaten her so brutally that her people laid a charge against him at the Commissioner's court and he was sentenced to prison for six months. His older brother agreed that the woman should not return, and said her people could keep the cattle. Commenting on this case, old councillors insisted that the husband still had the right to any children she might bear. Only if a husband—or if he is dead, his heir—agrees to 'break the stomach' or 'to break the loin' can a woman marry a second time.

The second man pays a fine, usually ten head of cattle, of which half goes to the chief and half to the group of the first husband. Children born after this payment are the legitimate offspring of the second man, who gives a few *emabeka* to the girl's father, who does not return the animals given by the first husband.

A rigid etiquette of *hlonipha* (respect or shame) is demanded from a wife in her husband's home (*ekhakhakhe*). She is prohibited from using the names, or words similar to the principal syllable of the names, of her husband's nearest senior male relatives—his father's father, his father, his father's senior brothers, his own senior brothers—living or dead. If she forgets, she is threatened that her tongue will rot, and if she continues to speak the forbidden sounds, she is sent to fetch a fine from her family. A wife must also avoid certain places in the husband's home; she may not eat various foods, including milk, and she may not wear the style of clothing permitted to the girls of the family; finally she must behave with restraint and conspicuous humility on numerous occasions. The restrictions on her conduct *ekhakhakhe* are most marked during the first year of marriage, and, apart from the language taboos, decrease with the birth of children and years of service for the in-laws. When she is well established the husband, usually on the suggestion of the mother-in-law, gives her, if he can afford it, one or more animals known as *lipakhelo* (from *kupakhela*, to serve). The main purpose of these is to provide against destitution in her old age and to enable her to assist her children. Once she has the *lipakhelo* she is allowed to eat curdled milk *ekhakhakhe*. The laws of *ukuhlonipha*, apart from the language of respect, are considerably modified if a wife is already a kinswoman of her husband, or is attached as co-wife to one of her own relatives, in which case the first woman is said to 'have finished the *hlonipha*'.

The wife is subordinate to the husband in the family religion. Her ancestors may affect the health of herself and her children, but they can only be placated at the home of her own kinsmen and through her male line. The husband is the priest for his ancestors and it is his obligation to keep them well disposed towards his wife. Difficult birth is sometimes attributed to the anger of his ancestors because of 'bitterness' between himself and his wife. When the young couple have 'cleansed the heart', the baby is permitted to come forth.

Wives of a polygynist hold unequal status; during his lifetime they are graded primarily on the basis of seniority, the first taking precedence over the second and so on, but after his death the children's rights to inheritance and succession are determined by their mothers' rank and mode of marriage. The first wife of an important man is chosen for him by his senior paternal relatives and by his mother when they consider that he is ripe for marriage. The first wife is his *isisulamsiti* (wiper away of darkness) and will not be chosen as mother of the heir except in unusual circumstances. Her son is the *lisokancanti* (first circumcised), the adviser and confidant of junior brothers, including the heir.

Except in special circumstances, the successor to a polygynist is not known publicly during his father's lifetime. Only after the death of the husband does the family council choose the heir in accordance with the status of the wives.

The public behaviour of spouses is also regulated by rank and mode of marriage. Princes and chiefs exact more respect and obedience than commoners, and the king's wives are constantly guarded. On the other hand, daughters of the aristocracy are treated with exceptional honour and given considerable freedom.

Co-wives call each other *dzadze* or *fetu* (sister), but usually speak of each other by their different clan names or as mother of so-and-so. Co-wives participate in a number of joint activities in the daily routine; they each contribute to the main family meal and eat it in the yard of the 'great hut'; if the headman wants beer, all his wives must grind the grain, fetch the wood and water, contribute utensils; if he wants his fields weeded all the wives work in them. Between a woman and an *inhlanti*—junior attached co-wife—there is particularly close co-operation including the sharing of store- and cooking-huts.

On the whole, co-wives are on friendly terms with each other and it is not unusual for a woman to ask her husband to take a junior wife—particularly a sister—to help with the chores. But underlying the friendliness is always an undercurrent of suspicion; *bukwele* is the special word applied to the jealousy of co-wives, and the majority of accusations of witchcraft are levelled against these women, particularly the headman's favourite. The keeping of peace in the harem depends largely on the tact and wisdom of the mother of the headman and his first wife. Close relatives are considered useful allies as co-wives, and the kinship structure enables women to have as *tinhlanti* a range of kinswomen—full sisters, half-sisters, and brothers' daughters. The reasons for this selection will appear later.

(b) *Parent and child*

From the Swazi point of view the strongest affective relationship is not that between husband and wife but between mother and child. This is created in the first place by the child's physical dependence on the mother. She fondles and tends the baby, carries it around on her back, and suckles it until it is weaned in the third year. The husband may not cohabit with his wife towards the end of her pregnancy and for a few moons after she has given birth, and he is not allowed to hold the child before it is three moons old. His masculine interests keep him from being with the mother to any great extent and prevent him from giving the infant intimate care. In the polygynous home, in particular, the children regard the father from some distance, and with more respect

than love. The mother is 'soft', indulgent, a buffer between the child
and the father's 'hardness' and authority. (Throughout life, and
symbolized in ritual, the feminine is associated with 'softness', the
masculine with 'hardness'.) A mother has a strong influence on her
children's marriage, and will stand out against her husband if he tries
to force his daughter into a match which the girl finds objectionable;
a mother even goes so far as to encourage the girl to run away to the
maternal kin until the matter has been smoothed over. When a girl
marries, the mother's care and affection are recognized in the special
beast known as the 'wiper away of tears' (*imsulamnyembeti*) given her by
the groom. This remains the mother's property and may not be taken
by her husband; it is inherited by her youngest son, the accepted darling,
and not by the eldest who inherits the main property of her hut. Should
a woman die leaving only daughters, the *timsulamnyembeti* of the girls
should be used by her husband or his main heir to *lobola* a wife who will
be regarded as the 'mother' of the girls, though she may in fact be a
sister-in-law. She will feed them, when they visit the home, from the
late mother's gardens, and her son will be the heir of their hut.

A Swazi woman reaches fullest social stature as 'mother' in the home
of a married son, where she takes charge of his domestic affairs, and
lives in the great hut. A Swazi riddle runs: 'If your mother and wife
were drowning, which would you save first?' and the correct answer is:
'My mother; I can get another wife, but not another mother.'

There is a recognized preference on the part of Swazi, particularly
women, for male children. Herbalists tell me that pregnant women
often come to have the sex of the unborn child 'turned into' a boy, but
none of them could give instances of the desire for transformation into
a girl. On the death of an only son, the mother's stereotyped wail is:
'Who now will bury me? Who will care for me? I have lost my support.
I am abandoned on the veld.' For while a woman holds a privileged
position in the home of her married son, she cannot live at ease with a
married daughter and her son-in-law, especially if he has more than
one wife.

The grown son's behaviour towards his mother combines deference
with affection. For him to swear, uncover himself, or behave lewdly
in her presence is believed to evoke direct ancestral punishment, and
he will also be publicly rebuked and possibly fined by his family council.
The mother is expected to scold him if he neglects his duties as son,
husband, or father, and he must not answer back in anger.

The emphasis is always on the own mother—'the mother who bore
me'. Her hut is *ketfu*—our home. Though a casual European visitor
receives the impression that the children do not differentiate between
the various wives of their father, each of whom they address as 'mother',
and that the women treat all the children, whom they call 'my child', as
their own, to a Swazi there is no confusion. No co-wife may suckle

another's child; even if its mother is very ill, it will be sent to her own mother or to a full sister not in the same harem or to her father's sister. Children describe the 'mothers' by their status *vis-à-vis* their own mother. A senior wife will therefore be 'big mother', and a junior will be 'little mother'. A polygynist's grown children may be older than his youngest wives, but will always call them 'mother'. (Unlike the neighbouring Thonga, Swazi look with horror on the idea of a 'son' on the death of his father cohabiting with a young half-mother. In one case where this was known to have happened, the boy ran away to Johannesburg and refused to return. The woman fled to her own people.) Calling a woman 'mother' involves more than lip-service: the 'mothers' cook food which all the children share and when the real mother is ill or away her child still has its share. The element of personal affection is, however, important, and the real mother usually asks a special friend among her co-wives to look after her child so that it is not neglected—or bewitched.

The mother's interest in her own children often comes out in disputes over property, and the intensity with which she guards the interests of her own hut. A woman is so unwilling for the property of her hut and the marriage-cattle of her daughters to be merged with the general estate, that if she has no son she will urge her husband to put a motherless son 'in her stomach' or attach a junior co-wife to her for the specific purpose of providing a son. Women may not inherit property, but they are entitled to own it and pass it on to their youngest sons.

Succession and inheritance go hand in hand, and the fundamental principle underlying the selection of the main heir of a polygynous estate is that property and power are inherited from men and acquired by them, but are transmitted through women whose rank, more than any other factor, determines the choice. 'A ruler is ruler by his mother.'

Children are trained to regard the father as the legal and economic authority. It is hard to convey the extent of the subservience of the Swazi son to his father. He works for him, consults him in all his negotiations, refers to him as 'his head', takes legal oaths 'by father'. From infancy sons are taught to obey the father's word, and even married sons are never regarded as free from his control. As long as they live in his homestead they are expected to hand over to him whatever they may earn, and he may if he wishes give them back a portion. On the other hand, he must provide a son with cattle for his first wife, he must sacrifice on his behalf, and is responsible before the courts for any torts committed by his sons while in his homestead.

The status of the wives affects the behaviour between the father and his various sons. The first-born son of the first wife is the father's confidant—he is told about the allocation of family property and who the father considers a suitable heir. The father makes special provision for the first-born during his lifetime, and may also 'cut portions' for some of his other children, but the main distribution is only clarified after the father's death and the appointment of the main heir.

Daughters are removed from any legal title to the father's property, but a considerate father will provide them with a beast. The eldest daughter, the *inkosatana* (princess), usually receives special consideration. While close companionship between father and daughter is not expected, there is a recognized affection between them as a basis of reciprocal duties. A father keeps a watchful eye on his married daughter, anxious to secure her happiness and also to guard himself against any claim for return of cattle. On her marriage he provides her with a full bridal outfit and he periodically sends her gifts for herself, her children, and her in-laws. Should she be in need *ekhakhakhe* (at her in-laws) she seeks help from *kuɓo* (her own family), and this can never be refused without incurring the anger of the ancestral spirits at her father's home who remain actively interested in 'their child'.

(c) Siblings

The different claims of the children, dependent on seniority and sex, to family property and position affect their behaviour to each other. While they are still very young they sleep in the same hut, play together, and eat from the same dish, but at about the age of eight, when they have the lobes of the ear slit, the boys are separated from the girls, given masculine duties, and in the game of 'house house' learn not to choose their sisters as their wives. Together with the emphasis on sex and age differences comes an awareness of the importance of seniority of birth, which even overshadows the question of age. They learn to call people by their kinship terms, and on the classificatory system may find themselves addressing as 'father' or 'mother' children of their own age or even younger. No special term of address exists for older brothers or sisters, though in describing their position in a family they use such terms as 'older', 'younger', 'first-born', 'the entrails (last born)', and such.

The social identity of siblings is closest for children of the same sex by the same mother as well as by the same father. Swazi practise the levirate and the sororate. When a man dies, his younger full brother is expected to 'enter' the widows and bear children for the deceased. But should there be no younger full brother, the duty will fall on another junior kinsman rather than on a senior brother, the deceased's oldest brother in particular being treated with the respect and avoidance accorded to a father-in-law. Nor will the widows be 'entered' by the main heir, though he be junior in years to their own husband, for he assumes on the patriarch's death the role of 'father' in all practical affairs.

A man regards his brothers as essential members of his family council (*lusendvo*), and would not decide such important matters as the marriage

H

of a child, or the disposal of cattle or moving of a village, without consulting the senior members of the *lusendvo*.

The tie between sons of the same father undoubtedly depends largely on the status of the wives, and it is over succession and inheritance that cleavages between half-brothers come out sharply and bitterly. But the possibility of friction even between blood brothers appears from the injunction in the royal family that a queen mother should have only one son. 'The king is not followed' (by blood brothers). Swazi clan histories are marked by tragic instances of fraternal disputes.

While the main heir is supposed to assist his other brothers in the same way as a father, the unevenness in inheritance creates jealousies. The main heir receives far and away the major share—not only does he take the cattle of the main hut and of his mother's hut, but the *emabeka* of the first daughter of each independent wife as well as any unallotted property. Only if there is more than one daughter will the oldest son of an independent wife benefit directly by a sister's marriage. He will, however, receive the *emabeka* from the oldest daughter of any junior wife attached to his mother's hut. While the older brothers are thus usually provided for and the youngest son of each hut inherits the mother's property, the middle son is often left destitute unless the father makes special provision during his lifetime. Occasionally a father allots a particular daughter to such a son, and informs the family council that he will receive her *emabeka*, but this is rare: Swazi do not generally practise the custom of 'linking' brothers and sisters as do the Tswana tribes.

The relationship of sisters is not affected to the same extent by primogeniture. While an older sister nearly always marries before her younger full sister, the daughters of different mothers do not necessarily marry in order of age or status. In aristocratic families, moreover, the *inkosatana* (princess) has the privilege of retaining her girlhood freedom longer than other daughters of her father.

Affection and mutual help are the norm of sisterly behaviour. We have already mentioned the desire of an older sister to have a younger as her co-wife. If married to different men, and living long distances apart, the girls still try to keep in touch with each other through travellers and it is not unusual for them, and even for half-sisters, to 'borrow' each others' children, whom they call 'my children', as nursemaids and helps.

While brothers and sisters of the same father, albeit by different mothers, are taught from an early age that sex relationship between them is prohibited, they do not by any means avoid each other. They often walk along hand in hand (a demonstrativeness tabooed a man and his wife), call each other to drink from the same bowl, give each other gifts, and render each other many informal services. A sister acts as intermediary in a brother's love affairs and works for him the bead ornaments worn to make an impression on the girls. As usual, the degree of social distance varies with age and seniority: a boy shows more restraint towards his older than his younger sisters, and a girl knows that she will have to obey the main heir after her father's death.

Despite the difference of sex, the 'unity of the sibling group' appears in the marriage ritual when the groom makes a symbolic bid for another girl from the bride's family.[1] Should the bride have no younger full sister, but should there be a brother by the same mother, this boy is pointed out as providing her *inhlanti*. His daughter is a suitable junior wife for his sister—that is, for the girl's father's sister. While this arrangement is usually explained by the Swazi on the ground that the brother benefited by the sister's marriage-cattle and is therefore obliged to provide her with a co-wife if necessary, the underlying principle of the social equivalence of siblings is clear. It, and not the Swazi rationalization, accounts for the fact that a sister is the most suitable *inhlanti*, and only in the absence of a full sister does the obligation fall on the full brother. In finding a substitute for an independent wife who has died childless, and without a full sister, the choice of a daughter by the full brother is largely determined by her status. The strength of this obligation appears from a case in the royal family. The late king Bunu had a full sister Tonga Tonga, who married an important Ndwandwe chief who gave for her 100 cattle. Tonga Tonga was accompanied, as *inhlanti*, by a half-sister by a junior wife of Bunu's father. Tonga Tonga died childless soon after the marriage, and it fell to Sobhuza, heir of Bunu, to provide a substitute. Tonga Tonga had no full sister, and the family council selected as her substitute Bunu's leading daughter, Sencaβapi. Tonga Tonga's *inhlanti* then became Sencaβapi's *inhlanti*, though she, Sencaβapi, was her *inhlanti's* brother's child—an apparent reversal of the usual role, brought about through the emphasis on full status equivalence.

The extent to which a brother benefits directly by the bride-wealth of a sister depends on his place in the family, but all the brothers are considered to share in the increased family prosperity. This point was frequently made by informants—and so brothers by the same father help sisters when in need. A legal obligation rests on the heir or on the brother who received her marriage-cattle, and a moral obligation on all the brothers.

A sister enjoys a specially privileged position in the home of married brothers, and can take from their wives (her sisters-in-law) clothing, utensils, and other odds and ends, which may never be refused. The wives should appear glad, and only if articles of too great a value are removed may they complain against 'the girl of the home'. The difference between

---

[1] For a fuller description of marriage ritual see my article 'Marriage of a Swazi Princess', *Africa*, xv. 3, July 1945, pp. 145–55.

the position of a woman as wife and sister is very marked. Whereas she is always an outsider *ekhakhakhe*, when she comes *kuɓo* she is addressed as 'princess', 'our girl', or by her first name; she does not use the *hlonipha* language of shame and respect and has the free run of the home. Her children, described affectionately as 'the calves', often spend many years *kaɓonina* (at the mother's home) with their mother's brother (*umalume*, male mother). When the food is not cooked, or the fields are not hoed, the wife and not the sister is blamed, and when illness attacks a home the sister is seldom divined as a source of evil. Because of the trust that brothers have in their sisters being eager to promote their well-being, they are amongst the category of people to whom it is safe to send an heir till he reaches the strength of maturity.

PATERNAL AND MATERNAL KIN

Beyond the immediate family, which I have discussed primarily from the angle of behaviour, extends a range of kinsmen on both the father's and the mother's side. The way in which these are recognized provides the kinship structure which, albeit it hinges at each level on an immediate family, has a permanency and consistency greater than that of any particular family.

Though a Swazi retains links with the families of both his parents, the emphasis on the paternal kin (*kaɓoyise*) and maternal kin (*kaɓonina*) is not identical. The agnatic line has greater time depth, going back five to eight generations, and in the royal family even farther, while in the maternal group descent can be traced for only three or four generations, except in those cases where the mother belongs to the royal lineage.

The broad principles of the extended kinship structure can be seen from the chart of kinship terminology (Figs. 1, 2). It shows the typical feature of the classificatory kinship system in which a limited number of terms applied to lineal relatives are also applied to collateral. Thus the term *uɓaɓe* is not only applied to my own father, but to my father's brother (by the same or different mothers) and to my father's father's brothers' sons; and by a process of extension on the maternal side, it is also used for husbands of all the women I call *mage*—my own mother, my mother's co-wives, mother's sisters, mother's mother's sisters' daughters, and my mother's father's sisters' daughters as well as the wives of the men I call 'father'.

Swazi kinship terminology covers a range of five generations in all—two ascending, the contemporary, and two descending. Beyond the second ascending—the grandparent generation—everyone is classified as *ɓogogomkulu*, and beyond the second descending—the grandchild generation—as *ɓantfwaɓantfwaɓami*. If relationship with a person of the clan name of my mother or father cannot be traced, the generation

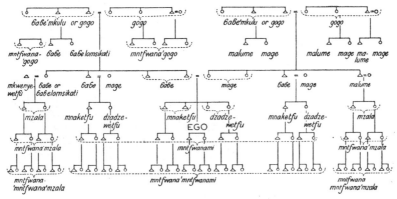

Each term is in the singular, and is in the vocative case

△ = male   ○ = female

FIG. 1. PATERNAL AND MATERNAL KIN

HUSBAND'S RELATIVES   WIFE'S RELATIVES

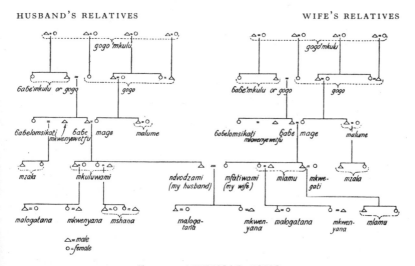

△ = male
○ = female

FIG. 2. AFFINAL KIN

kinship terms are usually applied, any one of roughly the generation of my father being called 'father', and so on.

Within each category of relations a distinction can always be drawn between close and distant kin. This is reflected in social obligations, the general rule being that the closer the tie the more precise and definite the obligations. The degree of distance will be elaborated in the descriptive term even though it does not appear in the term of address, which only indicates the broad category. Thus while a man will be able to describe accurately the 'huts' of his father's different wives, he will call them each *mage*, and while he describes his father's older brother as *babemkulu* (big father), he may address him, as well as his father, as *babe*.

Different terms of address for the same person do not all have the same emotional meaning, some carrying more affection and others more deference. There is a special word *kunambitsisa*, derived from *kunambitsa* (to have a pleasant after-taste from food), associated with the selection of the more demonstrative term. A woman will *nambitsisa* her brother's child if she calls him *mntfwanaketfu* (child of our place), but if she were angry she would reprimand him as *mntfwana' mnaketfu* (child of my brother), to imply his indebtedness to her, his father's sister. The word *kunambitsisa* is also used to describe the friendly familiarity permitted between various sets of relations, but the so-called 'joking relationship' is not developed among the Swazi.

(a) Paternal Aunt and Maternal Uncle

Swazi share with other Southern Bantu the custom of identifying each parent with his or her own siblings, with a slight differentiation according to sex. Not only are the father's brothers called *babe*, but his sister may be addressed as *babe* or by her descriptive term *babelomsikati* (female father). Similarly the mother's brother is *mage* or *malume* (male mother). The paternal aunt exercises the same type of authority over her brother's children as the father, and must receive respect and obedience from them. I remember when Sobhuza was visited by his paternal aunt in his modern office that she sat on the floor and he thereupon got off his chair and squatted beside her, explaining to me afterwards that he could not be 'above her'. The father's full sister takes part in the choice of her nephew's main wife as a member of his family council, and, as we have already stated, the paternal niece is a potential *inhlanti*.

The fact that the father's sister bestowed benefits on the father through her marriage cattle entitles her, by Swazi standards, to make various demands on him, on his wives, and on the children of the union which she made possible. On the other hand, the maternal uncle received advantages through the marriage of his sister, and she and her children may receive help from him. The *umalume* is always a great favourite; the *bashana* (sing. *umshana*, niece or nephew), may take beer from his hut without asking his permission, they bring him their troubles and seek his intervention in disputes with their own father. An *umalume* is under no legal obligation to assist even a full sister's son to collect bride-wealth, but he may do so from affection, and there have been a few cases where a man's own children resented the favours showered by him on a sister's children.

Marriage between an *umalume* and a niece is not favoured since it introduces the tension of sexual interest into an easy protective relationship. Furthermore, by such a marriage the man's sister becomes his mother-in-law, and familiarity following on the sibling tie is distorted by the avoidance imposed on a son-in-law. Even if the *umalume* is the brother of the wife of a classificatory father, the marriage is not encouraged. For this reason pressure was exerted, albeit in vain, against the marriage of Lamtana Dlamini, daughter of King Bunu's youngest brother, Lomvase Dlamini, to her *umalume*, Mzululeke Ndwandwe, brother of Bunu's main wife.

If a woman has no child or if she has borne only daughters, she may ask her brother to provide an *inhlanti*. The case of the late queen-mother Lomawa is usually cited as an example of this arrangement. Her mother, laNdlela (of the Ndlela clan), married Ngolotsheni Mkwatshwa and had three daughters, of whom Lomawa was the eldest. Ngolotsheni spoke to his wife and suggested she should get an *inhlanti* so that the cattle for her daughters need not be eaten by the great hut. LaNdlela had no sister, but her mother's brother of the Madlamalala clan had a daughter, and she was given to laNdlela (her cross-cousin—*umzala*) as an *inhlanti*, and bore the required heir.

Because of the father's sister's claim to her brother's daughter, her husband addresses her niece by the term of a potential spouse—*mlamu* —to which she responds with *mkwenyewetfu*. And because of the brother-sister obligation, the nephew is also called *umlamu*. The difference in generation is not important in husband-wife relationship in a polygynous society, where it is not unusual for a man's oldest sons to be senior to his youngest wives. Between *umlamu* and *umkwenyewetfu* is an easy familiarity more fully described in the account of the behaviour of a man and his wife's sisters and brothers, the bulk of his *balamu* (p. 108).

A Swazi idiom states 'The seed is begged from the kin' (*inhlanyelo iyacelwa esininini*). This is applied to cases such as those mentioned above in which a man marries more than one woman because of the women's relationship to each other.

It is also applied to marriages with women to whom the man is related in his own right. It is in the attitude towards such marriages that we see the influence of the Sotho on the dominant Nguni pattern. 'The Nguni', Mrs. Hoernlé writes, 'rigidly prohibit marriage, or sexual relations of any kind, with people related through any of the four

grandparents' (p. 74). 'The Sotho tribes all allow certain types of kin
to marry' (p. 86).[1]

(b) Cousins

Parallel cousins are classed as siblings and marriage between them
is condemned as incest; cross-cousins are distinguished as *bomzala* and
marriage between them is permitted. In the case of close cross-cousins
it is discouraged, but there is one instance in which marriage with a
maternal uncle's daughter is approved by a section of the people. If a
man's own mother is dead and he has no classificatory mother to put
in her place, some Swazi consider it a sign of filial affection to marry
a woman with the mother's clan name. Daughters of her full brothers
and half-brothers are considered 'too close', but the daughter of a 'clan
brother' is considered suitable 'to wake the hut of mother (*kuvusa indlu
yamage*)'. This gesture is usually made by a polygynist who puts the
woman into the 'mother's hut' of his main homestead. A cross-cousin
is never selected as main wife, but her link with the 'mother' gives her
the privileges of 'mother' during her 'son's' lifetime. It is interesting to
note that the Swazi are not agreed on the advisability of such marriages.
Some regard them as admirable, others look on them with disfavour.
The cleavage may originally have followed the division between Sotho
and Nguni clans, but to-day it seems largely a matter of personal
opinion. The discussion came out clearly when Timba Maseko, whose
own mother, Tana Hlophe, died, married Nkaniso Hlophe, daughter of
his mother's father's half-brother's son. Some informants considered
it a good marriage, others were very much against it and argued that
he should have put a 'cold' wife—a non-relative—into the hut of the
mother.

The kinship marriage which is generally approved is that with '*ugogo*'
—a woman of the family or clan of the paternal or maternal grandmother. This can be explained by the general behaviour between grandparents, parents, and grandchildren.

(c) Grandparents

The social inequality between proximate generations was illustrated
in the parent-child relationship, where it also became clear that the
generation distinction could be overruled by primogeniture as in the
promotion of the main heir to the status of 'father'. Marriage between
relatives two generations apart perpetuates the family links without
impinging on the parent-child behaviour.

Since marriage is patrilocal, a child often grows up in the home of the
paternal grandparents. The grandparents are said 'to teach the young

[1] *The Bantu-Speaking Tribes of South Africa*, edited by I. Schapera, Routledge,
1937.

to respect their parents'. Grandparents 'scold by the mouth', parents more often 'with the stick'. The law of the past issues in the voice of the grandfather, and he must give his sanction and opinion on any important event, such as the marriage of a grandchild. The power exercised by apparently decrepit ancients over sons and grandsons is partly explained by the fact that they are 'the nearest to the ancestors' and essential officiators in all domestic rituals. The grandmother—*ugogo*—is the main teacher of the young. She sees that the correct ritual is performed to ensure the health and proper development of the grandchildren and she supervises the numerous ceremonies which punctuate their growth in status. In many districts a woman, after she has borne a child, is not allowed into the great hut until the baby can crawl, when it is led to the supporting poles in the hut and then into the courtyard where the granny is waiting; she puts a little ash from the hearth on its forehead so that 'it will be one with its forefathers'. When the grandchildren are weaned they are usually put in her charge, and they sleep with her till approaching puberty, when boys and girls move to separate quarters.

So honoured and important is the paternal grandmother that any woman, irrespective of her generation, with the same clan name is addressed as *gogo*. Here the generation principle is violated and clan relationship triumphs over the family. Marriage with a woman of the paternal grandmother's clan gives her high status in a polygynous *ménage*, for she is said 'to wake the hut of granny' and also 'to wake the hut of father'. Such a wife is freed from most of the early restrictions of *hlonipha* since they were 'finished' by the dead grandmother whose place she revives.

The maternal grandparents show a proverbial affection and indulgence: 'at the home of the mother, the grandchildren are adored.' When a daughter is pregnant for the first time her mother usually pays her a visit bringing special beer, and the son-in-law kills a beast for her in return. Maternal grandparents beg the father to send the child to them on visits, and when it arrives lavish on it admiration and tenderness. 'It is the child of the calf.' If at all wealthy, the girl's father or brother gives the baby, whether boy or girl, an animal known as the 'beast to kiss'. The maternal grandparents also slaughter a goat to provide the babe with a carrying sling. The maternal kin must be kept informed of any illness, and if it is divined as caused by *lidloti lakuɓo* (the ancestor of the maternal home) the girl's father or brother must provide the sacrifice and officiate at his own hearth. Illness is attributed more frequently to the paternal than the maternal kin, while very often a woman and her children are said to be 'saved' by the 'ancestors of the maternal home'.

Marriage with a woman of the clan of the maternal grandmother (*ugogo otalamage*) is rated almost as high as marriage with a woman of the clan of the paternal grandmother (*ugogo otalaɓaɓe*). Such a wife is said 'to wake the hut of the mother's people', and she too is absolved from some of the taboos of other wives.

The position can be seen from the following diagram:

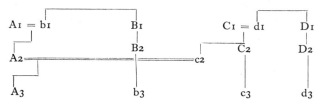

Capital letters represent males, lower-case letters females. For A_3 his mother's clan is C, his father's mother's clan is B, and his mother's mother's clan is D.

The grandparent–grandchild relationship has various repercussions. Thus, by the marriage of A_3 to b_3 (marriage into the paternal grandmother's clan), A_2 becomes the father-in-law of the woman b_3 who is his mother's relation. The cattle that left A_1's group for the woman b_1 made A_2 legitimate and created a bond with the B group, to give b_2's son the greater part of the estate of A_1's grandchild. A_3, as the meeting-point of the four clans A, B, C, and D, may obtain his main wife from B or D, the groups to which cattle were given by A and C. The men of B and D have no reciprocal claim to the sisters of A_2, though if they should intermarry many families rejoice that the 'cattle have returned home'. Other Swazi disapprove of such ties, saying that it is too like 'buying from each other'.

The order of preference in choosing a main wife of A_3 from amongst b_3, c_3, and d_3 would be b_3, d_3, c_3. (Other modes of marriage, such as that mentioned in the final section on rank, are rated even higher.) Since no Swazi desires to create unnecessary conflict it very rarely happens that anyone marries both a paternal and a maternal ugogo, and in such cases the paternal line has preference unless the mother be alive, when she may persuade the family council to favour her own clanswoman. This happened in the case of that forceful character, the queen-mother Gwamile Mdluli. Her younger son Malunge Dlamini included amongst his wives a woman of the Maßuzo clan and another of the Nkambule. Nkambule was the clan of his paternal ugogo, mother of the King Mbandzeni himself, and Maßuzo was Gwamile's own mother's clan name. Malunge died and the family council wanted to choose as main wife the Nkambule woman, but Gwamile, though her own father was not of great importance, argued so strongly in favour of ßakußo that they agreed to choose the Maßuzo wife.

In marriages with either a paternal or maternal ugogo the link may be through a common grandparent, as well as with more distant members of these clans.

AFFINES

In societies where marriages between kin are permitted the distinction between relatives 'by blood' and 'by marriage' is not usually sharp. But amongst the Swazi marriages with kinsmen are rare except in large polygynous homesteads. Of 35 monogamous marriages, 1 was with a maternal cross-cousin and 1 with a maternal uncle; on the other hand, 5 out of 12 chiefs whose genealogies I traced were selected as main heirs because their mothers were of the *ugogo* clan—2 paternal and 3 maternal (of the remaining 7, 3 were selected because their mothers were princesses of the ruling family; 2 were 'arranged' marriages (*ukwenzisa*); 2 were women of exceptional character).

Despite marriages between kinsfolk, the dominant pattern in affinal relations is set by the Nguni section of the population to which the royal clan belongs, and opposition between the two intermarrying groups is formally stereotyped. The husband's relatives, the *ɓekhakhakhe*, are put into a different legal and emotional category from the *ɓakuɓo*, and the husband draws a parallel distinction with the *kaɓomfati* (wife's folk).

(a) Parents-in-law

The restrictions imposed on a wife have already been mentioned, and since marriage is normally patrilocal the position of wife and daughter-in-law overlap locally. The strongest avoidance is manifested between the bride (*umkoti*) and her father-in-law, stressing the sexual barrier between them. In a polygynous home a father's young wife may be a contemporary of his son's wife, and a strong artificial sanction, based on maintaining peace between father and son, removes the son's wife from the range of potential mates of the old, dominant male. The young girl becomes the 'handmaiden' of the mother-in-law, whose own reproductive sexual life must cease when her oldest child marries.

The husband's behaviour towards his wife's parents is on the same pattern as hers to his group, but is eased by the fact that he does not live in their home. The difference of sex involves him in showing the strongest avoidance of his mother-in-law, his *umkwegati*. A man will be fined by his wife's family council if he makes lewd jokes or in any way misbehaves in her presence, and 'shame' prevents him eating (an act psychologically and verbally associated with sex) in her presence. She reciprocates with similar observances towards the son-in-law, whom she usually addresses as *mkwenyana*, or, if she wishes to *nambitsisa* him, as *mntfanami* (my child), but never by his personal name. Though some of the irksome taboos are absent in the case of kinswomen, and in any case decrease with the passing of the years, it is considered impossible for a man, particularly a polygynist, to live easily with his mother-in-law. 'She knows what I am doing to her child, who is a woman like herself.' One section of Swazi consider that the strongest prohibition against marriage, as strong as the law forbidding marriage with a person of one's own clan, is with a woman of the clan of the wife's mother, even though no relationship between the two women can be traced. We have seen that other sections, following the Sotho pattern, approve of this marriage in certain circumstances.

A man treats his wife's father with respect and courtesy, knowing that he is the person to whom the wife will appeal if badly treated. Being of the same sex, the relationship with the father-in-law is less strained than with the mother-in-law, but the *umkwenyana* is always on his best behaviour on his occasional visits. The father-in-law helps the situation by inviting him to eat and drink with him, and by extending opportunities for co-operation in male occupations. A good son-in-law is recognized as an asset in economic ventures.

The mother-in-law is the great *umkwegati*, but there are other women in a wife's home who are also tabooed and called *bakwegati*—they are the wife's brothers' wives. Though the social distance between a man and these women is not as irksome as with his mother-in-law, they are removed from all sexual contact. They are, in fact, potential mothers-in-law, because they may be called upon to provide his wife with an *inhlanti*.

(b) Sisters- and brothers-in-law

In sharp contrast to the avoidance of *bakwegati* is the familiarity between a man and his wife's sisters and brothers—the *balamu*. A wife's sisters can be taken as independent or subordinate wives, and until they are married they indulge in rough and often suggestive horseplay with the married sister's husband (*umkwenyewetfu*). Should he, however, make them pregnant without having negotiated marriage, he is fined and treated as an ordinary suitor. And once an *umlamu* is married, intimacy with her is regarded as adultery. The male *umlamu* will, if he provides a daughter as *inhlanti* to his sister, also be identified with a father-in-law, but the *umlamu* relationship is the stronger of the two.

The popularity of the marriage of a man with more than one woman of the same family appears from these limited figures: out of 24 marriages of commoners, each with two wives, 7 married two sisters. In the harem of the king Sobhuza II we find the following marriage types for his 43 wives: 14 women are unrelated to him and to each other; 4 women each have one full sister in the harem; 2 women have clan sisters; 8 women are of the Nkosi clan (one of them is linked with him through a common grandfather by different wives and this marriage evoked such criticism because of the 'closeness' that he set her up in a completely separate homestead from his other wives); 4 women are of the paternal grandmother's clan; 1 woman of the maternal grandmother's clan.

The husband's senior brothers receive some of the respect accorded to the father-in-law. Until his death all the husband's brothers and sisters are classed as *bomkulubakhe*, and they reciprocate with the same term. After his death the main heir becomes 'father-in-law'. By the custom of the levirate, the younger brothers are a wife's potential mates, and they may call her jokingly 'my wife', to which she will reply 'my husband'. But it is dangerous to show too much friendliness during the husband's lifetime lest they be accused of having caused the death. (The levirate relationship is fraught with difficulties and is in fact never gladly accepted by a brother, particularly if he has his own wives.) The term *umkuluwakhe* is also used of a woman and her brother's wives, and we have already described the right which she has to her husband's sister's daughter. *Umkuluwakhe* connotes mutual obligations and familiarities and a potential link through marriage.

(c) The groups

The two sets of parents-in-law address each other as *bakoti* and are polite and hospitable to each other. The man's people slaughter a beast when the girl's father or mother pays them a visit and the girl's folk send beer and presents. Naturally a great deal depends on how close the homes are to each other, distance making regular effective contact difficult. However, certain courtesies, particularly notification of births, illnesses, and deaths, are ritually enforced by the belief that their omission would evoke 'the bitterness of the ancestors'. To meet a person and call him or her *umakoti* is to *nambitsisa* that person exceedingly. The term *bakoti* is also extended to the grandparents of the young couple.

Apart from the relatives-in-law whom I have specially mentioned and to whom man and wife react in different norms, there are a number of in-laws to whom man and wife behave in similar fashion. Swazi say: 'My wife and I are one, through marriage, and her relations become mine', and vice versa. This explains the similar terms used towards each other's father's sister, mother's brother, and other categories evident on the chart (Fig. 2, p. 101).

RANK AND KINSHIP

An essay on Swazi kinship would be incomplete without special reference to rank, for Swazi kinship, like all other Swazi modes of behaviour, is characterized by the importance of rank by birth. Even within the immediate family the relationships reflect the pedigree of the parents: the mother of the king, for example, is married with cattle provided by representative sections of the people, making the king 'child of the country', and similarly chiefs of the district have the *emabeka* of their main wives contributed by their subjects.

The selection of a main heir is determined by the rank of the mothers, and we have indicated the preference given to women known as *ugogo*.

Even more important are women of the ruling clan, particularly sisters and daughters of the king. These women are sent as wives to important chiefs, spreading the network of the dominant aristocracy. When the polygynist Kambi Maseko died, his wives included a daughter of the king Mswati (by the levirate) and one with the clan name of the paternal grandmother. The family council appointed the latter as main wife, and announced their choice to the ruling king. When he found out that a royal princess had been overlooked, he told the council to reconsider their decision, for 'it is not law that the king should eat on the ground while the dog eats from the plate'.

To discuss fully the repercussions of rank on kinship would lead us into an analysis of the political structure, and we can in this essay merely indicate that the two are closely interlocked.

NYAKYUSA KINSHIP

By MONICA WILSON

INTRODUCTORY

THE Nyakyusa[1] are a Bantu-speaking group, numbering some 150,000, who live in a portion of the Great Rift Valley at the north end of Lake Nyasa. Their country is fertile, the rainfall is heavy and well distributed, and they are skilled and diligent cultivators, growing a great variety of crops. They also keep cattle, and fish in the lake and streams. Hence the land can carry a heavy population, averaging over 80 to the square mile, and in contrast to many of their neighbours the Nyakyusa are well fed and vigorous.

They are peculiar in that their villages consist not of kinsmen but of age-mates. Herd-boys of 10 or 11, who are the sons of neighbours, begin to build together at a little distance from their fathers. Gradually they are joined by younger boys, also from the village of their fathers, until the group covers an age-span of about five years; then the next set of boys is told to start a new village of its own. Most of these age-mates remain together all their lives. As they marry they bring their wives to the village and the children they beget live with them until the daughters marry, and the sons, in their turn, build new villages. Though the site of a village changes the group survives until the death of its members.

Once in each generation a great ceremony is held at which the chief-dom divides into two halves, each under a son of the chief, and authority is handed over to these sons and the leaders of the villages of young men. At this ceremony the old men within each half move aside, leaving the bulk of the land for their sons, who now rule the country. All the boundaries of the villages are redrawn, and the young men move from the site on which they built as boys to one which allows more room for their expanding families. Thus the Nyakyusa combine with chieftain-ship the formal handing of authority from generation to generation, so typical of the East African peoples organized in age-grades.

Being surrounded on three sides by high mountains, and on the fourth by the stormy head-waters of the lake, the Nyakyusa long remained isolated from the outside world. They were scarcely touched by slave-raiders and successfully repelled marauding bands of Ngoni. Not until 1891 did European missionaries settle in the country and the authority of the German Government was only established somewhat

[1] The material on which this essay is based was collected between 1934 and 1938 by my late husband, Godfrey Wilson, and myself. During that period he was a Fellow of the Rockefeller Foundation, and I a Fellow of the International African Institute. We are indebted to these bodies for making this research possible.

later. But by the middle of the nineteen-thirties (to which period this description refers) the Nyakyusa were doing a vigorous trade with the outside world in coffee, rice, and other local products, and many young men spent periods working on the nearby Lupa gold-diggings. Some 16 per cent. professed Christianity, and there were demands for more schools and trained teachers. Such is the group with whose marriage and kinship relations we are concerned.[1]

<h2 style="text-align:center">KINSHIP GROUPS</h2>

The basic unit of Nyakyusa society is the *elementary family* consisting of a man, his wife, and children. All families begin as elementary families and some remain so, but polygyny is permitted and honoured and the majority of men are able, as they grow older, to marry other wives, thus linking together a number of elementary families in a *compound family*.

There is no evidence of any marked difference in the survival rate of males and females, but there is a difference of ten years or more in the average marriage-age of girls and men, and it is this differential marriage-age which makes polygyny possible. A legal marriage is effected by the transfer of cattle from the groom to the bride's father, and the system is linked with a late marriage-age for young men and with a privileged position for the older men. Many men have not cattle with which to marry until they are well over 25, while their fathers may be able to afford more than one wife. The tax registers show in part of the district, among 3,000 men presumed to be 18 years or over, 34 per cent. bachelors, 37 per cent. monogamists, and 29 per cent. polygynists, and investigation proves that, generally speaking, it is the young men who are bachelors, and the men over 45 who are polygynists. Few commoners have more than 7 or 8 wives, but a chief may have as many as 40.

Within a compound family each wife and her children form a distinct segment. Each wife has either a hut to herself or else a separate alcove in a long hut with partitions, and there she has her fire for cooking. She fetches her own firewood and water, or sends an unmarried daughter for them. At meal times each mother eats with her own daughters and young sons apart; more rarely one or two women, either co-wives or neighbours, choose to eat together, but this group probably does not include all the wives of one man, for only those who are particularly friendly will join. Each mother provides food for her own sons, who, after 10 or 11, usually eat with friends of their own age, the group of age-mates visiting the mother of each member in turn. The husband eats alone or with neighbours of his own age, his wives each sending him a dish or taking turns to cook the whole meal.

---

[1] For an outline of Nyakyusa society see Godfrey Wilson, 'An Introduction to Nyakyusa Society', *Bantu Studies*, x, 1936, pp. 253–91.

The separate identity of each segment or *house* of the compound family is also reflected in the family names. Every man has three family names, that of his paternal grandfather, that of his father, and that of his mother, and a girl is referred to by her mother's family name as well as by that of her father. Thus the mother's name groups together the full brothers and sisters within a compound family, and if an individual in detailing his or her genealogy says, 'We were so many', the implication always is that there were so many children the offspring of one mother, sharing the mother's name.

Among commoners the first wife betrothed to a man while she is yet unmarried[1] ranks as the great wife (*unkasikulu*), and her eldest son is her husband's ultimate heir, inheriting the bulk of the family property. She herself takes precedence in ritual and she is entitled to the respect of her co-wives, but she has no authority over them, and the other wives are not ranked in order. A wise husband, it is said, divides his favours equally, visiting his wives in turn, and dividing what milk or meat there may be fairly between them; but in practice every man is thought to have a favourite with whom he sleeps more often, and to whom he gives more fine food or ornaments, than to the others. Often the latest bride ousts a former favourite and there is bitter antagonism between them—accusations of witchcraft against co-wives are frequent. Polygyny is thus correlated with jealousy and competition which involve a subordinate position for women in relation to their husband.

In a homestead (*akaja*) there commonly live together only a man, his wives, and their young children; sons, as we have seen, build for themselves at a little distance before they reach puberty; they work with their fathers and are cooked for by their mothers until they marry, but they live in a separate village. Girls also leave home early, for they are often betrothed and begin to visit their husbands from the age of 8 or 9, moving permanently to their husbands' homesteads at puberty. A man may build for an elderly mother in his homestead, but the obligation of a widow to go to the heir is insisted upon at least until she be past child-bearing; only in Christian families is it usual for a middle-aged widow and her son to live together. Occasionally a rich man with several wives may build two homesteads in different parts of the country, but this again is unusual except with chiefs.

Inheritance and succession in Nyakyusa society are dominantly patrilineal; genealogies are commonly traced farther in the male than in the female line, and economic and ritual co-operation extend farther among agnates than among matrilineal kin. Agnatic lineages of a span of three or more generations are concerned with the control and exchange of cattle, with inheritance, and with certain rituals, but for other purposes

[1] A divorcée ranks lower than such a girl even although marriage cattle have been given for the divorcée before an unmarried girl is betrothed.

I

it is not strictly lineages, but rather groups of cognates with a patrilineal bias, which co-operate. The Nyakyusa have no word for a lineage. All a man's kindred—the group of his cognates—make up his *ikikolo*. He distinguishes between his father's kindred (*ikikolo kya tata*) and his mother's kindred (*ikikolo kya juba* or *abipwa*), but both groups include relatives in the male and female lines; a child may participate in a ritual in his mother's sister's or his father's sister's family, as well as in those of his father and his mother's brother. The importance of links through females is brought out by the fact that at every point full siblings are held to be more closely related than half-siblings. For example, marriages between the descendants of a common great-grandfather are much disliked, but they are considered less bad if only one great-grandparent, not two, are common, i.e. if the related grand-parents are children of the same man by different wives.[1]

The span of lineages and groups of cognates co-operating varies somewhat with particular circumstances. Among commoners, lineages of three generations control cattle, inheritance, and prayers to the ancestors. Agnatic genealogies include six to nine generations, and genealogies of cognates for four generations are practically important, since marriage between the descendants of a common great-grandparent is disapproved, and when such marriages occur those concerned are made to drink protective medicines. Between the descendants of a common grandfather marriage is impossible,[2] and this is the group which, as we shall see, regularly co-operates.

Chiefs' genealogies occasionally include as many as nineteen genera-tions traced in the male line—an old chief Mwandesi, famous as an his-torian among the Nyakyusa, gave us such a genealogy—but more often they include no more than twelve or thirteen generations. Wider groups of kin do in fact co-operate among chiefs than among commoners, for the chiefs are reponsible for communal rituals in which the agnatic descendants of a common great-great-grandfather participate, and for the ordinary domestic rituals more distant kin are summoned than among commoners. Should a commoner's family claim kinship with a chief, that link is traced farther than a link with commoners; thus if the father is a commoner and the mother belongs to a chief's family there may be wider co-operation with her kin than with his. This is very noticeable when it comes to an analysis of the individuals avoided by a daughter-in-law in different kinship groups.

---

[1] Since divorce was rare in the traditional Nyakyusa system and the children of an inherited widow counted as children of the deceased, the children of one woman were practically always classed as full siblings. Should a woman have children by unrelated men, however, their grandchildren might possibly marry.

[2] There is a tradition among some sections of the Nyakyusa that very long ago they practised one type of preferential cross-cousin marriage—that between a man and his mother's brother's daughter.

KINSHIP AND LOCALITY

As we have seen, the Nyakyusa build not with relatives but with age-mates, and the age-span of a village (that is, the difference in age of its members) averages about five years. Now the spacing of births in Nyakyusa families was wide, for it was thought wrong for a woman to become pregnant again until her previous child was able to run beside her should the war-cry be shouted. No woman, it was argued, could flee carrying two children, therefore the elder child must be able to run before she was burdened with another. Hence four or five years between births was normal. This meant that full brothers (except for twins) were seldom in the same age-village, though half-brothers were often together. Since peace has been established births are less widely spaced, three years between them now being considered proper, so a pair of full brothers may well join the same village; but still the very close bonds which link together all the sons of one mother and father rarely include common residence in one village. It is, however, usual for affinal relations (*abako*) to inhabit the same village, for it is thought good to marry the sister or daughter of an age-mate.

The members of one chiefdom are not a kinship group any more than are the members of one village, and there is no myth of their common descent, but two factors tend to keep relatives within a chiefdom. First, a man has higher status in the chiefdom in which his father and paternal grandfather lived than he has outside it. Where his ancestors lived he is *umwilima*—an owner of the soil—a member of an old family, and as such entitled to greater respect and support from his neighbours than he will receive anywhere else. Old men explain that before the coming of the Europeans an 'owner of the soil' had much greater security of life and property than a stranger, for the latter, not being defended by his neighbours as one of themselves, was always liable to persecution by the chief. His wife might be taken by the chief and he himself murdered, or his cattle seized on some slight pretext. Moving from one chiefdom to another always occurred, but in recent years it has greatly increased. This is partly because land is becoming scarce, and men move to seek better gardens, but mainly because the traditional methods of dealing with accusations of witchcraft have been prohibited, and when a man suspects that he or his family or cattle are being attacked by witchcraft he thinks his only safeguard is to move. Probably 80 per cent. of Nyakyusa men now move at least once during their lifetime, but of these many return later on to their home chiefdoms, for the prestige of being an 'owner of the soil' is still a strong inducement to do so.

The second factor which tends to keep relatives within a chiefdom is that marriages within a chiefdom are preferred to those beyond. Marriage with a woman of a neighbouring chiefdom was permissible but beyond that it seldom occurred, since the danger of travelling made it impossible for a wife to visit her parents. To-day the range of marriage is increasing, but parents still object to their children taking partners from forty or fifty miles away, on the ground that such a distance prevents that easy exchange of visits and gifts between in-laws which is held to be essential to a successful marriage.

THE BONDS OF KINSHIP AND AFFINITY

Relations within and between the kinship groups we have defined are articulated in co-operation in cultivation and the sharing of food, in building, in the passage of cattle, and in participation in common rituals; these activities we must now consider.

In an elementary family husband and wife co-operate in cultivation, the man hoeing, his wife sowing, weeding, and reaping. Each wife in a compound family has her own fields in which she works with her unmarried daughters. Unmarried sons hoe with their fathers, working in some households only in the fields of their own mothers, while in others they work as a group with their father, hoeing each woman's plot in turn. Often a boy brings his friends—usually only two or three, but sometimes as many as ten—to work in his mother's fields, and he in turn will assist these friends. Those who have been working together always eat food prepared by the woman whose field they have been hoeing, for the produce of a woman's fields is used to provide food for her husband, her own children, herself, and any others who have been working in her fields for the day on which they have worked. The relative rights of husband and wife to dispose of crops vary with the different crops,[1] but no co-wife has any rights over another's food. A woman may, and often does, ask her co-wives to help her in her fields, and sends them presents of cooked food from her own fire; she may help them and receive presents in return; but they have no rights over her fields or her food.

From the time he is betrothed a young man begins to work in the fields of his mother-in-law (for so she is called from the time he has handed over the betrothal gift), dividing his time between her fields and those of his own mother, and bringing friends to work in both sets of fields. Often also he hoes a field near his own house which his 'mothers-in-law' (that is, his betrothed's mother, her co-wives, and possibly some of her sisters or neighbours) plant and weed and reap. The crop from this field belongs to his mother-in-law until his betrothed reaches puberty and comes to live with him permanently as his wife. Then the field is hers, and though her 'mothers' come to help her in the field the food belongs to the young people.

After marriage the young husband continues to help both his father

[1] For an analysis of these rights see Godfrey Wilson, *The Land Rights of Individuals among the Nyakyusa*, 1938, Rhodes–Livingstone Paper No. 1, pp. 16–29.

and father-in-law in hoeing, while both his own 'mothers' and his wife's 'mothers' help her with planting and weeding and reaping; gradually, however, the amount of such co-operation diminishes. A man spends less and less time in the fields of his mother and mother-in-law as he grows older and has an increasing family of his own to support, while the help from his mother and mother-in-law diminishes correspondingly. As one newly married informant explained: 'My wife's mothers still help her a lot in cultivation; they say, "She is a child, let her dance and enjoy herself." But when a girl gets older and has borne one or two children, then her mothers stop helping her so much. They say, "We helped you before because you were only a child. Now you are a woman, do your own work." '

In building there is co-operation of the same sort. A young man helps his father, bringing with him a group of age-mates if a heavy job is on hand, and similarly he works with his father-in-law. His mothers and mothers-in-law in their turn help him with the women's tasks of carrying bamboos and grass, and plastering. We once watched a party of twenty-one women and girls, 'mothers' of the wife of a chief, come to help their 'daughter' build.

To grasp the significance of all this co-operation it must be realized that the Nyakyusa get the great bulk of their food from their fields, and that skill and diligence in cultivation bring prestige to both men and women. House-building is also very important in this climate of torrential storms and cold mists. The rainfall (averaging 100 to 130 inches in the year) makes substantial houses a condition of survival.

But not only do Nyakyusa relatives work together in field and in homestead, they are also continually handing on from one to another their dearest possession, cattle. Indeed, the giving of cattle is involved in all the closest relationships, and their reciprocal transfers of cattle are what hold families together. Cattle are prized not only because they provide two favourite foods, milk and meat, a supply of which makes it possible for a man to feast his neighbours, but also because they are necessary to an honourable marriage and a pious funeral.

Cattle are not the exclusive possession of one individual; rather they are property in which all the male members of a lineage of a span of three[1] generations have certain rights. A man who is the senior son of a senior son, and whose grandfather's and father's full brothers are all dead, controls not only the cattle inherited from his father, and those from the marriages of his own full sisters and daughters, but also those from the daughters of his full brothers and the daughters of his sons.

---

[1] Since the average marriage-age of men is about 25, agnatic lineages of full brothers of more than three surviving generations of married men are rare. Agnatic lineages of half-brothers of four surviving generations of married men are common enough, but exchange of cattle is not maintained to the fourth generation between the descendants of half-brothers.

At the same time he is responsible for providing marriage-cattle for his sons and sons' sons, and for his younger full brothers and their sons and sons' sons. He is also responsible for providing one or more cows to kill on the death of any dependant on whose account he provides or receives marriage-cattle, and on the death of the husband or wife of any of these. On the other hand, the rights of disposal of the 'father' of the lineage are limited, firstly, by the strong claim every group of full brothers has to the cattle from their own full sisters and daughters, and secondly, by the practice of giving cows to younger brothers and sons over which they have ultimate rights. Certain individual rights thus exist, but the unity of a group of full brothers and their interest in a common stock of cattle are maintained through three generations.

Relations between half-brothers vary somewhat. Those whose mothers are sisters, or otherwise closely related (for, as we shall see, it is common for a man to marry kinswomen), share the same reciprocal rights over cattle as full brothers, and half-brothers who are not linked through their mothers may yet be linked by cattle. As we have noted, each group of full brothers has a special claim to the cattle that come from the marriages of their full sisters, but their father or grandfather disposes of them as he wishes. If he gives some of their cows to a half-brother he thereby creates between the eldest of the group and this man the special relationship of 'milking each other's cows' (*ukukamanila*), and it is expected that the cows given will in time be returned by this half-brother from the marriage-cattle of a full sister or a daughter of his own. A similar link is established between half-brothers if a father uses the cattle from a daughter's marriage to marry another wife himself. The new house thus begun is linked to the house from which the cattle originally came, and at least one cow must be returned when the eldest daughter of the new house marries.

The exchange once begun goes on; as their sisters and daughters marry, linked half-brothers continually give each other cows; between their respective sons also the exchange usually continues, but between their grandsons it lapses. Reciprocity is expected and can be legally enforced, but it is not insisted upon so long as the two men concerned are friends, and its legal enforcement at once breaks the relationship. If two such half-brothers (or their sons) quarrel one may take legal action for separation against the other. The cows that have been handed over by both sides since the beginning of the relationship (perhaps twenty or thirty years before) are counted up, and one or the other is ordered to pay over the balance to make the numbers equal. After this the two are 'no longer kinsmen', they have no mutual obligations, and do not attend each other's funerals.

It is usual for a father to create this relationship between his senior son and the eldest son of each of his other houses, so that by this exchange of cows the family is held together. Its continuance depends very largely on personal friendship. Good relations between half-brothers and their sons are valued, but quarrels leading to legal separation occur. By contrast, quarrels between full brothers seem rarely to be serious and never to go to the length of a lawsuit; the unity of a group of full brothers is in fact maintained by their distinction from, and in some situations by their opposition to, their half-brothers.

The separation of each house and the importance of links between houses through 'milking one another's cows' is apparent in the rules of inheritance. A man's heir is his next living full brother, or failing a full brother, a half-brother linked through their mothers. Should such an heir be lacking, the eldest son of the dead man inherits, provided he is grown up. If he is still a child a half-brother linked by cattle inherits, failing that a half-brother with whom there is no such bond.

The heir, if he be a brother, takes all the widows of the deceased; if he be a son he takes all save his own mother and her kinswomen who must go to the son of another house. Whether he be brother or son he inherits the cattle of the deceased, and has the right to move into his homestead and take his gardens if he chooses to do so. He succeeds to the position of 'father' (*tata*), and as such is not only entitled to the respect and obedience of his younger brothers and brothers' sons, but also has the same obligations to them as the dead man had. The heir is avoided by those affines who avoided the dead man; often he takes the dead man's name. Indeed so close is the identification that even the barrier between succeeding generations is leapt, and a son who is his father's heir may be welcomed to the village of his father as the equal of his father's age-mates.

Now this form of inheritance operated in a society in which there was little opportunity for individuals to acquire wealth. Occasionally a poor man would hoe for a chief and, after many seasons' work, gain cattle with which to marry; young men also may sometimes have acquired cattle in war. But the great bulk of property was family property which every male, provided he lived long enough, enjoyed in his turn. The eldest son of an eldest son married earlier than did his juniors, and if he lived he acquired more wives and begat more children than they did, but each man lived in the expectation of one day enjoying the possessions, in wives and cattle, of his seniors.

Since the coming of the Europeans the situation has changed. Opportunities for the individual to acquire wealth either in employment or by the sale of produce are considerable, and the property of an energetic and capable man is often very much greater than that which he has inherited. Correlated with the change in the economy there is in process a change in the traditional law of inheritance. A younger full brother still has the right to claim his elder brother's property on the latter's death, but not uncommonly he relinquishes this right in favour of the deceased's senior son (provided that son is grown up) on the ground that if he takes his elder brother's property, then, when he himself dies, that brother's senior son will claim all that he, the uncle, held, including property he earned himself as well as that which he inherited. It was explained that if a younger brother, who already has considerable property in his own right, accepts the inheritance of an elder brother, there will almost inevitably be quarrelling between their sons over the division of the property when the younger brother dies. This tendency towards the direct inheritance of sons is further emphasized in Christian families, where there is no polygyny, and consequently no group of wives to be inherited, and where the right of the one widow to refuse to be inherited is recognized.

We have shown that a man's heir is commonly either his own younger full brother or else his senior son; now a distinction must be drawn between the positions of these two possible heirs. A man's younger brother inherits all his powers and responsibilities, and exercises authority over all the dead man's children; but when the heir is the senior son his authority is more limited. He is without a rival in the position of 'father' to his younger full siblings, but in relation to his junior half-siblings that position is shared with the eldest of each group of full brothers.

A separate inheritance for each house is not so clearly marked among the Nyakyusa as among the Nguni people of the south. Though gifts of cattle are sometimes made to individual sons, the estate is not apportioned to each house, nor are the cattle of each house milked for the benefit of that house, as is common in Pondoland. Neither are land rights inherited by houses, for all the land falls to the heir who moves into the dead man's homestead. Indeed inheritance of land rights was relatively unimportant, since village boundaries were redrawn and homestead sites and most arable lands redistributed in each generation, at the great 'coming out' ceremony.[1] Nevertheless the eldest son of each house inherits certain rights on the death of his father and of his father's full brothers. He then gains the right of disposing of the cattle of his own full sisters, of his daughters, and of his full brothers' daughters. As we have seen, a senior son who inherits from his father (or father's brother) may or may not exchange cattle with each group of his half-brothers; if he does so at all his dealings are with the eldest of each group, who receives the cattle for full sisters and daughters of the group, to whom his younger full brothers look for cattle to marry, and for whom they hoe. Thus in each generation there is some separation of property between the different houses of a compound family.

The precedence of the senior son appears most markedly in ritual, for although in minor matters the eldest of each group of brothers may officiate as priest, whenever serious trouble comes the prayers of the senior brother must be sought on behalf of all his junior half-brothers,

[1] Cf. Godfrey Wilson, *The Land Rights of Individuals among the Nyakyusa.*

unless they have been legally separated from him. So much for the control of cattle within the lineage, and their part in binding together its members.

The exchange of cattle is also one of the main bonds between lineages. A legal marriage is effected by the handing over of cattle— traditionally 1 to 3 head, now 5 to 20—by the representatives of the bridegroom to the father of the bride. It is the transfer of cattle which makes it possible for a woman to bear legitimate children, and which gives the husband legal control of these children. If a father refuses to accept cattle on behalf of his daughter she cannot be married and is greatly disgraced, since it is considered very shocking for an unmarried girl to bear a child. Indeed, such an occurrence is still rare. If no cattle pass there is no relationship (*ubukamu*), the Nyakyusa say, between the husband's people and the wife's people. 'A wife for whom cattle have not been given is not my relative (*unkamu*)', and 'since you (Europeans) do not give cattle at marriage where does the relationship (*ubukamu*) come from? With us relationship is cattle (*Uswe ubukamu syo nombe*).' Such were typical Nyakyusa comments on the passage of cattle at marriage. And should a woman make a runaway marriage she cannot visit her parents at all, not even to attend a funeral, until her husband takes a cow to her father to create relationship.

In fact, a legal form of marriage without cattle did exist traditionally, but the status of those who married in this way was much lower than the status of those who married with cattle. Informants explained that since in the old days cattle were scarce and owned only by the richer families, a father might agree to the marriage of his daughter in return for labour. 'If a poor man had hoed for me, the father, and built a house for me, then I said, "I am satisfied; because he does not speak proudly, he was my servant, I'll give him my child".' The consent of the bride's father made the union a legal one, but some, at least, of the children, including the first-born daughter, belonged not to the husband but to his father-in-law, and the husband was referred to scornfully as 'a cock' since 'chickens are the hen's, the cock goes about alone'. Thus marriage by service was traditionally an alternative, albeit a less honourable one, to marriage with cattle.

Even when cattle are given at a marriage the son-in-law is expected to do a certain amount of hoeing for his father-in-law, as we have seen, and a connexion is made between his diligence in hoeing and the demands for cattle. If he hoes satisfactorily he is not pressed for the cattle outstanding, but if he is lazy they are demanded very quickly. And however many cattle he gives, hoeing is spoken of as an essential part of his obligation to his affines. Indeed nowadays, when a young man in paid employment is unable to hoe, he often gives two or three shillings to his father-in-law in lieu of labour.

A legal marriage was commonly (and now is always) created by the transfer of cattle, and it is dissolved by the return of those cattle. Traditionally a husband could claim back all his cattle together with their progeny if the wife leaving him had borne no children, but if she had borne even one child one cow was left, for, the Nyakyusa say, 'If we left no cows the children, when they went to visit their mother's people, would be in a difficulty. Their mother's people would say to them: "You are not our relatives. Where are your cows?" ' Nowadays, if a woman has borne several children, two cows are left, but there is no exact balancing of the number of children against the number of cows left. And since 1935 calves have no longer been returned; the difficulty of tracing all the calves, when an increasing number of cattle is being given at marriage, was such that the British Administration pressed the chiefs and councillors to agree to a change in the law regarding progeny.

No matter who has initiated the divorce the children belong to the husband, and he can even claim the child yet unborn, if the divorce takes place while his wife is pregnant. Did he not give cattle for her?

The importance of cattle in creating a marriage is shown by the fact that formerly a husband might be compelled to divorce his wife solely on the ground of his poverty, irrespective of their personal relations. Traditionally, when a fine was imposed for theft or manslaughter, a man might be compelled to divorce his wife in order to pay the fine, or if his sister with whose cattle he had married left her husband, he might have to divorce his own wife in order to return the cattle to his sister's husband. Old men explained that a father might refuse a young man reputed to be a thief, or quarrelsome, 'because the father did not want that man's cows in his homestead'. The father thinks to himself, 'If this youth's cows are finished they (his creditors) will come and take those he gave me. They will say, "Fetch back your daughter and return the cows." ' Nowadays the courts have no authority to compel a divorce in order to enable a husband to pay a fine, but there is still the feeling that 'a man's property is with his father-in-law' and may be recovered there.

Despite the possibility of divorce on account of poverty marriage was traditionally stable. Informants are unanimous on this point. The sanction against adultery was spearing or impaling the man. A husband finding his wife with another man speared him, or, if the couple had run away to another chiefdom, he followed them up, along with two or three of his own kinsmen, and sought to kill the adulterer and bring his wife back. Sometimes fleeing lovers got away, but often they were over-taken by the enraged husband and his kinsmen. An adulterer could hope for no support from his neighbours if his lover were a woman from his own chiefdom, and even if she came from another chiefdom he was not secure, for his fellow villagers might drive him out lest they should all be attacked by the injured village. 'Men were afraid; they said, "An adulterer brings war." ' Hence, the Nyakyusa say, men seldom ran off with married women. Divorce which did not begin with an elopement was equally rare. A woman could secure a divorce from her husband for consistent ill treatment, if her kinsmen agreed, but they were slow to do so; more often her father and brothers would catch the husband and beat him for ill treating their daughter and sister; and if a wife behaved badly her husband would beat her rather than divorce her.

To-day the situation is very different. More than half the pagan women have been divorced at least once (some of them three or four times) and these divorces are commonly initiated by running off with a lover. An attack on an adulterer (not caught *in flagrante delicto*) is treated as a criminal assault or homicide; instead adultery is punished by a fine of three cows, two being paid by the man found guilty of adultery to the husband of the woman concerned, and one by the father of the woman to her husband, since the father is regarded as being in some measure responsible for his daughter's conduct.

But formerly divorce was relatively infrequent, and even if a husband or wife died, the affinal relationship between their families was not dissolved; instead a younger brother or sister took the place of the deceased. A widow was inherited by her husband's heir, and this right of inheritance was insisted upon even though the 'widow' was a child, not yet initiated though betrothed. For a widow to refuse the heir was comparable to deserting her husband; if she ran off the heir pursued her as her husband would have done, and indeed he was regarded as her rightful husband. Nowadays if a widow refuses the heir and returns to her father no damages can be claimed by the heir—he only gets back the cattle given for the woman—but still there is a very strong feeling that widows *should* accept the heir as husband. We heard one father, persuading his daughter to remain with the heir, say to her: 'See, he also is a husband who married you.' And in fact many pagan widows agree to be inherited because they wish to remain with their children; if they refuse the heir they are parted from their children like divorced women. Only in Christian families may a young widow remain with her children without accepting the heir as her husband, and without causing her father to lose the cattle given for her. And even among Christians a widow who remarries must leave her children with their father's heir.

If a wife dies she is very often replaced by a younger sister (*unuguna*) or by a daughter of her brother (*umwanasenga*). Should she die childless such a substitute must be provided, or else all the marriage cattle have to be returned. If she has borne children a sister is, in Nyakyusa eyes, the best person to mother these children; indeed it is often the children who go to their maternal grandfather or uncle to ask for 'another mother to care for us'. In the old days if the wife who died was young no further cattle were asked for the sister given in her place, but now the father often claims marriage-cattle all over again. Fathers argue thus: 'These cattle have gone with her who died. Do you wish men to say of the younger sister, "They gave no cows for her, they just took her"?' Nevertheless a smaller number of cattle is often accepted for the second sister than for the first.

And here we come to the crux of Nyakyusa ideas of marriage: relations between affines (*abako*) are ideally permanent—a divorce should never occur; a dead husband should be replaced by his heir, a dead wife by her younger sister or brother's daughter; the individuals concerned may change but the relationship between the families remains. This idea of permanence is pushed to the point at which some say that *whenever* a woman dies she should be replaced, no matter what her age is; in fact women who have borne children are not replaced if they die after their own husband and his brothers have died. But marriages between two families already linked are strongly encouraged, provided that it does not mean marriage between the children of a common grandfather. Very frequently a man does not wait for the death of his wife to marry her younger sister or brother's daughter. *Ukusakula*—to bring a younger relative to one's husband as wife—is the form of polygyny generally preferred and is the mark of successful marriage relations, for a man will not marry the younger kinswoman of a wife with whom he is on bad terms, nor will a wife consent to bring her little sister or niece to him if he is a harsh husband. Instead she will advise her father to refuse the offer, should the husband suggest it, for the initiative in such a marriage may come either from the husband or from the elder sister already his wife.

Sometimes two brothers marry two sisters, or a young man may seek a wife in the family from which one of his stepmothers came. 'He marries from where his father married.' Now, as we have mentioned, there is a tradition among some of the Nyakyusa of a former custom of cross-cousin marriage (with the mother's brother's daughter), but one informant argued that it had never been real cross-cousin marriage, but only marriage with the half-brother of a father's sister's son. 'I call my mother's brother's sons my cousins (*abatani*), but his daughters are my sisters (*abilumbu*). It never was the custom to take them to wife, but it was, and still is, the custom to give them to my half-brothers. I am the owner of these women (*ndi mwene bakikulu aba*), I may take one of my brothers by a different mother to my mother's brother's place and say to my brother, "There is the girl for you." ' Whatever the traditional practice, cross-cousin marriage does not now occur, but marriage with the half-brother of a cross-cousin does, though less frequently than marriage with a wife's brother's daughter. It is to be noted that marriage with a wife's brother's daughter is incompatible with cross-cousin marriage, and that it operates in a system in which the older men have first right to women. The girl who, under a system of preferential cross-cousin marriage, would become the wife of a young man, often, under the present Nyakyusa system, becomes the wife of that young man's father.

The suggestion that a man has some rights over his mother's brother's daughters fits in with other facts, for the passage of cattle creates a special relationship not only between a husband and his affines but also between his children and his wife's people, more particularly with the brother who benefited from her cattle. From this uncle (*umwipwa*) a nephew, when he grows up, can claim a cow (*ijabwipwa*), and, as one informant put it, 'This custom of getting the cow, *ijabwipwa*, is to show the relationship of the mother's people to the young man and his father, and also to the mother of the young man. Especially we think it is to honour their daughter, the mother of the youth; it is to say, "Thank you, we have received cattle on your behalf, you have borne a child for us." ' Mother's brothers who did not receive cattle on her account are *abipwa* too, but 'that which makes this relationship important is cattle. It is an insignificant relationship if the uncle is not milking the cows from the young man's mother.' Because of the cows a nephew can take food, especially the prized thick milk, in his uncle's homestead, without asking permission, and should he quarrel with his father it is to his linked mother's brother that he goes. He also has certain rights of inheritance, for should the uncle to whom he is linked die without a brother (own or classificatory) or a son to inherit, the nephew claims the cattle given for his mother.

Between the sons of brother and sister (*abatani*) there is freedom and friendship as between equals, and a mother's brothers' daughters are almost as sisters; we heard no suggestion of unusual jocularity between cross-cousins.

We have explained the Nyakyusa view that relationship (*ubukamu*) between two lineages is initially created by the passage of cattle. It is maintained by co-operation in cultivation and building, by the occasional exchange of gifts of food, and above all by coming to mourn and bringing cows to kill at each other's burials. Unless he is utterly destitute a son-in-law must bring a cow to kill at the death of his wife's father or mother, and his wife's father (or this man's heir) must, on his part, bring a cow to the burial of his daughter or her husband. Thus we come to the religious interdependence of relatives which is so important to the Nyakyusa that relationship is often defined by them in terms of attendance at each other's rituals—to say of a man 'we do not go to each other's burials' is to imply that he is not counted as a relative.

The rituals in which relatives join are those celebrated at puberty and marriage, at birth (especially at a twin-birth), at death, and in case of sickness or misfortune, particularly if blood has been shed or if one of the family has been bound with ropes. Here we can only indicate very cursorily the nature of these rituals, for the description of them and an analysis of their symbolism would make a book in itself.

The overt purpose of the rites in each case is fertility and health; neglect of them is believed to result in sterility, sickness of one type or another, and 'madness' (*ikigili*), or, more accurately, specific neurotic symptoms. Different pathological conditions are associated with the neglect of different rituals. From the point of view of kinship and marriage the essential fact is that relatives are believed to be mystically affected by the very fact of their relationship. Should a son not take part in the death ritual for his father he is in danger of going mad; should a sister's son not be called to drink medicines at the birth of twins to his mother's brother the nephew's children may swell up and die; should the wife of a murderer eat with the widow of the victim before purification both will begin to cough blood. It is not the same set of relatives which is concerned each time, for the range varies with the ritual. The previous experience of individuals also affects attendance, for once a person has gone through the death or twin ritual as a principal he is not required to take part again.

A large group of cognates is concerned in a twin ritual. At one we watched, all the descendants of the father of the twins, all his full siblings and their descendants, his half-brothers and their agnatic descendants (but not his half-sisters), his father's full siblings and half-brothers and their agnatic descendants (but not his father's half-sisters), as well as his wife's brother and sister and their children, were treated. The wives of all the men concerned took part, but not the husbands of the women, and it was noticeable that while links through both males and females counted with nearer relatives, more distant connexions were traced only through males. For example, the children of full siblings' daughters were treated, but not the children of half-siblings' daughters—only the children of half-brothers' sons. The only distant relative connected through females who was treated was the baby of the daughter of the principal's father's sister's son.[1]

At a burial a similar large group of cognates and their wives is expected to attend, along with the sons-in-law, sisters' husbands, and fathers-in-law of the deceased, if he be a mature man; but when it comes to the death ritual (*ubunyago*) for purifying the chief mourners and driving away dreams of the dead from their minds, only a small group of kin—siblings, own children, and grandchildren—together with the widows or widower, of the deceased, is concerned. Similarly, after the shedding of blood it is only these relatives of the slayer and slain who drink medicines.

One further principle which is necessary to an understanding of kinship and marriage emerges from a study of the rituals: it is the separation of sexual activities and the parent–child relationship. The Nyakyusa believe that the sexual fluids are extremely dangerous to children, hence (they say) the restrictions on the parents of a young child sleeping

---

[1] Possibly because infants are identified with their mothers.

together. The mother may not conceive again until the child is weaned, and she must always be in a position to wash scrupulously before going from her husband to the child.

At the same time a newly married wife who is 'hot from her husband' is held to be dangerous to her own parents, and she must not go into the inner part of her mother's house where the bed is, though before puberty she was free of the house; likewise a widow who has been inherited cannot eat with her parents until they have drunk a medicated beer together, lest they fall ill on account of the 'dirt' of her new husband on her. For a son to sleep with his father's wives is believed to be mystically dangerous to both men, and if, as sometimes happens when the father is old, permission has been given to the son to take those wives who will be his inheritance, elaborate ritual precautions are taken. And when the father does die one of the overt purposes of the death ritual is to make it safe for the heir to sleep with the widows.

So strong is the feeling that the sexual activities of succeeding generations must be separate, that it is forbidden for a woman to bear children after the marriage of her son, and she must not risk conceiving a child from the time of her daughter's puberty until her daughter has conceived. If the mother 'oversteps' her daughter in this way it is thought that the latter will be barren.

The separation reaches its greatest elaboration in the avoidance of father-in-law and daughter-in-law (*abakamwana*). A woman may never look at her father-in-law nor enter his house, nor meet him on a path, nor mention his name, or words like it. She avoids even the cow which looked into his grave, and the flesh of a cock which was in his homestead, and the banana grove where her husband prays to his dead father. This avoidance of the father-in-law (*ukutila unkamwana*) is extended to his brothers, half-brothers, and male cousins, the sons of full siblings of his parents. For example, a woman avoids the sons of her father-in-law's mother's full sisters and brothers, but not those of her half-sisters and half-brothers. It is extended in a modified degree to the father-in-law's sisters, half-sisters, and female parallel cousins, for all are *abakamwana*. She cannot look at these women or greet them directly, though she does not fly at their approach as she does at the approach of her father-in-law or one of his brothers, own or classificatory; to veil her face before a female *unkamwana* is sufficient. And when the father-in-law dies his heir is avoided in his stead, though less strictly than the dead man was, and the wives of the heir (if he be the son of the deceased) go through a special ritual to enable them to meet their husband, who is now also their 'father-in-law'.

But it is not only the father-in-law's siblings and heir that a wife must fear; though she can talk freely with her mother-in-law, the latter's brothers and half-brothers, and the husbands of her full sisters (but not of her half-sisters) are treated as fathers-in-law, though again the avoidance is less strict than it is towards the husband's own father. And the extensions apply to those identified with the daughter-in-law as well as to those identified with the father-in-law—a wife avoids not only her own 'fathers-in-law' but those of her sisters and half-sisters also.

These general rules are modified by particular circumstance, for the range of avoidance varies somewhat with proximity, friendship, and social status. A parallel cousin of the husband's father, who lives at a distance, may well not be known and so not avoided, whereas a more distant relative with whom the family is friendly, or who is a chief, may be treated as a father-in-law's brother. All who are reckoned as kinsmen of the father-in-law and of his generation are in fact avoided; indeed the Nyakyusa themselves take the range of avoidance as a criterion of kinship. Often a man will say: 'I am related to so and so, though distantly; *my wives avoid him.*' But avoidance shows relationships in consecutive generations only, for a woman conspicuously does not avoid her husband's grandfather and his siblings.[1]

When the Nyakyusa are pressed to give their reasons for insisting on so strict an avoidance between father-in-law and daughter-in-law they relate a myth concerning a chief who looked on his son's beautiful young wife, and coveted her and took her. 'People thought this so bad that from that day they forbade father-in-law and daughter-in-law to look on one another.' And any familiarity whatever between father-in-law and daughter-in-law savours of incest or indecency to the Nyakyusa. As one old woman put it: 'If a girl looks on her father-in-law she compares him with her husband; she sees the physical resemblance between them. It is as if she had looked on her parents-in-law sleeping together.'

The great elaboration of avoidance is correlated with the age-village organization; were father and son to be near neighbours such strict avoidance between father and daughter-in-law would not be possible, and indeed the necessity for avoidance between them is given as a reason for fathers and sons building apart. Only among those Christians who relax the rules of avoidance are the homesteads of father and son found near one another. It is to be noted also that this emphasis on avoidance occurs in a society in which polygyny is approved, and in which the cattle with which to marry are mostly controlled by middle-aged and elderly men who customarily marry young girls.

Between mother-in-law and son-in-law (*abako*) there is reserve and a measure of avoidance—he may never go into the inner part of her hut where her bed is, and the food she cooks for him will be brought by someone else—but the restrictions on his behaviour are slight compared to those imposed on his wife.

---

[1] Here the Nyakyusa system differs from that of the Pondo.

EXTENSIONS OF KINSHIP BEHAVIOUR

The forms of behaviour primarily appropriate to kinsfolk are extended in some measure to neighbours who, owing to the age-village organization, are very often not related at all. All one's father's mates in his village are 'fathers in the village' (*batata pa kipanga*), their wives are all 'mothers in the village' (*abanna pa kipanga*), and their children of opposite sex are 'sisters (or brothers) in the village' (*abilumbu pa kipanga*). Neighbours co-operate in herding, those who live next door to one another sending out their cattle to pasture together, and they join also in cultivating and building. We have shown that a young man working for his father or father-in-law is very often accompanied by a group of friends, neighbours from the boys' village, and with this group he eats after work. So also with the older men and women: for any major undertaking, such as hoeing or reaping a big field, or building a house, at least one work-party is usually held to which close neighbours as well as relatives are expected to come. An investigation of any working group will show that some of the members are there because they are relatives of the organizer, others because they are village neighbours of his own or of his son or son-in-law.

But such economic co-operation stops short at the exchange of cattle. Very occasionally an intimate friend, who is also rich, may bring a cow to a funeral, but there is none of that circulation of cattle which binds together kinsmen and affines. Nor is the assimilation of neighbours to kinsfolk pushed to the point of village exogamy. Marriage within the village is and always has been permitted, though traditionally, it is said, a man would not readily marry the daughter of a next-door neighbour, with whom he ate, and with whose cows his were herded. For the daughter of a next-door neighbour is 'like your own daughter'. But there could be nothing against marriage with the daughter of a fellow villager living farther off, and marriages between the children of fellow villagers are felt to be particularly appropriate. 'It is good to marry a sister of the village', the Nyakyusa say; 'our fathers were friends and built together'.

As in the material, so in the religious aspect, there is a measure of co-operation between neighbours. At the great events in life—marriage, birth, and death—neighbours are expected to show sympathy and to rejoice or mourn with their friends as may be appropriate. Not to attend a burial in the village is to incur suspicion of having killed the dead man by witchcraft; not to dance at a wedding feast is likewise unneighbourly. At the initiation of a girl her age-mates—half-sisters and neighbours—keep her company, women neighbours share with her senior female relatives the task of instructing her, and both neighbours and relatives are included in the party which formally takes her to her husband. When food and firewood are required to provide for the guests at

K

initiation and marriage feasts, and at burials, neighbours as well as relatives contribute, food at a burial being provided on the first day by the bereaved household, on the second by relatives, and on the third by neighbours.

But when it comes to the domestic rituals—the treatment with medicines and the prayers to the ancestors—then, with one exception, it is relatives alone who are concerned. No neighbour is purified and protected from dreams of the dead at the ritual after death, nor washed from the contamination of blood and ropes; no neighbour is concerned in the fertility rites of initiation and marriage. Only in the fearful event of a twin-birth do next-door neighbours come with their children and their cattle to drink or be sprinkled with medicines, to save the cattle from purging and the humans from monstrously swollen legs. Even in this case fellow villagers living at a little distance and herding their cows in another group are not affected, whereas all relatives, no matter where they may live, must be treated. Thus neighbours play a small part in the domestic rituals though, as we shall see in the following section, they are believed to exert a mystical power to enforce obligations between relatives, including the performance of the rituals.

We have dealt with the extension to fellow villagers of the forms of behaviour primarily appropriate to kinsfolk; it remains to note the part which kinship plays in the political organization.

KINSHIP AND POLITICAL ORGANIZATION

As has been shown, there is no all-embracing kinship bond between the members of one village or one chiefdom, and, according to tradition, chiefs and people are of different stocks; but relationship is traced between the chiefs of different chiefdoms, and by virtue of their relationship various groups of chiefs share in common rituals. The welfare and fertility of a country is held to be bound up with the health of its chief, and, just as a living chief has mystical power over his land, so dead chiefs are thought to have power over the countries they ruled. Thus half-brothers who divide their father's chiefdom pray together at the grove in which he is buried on behalf of both their countries, and in certain circumstances a number of chiefs combine to pray at the grave of a reputed common ancestor. The religious obligations of kinship are then a bond linking chiefdoms; nevertheless, participation in common rituals did not in practice exclude war.

Despite the fact that chiefs and people are believed to be of different stocks there is no cleavage between the descendants of chiefs and commoners, the descendants of the junior sons of chiefs being quickly assimilated into the group of commoners. The headmen of the age-villages (*amafumu*) cannot be the sons of chiefs or of former village headmen; they are commoners *par excellence*, and the Nyakyusa insist that were son to succeed father in the office it would become a chieftainship. Thus, although there are hereditary chiefs, kinship does not play a dominating part in the political organization.

GENERAL PRINCIPLES

We are now in a position to summarize certain general principles embodied in the Nyakyusa organization. It is clear that the older generation, especially the men, have a privileged position. The older men control cattle and labour; the majority of them have more than one wife, and the possession of many wives, together with unmarried sons and young sons-in-law who hoe for him, means that a man has at his disposal plenty of food; and food makes lavish hospitality, the foundation of prestige, possible. Along with the control of wealth goes religious authority, for not only do men have mystical power over their descendants, they are also the mediators between them and their ancestors.

The privileges of seniority accrue not only to the senior generation but also in some measure to a senior son—the eldest son of a great wife —and in a lesser degree to the eldest son of each house. Though inheritance passes from brother to brother there is an ultimate, albeit delayed, efficiency of the principle of primogeniture. The senior line of any family is likely to be the most wealthy and the most numerous, for the senior son of a senior son is likely to marry earlier and have more wives than his juniors. In ordinary everyday speech the differences between senior (*unkulu*) and junior (*unuguna*) siblings of the same sex are marked.

Secondly, we can observe a certain identification of siblings, half-siblings, and father's brothers' children of the same sex, all of whom are *abakulu* or *abanuguna*.[1] The identification appears further in the extension of the term for father (*tata*) to his brothers, half-brothers, and father's brothers' sons, and a similar extension of the term for mother (*juba*), and in their reciprocal use of 'my child' (*mwanangu*) both in address and reference. It appears in the replacement of a dead husband by his younger brother, half-brother, or father's brother's son, and the similar replacement of a dead wife; and it appears in the extension of the rules of avoidance to include all those whom the husband calls father, and whom the daughter-in-law calls sister.

Even between siblings of the opposite sex (*abilumbu*) there is a measure of identification. A man's wife must be deferential to his sister (*ugwifi*), for this sister is very close to her husband. As one informant put it, 'our sisters are as men, those who married our wives'. On the same principle a woman avoids her husband's father's sister. One day an old woman in a crowd drew our attention to this fact: 'See, I do not

---

[1] Mother's sisters' children are referred to as brothers and sisters, not as cousins (*abatani*), but when it comes to the control of cattle, inheritance, and rituals they are not treated as siblings.

go to greet them, my brother's son's wives. I am like the father of their husband.' And a girl is very respectful to her father's sister (*unnasenga*), even though the latter is a mere child; she fetches and carries for her, and never touches her back to smear her with ointment, as she would a mother, for 'father's sister is father'.

A sister is felt to be more nearly the equal and intimate of her brother than a wife can ever be—indeed one day the Nyakyusa, seeing a European woman brush a caterpillar off her husband's sleeve, laughed and said: 'Why, she behaves like a sister! A wife would never take such liberties.' A father's sister may even be asked to arbitrate between her brother and his son, in case of dispute, which the wife and mother could never do. And the assurance which a sister has in dealing with her brother is extended in some measure to her children, a man being free with his mother's brother (*umwipwa*) in a way in which he cannot be with his father.

But the tendency to identify brother and sister is limited at every turn by the sex difference. Brother and sister are much less familiar than brother and brother, or sister and sister; much more freedom is possible with a father's sister than with the father himself, much less with a mother's brother than with a mother herself. The sex difference appears vividly in the rules of avoidance: a woman does not greet the sister of her husband's father, or look her in the face, but she may be in the same company; whereas should word come that her father-in-law or his brother is approaching she disappears immediately; and she avoids her mother-in-law's brother only a little less strictly than her husband's father, but with her mother-in-law she can talk and work.

We have shown that siblings, half-siblings, and father's brother's children are grouped together, but at the same time very clear distinctions are made between each group of full siblings. How these appear in family names, in the distribution of cattle, and in inheritance has already been discussed (*vide supra*, pp. 114, 117–18). It remains to note that precise terms exist for the distinctions. *Unkulu, unuguna,* and *ulilumbu* (*vide supra*) may all be qualified thus:

unkulu munna   elder full sibling of the same sex.
  ,,   *mbannabo* senior half ,,   ,,   (mothers related).
  ,,   *munumba* ,, half   ,,   ,,
  ,,   *mbisabo*   father's elder brother's son (or daughter, woman speaking).

Along with the grouping together of those of the same generation goes the separation of those of succeeding generations, which is carried to the point of territorial segregation. Fathers and sons *must* live in different villages. They do not eat and drink together, sharing those urbane conversations over a well-cooked meal which to the Nyakyusa are the essence of the good life; in a word they do not *ukwangala*, for that is only possible between equals; it is not possible between men and women or between fathers and sons. The separation is especially marked in the field of sex. One of the reasons given for sons building apart is that they should not hear lewd conversation and see sexual play between their parents; for children to learn anything about sex from their parents is shameful; such instruction must come from their immediate seniors, older brothers and sisters, not parents; and, as we have seen, elaborate precautions are taken to prevent any action felt to symbolize an association of the sexual activities of parents and children.

This separation of the generations is broken by inheritance, for a senior son may inherit most of his father's wives and, joining the village of his father, be treated almost as his father. The parallel among women is the custom of replacing a dead woman by her brother's daughter should no younger sister be available. Among women, indeed, the differentiation between the generations is much less marked than among men, for co-wives are commonly of different ages, and a brother's daughter may well join her aunt as a junior co-wife. Even mothers and daughters will eat together.

Unlike parents and children, grandparents and grandchildren (*abisu-kulu*) are expected to be familiar. As one man explained when asked if his wife avoided his grandfather: 'No, he is my comrade. I am Mwakalambo and he is Mwakalambo.' And significantly the words 'husband' (*undume*) and 'wife' (*unkasi*) are used between grandparent and grandchild of opposite sex.

Lastly, we repeat that the effective range of Nyakyusa kinship varies with personal friendship, proximity, and social status, and that there is some correlation between range in the contemporary and historical moments, those who recite the longest genealogies recognizing the widest connexions among the living.

THE MAINTENANCE OF KINSHIP AND MARRIAGE RELATIONSHIPS

Some indication has already been given of the types of social pressure which maintain these relationships. Now we shall consider more closely the nature of that social pressure. In all the kinship and marriage relations of the Nyakyusa we find that there are mutual economic obligations, and some of these are enforced by reciprocity, that is, if one party neglects its obligations, the other does likewise.

Both boys and girls owe their parents, the Nyakyusa think, a material recompense for the trouble and expense of feeding and bringing them up; while a boy, in addition, must make some return for the cattle his father gives him to marry with. A girl fulfils her obligations mainly by getting and staying married. Since marriage involves a transfer of cattle to her father, and divorce involves their return to her husband, it is above all by behaving well in the relationship of marriage, and so avoiding divorce, that a woman discharges her obligation to her parents.

'If a daughter ran home in the old days', we were told, 'and said that her husband had beaten her, then her father sent to inquire among the neighbours about the quarrel; if they said that it was she who was in the wrong, then her father would beat and scold her, saying: "I thought you were a grown woman and were supporting me, but instead of this you spoil my wealth." ' The word which we translate 'were supporting me' is a form of *ukuswila* which usually means 'to feed a child', and it thus brings out very precisely the element of economic reciprocity in the relationship of father and daughter. We asked our informant what was meant by 'spoiling my wealth'. 'Would not her husband come to fetch his cattle back (i.e. divorce his wife)?' he replied.

The obligation to the parents which a daughter thus fulfils by an unbroken marriage is discharged by a son in the fields; he earns the cattle for his marriage and repays his parents for his food and upbringing by hoeing, and nowadays by earning money for them as well. The labour of an unmarried son is one of the most important sources of wealth in Nyakyusa society, and it is directly secured to his parents by his dependence on his father for marriage-cattle. A boy's economic value to his parents is increased by every year he stays unmarried, but the quicker a girl gets married the better for them. And it is an essential condition of the economic value of children that the marriage-age of young men is, on an average, ten years older than that of their sisters. For a father pays out as many cows for a son's marriage as he receives for a daughter's; it is because he has time, between receiving and paying out, to keep the cattle and let them increase in his house that the transfer of cattle benefits him, while this interval of time is also filled by the useful labour of his son. Now the length of this interval depends partly on the diligence of the son in hoeing. For a son who is lazy a father will be slow to give marriage-cattle,[1] whereas for a diligent youth the father should provide cattle as soon as he can. And should the father, having cattle, not provide for his son's marriage, that son may take his strength elsewhere, going to hoe for his mother's brother, or even for a kinsman of his father, in the expectation that in due course the man for whom he has worked will repay him, like a father, by finding the marriage-cattle. Or nowadays he goes off to work for Europeans and keeps his earnings for himself.

This example brings us to the kernel of our argument. Between father and son there is direct reciprocity, a balancing of labour against early nurture and cattle, and should one neglect his obligations the other may do likewise. Between father and daughter the case is somewhat different: the economic obligations of the father are largely fulfilled before his daughter marries, and the return she owes him is enforced by religious and conventional rather than by economic sanctions. Everyone agrees

[1] For an example see Godfrey Wilson, 'An Introduction to Nyakyusa Law', *Africa*, x. 1, Jan. 1937, p. 33.

that a girl *ought* to stay married so that her father may benefit from her cattle; she is urged to do so by the fear of losing the power to bear healthy children, owing to the anger of her parents, and by the fear of being shamed by the refusal of her father to receive cattle on her account. She does not fear much direct economic loss; only indirectly in the food given her by her father to present to her husband and in the food and cow given to her son by her brother, may she be said to get some return for the cattle given on her behalf. It is noticeable that while the divorce rate has risen sharply, sons, for the most part, still hoe diligently for their fathers.

In all the relations in which cattle pass there is direct economic reciprocity between the men who give and those who receive them; brother gives to brother in the expectation of a return and, should no return be made when the occasion for it arises, a legal separation with a careful balancing of accounts—a counting of cattle given and received—follows. Between son-in-law and father-in-law there is a similar balancing of obligations: the son-in-law works and gives cattle in return for a wife and children; if his wife leaves him, or dies, or is sterile, she must be replaced, or the cattle returned. Cattle killed at in-laws' funerals are carefully reckoned in the tally of those owing from one family to the other, and even in the exchange of gifts of food a rough balance is enforced.

Between husband and wife also there are reciprocal economic obligations. Traditionally a wife planted, weeded, reaped, cooked, and did the housework, while her husband saw to the stock and hoed. Nyakyusa women are aware that one road to a man's heart lies through the kitchen, and good cooking and cleanliness are recognized means of becoming the favourite wife; while the diligent man who hoes ample fields for his wives is honoured by them on that account. Should a man fail to hoe for his wife she has grounds for divorce, while should she be lazy he is considered justified in beating her.

This illustrates a second type of pressure very important in the old Nyakyusa society, the right of private people to use force. A father or one of his village neighbours might beat a child for doing wrong; a husband beat his erring wife; a father-in-law and his sons beat a son-in-law who was ill-using his wife, their daughter and sister; and a husband, aided by his brothers, tortured and killed the seducer of his wife. If cattle were owing from a man in another chiefdom the creditor might go armed with one or two kinsmen to collect his debt. Such a use of force was considered perfectly legitimate, though for a junior to strike a senior, or a wife her husband, or for one to seize another's cattle without good cause, provoked further punishment.

This right of using force without reference to any court is becoming more and more circumscribed. The man who beats his neighbour's son is liable to be summoned to court by his neighbour, and a Christian may be reprimanded by his Church even for beating his own wife when she has done wrong. The man who goes armed to collect his debts or who pursues the seducer of his wife and kills him is punished, for the right to use force has become the prerogative of the courts. As one Nyakyusa put it: 'Of old if a boy insulted me I'd beat him; now if I do so his father summons me to court and the judge says, "Are *we* not here?" '

But it must not be thought that courts did not play a great part in the traditional Nyakyusa society. Constantly the Nyakyusa take quarrels to older relatives or respected neighbours for arbitration; this was the traditional custom, and traditionally there was a chief's court with power to enforce its judgements within the chiefdom.

Quarrels between relatives are most often taken to senior relatives to be settled; disputes between brothers or a brother and sister, or between a man's wives or his children, are taken to the father, and one between kinsmen or brothers whose father is dead is referred to the senior kinsman of the lineage; but the exact relationship of the arbitrator to the quarrelling parties does not matter so much as that they should both respect him, and indeed relatives may take their cases to a respected neighbour as they would do if they were not related at all;[1] it is only thought more appropriate to go to a fellow kinsman. What is considered bad is that a dispute between kinsmen should go to the chief's court; they should always settle the case privately if possible; though, as we have seen, half-brothers or parallel cousins who are on bad terms may come before the chief's court for a formal separation and sorting out of the cattle they have exchanged.

Quarrelling between relatives is not, however, merely a secular matter, for pagan Nyakyusa (and many Christians also) believe implicitly in the mystical power of senior relatives, living and dead, over their descendants, and the neglect of kinship obligations which angers the seniors is believed to bring sickness or misfortune.[2] This power is most commonly spoken of as operating within the agnatic lineage, a father having mystical power over his children and sons' children, and the senior son inheriting power over his sisters and half-sisters, his junior brothers and half-brothers, and their children and sons' children. The anger of a father-in-law with his son-in-law is thought to affect the latter's children, i.e. a man has power over his daughter's children, and in case of sickness may pray on their behalf, but there is never any mention of power over more distant descendants in the female line. A woman remains under the mystical power and protection of her own kinsmen, living and dead, all her life, and she is also affected by the anger of her husband's kin.

---

[1] For an example see Godfrey Wilson, 'An Introduction to Nyakyusa Law', *Africa*, x. 1, Jan. 1937, p. 27.
[2] Cf. Godfrey Wilson, 'An African Morality', *Africa*, ix. 1, Jan. 1936, pp. 83–5.

The sins commonly spoken of as bringing down the wrath of senior relatives are unfilial behaviour, such as a son speaking angrily to his father, or actually striking his father, or wasting his father's substance by committing adultery, so that his father is forced to pay the fine, or failing to give his father a share of his earnings. 'If a married man, married with his father's cattle, goes away to work and gains much wealth and does not send any home to his father, he will fall sick. The ancestors will be angry and say: "He is not wise, he has given his father nothing!" He will fall sick there at his work. But if he is an unmarried man it is different; his father has given him nothing, he may keep the cows to get himself a wife and nothing will happen; only the first cow he gains he should send home to his father. If he does not do this he will fall sick. The other cows he can keep.' And if a daughter leaves her husband without good cause she risks her father's wrath, which, it is believed, may cause her to be barren. In the same way the heir who inherits the position of 'father' is believed to suffer if he neglects his dependants. If he refuses to provide marriage-cattle for a younger brother or the deceased's son, or if he refuses to give bananas to the daughter of the deceased when she comes 'home' to him so that she may have a gift to take back to her husband, it is said that the heir's children will fall ill.

Quarrelling between husband and wife, quarrelling between kinsmen, adultery of women, incest, neglect of rituals (including failure to summon relatives to rituals), and breaches of the rules of avoidance, all these are thought to rouse the wrath of senior relatives and bring on the wrongdoer or his children some such evil as sterility, illness, thin and sickly children, a lingering death, or solitude in the world of the dead. For if an heir has neglected his wards it is said that his kinsmen will not come to meet him on the road when he makes the journey to the land of the dead. Painful periods and difficult labour are also directly related to sin, and if a brewing of beer—the pride of a good housewife—goes sour, immediately it is whispered that she who brewed has been quarrelling with her husband. Have not the ancestors manifested their displeasure?

But it is not only relatives who are believed to bring sickness and misfortune for breach of kinship obligations; whenever fellow villagers are shocked (*ukuswiga*)[1] at some breach of customary behaviour their breath—'the breath of men' (*embepo syabandu*)—is believed to fall on the culprit and cause him (or her) to fall ill. Villagers are shocked, not only at the neglect of obligations towards themselves, but also at breaches of the laws of kinship and affinity, such as incestuous unions, neglect of avoidance, unfilial behaviour, neglect of his wards by an heir, and so on. Here we see the importance of the 'fathers of the village', for if a son has insulted his father it is not only the father and the ancestors

[1] Literally 'to be astonished', but often with the implication of disapproval.

who must be appeased, but also the father's fellow villagers. An erring son who has quarrelled with his father and later falls ill will bring a bull to kill at his father's homestead for the father and his neighbours to eat, so that the curse of the village may be removed. The exact nature of the supposed mystical power of neighbours need not concern us here; it is related by the Nyakyusa to the power of witchcraft rather than to the power of the ancestors,[1] but the 'astonishment' of villagers is considered to be a legitimate use of mystical power, and it operates as one of the main sanctions for the maintenance of obligations between relatives as well as between neighbours.

While emphasizing the mystical danger, in Nyakyusa eyes, of angering relatives and neighbours, we must not overlook the fact that shame also operates. Informants spoke of actions which would cause one 'to die of shame' (*ukufwa nesoni*), and to tax someone with being 'shameless' is one of the commonest forms of reproof. The line between being ashamed and fearing that the shocked astonishment of one's neighbours will affect one's health is ill defined, but it is quite clear that the Nyakyusa dread being shamed by comments on their stinginess, quarrelsomeness, or ill manners. Generosity and urbanity in kinship relations carry prestige in the same way as they do in village relations. One rich man, whom we knew intimately, provided marriage-cattle for several sisters' sons; he had no obligation to do so, but he gained great honour among his relatives as well as among neighbours by his generosity.

It is apparent that these various types of social pressure were effective, in the traditional Nyakyusa society, in maintaining the form of kinship and marriage relations we have described. To-day they are not wholly effective and the form is changing. The most obvious breakdown is in marriage. The high degree of polygyny among elderly men and the large number of young bachelors unable to marry for lack of cattle make the temptation to adultery, often followed by divorce, very strong. The Nyakyusa themselves say that the most common reason for a woman to leave her husband and elope with a lover is sexual neglect. Some speak of their husband's laziness in hoeing, or his unfair division of milk and other food, but most often the complaint is sexual neglect, and it is possible that the lower divorce rate among Christians (18 per cent. as against 59 per cent. in a small sample) is related to the fact that they are the one group of families which remain monogamous.

The sexual privileges of the older men were maintained by the right of the aggrieved husband to pursue and kill an adulterer and by the denial to women of any right of personal choice. It is clear that formerly, unless a woman could prove by the witness of neighbours that she was being severely ill treated by her husband, her father would refuse to countenance a divorce, nor would he agree to her refusing the heir on the death of her husband. Nowadays, under the influence of the British

---

[1] Cf. Godfrey Wilson, op. cit., pp. 85–92.

Administration, the courts uphold a woman's right of choice in marriage
or inheritance, and her right to a divorce in certain circumstances.
This new freedom for women, and the denial of the right of an individual
to wreak private vengeance on an adulterer, are incompatible with the
traditional form of marriage.

RELATIONSHIP TERMS

(*U*) *tata*[1]	My father, father's brothers and male parallel cousins. Also mother's brother in address.
(*U*) *juba*	My mother, mother's sisters and female parallel cousins, father's wives. Also father's sister in address.
Umwanangu	My child, son or daughter; sister's son or daughter (woman speaking); brother's son or daughter (man speaking). Brother's son or daughter in address (woman speaking). Sister's son or daughter in address (man speaking).
Undume	Husband and all his brothers, sisters' husbands, grandson, grandfather (woman speaking).
Unkasi	Wife and all her sisters, brothers' wives, granddaughter, grandmother (man speaking).
Ulilumbu	Sibling or parallel cousin of opposite sex. Used in some contexts of a cross-cousin of opposite sex.
Unkulu	Senior sibling or parallel cousin of the same sex.
Unuguna	Junior sibling or parallel cousin of the same sex.
Untani	Cross-cousin.
(*U*) *jubasenga*[2]	Father's sister or female parallel cousin.
Umwanasenga	Brother's child or male parallel cousin's child (woman speaking).
Umwipwa	Mother's brother or his male parallel cousin. Sister's child or female parallel cousin's child (man speaking).
Umwisukulu	Grandparent, grandchild; sibling of grandparent, sibling's grandchild.
Unko	Father-in-law and his brothers, mother-in-law and her sisters (man speaking), son-in-law and his brothers.
Unkamwana	Father-in-law and his siblings and parallel cousins, brothers of mother-in-law and husbands of her sisters, fathers-in-law of sisters (woman speaking). Daughter-in-law and her sisters and parallel cousins (man speaking).
Undamu	Wife's brother, sister's husband (man speaking).
Ugwifi	Husband's sister, brother's wife (woman speaking).
Unjimba	Father of son-in-law or daughter-in-law (man speaking).

[1] The initial *u* is always dropped in the vocative case; it is seldom heard at all
with *juba*, *jubasenga*, and *tata*.

[2] *Esenga* is an avoidance word for cattle. The father's sister is sometimes called
umwenesenga which might be translated 'the owner of the cattle'.

KINSHIP AND MARRIAGE AMONG THE TSWANA

By I. SCHAPERA

THE Tswana tribes of the Bechuanaland Protectorate seem to have fewer marriage restrictions than any other group of Bantu-speaking peoples in southern Africa. They lack exogamous units such as are commonly found elsewhere (e.g. among the Nguni, Venda, Tsonga, and Shona), and they allow marriage between first cousins of all kinds and various other close relatives. In addition, they practise the levirate and the sororate. However, the rules of mating are not always identical, and a union permitted in some tribes is forbidden in others. In this paper I shall compare briefly the marriage regulations of nine different tribes that I have studied in the field.[1] My main objects are to determine if those regulations conform to a single fundamental type, and to see how far they can be related to other aspects of Tswana social structure. I shall comment also upon the local variations that occur, and discuss the problems that they present for explanation.

THE SOCIAL SETTING

I have already described elsewhere the main features of Tswana social organization.[2] For our present purpose it is enough to note that each of the tribes dealt with here has its own territory, and forms a separate political unit under the leadership and authority of a chief who is subordinate only to the British Administration. In size they vary greatly, the extremes being represented by the Tlôkwa, with about 2,000 people, and the Ngwato, with about 110,000. Their members have been recruited from many different stocks; the proportion of 'aliens' is largest in the north, smaller but still fairly high in the south, and smallest in the east.[3] This ethnic diversity is sometimes reflected in the occurrence within a single tribe of several different languages and other cultural variations. But the Tswana proper, who are the ruling community in each tribe, all speak the same language and have much the same culture;

[1] The tribes are the Kgafêla-Kgatla, Malete, and Tlôkwa (Eastern Tswana), Tshidi-Rolong, Ngwaketse, and Kwena (Southern division of Western Tswana), and Ngwato, Tawana, and Khurutshe (Northern division of Western Tswana). There are in the Union of South Africa many other Tswana tribes, but the relevant information about them is not available.

[2] See especially *Handbook of Tswana Law and Custom* (Oxford University Press, 1938), chap. i; *Married Life in an African Tribe* (Faber, 1940); and 'Some Features in the Social Organization of the Tlôkwa', *Southwestern Journal of Anthropology*, ii, 1946, pp. 16-47.

[3] See note 1 above for the geographical distribution of tribes.

unlike most of their alien subjects, moreover, they tend to concentrate in large compact villages containing several hundreds or even thousands of inhabitants. In this paper I shall deal with them alone and ignore the other elements of the tribal populations.

The smallest well-defined unit in the social system of the Tswana is the household, a group of people occupying the same enclosure of huts. It consists basically of a man with his wife or wives and their unmarried children, but often also includes one or more married sons, brothers, or even daughters, with their respective spouses and children. It may contain up to fifteen people, occasionally more, but the general average is from five to seven.

Several different households, living together in the same part of a village or ward settlement and acknowledging a common 'elder' (*mogolwane*), constitute a family-group. This group consists basically of families whose men are all agnatic descendants of the same grandfather or great-grandfather; the man senior to the rest by right of birth is their accepted leader. However, it may also contain married sisters or daughters of those men, with their husbands and children; possibly one or more uterine nephews who have come to live permanently with their mother's people; and in rare instances even siblings of a woman married into the group. In effect, it is a form of extended family, dominantly but not exclusively patrilocal in character. It usually has from twenty to fifty members.

A number of family-groups, living together in a distinctive portion of a village, or sometimes even in a separate village, make up a ward. The ward is the basic unit in the administrative system of the tribe, its members being subject to the authority of a hereditary headman with well-defined judicial and executive powers. The number of wards varies roughly with the size of the tribe; the Tlôkwa, for instance, have only five, and the Ngwato approximately 300. The number of people in each also varies considerably, some containing less than 100 and others well over 1,000.

Occasionally the men belonging to a ward all have a common agnatic ancestor, the headman being senior to the rest in line of descent. But the great majority of wards now also contain people of alien origin. Some may have been placed there by the chief to help the headman and strengthen the ward when it was founded; others may have been allowed to transfer from their own ward because of internal dispute; or, if a group of new-comers to the tribe is considered too small to form a separate ward, the chief will attach it to one already existing. Such recruits are seldom related by birth to the nuclear lineage of the ward, but they may subsequently marry into it. Neither the ward nor even the family-group is exogamous, and marriages between members are in fact fairly common. However, should a wife be an outsider, she must normally be brought to live among her husband's people, and the children all belong to his group.

related to father's sis

THE KINSHIP SYSTEM

It will have been gathered that most of a man's neighbours may be closely related to him, especially in the agnatic line. His immediate maternal relatives and/or relatives-in-law are sometimes also of his own ward, but they generally belong somewhere else. In addition, he has more distant relatives of all kinds widely scattered over the tribe and even in other tribes, for the Tswana carry recognition of relationship much farther than is common in our own society. Almost everybody with whom genealogical connexion can be established, no matter in how remote a degree, is considered a kinsman. Even if no direct link can be traced the mere fact that someone belongs to the same group as a close relative may lead to his inclusion within the body of kin; thus, all members of the ward from which one's mother comes are loosely classed as 'maternal relatives' (*ba ga etsho mogolo*), and all members of the ward into which one's sister or daughter is married are classed as 'sons-in-law' (*bagwê*).

In general, relatives are expected to be friendly and to help one another: a man looks to his kinsmen of all kinds for hospitality, assistance in work, and support in times of trouble. But he relies above all upon the members of his own family and such other close relatives as his parents' siblings with their spouses and children or his wife's parents and siblings. These people advise and help him in all his problems and undertakings, a special 'family council' being summoned if necessary; according to their particular status they make him prescribed gifts of food and other commodities, and have certain duties to perform at the ceremonies that he organizes; and they also are the only ones directly affected by the marriage regulations. His more distant relatives, unless they are actual neighbours, seldom figure prominently in his life, and even on special occasions of festivity or mourning, when all the available kindred are assembled, his close relatives invariably take pride of place.

The importance of close relatives is reflected particularly in the system of 'linking' (*go rulaganya*) that is so conspicuous a feature of Tswana kinship. In almost every family of any size the children are usually paired together—elder brother with younger brother, elder sister with younger, and brother with sister. Those of the same sex are paired together alternately (first and third, second and fourth, and so on), those of opposite sex go in relative order of birth (eldest brother with eldest sister, second brother with second sister, and so on).[1] Moreover, a man's linked sister is also the linked paternal aunt of his children, just as he is the linked maternal uncle of hers; and linked brothers (or sisters) are the linked senior and junior paternal uncles (or maternal aunts) respectively

[1] The arrangement depends mainly upon the actual composition of the family and the decision of the parents, and many variations are found from the order given above.

of each other's children. Among his immediate relatives, therefore, a man may have one of each kind to whom he is specially attached, and with whom he is said 'to work together for life'. It is with them that he is most closely associated in kinship obligations, and it is they who above all are expected to carry out the roles conventionally assigned to relatives of their class. Should they be living elsewhere, a sibling of the same sex who is close at hand will do as a substitute, but on all important occasions they are specially summoned.

The Tswana themselves habitually group their closer relatives into three major categories: *ba ga etsho*, agnatic relatives; *ba ga etsho mogolo*, maternal relatives; and *bagwagadi* (m.s.) or *bo-mmatsale* (w.s.),[1] the kinsmen of one's spouse. The first is the most directly important, for many social institutions are organized on a patrilineal basis. Membership of tribe, ward, and family-group is determined primarily by descent traced through the father; property and rank normally pass from father to son, or, failing a son, to the next male member of the same lineage; a man's surname is usually the given name of his father or paternal grandfather, and wards or family-groups often bear the name of their leader's agnatic ancestor; if a marriage is dissolved the children (especially the sons) always remain with the father; and, in the old days, people worshipped the spirits of their deceased paternal ancestors. In genealogies, too, the father's relatives are invariably remembered farther back and in greater detail than the mother's (unless she is descended from a chief).

Moreover, as already noted, a man's close agnatic kinsmen usually belong to his own family-group and ward. Consequently they are the relatives with whom he habitually associates and from whom he expects immediate support and protection. Their mutual dependence unites this localized category of kin into a co-operative body whose solidarity is generally recognized. *Fa gare ga bana ba mpa ga go tsenwe*, says the proverb, 'Outsiders should not intrude upon children of one womb.'

But the relations between individual members of the group are also governed by well-defined principles of discipline and authority. The head of a household is responsible in tribal law for the conduct and liabilities of his children and other dependants, from whom he accordingly demands unfailing obedience and respect.[2] A mother, although entitled to similar consideration, is more openly affectionate and lenient than the father, and is usually the medium through whom he is approached. A younger brother, again, should defer to and serve his elders,

[1] Throughout this paper I shall use the abbreviations m.s. for 'man speaking' and w.s. for 'woman speaking'.

[2] It should be understood that the summary descriptions given here of behaviour patterns embody the substance of what informants defined as the recognized norms; there are many individual instances in which the norms are not observed. See *Married Life in an African Tribe*, chaps. ix and x.

who in turn control but also advise, support, and protect him. A similar pattern of behaviour obtains between sisters. Siblings of opposite sex are not so rigidly differentiated according to relative age, nor are the rules of conduct between them well defined. In general, a brother should look after the welfare of his sisters and help them in their troubles, especially once the father is dead; they in turn render him such domestic services as fall within their scope. All such obligations apply chiefly to linked brothers and sisters, but in a lesser degree they are observed by other siblings also.

The behaviour patterns obtaining in the family are extended to the other close relatives, but with modifications for age, sex, and seniority. Among those living in the same group the paternal grandparents and especially the grandfather share in the obedience and respect due to one's seniors generally, but they tend to be kindly and tolerant rather than insistent on strict discipline. The father's elder brothers have greater authority than even he, and are if anything more esteemed; his younger brothers, on the other hand, are the recognized auxiliaries of their nephews, to whom they are much more affable and friendly. Paternal aunts are also respected, but seldom figure as prominently in a man's life as their brothers, especially if, as often happens, they leave the ward after marriage. They certainly do not command anything like the great authority that they are said to possess among the Venda and some of the Northern Sotho. The children of paternal uncles, again, are regarded much as brothers and sisters, and are one's usual playmates in childhood; in later life, however, they are differentiated according to the relative status of their father and the appropriate conduct is applied to them. More remote agnates are distinguished mainly according to line of descent: if senior to one's father by birth, they are entitled to obedience and respect; if junior, their services can be freely commanded. The saying that a man's 'elder brother' is his chief, and his 'younger brother' his subject, summarizes adequately the accepted relationship.

In everyday life the hierarchy of age and seniority is seldom considered oppressive, and most people remain on good terms with their agnates, co-operating willingly and harmoniously with them as occasion arises. But disputes sometimes occur owing to arbitrary exercise of authority and rival claims to property or position, and it is not fortuitous that most accusations of sorcery are made against one's relatives in the same ward. The close proximity in which they live, and the rules of patrilineal succession and inheritance, breed jealousies and conflicts that may prove stronger than the ties of mutual dependence.

One's maternal kinsmen (ba ga etsho mogolo) are not as a rule involved in situations of the kind just described; they cannot be rivals for property or position, and they generally (although by no means invariably) belong to some other ward. In consequence, perhaps, they are notoriously more affectionate and devoted than agnates. Children when small are often

KINSHIP AND MARRIAGE AMONG THE TSWANA 145

sent to live for a while at their mother's parental home, which they are afterwards encouraged to visit frequently; there they are assured of a warm welcome and generous hospitality, and enjoy many privileges. *Ngwana mogolo kwa gabo-mogolo*, says the proverb, 'A child is important at the home of its mother's people.'

A linked maternal uncle, in particular, must be consulted in all matters specially affecting his sister's children; his opinion is so important when their marriages are being arranged that his veto is sometimes decisive; he helps with food, clothes, and other gifts at all their *rites de passage*; special exchanges of property are common between him and his nephews; and he (or his successor) also has the ritual duty of preparing their corpses for burial. It is to his maternal uncle perhaps more than anybody else that a man looks for disinterested advice and aid in times of difficulty; and when disputes arise between father and son, or brother and brother, it is often also the uncle who reconciles them or with whom the oppressed child or younger brother goes to live if peace cannot be restored. The mother's parents and sisters, similarly, are commonly said to be more affable and indulgent than the father's.

Cross-cousins are expected to associate together on terms of the greatest intimacy. They are regarded as the most suitable mates for each other; but even if they do not marry, or are of the same sex, they are entitled and encouraged to be very familiar. In speaking to each other, for instance, they can use obscene or insulting language which, if addressed to any other person, would be a just ground for offence; they can help themselves freely to each other's personal belongings, and behave without restraint in various other ways. *Mmapa le ntsalaê moakodi*, says the proverb, 'Beside his cross-cousin a man is happy.' This joking relationship, known as *go tlhagana*, prevails symmetrically between cross-cousins of both kinds, no distinction being made according to line of descent.

The behaviour patterns between relatives-in-law are not as formalized as some of those already mentioned. When a man marries one of his relatives his original kinship ties with her family tend to persist. A father-in-law who is also an uncle, or a brother-in-law who is also a cross-cousin, continues to be treated along much the same lines as before, except perhaps when questions arise affecting the stability of the marriage. Most men and women, however, marry outside their kindred, and thus enter into special relationships with a new series of people. Those who concern them most are the parents and siblings of their spouses; other relatives, such as uncles, aunts, and cousins, come into prominence only on festive or other special occasions.

The basic attitude in all instances is one of friendship and co-operation. A woman often continues to live at the home of her parents for some time after marriage, her husband going there to sleep with her at night. As a result, he sees much of her parents and other close relatives,

L

who, without being familiar, treat him cordially and with respect. After taking his wife to his own home he is expected to visit his relatives-in-law frequently, help them at work, and invite them to all his domestic celebrations. They reciprocate in the same manner. A woman's relations with her husband's people may at first be characterized by mutual politeness, accompanied perhaps by a show of authority on their part, but if she proves a good wife they gradually unbend and she is accepted and treated as a daughter. There is no form of taboo or other prescribed avoidance between relatives-in-law of any kind.

KINSHIP TERMINOLOGY

The kinship terminology reflects many, but not all, of the social distinctions. The basic pattern is set by the terms used within the family. Husband and wife call each other *mosadi* (woman) and *monna* (man) respectively;[1] there is also a term for spouse, *mogatsa*, but it is used mainly in descriptive formations. Parents are distinguished according to sex: father is *rrê* (dial. *ntatê*), and mother is *mmê*. Children can also be distinguished according to sex, a son being *morwa* and a daughter *morwadi*, but the common term for either is simply *ngwana*, child. Siblings of the same sex are distinguished according to relative age: older brother (m.s.) or older sister (w.s.) is *mogolole* (dial. *nkgonne*), and younger brother (m.s.) or younger sister (w.s.) is *nnake*. Those of opposite sex, i.e. brother (w.s.) or sister (m.s.), call each other *kgaitsadi*.

The terms just given are generally also used in compound families, but, if necessary for purposes of reference, distinctions can be made by means of descriptive terms. A stepfather, for instance, may be called *mogatsa-mmê*, mother's husband; a stepmother *mogatsa-rrê*, father's wife; and a half-sibling *ngwana-rrê*, father's child, or *ngwana-mmê*, mother's child. Co-wives of a polygynist call each other *mogadikane* (said to be connected in origin with the word *bogadi*, bride-wealth); alternatively, they may use *mogolole*, older sister, or *nnake*, younger sister, according to their relative status. Similarly, a woman may call her senior co-wife's child *ngwana-mógolole*, older sister's child, and her junior co-wife's child *ngwana-nnake*; the child reciprocates by calling her either *mmangwane*, mother's younger sister, or *mmê-mogolo*, mother's older sister.

The distinctions made between siblings are extended to parent's siblings and to siblings' children. The terms for father's siblings all have the root *rrê*, and those for mother's siblings all have the root *mmê*, but the appropriate distinctions are made for sex or relative seniority. Father's older brother is *rrê-mogolo* ('great father') and father's younger brother *rrangwane* ('little father'), but any father's sister is *rrakgadi* ('female father'); similarly, mother's older sister is *mmê-mogolo* and mother's younger sister *mmangwane*, but any mother's brother is *malome* ('male

[1] All Tswana terms are given here in their simplest form; various modifications can be made to indicate person or number.

mother'). Reciprocally, older brother's child (m.s.) or older sister's child (w.s.) is *ngwana-mogolole*, and younger brother's child (m.s.) or younger sister's child (w.s.) *ngwana-nnake*, but brother's child (w.s.) is *ngwana-kgaitsadi* and sister's child (m.s.) *motlogolo*. Here all the terms used are descriptive, except the last, and no sex distinctions are made.

As already noted, father's siblings are distinguished from mother's. In the second ascending generation the two lines are merged; father's father and mother's father are both *rrê-mogolo*, and father's mother and mother's mother are both *mmê-mogolo*. These are also the terms for father's older brother and mother's older sister respectively, so that here we have persons of different generations being classed together. Reciprocally, son's child and daughter's child are also merged together; the usual term is the descriptive *ngwana-ngwana*, although *motlogolo* (sister's child, m.s.), is occasionally heard as an alternative.[1] Here again, as with other relatives of descending generations, sex distinctions are lacking.

Parallel cousins are sometimes classed with siblings. This usage is especially common for agnates (the children of paternal uncles), although the descriptive terms *ngwana-rrê-mogolo* or *ngwana-rrangwane* also occur everywhere. The children of maternal aunts, however, are habitually called by descriptive terms, sometimes abbreviated in address to *mmê-mogolo* or *mmangwane* respectively; their classification with siblings is a less common and apparently not even universal alternative.[2] On the other hand, cross-cousins, regardless of sex or relative age, always call each other by the special term *ntsala* (dial. *motswala*).

The children of agnatic cousins, again, are classed with the children of siblings; those of materterine cousins are called by descriptive terms (e.g. *ngwana-ngwana-mmê-mogolo*), sometimes abbreviated in address to simply *mmê-mogolo* or *mmangwane*; and those of cross-cousins are also called by a descriptive term, *ngwana-ntsala*.

The terms for other remote relatives are of the same pattern. The siblings of grandparents are classed, not with the grandparents (as is usual in other Bantu systems), but with uncles and aunts, i.e. they are called by the same terms as are applied to them by one's father or mother respectively. In reference, line of relationship is generally distinguished by adding the words *a rrê*, 'of my father', or *a mmê*, 'of my mother'; thus, the younger brothers of father's father or of mother's father are both addressed as *rrangwane*, but the former is referred to as *rrangwana-rrê* and the latter as *rrangwana-mmê*. The agnatic cousins of one's parents are also classed with uncles and aunts; the materterine cousins, however, are simply called either *mmê-mogolo* (mother's older sister) or *mmangwane* (mother's younger sister), regardless of sex; and the cross-cousins

---

[1] The use of this alternative has been noted only among the Rolong, Ngwaketse, and Ngwato.

[2] I did not find it among the Kwena, Tawana, and Tlôkwa, although I would not say that its use is completely unknown to them.

are addressed as *ntsala*, but referred to as *ntsala-rrê* or *ntsala-mmê* according to line of relationship. The children and other descendants of all these people are referred to descriptively but addressed by the same terms as their parents; the only exception is that the terms for siblings and brothers' children (m.s.) are occasionally applied to agnates.

The general effect of these linguistic usages is that one's remoter kinsmen tend to be grouped into three major categories: (*a*) agnates, for whom descriptive terms may be used but who are sometimes also classed, according to generation, with paternal uncles and aunts, siblings, or brother's children (m.s.); (*b*) materterine relatives (including those of one's father), all of whom, regardless of sex or generation, are normally addressed as mother's sister, and (*c*) 'cross' relatives (*ntsala*), including the descendants of anybody called father's sister or mother's brother.[1]

The terms for relatives-in-law vary considerably and are difficult to summarize briefly, since alternative usages occur even within a single tribe. Distinctive terms are found everywhere for husband's father and mother (both called *mmatsale*), wife's father and mother (both called *mogwagadi*), daughter's husband (*mogwê*, dial. *mokgonyana*), and son's wife (*ngwetsi*). *Mmatsale* and *mogwagadi* (or the descriptives *ngwana-mmatsale* and *ngwana-mogwagadi*) are often also applied to the siblings and other close relatives of one's husband or wife respectively, although it is equally common for these people to be called by the same terms as are used for them by one's spouse. The eastern tribes, however, have a special self-reciprocal term, *mogadibô*, for husband's sister and brother's wife (w.s.), and the Kgatla further use *molamo* for wife's brother and sister's husband (m.s.). Elsewhere sister's husband (m.s.) is generally classed with daughter's husband. The same usage occurs in the western tribes for the husbands of nieces and other junior relatives, but the more common tendency, both here and in the east, is to class them with their respective wives. The wives of brothers and nephews, again, are either classed with their respective husbands or called by descriptive terms.

The terms for the spouses of uncles and aunts are still more varied. The eastern and southern tribes class father's sister's husband with his wife; the northern tribes prefer the descriptive *mogatsa-rrakgadi*. The eastern tribes, again, class mother's older sister's husband with father's

[1] The basic pattern may be represented by the following diagram:

	Ascending	Contemporary	Descending
Paternal	△ rrêmogolo	→ mogolole	→ (ngwana-)mogolole
	△ rrangwane	→ nnake	→ (ngwana-)nnake
	○ rrakgadi }	→ ntsala	→ (ngwana-)ntsala
Maternal	△ malome }		
	○ mmêmogolo	→ (ngwana-)mmêmogolo	→ (ngwana-ngwana-)mmêmogolo
	○ mmangwane	→ (ngwana-)mmangwane	→ (ngwana-ngwana-)mmangwane

The words in brackets are often omitted in address.

older brother and mother's younger sister's husband with father's younger brother; this usage occurs also in the northern tribes, but more commonly both they and the southern tribes call such a man either by the same term as his wife or by a descriptive term. The wives of paternal uncles are usually classed with maternal aunts, but in the north descriptive terms are the more common alternatives. The northern tribes also use a descriptive term for mother's brother's wife; the eastern tribes, surprisingly, class her with grandmother; and the southern tribes have both usages.

In general, one is left with the impression that the terminology for relatives-in-law, and even to some extent for blood relatives, is nowadays going through a process of change. Such special terms as *mogadibô* and *molamo*, for instance, seem to be known only to elderly people; the abundance of alternative usages indicates a lack of standardization; and there is also a marked tendency for both siblings and siblings-in-law of all kinds to call each other *mogolole* or *nnake*, terms that correctly should be used only for persons of the same sex as the speaker, or, especially among the eastern tribes, to substitute terms of Afrikaans origin, such as *sebara* (brother-in-law) and *ausi* (elder sister).

PROHIBITED AND PREFERENTIAL MATING

Apart from being expressed in the behaviour patterns already noted kinship affects sexual relations. The Tswana prohibit marriage or cohabitation between relatives of certain categories; they also approve or even encourage the mating of others. These regulations apply to both 'marriages' and 'secondary unions'. By a 'marriage' I mean here a form of mating in which the man and woman are legally recognized as husband and wife, and are subject to all the rights and duties that the relationship entails. The woman's people, for instance, are entitled to receive *bogadi* (where the practice still prevails), and the children that she bears belong to the man. A 'secondary union', on the other hand, is merely an extension of an existing marriage. Its essential character is that, for purposes of child-bearing, one of the original parties to that marriage is replaced by another person of the same sex, who is regarded as a bodily substitute, and not as an independent spouse. Thus, if a woman is childless, her younger sister (or some other relative) may be provided to bear children on her behalf, such children ranking according to the status of the barren wife; or, when a husband dies, his younger brother may cohabit with the widow in order to raise seed to the deceased. The original marriage, in such cases, still persists, even although it is no longer the same people who cohabit. The distinction between the two forms of mating will appear more fully in the course of our discussion. It is important in the present context because a man is sometimes allowed to form a secondary union with a woman whom he may not marry.

Before I deal with the actual rules of mating something should be said about Tswana marriage generally. For a marriage to be valid, under old tribal law, two essential conditions must be satisfied: (*a*) a formal agreement, reflected in the betrothal ceremonies, must be made between the two family-groups concerned, and (*b*) the bridegroom's family must give cattle to the family of the bride. These cattle are known as *bogadi*. Their number, which in practice usually ranges from four to ten head, is decided by the boy's people alone, the girl's family having no say in the matter. In the old days, once the betrothal had been confirmed, the boy was allowed to cohabit with the girl at her parents' home, and it was only after a year or more, perhaps when she had already given birth to a child, that she would be taken formally to live among his own people. This custom of temporary matrilocal marriage, known as *go ralala*, has been abandoned among the Ngwato and Tawana, but is still found in most other tribes. The *bogadi* cattle should normally be given by the time that the girl leaves her own home to join her husband's people; in fact, they are seldom produced until much later.

There have been several other changes in marriage law, owing mainly to contact with Western civilization and especially with Christianity. As we shall soon see, the rules governing the choice of a mate have altered in some tribes. Again, the adoption of European civil marriage introduced various consequences and implications not found in old Tswana life, but this form of marriage is practised by only a small proportion of men. More important, perhaps, was the abolition of *bogadi* among the Ngwato and Tawana towards the end of last century, and its abandonment by many Christians in other tribes.[1] The giving of *bogadi* is accordingly no longer a universal condition of marriage. Greater stress is laid nowadays upon the consent of both family-groups, which must still be obtained before the tribal courts will regard a marriage as valid.

Marriage Regulations

The rules stipulating whom one may, or may not, marry apply to both kinsmen and affines. The kin whom a man is specifically forbidden to marry include, firstly, all women to whom he is related in the direct line of descent (grandmother, mother, daughter, granddaughter, &c.). The same prohibition applies everywhere to his full sisters, and nowadays also to his half-sisters (both paternal and maternal). Marriage with a half-sister was formerly permitted among the Ngwaketse and Rolong, but apparently nowhere else. Among the Ngwaketse it is said to have been abolished by Chief Bathoeng I (1889–1910). I do not know how or when it ceased among the Rolong.[2]

[1] This topic is discussed more fully in my *Tribal Legislation among the Tswana*, pp. 44 ff. (London School of Economics Monographs in Social Anthropology, No. 9, 1943.)

[2] Z. K. Matthews writes as if marriage with a half-sister is still allowed ('Marriage Customs among the Barolong', *Africa*, xiii. 1, Jan. 1940, p. 11); my own informants said that it is nowadays considered wrong.

The only other kin whom a man is generally forbidden to marry are his parents' sisters and his sisters' daughters. Instances are known among the Kwena of marriage with a father's half-sister, and among the Ngwaketse of marriage with a mother's half-sister, but both were considered irregular. Such marriages have not been recorded in any other tribe. Among the Ngwaketse, too, and among them alone, a man was formerly allowed to marry his half-sister's daughter, but this also was forbidden by Bathoeng I. In the other tribes it has apparently always been considered incestuous.

The rules about marriage with a brother's daughter vary considerably. The Kwena, Ngwato, Tawana, Malete, and Tlôkwa permit marriage with any brother's daughter. The Ngwaketse and Khurutshe say that a man may marry his half-brother's daughter, but not his full brother's. The Rolong and Kgatla, finally, prohibit marriage with both varieties.

Except for the women just mentioned a man may marry any of his kin. Such marriages are indeed strongly encouraged, especially with a cross-cousin. My informants in all tribes said that cross-cousin marriages are preferable to any other. *Ntsala wa motho ke mogatsê*, states the proverb, 'A person's cross-cousin is his (rightful) spouse.' In principle this applies especially to the daughter of the linked maternal uncle. Failing her, the daughter of any other maternal uncle will do. Then come, in stated order of preference, the daughter of the linked paternal aunt, and, failing one, the daughter of any other paternal aunt. Marriage with an agnatic cousin is also approved of everywhere. Here again the union is sanctioned by a proverb: *Ngwana rrangwane, nnyalê, kgomo di boêlê sakeng*, 'Child of my father's younger brother, marry me, so that the (*bogadi*) cattle may return to our kraal.' Despite the wording, one may also marry the daughter of a senior paternal uncle. On the other hand, my Kwena informants spoke disapprovingly of marriage with a materterine cousin; they said, too, that it was extremely rare among them, and would probably not be allowed nowadays, 'because your mother's sister's daughter is very much like your own sister'. Some of the Ngwato, too, said of such a marriage that 'it is unbecoming' (*go a rona*). But the same objections were not voiced in any other tribe, and certainly none, with the possible exception of the Kwena, prohibit a marriage of this kind.

In the old days, according to my informants, so much importance was attached to cousin marriages that a boy's parents almost invariably first sought him a wife among the daughters of their own brothers and sisters; if they did not, they were said to have 'violated our law' (*ba tlotse molaô wa segarona*). Priority was given to the daughters of maternal uncles, and it was mostly with them that child betrothals occurred. A girl's cousin, moreover, could generally obtain preference over any other suitor, and if no one at all seemed anxious to marry her, her maternal uncles or paternal aunts were expected to find her a husband among their sons.

Segôlê se tsholwa ke ba-bo-sona is the proverb quoted in this connexion,
'A cripple is looked after by his own people.'

However, cousin marriages are not compulsory. The claims of
relationship can be offset by the lack of other desirable qualities, and if
either the girl or her parents fail to reach satisfactory standards of
conduct and character a wife will be sought somewhere else. Her own
people, similarly, may refuse to hand her over to some cousin of whom
they disapprove or with whose parents they have quarrelled. And, of
course, it happens often enough that no suitable cousin is available. In
such cases it is held that a more remote relative should be married if
possible, but there is no special category for whom preference is
expressed.

We come now to relatives by affinity. As regards marriage regulations
we may group them into three classes: those whom a man is allowed to
marry, those with whom he may neither marry nor cohabit, and those
whom he may not marry but with whom he is allowed to contract a
secondary union should the occasion arise. I shall for the moment
confine myself to the first two, and will discuss the other below.

Among all the Tswana a man is to-day not allowed to marry or cohabit
with his mother-in-law or his stepdaughter. The Ngwaketse formerly
permitted marriage with the latter, provided that the man himself had
not begotten children by her mother; however, this also was prohibited
by Bathoeng I. Except for these two, a man may marry any of his wife's
relatives, but there is no special preference, e.g. for her brother's
daughter, such as is found among some other Southern Bantu. He may
also marry the widows or divorced wives of any of his male relatives,
excepting only his stepmother and daughter-in-law; but he may enter
into a secondary union with the former, and in some tribes (formerly)
also with the latter. Among the Kwena and Ngwaketse, finally, one is
allowed to marry a step-sister (the daughter of the father's wife or
mother's husband by another marriage). In all other tribes such a union
is considered incestuous, although instances are on record among the
Ngwato and the Rolong.

Secondary Unions

So far I have been dealing with unions where the man and woman
become full husband and wife. However, marriage among the Tswana
is not merely a relationship between husband and wife; it also establishes
certain rights and duties between their respective families. One obligation, common to both, is to ensure that the marriage shall be fruitful.
Hence, if the wife is barren or dies fairly young, her parents may have
to provide another woman to bear children on her behalf. This substitute is known as *seantlo*. She does not rank as an independent wife, but
is attached to the 'house' of the woman whose place she is to fill; and, in
the absence of a direct heir, her eldest son succeeds to the status and

property of that house. Again, should a husband die, his widow if young enough is expected to cohabit with one of his kinsmen in order to continue bearing him children. This man is not regarded as a new husband; the children he begets by the widow are legally those of the dead husband, and they call their genitor, not 'father', but by the relationship term appropriate to his original status in their circle of kin, e.g. *rrangwane*, father's younger brother. No *bogadi* is given either for a *seantlo* or for 'entering the hut' (*go tsêna mo tlung*) of a dead husband.

The choice of a seed-raiser is governed partly by the nature of his relationship to the dead husband; only certain relatives are eligible, others being debarred by the rules of incest. The man who above all is expected to cohabit with a widow is her husband's younger brother, preferably the next in order of seniority.[1] Failing a younger brother, the seed-raiser can be a junior paternal uncle, the son of a paternal uncle, or some more remote relative of approximately the same standing, e.g. an agnatic second cousin. The eldest son of a polygynist is also allowed to raise seed to his father, but only by junior widows, not by his own mother. This form of levirate is specifically sanctioned by the proverb, *Molala le mmaagwê ga a bolawe, o itsala monnawê*, 'The man who lies with his "mother" is not killed, he is begetting his (own) younger brother.' The Ngwaketse say that Chief Bathoeng I prohibited its practice among them, but it is still recognized in all the other tribes.

In the two varieties just mentioned the seed-raiser is junior in status to the dead husband. However, an elder brother may also take on the role. This form of levirate, although not prohibited by any of the Tswana, is regarded with disapproval by the Ngwato, Rolong, and Kgatla. Their objection is due mainly to the difficulties its practice raises about the status of children. The proverb says, *Kgosi ga e tsalele*, 'A chief does not beget children for others.' Hence, it is pointed out, if a man begets children by his younger brother's widow they may tend to claim a higher status than that to which they are entitled. In law, they are the children of the younger brother, but, owing to the senior status of their genitor, they will prefer to claim him as their father instead. It is because of such possibilities of conflict that this form of levirate is disliked. There is apparently no objection on grounds of incest to cohabitation between a man and his younger brother's widow.

All the tribes to-day forbid and condemn a man's 'entering the hut' of his son's widow, i.e. of his daughter-in-law. But this was formerly an accepted usage among the Kwena and Kgatla, and instances are also known of its having occurred among the Ngwato and Rolong (as well as among the Mmanaana-Kgatla, a formerly independent tribe now subject to the Ngwaketse). I lack the relevant information for the Tawana, but in the four remaining tribes I was told that the practice had never been permitted (although my Tlôkwa informants said that it

[1] The Tawana say that he should be the husband's linked younger brother.

was beginning to occur nowadays). Even among the tribes where it formerly existed it did not have the same recognized status as the fraternal levirate; the husband's father was not formally chosen as seed-raiser, but entered his son's hut surreptitiously and of his own accord.

The only other recognized form of levirate is with a maternal uncle's widow. This variety is allowed by the Khurutshe, Kgatla, Malete, and Tlôkwa, but is said to be relatively infrequent and to be practised only when no one else is available. The Rolong stated that they formerly also had the custom, but that it was forbidden long ago by Chief Tawana (c. 1805–49). The Ngwato, Kwena, and Ngwaketse say that it has always been prohibited among them as incestuous. I lack the relevant information for the Tawana.

The substitute (seantlo) for a dead or barren wife must also be one of her close relatives. The most favoured is her younger sister, especially the one linked to her. Failing a younger sister, an unmarried elder sister may be provided instead. If no sister is available some other close relative will do, who should be of the husband's own or a younger generation. Preference is given to a matrilineal relative (a sister's daughter or maternal aunt's daughter), but an agnatic niece or cousin is also considered suitable. A cross-cousin is generally excluded; only among the Kgatla and Rolong was I told that a maternal uncle's daughter could be provided if the wife had no other available relative.

However, although if need be some such relative may be substituted, the wife's sister is always considered by far the most suitable person to take her place. This is reflected in a custom that was formerly universal, but has now been abandoned everywhere (among the Ngwaketse it was specifically abolished by Bathoeng I): if a dead wife had no unmarried sister her parents might give the husband a younger sister who was already married to someone else. This form of sororate was practised especially when a man had married his cross-cousin. The husband of the woman who was thus taken to become a seantlo could keep the children she had borne him, but he could not recover his bogadi nor claim any later children as his own.

It may be added that the sororate in general was never obligatory. Where the two families were previously related, or if they were on friendly terms, they might agree to substitute another woman for a dead or barren wife; but the wife's people were not bound to provide such a substitute, nor the husband to seek one. Greater importance was attached to the levirate, and although the custom is admittedly decaying, especially among Christians, public opinion even to-day still tends to condemn a man who fails to raise seed to his dead brother.

THE FREQUENCY OF KINSHIP MARRIAGES

The description just given embodies the substance of statements made by informants. It remains for us to see how far the Tswana do actually marry relatives and what categories they then prefer. The material upon which the following discussion is based consists of genealogies collected in eight tribes.[1] For three (Rolong, Tawana, and Khurutshe) I have the genealogies of the royal families only; in the others I also obtained genealogies of people who do not belong to the ruling line, but who are of true Tswana stock.

As will be shown in a moment, the proportion of marriages with near kin is markedly higher among members of the royal family than among commoners. Accordingly, I shall deal first with the five tribes where I obtained genealogies of both groups, and where my figures are consequently more representative of the population generally. These genealogies embrace altogether 2,574 marriages. For preliminary discussion we may classify the marriages into two major categories: (a) those where husband and wife had a common grandparent or were more closely related, and (b) those where they were more distantly related or not at all. The following table gives the number and percentage proportion of marriages of type (a) found in each tribe. (The heading 'Nobles' covers marriages recorded in the royal genealogies, and 'Commoners' the others; 'S' is the size of the sample in each case, and 'No.' the number of marriages between close relatives.)

TABLE I

Proportions of Marriages with Near Kin

Tribe	Nobles			Commoners			Total		
	S.	No.	%	S.	No.	%	S.	No.	%
Ngwaketse	180	23	12·8	799	46	5·8	979	69	7·0
Kwena .	238	27	11·3	250	13	5·2	488	40	8·2
Ngwato .·	169	27	16·0	113	7	6·2	282	34	12·1
Kgatla .	170	15	8·8	282	13	4·6	452	28	6·2
Tlôkwa .	218	19	8·7	155	9	5·8	373	28	7·5
Total .	975	111	11·4	1,599	88	5·5	2,574	199	7·7

The figures show that, in general, the proportion of marriages between near kin is just about one in thirteen. There is fairly close agreement among all tribes except the Ngwato, who are well above the average. However, since the genealogies do not constitute a true random sample, the tribal variations need not be stressed. On the other hand, the class variations are significant. Among the Ngwaketse, Kwena, and Ngwato the proportion of marriages between near kin is roughly two to three times greater among nobles than it is among commoners, and even among the Kgatla and Tlôkwa it is appreciably greater, although not to

---

[1] I have omitted my Malete genealogies, since they are not detailed enough for the present analysis.

the same extent. The general average for nobles is one in nine, and that for commoners one in eighteen.

In the three tribes for which I have genealogies of the royal families only, the corresponding figures are:

Tribe	S.	No.	%
Rolong . .	260	19	7·3
Tawana . .	245	41	16·7
Khurutshe . .	66	6	9·1

Including the figures already given, we get a total of 1,546 marriages of nobles, of which 177 (11·4 per cent.) were between close relatives.

The two sets of genealogies together embrace 265 marriages between people who had a common grandparent or were more closely related. We must now analyse these marriages to see if they indicate any special form of preference. To facilitate discussion I shall combine the figures for all the tribes, but where necessary I shall refer to significant local variations.

TABLE II

Types of Marriage between Near Kin

Wife's relation to husband	No.	%
Sister	4	1·5
Mother's sister	2	0·8
Sister's daughter	3	1·1
Brother's daughter	34	12·8
Mother's brother's daughter . . .	83	31·3
Father's sister's daughter	32	12·1
Father's brother's daughter . . .	84	31·7
Mother's sister's daughter . . .	23	8·7
	265	100·0

Before we consider the details it may be noted that marriages of the first three types together constitute less than 0·3 per cent. of the grand total (3,145), those with a brother's daughter 1·1 per cent., and those with first cousins 7·1 per cent. (cross-cousins 3·7, parallel cousins 3·4).

Marriages with a sister occurred only among the Ngwaketse (3) and the Rolong (1); the woman, in each case, was a paternal half-sister. As already noted, such marriages were formerly permitted in both tribes, although nowadays they are considered incestuous. The marriages with the mother's sister and the sister's daughter were confined to the Ngwaketse, and here again, in each case, the connecting link was a paternal half-sister and not a full sister. Marriage with the sister's daughter, although nowadays prohibited, was formerly permitted, but marriage with the mother's sister is said to have always been regarded as incestuous; I failed to inquire why the two in question had been recognized. It may be added that with one exception (a marriage with the sister's daughter) all the marriages in this group took place last century and the people concerned have long been dead; among the Ngwaketse, moreover, two instances of marriage with a sister and one of marriage with a mother's sister were found in a single collateral branch of the royal family.

Marriages with a brother's daughter occurred in all tribes except the Kgatla, where, as already noted, they are prohibited. The Rolong, according to my informants, also prohibit them, but one early instance is found in the genealogy of the royal family; and among the Ngwaketse, where it was said that a man may marry his half-brother's daughter but not his full brother's, there were two instances (out of twelve) of marriage with the latter.

The figures for cousin marriages show a marked difference between stated preferences and actual practice. The order of preference, as laid down by informants, is mother's brother's daughter, father's sister's daughter, father's brother's daughter, mother's sister's daughter. The actual order of frequency, as shown in Table II, is father's brother's daughter, mother's brother's daughter, father's sister's daughter, mother's sister's daughter. There is, however, very little difference between the first two, although they are far more common than the others. Moreover, they occurred in every tribe. No instances of marriage with a daughter of either father's sister or mother's sister were found in the Khurutshe genealogy, but this may be due partly to the smallness of the sample. The Rolong also lacked instances of mother's sister's daughter marriage. On the other hand, one was noted among the Kwena, who it will be remembered spoke disapprovingly of such a marriage; but it should be added that the man in question, a member of the royal family, had settled and married among the Tlôkwa, whose chief was his maternal uncle.

Further analysis of the cousin marriages reveals another important feature. In the five tribes where I have genealogies of both nobles and commoners the various forms were distributed as follows among the two classes:

TABLE III

Class Variations in Cousin Marriages

Type	Nobles		Commoners	
	No.	%	No.	%
Mother's brother's daughter . .	43	30·3	40	50·0
Father's sister's daughter . . .	20	14·1	12	15·0
Father's brother's daughter . .	68	47·9	16	20·0
Mother's sister's daughter . .	11	7·7	12	15·0
	142	100·0	80	100·0

Among nobles nearly half the marriages are with the father's brother's daughter; the mother's brother's daughter comes next, but is obviously less favoured; and then, much lower in the scale, are the father's sister's daughter and, finally, the mother's sister's daughter. (In the three tribes for which I have genealogies of the royal families only, the corresponding proportions, out of 52 cousin marriages, are: father's brother's daughter, 48·1 per cent.; mother's brother's daughter, 36·5; father's sister's daughter, 9·6; and mother's sister's daughter, 5·8.) Among commoners, on the other hand, there were as many marriages with the mother's brother's daughter alone as with all the other types of cousin combined; only one-fifth were with the father's brother's daughter, and the mother's sister's daughter ranked equally with the father's sister's daughter, both nearly as common as the father's brother's daughter.

The genealogies of the commoners are not sufficiently extensive for further detailed analysis, but those of the nobles allow us to determine the proportions and kinds of marriages with more remote relatives than those already discussed. Of the 1,546 marriages in this group (the figures are for the eight tribes combined), 177 (as already noted) were between people related through a common grandparent or more closely. There were another 200 (12·9 per cent.) in which husband and wife had a common great-grandparent, 408 (26·4 per cent.) in which they were still more remotely connected, and 761 (49·2 per cent.) in which there was no discoverable relationship. In all, that is, about half the noble marriages are between people genealogically connected. Among commoners I was able to establish genealogical relationship in only 331 out of 1,599 marriages (20·7 per cent.).

The only figures calling for further comment are those for marriages among nobles having a common great-grandparent. Of the 200 marriages in this group, no fewer than 112 (56·0 per cent.) were between agnates (father's father's brother's daughter, 15; father's father's brother's son's daughter, 58; father's brother's son's daughter, 36; brother's son's daughter, 2). If we add the marriages of type (a), we find that of 377 marriages in which husband and wife had a common great-grandparent or were more closely related, there were altogether 213 (56·5 per cent.) with an agnatic relative, 80 (21·2 per cent.) with a paternal 'cross' relative, 67 (17·8 per cent.) with a maternal 'cross' relative, and only 17 (4·5 per cent.) with a matrilineal relative. It seems evident that men of the royal family, when they do marry fairly close relatives, prefer women of their own lineages. Some possible reasons will be suggested below.

We may now turn to affinal marriages or secondary unions. The incidence of the sororate is easy to determine from the genealogies. In all, 347 men had married more than once, the total number of their wives being 889. Of the 542 additional wives 16 were explicitly stated to have been taken as substitutes for a childless or deceased relative. There were

36 other instances in which a man had married independently a close relative of an earlier wife. This gives a total of 52 marriages (9·6 per cent.) in which the additional wives of polygynists or widowers were closely related to predecessors. The actual relationships were as follows:

Relationship	Sororate	Marriage	Total	%
Older sister	..	4	4	7·7
Younger sister	12	9	21	40·4
Mother's younger sister . .	..	1	1	1·9
Sister's daughter . . .	1	4	5	9·6
Brother's daughter . . .	..	· 2	2	3·8
Mother's sister's daughter . .	..	2	2	3·8
Father's brother's daughter . .	2	10	12	23·1
Mother's brother's daughter .	1	2	3	5·8
Father's sister's daughter . .	..	2	2	3·8
	16	36	52	99·9

It will be seen that almost half the unions were with a wife's sister, and almost a fourth with her father's brother's daughter. The one instance of true sororate with a mother's brother's daughter occurred among the Kgatla.

Information about the extent to which the levirate is practised is seldom available in the genealogies. Since the widow's children in such cases are held to belong to her late husband, the name of the actual father if (someone else) would not necessarily be mentioned; nor, I must add, did I when compiling the genealogies think of inquiring into the point. However, the relevant information was occasionally volunteered, especially about the widows of chiefs. In all, I learned of 16 instances. The seed-raiser's relationship to the dead husband in these instances was as follows: son, 5; younger brother, 4; brother's son, 3; father's brother's son's son, 2; older brother, 1; mother's sister's son, 1. The last, which occurred among the Tlôkwa, is perhaps the only one calling for special comment; here the husband had been adopted as a child by his maternal aunt, and the man who subsequently acted as his seed-raiser was therefore also his foster-brother.

There were also 129 women who had married again after being widowed or divorced. The total number of their husbands was 274. Of the 145 additional husbands, 20 (13·8 per cent.) were closely related to a predecessor. The exact relationships were as follows: father's brother's son, 8; younger brother, 5; father's younger brother, 2; brother's son, mother's brother, sister's son, father's sister's son, and mother's brother's son, 1 each. The one instance of marriage with the husband's sister's son (i.e. of a man with his mother's brother's widow) occurred among the Ngwaketse, where it is said to be forbidden; the man was subsequently overwhelmed by a series of misfortunes, which were piously attributed to the breach of the taboo.

CONCLUSIONS

The material presented above shows that, in general, the Tswana prohibit marriage only between kin of the first and second orders, excluding a brother's daughter; there are also only a few affines whom a man may not marry (his wife's mother, wife's daughter, father's wife, son's wife, and stepsister). Marriage is allowed with any first cousin, but preferably with a cross-cousin; various forms of levirate are practised (junior fraternal, senior fraternal, and filial), and so is the sororate, especially with the wife's sister.

However, there are several local variations of the general pattern. The Rolong and Kgatla prohibit marriage with any brother's daughter, the Ngwaketse and Khurutshe with a full brother's daughter; the Ngwaketse and Kwena allow marriage with a stepsister; the Ngwaketse formerly permitted marriage with a half-sister, half-sister's daughter, and step-daughter, and the Rolong with a half-sister; and the Kwena and Kgatla formerly recognized the paternal levirate (cohabitation with a son's widow). The Khurutshe and the three eastern tribes (Kgatla, Malete, and Tlôkwa) also allow cohabitation with a mother's brother's widow, which is prohibited elsewhere, although it was practised long ago by the Rolong.

Genealogical and other data show that the mating prohibitions have occasionally been violated, although on the whole instances are rare.[1] In addition, the cousin marriages that have actually occurred do not conform to the stated order of preference. Among commoners the mother's brother's daughter is by far the most frequent choice, but the father's brother's daughter comes next, ahead of the father's sister's daughter; among nobles the father's brother's daughter is preferred to even the mother's brother's daughter, and both are married more commonly than the two other types of first cousin. Nobles also show a definite bias towards marriage with agnates among their more distant kin.

These facts pose various problems for discussion. Can we account for the tribal variations in rules of mating? Why do cousin marriages differ in actual order of frequency from the order of preference laid down by informants, and why do nobles, in contrast with commoners, marry agnatic relatives more frequently than others? How are the rules of mating, in general, related both to other aspects of the kinship system and to the social structure as a whole, and, in particular, can we explain why the Tswana have such a limited range of restrictions?

It may be said at once that the Tswana material does not fully support Rivers's well-known contention that 'the terminology of relationship has been rigorously determined by social conditions', including especially

---

[1] I have dealt with this topic more fully in a paper on 'The Tswana Conception of Incest', in *Social Structure* (ed. M. Fortes, 1949), pp. 104–20.

forms of marriage.[1] It is true that relatives to whom different patterns of behaviour apply are often also called by different terms, e.g. paternal and maternal uncles, elder and younger brothers, cross-cousins and parallel cousins. On the other hand, the same term of relationship is sometimes used both for people with whom mating is forbidden and for those who may be married or taken as secondary consorts. Thus, *kgaitsadi* = (*a*) sister (prohibited), (*b*) father's brother's daughter and mother's sister's daughter (permitted); *rrakgadi* = (*a*) father's sister (prohibited), (*b*) father's father's brother's daughter (permitted); *mmangwane* = (*a*) mother's younger sister (prohibited), (*b*) junior step-mother and father's younger brother's wife (both permitted); and *mogwagadi* = (*a*) wife's mother (prohibited), (*b*) wife's sister (permitted). In such cases there is generally an alternative term for the woman who may be married. A parallel cousin, for instance, may be called by a descriptive term, and a wife's sister by the term for 'sister (w.s.)'. But, with parallel cousins descriptive terms are far more commonly used for the mother's sister's daughter than for the father's brother's daughter, although marriage with her is much less frequent; on Rivers's argument, we should have expected the opposite tendency to prevail. Again we may find all tribes using the same term for a certain relative, but differing in the rules about mating with her. The best example is the brother's daughter, who may be married in some tribes but not in others, yet who is called by the same term throughout.

The mating regulations also do not conform exactly to the other rules of behaviour between relatives. Parallel cousins are said to be treated 'much the same as sisters', but, unlike them, may be married; and the practice of the levirate with the widows of one's father or paternal uncles does not accord with the respect that should be shown to such women as 'mothers'. It can of course be argued, and correctly, that in these instances the behaviour patterns are not really the same, the rules varying in intensity with the nearness of the relationship. But the same argument will not explain why some tribes allow and others prohibit marriage with the brother's daughter, although in all she is regarded 'as a daughter'; nor does the formal attitude towards the mother's brother's wife in other respects differ according to whether or not she is a potential mate. Again, the symmetrical joking relationship between cross-cousins fits in well enough with the preference expressed for marriage between them, but this does not explain why the mother's brother's daughter is married far more frequently than the father's sister's daughter.

The observations just made suggest that among the Tswana there is apparently little causal connexion between kinship terminology, mating regulations, and the other rules of kinship behaviour, i.e. we cannot say that one of them necessarily 'determines' the others. The kinship

[1] W. H. R. Rivers, *Kinship and Social Organization*, 1914, p. 1.

M

terminology is not derived from the rules of mating, nor are the latter always consistent with the other rules of behaviour between relatives. To explain why the Tswana marry as they do we must therefore look also to other features of their social system.

We must note, firstly, that marriages are usually arranged, not by the young couple themselves, but by their parents and other close relatives; formerly, indeed, it was not uncommon for girls to be betrothed during infancy or even before they were born. Moreover, in choosing a bride people look for the qualities likely to ensure a stable marriage: the girl herself should be industrious, modest, chaste, obedient, and amiable, and her parents should be of respectable ancestry and good character, free from any suspicion of practising sorcery.

It is largely because parents wish to find a good wife for their son that they prefer to marry him, if possible, to the daughter of some close relative, with whose conduct and reputation they are themselves well acquainted. Near relatives, informants also argue, are apt to be more tolerant of each other than strangers, and, because of the pre-existing ties, their kin will take greater interest in the welfare of the marriage and try to ensure its success. Such marriages, moreover, bind the two families together even more closely than before and make for increased harmony and co-operation—a factor of much importance in a society where people depend greatly upon their relatives for help in major household activities.

These statements help us to understand why among the various types of cousin marriage those with the daughters of uncles predominate. A man's brothers normally live in his own family-group and ward, so that he sees them daily, whereas his sisters will generally have moved away after marriage. A married woman, similarly, maintains closer contact with her brothers, who as the male representatives of her own family continue to have some responsibility for her welfare, than she does with her sisters, whose husbands are not so directly concerned. In both instances a child's parents are apt to associate more intimately with his uncles than with his aunts, so that the former's daughters tend to be considered first, because they are better known, when a wife has to be chosen for him.

Several other factors determine the preference shown by commoners for marriage with the mother's brother's daughter. A man whose own wife has proved satisfactory readily turns to her family for a daughter-in-law, because experience has shown him that they train their children well. The *bogadi* cattle received by a man when his sister is married are also held to give her sons a prior claim to his daughters, and he himself, since he has an important say in choosing a wife for his nephew, may succeed in arranging a marriage with his daughter. The joking relationship between cross-cousins is another reason often given: the familiarity that it encourages and even enjoins, some informants state, makes for tolerance and indulgence between husband and wife and thus helps to ensure a stable marriage.[1]

Similarly, in explaining the relative popularity of marriage with a father's brother's daughter, the Tswana often add that it keeps the *bogadi* cattle in the same family circle and prevents them from passing into the hands of outsiders.[2] In the old days, when polygynous marriages were much more common than now, this may have been an important factor, since *bogadi* would have to be given for several wives. But even then the cattle received when a girl married did not remain the sole property of her father or brother; they were divided among her close relatives generally, including especially her maternal uncle, who in some tribes had the first claim upon them. The economic argument must therefore not be stressed unduly; moreover, as we have seen, among commoners the father's brother's daughter is married far less commonly than the mother's brother's daughter, in whose case it is not relevant, since marriage with her again involves the alienation of cattle from the family-group.

Among nobles, where marriage with the father's brother's daughter is actually the most common form of cousin marriage, the dominant factor is certainly not *bogadi* but status. It is considered highly desirable that the chief's heir and other senior children should marry persons of rank. The motive is not so much 'to keep the blood pure' as to secure the political advantages attached to union with powerful or influential families. Hence the choice of a mate is in effect restricted to the royal families of other tribes, the leading families of important subject communities within the same tribe, or collateral branches of the royal family itself. There is another reason why agnates are preferred. Since, in the Tswana social system, a man's maternal relatives are expected to be his main partisans, a chief by marrying into his own lineage can ensure that his sons, especially the heir, have a powerful backing close at hand. There are several instances in tribal history where a claimant to the chieftainship, whose maternal relatives were of the same tribe, succeeded against a rival whose mother was a foreigner. A man whose maternal uncles were also his agnates was thus in a particularly favourable position. The fact that he was their sister's son would probably also help to remove the sources of conflict which, as we have seen, sometimes enter into the relations of agnates.

So far I have been trying to show why the Tswana, in general, tend to marry certain types of relatives more frequently than others. It is more difficult to explain why some tribes allow kinship marriages that others prohibit. As I have already indicated, except for the rules of

---

[1] Other informants, however, maintained that the joking relationship has the opposite effect, since a wife may presume upon it to be cheeky and even impertinent to her husband instead of showing him due deference and submission.

[2] Cf. the proverb quoted above, p. 151.

mating there appear to be hardly any significant tribal variations in either formal behaviour patterns or terminology for the relatives concerned; we cannot, therefore, connect the differences in mating regulations with other differences in the kinship system. This applies not only to the sister, sister's daughter, and stepdaughter (with whom marriage is now prohibited in the tribes where it was formerly allowed), but also to the stepsister and brother's daughter, about whom usage still differs. The only relative for whom kinship terms vary is the mother's brother's wife. The eastern tribes call her 'grandmother', the northern tribes use a descriptive term, and the southern tribes have both usages. This may be associated with the fact that it is also only among the eastern tribes, and the Khurutshe,[1] that one may cohabit with her; but, here again, there is nothing to indicate that the conventional behaviour patterns differ in other respects.

It may well be that I did not investigate these variations deeply enough while in the field; I certainly did not inquire, as I should have done, into the formal reasons for every individual type of marriage prohibition, a procedure that would possibly have thrown light upon some of the inter-tribal differences. At present I can only suggest that the variations must be attributed, at least partly, to independent local developments due to specific historical incidents. I cannot account in any other way for the former occurrence and subsequent abolition among the Ngwaketse of some types of marriage that were prohibited everywhere else, nor for the complete prohibition of marriage with the brother's daughter among both the Rolong and the Kgatla, who belong to different divisions of Tswana and have never been intimately connected. It is possible also that diffusion among neighbouring tribes may account for the former existence of sister marriage among the Rolong and Ngwaketse, and of the paternal levirate among the Kgatla and Kwena. On the other hand, it should be noted that the Rolong and Kgatla are both marginal tribes, who have closer affinities with the Tswana peoples of the Union than with those of the Protectorate. It is possible, therefore, that comparison with the Union tribes may help to explain some of the differences noted. However, detailed information is not at present available about the mating regulations of those tribes.

This brings me to the final point. I have shown that the Tswana tribes (of the Bechuanaland Protectorate) permit marriage with all but a few very close relatives; but I have not tried to explain this feature of their kinship system. In other Sotho groups, such as the Pedi of the Transvaal, marriage is prohibited with the mother's sister's daughter, and in still others, such as the Lobedu, marriage is permitted only with cross-cousins, especially the mother's brother's daughter. There are other southern Bantu, such as the Nguni, who prohibit marriage with

---

[1] I failed to get the kinship terminology of the Khurutshe, and am therefore unable to say what they call the mother's brother's wife.

any first cousin at all, and who are also organized into exogamous patrilineal clans. It seems evident that for an adequate explanation of Tswana mating regulations we need a still wider comparison than I have suggested above. We must compare the Tswana with other groups of Sotho, and the Sotho generally with the Nguni and other groups of Southern Bantu. Only then, I think, will it be possible for us to state why the Tswana regulations differ from those of other groups. This I hope to show more fully in a later publication.

KINSHIP AND MARRIAGE AMONG THE LOZI OF NORTHERN RHODESIA AND THE ZULU OF NATAL

By MAX GLUCKMAN

INTRODUCTION

IN this essay I contrast the marriage and kinship systems of the Lozi, the dominant tribe of Barotseland, with those of the Zulu.[1] I make this comparison because it brings out clearly the attributes of the Lozi system, and these attributes are characteristic of a large number of Central African systems which I consider have not yet been defined. On our present information I tentatively define these systems negatively, by the absence of a corporate lineage (i.e. of any organized kinship group of several generations depth reckoned in one line, which is internally segmented on a genealogical system, the whole and each segment having identity and unity against corresponding groups). The Zulu system is of this latter type, wherein the corporate lineage and its segments endure in time irrespective of changes in personnel, and form the nuclei of villages and local groupings.

In Central Africa villages are also corporate groups of kindred, but

[1] I worked among the Lozi as a research officer of the Rhodes–Livingstone Institute of Social Studies, Northern Rhodesia (1940–2, 1947), and among the Zulu on a grant from the National Bureau of Educational and Social Research (Carnegie Fund), Union of South Africa Education Department (1936–8). I thank Dr. Elizabeth Colson and Professor A. R. Radcliffe-Brown for criticisms of an early draft of this essay. It was written at the Rhodes–Livingstone Institute in Livingstone and I was restricted in making comparative reference to the books available there and at libraries in Johannesburg which I visited.

The argument advanced in this essay arose directly from E. E. Evans-Pritchard's *Some Aspects of Marriage and the Family among the Nuer*, Rhodes–Livingstone Paper No. 11, 1945 (reprinted from *Zeitschrift für Vergleichende Rechtswissenschaft*, 1938). I acknowledge gratefully the stimulus I received from this analysis, though I have only referred to it occasionally in my text, and from discussions with Professor Evans-Pritchard himself.

The best available descriptions of the Lozi are my 'The Lozi of Barotseland' in *Seven Tribes of British Central Africa*, London: Oxford University Press for the Rhodes–Livingstone Institute (forthcoming); *Economy of the Central Barotse Plain*, Rhodes–Livingstone Paper No. 7, 1941; and *Essays on Lozi Land and Royal Property*, Rhodes–Livingstone Paper No. 10, 1943. A general account of the Zulu, not based on field research, is E. J. Krige's *The Social System of the Zulus*, London: Longmans, 1936. See also my 'The Kingdom of the Zulu of South-East Africa' in M. Fortes and E. E. Evans-Pritchard (editors), *African Political Systems*, London: Oxford University Press, 1940. In general I describe Zulu law as practised by the Zulu, not as laid down by the Natal Native Code and Native Appeal Court decisions (see W. G. Stafford, *Native Law as Practised in Natal*, Johannesburg: Witwatersrand University Press, 1936).

they are formed on a different framework. The villages move frequently in search of virgin woodland for cultivation and their membership changes at each move and between moves. Villagers constantly alter their residence. A village is constituted by the attachment of small groupings of kindred, of families, and of individuals, to a headman with whom they are linked in various ways. In many matrilineal and matrilocal tribes of Northern Rhodesia and Nyasaland a series of small groups of matrilineal kin are linked to the headman, who is a member of one, by various cognatic ties (e.g. Yao and Cewa, and perhaps Bemba and Lamba).[1] Other kinsmen and kinswomen also attach themselves to a popular headman. Bemba may move through four villages during their lives. Among the Ila and their neighbours, the Tonga, who are matrilineal but dominantly patrilocal, the links of villagers to headman are more varied. With a headman will be some of his sons, some of his uterine nephews, and some of his sons- and brothers-in-law, as well as other relatives, with some of whom he cannot trace genealogical connexions. In both these matrilocal and patrilocal complexes the inhabitants of neighbouring villages are not related to one another by links which form them into a kinship grouping standing against other kinship groupings. Nor is it clear from anywhere that the relations of groups of kin are determined by their positions relative to one another in a genealogical system. The only corporate group of kindred is the village.

Associated with this type of village are kinship systems which are shallow (1–4 generations from adults) but ramify widely in all lines. Shallow kinship systems ramifying in all lines, short-lived villages of varied constitutions, and slash-and-burn shifting cultivation form a single coherent complex. However, I believe that Central African kinship systems may have a common pattern, independent of this environmental setting. It appears in an unusual form among the Lozi largely because in their environment the size to which their villages can grow is limited and kinship groupings cannot expand in one locality, though each village may endure through centuries. Initially, we may note that the Lozi and their related sub-tribes are dominantly patrilineal and patrilocal (like their Lunda forebears), though the surrounding tribes are matrilineal and often matrilocal. Part of the Lozi kinship system is a marriage complex differing in almost every rule and consequence from that of the Southern Bantu.

The Lozi live mainly in the great flood plain of the upper Zambezi river. Most Lozi build their villages on 'mounds', higher parts of the plain, which stand above the waters of the summer floods. Towards the

---

[1] See on the constitution of these villages M. Gluckman, J. C. Mitchell, and J. A. Barnes, 'The Village Headman in British Central Africa', *Africa*, xix. 2, 1949, pp. 89–106; and essays by J. A. Barnes on the Ngoni, E. Colson on the Tonga, M. Gluckman on the Lozi, and J. C. Mitchell on the Yao in *Seven Tribes of British Central Africa*.

height of the flood the Lozi move for a few months to other homes, built above the water-line on the margins of the plain, where they remain until the fall of the waters in winter enables them to return to their permanent homes. Not all the members of one plain village go to the same margin village. Especially since the 1890's, many Lozi have made their permanent homes on the margin near markets created by missions and administrative posts. The flood, and the movements of people, cattle, and fish associated with it, dominate Lozi life. Gardens are covered and uncovered, watered and fertilized, by it; it fixes the pasturing of cattle; it conditions methods of fishing.

The Lozi have a mixed economy. They are proficient gardeners and fishermen, planting and reaping crops and catching fish in various sites during almost every month of the year. Their gardens and fishing-sites are dispersed in the plain, from its centre at the river into the encircling woodlands. Often different activities have to be pursued at the same time in widely separated places. They have to send their cattle to flood-season grazing in the woodland and the small plains within it when they are gardening and fishing on the Zambezi plain; the cattle return to graze on pastures in the plain when the flood falls, before the people move back to their homes.

The flood compels the Lozi to build their homes on the mounds in the plain and therefore these are the basis of their social organization. To each mound are attached certain gardens and fishing-sites which in general can only be used by the residents of the village built on the mound. The villages are of different types. Some villages are inhabited by groups of kinsmen, consisting usually of a small core of agnates and other cognates with their wives and children, and possibly an occasional male affine or stranger as well as serfs. The limited area of the building-space on a mound, and of the resources centred in it, restricts the size to which villages can grow. Some have only a couple of men in them and the average village varies from six to ten men. The other type of village belongs to the royal family and to the titles of councillors at court. These are inhabited by members of different tribes, both Lozi and subject peoples, collected by kings. Their size runs from tens of people into a couple of hundred, and thousands at the capitals. Royal villages are aggregations of small groups of kindred which resemble the groups in family villages, so that in effect a royal village is like a number of family villages concentrated together. Inhabitants of a royal village have permanent rights of holding in it. The Lozi imposed Lozi rules on members of subject tribes brought into their villages, and to-day it is impossible to distinguish their descendants by behaviour from true Lozi, of whom indeed there are admitted to be very few, because of intermarriage.

The Lozi villages therefore have histories running into hundreds of years, for since they came to the plain they have built on the same mounds. Yet because mounds are small and scattered in the plain, members of each village as its population grows must seek new land at a distance; perhaps, therefore, they have not been able to develop extended unilineal kin-groups. In addition, I believe this pattern is generally foreign to Central Africa.

The Lozi have not remained in undisturbed possession of their plain. In 1836 the Kololo, a people with a Basuto nucleus, conquered them. Some Lozi remained under the Kololo. Others retired to northern swamps whence, in 1866, they annihilated the Kololo and regained their homeland. I consider that the Kololo conquest did not affect the Lozi kinship system.

The Zulu cultivate their gardens and graze their cattle on the hills and in the valleys of south-east Africa. They live in small villages inhabited by groups of agnates and their wives. Often the members of a number of neighbouring villages are related to one another by patrilineal ties to form a group (*umdeni*) within a lineage system (*ulusendo*), in which a genealogically senior headman, descended by primogeniture from chief wives of his ancestors, is recognized as superior by other headmen. The people practise shifting cultivation, but villages tend to be settled in one area for many decades. As a village grows it splits into patrilineal branches, which normally establish independent villages within the lineage land-area.

Both Lozi and Zulu are organized in powerful kingdoms.

KINSHIP STRUCTURE AND THE AFFILIATION OF CHILDREN

The Zulu kinship system is similar to that of the Swazi, described by Dr. Kuper elsewhere in this book. The Zulu are divided into a number of exogamous clans (there is a word, *isibongo*, for clan name, but not for the group) each of which is an association of dispersed agnatic lineages which are corporate groups of kinspeople who to-day trace common descent in a putative patrilineal line over six to nine generations. Thereafter there is a genealogical gap before clan founders are referred to. However, this genealogical gap dates from the establishing of the Zulu kingdom in 1818–28; before that the people of the Zululand region were organized in small tribes whose nuclei were lineages with a genealogical framework of some twelve generations depth, since these nuclei were then localized groups.

The lineages within the clan are usually residential units. Their segments are cores of villages and a number of segments living in one neighbourhood form a recognized group (*umdeni*) against other similar groups, in their own and other clans. The segments are placed in a genealogical structure. Members of a segment hold rights in each other's herds and lands, consult on personal questions, and arbitrate in quarrels between members. The *umdeni* exists even when its constituent villages are divided by political boundaries between provinces of the nation or between nations. There are also rights and obligations between fellow-clansmen. They have residual inheritance rights; they should be hospitable to and help one another; they may drink milk with each other; they may not marry each other's sisters; they share a common clan-head and his ancestors and a sacred clan-song, and in some clans common ritual and taboos.

Each exogamous clan obtains wives from other clans by giving cattle which transfer to the husbands and their agnates rights to all the children of the wives, whoever are their genitors. A child is absolutely a member of his mother's husband's lineage and all his rights of inheritance lie in it. He has also certain rights and duties in his mother's lineage: he cannot marry in it and he can drink its milk, but he does not inherit in it or normally come under its ancestors. An illegitimate child, unless redeemed by his genitor with cattle, or by his or another's subsequent marriage to the mother, belongs to his mother's agnatic lineage.

In the kinship terminology relatives of the father's and mother's sides are clearly distinguished, and lineal and collateral kin on either side are identified with one another in the first ascending generation. The father's brothers (real and classificatory) are 'fathers' and his sisters are 'female fathers'; the mother's sisters are 'mothers' and her brothers are 'male mothers'. In the grandparents' generation the same terms are used on both sides, but the behaviour pattern to the father's father is of submissive respect, against familiarity on the other side. Kinship farther back is traced in the patrilineal line only. In ego's own generation there is no distinction on a lineage basis: all of the ortho-cousins are brothers and sisters and both sets of cross-cousins are called by one term (*umzala*). Marriage is not allowed with any member of one's father's or mother's clan, nor with anyone who shares a common grandparent. The unity of the lineage does appear to some extent in the terminology. Besides using the terms set out in Fig. 6 for siblings, a man or woman calls all siblings and cousins of both sexes in his or her lineage 'brother' (*mfowethu*). This fits in with the identification of father and father's sisters who are also members of the lineage. Children of all siblings, half-siblings, and cousins, are called 'my child', and all their children are grandchildren. Descriptive phrases indicate sex difference and the exact linkage.

The husband calls his and his brothers' and sisters' affines *umlanda*, except his wife's father and mother who are *mamezulu*. The wife and her family call her husband's kin *mkwenyana*, or the wife may say *ekhakami*. But, in addition, both spouses use specific and distinctive terms for certain of their affinal relatives. In the grandparents' and senior generations they use the same terms as for their own kin, and similarly in the grandchildren's and junior generations. The husband can courteously use the term for parents to his wife's parents, but there are distinctive terms. The wife also has distinctive terms for her parents-in-law, but she, resident in her husband's village, tends to adopt the terms he uses.

The influence of lineage categories is seen in that the husband calls his wife's brothers and sisters, and also his wife's brother's child, *mlamu*. They are members of his wife's lineage. But the same term is also applied to wife's brother's wife. The wife adopts the term used by her husband for his siblings of both sexes, and all their children are her children, as he calls her sister's child 'my child'. In short, a wife calls all her husband's relatives by the same terms as he would use, allowing for sex differences; thus the wives of her husband's brother are her fellow-wives, while her husband calls them 'my wives'.

The relationships of affines are marked by restraint and avoidance. A wife avoids the milk and meat of her husband's home until a special ceremony is performed for her. She must not go to certain parts of the village, must cover her body before her senior male affines, and avoid using the radicals of their names. As she bears children the relationship gradually eases, and when her sons grow up her position as 'mother (father) of the village' is powerful. A man avoids his mother-in-law, but is freer than his wife. He cannot eat meat at her home unless a beast is especially killed for him.

A man calls his wife's sister's husband *mnawethu* (my comrade). Their children by the sisters cannot marry, but their children by other wives may.

Zulu chiefs in the past could marry in their clans, thus splitting them and producing new clans, but this belongs to the study of political organization, as does the rule that a Lozi paramount chief can marry his half-sister.

No corporate unilineal group of kinsmen exists among the Lozi. Every child, legitimate, illegitimate, and adulterine, has a right to make its home in a village of either of its mother's parents and to inherit there. It also has these rights with the kin of its father, who in Lozi law is the genitor. The difference among the Lozi in a child's relations with its father's and mother's kin is one of emphasis. There is no dominant unilineal kin-group, either in father's patrilineal or mother's matrilineal lines. A child's proper home is with its father and it should go to his village to live and inherit; but this may be the village of his father's father or his father's mother. If a child does not get on well with his father, if his father fails to provide properly for him, or if he quarrels with his paternal relatives, he will go to live at his mother's home, which again may be his mother's father's or his mother's mother's. I have even recorded Lozi growing up and establishing themselves at their father's mother's mother's and their mother's mother's mother's homes. While in Zululand there are very many cases in which there are disputes over the guardianship of children, which hinge on the question of who paid marriage-cattle for the mother and whether it was delivered, similar cases are practically unknown among the Lozi. Lozi say 'the child belongs to both sides', and the courts will not constrain a young boy (or girl) to leave his mother's home to go to his father. In any case, when the child grows up, it will itself choose freely where it wants to live.

Manner of residence and rules of inheritance are consistent with the environmental situation of Lozi settlements. The small size of mounds means that Lozi villages can be inhabited only by small groupings of kindred, though usually villagers are related to one another. In a small family village on a mound, or in a family's part of a royal mound, it is impossible for the headman to place all his own sons and brothers' sons on land. Therefore some of them seek new land from the king or beg land from other relatives. Owing to the dotting of mounds in the plain, and because they are all owned, this may be far away. Frequently the king moves people into his royal villages. It happens thus that a village may fall below its full strength. Other relatives then move in to the vacant places. They have rights to inherit. When an elder dies no successor is definitely indicated. Men and women in all branches of the kindred meet to select an heir on the basis of his character—his wisdom and generosity and above all his ability to keep the village contented. They prefer to select a son, but he may be born of any wife of the husband and be one of her younger sons. If there is no suitable son they will choose a brother, a brother's son, a son's son, a sister's son or a daughter's son. The heir then replaces the dead man: he takes over all his land and cattle, including land and cattle allotted to wives, and divides them among the dead man's sons, grandsons, and nephews, in all lines, while retaining the largest portion for himself. The wives are not inherited; they may remain with their children, but they cannot claim land from the new headman, or they may return to their homes and marry again. Only succession to the chieftainships is by selection from agnatic descendants of ruling chiefs.

The large choice of homes which is open to a Lozi is reflected in the mode of tracing descent. Instead of having a single important kin-group, reckoned from father through all his male ancestors, as among the Nuer, Swazi, and Zulu, or from the mother through all her female ancestors, as among the Ovambo and Ashanti, or in two lines, matrilineal and patrilineal, as among Herero and Yakö, the Lozi reckon descent theoretically in all, including mixed, lines, and in practice in every line with whose members they maintain connexions. They have no clans, but they have *mishiku* (sing. *mushiku*), which I translate as 'descent-names'. This defines their attributes clearly, for the people sharing a single descent-name are not considered to be a group, nor do they have any specific obligations to each other, nor are there any ritual beliefs or practices attached to any descent-names. Nevertheless, people who share a descent-name feel that they are kinsfolk. The descent-name indicates that somewhere in his ancestry a man has a male or female ancestor or ancestors who, again in any one or more of his or her or their lines, had that descent-name. Lozi say everyone has eight descent names, but admit that everyone might ultimately be able to claim all the Lozi descent-names. A Lozi will remember the descent-names of those kinsmen with whom he lives and co-operates. Thus, where a man's mother comes from near by, when asked he will give spontaneously the descent-name of his mother as well as his father; if her mother, his maternal grandmother, lives so far away that he never sees her family, he readily forgets her descent-name. I have found in questioning Lozi about their descent-names that most remember two, the father's in the paternal line and the mother's in the paternal line, while next most frequently they remember the father's in his mother's paternal line. Some Lozi give five descent-names, but very many know only two and others only one.

People who share descent-names certainly do not expect to trace genealogical relationship. The Lozi, except for the royal family, trace their descent genealogically for only three or four generations from adults. There are no broadly based unilineal groups associating in common rights of residence, ownership, inheritance, production, &c., and consequently the structural depth of the kinship system is shallow, while it ramifies widely in all lines. The Lozi is interested in tracing his genealogical relationship with particular kin through any of the many lines of his descent rather than to claim or trace a distant relationship with someone in one special line. The patrilineal bias shows, however, in a tendency to change matrilineal links into patrilineal links by treating women in genealogies as men, or maternal uncles as fathers, where they link people with a village.

A Lozi may marry a woman with the same descent-name as himself. He should not marry a woman with whom he can trace genealogical relationship in any way, and we have seen that Lozi fail to trace genealogical relationships beyond four generations. In fact intermarriages occur earlier, while relationship can still be traced. The Lozi say, *sikowa sakukwata okusatunda kasapula*, 'a kindred gets so big that relationship is broken with time'. They apply this saying when a young man wants to marry a girl whom his elders consider is related to him. The elders protest, the young man counters with the maxim and marries her. It is significant for my later analysis that the couple will be cursed: 'You have chosen to marry. Only death may now divorce you; you may not separate from each other.' They establish a new relationship by affinity which ultimately produces new cognatic ties between the two kindreds. Lozi say that a man should not marry a woman with whom he is linked only by patrilineal ties, but such marriages occur.

Most Northern Rhodesian tribes have matrilineal exogamous clans but also forbid intermarriage with ortho-cousins on the father's side. They allow, and often prefer, marriage of cross-cousins. Among the Lozi, as shown on the genealogical chart (Fig. 6), all cousins are classed as brothers and sisters and marriage with them is forbidden. Thus, if the relationship is remembered, a man will call his mother's father's mother's daughter's son's daughter 'my sister' (*kaizeli*). Here I have deliberately given an example in which there is a jump from maternal to paternal line at almost every step, which is the most complicated combination. He should not marry her, though he may force the marriage by claiming that the relationship has grown old. That is, while the older people still call each other 'brother' and 'sister', the young people say in effect, 'There is no longer relationship between us.' By marrying they establish a new set of relationships. They no longer call each other 'brother' and 'sister' but 'husband' and 'wife'. The husband's and wife's siblings also stop calling each other, and the spouse of their sibling, 'brother' and 'sister', and they become 'brothers- and sisters-in-law' (*balamu*) to each other. Their fathers or their mothers, or their father and mother, depending on through whom the old relationship was traced, are no longer siblings (brothers and sisters), but call each other 'the other parent' (*mukwange mushemi*). The spouses no longer call the parents 'my father' or 'my mother', but 'my relative-in-law'. Thus the marriage breaks cognatic, and establishes affinal, relationships. The children of this couple will call the children of their parents' siblings 'my brother' and 'my sister', and though the marriage ban is broken for the one generation, it is renewed in a lower generation by the creation of new cognatic relations between their descendants. Since the spouses were related they will probably share at least two descent-names, and their children will have the same descent-names in more than one of their ancestral lines. I frequently found this in recording genealogies. In this dominantly patrilocal and patrilineal society relationship is obviously more easily broken where there is a female at some point in the chain of genealogical connexions; and more easily broken where there is descent from one man through two wives than where it is through one wife.

Even where there is no blood-relationship but there are certain marriage connexions marriage is banned, but here relationship becomes weak earlier. The Lozi say *mwaboyu ta mwaboyu*, 'the relatives of a man's relatives are his relatives' (see Fig. 7). Since divorce is frequent and a widow is rarely married again by one of her husband's kinsmen, a man's half-siblings through his mother or father are related through his mother's or father's other marriages to people who have not even putative blood-connexions with him, but through his half-siblings he claims them as relatives. Men and women related thus call each other 'brother' and 'sister' and do not marry. Similarly, a man calls his wife's brother's wife 'my sister', and most of my informants agree that he should not marry her if his wife's brother divorces her or dies. A woman calls her co-wife's brother 'my brother' (see Fig. 8), and again most informants say that he should not marry her if she is divorced or widowed. I know of one marriage in the former set of relationships; the man's earlier wife, sister of his new wife's divorced husband, left him and he did not appeal to the court.

Men who marry related women, or have sexual relationships with the same woman, are regarded as related and address one another by the special term *mufubalume* ('fellow-husband)'. This denotes a man who has slept with the same woman as oneself, and it applies between two lovers of one woman, between an adulterer and his cuckold, and between a man who has married a divorcee and her former husband. Lozi explain it as 'a man who quarrels with you because of sexual intercourse'. It is extended, on the principle of the equivalence of siblings, to apply between a man who has married a widow and the brothers of her dead husband, and between men who have married classificatory sisters. In general, the descendants of these men should not marry, but though their marriages will be resisted, it will not be as strongly as where there is a real cognatic relationship.

Thus in all lines except the purely patrilineal the Lozi allow marriages where a distant genealogical connexion can be traced, and ultimately welcome them, to renew the relationship. Perhaps, therefore, these marriages are cursed with a ban on divorce. This process also occurs in some Zulu lines; it is approved for a man to renew relationships by marrying a woman of his father's mother's or mother's mother's clan with whom he cannot trace links. He cannot marry a known cognate. Nor can he marry a woman of his father's or mother's clan, even though she belongs to a different lineage with which genealogical links are no longer remembered.

The Lozi thus tend to trace and merge relationships as widely as possible in the present living generations of immediate cognates, and not to trace relationship between kinsmen in one line who may be widely dispersed over the country. Nor does the Lozi system generally differentiate between the lines. This appears clearly in Figs. 6, 7, 8. In the same generation siblings are distinguished by sex: a sibling of the same sex is *muhulwani* if older, *munyani* if younger, but *kaizeli* is a self-reciprocal term between siblings of opposite sex. This sex distinction is not maintained downwards, where there are only two terms used: child (*mwana*) and grandchild (*mwikulu*). Descriptive terms, 'of boy' and 'of girl', are used to distinguish between them, and descriptive combinations are necessary to distinguish the exact linkage. Great-grandchildren are again 'children', great-great-grandchildren again 'grandchildren', and thereafter in theory the alternation proceeds regularly, though the relationship is rarely traced. The same process occurs in the senior ascendant generations: all grandparents and great-great-grandparents are *kuku*, irrespective of sex. In the parent's generation all the father's brothers and sisters are *ndate* (my father) like the father, though the father's sister can be called 'female father' (*ndate wamusali*). Similarly, the mother's sisters and brothers are all *me* (my mother), though the mother's brother may be called *malume* ('male mother'). The terms of the parents' generation are extended to the great-grandparents and great-great-great-grandparents, but the distinction between father's or mother's sides is overridden: all males are *ndate* (father) and all females are *me* (mother) on both sides.

This merging also extends to the spouse's relatives in lower and higher generations. People whom your spouse calls 'child' or 'grandchild' or 'grandparent' or 'great-grandparent' are similarly related to you, and you may not marry them. You primarily distinguish your parents- and children-in-law by the self-reciprocal term *mukwenyani*, but you also call them respectively 'father' and 'mother' and 'child', and your spouse's more distant connexions, such as mother's brother, you address by the same terms as your spouse does. His or her siblings, irrespective of sex, are *balamu* (sing. *malamu*), or husband (w.s.) or wife (m.s.), again irrespective of their sex. Beyond that a man or woman takes over the terms of address which his or her spouse uses for kinsfolk.

Thus among the Lozi relationships in all lines of descent tend to be merged by generations. The actual importance of the different lines varies from individual to individual, with a general bias to the paternal. But the mother's immediate home is more important than the home of someone distantly connected in the patrilineal line. Nearness of cognatic relationship, and not membership of a unilineal kin-group, is emphasized. There are slight differences in the behaviour patterns to father and mother's brother, and to mother and father's sister, but in general they are similar. Father and mother's brother are both treated with affectionate respect, but the relationship is easier with the latter. However, while among the Southern Bantu a man may claim something he wants from his mother's brother, among the Lozi a man could take anything of his father's or mother's brother's or of any other relative (*kufunda*: this has now been declared theft). A man can claim help from his mother's brother as from his father, and father and mother's brother share marriage payment of girls equally. My impression is that generally a man is friendlier with, and takes more care of, his sister's children than his brother's children. The father's sister is treated with considerable respect, while people behave with more ease to mother's sister.

There is one variation in behaviour to parents' siblings of the same and different sexes. A mother's brother also calls his sister's daughter 'my wife' and his sister's son 'my fellow-husband' (*mufubalume*), and father's sister also calls her brother's son 'my husband' and her brother's daughter 'my co-wife' (*muhalizo*), as well as 'my child'. Grandparents and grandchildren of opposite sex can address each other similarly. Between persons of opposite sex this form of teasing ceases when the youngsters, who find it embarrassing, grow up: they use the terms grandparent, father, mother, and child, out of respect. But mother's brother and sister's son still call each other 'fellow-husband' because the nephew can sleep in his uncle's hut, fondle his uncle's wife's breasts, and marry her if she wants to when his uncle dies. Lozi also say that these terms are used because these relationships are friendly and easy, and the young-sters can consult their elders on sexual matters (e.g. about the impotence of niece's husband or frigidity of nephew's wife); but clearly they fall into the pattern of joking relationships, since we have here a woman who is a father, and a man who is a mother. Similarly in the case of grandparents there is conflict because the terms of nomenclature iden-tify odd and even generations despite the great difference in age.

Behaviour to affines varies markedly according to generation. Parents-in-law and children-in-law, who address each other by a self-reciprocal term (*mukwenyani*), are treated with great respect. Son-in-law and mother-in-law, and father-in-law and daughter-in-law, practise mutual avoidance and if they touch each other must pay damages 'to wash away the fault'. They must not sit alone in a hut or use bad language before each other. A son-in-law should not sit on the same mat as his mother-in-law. This respect is not, however, carried as far as among the Zulu, where the daughter-in-law must avoid using any word like the names of her senior male relatives-in-law, and must not walk through the cattle-kraal or the men's place.

Directly related brothers- and sisters-in-law behave freely to each other. They are 'man and wife', even when of the same sex, though they more often call each other *mulamu* than 'wife' and 'husband'. But they should not marry. They joke and tease each other. A spouse takes over from his or her partner behaviour patterns to grandparents, nieces, and nephews.

The corporate groups of kindred which in theory have lasted from the beginnings of Lozi history are the villages. Since people have constantly moved or been moved by the king between villages and neighbourhoods, the pattern of kinship links in local communities is constantly altering. No unilineal framework exists to which they can be referred; only royal people close to ruling kings can trace their descent from Mboo, the founder of the Lozi kingdom, son of God and His daughter. This agnatic line is the core of the whole nation's history. Nevertheless, for commoners, too, kinship links are all-important in defining membership of a village and rights in it, and denoting relationships with and claims in other villages. Descent-names provide the ultimate reference for common origin by blood. By whatever links cognates are united they express their kinship by citing their descent-names. Correspondingly, strangers who find they share a descent-name feel that they are kin. The descent-names have this high value because they originated with the first Lozi who lived with King Mboo. They symbolize the notion that kin-ship, relationship by blood as such, comes from the beginning of time, even though the Lozi can only remember their genealogical ties back for a very few generations. They give historic depth to the shallow genealogi-cal system. Every descent-name is related to some stage of Lozi history: the Lozi names are those of the first inhabitants of the plain, those of

N

foreign tribes date to the absorption of these tribes in the nation. The villages which are the corporate groups of kindred are built on mounds which provide the only sites for homes in the plain. Certain of these mounds are known as those of the Lozi's distant forebears, and each Lozi descent-name is referred to an ancestral village on one of these mounds. The possession of a Lozi descent-name enables a man to point to his ancestral village, and claim to be a true Lozi, a true inhabitant of the plain, a descendant by blood of the original settlers related to the daughter of God, a kinsman of all Lozi.

The Lozi kinship is thus largely consistent with their modes of residence and production. We have seen that it is physically impossible for large groups, tracing unilineal relationship, to live on the mounds in the plain or on neighbouring mounds. As the group on a mound increases some members must seek land at other mounds far away, while the people at each mound must depend on their neighbours for help in prosecuting their many dispersed and contemporaneous activities. With these they intermarry and become related in a variety of ways. Cognatic relationships are periodically broken by marriages between people who can still trace relationship. These marriages establish new cognatic ties, and, I repeat, it is these marriages alone which are cursed by a ban on divorce.

Nevertheless, the Lozi pattern of kinship, despite its unique environmental setting for the region, has attributes which are characteristic of Central Africa. The system of nomenclature of the Bairu of Ankole, in distant Uganda, is more like the Lozi system of nomenclature than any other African system I know of,[1] but the free choice of homes for children, and the inability of either set of kin to claim children against the other, produce similar results in many of the tribes of Central Africa.[2]

I summarily contrast the Zulu system. There a man's rights of inheritance reside only in his agnatic lineage. His mother's and his grandmothers' homes and people are very important in his life, but his major ties of kinship and his economic interests pull him to his agnatic lineage. A Zulu inherits only from his agnates and he usually lives with and obtains land from them. For purposes of inheritance and familial pride Zulu are more interested in their distant patrilineal relationships than in close relationships in other lines.

[1] K. Oberg, 'Kinship Organization of Banyankole', *Africa*, xi. 2, April 1938.
[2] See e.g. A. T. and G. M. Culwick, *Ubena of the Rivers*, London, 1935; G. G. Brown and A. McD. B. Hutt, *Anthropology in Action*, Oxford, 1935, pp. 82 ff.; A. I. Richards, *Land Labour and Diet in Northern Rhodesia*, London, 1940, chap. viii; and W. Allan, M. Gluckman, D. U. Peters, and C. G. Trapnell, *Land-holding and Land-usage among the Plateau Tonga of Mazabuka District, Northern Rhodesia*, Rhodes–Livingstone Paper No. 14, 1948, chap. iii.

FORMS, CONDITIONS, AND PERSONAL CONSEQUENCES OF MARRIAGE

There are thus four striking differences between the Lozi and Zulu systems: the presence of the agnatic lineage among the Zulu and the Zulu distinction between ortho-cousins and cross-cousins, neither of whom they can marry, against the absence of this lineage among the Lozi and their merging of all cousins as brothers and sisters; the Lozi alternation of descending and ascending generations as children and grandchildren, and as parents and grandparents, respectively; and the Lozi merging of cognatic kin in numerous lines, and these kin with affines, to a greater extent than do the Zulu.

I observed no important differences in the psychological relationships of husbands and wives, though their social relationships differ widely. Zulu and Lozi marriages do not generally spring from romantic attachments, and their concept of love between the sexes is on the whole restrained, though sexual attraction between men and women may make them brave severe sanctions. In both societies there is only a limited field in which men and women can associate. They sleep together and produce children together, and their union founds an economic unit, but in general social and public life their contacts are limited. A man seeks companionship with his fellow men, a woman with her fellow women. Except in the intimacy of the marriage bed it is difficult for a man to enjoy the company of a woman. Here a Zulu is freer than a Lozi: he can spend his time with his sister, whom he can call 'my brother'. A Lozi may not touch his sister or a female affine without committing *sindoye* (a breach of the sexual ban) and he must not be alone with her in a hut. If he is, he is accused of sorcery. At beer-drinks men and women sit apart, and at dances they stand on opposite sides of the circle. By Lozi standards if a man walks along a path with another's wife who is not related to him, or gives her snuff or a drink of beer, or even speaks to her when no one is by, he commits 'adultery', even if he does not sleep with her. Men are often afraid to work gardens for, or help, the wives of their brothers who are labour migrants, lest their brothers charge them with being lovers of their sisters-in-law. In this background Lozi marry for sexual satisfaction, to secure an economic partner, to obtain children, but not to find a companion. This applies in general terms to the Zulu, save that, as marriage is far more stable among them, suspicions of adultery do not arise so easily. For example, men always help their absent brothers' wives.

However, the importance of the marital relationship must not be underestimated. Lozi trust and confide in their mothers and sisters, with whom their ties are enduring, rather than in their wives, with whom their ties are ephemeral. But a wife has a right to know all her husband's affairs and she is, with him, 'lord of the home'. If he neglects to treat her thus, and favours his kinswomen, she will be granted a divorce.

Both societies are polygynous, and jealousy between the co-wives of one man for his sexual and other favours is pronounced. It is recognized in proverb and saying and appears in charges of sorcery. In this similar background they evaluate sororal polygyny in opposite ways which reflect graphically the difference between the two marriage systems.

The Zulu approve of marriage to two sisters. Often a woman will urge her husband to marry her younger sister, who will become subordinate to her, so that she may have a 'companion' who will share her labours and her loving care for her children without the jealousy of a stranger co-wife. 'The love of sisters overcomes the jealousy of polygyny.' The husband cannot marry his wife's senior sister, but this is because she cannot be a subordinate wife to her own junior. Among the Lozi it is considered very bad to marry even a classificatory sister of your wife while the latter is alive. Your wife and relatives will protest strongly, and I have records of wives who walked out on their husbands when they married thus. Lozi say, 'The jealousy of polygyny spoils the love of sisters. It will break up their family.' They must not be put in the position of competing for a man's favours or their children in the position of competing for their inheritances in both their lines. Among the Zulu their inheritances and relative status would be fixed.

This variant approach to sororal polygyny is one of many differences in the family complexes of Zulu and Lozi. The Lozi family of parents and children is very unstable as a domestic grouping, and in addition divorce is frequent and easily obtained by both man and wife. A man who wishes to divorce his wife merely sends her home and need give no reason. The wife, unless she can persuade her husband to divorce her, must seek release in court, but she can gain it on many grounds. Moreover, she will be released by the court if the husband does anything which can be construed as 'driving her away'. If he says 'get out' to her, if he pushes her, if he takes from her any article which he may have given her, if he favours another wife, if he does not sleep with her, she will get a divorce. A woman has very little security in marriage; a man has not much more, unless he is patient, controlled, and careful not to act unguardedly in a way the courts can interpret as dismissal of his wife.

In Loziland to-day people discuss divorce all the time. On the other hand, divorce is almost unknown in Zululand. It can be obtained in a magistrate's court, but men do not want to divorce their wives and women rarely seek divorce. In native opinion a woman should only be released if her husband is intolerably cruel. I never heard divorce discussed as a social problem in Zululand: the problem was always illegitimacy.

Obviously it is difficult to eliminate the effect of modern conditions on the stability of marriage. We can say that marriage has always been stable in Zululand, and old records on the Zulu[1] indeed affirm that they were a 'moral' people among whom divorce, adultery, and illegitimacy were rare. Chastity was highly valued, and was part of the ethical code enforced by the age-set regimental organization which was directly under the king. Regiments could only begin to marry when the king gave them permission as a set to marry a younger age-set of girls, who by this time would be well in their twenties. A man in an older regiment could marry a girl whose set had not yet had its mates indicated. Intercourse *intra crura* by youngsters was allowed. If an unmarried girl became pregnant by a young warrior, both they and their families were liable to be killed. Therefore she would be hurriedly married to a man whose regiment had leave to marry. Zulu themselves attribute the high and increasing illegitimacy rate to Government's banning of this sanction. Girls, be it noted, still do not marry till they are in their twenties. Adultery too was severely punished, with death, or flogging with thorny branches, or cacti were thrust into the woman's vagina.[2]

On the other hand, early travellers to Loziland, and every missionary and administrative record, describe men and women as promiscuous and marriage as unstable. Holub, one of the earliest visitors to the country, reported that marriage was lax and particularly that women, including the queens, looked upon the marriage tie as loose. Macintosh wrote that 'marriages are unmade at a moment's notice . . . the wife being deprived of everything, even her beads, blankets, and clothes, and told to go. . . . Should a man take a liking to someone else's wife he will have an interview with her and bring her home.' Texts, life-histories of old men, and genealogies, confirm this. The evidence contradicts Lozi assertions that girls, who are now usually married shortly after puberty, used in the past to be much older before they married, and grew up, unspoiled, with boys at cattle-posts where strict morals were inculcated. Seduction, adultery, and abduction of wives were undoubtedly rife. The quotation from Macintosh bears out what Lozi told me: that adulteries, divorces, and abductions did not come to court at the capital until 1918–20, when the paramount chief issued an edict saying that his court would hear these cases. To-day it does little else. Previously cases of adultery and abduction of wives were settled by the kindreds involved. The wrongdoer hid from the wrath of the cuckold and his kin, who came armed and had to be appeased with gifts. Only if blood were shed did the king intervene.

Therefore it seems reasonable to assume that divorce was always relatively frequent in Loziland. Old men bemoan the looseness of modern

[1] I must emphasize that I am writing here of the Zulu proper, and not of Natal or Cape Nguni.

[2] See M. Read, 'The Moral Code among the Ngoni' (of Zulu stock), *Africa*, xi. i, Jan. 1938.

women in contrast to the fidelity of their mothers, and undoubtedly modern conditions have increased marital laxness. But modern conditions have borne more severely on the Zulu. Nevertheless, despite the abolition of their kingship, and the effects of labour migration, &c., Zulu marriage is firm and enduring. However long a labour migrant is away, his wife should not be divorced: she can bear children for him by his kinsmen or a lover. If a Lozi is away for three years, now, his wife is entitled to a divorce: the period has been steadily reduced from seven years. I argue therefore that modern conditions have given full rein to tendencies already present in Lozi society, and that when the paramount chief tried to control divorce and abduction he was not tackling a newly created problem.

I begin my analysis from the dissolution, and not from the contracting, of marriage because its instability among the Lozi and its stability among the Zulu set the fundamental difference between the marriage complexes in the two societies. On this hinges a whole set of rules. Initially, we may see here why there is a different reaction to sororal polygyny. Among the Zulu this is approved because the sisters help one another and it is unlikely that divorce of one sister will spoil the marriage of the other or that their competition for their husband will lead to a divorce. Marriage to two sisters binds the lineages involved more firmly together. Among the Lozi, each marriage is potentially so unstable that a sister co-wife would very likely get involved in trouble with her husband arising from a quarrel with her sister, and their competition is likely to lead to the divorce of one or other. We have seen how widely the concept of 'sister' extends. The Lozi also disapprove of a marriage which gives rise to two sets of kinship terms for the same people, and which produces two sets of children with identical attachments in all their lines. They are interested in spreading the net of their cognatic and affinal connexions as widely as possible. Marriage to two women who are sisters would prevent this. However, a man can marry, though not claim, the sister of his dead wife. Here her interest in her dead sister's children is emphasized, and he renews his relationship to his affines. It is also proper for a woman to marry her sister's husband's brother, especially a half-brother.

In brief, among the Zulu marriage moves a woman from her kin-group to her husband's; the 'love of sisters' is an additional tie between co-wives. Among the Lozi a woman's main tie remains with her kin, and is not with her husband's: 'the love of sisters' must not be endangered.

The Zulu in Natal have the same types of marriage-forming families as are reported by Evans-Pritchard from the Nuer in the far distant Sudan[1] and I follow his definitions.

1. Outside of marriage, there is the *natural family*, which is formed by

[1] Op. cit., pp. 5 ff.

a man living with his concubine and her children. This is rarely found in Zululand.

2. There is the *simple legal family* formed by a man and a woman for whom he has given marriage-cattle, and her children. If a man has more than one wife his household constitutes a compound family. Among the Zulu these wives are graded. One, the chief wife of the great house, who may be married late in life, will produce the main heir. She has placed under her a number of subordinate wives. Another wife is head of the left-hand house which also contains subordinate wives, and another group of wives in very big families may form the right-hand house. A separate wife is sometimes set apart in the chief house to bear an heir to it if it has no sons. Finally, the first wife married (who may be called *mame*, my mother) becomes mother of the *uyise wabantwana* (father of the children), a son who ritually replaces the father on his death. These are indigenous gradings. The Natal Code of Native Law hoped to reduce litigation by ruling that the first wife married is the great wife.

3. Where the husband dies and an approved relative of his lives with the widow and the children, he begets more children for the dead man; this is the *leviratic family*. The pro-husband does not pay marriage-cattle. Evans-Pritchard has emphasized the important difference between *leviratic marriage*, where the dead man is still the husband of his widow and her future children are his and do not belong to the man living with her, and *widow inheritance*, where the widow is expected or even compelled to marry a relative of the dead man. This is a new union and future children belong to the new husband. In leviratic marriage future children address their genitor by the same term as do their mother's other children; in widow inheritance he is their father, so that they and their mother's other children may address him by different terms. The Zulu have leviratic marriage. Sometimes a Zulu widow goes to live with a stranger; then, in Evans-Pritchard's terms, she is living in *widow concubinage*. But, as among the Nuer, the children still belong to the dead man. Until the reign of King Mpande (1840–72) a woman's person was also permanently transferred to her husband's agnatic lineage. A widow could never go to a man not related to her husband without his being prosecuted. Mpande passed a law allowing a widow to go to any man she liked, but the children were to remain the dead husband's. Her lover, their genitor, could claim one beast from the marriage payments for his daughters, 'the beast of the knees', since he had gone on his knees to beget them, but correspondingly he should contribute one beast to the marriage payments given by his sons for their wives. Latterly, under Government regulation which prevents women from being compelled to marry against their will, widows can marry other men, but the new husband must return the marriage payments to the heirs of the widow's dead husband, less one beast for each child born.

4. The Zulu, like the Nuer, also have *ghost marriage*. There are two

forms of this: (*a*) if a man was betrothed and died, his fiancée should marry one of his kinsmen and bear children for the dead man, as if she were a widow; and (*b*) a man may 'waken' a dead kinsman who was never betrothed by marrying a wife to his name and begetting children for him.

5. As among the Nuer a rich and important Zulu woman can marry another woman by giving marriage-cattle for her, and she is the pater of her wife's children begotten by some male kinsman of the female husband. They belong to the latter's agnatic lineage as if she were a man. If a man dies leaving only daughters and no son, the eldest daughter should take his cattle and marry wives for her father to produce sons for him. This and the preceding forms of marriage are weighty customs enforced by ancestral wrath, and they arise from the importance of continuing the agnatic line.

6. An impotent Zulu man can marry wives with whom he asks a kinsman to have intercourse, so that he can get children. This is a simple marriage.

7. Among the Zulu in addition it is considered proper that when a chief or important man marries his chief wife, the heads of all the subordinate social groups under him should contribute the marriage-cattle. Her son is then a child of the group who gave the cattle, and therefore should rightly succeed to the heirship.

These forms of marriage all depend on the legal consequences which flow from the cattle which a Zulu gives for his bride. The cattle make him pater of all her children, whether or not he is their genitor. The Zulu says 'cattle beget children', which means that the marriage-cattle given for a woman indicate the giver (usually her husband) to be the pater of her children. Once a man has given marriage-cattle for a woman he is pater of all her children, even if she deserts him or if he dies. Therefore men who are dead or impotent, and women, all physically incapable of begetting, can be paters of children who have been begotten by other men, and a whole group can be pater to children whose mother's marriage-cattle it has contributed. A man secures his illegitimate children either by giving cattle for them separately or by securing all an unmarried woman's children by subsequent marriage (giving of cattle); otherwise they belong to the mother's agnatic lineage. The purpose of the cattle is to procure children, and Zulu say that in the past they began to pay cattle only when a child had been born.

The effect of this rule is to give great permanence to legal marriage, and to ensure that the members of the simple legal family live together. Marriage endures beyond the death of the husband and father, for he is still married to his widow now living either in leviratic marriage with a kinsman of his, or in widow concubinage, and he is still father of her future children. These children take his clan name and have rights to live and inherit in his agnatic lineage; they have not those rights elsewhere. The death of the wife may break the marriage, but, though it is not compulsory, it is considered proper, if the husband has been a good spouse and son-in-law, that she should be replaced by a younger sister who steps into her place under the sororate. The sister is now the dead woman and the family is reconstituted. If a woman dies before bearing children she has not fulfilled the purpose for which the marriage-cattle were given, even though she has worked and given sexual services, and her family must replace her with a younger sister or else they must return the marriage payment. A younger sister should also be sent to bear children for a barren woman, or her parents must return the cattle. If they do the latter, a good Zulu does not necessarily send his barren wife home; he may use the returned marriage-cattle to obtain a wife whom he puts 'into the house' of his barren wife to bear children for her. Thus even maternity can be fictitious. I suggest that the low rate of divorce is another aspect of this general permanence of marriage, the effect of which is to bring in a woman from another clan to bear children for the agnatic lineage which, under exogamous patriliny, is unable to reproduce itself.

Zulu marriage thus constitutes a long enduring union between the spouses, which extends to their kin, above all their agnatic lineages. This is still the position in Zululand now when European statute has fixed the amount of the marriage payment, but in the past these consequences were even clearer. Then there was no fixed amount of marriage payment: bridegrooms were proud to give what they could. The first beast was sent after the birth of a child, and thereafter the son-in-law, known as 'the handle-of-a-hoe', gave a beast to his father-in-law every time one of his wife's brothers got married. He was also supposed to help his father-in-law with cattle whenever the latter was in need. Zulu say that cattle continued to pass as long as the relationship between the families was remembered, in both directions but chiefly to the woman's home, even after the original spouses had died.

Evans-Pritchard's description of Nuer marriage and the family emphasizes that the legal bonds resulting from marriage are very strong, though often a man's wife may not live with him or his proxy. Nuer women do desert their husbands and many widows live in widow concubinage and not in leviratic marriage. Nevertheless, the cattle given at marriage always make the giver pater of a woman's children, and lineage ties and rights of inheritance draw the children back to their pater's home. The same rule determines the affiliation of children in Zululand. There, in addition, the members of a legal family almost always live together. Most widows go into leviratic marriage and few wives desert their husbands. Courts order deserting wives to return to their husbands.

We may say then of the Zulu, as Evans-Pritchard did of the Nuer, that 'the social principle of agnatic descent is, by a kind of paradox, traced through the mother, for the rule is that in virtue of payment of bride-wealth all who are born of the mother are children of her husband. Thus all the children of a woman may be children of a man whom their mother has never seen. Or a woman may bear children by many men yet they all have one father.'[1] The principle is expressed in Zulu, where the word *isizalo* means both the womb of a female and a man's origin, i.e. his tribal or clan name, which is derived from the pater.

In ranked Zulu society the principle that 'agnatic descent is traced through the mother' is additionally important, because the status of sons depends on the status of their mothers in the compound family. Hence the importance of the levirate which, as among the Nuer, places the children in a genealogy which reflects the segmentary lineage system.

The Lozi do not have leviratic marriage, ghost marriage, woman-marriage-to-a-woman, and do not contribute to the marriage payments for the wives of their leaders. A woman is always released from marriage to an impotent man, who is 'another woman'. Wives are not graded in any special status. By order of marriage, irrespective of their relative ages and tribal status, they are referred to as the first, second, &c., wife, and senior wives are supposed to be treated respectfully by junior wives, and have greater rights and obligations. But no wife has instituted authority over another, despite the fact that the Lozi is a ranked society, and no wife has status conferring special rights in inheritance on her son or sons. The main heir selected may be the son of a young wife, and among one wife's sons a younger may be preferred to an elder son. A Lozi wife and her children have no status to persist after her divorce; even if a Zulu wife is divorced her children retain their positions derived from her status in the household.

Until the 1900's, when the average Lozi commoner married he gave the bride's parents a few hoes and mats. It is comparatively recently (1900–10) that their paramount chief Lewanika issued a law that two beasts or £2 should be given for a virgin and one beast or £1 for a girl who is not a virgin (a widow, a divorcee, an unmarried girl who has had a child, or an unmarried woman who is so long past puberty she should not be a virgin). To constitute legal marriage now there must be consent of the parties and consent of the bride's parents or guardians, which is implicit in their accepting the marriage payment. The last is the most important indicator of a legal marriage, at which a Lozi court looks to see if it will award adultery damages if another man sleeps with the woman. If her parents have consented to the union but the man has not delivered the cattle or money, the court will not award him damages. It will say that she is his concubine, 'a wife of the country'. Thus the marriage payment gives a man the right to exclude other men from his wife, and the right to control her. Though divorce is frequent and a woman can get it easily, if her husband resists she must go to court. If she refuses point-blank to live with her husband, neither he nor the

---

[1] Op. cit., p. 64.

courts can compel her to do so. If she deserts him he can always in this polygynous society take other wives or concubines, while she can only lie with or go to another man under threat of an adultery charge, when her lover will pay damages of two cattle to the husband, or three if she has come to him as a wife, and she will have to pay a fine of one head to the court. (These fines were raised by £2 in 1947, after this essay was first written.) Thus ultimately a woman, if her lover is eager to have her, can force a divorce from her husband. When an abductor pays damages to the husband the latter loses his rights over his wife. If she agrees to return to her husband she remains his wife; but she can remain with her abductor. The third beast he gave to the husband counts as a marriage-beast. This usually happened in the past. To control these moves the Lozi have made it a criminal offence for a woman's abductor to give her parents the fine she must now pay the court.

In Lozi law delivery of the marriage payment is essential to pass these rights over the wife's person; in Zulu law agreement to deliver is sufficient. This does not affect the issue that the husband gets these rights in both societies, though it means that what is a proper marriage in Zulu eyes is not reckoned to be so by the Lozi.

Payment of the marriage-cattle does not give the Lozi man the right which a Zulu has to all the woman's children. In general, under Lozi law the pater is the genitor, not the mother's husband. The difference between the two sets of rules appears clearly in rights to illegitimate children. A Zulu must redeem his illegitimate children with cattle and also pay seduction damages to the girl's father and mother as well as a fine to the chief, and he can never claim his adulterine children. If a Lozi gives an unmarried girl a child he pays her father a beast, to compensate for the one that will be lost from the marriage payment. Formerly he paid no damages for giving a child to a non-virgin, but these were imposed by a Native Authority law in 1947. In both cases the child is always his, even if he does not deliver the damages for seduction. The Lozi say one beast is paid at marriage for the bride's untouched fertility if she is a virgin, and one is 'the beast of shame because husband and wife know each other', i.e. it is paid for sexual rights. In theory, the marriage-cattle do not give rights to the woman's children who, if adulterine, may belong to the adulterer and not to the husband. However, the husband has in practice a limited right to all her children. He is 'the owner of the hut' and it is assumed that all the woman's children are his. He may suspect a child is adulterine and overlook this. If he claims damages for adultery on the grounds of birth of a child he loses the child, unless he too was sleeping with his wife when she conceived. An adulterer can claim that a married woman's child is his if he alone had access to her. If she admits it he takes the child, though he will have to pay damages. Before men went to labour centres or jail for long periods it is unlikely that this question arose, but the Lozi reaction in this situation is the opposite of the Zulu's. One man noted for his many children told me he had gone into the huts of his infertile friends, at their requests, to give children to their wives. He could claim the children. Usually, however, sterile men ask this favour of kinsmen to avoid the claims.

Adulterine children are related to their mother's husband and other kin under the rule that the relative of one's relative is one's own relative.

Barrenness in a Lozi wife is not a breach of an essential condition of the marriage contract. The husband cannot claim a sister in marriage or a refund of the marriage payment. He can divorce her, and if she was a virgin at marriage get back half the payment if she has not conceived, but divorcing a woman for sterility is very different from having the right to demand a female relative to produce for her.

When a Lozi dies his kinsmen have no rights to keep his wives. These are free to go and marry where they please. They will be approved of if, having children, they marry his brother, or resident uterine nephew, so as to prevent the children being drawn from their paternal home, but it is a new marriage for which a new marriage payment must be given and its children are of the new husband, not of the dead man. Though the Lozi lack the levirate, they do have a limited sororate. Until 1946–7 if a man married a woman and she died shortly after marriage, leaving no children, he could not claim her younger sister or the return of the marriage-cattle as a Zulu can. He had no case in law; the Lozi held that God took the woman and she and her parents were not at fault. The parents might of their own good heart, if they approved of him, give him another sister to replace the dead wife, or he might beg for one. Then he paid no cattle. If his wife died leaving a child he had no right even to beg. If he wished to marry her sister he had to pay marriage-cattle again. However in 1946–7 the High Court held that if either wife or husband died and the wife had not conceived, according to Lozi law (on which it was misinformed) one beast must be returned, and Lozi courts now follow this decision.

We have seen that if a Zulu wife dies childless, and is not replaced by a sister, the marriage-cattle return, because she has not fulfilled an essential part of the contract. Some cattle return if the wife has only one or two children, none if she has three. Similarly, in the rare event of divorce, no cattle are returned if there are three children, but some are returned if there are only one or two children. Under the European-imposed Natal Native Code an erring Zulu husband can be deprived of the cattle as punishment. If a divorcee or widow marries elsewhere, the new husband may pay cattle to her house within her former husband's compound family. Among the Lozi no cattle used to return on the death of a childless wife. On divorce, the beast given for a non-virgin does not return; one of the two beasts given for a virgin returns if she has not conceived, i.e. if she has miscarried the husband loses his rights to it.

The long enduring rights conferred on the Zulu husband extend forward to betrothal. If a girl breaks an engagement she must return the gifts given to her, and her family must return most goods transferred during the negotiations. The court would, were it not for Government, compel marriage. If the boy is in the wrong, he forfeits the gifts and may have to pay compensation for wasting the girl's time. Among the Lozi, if an engagement is broken by the girl any gifts given by the boy to the girl do not return. Lozi courts do not therefore recognize infant betrothals. The Zulu do.

To sum up, in both societies marriage gives the husband the right to claim damages from an adulterer, and to some extent to control his wife's movements. Among the Zulu he also gets the right to all the woman's children, and this right vests for ever in him and his agnatic group, even after his death. If she is childless she must be replaced or the cattle returned, and the amount of cattle returnable on divorce depends on the number of children the wife has had. Once a woman is betrothed her fiancé's kin have a right to claim her in ghost marriage. A man redeems his illegitimate children with cattle. Thus Zulu marriage transfers a woman's fertility absolutely to her husband's agnatic kingroup, and an essential element in the contract is that she have children. Associated with this situation we have rare divorce. Among the Lozi a child should go to its genitor.[1] Children belong automatically to their mother's and their genitor's families. Therefore the Lozi do not have Zulu forms of marriage in which women and dead men can marry wives. An illegitimate child goes to its genitor independently of payment. When the husband dies his widow is free to marry elsewhere, though she would be approved if she entered into a new marriage with one of his cognatic kinsmen. The children of this new union belong to the new husband. A man's kin have no claim on his fiancée if he dies. That the woman should produce children is not an essential part of the contract. While she lives, if she is childless her husband should not be given a sister, and he cannot claim refund of the marriage-cattle unless he divorces her and she was a virgin. If she dies childless shortly after marriage her parents can of their goodwill replace her; the husband has no claim in law. With this is associated a high rate of divorce.

[1] My reading so far reveals a similar rule only among Hehe, Bena, Kikuyu, and Ganda: Brown and Hutt, op. cit., p. 102; G. Gordon Brown, 'Legitimacy and Paternity amongst the Hehe', *American Journal of Sociology*, xxxviii, 2, Sept. 1932, pp. 184–93; A. T. and G. M. Culwick, op. cit., p. 372; J. Kenyatta, *Facing Mount Kenya*, London, 1938, p. 184; J. Roscoe, *The Baganda*, London, 1911, p. 61; L. Mair, *An African People in the Twentieth Century*, London, 1943, [on Ganda] p. 57. Among the Tallensi a child belongs to the woman's husband, but he may run to his genitor's home where he will be received: M. Fortes, *Marriage Law among the Tallensi*, Accra: Gold Coast Government, 1937, pp. 12–13; so too with the Shona, see C. Bullock, *The Mashona*, Cape Town, 1927, p. 328.

The fact that divorce hangs over every marriage in Loziland, but not in Zululand, appears in the marriage ceremonial. The Lozi ceremony, if it is performed, is simple and attended by few people. The bride's senior relatives do not come to the bridegroom's village, and the bridegroom's senior male relatives do not attend the ceremony if there is one. 'It is a play of children.' A Zulu bride should be escorted by many senior relatives, though her own parents do not attend. The bridegroom's parents participate in the complicated ceremonial which spreads over many days. The ceremonial chiefly expresses the hostility and conciliation of the two lineages concerned.[1]

I have analysed two contrasting types of marriage complex as they appear among Zulu and Lozi. Among other things, we see that the divorce rate is only one index of the general durability of marriage which, I suggest, is a function of the kinship structure as a whole. Recent researches have shown that a high rate of divorce is not always an indication of general social instability. In many tribes the family is unstable; in some (e.g. Nuer) as a domestic unit, despite strong marriage ties, while in others the marriage tie also is fragile. Stability inheres in the extended kinship groupings and relationships which form the structure of the society.[2]

I have surveyed the literature on many African tribes[3] and affirm tentatively that divorce is rare and difficult in those organized on a system of marked father-right, and frequent and easy to obtain in other types. The correlation has been stated, without explication, by Loeb for Indonesia:

'Nowhere does the form of social organization show influence more than in the laws of divorce. In a strict patrilineal society divorce can be obtained at the will of the husband, since the husband would not wish to lose the bride-price. An exception is made in the case of adultery. In the sibless or bilateral families of Indonesia (Mentawei excepted) divorce is frequent, and where there is a bride-price the rule almost everywhere holds that the bride-price must be paid back if the fault lies with the woman and not paid back if the fault lies with the man. The village or family head checks too frequent divorces. Among people with matrilineal sibs, as the Minangkabau, there is no bride-price and divorce is very frequent and can be obtained at will by either party.'[4]

[1] A. W. Hoernlé, 'The Importance of the Sib in the Marriage Ceremonies of the South-eastern Bantu', *South African Journal of Science*, xxii, 1925.

[2] See e.g. Evans-Pritchard, op. cit., pp. 64–5; D. Forde, *Marriage and the Family among the Yakö in South-Eastern Nigeria*, London, 1941, pp. 113–14; M. Fortes, 'The Significance of Descent in Tale Social Structure', *Africa*, xiv. 3, July 1944, at pp. 362, 373–4, 382.

[3] As stated earlier, my comparative survey was limited by library facilities. Here I quote only on tribes whose marriage rules indicate the lines which guided my hypothesis, or whose marriage rules are against my hypothesis. The literature is not clear on most points.

[4] E. M. Loeb, *Sumatra: Its History and People*, Vienna, 1935, pp. 68 ff.

Loeb here relates the relative frequency of divorce to the amount of the marriage payment, and this is still commonly done in books on Africa.[1] Evans-Pritchard strongly criticized this correlation: the assumption that the maintenance of marriage relations is due to economic motives

'is at the basis of the assertion often made that the function of bride-wealth is to stabilize marriage. The word "function" carries no meaning in this context. Is it true, moreover, that the relations between husband and wife persist through what amounts to economic blackmail? No evidence is adduced to justify belief in a functional relationship between the amount of bride-wealth paid to the bride's group and the durability of her union with her husband. No one would deny that the difficulty of returning a very large amount of wealth may be a motive in the pressure which the parents of a girl bring to bear on her to remain with her husband, but it is a hopeless distortion of social realities to regard this as an explanation of bride-wealth. . . . This point of view also neglects the fact that the relations between husband and wife are not of primary importance, and that the stability of marriage rests on the goodwill of a man's father-in-law or brothers-in-law . . . it is evident that the stability of the family is not really a function of economic motives, but of moral and legal norms from present-day conditions in Zandeland, for, in spite of payments, divorce is rife. It is morals that censure divorce and law that refuses to recognize grounds for divorce which ensure the stability of the union of husband and wife. It derives its stability from the restraint imposed by law and morals and not from economic blackmail. In the past Azande regarded marriage as an indissoluble union between man and wife, and as unseverable relations between their affines, and divorce was allowed only for a flagrant breach of obligation on the part of the husband towards his wife's father or brothers.'[2]

As Evans-Pritchard says, individuals when they contemplate divorce may consider difficulties about marriage payment. I suggest that this is the least important side of a complex relation. The frequency of divorce is an aspect of the durability of marriage as such, which in turn is a function of the kinship structure. I have no space to cite all my support-

[1] See e.g. A. I. Richards, *Bemba Marriage and Present Economic Conditions*, Rhodes–Livingstone Paper No. 4, 1940, pp. 53–4; A. T. and G. M. Culwick, 'The Function of Bride-wealth in Ubena of the Rivers', *Africa*, vii. 2, April 1934, p. 151; G. G. Brown, 'Bride-wealth among the Hehe', *Africa*, v. 2, April 1932, p. 146. A Nyasaland Government inter-departmental memorandum states the correlation of high divorce rate with patriliny and low divorce rate with matriliny, and refers it to the difference in quantity of marriage payment: see summary in *Nada*, xvi. 1939, pp. 43–4.

[2] E. E. Evans-Pritchard, 'Social Character of Bride-wealth, with special reference to the Azande', *Man*, xxxiv, 1934, No. 194, pp. 172 ff. M. Fortes refers to this statement and says his Tallensi data support it: 'Kinship, Incest and Exogamy of the Northern Territories of the Gold Coast', in *Custom is King: Essays presented to R. R. Marett*, London, 1936, p. 250. It seems from C. R. Lagae, *Les Azande*, 1926, p. 155, that divorce is also now common among the Belgian Congo Azande. Schwernfurth (*The Heart of Africa*, 1873, ii, p. 28) praised the stability of marriage among the Azande.

ing data from other tribes, but it seems that rare divorce goes with levirate, sororate, rights to claim a betrothed girl, &c., and with them it is found in father-right societies. Marriage is for a woman's lifetime even if her husband dies. The marriage payment transfers the woman's pro-creative power absolutely to her husband's agnatic lineage for her life, and therefore divorce is rare. This emerges most clearly among the Nuer, where with constant changes of households the legal bonds in the family resulting from marriage are very stable. If the society has many goods marriage payment can be high. Among the Lozi and other tribes, who recognize inheritance in all lines, the marriage payment gives the husband rights over his wife, and indicates generally the children's paternal attachment while the marriage lasts, though in some tribes children should go to their genitors. Divorce is frequent, for the woman produces for her own line as well as her husband's. In matrilineal societies the woman produces for her own matrilineal line and the marriage payments do not transfer her fertility. Divorce is frequent. Therefore the marriage payment tends to be low; there is none among the cattle-owning Ovambo. On this hypothesis, which needs more testing, the amount of goods transferred and the divorce rate tend to be directly associated, but both are rooted in the kinship structure. It is rare divorce which allows high marriage payment, rather than high marriage payment which prevents divorce.

The amount of goods transferred at marriage will obviously be influenced by factors extraneous to the kinship-marriage complexes. Thus the types and quantities of property available, and the proportions of the sexes and their relative marriage-ages, may by the laws of supply and demand affect the marriage payment and the divorce rate.[1] I give a few examples to support my hypothesis that the influence of property is secondary. The patrilineal-patrilocal Azande with no cattle had initially low payment in spears and in the past rare divorce. I think the Ganda may also be taken as a propertyless people with father-right and rare divorce,[2] but data on this type of tribe in Africa are too confused to be cited. On the other hand, there are several African peoples who had large herds of cattle but did not use them for marriage payments, and they are all peoples with mother-right or an unspecified or double descent system of succession. The Lozi fall into this category, as do the Ovambo and Herero.[3] If property transfers determined the stability of marriage, these cattle-owning tribes could have used their herds to effect

---

[1] See e.g. Oberg, op. cit., p. 136.

[2] Roscoe, op. cit., p. 97.

[3] C. H. L. Hahn, 'The Ovambo', in *Tribes of South-west Africa*, Cape Town, 1928, pp. 32–5; M. Rautenan, 'Die Ondonga', in *Rechtsverhältnisse von einge-borenen Völkern* (ed. S. R. Steinmetz), Berlin, 1903, pp. 330 ff. On Herero see G. Viehe, 'Die Ovaherero', in ibid. at pp. 305–6; B. von Zastrow, 'Die Herero', in E. Schultz-Ewerth and L. A. Adam, *Das Eingeborenenrecht*, Stuttgart, ii. p. 254; E. Dannert (jun.), *Zum Rechte der Herero*, Berlin, 1906, p. 46.

this, since they all approve of stable marriages. Indeed, the mother-right Ila, who are patrilocal, have high marriage payments from large herds, but among them divorce is frequent.[1] They may have high payments because they are said to have few young women. I lack space to cite further examples, but those given clearly refute the explanation put forward by Loeb and others. Therefore I suggest that the divorce rate is a reflex of the kinship structure itself. The morals and laws which, as Evans-Pritchard says, sanction the stability of marriage, and the relations between affines which affect it, are aspects of that structure, even where, as among the Zulu, chastity and fidelity are also enforced by the ethical code of the regiments in a military nation.

However, it is important to stress that even where marriages are unstable, they always exist. Theoretically there is no reason why, given the ban on incest, the men of a matrilineal group should not keep their sisters and daughters and allow strangers to impregnate them in casual encounters, as was in effect believed to be the position among the Nayar. Always, however, even among the Nayars as we now know, the association for begetting children is institutionalized and important. Marriage cannot be referred altogether to the kinship structure.

THE PROPERTY CONSEQUENCES OF MARRIAGE

Lozi and Zulu families are economic units. The husband must give his wife land for gardens, feed her from his own gardens and herds (and fishing-sites among the Lozi), and provide her with a hut and clothing. The wife must work her gardens and do household duties.

In Lozi law husband and wife have equal rights in the crops she has worked—the land is his but the labour is hers. They and their children feed from these crops. On divorce they share the crops equally. If he dies and she leaves his home she takes half the crops. If she dies her heirs, who are her sons and daughters, her parents, and her siblings, can claim her share against her husband, his sons by other wives, and his brothers and parents. If the husband lived in one of her homes in affineship (*bukwetunga*) he has no rights in the crops: neither the land nor the labour were his.

Similarly, father and mother each have a right to half the marriage payments for their daughters. 'They are both parents, they both gave birth to the child', say the Lozi. If £2 or two beasts are given for a virgin daughter, each should get one. When £1 is given for a girl who is not a virgin they share the money, and if a beast is given and it is killed the two families share the meat. However, usually the father keeps it and gives the first and all odd calves to the mother and her kindred. Each kindred should divide the cattle, or money, or meat, which it receives among its own members. The bride herself has rights in both portions,

[1] E. W. Smith and A. Dale, *The Ila-speaking Peoples of Northern Rhodesia*, London, 1920, i, p. 298; ii, pp. 50 ff.

O

which is inconceivable to a Zulu. Lozi say 'the bride brought the cattle'.
If either kindred ever kills a descendant of a marriage-beast the bride
who brought the beast should be given the tongue, and specific portions
should be sent to the other kindred.[1] Frequently a father, or maternal
uncle if the bride lives with him, does not share the marriage payment
with the other kindred as he should, or share his portion with his own
relatives. People can sue the other kindred for their rights in the
marriage payment, but rarely do so 'for it will spoil their relationships'.
They content themselves with the reflection that if there is divorce of
a virgin who has not conceived or if the woman is fined for adultery,
which are both very likely to occur, they will be under no obligation to
contribute to the return of a beast or to her fine. 'We knew nothing of the
marriage.' If they have shared in the payment they should contribute.
Whichever kindred the man pays the woman is legally his wife.

The mother's own cognates are heirs to her rights as against the
father's relatives, i.e. failing her own sons, her parents, siblings, and their
children inherit. The father, his sons by other wives, and his brothers
have no rights in the maternal portion of a dead woman's daughter's
marriage payment. If both parents are dead their sons inherit both sets
of rights, but they should divide the payment in half and distribute one
half among their paternal kindred and one half among their maternal
kindred.

If the chief or any other person gives a man the marriage payment for
his wife he gets no rights in the payments for her daughters.

Since divorce is rare the Zulu have no fixed rules about the division
of the crops, but on my information I should say they would belong
altogether to the husband. Since widows should remain in leviratic
marriage there is no law about the division of crops on the death of one
or other spouse, and I incline to think that if the widow left her husband's
kin they would not allow her to take any of her crops. I did not inquire
carefully. Certainly, the mother and her kin have no rights in her
daughter's marriage-cattle, if marriage payment has been given for her.
All go to the bride's father who may divide them among his agnates.
A separate beast, which is not reckoned part of the marriage payment
(*ilobolo*), is given by the groom to her mother for his bride's virginity
and for her mother's care. The mother usually eats it with other women.
The same beast is paid by a seducer of a virgin to his love's mother. The
bride's maternal uncle can claim a beast if he reared the girl.

The extent to which the marriage-cattle are owned in the agnatic
lineage appears in a very complicated set of rules about their distribution.
In a simple legal family, if a man gave the cattle himself, he or his sons
are entitled to all the cattle of his daughters. But if he borrowed the
cattle and has not repaid the loan, the lender can claim the cattle of his

[1] I give examples of actual divisions of the marriage payment in my *Essays on
Lozi Land and Royal Property*, pp. 65–7.

eldest daughter. If the lender is the father's chief, the father would not offer to return them, because it is an honour for his eldest daughter to 'belong' to the chief. If the husband did not deliver the marriage-cattle to his affines they claim the eldest daughter's cattle; and a poor man can marry a wife by pledging his eldest daughter thus. If he has no daughter, there is no liability. While the father is alive the cattle of other daughters are his and he can deal with them as he pleases. However, if he uses the cattle to marry other wives, these become subordinates of 'the house' (i.e. the wife) from which the cattle came. The junior wife and her children are under the authority of the senior wife and her children. The eldest son in that house can claim the cattle of the subordinate wives' eldest daughters. The chief heir of the great house can claim the cattle of the eldest daughter of each constituent house. He can also claim the cattle of the eldest daughter of the left- and right-hand houses, to establish his seniority, even though the left- and right-hand houses are established with independent herds. Their heirs have rights within their own houses similar to those of the main heir in his house: they take the cattle for eldest daughters of houses established from their herds. Subject to these rights of senior sons, cattle of a woman go first to her father and own brothers, failing these to the main heir of her house, and, failing one in her house, to the main heir of the compound family. Beyond that inheritance is in the agnatic lineage. The mother's kin have no claim once marriage-cattle have been given for her, save for the beast of virginity. Their rights to the marriage-cattle of the eldest daughter if her mother has not had cattle delivered for her do not affect this principle.

Marriage-cattle among the Zulu are thus definitely property of 'the house of the woman', subject to certain contingent claims, but only within the agnatic compound family. What we may call 'the house-property complex' has wider implications. A Zulu allots land and cattle to each of his wives. Land and cattle thus allotted become irrevocably property of the house, even if the woman is divorced or demoted in status. This property can be used by the father, subject to the rules set out above, but it is inherited by the sons of that wife against their half-brothers by their father's other wives. As widows usually remain attached to their dead husband's agnatic lineage, even if they are 'entered' (*ukungena*) by a sister's son of the dead man, they retain the land allotted to them for gardens; when a woman or widow dies her land goes to her own children, as do the cattle. If the husband while alive uses these cattle or this land for another wife, she becomes subordinate to the first wife. My notes are not clear about a woman's own property. Zulu law says a woman cannot own anything, and if she earns property as a doctor it is in the care of her male guardian. It is property of her house and on her death should go to her sons, and failing them to sons of a sister married in sororal polygyny. I am uncertain if after this it goes to her agnatic kin or her house in her husband's family. Where a woman has herself married a wife with cattle, she is treated as a man and her property passes to 'her' sons by her wife or wives on regular rules of agnatic succession.

Any land or cattle which the father did not allocate go to the main heir, who must use them for the benefit of all his father's sons, just as the heir in each house must help his siblings. If an agnatic line dies out for lack of sons, an heir is raised by marrying a wife with the cattle left or they pass in the agnatic lineage. The chief enters into heirless estates before maternal kinsmen.

That is, while a woman gets no rights of ownership in the cattle and fields allotted her by her husband, save during her marriage, she has rights of holding which vest through her in her sons. But they do not through her get any rights in the property of her family. Thus though Zulu descent and succession to property and status are strongly patri-lineal, they are reckoned through an unrelated woman: 'the social principle of agnatic descent . . . is traced through the mother' (Evans-Pritchard). The sons' rights and positions in their father's home and in their agnatic lineage are determined by the positions of their mothers. Some of the main sources of litigation among the Zulu are disputes between half-brothers about their rights arising from the respective status of their mothers, and what cattle and fields and other goods were allotted to their mothers while the father was alive. The positions of wives' huts in the village, their status in the tribe, the order of their marriage, their wedding ceremonial, the source of their marriage-cattle, are all considered in evidence.

Among the Lozi the inheritance of property and status goes by very different rules. Here the mother does not fix agnatic descent; the child goes to its genitor. Correspondingly, her sons inherit no property rights from their father through her. The Lozi man, like a Zulu, allocates some of his cattle and gardens to each wife. He also gives cattle, gardens, and fishing-sites to his sons and daughters as they grow up, and they are entitled to these against his selected general heir. They transmit this property to their own heirs, agnatic or uterine. They are not entitled to claim the fields and cattle allotted to their mothers, against the general heir, who takes them all, and the marriage-cattle of his half-sisters, though he is under an obligation to give some to his siblings and half-siblings and cousins. Here a woman does not transmit property rights to her children in her husband's home, but she transmits to them pro-perty rights in her own homes, paternal and maternal. Not only are they heirs to property she may herself have acquired, as among the Zulu, but they may also succeed to her brother, their maternal uncle, or to her father, their maternal grandfather, or even to their matrilineal great-grandfather, their mother's mother's brother. The contrast emerges clearly in the Lozi institution of 'the beast of the fire'. If a woman has lived for some years with a man, cooking and gardening well, preferably bearing children, her husband will give her a 'beast of the fire' in thanks. This is hers, and is inherited by her children; failing them it goes to her parents, her brothers or sisters, or even more distant relatives in her paternal or maternal family, as against her husband's sons by other wives or his brothers. The husband will warn her to send 'the beast of the fire' to her own home lest his general heir claim it, as he is entitled to claim cattle given for her nurture and use, against her sons.

Further, among the Zulu, when the husband dies the widow is expected to remain in his home to bear more children in his name, and therefore is entitled to retain and work the gardens he gave her; but among the Lozi, as soon as the husband dies the widow loses rights to land at his home. She takes half the planted and reaped crops, but even if she has children in the village and elects to remain with them, the general heir is not bound to give her land to cultivate for herself. She must get land in the portion allotted to her children under their right to land at their father's home. Thus among the Lozi the place of a married woman is not fixed in her husband's village by her marriage; she does not pass with her fertility to bear children for them only. Her position and her rights to property remain in her own paternal and maternal homes, and therefore she transmits rights of succession and inheritance to her children there, while they get no rights through her in her husband's home. I must stress that I refer here under 'house-property complex' to the inheritance of rights through the mother. In practically every Bantu society each wife's house has its own property while the husband lives, as among the Lozi. The wives do not pass rights in this property to their sons. I suggest that this is why wives do not have fixed status in ranked Lozi society as they do among the Zulu. Even the Lozi Paramount's widows become nonentities save through their children. The Zulu king's widows have status in their own right.

These differences in Zulu and Lozi laws of property are consistent with the internal structure of their marriage complexes. However, we cannot assert that in African societies organized in corporate agnatic lineages a woman transmits to her sons specific rights in their patrimony, and no rights in her own family property. On present information, it can only be claimed that it is not recorded from a single tribe without the agnatic lineage, that a woman passes rights in the patrimony to her sons against their father's sons by other wives. Clearly in purely matrilineal tribes the rule would not be found, but neither does it exist in any account of tribes organized 'bilaterally'.[1] On the other hand, what I have called the 'house-property complex' in patrilineal societies seems to have a twofold geographical distribution. First, it is found in South Africa among all Nguni, Sotho, Tswana, and Venda peoples, roughly as far north as the Limpopo. Offshoots of these, like Ngoni, Ndebele, and

[1] See e.g. Forde on the Yakö, op. cit., pp. 45, 56, 70; H. Vedder, 'The Herero', in *The Native Tribes of South-West Africa*, p. 195.

Shangana, have carried the complex with them. Generally the complex stops north of the Limpopo. Bullock says specifically that, in contrast with the Southern Bantu, the Shona (who have an agnatic lineage system) do not pass property through the wife. Jaques's description shows that Junod's Thonga do not have it. Among Shona and Thonga a general heir is appointed who divides the patrimony[1] as in the patrilineal and bilaterally organized tribes in Central and Eastern Africa.[2] This seems from Roscoe's account to be the position among the interlacustrine Bantu.[3] In north-eastern Africa, however, the complex is found again among the Chaga,[4] probably the Kikuyu and Kamba,[5] and to some extent the Bantu Kavirondo.[6] Driberg reports it among all Nilo-Hamites and Nilotes, and individual records confirm this.[7] In West Africa the complex does not occur among the Tallensi, Ibo, or Dahomey, all of whom have agnatic lineages.[8]

The absence of the house-property complex appears to be associated among the Shona and Thonga, and the West African peoples cited, with the rule that inheritance of a deceased man's inherited estate passes through his brothers before it drops a generation to their sons and nephews, all of whom hold it before it drops again to the grandson

[1] C. Bullock, *The Mashona*, p. 370, and A. A. Jaques, 'Terms of Kinship and Corresponding Patterns of Behaviour among the Thonga', *Bantu Studies*, i, 1927–9, pp. 327–48. H. A. Junod, *The Life of a South African Tribe*, London, 1927, is not clear, but as he does not describe 'the house-property complex' it is unlikely that it is present. However, A. Clerc implies that the kindred Ronga devise property through their wives ('The Marriage Laws of the Ronga Tribe', *Bantu Studies*, xii, 1938, at pp. 103–4).

[2] See e.g. Brown and Hutt, op. cit., pp. 82 ff.; A. T. and G. M. Culwick, op. cit., pp. 275 ff.; G. Wilson, 'An Introduction to Nyaklyusa Society', *Bantu Studies*, x. 3, Sept. 1936.

[3] J. Roscoe, *The Baganda*, *The Northern Bantu*, 1915; *The Banyankole*, 1923; *The Bakitara*, 1932; *The Bagesu*, 1924.

[4] C. Dundas, *Kilimandjaro and Its Peoples*, London, 1924, pp. 304 ff.

[5] C. Dundas, 'The Organization and Laws of Some Bantu Tribes in East Africa', *J. Roy. Anthrop. Inst.*, xlv, 1915, at p. 294; Kenyatta, op. cit., pp. 32 and 177; and W. S. and K. Routledge, *With a Prehistoric People, the Akikuyu*, London, 1910, p. 47 and pp. 142 ff. But G. Lindblom, *The Akamba*, Upsala, 1920, is not clear: see pp. 162 ff.

[6] G. Wagner, *The Changing Family among the Bantu Kavirondo*, Supplement to *Africa*, xii. 2, 1939, pp. 19 ff.: marriage payments go to the bride's full brothers, other property is given out as sons grow up.

[7] J. H. Driberg makes a general statement for the Nilotes and Nilo-Hamites: 'The Status of Women among the Nilotics and Nilo-Hamitics', *Africa*, v. 4, Oct. 1932, at p. 419. See also J. H. Driberg, *The Lango*, 1923, pp. 174 ff.; J. G. Peristiany, *The Social Institutions of the Kipsigis*, London, 1939, pp. 211–12; M. Merker, *Die Masai*, Berlin, 1910, p. 203; Evans-Pritchard on the Nuer, op. cit., p. 49; C. G. and B. Z. Seligman on the Dinka, *Pagan Tribes of the Nilotic Sudan*, London, 1932, pp. 172 ff.

[8] M. Fortes, *Marriage Law among the Tallensi*, pp. 9 ff.; C. K. Meek, *Law and Authority in a Nigerian Tribe*, London, 1937, pp. 319 ff.; M. Herskovits, *Dahomey*, New York, 1938, pp. 87 ff.

generation. Clearly in such a system the estate could not be divided into sections passing directly to groups of sons demarcated by their mothers. Nevertheless in these systems each man creates also his own estate. His inherited estate passes to his brothers before vesting in the generation of sons; his earned estate vests immediately in his sons and passes from one to the other of them before vesting in his grandsons. Among the Southern Bantu the house-property complex is part of the graded organization of the component families within the compound polygynous family. In north-eastern Africa, too, it seems that inheritances pass directly to sons and not through a generation of brothers first.

I have described these two contrasting sets of inheritance rules because, as stated above, they fit logically into the various kinship and marriage systems respectively. I have also indicated the geographical distribution of the types of rules, and the occurrence of other associated rules. Though the comparative data do not yet allow us to generalize firmly about them, I draw attention to them because the significance of the difference has been missed in regional surveys in the past,[1] and because information on this point is not always clear in the literature.

MARRIAGE PAYMENT AND THE SOCIAL STRUCTURE

The evidence from the Lozi and Zulu indicates that we may have to distinguish different types of marriage payments. There are several aspects of marriage. It breaks or modifies certain existing social relationships and creates new social relationships: the union of a man and his wife, and an alliance between the kinsfolk of the two spouses. It unites men and women to produce children to occupy specific positions in the kinship system, since normally it is through the marriage of their parents that children acquire their kinsfolk on both sides. But clearly the structure of the kinship system primarily determines the conse-

[1] e.g. in I. Schapera's (editor) *The Bantu-speaking Tribes of South Africa*, London, 1937, especially essay on 'Work and Wealth' by I. Schapera and A. J. H. Goodwin, at pp. 162 ff. The Seligmans in discussing what I call the house-property complex among the Dinka call it 'not an inheritance with female descent. . . . It would appear to be a compromise between patrilineal and matrilineal descent, and to be associated with the Nilotic relationship system in which brothers and sisters, children of the father and mother, are distinguished from one another' (loc. cit., p. 174). E. Torday ('The Principles of Bantu Marriage', *Africa*, ii. 3, 1929, at p. 263) sees the legal position correctly: 'For inheritance of property, every house has its own rights as far as these fields and stock are concerned, and, even where the patriarchal system prevails, inheritance is by the mother.' But he wrongly applies this rule to all Bantu, though he cites only Dundas, *Kilimandjaro*, pp. 304–9, on the Chaga, and Routledge, op. cit., p. 47, on the Kikuyu, in support. He also refers to Van Wing, *Études Bakongo*, pp. 223 ff. (misprinted pp. 233 ff.), and Torday and Joyce, *Les Bushongo*, p. 272, for the allocation of property to wives. Van Wing and Torday and Joyce do not state that these allocations are inherited by wives' sons.

quences of marriage in the affiliation of children and therefore the attributes of the marriage payment.

Marriage in most societies transfers to the husband a certain common minimum of rights: almost always an exclusive right to the wife's sexual services, or to the lending of them, certain powers over her person, rights to the produce of her economic activity balanced by economic obligations to her, and a prima facie right to be pater to her children. The extent and duration of these rights varies greatly. We have seen that Lozi marriage payment is low, considering their wealth in cattle, and that even then it dates from a recent enactment. It does not transfer the woman's fertility altogether to her husband, let alone to her husband's kindred. Comparative data show that in general marriage payments fall with the decreasing dominance of patrilineal descent until very little is given in purely matrilineal societies. In Central Africa a son-in-law may give some years of service, but it is in matrilocal marriage. The matrilineal Ovambo are rich cattle-owners, but a husband gives for his wife only a present to her mother, and it is killed for the wedding feast. That is, when children are not dominantly joined to the husband's line he tends to give but little for his wife, whose economic and sexual services alone are transferred to him. In almost every African tribe he does give something to get these rights and prima facie rights in relation to her children. On the other hand, in patrilineal societies of the Zulu type the marriage payment permanently transfers the woman's procreative capacity to her husband's lineage. Therefore, relative to the society's wealth, the payment tends to be large.

I suggest that it may no longer be wise to name the common institution of transferring goods by a single term (marriage payment, bride-wealth, bride-price). This leads to disputes about whether the attributes ascribed to it, e.g. by Evans-Pritchard in East Africa, apply to the transfer of goods among the Yakö or Lozi or some other tribe. The Lozi institution, on the surface a similar transfer of property, is not the Nuer or the Zulu institution when we come to examine their structural relations. For the common element, the rights transferred in all societies, we may follow Radcliffe-Brown's use of the term marriage payment, but it may be necessary to distinguish at least marriage payment Type A, Type B, &c. I have analysed two types, and there are likely to be more. Certainly my crude categories will not cover every variation, and further analysis requires to be done in many tribes.

I consider that the data we have indicate that the basis of the variation in the complexes is probably the different affiliation of the children. Zulu society is chiefly distinguished from Lozi by its structure of unilineal agnatic groups, which are exogamous, and which are associated with a marriage rule by which the giving of cattle to a woman's father transfers her fertility for all her lifetime to the agnatic group of her husband, who may indeed have been dead before she was married to his name, or who may be a woman or an impotent man. If the wife goes off in adultery, the children are her husband's; if he dies, she continues to bear for him; if she is barren, or dies before bearing, a younger sister should replace her. The outstanding fact is the extreme endurance of the husband's rights and their passing on his death to his agnatic heirs. Legal marriage and the domestic unit it establishes are thus very stable, though there may be frequent adultery. The legal emphasis is the same among the Nuer, even though they have frequent changes in the constitution of households. Marriage is stable in that wherever the woman is her husband accompanies her, even after his death, to be pater of her children, for whoever their genitors are, they belong to the man or group which gave cattle for her. The husband or his heirs may let his wife go and not reclaim the marriage payment, since they get the children even though they lose her other services as wife. In these tribes marriage payment thus binds the woman's reproductive capacity to the perpetuation of the extended agnatic lineage. Each such group loses its daughters, but insists on its rights to the fertility of its daughters-in-law.

Moreover, rights of inheritance vest in children exclusively from the agnatic lineage of their pater. They have no rights in their mother's family unless they are unredeemed illegitimate children, when they rank as if they were members of her agnatic lineage. Therefore economic and other interests pull the children almost entirely to the home of their pater and his agnatic lineage.

The Lozi have no extended unilineal kin-groups. Among them the corporate groups which endure in time are the cognates in family villages or in sections of a royal village, based on the mounds which dot the plain and which are centres of surrounding gardens, fishing-sites, and pastures. Lozi's relatives in the patrilineal and matrilineal lines may be scattered at many places far over the surface of the great flood-plain. Because their productive activities are varied, and many fall in distant places in the same month, they require co-operation and help from many people. Kinship provides the framework for getting this help, but since neighbours in the various parts where they have economic resources are linked to them by patrilineal, matrilineal, and mixed ties, they emphasize relationship in all of their lines of descent. For them it is not important to fix an individual's relationship to a single line, but to emphasize his links with many lines; therefore marriage does not tie a woman's procreative power to one line. She produces for many lines. Among the Zulu economic and other interests coincide with the pull of agnatic lineage ties; among the Lozi, with their limited resources centred in restricted dwelling-mounds, economic interests may pull a man to settle with his mother's kindred, in either of her lines of descent. As a woman's productive capacity is not tied to a single lineage group, the child goes to its genitor, not to the legal husband of the woman. This removes the main buttress of marriage; since the children can shift their allegiance and emphasize that relationship which most pleases or profits them, the family as a whole is an unstable association. I am not here referring only to the instability of households: this is also marked among the Nuer, but among them lineage ties always draw the family together about the woman's husband. Among the Lozi, too, a large proportion of children grow up elsewhere as foster-children and not in the villages where they will ultimately settle. There is no dominant pressure of interests and law to induce them to return to their father's home, though most do. They may go to the home of any of their near ancestors. Adulterers can claim their children, and adultery is incessant. Men divorce their wives easily and at personal will; women are always straining to be released. Marriage, as well as domestic association, is unstable. I have suggested that the reason for this is to be sought in Lozi kinship structure, which is of a pattern common in Central Africa, but which here is directly related to their modes of production and settlement in their physical environment.

We see then that in these societies the types of marriage and the forms of the family, with inheritance of property, rights of children in father's and mother's lines and the rights of these lines to claim them, laws of betrothal, destination of widows, rates of divorce, status of wives in their husband's homes, are all consistent with certain types of kinship system. In some societies the household group which is usually designated as the family may be unstable. The structural stability of the society rests in the extended kinship lines, one of which may be the nuclear framework on which local communities are organized as corporate groups. These reach back into the history of the tribe through all changes of personnel, while the domestic family itself is always an ephemeral, and often an unstable, association.[1]

I have presented my argument more strongly than I myself feel is justified at present, in order to make clear the type of data and analysis I consider likely to be most fruitful. I should have preferred to do further comparative research before publishing it, had it not been for the opportunity of presenting it in this symposium. I am fully aware of the difficulties of establishing the validity of the hypothesis, but even if it is wrong it may be useful. Some of the difficulties are inherent in sociological analysis, since in this there are always complicating variables. Others arise from the vague and embracing use of categories and concepts (of which I too am guilty) such as patrilineal, lineage, marriage, divorce, &c. When is a marriage complete, and when can we class the separation of a cohabiting couple as divorce?[2] Are the Bena patrilineal

---

[1] See references p. 166, n. 1, especially Evans-Pritchard, *Nuer Marriage*, pp. 64–5.

[2] For example, on the difficulty of establishing when there is a marriage and when divorce, see Richards, *Bemba Marriage and Modern Economic Conditions*. It is difficult to tell what Fortes means by divorce (see his *Marriage Law among the Tallensi*, 1946). He speaks of a high divorce rate but divorce from a 'proper' marriage is obviously a most serious ritual and social step (see his *The Dynamics*

and the Ila matrilineal, and have they lineages? The literature is generally confused and imprecise, and the posing of problems may help to clarify descriptions.

I am myself uncertain whether it is the stability of people's attachment to specific areas, or patriliny or father-right itself, or the agnatic lineage, or all of these together, which, whatever the other variables are, tend to be associated with a strong marriage tie. That any or all of these are significant seems definite to me. Evans-Pritchard has stated that the Azande, organized on father-right but without the agnatic lineage, had rare divorce in the past. He has not reported on the problem fully, but it might be that the State power prevented women from leaving their husbands if they wanted to, i.e. there was instituted authority to compel them to remain in marriage. When that authority was restricted by British occupation divorce became rife. On the other hand, despite European support for women against men in Zululand, something there, I suggest the agnatic lineage, has maintained the stability of marriage; while in Loziland the marriage tie has become looser and looser, even though tribal ethics approve of firm unions, while not condemning divorce. However, as we have seen, the code of the Zulu age-set regiments, backed by the State, punished severely unchastity and infidelity: perhaps these codes are still the main sanctions on marriage despite all structural changes. Yet the ban on prenuptial conception does not seem to have retained similar force. Illegitimate births are frequent while divorces are rare. According to old records and modern field-workers this seems to be the position among all Southern Bantu tribes who had tribal initiation into age-regiments,[1] save for the Thonga of Portuguese East Africa. In his book Junod implies that divorce is frequent, though this seems to contradict an earlier article on another group of Thonga, and Clerc states explicitly of the related Ronga that divorce is impossible once the wife has borne a child: 'she is forever bound to her husband's village'.[2]

I give these references in detail for, while all the Southern Bantu have

of Clanship among the Tallensi, 1945). In Dahomey (Herskovits, op. cit.) the divorce rate varies according to which of the thirteen types of marriage is contracted, but it seems to vary according to my postulate.

[1] H. Kuper, paper on the Swazi in this book, and An African Aristocracy, 1947, p. 104; Read, 'Moral Code of the Ngoni', pp. 16–18; E. Casalis, Les Bassoutos [written 1859], Paris, 1930, pp. 231–2; D. F. Ellenberger and A. Macgregor, History of the Basuto, 1912, p. 273; E. H. Ashton, unpublished thesis on the Southern Sotho, University of Cape Town, quoted with his permission; C. L. Harries, The Laws and Customs of the BaPedi and Cognate Tribes, 1929, p. 36; H. Stayt, The Bavenda, 1931, p. 152; I. Schapera, Married Life in an African Tribe [Tswana], 1940, p. 294.

[2] H. A. Junod, op. cit. i, pp. 198–9. Cf. his 'The Bathonga of the Transvaal', Addresses and Papers, British and South African Associations for the Advancement of Science, 1905, iii, pp. 258–9, together with Harries, loc. cit., previous footnote; A. Clerc, 'The Marriage Laws of the Ronga Tribe', p. 89.

agnatic lineages, it is of tribes without age-sets that a few records state there is frequent divorce. It seems clear that among the Natal Nguni and the Shona divorce was rare.[1] Hunter on the Pondo says 'dissolution was usual [though disapproved]. . . . Very many of the married women whom I knew had been married more than once, and the number of [unmarried divorcees] is considerable.' Cook implies that Bomvana divorces are frequent, but while divorced women are free to remarry, he had 'been unable to find a woman married again. There seems to be a strong aversion to this. Further, a woman who has returned from her husband's [village] is in the nature of a byword for female frailty.' Soga states that among the Xhosa 'divorce is not so common as might be supposed', and a deserting husband can return after many years to claim his wife and children.[2] Most of the old writers on these Cape Nguni peoples who dealt with the subject stated explicitly that divorce was not frequent, was not easy to obtain, and required the sanction of the chief; but a few imply that a man merely sent his wife home and women could run away, without stating how frequently this happened.[3] Generally writings on this part of Africa did not state the frequency of divorce, and were concerned to examine, as were the 1883 Cape Commissioners on Native Law and Custom, whether it was possible for a woman to escape from a marriage which they regarded as a sale into slavery. However, since a competent authority states that the Pondo have frequent divorce and I have been unable to find a specific reference to them in the early literature, it is perhaps worth recording that Sir Theophilus Shepstone told the 1883 Commission that the Pondo, unlike the Zulu, had become 'far more immoral' than they were fifty years before. He ascribed this to

[1] C. T. Nauhaus, 'Familienlieben, Heirathsgebräuche und Erbrecht der Kaffern', *Zeitschrift für Ethnologie*, xiv, 1882, at p. 210; L. Marx, 'Die Amahlubi', in S. R. Steinmetz (ed.), *Rechtsverhältnisse von Eingeborenen Völkern*, p. 353; and information from Dr. S. Kark who kept extensive records for a southern Natal grouping over seven years recently and noted one divorce. On the Shona, Bullock, op. cit., p. 367.

[2] M. Hunter [Prof. M. Wilson], *Reaction to Conquest*, 1936, p. 212; P. A. W. Cook, *Social Organization and Ceremonial Institutions of the Bomvana*, 1932, pp. 156–7; J. H. Soga, *The Ama-Xosa*, 1932, pp. 283 ff.

[3] Clear statements on the rarity of divorce are: H. Lichtenstein, *Travels in Southern Africa in the Years 1803, 1804, 1805, and 1806*, 1930, i, p. 322 and p. 326, at pp. 322–3 quoting L. Alberti, *De Kaffers aan die Zuidkust van Afrika*, Amsterdam, 1810—on the Xhosa; Warner, Dugmore, and Brownlee in J. Maclean (ed.), *A Compendium of Kafir Laws and Customs*, 1858, pp. 53–4, 70, and 163—on Xhosa, Tembu, Fingoes; J. Macdonald, 'Manners, Customs, Superstitions and Religions of the South African Tribes', *J. Roy. Anthrop. Inst.*, xix, 1889, pp. 271–2—chiefly on Xhosa; A. Kropf, *Das Volk der Xosa-Kaffern*, 1889, pp. 154–5. Note that none of these refer to the Pondo. The strongest indication that divorce was frequent is in the report of the *Cape Government Commission on Native Law and Custom*, 1883 (Parliamentary Paper G. 4–1883), Cape Town: W. A. Richards, p. 37, para. 95. D. Kidd did not specify the tribes to which he applied his contradictory statements: *The Essential Kafir*, 1904, 2nd edit. 1925, at pp. 225 and 358.

the removal of the threat of attack by the Zulu which led to a decline in military virtues.[1]

I have referred to the Southern Bantu material in some detail partly to indicate the difficulty of assessing the data on these problems. It must be emphasized that records on the Southern Bantu, especially on marriage, are better than those on most regions of Africa. But I feel I must also, even in this compressed essay, cite the Pondo and Thonga as peoples who are said to have unstable marriages, since they not only have the agnatic lineage but are close to being neighbours of the Zulu. I indicate that it is possibly the moral code of the age-sets which helps to stabilize Zulu marriage, to show that I do not discount the influence of ethical rules themselves. It is clear that special variables have to be examined in each tribe.[2]

I have considered briefly some of the possible influences that the types and quantities of property available to particular peoples may have on the marriage payment and hence on marriage. We have seen that the presence of considerable movable property in the form of cattle among Lozi, Ovambo, and Herero is not itself sufficient to produce high marriage payments; and where it has done so among the Ila, marriage is not thereby stabilized. I suggested that the Azande and Ganda are father-right peoples who lacked property which could produce high marriage payments, but nevertheless had stable marriage. However, I have not had space to examine whether a kindred group becomes stable about a fixed piece of land, or herds of cattle, and whether this and the rights of the children to the property, are not what stabilize marriage, rather than agnatic descent and father-right themselves. It appears to me that property in this form is by itself insufficient, since we have many records of peoples with matrilineal succession to valuable lands or herds among whom marriage is very unstable.[3]

In this essay I have restricted my survey in general to Black Africa. I believe that for this region my argument is likely to be validated as a demonstrable tendency. So far I have been able to make only an even more cursory survey of the literature on other primitive groups. I have

[1] Report of the Commission cited in previous footnote, p. 31, Q. 564.

[2] e.g. why do the Xhosa not practise sororal polygyny, the levirate, divorce for barrenness, though their marriage rules are so similar to those of the other Nguni? (*Opera cita*, Lichtenstein, i, pp. 319–25; Ayliff in Maclean, p. 163; Macdonald (on Gaika and Tembu), p. 272; Soga, p. 139; 1883 Cape Commission, pp. 114–15).

[3] See e.g. M. Fortes, 'The Ashanti Social Survey', *Rhodes–Livingstone Journal*, vi, 1948, p. 19 on the attachment of the Ashanti matrilineage to village and lands, and J. B. Danquah, *Akan Laws and Customs*, 1928, at p. 156: 'it cannot be exaggerated how easily and rapidly marriages may be dissolved with little trouble'. e.g. also K. M. Panikker, 'Some Aspects of Nayar Life', *J. Roy. Anthrop. Inst.*, xlviii, 1918, at pp. 266 ff. See also various works on the Pueblo Indians, as F. Eggan on 'The Hopi Lineage' in *Studies in Social Structure: Essays presented to A. R. Radcliffe-Brown*, 1949.

cited Loeb's statement of the one part of the correlation, the divorce rate with the kinship structure, for Indonesia,[1] and the thesis seems to be borne out generally in North America and Oceania. The largest group of peoples which can by most criteria be classed as at all primitive, for whom the thesis appears to be incorrect, is the Bedouin. Under Islamic law divorce is simply effected and most records on the Bedouin state that it is frequent. There are contrary statements, and it is impossible for me to give a decision on this set of peoples who, having agnatic lineages, should on my theory have stable marriage. I record that the present bias of the data is against my argument.[2] It is, of course, doubtful whether an Islamized people can be considered primitive.

I do not even venture to express an opinion on the stability of marriage in more developed communities, in towns and complex rural economies, for here many complicated variables enter. I am aware that my analysis ultimately involves the question of what is the relation of the family to the total social structure, of how far the stability of the family is related to the stability of that structure, of what effects moral rules have as compared with structural determinants, &c. In defence of my attempt to penetrate these intricate problems I plead that we must isolate a few of them at a time. Among Lozi and Zulu the kinship system, and the marriage payment and its consequences, form complexes which are internally consistent and which differ in practically every relation. Therefore they offer ideal material for initial comparison.

[1] I read this after I formulated my argument.

[2] H. Granqvist (*Marriage Conditions in a Palestinian Village*, Helsingfors: Societas Scientarium Fennica, 1931, pp. 268 ff.) made a quantitative analysis of divorces and concluded: 'as far as I can see there is little which goes to prove that divorce is so frequent among Muhammedans'. Otherwise all statements on the urban and peasant fellahin emphasize a very high divorce rate, though Blackman's description implies that divorce is a serious business (*The Fellahin of Upper Egypt*, p. 95). The typical statement on the desert Bedouin is that of G. W. Murray (*Sons of Ishmael. A Study of the Egyptian Bedouin*, London, 1935, at pp. 225–6) that 'divorce is very common among the Bedouins, for a variety of reasons'. A. Kennett (*Bedouin Justice: Laws and Customs among the Egyptian Bedouin*, 1925, p. 100) writes that 'divorce, although a very much simpler business than in civilized countries, is by no means as easy as is popularly believed; and Bedouin public opinion is usually sane and healthy'. I dare affirm that modern studies will show Bedouin marriage to be stable.

SOME TYPES OF FAMILY STRUCTURE AMONGST THE CENTRAL BANTU

By A. I. RICHARDS

CHARACTERISTICS OF MATRILINEAL KINSHIP ORGANIZATIONS IN CENTRAL AFRICA

MOST of the Bantu peoples of Central Africa reckon descent in the matrilineal rather than the patrilineal line, and many of them practise some form of what is usually known as matrilocal marriage. In fact, it is the matrilineal character of their kinship organization which distinguishes them so clearly from the Bantu of East and South Africa, and for this reason the territory stretching from the west and central districts of the Belgian Congo to the north-eastern plateau of Northern Rhodesia and the highlands of Nyasaland is sometimes referred to as the 'matrilineal belt'.[1]

Within this group of 'matrilineal' tribes there is a remarkable degree of uniformity as to the principles governing descent and succession and the various ideologies by which people explain their adherence to the mother's rather than to the father's line, and stress their community of interests with their maternal relatives.[2] Blood is believed to be passed through the woman and not through the man. The metaphors of kinship stress the ties between people 'born from the same womb' or 'suckled at the same breast', and in some tribes the physical role of the father is believed to be limited to the quickening of the foetus already formed in the uterus. The duty of the woman to produce children for her lineage is emphasized, and descent is traced from an original ancestress or a series of ancestresses known as 'mothers' of the lineage or clan, and also in some cases from the brothers of these founding ancestresses. The ancestral cult centres round the worship of matrilineal rather than patrilineal ancestors, although spirits of the father's line are sometimes the subject of subsidiary rites.

A child belongs to his mother's clan or lineage, and succession to office follows the common matrilineal rule, that is to say, authority passes to the dead man's brothers or to his sisters' sons, or to the sons

---

[1] There are, of course, a number of patrilineal or mainly patrilineal tribes in the Belgian Congo, including most of the Luba (as distinguished from the Luba-Hemba), the Songe, and the Nkundo.

[2] Matrilineal is used here in inverted commas because it is generally recognized that no society is entirely matrilineal or patrilineal as regards descent, inheritance, succession, and authority, but that the family system provides a balance of interests and rights between the two sides of the family with a predominant emphasis on one side or the other, and it is in this sense that I shall use the term in this article. See my 'Mother Right in Central Africa' in *Essays presented to C.G. Seligman*, 1930, for a description of Bemba kinship from this point of view.

of his maternal nieces. Among some of the Central Bantu women succeed to the titles of royal ancestresses, or hold positions as chieftainesses, with special ritual functions.

But with these principles of descent and succession the similarity ends. The Central African people differ in a rather striking way as to their family structure, and in particular as to the various forms of domestic and local grouping based on the family.

These variations in the family structure depend largely on the nature of the marriage contract and the extent to which the husband is able to gain control over his wife, who belongs, by virtue of matrilineal descent, to the lineage and clan of her mother and of her brothers and sisters; and also on the extent to which he manages to achieve a position of authority over the children she bears. In matrilineal societies the man's control over his wife and her children can never be complete, except in the case of a union with a slave woman, but he can gain considerable power over his wife's labour, her property, and her child-bearing powers, as well as rights over his children's work and their marriages, by virtue of the service or payments he makes to his father- or brother-in-law. Moreover, the ways in which domestic authority is divided between a man and the head of his wife's kinship group are surprisingly varied. In some cases there is a formal allocation of rights and privileges between father and mother's brother in return for service and payments. In other cases the balance is less well defined, and every marriage produces what can only be described as a constant pull-father-pull-mother's-brother, in which the personality, wealth, and social status of the two individuals or their respective kinsmen give the advantage to one side or the other, and a number of alternative solutions are reached within the same tribe.

In this balance of privileges and duties between the patrikin and the matrikin the crucial point is obviously the husband's right to determine the residence of the bride. If she and her children live in the same homestead or village as his kinsmen, his domestic authority is likely to be greater than where they remain with the wife's relatives.

Throughout this area, at any rate, the rule of residence at marriage seems to me to be the most important index of the husband's status. It also provides the most convenient basis for the classification of these different forms of matrilineal family. In Central Africa we find every gradation from the marriage in which the husband has the right to remove his bride immediately to his own village, to varieties of trial marriage, temporary unions, or customs by which the husband takes up more or less permanent residence in the wife's group.

For this reason I have found the old terms 'matrilocal' and 'patrilocal' of little use for comparative purposes. Many writers have pointed out that the words are in themselves confusing, since there are two parties to a marriage and what is 'residence with the mother' for the one is 'residence with the mother-in-law' for the other. If the terms are to be retained for purposes of classification it would be necessary to adopt a convention by which, for instance, they were always used with relation to one sex. Firth and Adam suggest as an alternative the use of the words 'viri-local' and 'uxori-local' to meet this difficulty,[1] and I shall use these terms from time to time.

Another difficulty with regard to the Central African area is the variety of forms of marriage relationship which could reasonably be included under the title 'matrilocal'. In societies practising matrilineal descent a man may live with his wife's people because the marriage is on trial; because he is fulfilling a marriage contract by service instead of the payment of goods; or because he means to settle permanently in his wife's group.[2] He may have sex access to his wife at night and work in her fields, but act as head of his sister's house and spend a large part of his day with the latter. This is the practice of the matrilineal Menang-kabau of the Padang highlands of Sumatra and the kindred peoples of Negri Sembilan.[3] A similar position holds good among the Hopi of Arizona. Alternatively a husband may live at his wife's village but often be away visiting his own relatives, as amongst the Yao (see p. 233); or he may spend alternate years in his own and his wife's village, as in Dobu Island. In any of these cases there will be some years, some months, or some hours in which the marriage may reasonably be called matrilocal. The term gives no indication of the length of time a man spends in his wife's village, or the degree to which he is incorporated with her matrikin, or isolated from his own family.[4] For this reason I have found it better to use the phrases 'marriage with immediate right of bride removal' or 'marriage with delayed right of bride removal' or 'marriage without bride removal' in describing the family systems of the Central Bantu.

The terms 'matrilocal' or 'patrilocal' are similarly lacking in precision

[1] See R. Firth, *We, the Tikopia*, 1936, p. 596, and L. Adam, in *Man*, Jan. 1948, p. 12. N. W. Thomas, who suggested the terms patrilocal and matrilocal in 1906, put them forward 'not as being specifically appropriate but as being parallel to patrilineal and matrilineal, denoting descent in the female or male line respectively' (*Kinship and Marriage in Australia*, 1906, p. 108), thus showing that he realized from the start the ambiguity of the terms.

[2] Rivers points out, in his article on 'Kinship', in Hastings's *Encyclopaedia*, that marriage by service 'passes insensibly into the matrilocal form of marriage' and trial marriages 'shade insensibly into trials before marriage on the one hand and into ease and frequency of divorce on the other'.

[3] Cf. Verkerk-Pistorius, *Studien over de inlandische Houshouding in de Padang-ische Bovenlander*, 1871. Quoted by Taylor in 'Matriarchal Family System', *The Nineteenth Century*, xl, 1896, p. 96, where he describes the 'Chassez Croisez' which takes place at dusk when each man leaves his sister's house where he has been by day, to join his wife and children at night; cf. also F. C. Cole, *The Peoples of Malaysia*, 1945.

[4] R. Linton stresses the importance of the propinquity of the two settlements in determining the character of the descent system in *Study of Man*, 1936, p. 168.

P

when used as a means of classifying types of family and domestic unit. According to the terminology adopted in this book, a parental family is a household or homestead composed of a man, his wife or wives, and their children. Such a unit naturally grows in size in societies where it is customary for either the sons or the daughters to live with their parents after marriage. This wider group, usually based on the principle of unilineal descent and composed of members of three generations, is here described as an extended family.[1] Members of extended families of this kind usually live in a separate kraal or homestead or they may form the nucleus or core of a village or a section of a village. They tend to co-operate in economic affairs, to exercise some common rights over property, to accept their genealogical senior as a common authority, and to practise some joint ritual. Where it is a common practice for a man who has married sons to separate off from his father's homestead to start a new community, and where the land situation makes this possible, a three-generation extended family of this kind becomes the normal pattern of residence as it is, for instance, amongst the Zulu. Where, however, the villages are more permanent and the splitting off of new extended families is not so easy, the residential pattern is naturally much less uniform. The eldest brother of a group of siblings may succeed to the position of his father in a patrilineal society or to that of his mother's brother in a matrilineal society, and various other changes of this kind may take place. Thus in the more or less permanent villages there may be two or three extended families or remains of extended families. There may also be two or three alternative types of marriage in the same community, and a number of principles of residence. Such larger residential units, usually based on a nuclear extended family but with a number of additions, I have called local kin groups, specifying whether they are predominantly matrilineal or patrilineal in composition.

In such extended families or local kin groups extension takes place on the basis of certain nuclear or pivotal relationships. For instance, according to the rules of residence at marriage, the children of one sex marry out of the homestead, whereas those of the other remain within it. Rules of succession and inheritance similarly determine the incidence of authority and economic privilege within the local community. Property rights and authority may go from father to son, from mother to daughter, from brother to sister's son, and so forth. I find it convenient to classify the different types of extended family by means of these nuclear relationships, even though the categories constantly overlap. Thus I use the term 'father-son extended family' for a Zulu homestead;

[1] I have found it useful to employ the term 'grand-family' suggested to me by R. Firth to indicate a three-generation family descended in the direct line, patrilineal or matrilineal, when it is necessary to distinguish between this and other forms of extended family. See pp. 218, 227, 228.

or the 'mother-son extended family' for a local unit which is a common pattern amongst the Swazi, where the woman leaves her husband's kraal at the time of her son's marriage and lives with him in a position of authority to the end of her life. Parent-daughter extended families of one kind or another exist where uxorilocal marriage is practised. These include the mother-daughter family of the Hopi, where property in land or houses is passed through the woman; the sororal family, where a group of married sisters and their daughters live together, usually under the care of an elder brother (see p. 232); or the sibling family found amongst the Nayar of Malabar, where a man lived with his sisters and the latter were visited by their husbands at night; or a father-daughter family, where married daughters live with their parents, but their father is very much the head of the group and may determine residence instead of the mother (see p. 227). Other types of extended family include the matrilineal fraternal family, where a group of brothers live with their wives and their sisters' sons.

It is obvious that in the case of residential units such as these the nuclear relationships vary from one type of extended family to the other; that is to say, one homestead is based on the close relationship of a group of the men of the family, as in the case of the patrilineal father-son family or the matrilineal fraternal family; while another is founded on the kinship of women, as in the mother-daughter family of the Hopi. The interests of brother and brother, brother and sister, or mother and daughter may be identified by one marriage system or the other, while the extended families so formed may attract to themselves additional households of kinsfolk or slaves, according to fixed rule or more casual association.

I hope to distinguish four different types of family structure amongst the Central Bantu by means of the criteria indicated, that is to say, the type of marriage contract, the distribution of domestic authority, the residential units, and the primary kinship alinements.

The literature on this area is as yet scanty. When further material is available I expect to find a range of variation between these types and even the appearance of new forms. It is my thesis that the balance of interest between the two sides of the family is bound to be an uneasy one in the case of matrilineal communities, and for this reason variation between neighbouring societies within the region is to be expected as well as different types of marriage and family within each tribe itself.

VARIETIES OF FAMILY STRUCTURE
(Type A) The Mayombe-Kongo Group

I have selected the Mayombe and the Kongo as typical of a group of western Congo peoples which practise matrilineal descent, succession, and inheritance, and give high marriage payments with the right of immediate removal of the bride, but with the return of her children to her brothers' village at puberty. To the same group of people belong the tribes of the Kwilu basin such as the Huana, Yaka, Yanzi, and Sakata, as well as the Songo of the Luniungu and Gobari areas and the Ambundu to the extreme south-west of the district.[1]

The Mayombe inhabit the lower Congo area between Shiloango and the Luakula basin, south-west of Brazzaville. The Mayombe were described by Van Overbergh in 1907, but since that date our information has been supplemented by a series of articles by N. de Cleene, as well as an important study by F. P. Van Reeth.[2]

The Kongo inhabit the region of the cataracts south of the Congo between Matadi and Stanleypool. Van Wing's study of the Mangu tribe of the Kongo group was written in 1921. Further material appeared in Torday's article in 1933.[3] I shall base my description on the Mayombe material in the first instance.[4]

Economic Determinants

The peoples of the lower Congo area appear to have more economic resources at their disposal than the other selected tribes. Their material culture was more highly developed than that of most other Bantu peoples, and ironwork, copper, wood- and ivory-carving as well as weaving, reached a high level. This was particularly the case among the Kongo. Copper and iron objects were used for marriage and other payments. Trade in ivory and slaves seems to have been established for some hundreds of years. This area has also been longer in contact with Europe than have Northern Rhodesia and Nyasaland, since the Portuguese occupation of the western coast district dates from the fifteenth century. Under present-day conditions these people are described as producing almost all the palm oil and coconut oil of the Congo and they

[1] E. Torday and T. Joyce, 'Notes on the Ethnography of the Bahuana', *J. Roy. Anthrop. Inst.* xxxvi, 1906; P. J. Denis, 'L'Organisation d'un peuple primitif', *Congo*, i. 4, 1925, pp. 481–532; De Beaucorps, 'Le Mariage chez les Basongo de la Luniungu et de la Gobari', *Bull. Jur. Indig.*, xi. 6., 1943, pp. 109–26; G. Week, 'La Peuplade des Ambundu', *Congo*, ii, 192, 1937.
[2] N. de Cleene, 'La Famille au Mayombe', *Africa*, x. 1, Jan. 1937, pp. 1–15; 'L'Élément religieux dans l'organisation sociale des Bayombe', *Congo*, i. 5, 1936, pp. 706–11; 'Individu et collectivité dans l'évolution économique du Mayombe', *Inst. Roy. Colon. Belge Bull.* xvi. 2, 1945, pp. 254–60; Van Overbergh, *Les Mayombe*, 1907; F. P. Van Reeth, *De rol van dem moederlijken oom in die inlandsche familie*, Inst. Roy. Colon. Belge Mémoires, 1935; 'De bruidsprijs bij de huwelijken in Congo', *Semaine de Missiologie*, Louvain, 1934, pp. 192–215; M. Nauwelaert, 'Note sur la Société Yombe', *Congo*, i. 4, 1938, pp. 504–9; L. Bittremieux, *Mayombsche idioticon*, 1923; H. Deleval, *Les Tribus Kavate du Mayombe*, 1913.
[3] Van Wing, *Études Bakongo*, 1921; E. Torday, 'Dualism in Western Bantu Religion', *J. Roy. Anthrop. Inst.* lviii, 1933, pp. 225–45; *Causeries Congolaises*, 1925.
[4] N. de Cleene, 'Les Chefs indigènes au Mayombe', *Africa*, viii. 1, Jan. 1935, pp. 63–75.

seem to have considerable wealth in money. Agricultural land is fertile, although there appears to be considerable pressure of population in some districts, and rights over forests, garden and house sites, and palm-trees will be shown to be important determinants of kinship ties. Small stock such as goats and sheep are kept in some districts and are used for marriage payments, but the ritual attitude to stock which is characteristic of the Eastern and Southern Bantu does not exist. Differences in economic and social status were evidently marked at the time of the arrival of the Belgians. Slavery was such an important institution in pre-European days that the people are described as falling into three groups, chiefs, freemen, and slaves,[1] and this high incidence of slavery affected the balance of the kinship system, since rules of descent differed for slaves and for freemen. Chiefs and commoners were differentiated according to their wealth in material possessions.

Ideology and Principles of Descent and Succession

The Mayombe believe that blood passes through the woman and not through the man. The child belongs to a series of kinship groups based on matrilineal descent: the clan (*mvila*), which is an exogamous division tracing descent to a legendary founding ancestress and associated with a territory; a major matrilineage (*dikanda*), a subdivision of the clan, which is also exogamous and which reckons direct descent to a depth of about six generations from a known founding ancestress, and which is associated with a district; a minor matrilineage (*mvumu*, pl. *bivumu*), which is a local group forming a village or section of a village and is composed of a group of brothers and their sisters' sons, with sisters who marry elsewhere but contribute money obtained by their work to the *mvumu* funds.[2]

The descent system of the Kongo is similar. Van Wing speaks of matriclans (*dikanda*), tracing descent from a legendary ancestress, and matrilineages (*luvila*), which he describes as 'lignées'. The matrilineage traces descent to an actual ancestress, acknowledges a common head, and shares rights over a strip of territory, but the institution of chieftainship is more pronounced in this tribe and De Jonghe speaks of 'crowned

---

[1] Van Overbergh, op. cit., pp. 383, 405, 409.

[2] I use the term 'clan' for the largest group which traces unilineal descent, usually putative, from a common ancestress, and 'lineage' for a named group tracing actual descent from a known ancestress. I use this term for a variety of kinship groups based on the tracing of direct descent in one line, and distinguish different types by qualifying terms such as 'patrilineage' or 'matrilineage'. I find Evans-Pritchard's use of 'maximal', 'major', 'minor', or 'minimal' lineages a very convenient one where two or three levels of subdivisions of the clan exist and they remain structurally connected. I am using the term 'lineage' to cover a number of different unilineal descent groups such as the Ramage described by Firth in Tikopia, the sub-clan as used by Malinowski in the Trobriands, and the 'section' employed by Nadel in accounts of the Nuba.

chiefs', 'clan chiefs', 'lineage chiefs', and village headmen.[1] The clans are also arranged in something like an order of hierarchy according to traditions of first arrival in the area. The Kongo also recognize as a special category the father's people or *kitata*. There is no legal identification of a child with his father's matrilineage, but the ancestors of this line are remembered for four generations and are honoured 'by respect'.

The descendants of the same father are described as having a fraternity from 'the grave of the father',[2] that is to say they were brought up in their father's village and return to bury him there. They are also described as being 'brothers of the same village'. A similar recognition of paternal ancestors is clearly marked at the time of the marriage of a girl, since she then calls on the spirits of her father's matriclan, her paternal grandfather's matriclan, and then her maternal grandfather's matriclan.[3] It is for this reason that Torday speaks of dual descent amongst the Kongo, but the term *kitata* seems merely to mean the father's people. It is the name of a category of relations who are honoured and remembered with affection. The Kongo peoples similarly use a collective term for their matrikin (*kingadi*), for the brothers and sisters of a man's wife (*kinzadi*), or for the father and mother of a son's wife or a daughter's husband.[4]

The rule of matrilineal descent was formerly associated with the developed cult of the maternal ancestors. De Cleene points out that the chief of the Mayombe clan formerly had religious functions and his village was the centre of an ancestral cult;[5] the same kind of cult, associated with clan and lineage ancestors, was definitely marked amongst the Khimba.[6] In the case of the Kongo, ceremonies performed for the illness or death of a member took place within the clan and occasionally the lineage, but this type of cult seems to have largely lapsed amongst the Mayombe and the Kongo at the present day. Mayombe chiefs are mentioned as possessing fetishes, and the heads of local lineage groups are said to have magic powers or *kindoki*, but it is expressly stated by both De Cleene and Van Reeth that they have no significant part to play in an ancestral cult.

The principles of descent and affiliation are clear. All freeborn Mayombe belong to matrilineal descent groups, and it is only the children of slave wives who belong to their father's matrilineage, or descendants of immigrants who have attached themselves to a chief and intermarried with women of his matrilineage. Children may also

---

[1] De Jonghe, Preface to Van Wing, op. cit., p. vii.

[2] Van Wing, op. cit., p. 134; also E. Torday, *J. Roy. Anthrop. Inst.* lviii, 1933, p. 238.

[3] Van Wing, op. cit., p. 201.

[4] De Jonghe, Preface to Van Wing, op. cit., p. x.

[5] De Cleene, 'Le Clan matrilinéal dans la société indigène', pp. 12 and 13; Van Wing, op. cit., pp. 122, 271, 272.

[6] Bittremieux, *La Société secrète des Bakhimba*, 1936.

be obliged to belong to their father's clan if their matrikin have been unable to return the marriage payment when the father has asked for a divorce. The children in this case will be kept as hostages until the repayment has been made, but they will always be reckoned as socially inferior members of their father's clan.[1]

Succession to office amongst the Mayombe follows the matrilineal rule, that is to say, it goes from brother to brother to uterine nephew and then to uterine grandson. The offices which are hereditary are those of chief, head of a village or village section, or senior brother (*khazi*) of a matrilineal fraternal family. De Cleene states that the chiefs, whose powers seem to have been rather exiguous, were always succeeded by their brothers, but with regard to the post of head of the kinship village or village section, there seems to have been considerable room for exercise of choice within the 'filiation uterine'.[2] This post is so important that young men are trained for it. Van Reeth describes the careful selection of two or three uterine nephews by the head of the village, and the education of these boys for their future work.[3] The succession is usually matrilineal, but a complete stranger may be appointed to the village headship for want of a sufficiently intelligent hereditary candidate.

Rules of inheritance and ownership of property are exceedingly important in the maintenance of kinship ties. Property consists of houses and garden sites, palm-trees, household goods, and wealth in money. Each man has individual rights to cultivate land allocated to him by the head of the minor matrilineage (*mvumu*), but the property of this group of brothers and sisters is held jointly and administered by the senior brother. Women who leave their village to marry keep their possessions distinct, and money made from the sale of produce or in other ways is handed over to their senior brothers, and hence is finally inherited by their children. It is not clear from the evidence whether any forms of property could be passed from father to son or father to daughter, but this seems unlikely.

The Marriage Contract

Marriage amongst the Mayombe is described as a system by which a man acquires sex access to a woman, and certain clearly defined rights to her services and those of her adolescent children, in return for a substantial payment in money or goods. The Mayombe husband never acquires full authority over his wife or children, as we shall see, but the marriage payment enables him to remove his bride to his own village immediately on marriage; his sex rights over her are exclusive, and

[1] De Cleene, *Africa*, x. 1, Jan. 1937, p. 6; Deleval, op. cit., p. 29.
[2] De Cleene, *Inst. Roy. Colon. Belge Bull*. ix, 1938, p. 68; Van Reeth, op. cit., pp. ii, 20.
[3] Ibid., p. 11.

payments as damages for adultery are heavy. In the old days, in fact, adultery was a crime punishable by death.

The marriage payments can be described as substantial in relation to the tokens and gifts passed at marriage in the other selected type societies. Van Reeth speaks of 50 lengths of cloth valued at 12 francs each in the old days; 400 to 500 francs in money after the 1914–18 war and a rate in 1936 of 3,000 francs.[1] Weeks gives figures for the lower Congo area in general as follows: 55 beads (very scarce and dear) in 1885; 30 pieces of cloth to the value of £9 in 1883; and beads or money to the value of £20 in 1914.[2] Van Wing gives figures of 40 to 60 francs to 100 francs amongst the Mpungu in 1910 to 1915.[3] Interesting material is given by Mertens for the Banbata group in 1948, in which he compares the marriage payments with the average wage for an unskilled worker, e.g. 1,500 to 2,000 francs for the total marriage payments for a man earning 50 francs a month.[4]

The Mayombe woman, although she is potentially the founder of a lineage, is definitely in an inferior position when she marries into her husband's village. She is there a stranger. De Cleene describes her as a servant in her husband's village ('Elle n'est d'ailleurs qu'en service chez son mari').[5] Whether she is ever finally incorporated in any sense of the word in her husband's group is not clear. When she first marries it is evident that she is definitely an outsider in her husband's *mvumu*. On the other hand, the services she must do for her husband are limited by custom. If she is asked to do anything beyond these prescribed tasks for her husband or his brothers, she must be paid something additional for her work; in fact a Belgian ethnographer uses the word 'wages' when describing such payments. Moreover the wife, as has been pointed out, keeps her own property distinct. She has her own gardens from which she is only obliged to give half the produce to her husband, while she controls the rest herself, and she usually gives it to the members of her own *mvumu*. Both in terms of economic interests and principles of affiliation she is evidently very closely identified throughout her life with her matrikin.

The marriage payment here performs different functions from those ascribed to the *lobola* of the patrilineal Bantu of East and South Africa, but it is an equally significant element of the contract. Van Reeth shows that where a girl marries without the permission of her own *mvumu* her husband will give an unusually high marriage payment to her *khazi*, and will thus gain complete possession over her and her children. She then abandons all property rights in her matrilineal inheritance.[6] The bride-

---

[1] Van Reeth, op. cit., p. 196.

[2] Weeks, op. cit., p. 142.   [3] Van Wing, op. cit., pp. 205–9.

[4] V. Mertens, 'Le Mariage chez les Bambata (Bakongo) et ses leçons sociales', *Zaire*, ii. 10, déc. 1948, pp. 1099–126.

[5] De Cleene, *Africa*, x. 1, Jan. 1937, p. 4.   [6] Van Reeth, op. cit., p. 27.

wealth is provided by the men of the bridegroom's matrilineage and this seems to give them certain residual rights over the bride. A husband's brothers may produce children by the wife if the husband is impotent, and may inherit her, if she becomes a widow, with only a slight addition to the original payment made.

The father has certain rights to his children's services during their early youth. A young man pays his earnings to his father until his marriage when he returns to his own *mvumu*, but it is probable that these rights are considered as a return for the amount a man pays for the upkeep of his wife's children and the fact that he is responsible for paying their debts and providing magicians to cure them if they are ill. In the case of divorce the marriage payment is returned, either wholly or in part, and in that case the children are immediately removed by their mother's brother. In fact it is said that the *khazi* comes to fetch his sister's children as a sign that he wants a divorce to take place.[1]

Authority

The children remain under the authority of the father until an age described variously as puberty, or even earlier, or at marriage.[2] While they are small the father has considerable powers over the children, and if the *khazi* wishes to take two or three of his sister's sons to train as heirs at an early age, he must do so with the father's consent.[3] But De Cleene states that the father can get obedience by appealing to his children's goodwill or using 'artifices'. If he is dictatorial, the mother reminds him that the children do not belong to him, and that they will leave him at once for their maternal uncle if they are badly treated.[4] Deleval comments on the affection felt by children for their father, but says the mother is usually the disciplinarian.[5] Van Reeth says that if a child runs away to his *khazi* the father will have to make a formal request to get him back again. In any case, whatever the temporary powers of the father, the mother's brother always has overriding rights. An intractable boy is sent by the father to his mother's people to be corrected. The *khazi* appears if one of his nephews or nieces is ill, especially if sorcery is suspected. When they are adolescent and have come to live in his village he has absolute rights over their services and he can sell them into slavery and determine their marriages. He provides for the marriage payments of the boys, with the aid of the men of his *mvumu*. He receives those given for the girls. Neither boys nor girls can leave their *mvumu*

---

[1] Van Reeth, op. cit., p. 20.

[2] Van Wing gives a figure of 8–10 years for the Kongo, op. cit., p. 261; Van Reeth, op. cit., p. 20.

[3] Girls are also apparently selected for training in this way and are sent to a mother's sister. It is not clear what they are trained for and why they should be sent to a woman not living in the *mvumu*. Van Reeth, op. cit., p. 11.

[4] De Cleene, *Africa*, x. 1, Jan. 1937, p. 8.

[5] Deleval, op. cit., p. 31.

unless they have been enslaved or have refused to marry their selected spouse (see p. 216). Even when a man has chosen to live with his father during the whole of the latter's lifetime, which occasionally happens in the case of a father of high birth or great wealth, he returns to his mother's people once his male parent is dead. In these unusual circumstances he is referred to as 'a stranger chief' in his father's village (*fumu angani*) and is given particular respect.[1]

De Cleene quotes Mertens's account of an even more extreme form of the avunculate amongst the Badzing.[2] In this tribe a crowned chief could beat his nephews and nieces or sell his nieces for the benefit of the matrilineage or in order to liquidate his debts or accumulate wives for himself. In this area a father can buy back his son or daughter, but he can never secure for them clan membership, and when he dies they are scorned as slaves.

Residential Units

The basic domestic unit among the Mayombe is a parental polygynous family composed of a man and his wives and their young children. Such a homestead also included the huts of slaves in pre-European days. This polygynous family differs from those of the patrilineal Bantu of South and East Africa, however, since it can never become a grand-family. The sons and daughters of the head of the homestead always marry and settle elsewhere, and a Mayombe does not, therefore, normally live with any of his grandchildren, whether the children of his sons, as amongst the Ila, or those of his daughters, as amongst the Bemba (see p. 227).[3]

He has, however, young boys and married men dependent on him. These are his sisters' sons, who are described as his 'subjects'. Unmarried nephews apparently form part of the domestic unit and his wives cook for them, but it is not clear whether married nephews form part of the homestead in the sense of living in a cluster of huts marked off from the rest of the village or fenced around in any way. Nor is it clear whether all the sons of several sisters attach themselves to one eldest brother.

What is certain, however, is that the sons of one mother, together with their wives and young children, their sisters' grown sons, unmarried and married, and their sisters' unmarried but adolescent daughters form a

[1] De Cleene, *Africa*, x. 1, Jan. 1937, p. 8; also Deleval, op. cit., p. 32.

[2] J. Mertens, *Les Baldzing de la Kamtsha*, Inst. Roy. Colon. Belge Mémoires, 1935. See also De Cleene, op. cit., 1946, p. 36.

[3] I say 'normally' because it is quite clear that some sons remain with their fathers in some areas at any rate, both from Van Reeth's account of the selection of special maternal nephews as heirs, and De Cleene's statement that the sons of rich men may be tempted to stay with their fathers. This is obviously a point on which more detailed analysis of the composition of particular villages would prove useful.

compound family which acknowledges the authority of the senior brother (the *ngadi khazi*) and owns land in common from which individual gardens and trees are allocated. This matrilineal fraternal family is in the first instance the nucleus of the village, but an extended family naturally grows with the passage of years. The polygynous households of the brothers are increased by those of their married nephews until there are two, if not three, groups of married brothers residing in one village. New communities occasionally split off as in the case of other Bantu societies, but apparently this does not occur often, and some *bivumu* reach the size of 300 to 400 inhabitants.

It is possible to distinguish amongst the Mayombe a corporate matrilineage in the sense of a group of men and women who trace direct descent from a common ancestress, own land and property in common, which the men cultivate together and to which the women contribute money, and who all accept the authority of a senior brother. The men of this matrilineage and their wives and young children constitute the kinship settlement which is an extended fraternal family or several such extended families. Both the descent group and the residential group are described by the Mayombe as *bivumu*.

The *mvumu* is a very interesting type of residential unit on account of its joint activities and possessions and the marked authority of its head, the *khazi* or 'protector'.[1] This headman may be the eldest of a group of brothers, or he may be selected from amongst the most competent of the men who form the elders of the *mvumu*, or one of two or three boys chosen as potential headmen and educated by the existing *khazi* for the post (see p. 215). As has been seen, he may even be an outsider specially chosen for his gifts of leadership and brought into the *mvumu* for the purpose.

The *khazi* has supreme authority over the members of the matrilineage. According to Van Reeth's account he allocates land, palm-trees, and garden sites from those held in common by the men of the *mvumu*.[2] He is in charge of a joint purse composed of a levy on the earnings of the men and the contributions of the absent women who send him part of the money they earn by the sale of garden produce (see p. 216). This money is used to provide bride-wealth for the men and also dowries for the girls, and to pay for the expenses of the latter's weddings. It also pays for the services of magicians (*féticheurs*) or healers, if these are required by members of the group (see p. 234), and for funeral expenses. Van Reeth emphasizes the fact that the *khazi* is in charge of the labour of the members of his *mvumu* rather than their actual property.[3] They are his 'subjects' (*bilezi*), and he could, if necessary, sell them into

---

[1] De Cleene, *Inst. Roy. Colon. Belge Bull*. ix, 1936, p. 64. As distinct from the real eldest brother, the *ngadi khazi*.

[2] Van Reeth, op. cit., pp. 18, 19.

[3] Ibid., p. 14.

slavery in the old days. The *khazi* acts as judge in *mvumu* disputes and it is his job to prevent quarrels that might break up the group, and to act as arbitrator in marriage negotiations and discussions as to the amount of the bride-wealth to be returned in case of divorce. He must use the common purse carefully in order to keep the members of the *mvumu* united and must specially avoid wastefulness. Lastly, he protects the group against sorcery and does this by means of his own strong magic (*kindoki*).

The members of the *mvumu* usually constitute a village, but several *bivumu* may build together and in that case each retains its own centre and its own presiding *khazi*. The *khazis* of such a joint village or town together form a council.[1]

It will be seen from the following diagram that a matrilineal fraternal family composed of two brothers A and $A1$ and the sons of their sisters a and $a1$, and the sons of the latter's daughters $a2$ and $a3$, will grow in two or three generations to form a much wider group of matrikin in which new extended matrilineal fraternal families appear. $A2$ and $A3$ might well form the nucleus of such new extended families, and one or more of these may in time split off and form a new *mvumu*. Polygyny of course increases the number of residents in such a community but not the number of members of the matrilineage, since, however many wives a man has and however many children the latter may bear, they will not become members of the *mvumu*.

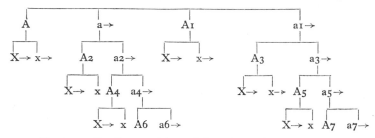

DIAGRAM I. Composition of the Mayombe *Mvumu*

The members of the *mvumu* are a (female) and A (male). X and x are sons and daughters of the male members of the *mvumu* who return to their own mothers' villages and are therefore not given special symbols. Succession passes from A to $A1$ and from $A2$ to $A3$, to $A4$ and then $A5$. a, $a1$, $a2$, $a3$, $a4$, and $a5$, $a6$, $a7$, leave the village to marry, as indicated by the arrows, but send back money contributions to the head of the family and sometimes return to live there in old age.

The strength and permanence of the *mvumu* is probably emphasized by the shortage of land which would tend to make young men anxious

---

[1] Corporate matrilineages with shared funds and a matrilineal fraternal family as the basic residential unit also exist amongst the Sakata and Songo (see ref. on p. 212, n. 1).

to return to their maternal uncles' villages to claim their rights to garden sites, and possibly also to the importance attached to the permanent ownership of palm-trees, which yield profits over a long period of years. The common funds of the *mvumu* seem mainly to consist of money, and it seems probable that the use of a money currency also makes for the corporate nature of the matrilineage, curious as this may sound. It is a convenient way in which the absent sisters can send contributions to the *mvumu* and it makes it possible to provide for all the needs of the *mvumu* from one source and therefore from one hand —the *khazi*'s.

The nuclear relationships in such a residential unit are plainly those between brothers and between brothers and their sisters' sons. It is a group based on the ties between men and not on those between women. A Mayombe boy is closely associated with his brothers all his life. He lives with them in his father's homestead; he moves with them to his own *mvumu* at the time of puberty. He is bound to them by ties of economic co-operation and joint ownership throughout life. With his paternal half-brothers, on the other hand, he has few links after the days of early childhood, since half-brothers go when the time comes to settle in their several *bivumu*.

(*Type B1*) *The Bemba-Bisa-Lamba Group*

A very different type of matrilineal organization is to be found among a group of kindred peoples who stretch from the Luapula basin across the plateau of north-eastern Rhodesia and parts of north-western Rhodesia. These tribes follow rules of matrilineal descent and succession. They contract marriage by service and token payments and a series of ritual acts which give the bridegroom ultimate, but not immediate, rights of removing his bride to his own village. There are thus variable rules of residence at marriage, and a divided authority between the father and the mother's brother.

The Bemba and Lala of the north-eastern plateau of Northern Rhodesia, the Bisa and other inhabitants of the Bangweulu swamps, and the Lamba on the Kafue river seem to have a very similar family system. The Kaonde and the Lunda of the Kasempa Province are probably similar in type, but we have only scanty information on their kinship system from Melland's work published in 1923.[1]

I have taken the Bemba as characteristic of the group, since I have the fullest material on this tribe, which I collected during two visits made in 1930 and 1933 respectively.[2] The Lamba were described by

---

[1] F. W. Melland, *In Witch-bound Africa*, 1923.

[2] I summarize here information contained in my 'Mother-right in Central Africa' in *Essays presented to C. G. Seligman*, 1936; *Land, Labour and Diet in Northern Rhodesia*, 1939; *Bemba Marriage and Modern Economic Conditions*, Rhodes–Livingstone Institute Paper No. 3, 1940; and an essay in *African*

Doke in 1931, but there is no information on the Lala, to the best of my knowledge.[1]

Bisa inhabit the Mpika district of north-eastern Rhodesia, and also some of the islands and adjacent mainland in the Lake Bangweulu area. These peoples have not been fully described. I visited the Bangweulu swamps in 1934 for a period of six weeks. Brief as my visit was, it enabled me to establish the fact that the kinship system of these people was more matrilineal in emphasis than that of the Bemba, whom they resemble very closely in other ways. I did not visit the Bisa settled farther to the east of the plateau.

Economic Determinants

The peoples of this group are poor in economic resources compared to those of the lower Congo. Their material culture is less developed and they have been in contact with Europe for a shorter period. The soil on which most of them live is poorer and the crops which they grow, mainly finger-millet, sorghums, and maize, have not yet been developed on a commercial basis and provide little by way of money income. Most of these people are shifting cultivators, moving their villages every four to seven years. Bemba, Lala, and Lamba are sparsely distributed over bush land with little or no shortage of land for cultivating. The Bemba population per square mile was reckoned as 3·65 in 1934. Tsetse-fly prevents the keeping of stock, except for occasional goats. There is thus practically no inheritable wealth amongst these peoples, either in the form of land, stock, or money, and this fact naturally influences profoundly the nature of their residential and kinship groups.

The Bisa, Ushi, and Unga, on the other hand, live in the Bangweulu swamps where cultivable land is scarce and where fishing-rights in the lake and the main river are valuable, and considerable trade in fish has been developed under modern conditions.

I think more exhaustive researches will show that some of the variations in the family structure of the swamp peoples are due to these differences in economic resources.

Ideology and Principles of Descent

According to Bemba dogma, blood passes through the woman and not through the man. The semen merely activates the foetus in the womb. Directly associated with this theory of procreation is the Bemba stress on the ties of a man with his sister 'born of the same womb' and her children, his uterine nephews and nieces. In the royal clan it is the duty of each woman to produce as many children as she can to succeed

Political Systems, 1940. My data on the Bisa and other swamp peoples have not yet been published.

[1] C. W. Doke, *The Lamba*, 1931.

her brothers, irrespective of the status of their fathers, and she is allowed, and even expected, to bear children by a series of lovers in order to carry on the line.[1] An ancestress is remembered by the number of children she bore, and even the consort of a princess, who is not a member of the royal clan at all, may appear as an important figure in tribal legend if he was the begetter of many children for the royal house.

With this theory of unilateral descent is associated the dogma of matrilineal guardian spirits attached to land. But guardian spirits of either line are attached to individuals. Ancestors enter the womb of a pregnant woman and become the guardian spirit of the baby to be born, and such ancestors may be of either sex. An interesting index of the differing patrilineal-matrilineal balance within the royal dynasty and outside it is the fact that in the case of commoners the guardian spirit may belong to the father's or mother's line, whereas in the royal clan it is the maternal ancestors and ancestresses only who return to act as guardians to the child. In the case of both commoners' and chiefs' matrilineages the injured spirits of the father's line may return to afflict the living with punishment, and the curse of the father or the father's sister is specially feared.

The child belongs to his mother's totemic clan (*mukoa*) and with this clan membership go rights of hospitality, blood compensation, reciprocal funeral offices within paired clans,[2] forms of greeting and joking relationships, and exogamy rules. The child also acknowledges ties of some kind with his father's clan, of which he will readily give the name when asked. The children of men who belong to the royal clan naturally try to stress their links with their father rather than their mother and are given special titles as 'sons of chiefs'. Children take their father's personal name, not their mother's.

The Bemba also reckon membership of a matrilineage or 'house' (*ŋanda*). This is a loosely organized group reckoning its descent from an ancestress 3 or 4 generations back in the case of a commoner, 13 or 20 generations in the case of hereditary court officials, and 25 to 30 in the case of the paramount chief himself. This matrilineage is composed of a man, his brothers and sisters, his sisters' sons and daughters, and the sons of his mother's sisters, and his mother and her sisters and brothers. The 'house' is not a local unit nor is it corporate in the sense of owning property in common or accepting common authority, but it is a group

---

[1] Note that among the Mayombe, with their corporate matrilineages, it is thought to be the duty of all women to produce as many children as possible for their brothers, whereas the insistence is only strong in the case of the royal women among the Bemba, and it is only the ruling dynasty that can be reckoned as a corporate matrilineage in any sense of the word. M. G. Marwick tells me that among the Cewa children were merely desired as providing future workers and as making for more stable marriages.

[2] Cf. my 'Reciprocal Clan Relations', *Man*, xxxvii, 1937, pp. 188–93.

in which positional succession is reckoned and which provides wives in the case of a default in the marriage contract. The authority of the genealogical senior of a 'house' is now of a rather tenuous kind. His word carries the preponderating weight in matters concerning marriage and other family affairs. He is summoned on all ritual occasions. Formerly he could sell members of the matrilineage into slavery.

The rules of succession follow the common matrilineal pattern. A man is succeeded by his brother, sister's son, or sister's daughter's son; and a woman theoretically by her sister, but actually by her uterine granddaughter.[1] I have not sufficient data to show clearly the span of the matrilineage which acts as the succession unit, but most genealogies of commoners are reckoned to a depth of three to four generations only, and the succession of brothers and classificatory brothers appears to take place within this unit.[2]

Succession to the chieftainship is only a special case of the characteristic 'positional succession' (*ukupyanika*) of the Bemba by which the social status and kinship position of each dead person, man or woman, is passed on to a selected heir or heiress. A successor must be found to acquire the guardian spirit of a person recently dead, and the bow of the man or the girdle of the woman, and to be addressed by the name of the dead and by the same kinship terms. In the case of an important man, the name of the departed will be regularly used by the successor, but where the dead man is a nonentity the name lapses, although fellow villagers will remember, if asked, which name has been 'eaten'.[3]

The inheritance of personal property is not an important determinant of kinship sentiment among the Bemba, since most possessions are perishable and the dead man leaves little more than his hereditary bow, the use of a house which will decay in a few years, or the produce of gardens that are soon to lapse into bush. Succession to office and positions of authority and the right of access to ancestral spirits are the significant links between one generation and another. Bemba succeed either to a position in a ruling dynasty or to the social status a commoner has acquired for himself by his individual efforts during the course of his lifetime. It is not the title of head of a clan or lineage that is inherited, but the particular individual status to which each man or woman has attained, and I found in fact that the names of insignificant people were quickly forgotten, whereas those of eminent men or mothers of large families were remembered for some generations.

---

[1] A daughter cannot succeed her mother or she would become the social equivalent of her father's wife.

[2] Cf. W. V. Brelsford, *The Succession of Bemba Chiefs*, 1944, and my essay in *African Political Systems*, 1940.

[3] Such a form of 'positional' succession appears to exist also among the Lamba (see Doke, op. cit.), as well as the Cewa and the Yao.

The Marriage Contract

By the Bemba marriage contract the man gives a series of small payments and a contribution to the initiation ceremony of his bride. He also works for his parents-in-law for an indeterminate period of years. The payments given by a bridegroom were, and are, small in relation to the high marriage payments for the Kongo area. They consisted of one or more barkcloths or some hoes in the old days and anything from 5s. to 10s. nowadays. £3 would be considered a very large payment.[1] Under modern conditions a bridegroom who is away working at the mines sends back money specifically 'to cut the trees for his father-in-law' if he cannot do the years' service.

Through his services the husband acquires various rights over his wife and children. In the first months of the marriage the girl merely sweeps his house and performs small services for him. Later she sleeps in his hut until the time of puberty when she is withdrawn until her initiation ceremony has been completed and the formal consummation of the marriage has taken place. The husband henceforth has complete sex rights over his wife, except in the case of the consort of a royal princess, and the penalties for adultery were very severe in the old days. A husband also has the right to the labour of his wife and she has very rarely a separate granary of her own, although she distributes the grain in the family granary. This is a male dominant society and, even though descent is reckoned through the mother, the wife is very much under the control of her husband even while he is an outsider in his wife's village.

The wife's parents give the son-in-law a series of 'gifts of respect' in the form of food, and these acts of politeness are very much valued and mark the different stages of his acceptance as a permanent son-in-law. Finally the rite known as the *kuingishya* or 'the entering in of the son-in-law' is performed, and by this ritual act the last in-law taboos are removed and the young man is definitely accepted as a member of his wife's *lupwa*—her family or group of closely related kinsmen. Paradoxical though it may seem, once the young man is admitted to the family he is free to remove his wife and children to his own village should he desire to do so. It is for this reason that I have described the marriage contract as marriage with delayed right of bride removal. The right is not always exercised, as some young husbands may have settled happily in their wives' village and wish to remain there. I did not make any quantitative estimate of the conversion rate of such marriages among the Bemba, but Barnes and Mitchell give the figure of 36 per cent. for the conversion of such marriages amongst the Lamba.[2]

[1] T. Cullen-Young in fact uses the term 'token-transfer marriages' of this type of union. See his 'Tribal Admixture in Nyasaland', *J. Roy. Anthrop. Inst.* liii, 1933, pp. 1–18; cf. also my *Bemba Marriage and Present Economic Conditions.*
[2] J. Barnes and C. Mitchell, *The Lamba Village: a Report of a Social Survey,* 1946.

Q

I should think it likely that the Bemba conversion rate is very much higher since the power of the father is stronger in this area.

Once the husband has been admitted to the wife's family he acquires various subsidiary marriage rights. He can, for instance, ask for his wife's sister in marriage and he gives no service to his father-in-law in respect of this union. On the other hand, even when he has removed his wife to his own village she will not necessarily be a permanent member of that group. She will probably return to her own people on the death of her husband or even when she has ceased child-bearing. Her husband's brother can inherit her if that is what she wishes; this is by no means considered a right, but rather something that may be a convenient arrangement for her support.

It will be seen that the marriage relationship in this area is one that is progressively established. A man builds himself a hut in his wife's village and lives there for four or five years or even longer. During this time he is gradually being made free to join in the activities of his wife's relatives by a series of ritual acts which bring to an end the taboos that kept him apart from his in-laws; but Bemba marriage in its early stages has many of the elements of a trial or temporary union. A bridegroom will leave his wife's village during the early stages of marriage if he does not think he is being treated with respect, and in this case no formal act of divorce seems to be necessary; Bemba divorce in the old days did not, in any case, involve the return of token payments or damages for services given. A man's parents-in-law might also refuse him the right to remove his wife and her children to his own village after three or four years' residence, and the wife herself occasionally refuses to follow her husband because she does not want to leave her own family. It is only in the case of a successful marriage, where the man has proved himself a good husband and son-in-law and has produced children, that he gains the right to remove his bride to a community of his own choosing, either to that of his mother's brother or even to that of his father or, in the case of a middle-aged man, to set up a village of his own.

Domestic Authority

Authority over Bemba children is divided between the father and the mother's brother. The maternal uncle formerly had rights of life and death over his sister's children, and could sell them into slavery or use them in payment of a blood debt incurred by a member of the matrilineage. He can still intervene in matters of marriage and can claim part of the girl's marriage payment. He still sometimes removes his sister's daughter from her husband and marries her to someone else to whom he owes obligation. But the father has authority over the children during their youth and can maintain this authority if he is a man of personality, birth, and status. Thus a chief will be able to keep his sons as well as his maternal nephews with him and will give some of them headmanships. It might be said in fact that all members of the royal clan contrive to gain control over their children as against the authority of their mother's brother.

A father is always consulted about the marriage of his daughter even if he has been divorced from her mother some time previously, and he can claim part of any marriage payment made for her.

The avunculate seemed to me to be much more strongly developed among the Bisa and other Bangweulu tribes, and this also seems to be the case among the Cewa according to Marwick. It occurred to me that this might be correlated with the absence of a strong centralized government and a ruling clan, and I was therefore interested to hear an educated Bemba volunteer the statement: 'The father is stronger amongst the Bemba than the Bisa. It is a matter of chieftainship. Members of the crocodile clan always try to get hold of their own sons as well as their sisters' sons.' Is there a correlation between divided authority, as between the father and mother's brother, and the existence of social differentiation and a hierarchical political system? It is a suggestion which needs testing in other areas.

Apart from the powers a man is able to gain over his wife and children as distinct from those of the mother's brother, every Bemba who establishes a permanent marriage builds up his authority in a variety of other ways. To begin with he gains, as a grandfather, what he loses as a father. The Bemba bridegroom starts his married life as a stranger in his wife's village, but since his daughters remain with him for some years after marriage he builds up a grand-family composed of his daughters, their husbands, and their children. In some cases he is able to persuade his sons-in-law to remain permanently with him, while in others he is even able to keep his sons in his own village. In time some of his sisters' sons, with their wives, will choose to come and settle with him, so that he will be head of a group of rather heterogeneous composition.

Residential Units

It will be seen that the basic domestic unit of the Bemba is a matrilineal extended family of the father-daughter type, that is to say, a group composed of a man, his wife, his young married daughters, and their husbands and children. This extended family is composed of separate parental families housed in huts in the same village and not fenced off in any way from the rest of the community; but it must be reckoned as forming one domestic unit, since the daughters' households are closely linked with those of their mother. When a young couple are married they have no garden or granary of their own for some years and the girl is not even allowed her own fireplace for a year or two. During the interval, cooking is done at her mother's house and dishes are supplied to her husband as he sits in the men's shelter. After the girl has been given her fireplace, much joint cooking will still be done and the gardens of mother and daughter will be made near to each other.

From some points of view the Bemba extended family might be described as patriarchal, since the authority of the grandfather over the little group of dependent households is so very marked. It is true that, according to Bemba theory, the important tie is the one between mother and daughter. If the father is dead, or divorced, the mother will live with her married daughters and her sons-in-law and will form a domestic unit as regards cooking and gardening; but where the father is alive, and the marriage has been stable for many years, he is very obviously the head of the grand-family. The house is described as his and not hers. He selects garden sites and supervises the work of his sons-in-law. The latter are described sometimes as 'working for their father-in-law' and sometimes as 'cutting trees for their mother-in-law'. It seems to depend on the relative social status and personality of the man and the woman concerned. But it is certain that the position of a Bemba grandfather is one that gives great power and authority and is in some respects more enviable than that of the grandfather in a typical patrilineal Bantu community, since the head of a Bemba grand-family has established his rule by individual effort and not through the help of his brothers or his patrilineage. The status of head of the grand-family is reflected in the spirit world. The names of maternal grandfathers are remembered in prayers as well as those of maternal uncles, by men as well as women, even though, as will be realized, these two belong by rule of descent to different clans. A man prays to his own ancestors on occasions of family affliction and in some cases he addresses those of his wife as well.[1]

The extended family is rendered an even more stable unit when cross-cousin marriage has taken place. Both types of cross-cousin marriage are practised in Bemba society, but I think the marriage of a man's daughter with his sister's son is the most common. Such a marriage brings into the village sons-in-law who are not strangers, but are closely identified by descent with the leading men of the group.

Though the father-daughter family is the basic domestic unit, it may exist in a number of different residential units since, as is common in matrilineal societies, there are several alternative forms of marriage. Chiefs or members of the royal clan send payments to their wives' parents for the cutting of their gardens and do not give service. Their superior status enables them to remove their brides to their own villages immediately. It is common in such cases for the girl's mother to move

---

[1] Ancestral spirits are of course associated with districts, and where a man is still living with his wife's family she or her brother tend to conduct the prayers. Where, however, a man has removed his family to his own village he may pray to his own and his wife's ancestors as I have described.

with her to the chief's village so that the son-in-law mother-in-law pattern is set up, but in other cases the girl goes alone to marry, and this is what would be described as a typical viri-local marriage. Polygyny, however, raises difficulties in this as in other matrilineal societies. Among the Bemba the second marriage is usually viri-local. Only very occasionally do the two wives live at separate villages with their own people, as is the case in parts of Nyasaland and the Congo. A man who marries a widow also generally has the right of immediate bride removal and the payment in goods and service is usually very small in such cases; but whatever variation there may be in the form of marriage, by the time the third generation has appeared some form of the father-daughter family exists.

The basic political unit of the Bemba is a village (*Umushi*) with a nuclear father-daughter grand-family and its numerous accretions. In some cases there are two or more of such nuclear households. A Bemba village comes into being when a man has sufficient dependants to warrant his asking his chief for permission to set up a new community; but the headmanship is hereditary and with the passage of years two or three grand-families, with their dependent households, become recognizable, and the village may have two or three cores.

The principles of accretion to the nuclear household are numerous. The headman's sister will very generally live with him if she is divorced or widowed or tired of married life. In any of these cases she will usually bring to live with her a few of her married daughters and in some cases her sons. The headman may also support some of his wife's relatives, or even his brother's wife.

From figures collected by Barnes and Mitchell in sixteen Lamba villages, 60·5 per cent. of the villagers were attached to the headman by matrilineal ties; 11·8 per cent. were more distant connexions; 19·7 per cent. were affinal relatives, and 8·2 per cent. connexions of different kinds.[1] It would be roughly true to say that the more important and popular a man is, the more different relatives he is able to attract to live with him, although a large village of this type, composed of more distant relatives, is likely to split into separate villages with the death of the headman in question. It must be remembered too that Bemba villages are rebuilt every four to five years, and each shift of the village site provides an opportunity for a change in the composition of the community. The more casually associated households drift away and join up with other senior relatives. The diagram on p. 230 makes some attempt to illustrate the different principles of association in a Bemba village.

It will be seen that the basic ties in the Bemba family are those of a woman with her daughters. This group of women co-operate closely in domestic activities for many years. Whereas the Mayombe girl

[1] Op. cit., p. 41.

changes residence from her mother's household to that of her maternal uncle and finally to that of her husband, the Bemba girl tends to remain with her own mother and sisters for a large part of her life. The Bemba girl is also closely associated in interest with her own brother, who will be her natural supporter in the first years of her married life and if she becomes divorced or wishes to leave her husband. The brother also shares with her husband control over her children as

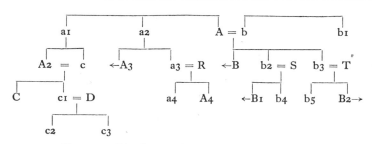

DIAGRAM II. Composition of a Bemba *Umushi*

A is a youngish headman living with two married daughters b_2 and b_3 and their husbands S and T and children and his wife's unmarried sister b_1. His son B had left to marry elsewhere. A's widowed sister a_2 lives with him with her married daughter a_3 and the latter's husband R and their children. His eldest sister a_1 is dead, but the latter's son A_2, and his married daughter c_1 and her husband D and children, have come to join A. Thus this village is composed of members of the clan of the headman A and that of his wife b. A_2 is his probable successor and heir.

has been described. The Bemba boy, in distinction, has few economic or residential links with his brothers, since the boys of one family tend to marry women in other villages and to go and live there. It is only when two brothers both decide to bring back their wives to the village of their mother's brother in later life that the two will be members of one village, and I do not remember a case in which this happened during my visit. The boy is linked with his mother's brother by the ties of matrilineal descent and the possibility of future succession. It is also possible that he may inherit his mother's brother's wife. He is afraid of his maternal uncle's authority and views him with much greater reverence than his father. However, there are few economic links between a man and his mother's brother and a boy is not attracted to the latter's village by the hope of inheriting cattle or land there, as is the case in the Congo and probably Nyasaland.

(Type B2) The Yao-Cewa Group

The kinship system of the matrilineal peoples of Nyasaland is very similar to that of their Northern Rhodesian neighbours, but the avunculate seems to be much more strongly developed and there are some interesting differences in the composition of the local group. Hence my decision to classify the Yao and Cewa as a separate sub-type.

Preliminary accounts of the social organization of the Yao were published by Stannus and Johnson in 1922.[1] Mr. Clyde Mitchell, of the Rhodes–Livingstone Institute, is at present at work on the Yao and I quote from his preliminary reports.[2] Mr. Max Marwick has also been working recently among the Cewa in the south-west corner of the Fort Jameson district and gives me permission to quote from an unpublished report.

Both the Yao and the Cewa differ from the Bemba in their lack of hierarchical forms of chieftainship and ruling dynasties. The Yao were scattered by the Ngoni from 1864 to 1870 and again by punitive raids of the British Administration during the anti-slave campaign from 1891 to 1895. The Cewa were even more dispersed. Both tribes seem to consist of a series of largely autonomous villages or groups of villages under the overriding rule of a chief.

The Nyasaland peoples form quite a marked contrast from an economic point of view also. The Yao were formerly great traders and were in contact with Arabs for some 200 years before the advent of the British. Their territory, mainly in the Liwonde, Fort Johnston, and Zomba districts, is accessible to the railway, making it possible for them to develop the sale of cash crops, and Mitchell gives figures of the annual average income from the sale of tobacco in two districts in 1943–4 as £4. 13s. 10d.[3] Wealthy individuals can make as much as £60 a year. This figure would be thought high in Bemba villages, where the rough estimate of yearly cash income that I made in one village during 1934 was about £2. Cattle are not numerous in the Liwonde district east of the Shire river where Mitchell has been working. Cattle have been kept by the Cewa described by Marwick for the last twenty to thirty years, although they are less wealthy than the Yao in other ways, and live too far from the railway to make it profitable for them to grow cash crops.

Another striking difference is the much greater population density in the Nyasaland area. Mitchell quotes a figure of 53·4 per square mile for the Yao as against 3·7 amongst the Bemba and 1·63 in some of the Bisa areas. In some of the Cewa districts there seems to be considerable land shortage. Marwick gives a figure of over 19 per square mile for the area with which he is concerned.[4] Both the type of cultivation and the land situation may account for the greater permanence of the Yao and

[1] H. Stannus, *The Wa-Yao of Nyasaland*, Harvard African Studies, 1922, and W. P. Johnson, *Nyasa the Great Water*, 1922.

[2] See J. C. Mitchell in 'The Village Headman', *Africa*, xix. 2, April 1949, and 'An Outline of Social Organisation of the Yao of Southern Nyasaland', in *Seven Tribes of Central Africa*, to be published shortly.

[3] Admittedly only a small proportion of the population here grows tobacco.

[4] R. H. Fraser, 'Land Settlement in the Eastern Province of N. Rhodesia', *Rhodes–Livingstone Institute Journal*, No. 3, June 1945.

Cewa villages, which in its turn influences the type of kinship tie developed in the local group. It is true that new villages hive off from the old amongst the Nyasaland peoples, but Mitchell states that many settlements have a history of thirty years in one place and of five generations of hereditary headmen. This must be compared with an average life of four or five years for the Bemba village with three generations of headmen at the most. It would seem, therefore, that the Yao have far more inheritable possessions than the Bemba, including valuable garden sites, house sites, houses, and money, while the Cewa have cattle to leave to their descendants as well.

A Yao belongs to his mother's clan. These clans have a name (*lukosyo*). They were formerly exogamous, but are so no longer. They are now widely dispersed and seem to fulfil few important sociological functions in the present-day life of the people. Clan names are pronounced after sneezing, and there was evidently some recognition of kinship between immigrant Yao bearing the same clan names as resident Nyanja, since the *lukosyo* name was used by the Yao as a means of claiming help.

Within the clan the Yao distinguish major matrilineages or houses known as *mawele* (sing. *liwele*) (breasts) or *milango* (doorways). These groups trace descent from a founding ancestress (*lipata, likolo*). They are similar to the 'houses' of the Bemba, but each house reckons seniority according to the position of its founding ancestor or ancestress and is described as being 'of the large breast' or 'of the small breast' respectively.

The effective descent group is the *mbumba*, a small unit consisting, in theory at least, of a group of sisters and their children under the leadership of their eldest brother.[1] The *mbumba* traces its descent to a common grandmother or great-grandmother, but apparently the matrilineage rarely has a greater depth than four generations. Succession to office follows matrilineal rules. A man is succeeded generally by his eldest sister's son and not by his brother. The most important type of succession is to the semi-autonomous and more or less permanent headmanships, which are coveted positions giving a man the right to rule over a group of his married sisters and their descendants. The installation ceremonies for headmen in this area are much more elaborate than those found among the Bemba, where the most important ritual of this kind centres round the installation of chiefs of the ruling dynasty, and this fact reflects the greater importance and permanence of the Yao headmanships. The people also practise a form of positional succession similar to that of the Bemba. Property is inherited by sisters' sons apparently.

Clan membership among the Cewa presents some differences since the *viwongo* or clan names are now inherited patrilineally as the result of Ngoni influence, although lineage descent and succession are matrili-

[1] Bemba use the word *bumba* for any group of kinsfolk who are under the leadership of a senior man.

neal as among the Yao. Further details on the functions of the Cewa clan are not available.

The marriage contract differs from that of the Bemba in that the ceremonial is less protracted and elaborate. Amongst the Yao the exchange of presents between the two families is insignificant and the bridegroom is not obliged to make gardens for his father-in-law. He merely makes a garden for his own wife, and these services do not entitle him to remove his bride to his own village in the majority of cases. Mitchell states that two types of marriage are recognized by different names: *kulombela*, or marriage without removal of the bride, and *kulowosya*, or marriage with immediate removal; but he suggests that the latter form only takes place in the case of the marriage of a headman. Transfer marriages also occur when a man succeeds to a position of headmanship and is obliged to leave his wife's village.

A significant feature of Yao marriage is the importance of the four 'sureties' or witnesses of the contract—senior and junior representatives of the husband's and wife's matrilineage respectively. These sureties, who watch over the success of the marriage and adjudicate in cases of dispute or divorce, seem to be a sign of the much more corporate nature of the Yao matrilineage as compared to that of the Bemba.

Among the Cewa, service is given to the parents-in-law for a year or so, as occurs in Bemba country. Native authorities have recently tried to enforce a marriage payment of 30s. to be given to the witnesses of a marriage, usually the mother's brother (*tsibweni*) or the brother of the girl, in order that claims may be made in the case of adultery; but the practice is not often followed and this group of Cewa reject the Ngoni custom of giving bride-wealth, here described as *ciwololo*, since this would give the father control over the children of the marriage. In fact they refuse *ciwololo* in the case of a marriage between a Ngoni man and a Cewa woman. The Cewa headman is allowed to remove his bride immediately at marriage. The commoner can remove his wife to his own village at the end of a year's service and after the birth of one or two children, as among the Bemba, but it is not clear how frequent these conversion marriages are.

In both these tribes the degree of incorporation of the son-in-law is never so great as amongst the Bemba apparently. Mitchell says that unsuitable husbands are dismissed with compensation and sent away. He adds that the husbands of the women of a village are often away visiting and are definitely not reckoned as members of the community. Stannus states that a widower is usually given a present with the suggestion that he go elsewhere since he no longer has any standing in his wife's village. Marwick indicates that Cewa marriage ties sit loose and speaks of a man and his sister and 'her current husband'.

The Cewa talk of the father as a stranger. 'He is as a beggar; he has simply followed his wife.' At divorce he leaves his wife's village with his hoe, his axe, and his sleeping-mat and has no right to any of the children of the marriage, even if he may have begotten as many as seven children.

The authority of women seems to be higher in Nyasaland than in Northern Rhodesia. Johnson notes that in Yao villages 'the woman head of the family is the main outstanding person',[1] and Mitchell speaks of women acting as heads of hamlets composed of their daughters and the latter's children, or of two sisters with their children. This would be an unusual phenomenon in Bemba society and may possibly be correlated with the fact that men have always tended to be absent for long periods in the year, as Mitchell points out, formerly raiding or trading and now doing wage labour. Nevertheless a woman and her children, or a group of sisters and their children, are normally under the authority of their eldest brother, who is the *asyene* or owner of their *mbumba*, which Mitchell translates as 'sorority group'. He is referred to by a special kinship term by his sisters and younger brothers and definitely treated as the head of a group of siblings. As a young man the eldest brother probably lives in his wife's village, but later in life he may succeed to the headmanship of his sisters' village and live with them and their married daughters. The head of the *mbumba* settles disputes between members of the group, represents his sisters in a court case, pays their fines, makes decisions as to the marriage of his sisters' sons and daughters, and pays for diviners in the case of illness. In the old days he presumably had the right to sell his sisters' children into slavery, as in other parts of Central Africa, and Johnson states that a man might choose one of his sisters' sons to live with him from the age of 8 or 9 if he wanted to do so. The Cewa *tsibweni*, or mother's brother, under present conditions has the duty of correcting and punishing his sisters' children, whom their father, in theory at any rate, should never beat. He is also responsible for sending them to school. He can get his maternal nephews to herd his cattle for him, and they are glad to do so because they hope one day to inherit these cattle. So far the duties of the maternal uncle of the Yao and the Cewa do not differ very much from those of the. mother's brother in Bemba society, but primogeniture is evidently much more marked amongst the Nyasaland peoples. The eldest brother amongst the Bemba is not distinguished linguistically from his juniors and is not regarded specifically as head of a group of siblings. He may succeed to his mother's brother's position and so become the head of a house, and possibly also of a village, but if he does not so succeed I do not think he is regarded as having specific powers or rights over his brothers and sisters.

The rights and duties of the Yao father have not yet been clearly described. Johnson says that a boy remembers his obligations to his father, 'but this is often from a good feeling of pity or of family regard' rather than from duty.[2] It is clear, however, that some fathers become

---

[1] Johnson, op. cit., p. 68.   [2] Ibid., p. 87.

heads of large households, and achieve considerable domestic authority over their wives' children, although not, of course, ultimate control over their destinies. In the old days the head of a polygynous family with incorporated slaves must have wielded authority over a domestic unit of considerable size. But even under present conditions it seems that whenever a marriage relationship has been maintained for a number of years and daughters have been born, have married and produced children, some kind of father-daughter grand-family of the Bemba type is bound to appear, and a middle-aged Yao who is the father of married daughters probably achieves much the same position as that of a Bemba father and grandfather. The difference, apparently, is that this grand-family is less permanent amongst the Nyasaland peoples, since it falls to pieces immediately the father or the mother dies, and the children and grandchildren then return to their own matrikin. There is also a linguistic distinction which indicates the different emphasis: a Bemba son-in-law is said to be working for his father-in-law, whereas the Cewa is said to be working for, or living with, his mother-in-law.

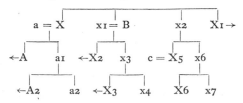

DIAGRAM III. The formation of Yao *Mbumba*

X lives with two married sisters, $x1$ and $x2$, and their married daughters, $x3$ and $x6$. X, $x1$, and $x2$ represent one *mbumba*. As $X2$ grows up he assumes the guardianship of $x3$ and $x6$ thus making another *mbumba*. The residential group here consists of X, his sisters and their married daughters together with X's wife a and her married daughter, $a1$.

Cross-cousin marriage between a man $X2$ and his mother's brother's daughter $a1$ will keep $X2$ in the group in which his sisters live.

In the case of a senior brother who is selected for the position of head of a sororal family, he takes his wife with him and marriage therefore becomes viri-local. The head of a Yao village of this sort thus has authority over his wife's children and over those of his sisters, but the position of the wife's children seems to be clearly differentiated from that of the sisters' children, and Mitchell speaks of a traditional hostility between them. I never saw evidence of such hostility in Bemba villages, which also often contain a man's children and his sisters' children.

Both Yao and Cewa villages can contain a number of extraneous units. Johnson speaks of settlements composed of kinsmen, incorporated refugees, traders, and slaves, and Mitchell shows the number of separate sororal families which are to be found in a village of long standing. Marwick describes a village as possibly combining several groups composed of the married daughters and one or two sons of an old woman, dead or alive, and additional extraneous simple families attracted to the village for economic reasons.

The matrilineal system of Nyasaland therefore differs from those of north-eastern Rhodesia in the greater strength of the brother-sister group, the more pronounced avunculate exercised by the eldest brother in a society in which primogeniture is emphasized, and the growth of villages round a sororal extended family core rather than round a father-daughter grand-family. The ceremonial of marriage is less protracted, the services demanded of a son-in-law less severe, and marriage ties sit looser. Conversion marriages are common among the Cewa, but rarer, apparently, among the Yao. It is probable that the ties uniting members of the matrilineage are strengthened in these areas by the greater shortage of land, the greater permanence of villages, which are usually based on matrilineal ties, and the presence of inheritable wealth in the form of money, houses, and cattle; but full studies of land tenure and property inheritance have not yet appeared.

(Type C) The Ila Type

The Ila-speaking peoples of the Kafue river basin in Northern Rhodesia form the fourth distinguishable type of kinship organization in Central Africa. It is a system which is described as matrilineal since clan membership is reckoned through the mother, and the avunculate is strong, but there is some evidence that the individual belongs to double descent groups, one patrilineal and the other matrilineal; succession and inheritance may take place from the father as well as the mother's brother and in the ancestral cult the patrilineal ancestors have precedence. The man gives a high marriage payment in the form of cattle, which entitles him to remove his bride to his own village immediately and to maintain considerable authority over his sons, who remain living with him after their marriage, and who invariably inherit at least some of his cattle.

The Ila have linguistic and cultural similarities with the matrilineal peoples of north-eastern Rhodesia and Nyasaland, but they have traditions of origin from the east, and they keep cattle and express many of the ritual attitudes associated with the cattle cult as it is commonly practised among the Eastern and Southern Bantu. They apparently conquered their present territory about 200 years ago. Their history is one of internal warfare and raiding, and they never developed a centralized system of government. They are grouped to-day in a series of small semi-autonomous chieftainships.

The Ila were first described by Smith and Dale in 1922,[1] but have recently been revisited by Dr. Smith, who outlined some further features of their social structure in a paper read at the Royal Anthropological

[1] Smith and Dale, *The Ila-speaking Peoples of Northern Rhodesia*, 1922.

Institute, which he has kindly lent me. The Sala described by Brelsford in 1935 seem to be similar but more markedly matrilineal.[1] The Tonga, on which Dr. E. Colson is working, and the Lenje probably belong to the same group.

Principles of Descent and Succession

A man belongs to his mother's clan (*mukoa*). This is an exogamous unit with members who are dispersed throughout the various territorial divisions. The *mukoa* is associated with legends of origin and a totemic name and taboos. It is also named after its place of origin and prominent ancestors. Its members have certain common rights and duties, such as the payment of blood compensation and the giving of mutual aid, and they are described as taking decisions in the case of the marriages of members. The Ila also recognize allegiance to other descent groups known as *kameko*, amongst these the matriclan of the father and those of the grandfathers.[2]

Spirits from both sides of the family can be re-born in a new child, although one statement shows that a woman's ancestors have the right to be born first and another that a man prefers sons to daughters because he can only be re-born through his sons,[3] while in a third case a child with guardian spirits from both sides of the family is described. Ancestors in both the father's and the mother's line are honoured, and it is expressly stated that 'All the deceased members of a man's family are his *mizhimo*' (family deities).[4] But it is an interesting and unusual feature of Ila ancestral beliefs that though clan membership is reckoned through the mother the ancestral spirits of the father are mainly responsible for the welfare of the children and are appealed to by him. We are told that 'The wife's (spirits) are her own and only to a certain degree of the children, in that they help the father's a little in shepherding and guarding the children.'[5] A man continues to worship his ancestral spirits and a woman hers, and there are separate spots on each side of a hut door for prayers of this sort—a feature not recorded elsewhere in the area.[6]

According to Smith's new material a man also belongs to a local descent group (*lunungu*) which is composed of a man, his sons, and their children, and which therefore might be described as a patrilineage. Hence we get a three- or four-generation local patrilineage which practises the worship of the patrilineal ancestors, which gives rights to the inheritance of some cattle and which is also exogamous, as well as a matrilineal exogamous clan. Smith was also told that women can start their own *lunungu* composed of their daughters and the latter's children

---

[1] W. V. Brelsford, *J. Roy. Anthrop. Inst.* lxv, 1935, pp. 205–15.
[2] Smith and Dale, op. cit., vol. i, p. 295.
[3] Ibid., vol. ii, p. 2.
[4] Ibid., p. 165.   [5] Ibid., p. 173.
[6] Presumably a woman worships her father's spirits or her mother's.

which looks as though there may be local matrilineages as well as patrilineages. This is obviously a matter on which further research is necessary.

Succession to chieftainship follows the matrilineal line amongst the Nanzela group,[1] and Smith gives an instance of a line of descent of twelve chiefs; but there is considerable elasticity in the case of the succession to chieftainships and nothing like a fixed order of succession, as is found amongst the Bemba for instance. Amongst the Bwila a brother's son or sister's son may succeed to the chieftainship, or even an unrelated man chosen by the elders as successor to a vacant post.[2] There seems, however, to be some effort to get a chief from the same clan as his predecessor, and if this is not possible the new chief may take the clan of the old as a courtesy title.

Amongst commoners there is evidently a form of positional succession similar to that amongst the Bemba. It is expressly stated that each man and each woman has an heir 'to eat the name'. The heir is selected after considerable discussion and it is not clear whether he is necessarily a brother or a sister's son. The heir inherits a large proportion of the property but not all, since a dead man's sons, his sisters' sons, and others have a right to a share in the dead man's goods (kukoma).[3]

A characteristic of this type of kinship system is the wide group that shares in the inheritance and the fact that they are called from both sides of the family. Property consists of the dead man's wives, cattle, and formerly, slaves. In some of the divisions made the cattle of a dead man went to his heir, to his younger brothers, to his sons and daughters, and to his sisters' sons. In one case three widows went to the heir, one to the sister's son, and one to the deceased mother's family.

The allocation of cattle as between the different wives of a polygynous household is not described and we do not know whether these herds remain distinct, as amongst some other Bantu peoples, so that the heirs of these herds form a separate subsidiary line of descent as amongst the Swazi for instance.

It is important to note, however, that women can inherit property in their own right and can acquire wealth individually. Foodstuffs are divided between husband and wife on divorce, and a woman can make a private garden or can get cattle from her father, presents from her husband, or a tithe of the cattle obtained as compensation by the husband when she has committed adultery. A woman in fact can become so wealthy that she is chosen as a chief.[4] It may therefore be that a lunungu composed of a man's daughters and their children arises in the case of women who have acquired or inherited cattle which they wish to pass

---

[1] Smith and Dale, vol. i, p. 304.
[2] Ibid., pp. 300, 304, 305; we are even told of a competition to select the best man.
[3] Ibid., p. 303.   [4] Ibid., pp. 380–1.

on to their own children. If this is the case the *lunungu* is in fact a cattle inheritance unit based on inheritance either through a man's sons or, in some instances, through his daughters, and it is distinct from the matrilineal unit of descent, the clan. The inheritance of residence and the inheritance of property in cattle seem, in every case, to take precedence over the clan affiliation.

The Marriage Contract

A *Mwila* pays a substantial sum in bride-wealth. This was formerly composed of mixed goods (blankets, shells, hoes, and cattle). It is now normally paid in cattle and was reckoned as four to five head, or about £12. 15s., in 1922—a high payment, since wages must then have been not more than £1 to £2 a month. By this payment he secures the right to remove his bride immediately to his own village and to possess the children, who remain his in case of divorce, even though by clan membership they belong to their mother's *mukoa*. Because of the bride-wealth, the woman remains the property of the husband's family, and is inherited in the event of her husband's death. Cattle are returned in the case of divorce. They are provided mainly by clan members with some contribution from the patrikin. The *chiko* is returned in the case of divorce, or where the woman proves barren, unless another woman can be provided in her place. The *chiko* cattle are divided amongst an unusually wide group of relatives, mainly the maternal kinsmen. The parents are expressly stated to get a very small share.

Domestic Authority

The question of authority over the children is a complex one. A man could apparently sell his sisters' children into slavery in the old days or use them for blood compensation or plan their marriages. Smith and Dale say: 'If the interests of the clan conflict with those of the family, the former prevail over the latter.'[1] On the other hand, as has been said, the children belong by right of marriage payment to the father and remain with him in the case of divorce. They are associated with him by ties of residence, economic co-operation, and hopes of inheritance.

Residential Unit

The basic domestic unit amongst the Ila is an extended family, composed of a man, his wives, his married sons, and the latter's children, his unmarried children, and his servants and slaves. This extended family has a title—the *mukwashi*. It is separated from the rest of the village houses by a fence, and its members share in economic activities, in particular the care of the joint cattle of the establishment. It is not clear how often the *mukwashi* divides into new groups, but it is

---

[1] Smith and Dale, vol. i, p. 284.

expressly stated that it is 'not large' and a unit of twenty-five was described as unusually big.[1] There is thus an anomalous situation of a typical patriarchal extended family as a basic residential unit of a society with matrilineal descent, and the ties of joint residence and ownership of cattle are recognized to be as strong as, if not stronger than, those of matrilineal descent, common legends of origin, the keeping of taboos and rights of mutual help.

Nevertheless, membership of the clan gives a man a special position in the village from which his mother came and where he has rights of succession, and he is here described as 'a possessor of the land'[2] rather than as 'treading the land of others'. The Ila recognize the difference between the domestic unit under the authority of the father and the descent unit of which the mother's brother is head. 'The clan is your mother's, the family is your father's.'[1]

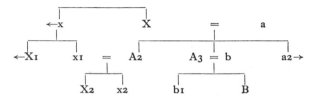

DIAGRAM IV. The Ila *Mukwashi*

X lives with his married sons A_2 and A_3 and the latter's children. He does not live with a member of his own clan unless his son A_2 marries the daughter of his sister x. The children of this union X_2 and x_2 will then be members of his clan; his daughter a_2 marries out.

A man's daughters of course leave the *mukwashi* to marry elsewhere. Men of the *mukwashi* marry women of different clans, and thus the children brought up in the village may belong to a variety of different clans and the residential unit is not based on descent at all. However, cross-cousin marriage with the father's sister's daughter is practised and this will reduce the number of alien clans within the *mukwashi*.[3] It would appear in fact that here, as elsewhere in the area, a cross-cousin marriage obviates some of the difficulties of patriarchal rule combined with matrilineal descent.

It will be seen that the nuclear relationships in this residential unit are those between father and son. A boy is linked with his brothers from his earliest years. He lives with them and shares in the care of the same herd of cattle, and hopes to inherit some of these cattle. He is, however,

---

[1] Smith and Dale, vol. i, p. 284.
[2] Ibid., p. 286.
[3] Miss Mary Tew has pointed out to me that the Ila and the Yao practise opposite types of cross-cousin marriage in conformity with this residential pattern.

dependent on his matrikin for his bride-wealth, and has rights of succession in the village of his mother's brother, where he is 'at home'. He
has a number of rights and obligations associated with his membership
of a matriclan. Girls are identified with the members of their *mukwashi*
by right of residence and are also 'at home' in the village of their mother;
but they live in their husband's village and will usually be inherited by
one of the latter's brothers if they become widows. Thus both boys and
girls have a double allegiance as regards local affiliation and economic
co-operation, and this is reflected closely in the ritual and ideology of
kinship.

I realize that many points in this analysis are of the nature of hypotheses since further data on descent and residential grouping amongst
the Ila-speaking peoples are required. I thought the material worth
including, however, since it shows an extreme case of the variety of
residential pattern which can exist in a society which practises matrilineal
descent, and of the power the father can obtain in such societies. It also
provides an example of a type of social structure in which the principles
of unilineal descent are less important as a basis of grouping than
residential kinship ties.

VARIATIONS IN LINEAGE STRUCTURE

The lineage structures correlated with these types of family system
cannot be fully analysed in the compass of this article and with the
present gaps in our knowledge, but it will be useful to summarize some
of their salient characteristics.

The lineage system of the Mayombe and Kongo could be described
as a segmentary type, using the term in the way that Evans-Pritchard
has employed it in his descriptions of Nuer kinship and political
organization, although there are many irregularities due to the intrusion
of foreign elements.

The Mayombe are divided into nine exogamous matriclans (*mvila*),
of which the members trace descent from a putative ancestress and
remember a common legend of origin. The *mvila* are divided into
major matrilineages (*dikanda*) the members of which trace actual
descent from a common ancestress. Van Reeth shows one such division with a six-generation span.[1] The *dikanda* are associated with
named territorial districts and their members have ultimate rights over
all the land in the district, although each minor matrilineage (*mvumu*)
actually exercises cultivating and hunting rights over its own particular
area. The head of the senior minor matrilineage in each *dikanda* is
recognized as chief (*pfumu dikanda*). Such a man would rule over his
own *mvumu* and others attracted to him, such as immigrant *bivumu* or

[1] Van Reeth, op. cit., p. 4; cf. also De Cleene, *Inst. Roy. Colon. Belge Bull.*
ix, 1938, p. 68.

R

those of slaves. He would take a leading part in councils of lineage elders and is described as forming a centre of political organization in the territory rather than as being its chief.[1]

Disputes over authority and land have apparently led to a further process of division, and the split off of minor matrilineages, the *bivumu*, which trace direct descent from an ancestress, practise exogamy, and own land and property in common in the way that has been fully described.[2]

The Kongo system is similar except that the lineages are of a dual and not a triple order and there is a certain linguistic difference, since the *kanda* are here the exogamous matriclans and the *mvila* the matrilineages. The Kongo clans are arranged in some kind of hierarchy of genealogical seniority as are the matrilineages. There are usually three such matrilineages, known respectively as the children of the eldest sister, those of the middle, and those of the youngest born, but Van Wing records cases of five, seven, and even nine such constituent matrilineages of a clan.[3] The men of the *luvila* may form a village, or two or three may combine, in which case each will obey its own head and keep its own land rights distinct.

In both these sets of tribes a group of brothers and their sisters form a corporate matrilineage accepting the rule of a senior brother. The men and their absent sisters are kept closely united by joint ownership of land and permanent trees yielding a cash income. Where a split occurs and one brother leads off his descendants to form a new *mvumu*, it remains structurally connected with its parent body and with the other *bivumu* in the *dikanda* in which it can claim residual rights to land; it acknowledges the precedence of descendants of genealogically senior ancestresses ruling over other *bivumu*, and accepts the political authority of the head of the senior lineage known as the *dikanda* head, the crowned chief or the senior clan elder.

The Bemba-Bisa system differs widely. Here there is no corporate matrilineage owning property rights in common, and the residential unit is not based on the co-operation of a group of siblings of one sex. The Bemba are divided into forty exogamous totemic clans (*mikoa*) which have the name of an animal or plant, a legend of origin or separation from the parent stock, greetings and praise titles, and reciprocal burial obligations and joking relationships amongst paired clans.[4] Founding ancestresses and ancestors are remembered in the case of the royal crocodile clan and senior clans of which the members claim

---

[1] Nauwelaart, op. cit., 'formant des noyaux de groupements politiques voisinants', p. 406.
[2] The 'sub-clan' of De Cleene and the 'schoot' (literally 'womb') of Van Reeth.
[3] Van Wing, op. cit., p. 119.
[4] Cf. my 'Reciprocal Clan Relationships', *Man*, Dec. 1937.

descent from warriors and councillors who accompanied the first chief
when he occupied Bemba territory some 200 years ago. Otherwise
ancestresses of clans are not remembered with great interest, if they
are called to mind at all.

Clans are arranged in a certain order of precedence and are attached
in people's minds to particular districts which their ancestors first
occupied and where their descendants are still numerous, at any rate
according to the prevailing belief.[1] Clan members still acknowledge
obligations of hospitality and mutual help. Senior clans provide hereditary officials for the chiefs' courts. Where a woman is required to
fulfil a marriage obligation or to perform a ritual act of intercourse, as in
some of the ceremonies connected with chieftainship, she may be sought
within the clan, if there is none suitable within the matrilineage. The
mukoa has no recognized heads except the holders of hereditary offices
at the paramount chief's court, who are heads of matrilineages which
have become established in the vicinity of the Citimukulu's village. These
are sometimes loosely described as 'heads of clans'.[2]

Within the clan there are a number of matrilineages or 'houses'
(*ŋanda*). These are loosely organized groups reckoning descent from an
ancestress 3 or 4 generations back in the case of a commoner, 13 to 20
in the case of a hereditary court official, and 25 to 30 in the case of the
paramount chief himself. The 'house' is not a corporate unit in the sense
that it owns property in common, but it is the unit in which positional
and office succession is reckoned and which provides wives in the case
of a default in the marriage contract. There is no structural inter-
connexion between these small three- to four-generation matrilineages,
and they perform no political functions. It is only the royal dynasty
that acknowledges a common authority and exercises common rights
and privileges.

The Yao clans seem to have survived only as distinguishing names
associated with exogamous rules. They have no local attachment or clan
head. The effective descent group is a corporate matrilineage consisting
of the descendants of a common ancestress who acknowledge the
authority of a senior mother's brother or brothers. Of this group the
married sisters and the eldest brother form the core of a residential
group. These small matrilineages are not structurally inter-connected
in any way.

The Ila are grouped into ninety-three exogamous matriclans (*mikoa*).

[1] I have collected no statistical data on this point, but the connexion is so
clear that I found I was able to guess the probable district from which men came
when I knew their clan.
[2] The Lamba are divided into thirty-two exogamous clans and Doke states
that 'property must remain within the clan' (op. cit., p. 193). The Kaonde are
divided into sixty-two exogamous clans, but their functions are described as
insignificant except for the performance of reciprocal burial rights (Melland,
op. cit.).

These clans form the unit in which blood compensation used to be paid and which still entails obligations of mutual aid and the payment of the bride-wealth of its members. Clan members exercise common rights over fishing-pools and are 'associated in the minds of people with certain localities or places of origin'.[1] They could claim the right to parcels of land in such localities and an eminent member of a *mukoa* could be buried there. But clan members were dispersed throughout the various territorial divisions and exercised no political authority. They performed no joint ceremonial, although they occasionally gave competitive displays at feasts for the exhibition of cattle.

The Ila also recognize another more restricted descent group, the *lunungu*, of doubtful structure which is the unit of succession and ancestor worship.

These units are also exogamous. Dr. Smith's recent account suggests that a man and his sons and their children form such a unit, which would in this case be a patrilineage in a matrilineal society. He also suggests that women may start their own *lunungu* composed of their children. I have suggested elsewhere (p. 239) that these are in reality units of cattle inheritance which have formed themselves in a society in which clan membership is matrilineal, but marriage payments give the right to viri-local marriage, and cattle are left to a man's sons and daughters as well as to his maternal nephews. The *lunungu* are not apparently structurally inter-connected at all.

THE LINEAGE STRUCTURE OF THE SELECTED TRIBES COMPARED

Tribe	Lineage structure	Mechanism of identification	Rights and obligations
TYPE A. LOWER CONGO. *Lineage system with triple segmentation*			
Mayombe	1. Clan (*mvila*)	Name of ancestress. Legend of origin.	Exogamy.
	2. Maj. lineage (*dikanda*)	Name of ancestress. Legend of split off.	Exogamy. Named territory. General territorial rights. Political authority by senior lineage head.
	3. Min. lineage (*mvumu*)	Name of ancestress.	Exogamy. Authority with senior brother. Joint land and property rights. Men form residential unit.

[1] E. W. Smith (unpublished manuscript).

Tribe	Lineage structure	Mechanism of identification	Rights and obligations
	Lineage system with dual segmentation		
Kongo	1. Clan (*kanda*)	Name of ancestress. Legend of split off. Praise-names in archaic language.	Exogamy. Arranged in precedence. Authority over named territory with clan head. Cult of clan ancestors particularly at illness or death.
	2. Lineage (*luvila*)	Name of ancestress. Legend.	Corporate rights as with *mvumu* above. Joint participation in burial rites with other lineages.

TYPE B. N. RHODESIA AND NYASALAND. *Dispersed clan with local 3–4 generation lineages*

Tribe	Lineage structure	Mechanism of identification	Rights and obligations
Bemba-Bisa-Lamba	1. Clan (*mukoa*)	Totem symbol. Legend of origin. Greetings. Food taboos.	Exogamy. Mutual help. Reciprocal burial relationships. Provide chiefs, councillors, and priests.
	2. Min. lineage (*ŋanda*)	Name of ancestress or her brother.	Exogamy. Unit of succession. Unit of wife replacement and blood compensation.
Yao	1. Clan (*lukosya*)	Totemic symbol and name pronounced when sneezing.	Exogamy. *Formerly only.* Name used to claim help.
	2. Maj. lineage (*maŵele*)	Name of founding ancestress.	Recognition of senior and junior lines ('large or small breast').
	3. Min. lineage (*mbumba*)	Name of senior brother or group of siblings.	Brothers, sisters, latter's children under authority of senior brother. Residential group— sisters with selected senior brother.
Cewa	Clan (*ciwengo*)	*Ciwengo* name inherited patrilineally.	Not known.

Tribe	Lineage structure	Mechanism of identification	Rights and obligations
TYPE C. N. RHODESIA			
Ila	Clan (*mukoa*)	Totemic animal. Name of centre. Name of prominent ancestor.	Exogamy. Mutual help. Bride-wealth. Rights of burial in clan centres. Blood compensation. Displays at feasts.
	? Patrilineage (*lunungu*)	Common house.	Residential unit. ? Cattle ownership.

CONCLUSIONS

We have been able to distinguish at least three types of kinship organization among the Central Bantu. In all these tribes the matrilineal system makes for certain elements of conflict for which some kind of solution has to be found. The problem in all such matrilineal societies is similar. It is the difficulty of combining recognition of descent through the woman with the rule of exogamous marriage. Descent is reckoned through the mother, but by the rule of exogamy a woman who has to produce children for her matrikin must marry a man from another group. If she leaves her own group to join that of her husband her matrikin have to contrive in some way or other to keep control of the children, who are legally identified with them. The brothers must divide authority with the husband who is living elsewhere. If, on the other hand, the woman remains with her parents and her husband joins her there, she and her children remain under the control of her family, but her brothers are lost to the group since they marry brides elsewhere and they are separated from the village where they have ‑rights of succession.

There is the further difficulty that in most societies authority over a household, or a group of households, is usually in the hands of men, not women, as are also the most important political offices. Thus any form of uxori-local marriage means that an individual of the dominant sex is, initially at any rate, in a position of subjection in his spouse's village, and this is a situation which he tends to find irksome and tries to escape from.

There are, of course, a number of solutions to the matrilineal puzzle. The first of these may be described as the matriarchal solution, in that property, and particularly houses and lands, pass through the woman as well as the line of descent. The eldest brother usually acts as manager of the estate. This is achieved either by the institution of the visiting husband or by that of the visiting brother. The women of the *taravad* or matrilineal joint family of the Nayar of Malabar live with their brother or brothers and are visited by their husbands at night. In the case of the Menangkabau the men were members of their sisters' joint household (*rumah*) and spent much of the day there, but they returned to their wives' households at night.[1] Among the Hopi the situation is slightly different, in that a group of married women live together and own land and houses jointly, but each husband acts as manager of his wife's land and chief worker on it, while the brother acts as spokesman and ritual officiant for his sisters and as host in their houses.[2]

Such solutions only seem to me to be possible in big settlements with permanent housing, where a man can walk easily from his own household to that of his sisters and perform his two functions without clash. This is the case amongst the Nayar and something similar occurs in the large towns of Ashanti Province in the Gold Coast where a woman visits her husband at night. But Central Africa is much less closely settled. In Northern Rhodesia shifting cultivation is practised, and villages not only move, but are more sparsely distributed, often at a distance of 17 to 30 miles apart. In these circumstances either the wife or the husband may have to live some distance away from the group to which they are legally affiliated. The more densely occupied Yao area allows husbands to be away visiting their own relatives more easily and it appears that they often do so.[3]

The second solution is that of the fraternal extended family with sisters and children 'loaned away'. This is the solution adopted by the Trobriand islanders and the western Congo people. Here viri-local marriage makes it possible for a group of brothers to live together and to exercise full male authority over the community, while their sisters are loaned out to men in other communities and the children of the matrilineage are reclaimed at puberty.

The third solution might be said to be that of the borrowed husband. These are the various forms of uxori-local marriage described in this area. The conflict of interests in these societies is probably the most extreme, since all the men of a community cannot at the same time act as mother's brothers with authority over their own local descent group and also as husbands living in their own wives' villages, as the rule of uxori-local marriage demands. Amongst the Cewa and Yao it seems that the majority of marriages are uxori-local but that marriages are easily broken. A man who cannot stand the situation in his wife's village

---

[1] F. C. Cole, op. cit., pp. 253, 266.

[2] Verbal communication from Mrs. Aitken; cf. also Daryll Forde, 'Hopi Agriculture and Land Ownership', *J. Roy. Anthrop. Inst.* lxi, 1931, pp. 357–99.

[3] Daryll Forde suggests to me that the necessary factor is not the size of the settlement but its compact and endogamous character. A man can act simultaneously as husband and manager-brother where he has married within the same community. Both the size and the endogamous character of the local unit seem to me to be relevant factors.

leaves and goes elsewhere. This might in fact be described as the solution of the detachable husband. Added to this certain senior men have a right from the start to practise viri-local marriage since they are selected as heads of villages or inherit such positions. They thus escape from the difficult position in which their younger brothers are placed. In other words, there is here a stress on primogeniture with viri-local marriage as one of the privileges of the first-born. The Bemba deal with this difficulty by the transfer or removal marriage, by which the young man is dependent on his father-in-law in youth but gains authority as the head of a father-daughter grand-family in his old age; this is a solution which is possible in areas where land is plentiful and the setting up of new homesteads and villages is easy, and where the political system allows of the constant creation of new units.

Still another way out of the difficulty is the solution of the selected heir, which allows the head of the matrilineage to choose one or more of his sisters' children to succeed him and to transfer these boys to his own village while the remaining children are allowed to stop with their father. This seems to be the practice among the Mayombe, according to Van Reeth (see p. 217). Kirchoff quotes the similar custom of the Tlingit by which one or two sons of a woman marry their cross-cousins and go to live with their mother's brother, whereas the rest of the children marry viri-locally. The Nuba often adopt one or two sisters' sons to be brought up as their own sons in the same way.[1]

In every case there are constitutionally recognized alleviations for the socially childless father in these matrilineal societies. Slavery allows him to gain control over the children of slave wives who thus join his clan, and Torday speaks of Kongo fathers choosing slave wives for preference for this reason.[2] Cross-cousin marriages may give the father control over some of his grandchildren that he cannot maintain over his children, or bring into his village members of his clan. By the mother's brother's daughter marriage of the Yao the son of one of the married sisters belonging to the sororal family marries the daughter of the manager-brother and therefore contracts what is virtually a viri-local marriage.

Polygyny and the marriage of widows also allow men to contract at least some viri-local marriages in most of the Central African tribes, and, whatever the rule of descent, a man who has succeeded in becoming the head of a polygynous household is in fact a patriarch over his wives and young children. Lastly men of wealth and distinction are able to reverse the usual rules of residence.

---

[1] P. Kirchoff, 'Kinship organisation', *Africa*, v. 2, April 1932, pp. 184–91; S. F. Nadel, *The Nuba*, 1948, p. 31. This list does not of course exhaust the logical possibilities. The solution of alternating residence among the Dobu has been mentioned already. There is also the separate men's and women's houses of the Ga of the Gold Coast.

[2] E. Torday, *Causeries Congolaises*, p. 103.

Authority over the children of a marriage consists of a series of rights and privileges, and many kinship systems allow for the exercise of different types of authority by different members of the patrikin or matrikin. In Central Africa there may be a fairly complete severance between domestic authority exerted over the children brought up in their father's homestead and rights over their persons and the marriages they contract. These latter may be exerted by a man who lives some distance away. Domestic authority is a treasured asset in an area where local communities grow up round the core of the extended family and the head of such a family is actually or potentially the head of a village, and hence of the unit that is the basis of the whole political structure. On the other hand, this is an area in which slavery was formerly a very prominent institution, and, therefore, whatever hold the father may have gained over his children, the power of the mother's brother to sell them into slavery must have remained as a potential threat to be constantly feared. Even amongst the Ila, where the father is a patriarch ruling over a large polygynous homestead very similar to that found amongst the patriarchal Bantu, Smith and Dale describe the woman's brother as having 'power of life and death' over her children. The right to sell into slavery is apparently the power described.

A balance of rights and duties between the patrikin and the matrikin tends to produce secondary forms of descent. While it would be true to say that in every matrilineal society a man must know his father's clan and get some privileges from his patrikin, there are tribes in which both patrilineal and matrilineal relatives are organized in definite descent groups with names and corporate functions as amongst the Yakö. In Central Africa the existence of such double descent groups does not seem to be proved, but there is a secondary reckoning of descent in those tribes in which the patrilineal-matrilineal balance is most even. Amongst the Kongo the father's matrikin are known by a separate name and a man has sentimental ties with the men of his father's village in which he was brought up, and these informal ties seem to have led to the suggestion that the Kongo practise dual descent.

Ancestor worship also reflects the duality of the reckoning of descent. The Bemba commoner can inherit a guardian spirit from his father's side as well as his mother's, and will pray to his maternal grandfather as well as to his maternal uncle, although this would not be the case in the royal clan. The Ila pray to the ancestors both of the father and of the mother, and Kongo ceremonies honouring the father's ancestors have also been mentioned (p. 214).

In all these forms of family structure the crucial point, I have suggested, is the question of residence at marriage, and the determining factor in this regard is the marriage payment or the type of goods and services which the bridegroom gives. In Central Africa the tribes which give large amounts of goods or money in bride-wealth, as do the

Mayombe and the Ila, seem invariably to practise viri-local marriage; whereas those who give service or token payments, like the Bemba or Bisa, do not. The importance of the marriage payment is shown by the fact that even amongst the western Congo peoples, where the avunculate is most pronounced, a man who gives an unusually large sum to his bride's family is able to gain permanent possession of his wife and to keep her children with him instead of returning them to their maternal uncle at puberty. The passage of cattle as *chiko* amongst the matrilineal Ila is an equally important determinant. The *chiko* gives the father permanent possession of his children and enables him to keep his married sons with him to form the basic residential unit, the *mukwashi*. The division of cattle among his sons and his daughters sets up what seem to be a number of three- or four-generation patrilineages as well as similar groups united through rights of inheritance of cattle from their mother. In Northern Rhodesia there are no high marriage payments and a man cannot remove his wife and children to his village immediately. He may earn the permission to do so through service or joint residence, but he will never acquire complete possession of his wife and children.

As regards the stability of marriage in these different types of family, we have hints and impressions of various kinds but very little accurate quantitative data. The payment of bride-wealth is assumed to encourage a stable marriage since the wife's family is pledged to return cattle or goods received in this way if she breaks her contract. If this assumption is correct, divorce should be rare in the western Congo, where the marriage payments are considerable, but I have no figures to show whether this actually is the case or not. The divorce rate should also be low amongst the Ila, but as a matter of fact Smith and Dale say that it is frequent. It seems clear to me that the size of the bride-wealth and the way in which it is contributed are determining factors but by no means the only ones. Where the avunculate is strong the mother's brother usually has the power to take his sister's daughter away from the husband to whom she has been 'loaned' and give her to another man, and this must be reckoned as at least one of the causes of instability in marriage. It occurs amongst the Mayombe, the Ila, and the Bemba, and probably elsewhere. Moreover, where the residential units are based on ties of kinship through the woman rather than the man, the link between mother and daughter, or sister and sister, may become so strong that it can threaten the marriage of one of these women. Divorces sometimes occur in Bemba society at the time of the conversion of a marriage, that is to say when the husband has won the right to take his wife back to his own village. The woman may refuse to go with him because she wants to stay with her mother and sisters.

There are also positive inducements to permanent marriage. Bemba give token presents not bride-wealth, but a man stands to gain by a stable union because only by this means is he able to build up the basic domestic unit which puts him in a position of authority over several households and enables him to set up house where he wishes and ultimately to build his own village if he pleases. A stable marriage for a Bemba is the first step on the road to a headmanship. It is interesting to correlate different forms of family structure with greater or less stability in marriage in this way, but conclusive answers will have to wait until we have even some rough approximation to the differential divorce rates in these and contiguous areas.

Various economic and social determinants of family structure have been suggested in these pages, though fuller details of the economic organization of all the selected tribes would be required to test the hypotheses made. The presence or absence of inheritable possessions in the form of land, trees, cattle, or money have been correlated with the type of marriage, and the position of the father as against that of the mother's brother. It has also been associated with the corporate nature of a unit like the western Congo matrilineage, as against the dispersed descent groups of the peoples of Northern Rhodesia. It would no doubt be possible to start from the same set of facts and reach very different conclusions. Is it, for instance, the shortage of land and the value of the permanent palm-trees that make members of a matrilineage willing to live together in one closely organized group? Or is it the system of corporate matrilineages which makes them anxious to develop their land together instead of doing so alone, and encourages them to accept the rule of their genealogical head? No doubt there is something to be said from both points of view. Where the type of marriage makes it possible for a group of brothers to live together, an economic situation such as that of the western Congo increases their economic inter-dependence and counteracts centrifugal tendencies. Where, on the other hand, the family structure provides no basis for a group of co-operating men, and where the land supply is so ample that it is possible for men to set up new settlements easily, they do so and the matrilineage loses its corporate function. Detailed studies of contiguous people living in rather similar economic conditions are needed before we can generalize usefully on such questions. At present the variables are too numerous to permit more than likely guesses.

This article merely attempts to make some crude comparisons between four types of family structure associated with the rule of matrilineal descent in Central Africa, and to suggest some possible correlations between marriage type, residential grouping, economic and political organization.

KINSHIP AND MARRIAGE AMONG THE ASHANTI

By MEYER FORTES

INTRODUCTION

THE Ashanti are the most numerous[1] of the Akan-speaking peoples who occupy most of the southern half of the Gold Coast. Though they all speak dialects of a common language[2] and have a common culture, the Akan peoples were never politically united until they all came under the rule of the British colonial government in 1903.[3] Indeed the Ashanti are famous for the wars they fought against other Akan groups and against the British throughout the nineteenth century. During the eighteenth century Ashanti had emerged as a powerful national state consisting of a confederation of strong and semi-autonomous chiefdoms grouped round the kingship whose politico-ritual symbol was the Golden Stool.[4] The basis of this confederacy was war. It was first formed in order to throw off the yoke of Denkyera, an Akan state which held the Ashanti in subjection, and once established, it was strengthened and gradually expanded by wars of conquest against other Akan neighbours.

As the extent and power of the Ashanti confederacy increased, trade with the Europeans on the coast became a vital necessity, especially for the procuring of flintlock guns and ammunition. In attempting to gain control of the trade routes to the coast the Ashanti came into conflict with the coastal Akan, and subsequently with the British who had assumed the protection of the latter. The Ashanti fought six wars against the British. The last was the Ashanti revolt of 1901 which ended in defeat and annexation.

Though it was able to wage external wars with success, the Ashanti State was not internally altogether stable. The great chiefs guarded their regional autonomy jealously against encroachment by the king and this sometimes led to armed rebellion. The king's forces, aided by those of the other great chiefs, always, however, succeeded in suppressing a rebellious chief. The necessity of unity was recognized by the great chiefs of the confederation and had the backing of powerful religious sanctions.

[1] They now number approximately 750,000 people.

[2] See J. G. Christaller, *Dictionary of the Asante and Fante Language*, 2nd ed., Basel, 1933, Introduction.

[3] The standard history of the Gold Coast is W. W. Claridge's *History of the Gold Coast and Ashanti*, 1915. See also W. E. F. Ward, *A History of the Gold Coast*, 1948. The extension of British rule over all the Akan peoples was a gradual process which took half a century.

[4] Cf. R. S. Rattray, *Ashanti*, 1923, chap. xxiii.

The political history and structure of the State decisively influenced the whole social order of Ashanti. The large degree of autonomy reserved by the component chiefdoms of the confederacy led to emphasis on the local allegiance of individuals and groups as opposed to citizenship of the confederacy. Captives and fugitives from defeated tribes, added to slaves obtained by purchase, introduced alien elements into every chiefdom. Sometimes also many of the subjects of a rebellious chief sought refuge in other chiefdoms. And in spite of the legal priority of local allegiance, individuals often emigrated from one chiefdom to another for economic reasons, such as trade, as the result of marriage, for religious reasons, such as the desire to become an adherent of a nationally famous god, and so forth. In these ways kin groups often became dispersed. These influences are reflected in the kinship institutions of the Ashanti.

The main features of Ashanti social and political organization are well known from the ethnographic works of the late Captain R. S. Rattray.[1] Indeed the outlines of the Akan system were known to scholars long before Rattray first described it.[2] As regards Ashanti kinship institutions, in spite of rapid social and cultural change during the past forty years, the principles elucidated by Rattray still prevail.

In this paper I shall give a broad outline of Ashanti kinship organization as it emerges in their social structure to-day. It will be useful to give special consideration to certain aspects which Rattray did not sufficiently stress, in order to correct misinterpretations of Ashanti kinship based on his work. This applies particularly to the view that Ashanti kinship is characterized by the equal recognition of both matrilineal and patrilineal descent.[3]

[1] R. S. Rattray, *Ashanti Proverbs*, 1916; *Ashanti*, 1923; *Religion and Art in Ashanti*, 1927; *Ashanti Law and Constitution*, 1929. The accuracy and insight of Rattray's writings, based as they were on intimate contact with the Ashanti for nearly twenty years and a deep knowledge of their language, are acknowledged by Ashanti chiefs and elders. Dr. K. A. Busia, himself an Ashanti, has paid tribute to the quality of Rattray's data in his (unpublished) thesis on 'The Position of the Chief in the Modern Political System of Ashanti'; and my own inquiries in Ashanti during 1945–6 (vide my paper 'The Ashanti Social Survey: A Preliminary Report', in *Rhodes–Livingstone Institute Journal*, vi, 1948) fully confirmed his judgement.

[2] There is an excellent summary of what was then known of Akan kinship in Frazer's *Totemism and Exogamy*, 1910, vol. ii, pp. 553 ff. It was well known, from the writings of early travellers, that the Akan peoples reckoned descent in the female line. When Frazer wrote the *ntoro* divisions had also already been discovered by Mr. (later Sir) C. H. Harper; cf. reference in Frazer, op. cit.

[3] Cf. e.g. G. P. Murdock, 'Double Descent', *Amer. Anthropologist*, N.S. xlii. 4. 1, pp. 555 ff., who writes, *inter alia*, 'As is now well known, the Ashanti have both matri-sibs (*abusua*) and patri-sibs (*ntoro*).'

MATRILINEAL DESCENT

The Political Aspect

The rule of matrilineal descent, as Rattray made clear,[1] is the key to Ashanti social organization. This is due mainly to the fact that matrilineal descent is the basis of a localized lineage organization which is generalized through the social system as a whole by an organization of dispersed clans.

Every person of free matrilineal descent (an *odehye*) is by birth a member of his mother's lineage (*abusua*) and a citizen of the chiefdom in which this lineage is legally domiciled. A matrilineal descendant of an alien or slave woman is a member by right of birth of the lineage into which that woman was tacitly incorporated,[2] though he is subject to disabilities which not even the lapse of generations can altogether wipe out. Through marriage or, formerly, through flight or falling captive in war, a woman might live and have offspring outside her natal chiefdom. In such a case her matrilineal descendants still retain their connexion with her natal lineage and their rights of citizenship in her natal home, though they can exercise them only by taking up residence there. Dispersal does not deprive members of a lineage of their status, of rights to succeed to office or property vested in the lineage, or of their relationship to the lineage ancestors and gods. Thus one of the most prized rights of citizenship to-day is the right to occupy and farm virgin forest land freely in the chiefdom to which one's lineage owes allegiance. Nowadays it often happens that descendants of women who were captured in war return to their ancestral homes to claim land on this basis. Again, when a stool[3] falls vacant it often happens that a member of a branch of the lineage which has for several generations been resident outside their natal chiefdom is invited to return to take up the office. To the Ashanti themselves a lineage consists of all the descendants of both sexes by a known genealogy of a single known ancestress in the unbroken female line.

The localized matrilineage is found in its most precise and explicit form in those parts of Ashanti which have a tradition of permanent settlement over a long period. Every long-established Ashanti village or township was until recently divided into wards (*brono*), each of which was occupied by the majority of the members, both male and female,

[1] Rattray, 1923, and *passim* in his other works.
[2] As described by Rattray, 1929, chap. v.
[3] A chiefship, lineage headship, or other public office held by a man or a woman is always referred to as a stool (*konnua*). Carved wooden stools play a big part in Akan social life as symbols of office and of status and, duly consecrated, also serve as ancestor shrines. The holder of any public office is installed by being ritually presented to the ancestors of the group in the room which houses the ancestral stools. See Rattray, 1927, 1929, *passim*.

of a single lineage. In some cases this lineage would be a maximal lineage tracing common descent from an ancestress ten to twelve generations back; in others this unit would be a major segment of such a lineage, the main body of which occupied what was regarded as the original ward of the whole lineage. The lineage has a segmentary structure, each segment being defined in relation to other segments of a like order by reference to common and to differentiating ancestresses. This allows of both accretion to and differentiation within lineages. Thus non-local Ashanti women coming into a village as wives or captives automatically adhere to the lineage of their own clan. If their matrilineal descendants remain in the village they become an attached segment of the local lineage. For most social purposes they are treated as true members of the lineage; but they are not eligible for any office held by the lineage. Foreign slave women gave rise to many attached branches of authentic lineages, for the lineage principle is so dominant that a person or group cannot be completely absorbed by an existing lineage but is always treated as an actual or potential lineage segment. The norms of residence are the chief institutional means through which the lineage principle thus asserts itself (see below, pp. 261–2). Members of an attached lineage are known to be of alien origin and are not entitled to call themselves *odehye*. But it is a gross insult, actionable in law, for anyone to refer to their origins in public. This is in keeping with the maxim which has the force of a moral injunction as well as of a legal rule that no one should reveal another's origins.[1]

Though the lineage is segmentary in form it is dominated by the rule of inclusive unity. There is no hierarchy of jural status or religious authority corresponding to the hierarchy of segments. The corporate unit recognized for political, legal, and ritual purposes is generally the most inclusive lineage of a particular clan in the community. The solidarity of such a lineage in relation to the rest of the community is impressive. Ashanti are reluctant to admit to outsiders that lineage kinship is a matter of degree. They insist on the identification with one another of all lineage kin. But in personal matters and in the relations of lineage members among themselves, degrees of matrilineal connexion are closely observed.

Every such politically unitary lineage has a male head (*abusua panin*) who is often *ipso facto* one of the chief's councillors. He is chosen from among all the living male members (*adehye*), irrespective of age or generation, by consensus of the whole body of members of both sexes.[2]

[1] *Obi nkyere obi ase.* Rattray rightly emphasizes this in many places. This is one of the main reasons why genealogical inquiries are difficult in Ashanti and explains the apparent confusions one meets with in the ideas Ashanti have about their kinship system.

[2] In practice, of course, the decision rests mainly with the older men and women, especially with the former, and only mature men are chosen for the position.

Personal qualities of tact, leadership, intelligence, and knowledge of affairs determine the choice.

It is the duty of the lineage head, with the aid and advice of the older men and women, to watch over the welfare of the whole group. He has the power and the duty to settle private disputes between any of his fellow members so that peace and solidarity can prevail in the group. He is its chief representative in its political and legal relations with other lineages and with the community. He must take the lead in organizing corporate obligations, such as the funeral of a member, and he has to contribute the burial cloth. The crucial payment by the bridegroom by which a daughter of the lineage is legally espoused goes to him and his concurrence is essential for a divorce of any member of the lineage to be valid. Most important of all, both as a sign of his status and as sanction of his authority, is his custody of the male ancestral stools of the lineage. These ancestor shrines comprise the consecrated stools of his predecessors in office and they belong to the lineage as a whole. A subordinate segment cannot have its own ancestor shrines. On *Adae* days[1] he and his elders meet to pour libations and make offerings to the ancestral stools on behalf of the lineage. Individual members of the lineage may bring offerings to him for the stools in cases of personal misfortune or in expiation of sin or sacrilege. The heir of a deceased member must be formally approved by the lineage head and his elders, and a widow of any member cannot remarry without their consent. Such a lineage also has its god or gods (*obosom*) whose shrines are vested in the lineage.

The commonest occasion on which the unity and solidarity of the lineage receive public expression is the funeral of a member.[2] It is presided over by the lineage head. All the members of the lineage gather to take part in it. The expenses, which may be heavy, are shared equally by all the adult members—not, be it noted, among the segments of the lineage. This is nowadays one of the most important criteria of lineage membership. All are expected to observe mourning taboos, though distant lineage kin of the deceased will not do so as strictly as near kin. A death is felt as a shock and a loss by all members of a lineage wherever they may be.

In all these matters there is a very high degree of equality between male and female members of the lineage. It is common for the head to be assisted by a senior woman (*obaa panin*) informally chosen by him and his elders. This is extended to the State as a whole and to each chiefdom. The senior woman of the royal lineage is the Queen Mother of the chiefdom. Her duty is to watch over the morals of the women and

---

[1] For an account of the *Adae* ceremonies see Rattray, 1923, chaps. v–ix.
[2] Until quite recently every maximal lineage in a village or township had its own cemetery, which was sacred ground used for burial only by its own members. Christianity has changed this.

girls, to supervise such feminine matters as girls' puberty ceremonies, which are occasions for joint activities by most of the women of the lineage, and to help to make peace in family quarrels. In particular she is often the best genealogical authority in the lineage and this gives her great influence. The female ancestors of a lineage which owns a chiefship are also commemorated and paid ritual homage. The consecrated stools of the queen mothers are preserved in the custody of the ruling queen mother and she performs rites of worship similar to those of her brother the chief on *Adae* days. This does not apply to commoner lineages.

In these situations, moreover, all members recognized as belonging to the lineage are treated equally, irrespective of their true origin. It is only when it comes to the headship of the lineage that non-authentic members are excluded,[1] and this is because they have no direct access to the lineage ancestors.

Ashanti say 'one lineage is one blood' (*abusua baako mogya baako*); and again, that a lineage is 'one person' (*nipa koro*). This is not a question of physiological theories but a way of stressing the corporate unity of the lineage. It is symbolized in the rule of lineage exogamy and in the extension of the notion of incest (*mogya fra*—mixing the blood) to include the whole lineage. Incest is a crime and a sin. In the old days it was punished by death.[2] Nowadays the culprits are heavily fined and are obliged to provide sheep for expiatory sacrifice to the State ancestral stools. The public scorn they incur very often causes them to leave the community. The rule of exogamy is strictly observed, the apparent exception being that marriage is allowed with a descendant of an alien woman adopted into the lineage not more than four or five generations previously.[3]

Though all political offices, including the kingship, are vested in maximal lineages, ownership of land and other economically useful property is commonly vested in a segment of such a lineage. Yet in theory any member of a maximal lineage is eligible for selection as heir of a deceased member if he or she belongs to the appropriate kinship category. This rule also applies to the right to marry the widow of a lineage member. In practice inheritance and the levirate (which is thought of as a duty owed by the heir in return for the property he inherits) are restricted to a segment of the lineage. Mutual aid—as when a member gets into debt or funeral expenses have to be met—is extended

[1] Except when no true descendants survive, or, rarely, if none of the true members is deemed fit for the office. Cf. the right of slaves to inherit in the absence of true matrilineal kin, Rattray, 1923, pp. 43–4.

[2] Cf. Rattray, 1929, p. 304. *Mogya die*, eating the blood, is an alternative term for incest.

[3] Data on the marriages of 1,000 women in one chiefdom show only 4 per cent. of apparent intra-lineage marriages. In every case one partner was of alien maternal descent.

S

throughout the lineage, but the heaviest responsibility falls on this segment.

This segment, sometimes described as the children of one womb (*yafunu*), generally consists of the uterine descendants of an ancestress not more than four, or occasionally five, generations antecedent to its living adult members. That is, it consists of matrilineal kin whose female parents (and grandparents) usually grew up in a single matrilineal household as a group of siblings.

It is primarily within this segment that the jural authority of the mother's brother is effective. The segment has no appointed head, but one of the experienced senior males is accepted as the leading personality. As in all departments of Ashanti social life, any matter of importance that concerns the segment or one of its members is always dealt with after consulting the senior men and women. But the leading man will have the decisive voice. If the segment owns land, or fishing-rights, or other corporate property he administers it, and his successor will be chosen by reference to his capacity to act as leader in the affairs of the segment. In jural or religious matters (such as marriage or the swearing of an oath) in which the assent of the maximal lineage head is necessary, the procedure is as follows: the principal party goes first to his (or her) legal guardian, his mother's brother, who takes him to the segment leader, who then goes with them to the lineage head.

The maximal lineage found in a community is thought of as the widest local extension of the *yafunu* segment, and the kinship terms used in the matrilineal household are applied to all members of the maximal lineage. People of the same generation call one another 'sibling' (*nua*), irrespective of sex. Women of the mother's generation are called 'mother' (*ena, ni, mami*); men of this generation are addressed and spoken of as 'mother's brother' (*wofa*), and the men and women of the mother's mother's generation are called 'grandparent' (*nana*). A woman calls all the members of her children's generation *ba*, child, and a man calls them sister's child, *wofase*. Both men and women call their fellow members of their grandchild's generation *nana*, grandchild.[1] The conventional norms of behaviour symbolized by these terms apply throughout the lineage, but again more strictly within the *yafunu*. Much conduct felt to be absolutely binding within the *yafunu* is felt to be a matter of goodwill and decent standards outside that range. It is of great significance, too, that witchcraft (*bayi*) is believed to be effective only within the lineage. It is only within the lineage that amity and solidarity are binding in virtue of absolute sanctions, and the inevitable inter-personal hostilities and jealousies thus aroused are expressed in this belief about witchcraft.

[1] A very full list of kinship terms, including their variant usages, is given in Rattray, 1923. These terms are still in use, though the English loan-words *mami*, mother, and *papa*, father, are rapidly replacing the Akan terms in everyday speech.

The maximal lineages which constitute a township or village generally vary in numbers and in status. The lineage which provides the chief and queen mother ranks above the others and is usually the most numerous. My inquiries suggest that there are usually two or three maximal lineages which account for the bulk (half or more) of the population, while the remainder of the population is distributed among the other lineages. The significance of the lineage principle is clearly seen in the terms of address used towards the lineage kin of one's father and paternal grandparents. Any male member of one's father's lineage may be called or referred to as 'father' (*agya*), and a female member of his lineage may be called *sewa* (lit. female father). Similarly, any member of one's father's father's lineage may be called 'grandparent' (*nana*). These terms are used when the speaker wishes to show filial respect to members of these classes of paternal kin. Ashanti explain that this is because any member of one's father's lineage may become his heir, and the same rule applies to one's grandfather. Indeed, it applies to any kinsman or kinswoman.

A maximal lineage is regarded as the local branch of a widespread matrilineal clan. The same term *abusua* is used for the clan as for the lineage. It is believed that all the lineages of a clan are the matrilineal descendants of a single remote ancestress for whom a mythological emergence is generally claimed.[1] The local lineages of the same clan cannot, however, show their precise genealogical connexion with one another. Members of the same clan but of different local lineages behave towards one another as if they were distant kin of the same lineage. The rule of exogamy applies. A person coming to a strange place will receive hospitality from his clansfolk there, and will be accepted as one of them if he wishes to stay. He will be given kinship status in accordance with his age. If no suitable candidate for a lineage office can be found locally, the elders may seek out a clansman from elsewhere. But clanship does not, of course, automatically confer rights to property and office in a different lineage from one's own.

There are only eight clans in Ashanti[2] and every lineage belongs to one or other of these clans, and every clan is usually represented in every chiefdom. This is attributed to dispersion due to migration, wars, &c.

Rattray asserts that each Ashanti clan has a totemic avoidance, an animal or bird which clansmen are forbidden to kill or eat. I was unable

[1] Cf. Rattray, 1929, *passim*, for records of the mythological ancestry of Ashanti clans. As he (ibid., chap. viii) and other writers before him and since (cf. J. B. Danquah, *Akan Laws and Customs*, 1920) have pointed out, the same clan names and clan organization are found among all the Akan peoples.
[2] The correct list is given in Rattray, 1929, pp. 66–7. The 'dual organisation' he refers to appears nowadays only as an alternative naming usage for each clan. Cf. also M. J. Herskovits, 'The Ashanti Ntoro', *J. Roy. Anthrop. Inst.* lxvii, 1937, pp. 287 ff.

to obtain confirmation of this. It may be that the belief is dying out among the majority of Ashanti or else that it is an esoteric ritual secret (as Rattray implies) associated with chiefship and not readily divulged to a foreigner.

The clan system is important as a unifying force in the political organization and as an expression of the cultural unity of the whole people.[1] The fact that there are only eight clans and that one or more high-ranking chiefships are vested in each of them strengthens this effect. Every child knows that every Ashanti belongs to one of these eight clans and knows the name of his own clan. So, also, every child knows that the kingship is vested in a lineage of the Oyoko clan, and all members of this clan shine in the reflected glory of this connexion. This gives Oyoko lineages a little extra prestige; but every clan has claims to prominence in one area or another, for one reason or another. Hence all are considered to be of equal rank. An Ashanti is proud of the chiefships vested in lineages of his own clan.

Chiefs who belong to the same clan call one another 'brother' and this is not a mere title of courtesy. Often this connexion has the support of a tradition that the founders of the chiefships were the sons of one mother. Chiefs thus fraternally related often consult together over urgent public issues irrespective of their immediate allegiances. When one of them is installed, his brother chiefs send him obligatory gifts and he, in turn, sends gifts to thank them. They may have special ceremonial duties at his installation; and again, when a chief dies his brother chiefs must attend the funeral with special gifts and may have ceremonial duties in connexion with it. These ties are thought of as holding between chiefdoms—the stools—not as being personal, and they often in the past formed the basis of concerted political action.[2]

This is not the only way in which kinship norms enter into the political organization at the level of the chiefdom and the State. Marriage with daughters of other chiefly lineages as well as with daughters of commoner lineages has always been deliberately contracted by all chiefs, and especially by the Ashanti kings, as a means of creating and cementing political alliances. The lineage principle ensures the perpetuation of such ties as bonds between chiefly lineages and they are often invoked for political ends. Chiefs of different clans or of different sections of the national army[3] thus often had traditional ties of classificatory kinship. These links arose also from the practice of reserving certain subordinate chiefships coming under the jurisdiction of the

---

[1] The fact that the clan system is identical for all the Akan-speaking peoples is the most important symbol of their cultural unity.

[2] In a recent constitutional case collusion was suspected to have occurred between two chiefs on this score.

[3] See Rattray, 1929, chap. xv. The groupings followed in the national army still regulate procedure in big national gatherings and in the work of the Confederacy Council.

king or of the leading divisional chiefs for sons (*oheneba*) and sons' sons (*ohenenana*) of the king or the chief.

The Domestic Aspect

The rule of matrilineal descent governs the legal and moral relations of individuals as well as the structure and relations of politically significant groups. But its action is subject to limitations arising out of the other genealogical ties rooted in Ashanti family organization. This comes out graphically in the structure of the domestic group,[1] that is, the individual household occupying an independent dwelling. The household may be under a male head or a female head. If it is under a female head, it is normally a segment of a matrilineage consisting of the head and her children, her sister and her children, and perhaps her own and her sisters' uterine grandchildren. The household of a male head, on the other hand, may be either a parental family, consisting of a man and his wife or wives and their children, or it may include the head's sister and her children as well as his wife and his own children, with, sometimes, the children of his children or of his nieces. These domestic arrangements represent different ways of reconciling the potentially conflicting claims and sentiments characteristic of Ashanti kinship. On the one side are the overwhelming bonds of matrilineal kinship which embrace those arising out of motherhood; on the other, the ties of marriage and of paternity. Ashanti are much preoccupied with this problem and constantly discuss it; and though it has obviously been aggravated by missionary and modern economic influences, there is much evidence to show that it existed in the old days.

Missionary teaching lays special stress on the bonds of marriage and parenthood; and modern opportunities for accumulating private means and holding fixed property, such as cocoa farms and buildings, work in favour of the ties between parents and children. As a result the solidarity of the maximal lineage has declined in matters of a personal or domestic nature; but the strength of matrilineal kinship within the constellation of kinship ties crystallized in the domestic groups remains unimpaired. By Ashanti law the right of inheritance is confined to the matrilineage and men take precedence over women in the inheritance of a man's property. Brothers should take precedence over sisters' sons and the latter come before sisters. Formerly a mother's sister's son (a brother— *nua-barima*—in Ashanti terminology) inherited in preference to own sister's son. Nowadays this is not so and if no male heir descended from the deceased's mother is eligible, his own sister will demand acknowledgement as heir rather than permit the mother's sister's son to inherit. In inter-personal relations the trend is to stress lineal connexions in

---

[1] A detailed analysis is given in my paper 'Time and Social Structure—An Ashanti Case Study', in *Social Structure—Studies presented to A. R. Radcliffe-Brown*, 1949.

successive generations in preference to collateral connexions of higher genealogical status.

The relative strength of the potentially divergent family ties we have mentioned can be roughly gauged from data given in the paper just cited. It is unusual for people to reside permanently with distant maternal or paternal kin. In a relatively stable Ashanti community between 40 and 50 per cent. of the population live in matrilineal households under female heads, and only about a third of all married women reside with their husbands, the remainder living chiefly with matrilineal kin. About half of the children under 15 live with their fathers, a large proportion because their parents are living together, and the other half live in households presided over by their mothers' brothers. In Ashanti there are no avoidances between relatives-in-law. It is significant, therefore, that a man and his wife's brother (*akonta* reciprocally) are never found as members of a common household and that it is uncommon (though not unknown) for a woman and her husband's sister (*akonta* or *kunma*, lit. female husband) to reside together. On the other hand, it is not uncommon for a man to have both his own children and his sisters' children residing with him, but the preference of most men is to have only one class of filial dependants living with him. These are the arrangements found in practice, though the ideal of Ashanti men is for marriage and the domestic family to be patrilocal. It appears that the norm is for the ties of matrilineal kinship to be more or less equally balanced by those of marriage and fatherhood in inter-personal social relations; and this is achieved either by segregating their respective fields of action or by assimilating one class of social ties with its opposed class. This comes out clearly in Ashanti kinship usages and norms. The balance, however, is precarious, and the conflict and discord arising out of failure to reconcile antagonistic kinship rights and duties are chronic symptoms of the instability of Ashanti family relationships. The most general sign of this state is the resentment constantly expressed by Ashanti of both sexes and all stations in life against the restraints and frustrations which they attribute to the observance of the rule of matrilineal descent. Yet they continue to abide by this rule, acknowledging that its force derives from the political and legal system.

The Ashanti regard the bond between mother and child as the keystone of all social relations. Childlessness is felt by both men and women as the greatest of all personal tragedies and humiliations.[1] Prolific child-bearing is honoured. A mother of ten boasts of her achievement and is given a public ceremony of congratulation. As

[1] 'A barren woman (*obonin*) is looked upon with pity not unmixed with scorn. She feels an outcast. And the lot of the childless man (*okrawa*) is equally hard. However rich he may be he feels that there is something seriously lacking about him if he is sterile.' So writes Mr. T. E. Kyei (Dip. Ed., Oxon.), who was Principal Research Assistant to the Ashanti Social Survey.

intercourse between husband and wife is prohibited only during the seclusion and convalescent period of eighty days after delivery, children often follow rapidly after one another. By custom, still generally observed outside the big towns, birth must take place in the mother's natal home.[1] This not only ensures that the woman is under the care of her own close maternal kin, in particular her mother, at this time, but it fixes, in a very tangible way, the lineage affiliation and citizenship of the child. This custom greatly strengthens the inclination of women to reside with their mothers or close maternal kin rather than with their husbands during the early years of marriage. Moreover, the care of a young child falls almost wholly on the mother; and as she generally has her own farm to cultivate or other income-earning work to do, it is a great advantage if she can leave her children in her mother's care during her daily absences.[2] Maternal grandmothers (*naná*) play a great part in child-rearing. Indeed they can sometimes be very autocratic in this regard, arguing that a grandchild (*nána*) belongs more to the lineage (*abusua*) than to its parents and therefore comes most appropriately under its grandmother's care.

Mother and Child

But the critical feature, Ashanti say, is the bond between mother and child. They look upon it as an absolutely binding moral relationship. An Ashanti woman stints no labour or self-sacrifice for the good of her children. It is mainly to provide them with food, clothing, and nowadays schooling that she works so hard, importunes her husband, and jealously watches her brother to make sure that he discharges the duties of legal guardian faithfully. No demands upon her are too extreme for a mother. Though she is loath to punish, and never disowns a child, an Ashanti mother expects obedience and affectionate respect from her children. She is always spoken of and addressed as 'mother' (*maami, ena,* &c). To show disrespect towards one's mother is tantamount to sacrilege. Ashanti say that throughout her life a woman's foremost attachment is to her mother who will always protect and help her. A woman grows up in daily and unbroken intimacy with her mother, learns all feminine skills from her, and above all derives her character from her. This often leads to differences between husband and wife and so to divorce. For a man, his mother is his most trusted confidant, especially in intimate personal matters. A man's first ambition is to gain enough money to be able to build a house for his mother if she does not own one. To be mistress of her own home, with her children and daughters' children round her, is the highest dignity an ordinary woman aspires to. There are very many sayings and proverbs that express the attachment of

[1] Cf. Rattray, 1927, pp. 56 ff.
[2] Until weaned at the age of about one year, an infant is almost never separated from its mother. She carries it to her work and it sleeps beside her.

Ashanti to their mothers and indicate the importance of the mother in social life.[1] In the political sphere the concept of 'mother' is applied to the chief's female counterpart, the 'queen mother' (*ohemaa*), who is in fact usually his own or classificatory sister. Like a mother's control of her children, a queen mother's authority depends on moral rather than legal sanctions and her position is a symbol of the decisive function of motherhood in the social system. As Ashanti often point out, a person's status, rank, and fundamental rights stem from his mother and that is why she is the most important person in his life.[2] In the individual's life-history his or her mother stands for unquestioning protection and support against the world at large. It is of special theoretical interest, therefore, that she also stands for the source of the most dangerous occult force that can impinge on his life, that of witchcraft (*bayi*).

'Mother' to an Ashanti generally means his own mother. But the terms of reference and address used for own mother are widely applied, first of all to all women of his mother's generation in his lineage, and secondly to other women of her generation, as a term of courtesy. A person's own mother is, however, unique and his feelings and attitudes and modes of behaviour towards her are extended to no one else.

Custom, upbringing, and mode of residence decree very close identification of full sisters, and public behaviour towards one's mother's sister is indistinguishable from the behaviour one shows to one's mother. Indeed it is considered disgraceful to distinguish between them in public. An orphan left motherless in early childhood will generally be brought up by his mother's sister and in such a case she will be treated as if she were his own mother. But in normal cases it is accepted that people feel differently about their own and their proxy mothers.

PATERNITY

The Concept of Ntoro

Ashanti beliefs about the physiology of conception reflect the social values attached to the parents. The traditional ideas recorded by Rattray[3] are widely known and are still accepted among Ashanti who have had little contact with Western teaching. Even among the more sophisticated (but not necessarily literate) men and women, who maintain that a child has its father's blood (*bogya*) as well as its mother's, the belief that there is a closer physiological bond with the mother than with the father

---

[1] A very common saying is *Wo na awu a, wo abusua asa*—if your mother dies you have no lineage-kin left (cf. Rattray, 1916, p. 129). Other proverbs also stress the idea that one's mother is irreplaceable, that no one else can do for her child what she can do, that it is unthinkable for any person to disown his mother.

[2] Cf. Rattray, 1923, p. 79.

[3] Rattray, 1923, ch. xi; 1927, p. 51. As he puts it, conception is believed to be due to the blood (*bogya*) of the woman mingling with the spiritual (*ntoro*) element of the male.

prevails. Those who speak English say 'your mother is your family, your father is not'. But it is also generally accepted that there is a unique spiritual bond between father and child. This is what Rattray described[1] as the 'male transmitted *ntoro* (spirit)'. There is nowadays, as Herskovits has shown in a penetrating critical discussion of Rattray's statements,[2] some confusion among Ashanti about this concept.

According to my own observations (and these are confirmed by the independent inquiries of Dr. K. A. Busia and Mr. T. E. Kyei),[3] the account given by Rattray of the traditional complex of beliefs on this matter is substantially correct.[4] These beliefs are rapidly disappearing except among the older men and among lineages in which chiefships of superior rank are vested. A State's well-being is bound up with the health and well-being of its chief; and no matter what his private beliefs may be, a chief is obliged to ensure his and his State's good fortune by regular observance of all the religious acts connected with his position. The washing (i.e. ritual purification) of his *kra* is such an act. To know one's *ntoro* and perform its rituals is a hall-mark of free if not noble ancestry. It is a product, also, of the political importance attached to patrilateral ties among chiefs and councillors.

Father and Child

The crux of this aspect of Ashanti kinship lies in the great affective as well as jural weight attached to the recognition of paternity. The general rule that a child is considered by law to be the offspring of its pater prevails in Ashanti,[5] but the ideal is that pater and genitor should be the same person. It is a sin and a crime, for which both parties are nowadays liable to a heavy fine and to public obloquy,[6] for a girl to conceive before her puberty ceremony. But after this ceremony no

[1] Ibid.

[2] M. J. Herskovits, loc. cit.

[3] In unpublished memoranda kindly placed at my disposal by them. My own inquiries were made in several villages, including Asokore, where Herskovits worked.

[4] Herskovits states that 'according to the Asokore men then, Rattray's terms *ntoro* and *abusua* are to be replaced by '*kra*-washing group' and *ntoro* respectively'. This is certainly not standard Ashanti usage. The confusion arises to some extent because the ritual beliefs and practices associated with the *ntoro* concept are becoming obsolete. To most young people the term is a vaguely understood archaic word for kinship, hence they equate it with terms for the kinship groups which rule their life. But there is also deliberate misrepresentation. Only Ashanti of freeborn male ancestry have *ntoro*, in the traditional sense. People of slave descent in the male line have none. It is such people who sometimes insist, no doubt in self-defence, that *ntoro* refers to the clan.

[5] Thus an adulterine child belongs to its mother's legal husband, in accordance with the maxim *Okromfo nni ba*, a thief has no child.

[6] Part of the fine is used to procure sheep for a purification sacrifice to the community's ancestral stools. Formerly (cf. Rattray, 1927, p. 74; 1929, p. 306) both culprits were put to death or driven out of the village.

disgrace follows premarital pregnancy, if the girl has not been promiscuous. What is, however, reprobated and considered shameful, to the man as well as to the girl and her maternal kin, is refusal on his part to acknowledge paternity of the child. The latter is fully legitimate, as far as his status in his matrilineal lineage is concerned, but he carries a stigma which may be thrown at his head in later life in a quarrel. Paternity is acknowledged by the man's accepting the responsibility of maintaining his lover during her pregnancy and by his giving her and her child a number of customary gifts immediately after delivery.[1] On the eighth day after its birth (or nowadays, very soon after the eighth day) the child is named by its acknowledged father; and this is the critical assertion of fatherhood. If an unmarried girl's child and its physical parents suffer disgrace it is because the child was not named by its father.[2]

A man generally chooses a name for his child from among those of his forebears on either side of his parentage, but he is not bound to do so. Ashanti say that a man wants children so that he can pass on the names of his forebears. It is a very important filial duty as well as a source of pride. Hence the children of brothers and the children of a polygynist by different wives often bear the same names. The modern custom of using one's father's or one's own personal name as a surname (and not a name indicating one's lineage affiliation) goes back to the father's right of naming.

Ashanti connect this with the father's *sunsum* (his personality conceptualized as a personal soul) or his *kra* (his spirit, the source of his life and destiny), or, if they are versed in traditional religion, his *ntoro*. The ideas connecting the three ritual concepts thus associated with fatherhood cannot be discussed here.[3] It is enough to say that Ashanti believe that a child cannot thrive if its father's *sunsum* is alienated from it;[4] that its destiny and disposition are fixed by the *kra* which is transmitted by the father; and that this puts every person into one of a limited number of named quasi-ritual categories, the *ntoro* divisions. Each *ntoro* appears to be under the aegis of a god (*obosom*), from whom it takes its name, and whose abode is a river or lake.[5] The number of *ntoro* groupings recognized varies from seven to twelve in different areas, as the major nation-wide groupings have split up in

---

[1] Rattray, 1927, p. 6. Nowadays the gifts consist of imported toilet articles, clothes, soap, trinkets, &c., which may cost two or three pounds.

[2] Ibid. This rule applies as strictly to Christian as to pagan Ashanti. If the father refuses to name a love-child its mother's brother will do so and will accept paternal responsibility for it.

[3] Cf. Rattray, 1923, pp. 77 ff.; 1927, pp. 51 ff., 154. Cf. also Herskovits, loc. cit.   [4] Cf. Rattray, 1929, p. 8.

[5] This is seen from the names of the most widespread *ntoro*, e.g. Bosommuru —the god of the river Buru, Bosomtwe—the god of the sacred lake of the same name, &c. See Rattray, 1923, chap. xi.

adaptation to local circumstances. Each local *ntoro* division has its sacred day for the ritual purification of the *kra* of its adherents, specific totemic taboos, a distinctive form of response to a greeting from any of its members, and a number of names which are commonly though not exclusively found among its members. It is also believed that each *ntoro* goes with a particular type of character which its adherents are prone to have. The *ntoro* concept thus gives expression through ritual beliefs and sanctions, through etiquette and through names, to the value attached to paternity. Women as well as men are bound to honour paternity. A woman does so by observing her husband's *ntoro* taboos during pregnancy and nursing. If she does not, the child suffers injury through the anger and hostility of the father's *ntoro*. The *ntoro* concept emphasizes, in particular, the bonds of father and son which give continuity to the male side of family and kinship relations. Adherents of the same *ntoro* in any locality do not meet for ritual or social purposes and do not constitute an organized group analogous to the lineage. Nor, according to my information,[1] is membership of the same *ntoro* division a bar to marriage, as Rattray asserts. What is prohibited is marriage between patrilateral kin connected through males only not farther back than a common great-grandfather. As Ashanti put it, marriage is prohibited between the descendants of a man in the male line up to the fourth generation. The possession of a common *ntoro* is incidental in this connexion. It is the kinship thus symbolized which is the bar to marriage, not the ritual bond. This rule is asserted not by a count of generations but by reference to known ancestry; and paternal ascendants farther back than the great-grandfather (or descendants of a man beyond the fourth generation) are rarely remembered.[2] One of the main reasons for this is that there is no corporate organization based on the father's line, nor are jural or political rights (such as rights of inheritance) or duties derived from paternal descent.[3] The relations of father and child[4] are rooted wholly and solely in the fact of paternity. The bond is as unique as that of mother and child, though with very different emphasis. One's father's brother (i.e. any man whom one's father calls brother (*nua barima*)) is addressed and spoken of as 'father' (*agya, papa,* &c.) and his sister (any woman whom he calls sister (*nua baa*)) is one's 'female father' (*sewa*); but the respect and the frequent affection and goodwill shown

---

[1] I have records of cases of men marrying women of their own *ntoro*, and Dr. Busia has given me instances of this as well. Elders assured me that this is not due to modern changes.

[2] See, in this connexion, footnote 2 on p. 279 below.

[3] The exceptions are certain high palace functionaries serving the king whose titles are transmitted from father to son. This is explained either on the assumption that the original holder of a title was a slave or captive, or on the grounds that the duties involved can only be learnt by growing up with them, as a son grows up under his father's care and instruction.

[4] Rattray, 1929, chap. xi, discusses this subject with profound insight.

to them are said bluntly to be because of one's father. It arises from their mutual identification as siblings.

An Ashanti father has no legal authority over his children. He cannot even compel them to live with him or, if he has divorced their mother, claim their custody as a right. Ashanti say that children should grow up in their father's house[1] but investigation shows that not more than 50 per cent. of pre-adolescent children are found living with their fathers at a given time. Nevertheless it is regarded as the duty and the pride of a father to bring up his children, that is, to feed, clothe, and educate them, and, later, to set them up in life. Even after the divorce or the death of the mother, a conscientious father discharges these duties. This applies especially to sons. Their moral and civic training, in particular, is his responsibility and this gives him the right to punish them if necessary. If anything, Ashanti fathers (unlike mothers) tend to be over-strict in exacting obedience, deference, and good behaviour from their children. Nowadays it is strongly felt that a child's schooling, which is widely regarded as the most important preparation for gaining a living in the modern world, is his father's responsibility. Formerly he took his sons to farm with him or taught them his craft. Investigation shows that in practice approximately half of all children attending school are kept there by their fathers. Of the rest, half (25 per cent. of the total) are supported at school by their maternal uncles, and between 10 and 15 per cent. by their mothers.[2] An uncle, a mother, or other kinsman will only take on this responsibility if the father fails to do so.

The spiritual tie believed to unite father and child is a ritual symbol of the moral aspect of their relationship. Ashanti say that a man has no hold over his children except through their love for him and their conscience. A father wins his children's affection by caring for them. They cannot inherit his property, but he can and often does provide for them by making them gifts of property, land, or money during his lifetime or on his death-bed[3] (by written will nowadays). To insult, abuse, or assault one's father is an irreparable wrong, one which is bound to bring ill luck (*mmusuo*). While there is no legal obligation on a son or daughter to support a father in old age, it would be regarded as a shame and an evil act if he or she did not do so. And, as with all kinship ties, the bond with the father is given tangible expression in funeral rites. It is the sons and daughters (*mmaa mma*), own and classificatory,[4] of a man and the brother's sons and daughters of a woman who provide the coffin.

---

[1] The proverb says, 'A child grows up in its father's house but does not remain there.'

[2] Unpublished data based on a sample of nearly 700 children of all ages.

[3] Cf. Rattray, 1929, chap. xi.

[4] Generally those descendants of the deceased's father's father whom he called sons and daughters.

Parents have a very important part in the marriage of their children, for it is by marriage that a child is established as a socially responsible person. The consent of both parents, though not legally compulsory, is by usage deemed indispensable for any marriage to take place. A father should provide his son with a wife; and even if he seeks out a bride for himself, no respectable young man would marry her without his father's approval. Nor would a respectable girl marry without her parents' approval. In recognition of the parents' labours in nurturing her and of their concern for her well-being, special gifts are due to them from the bridegroom on her marriage. In this respect the father receives as much honour and consideration as the girl's legal guardian, her mother's brother. Indeed the former carries greater weight than the latter, as can be seen from statistics collected in 1945. It was found that in a sample of 525 women of all ages, about 33 per cent. had been given in marriage by their fathers, as compared with 28 per cent. given in marriage by their mothers' brothers; and though success in courtship depends to a very great extent on winning the girl's mother's favour, yet without the father's approval (if he is alive) the match would not be allowed. For it is the father's duty to make sure that the suitor is able to support his daughter. This appears from the sample just mentioned. Only 13 per cent. of the women interviewed claimed that their mothers gave them in marriage to their husbands.

The idea that a father is primarily responsible for his son's moral behaviour is seen in the rule that if a man commits adultery with another man's wife, the responsibility for paying the adultery damages falls on the father, not the mother's brother. Ashanti say that is why fathers take pains to get their sons married as soon as the boys are old enough. A girl's moral conduct is chiefly her mother's concern.

Ashanti say that no man loves his sisters' children as much as his own children. They say that sons are the support of their fathers. Chiefs, in particular, stress this. The more sons and sons' sons a chief has, the more secure does he feel. As their social standing depends on him and as they have no rights to his office, they will support him in all circumstances. They are his most trusted followers, and important chiefs appoint their own and their brothers' sons and sons' sons (*ohenemma* and *ohenenana*) as titled councillors to attend closely on them. In the old days, men say, a youth preferred to follow his father to war rather than his mother's brother.

Ashanti kinship, both from the point of view of the individual and from that of the system as a whole, is an arrangement of polar relationships. Where kinship is involved, a person is always looking two ways. The division between the sexes is a first consideration. Men have greater political power than women; but political status comes from lineage affiliation which is conferred by women, and this redresses the balance. The result, in practice, is that there is a high degree of equality between the sexes.[1] In terms of personal behaviour and attitudes, there is often no apparent difference between the relations of mother and children and those of father and children. The warmth, trust, and affection frequently found uniting parents and offspring go harmoniously with the respect shown to both. In terms of jural and moral relations, however, Ashanti contrast the parents who, as we have seen, very often live apart. Through one's father one is given access to social relationships in which voluntary choice can play a part. These affect one's personal life, not one's public character and roles. Men and women are usually very fond of their half-siblings by the same father; but there is no sense of inescapable obligation about this, as there is about all social ties through one's mother. And this is what Ashanti emphasize in regard to everything that concerns matrilineal kinship.

RELATIONS BETWEEN OTHER KIN

The Mother's Brother

Polar social roles in members of one sex give rise to sharper dichotomies. Ashanti bring out the characteristics of a father's role by contrasting it with that of the mother's brother.[2] A person's oldest living mother's brother (*wofa*)—using this term in the generalized or classificatory sense—within the lineage segment sprung from his mother's grandmother is the male of the parental generation in whom is vested sole legal authority over him. A *wofa* cannot discipline his sister's child (*wofase*) unless she or her husband asks him to; but he can command,[3] and in former times had the power to pawn, his *wofase*. Nowadays a man can demand financial assistance from his nephew but not from his son—though it is the latter who is most likely to help out of love and goodwill. A good uncle will help his nephew, e.g. by paying for his schooling or setting him up in business, in much the same way as a father often does with his son; but Ashanti look upon the former as creating an obligation to render an equivalent return either by doing the same in the next generation for their own nephews or by doing something for the generous uncle's other matrilineal dependants. For a marriage to be legal it is essential that the girl's *wofa* should accept the *nsa* payment and hand it to the head of his lineage. In divorce the wife's mother's brother's acquiescence and willingness to return the *nsa* payment is essential to make it legal.

The critical element in the relation of mother's brother and sister's son is the latter's status as the former's prospective heir. This comes out in the kinship terms used in addressing or referring to them by their

---

[1] Rattray showed this in many places in his books.

[2] Rattray's analysis (1929, chap. iii) of the mother's brother's position is still valid, and shows his usual deep understanding of the Ashanti.

[3] It is very significant that a slave called his master *wofa*, not father (*agya*).

non-lineage kin. Thus a man's children address his sister's son as father (*agya*) if they wish to show respect to him, since he might well step into their father's position some day. An honourable and conscientious man who inherits his mother's brother's property and position will treat the latter's children with the consideration due from a father. Again, a man can address his *wofa*'s wife as wife (*yere*) since he has the right to inherit her if his uncle dies. Cases of adultery with an uncle's wife occur now and then. The sister's son is fined and his action is a grave wrong against the uncle.[1] Though never condoned, it is explained by reference to the potential right of the levirate symbolized in the kinship terms used for a mother's brother's wife.

In theory nephews inherit in accordance with the seniority by age of their mothers; but as the heir has in every case to be approved by the lineage head and his elders, the claim of an incompetent or spendthrift man can be set aside in favour of a junior nephew of better character. For it is emphasized that the heir inherits not only property such as farms, houses, his uncle's gun,[2] clothes, &c., but also his debts and responsibilities. One of his chief responsibilities as heir, according to traditional custom, is to care for his predecessor's young children and widow. The simplest way to fulfil this duty is to marry the widow (*kuna aware*). Young people, both men and women, are averse to this nowadays. The women insist just as strongly as the men on freedom to go their own way after the death of a husband. But the formalities of inviting the widow to accept her husband's heir still form part of the final funeral ceremony on the eighth day after burial. Older men often honour the obligation,[3] which they describe as a just return for the benefits derived from the property inherited. Those who still adhere to traditional beliefs say that the uncle's ghost (*saman*) will punish the nephew who 'eats' (*di*) his property but refuses to care for (*fwe*) his wife and children.

Matrilineal inheritance is still the legal and customary norm, though it is denounced on all sides. The Confederacy Council has endeavoured to establish a rule first introduced by one of the Christian missions for its own members. According to this rule a man's estate is divided into three parts, one for the matrilineal heir, one for the children, and one for the widow's use during her lifetime, but reverting to the heir on her death. The Confederacy Council has, however, no means of enforc-

[1] It is said that certain branches of lineages owning chiefships were disinherited because of such a crime committed by sons of the women who founded these branches.

[2] The heir is described as the one who takes over his uncle's gun, this being the chief symbol of a man's status as citizen. An inherited estate belongs to the whole lineage segment descended from the original owner's mother and it is the heir's duty to manage it for the common benefit.

[3] In the previously mentioned sample of marriages, only 3 per cent. of the women admitted to being inherited wives and all were over 40.

ing such a drastic change, even though public opinion appears to support it, and the measure has remained a dead letter outside the Christian community referred to. Criticism is especially severe of the increasing tendency of matrilineal heirs to eject their predecessors' widows and children altogether from the enjoyment of properties in the building up of which they have often assisted. This is said to undermine the ties of marriage and of paternity which are, in any case, precarious by comparison with those of matrilineal kinship. Women prefer to work for themselves as an insurance against the future, rather than to assist their husbands. It is felt, also, to be inconsistent with the ideas of justice and of reciprocity which, in Ashanti thought, underlie the institution of inheritance. Nevertheless, only a minority of men take care to provide for their wives and children in the customarily lawful way by making gifts of property to them during their lifetime or by verbal (or, nowadays, written) testament. Inquiries show that three out of four cocoa farms pass from one generation to the next by matrilineal inheritance.

Ashanti say, as Rattray records,[1] that a sister's son is his mother's brother's enemy, waiting for him to die so that he may inherit.[2] But they insist equally on their common interests and axiomatic mutual loyalty. In fact, both aspects are observable in the relations of uncle and nephew. No social relationship in Ashanti is so ambivalent. The ideal is to assimilate the relationship, on the personal and affective side, to that of father and child. This, however, is achieved only by a minority of exceptionally conscientious men. Even men and women who grew up in the care of an uncle speak of him with respect but often without real affection. Adult nephews are often found living and working with an uncle in the most amicable way; but they are nevertheless very ready to find fault with the uncle for alleged selfishness in spending what should be preserved for the nephew to inherit, or for unfairness in the demands they make though they have a legal right to do so. If such criticism is levelled at a father the importunities of his sisters and their children are blamed.

The easiest solution is, as has been pointed out, to segregate potentially conflicting ties within the field of kinship. The more complete the segregation is the more satisfactory is the solution. A divorced woman or the mother of a love-child feels entitled to lean more on her brother than one who is married. The brother feels the obligation to provide for his sister's children as fully as he does for his own. Though their father is held by custom to be obliged to support them, divorce often makes him less amenable to their claims on the grounds that a wife and children of an existing marriage require prior consideration. A man whose sister's children live with him can more easily be a kind of father

[1] Rattray, 1929, p. 20. *Wofase eye dom* is the Ashanti saying.
[2] Hence it is a taboo for a man to sit on his living mother's brother's stool.

to them, as well as their legal guardian, if his own children are living elsewhere. And the same principle comes out again in the common Ashanti view that a child stays with its father till adolescence and then goes to his uncle, or, if a girl, to her husband. Many individual cases conform to this generalization, but it is not universal; indeed not more than 10 per cent. of adults fit the rule. As we have seen, a considerable proportion of children live with their mothers' brothers during childhood. It applies strictly only in the sense that after adolescence the influence of the mother's brother becomes preponderant in a person's social activities owing to the increasing importance of legal relations such as those of marriage, land holding, &c. The affairs of adults are considered to be the concern of the lineage and hence of their immediate legal guardians, not of their fathers. This is compatible with the Ashanti ideal that every married man should set up an independent household as soon as he is able to do so.

The obsolescence of widow remarriage is a symptom of the increasing divergence between the ties of fatherhood and marriage on the one hand, and those of matrilineal kinship on the other, which is found in Ashanti to-day. This is associated with the narrowing down of the lineage range within which precedent rights of inheritance are accepted —that is, the range within which the bond of siblingship is accepted as automatically binding.

Siblings

Next to the bond between mother and child none is so strong as that between siblings by the same mother. Ashanti see that it is simply the tie between mother and child translated to the level of generation equality. The most important difference socially recognized between siblings is that of age. An older sibling is entitled to punish and reprimand a younger brother or sister and must be treated with deference. He is, conversely, obliged to help his juniors in trouble. This applies especially to the mother's first-born (*piesie*) who is regarded as the head of the sibling group and also receives special consideration from his or her parents.[1] But in all other respects it is the equality and solidarity of siblings which Ashanti specially stress. The theme is common in discussions of the vicissitudes of marriage. 'Your brother or your sister, you can deny them nothing' is the way it is often put. Complete frankness and intimacy are possible only between siblings. Great as is the horror of incest, there are no avoidances between brother and sister. Ashanti are very particular about good manners and modesty of dress. It is

[1] It is the *piesie* whose birth transforms the woman into a parent (*obaatan*) and his or her position in the sibling group is unique for that reason. It is of interest that it is taboo for a *piesie* to have any contact with the medicine set up for twins. This accentuates his unique social position, the antithesis to which is a place in the sibling group that is shared.

T

only between siblings that easy informality of manners and dress is allowed. Brothers and sisters may joke with each other, tease each other, and even quarrel, as they are prone to do in childhood, without causing offence.[1] This accent on equality is not found in any other kinship relationship. It is felt to be immodest for adults of different generations to bath together; siblings of the same sex may do so. The attachment and mutual identification of sisters is notorious. Two sisters (in this case all women of the same generation in the lineage) cannot be the wives of one husband at the same time or in succession. They would quarrel incessantly—and so involve their immediate maternal kin in quarrels—because they cannot be kept separate in their relations with their husband. Sisters try to live together all their lives. A woman treats her sister's children so much like her own that orphan children often do not know whether their apparent mother is their true mother or her sister. This holds, though to a lesser degree (because of the legal inferiority of paternal ties), of brothers. Siblings think of one another's possessions as joint property. Borrowing between siblings cannot create debts[2] and, as we know, a sibling is a person's first heir.

The social identification and solidarity of siblings are particularly important and explicit in the relations of opposite sex siblings. Ashanti invariably contrast them with the relationships of husband and wife and of parent and child. The essential nature of the sibling tie lies, to most Ashanti, in its antithesis to conjugal ties. This is a bitter subject to many, both among the educated and among the illiterate folk; but it draws attention to the fact that the sibling tie shows its strength primarily in opposition to other ties, and in virtue of the constraint inherent in the rule of matrilineal descent. The pivot of the Ashanti kinship system in its function as a system of jural relations is the tie between brother and sister. A brother has legal power over his sister's children because he is her nearest male equivalent and legal power is vested in males. A sister has claims on her brother because she is his female equivalent and the only source of the continuity of his descent line. It is typical of the conflicts engendered by Ashanti kinship that men find it difficult to decide what is more important to them, to have children or for their sisters to have children. But after discussion most men conclude that

---

[1] Conventionalized joking is not customary in any Ashanti kinship relationship. The nearest approach to a joking relationship is the privileged familiarity that obtains between Ashanti and some neighbouring Akan peoples like the Nzima.

[2] This applies also to all lineage kin, by contrast with other kin; but siblings (including children of full sisters) may borrow one another's personal goods without asking permission; other kin, except parents, may not. The borrowing and lending of money is in a class of its own. It is a common complaint that irrecoverable 'loans' cannot be withheld from lineage kin, but this complaint is seldom made of siblings. A brother or sister must be helped even if the circumstances of his need are blameworthy.

sad as it may be to die childless, a good citizen's first anxiety is for his lineage to survive. That is why cohabitation without the legal formalities of marriage is not stigmatized.

Quoting their own experiences, men say that it is to his sister that a man entrusts weighty matters, never to his wife. He will discuss confidential matters, such as those that concern property, money, public office, legal suits, and even the future of his children or his matrimonial difficulties with his sister, secure in the knowledge that she will tell nobody else. He will give his valuables into her care, not into his wife's. He will use her as go-between with a secret lover, knowing that she will never betray him to his wife. His sister is the appropriate person to fetch a man's bride home to him, and so a sister is the best watch-dog of a wife's fidelity. Women, again, agree that in a crisis they will side with their brothers against their husbands. There is often jealousy between a man's sister and his wife because each is thinking of what he can be made to do for her children. That is why they cannot easily live in the same house. Divorce after many years of marriage is common, and is said to be due very often to the conflict between loyalties towards spouse and towards sibling.

But the basis of constraint in the sibling relationship is often felt to be irksome. There is much suppressed hostility between siblings. It is seen in the watchfulness of chiefs lest their sisters, the queen mothers, should plot to displace them in favour of their sons. It follows inevitably from the conflict of paternal love and avuncular duty or between a woman's loyalty as a sister and her dependence on her husband for sexual satisfaction and for the fulfilment of her purpose of motherhood. The high incidence of adultery among women is a consequence of this. It is no new thing, as the elaborate scale of adultery damages, which forms part of the traditional legal code, shows.[1]

Ashanti custom provides no collectively approved means of giving expression to the underlying hostility in the sibling relationship. It is rightly felt to be an inevitable result of matrilineal descent. It is therefore merged in the other suppressed hostilities aroused by these obligations. The accepted expression for these is the belief that witchcraft acts only within the lineage. Accusations of witchcraft are everyday occurrences in Ashanti, and their volume is increasing as claims based on lineage ties come to be felt as more and more onerous. Side by side with this is found a rapidly growing addiction to cults purporting to give protection against and to detect witches. Illness, death, barrenness, economic loss, and other misfortunes are often ascribed to witchcraft, and those accused are most often close matrilineal kin of the sufferer, especially a mother or sister.

Ashanti draw attention to the constraint inherent in the relations of maternal siblings by contrasting with them the relations of paternal

[1] Cf. Rattray, 1927, chap. viii.

half-siblings. Half-siblings are spoken of and addressed by the same kinship terms as full siblings.[1] They rarely grow up in the same household. But Ashanti say that one's father's child (*agya ba*) by another wife than one's mother is often one's most trusted and loved friend. It is a matter of one's own preferences. One has no binding obligations to him (or her) or to his (or her) children. It is purely a bond of sentiment based upon the feelings both parties have for their father;[2] thus it is a trusted half-sibling to whom a person in need of honest and disinterested counsel will go.

Grandparents

The grandparents (*naná*, reciprocal *nána*) on both sides are the most honoured of all one's kinsfolk. Their position and status are of very great importance in the social system. In Ashanti it is the grandparents who are the prototypes of persons and institutions commanding reverence and submission to the norms of tradition.

In terms of personal relations there is no distinction between paternal and maternal grandparents. In accordance with the principle of the identification of siblings, the terminology used and the correlated norms of behaviour are extended also to the siblings of the grandparents, and, by the lineage principle, to the lineage kin of the grandparents who are of different lineage from their grandchildren.

The maternal grandmother holds a special position as she is often the female head of the domestic group and this gives her great influence in the bringing up of children. She is the guardian of morals and of harmony in the household.

The young children are her special care; but the paternal grandmother also has this role. Grandparents (and their siblings) lavish affection on their grandchildren, who are their greatest pride. Grandparents can reprimand and punish their grandchildren for minor acts of disobedience or impropriety. In cases of serious misbehaviour they must call on the parents to take disciplinary action. It is from the grandparents of both sexes that children learn family history, folk-lore, proverbs, and other traditional lore. The grandparents are felt to be the living links with the past. They are looked up to with reverence, not only as the repositories of ancient wisdom but also as symbols of the continuity of descent. This applies particularly to the mother's mother's brother who is commonly the head of the lineage segment.[3]

[1] Indeed, the terms for sibling (*nua*), brother (*nua barima*), and sister (*nua baa*) are freely used in speaking of or to any kinsman on the mother's side or the father's side of one's own generation. All Ashanti kinship terms are used in this wide way.

[2] This is the present-day version. Old people still point out that there is the bond of common *kra* washing and the taboos that go with it.

[3] A full discussion of the status of grandparents would take us beyond the scope of the present essay. A few points, however, deserve to be noted. It is

The Father's Sister

The father's sister (*sewa*, lit. female father) receives the respect and often the affection due to a father, but there is not the deep attachment and trust felt for the father and his brothers. She describes her brother's child as 'my child (*ba*)' and she may scold but may not punish him. He feels at home in her house, and readily asks for and is given food or sleeping accommodation; but there are no binding obligations on either side. A *sewa* has no authority over or legal claim upon her brother's child. There is often an element of strain in the relationship owing to the actual or supposed influence of the *sewa* on her brother in the interests of her own children. She stands for the claims of his lineage on him, especially those of his potential heirs which conflict with those of his children. The affective distance and the stress on deference rather than on filial trust are increased through the position of the father's sister as potential mother-in-law by cross-cousin marriage. Formerly a sister usually acted for her brother in the ritual of naming his child,[1] but this is falling into disuse with the obsolescence of the name-giving ritual and the increasing emphasis on lineal relationships at the expense of collateral relationships.

As has been indicated before, all Ashanti kinship terms are used with a wide range of reference and there are often alternative terms for any one relationship.[2] Individuals are connected in more than one way owing to the high incidence of marriage within a community. The general rule that where there is kinship there is a bond of amity and goodwill, which may be invoked if necessary, applies to all genealogical connexions. And where circumstances lead individuals to wish to show

of great significance that the term for grandparent (*nana*) is also the title of respect used by a subject to a chief, and, indeed, is the general term of address or reference for a chief. It is used, similarly, to show respect to any person of rank, to old people, to the dead, to gods and fetishes, to priests and priestesses, &c. The reciprocal term (*nana*) is used by chiefs, elders, priests, &c., in addressing subjects or followers or suppliants to whom special consideration is being shown. The status of grandparents explains the importance so often attached to kinship within four generations. In brief, four generations is about the maximum extension of a descent line over which all the progeny of a man or a woman can remain united either under his or her authority (as sometimes happens in a matrilineal household) or through living contact with him or her. More usually four adult generations (the equivalent of five generations inclusive of children) embrace people of common descent strongly united by kinship sentiment focused on a progenitor or progenetrix who was the parent or grandparent of its oldest members. The 'grandparents' are decisive in this chain of living contact as they form the bridge between *their* grandparents and their grandchildren. By the sixth generation, except where the lineage principle is utilized to maintain the cohesion of the descent group, the chain is broken and kinship sentiment is no longer based on living contact. A great-grandparent is felt to be so near the ancestors that he or she is regarded with almost religious awe.

[1] See Rattray, 1927, pp. 62 ff.   [2] Ibid., 1923, chap. i.

special goodwill to or demand special consideration from each other, they find justification for this in kinship ties. As has been mentioned, on the principle of lineage unity any member of one's father's lineage may be addressed or described as father (*agya, papa, se*), or father's sister (*sewa*) if the filial relationship is stressed; or if the person concerned is of one's own generation and this is stressed, the term for sibling (*nua*) can be used. This rule applies to the lineage and generation alinement of all the kinsfolk of one's kin. But the jural and affective relationships associated with the use of these terms in their primary contexts are not automatically extended in this way. I may, half jestingly, address a daughter of a distant lineage brother of my mother as 'wife' (*yere*), but that does not mean I have a special claim to marry her. If, however, I court her successfully, he will probably explain his readiness to consent to the match on the grounds that I am his 'sister's son'.

MARRIAGE

The marriage customs of the Ashanti have been described in detail by Rattray.[1] In rural areas there has been little change in these customs, though greater latitude is nowadays allowed in their observance. The most important change has been the substitution of money payments for most of the gifts in kind customary in former days. The same rules apply to all ranks and classes, the only difference being that girls of chiefs' and high-ranking councillors' lineages are espoused with larger payments, graded according to their rank, than are commoners. Most educated men still marry in accordance with native custom.[2] Respectable citizens complain that illicit and casual unions are becoming a serious problem, and the older people blame disregard of parents' advice in the choice of a spouse for the notorious frequency of divorce. While there is evidence to support the view that shortlived illicit unions are increasing, especially in the towns, the data collected during the Ashanti Social Survey in 1945 indicate that a high divorce rate has been characteristic of the Ashanti for the past twenty to thirty years.[3]

A girl may be betrothed in childhood (*asiwa*), but cannot be taken in marriage until after her puberty ceremony. Girls marry between 16 and 18 years of age, youths between 20 and 25.

Ashanti marriage is restricted in accordance with the Ashanti concept of incest. Marriage is prohibited between individuals who would be committing the sin of incest if they had sexual relations. Thus marriage is forbidden between members of the same matrilineage, and this

[1] Rattray, 1923, 1927, 1929 *passim*, especially 1929, chap. iv.
[2] Church marriages and marriages in accordance with Colonial Civil Law are confined to a very small section of educated people.
[3] These data show that rather more than half of all men over 40 and about the same proportion of all women over 35 have been divorced at least once. The incidence is of course less with younger people.

includes accessory lineages which have been attached to the authentic lineage for four or more generations. This taboo extends to the clan throughout Ashanti.[1] Marriage is also prohibited with any 'patrilineal' descendant of one's father's father's father—i.e. of one's father's paternal *nanà* up to the fourth generation. This taboo is an extension of the taboo on sex relations with a father's brother's child (a sibling (*nua*) in Ashanti kinship terminology), which is regarded as a sin almost as heinous as incest with a full sibling. The basis of this is the identification of brothers. Thus the taboo applies to the children and sons' children of half-brothers by the same mother but different fathers. Lastly marriage with a lineal descendant to the fourth generation, or with a lineal ascendant (or the sibling of such an ascendant) to the fourth generation, is prohibited.[2] The ideal match is with a cross-cousin on either side, though there is a preference, for men, for marriage with a mother's brother's daughter (*wofa ba*)[3]—i.e. the daughter of a man of his mother's generation belonging to the lineage segment descended from her great-grandmother. Again, marriage with a member of one's own village or chiefdom is preferred to marriage with an 'outsider' (*ahoho*). The reasons given are that the character and family background of the parties are known to their respective parents and this enables them to make a careful choice. It is also said that such a marriage enables the parents and other kin of both spouses to take a personal interest in and help in the care of their children. But undoubtedly the most important factor is the strength of matrilineal ties in domestic organization. Intra-village marriage enables husband and wife to reside with their maternal kin if they wish to or have to. My investigations in 1945 showed that 75 per cent. and upwards of married people have spouses from the same village or adjacent villages. Chiefs still have two matrimonial prerogatives recorded by Rattray. Twin girls (*ntaa*) who are not kin to the chief of their place of birth within forbidden degrees are regarded from birth as his future wives and cannot marry anyone else unless he relinquishes his prior rights. Secondly, every ranking chief has a number of stool wives (*ayete*). These wives are obligatorily provided by various lineages of the chief's subjects; and if a stool wife dies she must be replaced by another girl of her lineage.[4]

A marriage may begin with a period of cohabitation approved by the parents of the couple and accepted as a proper marriage for all

---

[1] And, where clan affiliation is known, throughout the Akan-speaking peoples.

[2] The prohibited marriages listed by Rattray, 1923, p. 37, all fall under these rules. As has been pointed out, a common *ntoro* is not by itself a bar to marriage. Any attempt to defy these rules is nowadays treated as a crime subject to a fine. It should be noted that the count of four generations is always *exclusive* of the generation of *Ego*.

[3] Cf. Rattray, 1927, chap. xxix.

[4] This is the only form of 'sororate' practised in Ashanti. Cf. Rattray, 1929, p. 27.

practical purposes. The man, in such a case, has no right to demand adultery damages if his 'wife' has a lover and there is nothing to prevent the couple from separating by mutual agreement.

The decisive formality for the establishment of a legal marriage is the giving of the *tiri nsa* (lit. head wine), which Ashanti describe as a thanking gift (*aseda*). Most commonly this consists of two bottles of gin or an agreed equivalent in cash. It is handed over on behalf of the husband by the head of his lineage to the head of the bride's lineage through her legal guardian in the presence of representatives of both groups. Half of the gift is sent by the head of the bride's lineage to her father, and the remainder is distributed amongst the representatives of the two lineages.

The payment of *tiri nsa* gives the husband exclusive sexual rights over his wife and the legal paternity of all children born to her while the marriage lasts. It gives him, also, the right to essential domestic and economic services from her. He in turn is obliged to provide her and their children with food, clothing, and housing if she has none. He must give her sexual satisfaction and take care of her in illness, is responsible for debts she contracts,[1] and last but not least, must obtain her consent if he wishes to take an additional wife. These material rights and obligations are specifically recognized in Ashanti customary law. Chronic failure on the part of a spouse to fulfil any of them can constitute grounds for divorce which husband and wife have equal rights to demand. But the crucial right conferred on both spouses by the giving and accepting of *tiri nsa* is that of sexual satisfaction for procreative purposes. The husband thus acquires exclusive sexual rights over his wife. If she commits adultery he can, as we have seen, sue for compensation from the adulterer and claim the paternity of a child conceived in adultery. He has no such rights over a woman with whom he is merely cohabiting. A married woman can divorce a husband who neglects her sexually or who can be proved to be impotent or sterile. In such a case no efforts are made to reconcile the parties. This is generally attempted if divorce is demanded on other grounds. The rule that a man must get his wife's consent if he wishes to take a second wife is due to the fact that he is in effect asking her to share her sexual rights with another woman. The recognition of matrilineal descent is responsible for this high degree of equality between spouses in Ashanti marriage law and custom. It allows the conjugal relationship to be envisaged as a bundle of separable rights and bonds rather than as a unitary all-or-none tie.

Tiri nsa may be paid before or at any time after the couple begin to cohabit. In addition, the bride's father, mother, lineage head, and brothers are entitled to certain customary gifts from the bridegroom, but these may be waived. Offerings may have to be presented to gods

---

[1] But if she finds treasure trove her lineage takes possession of it.

(*obosom*) or medicines (*suman*) under whose protection the bride's parents have lived. The bride herself usually receives a gift of money from her husband when she first goes to live with him. This occasion is celebrated by her cooking a sumptuous meal for him and his kinsfolk and fellow villagers for which she herself and her mother supply the provisions.

Except for the *tiri nsa*, none of the customary gifts is returnable on divorce. For a divorce to be legal, *tiri nsa* must be returned through the same channels by which it was given.

A further payment may be demanded from the husband at any time during the marriage. If there is urgent need of money in the lineage segment to which the wife belongs, her mother's brother, as her legal guardian, can, with the consent of the other members of the segment, ask the lineage head to demand *tiri sika*, or head money, from her husband. Any amount may be asked for. It is in reality a loan for an indefinite period which serves as a pledge of the fidelity of the wife. It is returnable only on the termination of the marriage by divorce or by death of the wife. The husband may, however, make a free gift of the *tiri sika* to his wife and her lineage after some years of marriage, on divorce, or if she dies.

Polygyny is permitted, and chiefs often have large harems. It is, however, rare, nowadays, for commoners to have more than three wives at the same time; 80 per cent. of all married men have only one wife at a time. It is notorious that co-wives often show great jealousy of one another. They call each other *kora*, 'jealous one', and the usual practice is for a polygynist's wives to live separately. A polygynist must be scrupulously fair in sharing his time, his sexual attentions, and the material provision he makes for them, equally among his wives.

As has been mentioned, a cross-cousin is regarded as the most satisfactory spouse. At least this is still the view of the older people. Many young men take a different view. They say that a cross-cousin is 'too near', almost a sister, and so she is never as attractive as an unrelated girl. Some argue, also, that cross-cousin marriage reinforces the authority of the mother's brother, who is now also father-in-law, to an intolerable degree. But in rural areas there are many young men who approve of marriage with a mother's brother's daughter (*wofa ba*) on the grounds that it creates an additional bond with their maternal uncles and that it is a more secure marriage than a match with an unrelated woman. Women often argue in favour of the custom. They say it strengthens their claims on their husbands and their children's claims on both paternal and maternal kin. The older people—parents, mothers' brothers, and fathers' sisters—in whose interests and at whose insistence cross-cousin marriages are arranged[1] defend the custom on various grounds. The commonest argument is on the grounds of property and

---

[1] As Rattray points out, 1927, chap. xxix.

wealth.[1] Cross-cousin marriage most often occurs between the children of full siblings or of uterine first cousins. Such a marriage, it is contended, ensures that a man's daughter and her children derive some benefit from the property he is obliged to leave to his sister's son; or (where a man's son marries his sister's daughter) that his son's children get much benefit from his property. Importance is still attached, also, to the transmission of names, though not so much as when Rattray wrote.[2] Furthermore, parents praise cross-cousin marriage because there can be no mistake about the character or family background of one's child's spouse. They maintain, also, that such marriages are less liable to break up on frivolous grounds than marriage between non-kinsfolk. The kinship between all the parties concerned gives all of them a strong interest in smoothing out difficulties and supporting the marriage. But undoubtedly the strongest motive in favour of cross-cousin marriage derives from the conflicts latent in Ashanti kinship relations. Cross-cousin marriage offers a possibility of reconciling the conflicting influences of conjugal, parental, and matrilineal kinship ties.

The divergent opinions about cross-cousin marriage suggest, however, that there are strong tendencies working against it. In any case only a small proportion of all marriages can, at a given time, be cross-cousin marriages. My inquiries showed that this proportion has been decreasing over the past thirty to forty years,[3] and that cross-cousin marriages are not more stable than other marriages. This is in keeping with the general trend towards greater individual liberty of movement, of choice of occupation, and of selection of spouses due to new economic opportunities and new ideas derived from mission and school teaching. Chiefs and elders say that it is also one of the symptoms of declining parental and avuncular authority. But the chief factor working against cross-cousin marriage appears, to the outside observer, to be the increasing tendency to seek a solution for the tensions inherent in the Ashanti kinship system by segregating the field of conjugal and parental kinship from that of matrilineal kinship.

[1] Rattray, 1927, chap. xxix.

[2] Ibid. The belief that children sometimes reincarnate recent ancestors still prevails among pagan Ashanti. The point about the names, however, is that cross-cousin marriage ensures that a man's paternal antecedents may become the namesakes of his nearest lineage kin of the next succeeding generation. This is greatly desired.

[3] In a sample of 525 women from various parts of Ashanti who were or had been married, approximately 8 per cent. had been married to cross-cousins. A rough breakdown by age-groups gave the following approximate results:

Percentage of cross-cousin marriages

Among women under 30, approx. 2 per cent.
Among women aged 30–40, approx. 5 per cent.
Among women aged 40–50, approx. 9 per cent.
Among women aged 50 and over, approx. 14 per cent.

The status of parents-in-law (*ase*—the generic term for all in-laws) is not very precisely defined in Ashanti. There are no specific forms of etiquette or obligation between them and their son's wife or daughter's husband. There is only the general rule that they must be treated with special respect,[1] and must be given assistance and support whenever they need any. This is especially important in the early years of marriage. A man should go out of his way to help his mother-in-law or father-in-law with farm work, in house-building, or in other ways, and should not neglect opportunities of giving them small presents. These usages apply also, in an attenuated degree, to siblings-in-law. A woman should show deference and obedience to her parents-in-law. But it is accepted that there is constant danger of friction with parents-in-law. Both husband and wife are apt to resent the strong hold of a spouse's parents (in particular of the mother) and siblings over him or her. Ashanti, therefore, do not seek frequent contacts with their parents- or siblings-in-law. When a divorce occurs the spouse who feels wronged is apt to blame his or her parents-in-law or siblings-in-law. Men, in particular, are prone to lay a wife's failings at the door of her mother.

As has been mentioned before, there is a high incidence of divorce among Ashanti. This is due primarily to the strength of matrilineal kinship ties. Divorce usually makes little change in the domestic circumstances of a woman or in her economic situation, nor does it affect her jural status or that of her children. Though it may involve personal distress, it carries no moral stigma and no social penalties.

CONCLUSION

Kinship plays a very important part in Ashanti social life. It is not only the source of the critical norms governing the jural and personal relations of individuals in many fields of social life, but it also determines the structure of the corporate groups on which the political organization is based and influences political relations at all levels. The dominant principle of Ashanti kinship is the rule of matrilineal descent. In spite of nearly forty years of rapid social change under the influence of European economic, social, and cultural agencies, the Ashanti have tenaciously upheld this rule. The chief problem of kinship relations among them is to adjust the jural and moral claims and bonds arising out of marriage and fatherhood to those imposed by matrilineal kinship. Conflict between these rival claims and bonds is inherent in their kinship system. This problem is most acute for men and they seek a solution to it along two lines. Some attempt to assimilate the conflicting kinship ties to one another, and so to circumvent the dilemma of a choice of loyalties. Most, however, try to solve the problem by

[1] The proverb says *Ase fie, yenko no basabasa*—'The parent-in-law's house, we do not enter it carelessly'.

segregating the respective fields of the conflicting kinship ties. This method of dealing with the problem seems to be gaining ground under modern conditions. Though it appears to be an adequate method, it is undoubtedly uneconomical, imposing a heavy emotional and moral as well as material strain on the parties concerned. This is the crucial problem of contemporary Ashanti society.

DOUBLE DESCENT AMONG THE YAKÖ

By DARYLL FORDE

INTRODUCTION

THE relations arising from parenthood extend in all societies to form a wider system of kinship whereby, both for individuals and groups, rights of inheritance and succession, and ties of mutual obligation, are established on accepted principles of descent. But parenthood is dual, and if recognition were symmetrically accorded through both parents at each generation, kinship ties would proliferate indefinitely in ever widening aggregates. Moreover, the sex differences among both parents and siblings are a pervasive factor in differentiating cultural activity and attendant social status. In the process of establishing coherent and continuing social relations between kin, endless variety is possible in the stress and limitations set on the recognition of particular ties. The sex distinction may in some contexts be so dominant that women are grouped and succeed through their mothers, while men are grouped and succeed through their fathers.[1] But in the maintenance of groups of wide social relevance the sex difference between individuals is normally subordinated to the principle of affiliation of both sons and daughters through one of the parents to give rise to mutually exclusive kin groups of both sexes.[2]

Among many peoples one line of descent, either that through fathers or that through mothers, is stressed and a single system of unilineal groups is formed. But the ascription of status within groups based on one unilineal reckoning does not exclude the concurrent establishment of rights and obligations, if only between close relatives, with kinsmen in other lines of descent. The unilineal tendency itself contains the alternatives of patrilineal and matrilineal reckoning and these are not, as was once assumed, mutually exclusive. Both may be operative as principles of affiliation and group organization in distinct social fields, so that rights of succession and inheritance fall into distinct categories.

Systems of double descent or double unilineal kin-group organization have long been encountered in Africa, but they have often been misunderstood and few of them have been closely studied.[3] A people of

---

[1] This tendency, which gives rise to distinct descent groups among, for example, the Gê tribes of the Matto Grosso in South America, is exemplified over limited fields of inheritance in Africa; see, e.g., the paper by Dr. S. F. Nadel, in this volume.

[2] For a discussion of the range of conditions under which this tendency finds expression in the formation of a stable system of mutually exclusive unilineal kin groups, see my paper, 'The Anthropological Approach in Social Science', in *The Advancement of Science*, London, 1947.

[3] On the Herero system, which still awaits full analysis, see I. Schapera, *Notes on some Herero Genealogies*, University of Cape Town, 1945.

importance in this connexion are the Yakö, one of a number of 'semi-Bantu' speaking peoples[1] living some seventy miles north of Calabar on the eastern side of the middle Cross river in the Obubra Division of Ogoja Province, South-Eastern Nigeria (see map in Fig. 9). Their system affords an instance of full and simultaneous development of both patrilineal and matrilineal kin groups. Until the present generation, among whom many features are, as will be seen, being modified under the impact of Western institutions, matrilineal descent has been as outstanding in its sphere as patrilineal, and both are corporately organized.

The Yakö number about 20,000 persons grouped in five compact village settlements, one of them very large, situated at distances of from three to six miles from each other. The dwelling-area of the largest village, Umor, seven miles to the east of the Cross river, extends over a quarter of a square mile and had a population of nearly 11,000 in 1935. Six miles to the north lies Ekuri, smaller than Umor; the main settlement is again away from the river, although one of its wards has a waterside hamlet. Five and eight miles away to the east are two still smaller and closely neighbouring settlements of Nko and Ngkpani, while little more than three miles south of Umor is the fifth and smallest village of Idomi. A very high degree of linguistic and cultural homogeneity is maintained between the villages by a continual interchange of visitors, temporary residents, and permanent migrants. But there is no centralized political organization and sporadic, shortlived fighting between the villages, particularly between Umor and Ekuri, occurred in the past.

Yakö settlement has been comparatively stable. In the larger and traditionally older villages of Umor and Ekuri the house sites of important ancestors four generations back are pointed out and there are in places mounds several feet high said to have been formed by superposition of successive house floors. Of the smaller villages, Idomi and Ngkpani are held to have been established by migrations from Umor, the latter after a bitter quarrel between two Umor wards. But despite a rapid increase of population over at least the past two generations and the growth of Ekuri and particularly Umor into very large and crowded settlements, there is a very strong tendency for men to remain with their patrikin. When, as is increasingly common, dwelling areas in the village become fully occupied, the pressure is relieved by building hamlets (sing. *kowu*) on the nearest tract of farming land belonging to the group

---

[1] Others of these peoples which have a similar dual system of kin grouping are the Ekumuru, Abayong, Agwa'aguna, Enna, Abini, Agoi, and Asiga. The Agwa'aguna and Yakö share a common tradition of overland migration from an area further up the Cross river in what is now Ikom Division and trace their origin to Okuni. Among them both 'friendship' and social distance are expressed in taboos on fighting and intermarriage and in joking relations.

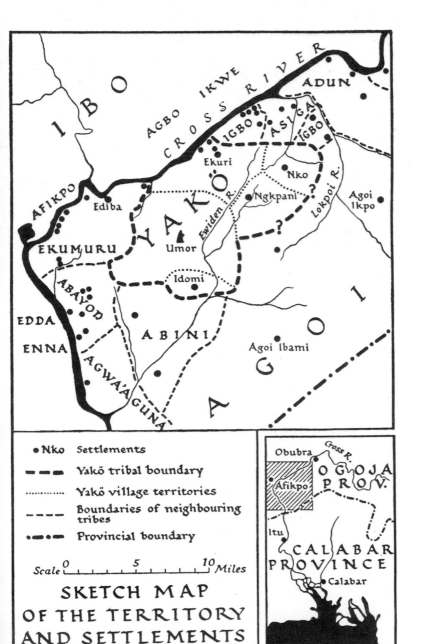

- ● Nko   Settlements
- ▬ ▬ ▬   Yakö tribal boundary
- ··········   Yakö village territories
- ‐ ‐ ‐ ‐   Boundaries of neighbouring tribes
- ·▬·▬·▬   Provincial boundary

Scale 0 _____ 5 _____ 10 Miles

SKETCH MAP
OF THE TERRITORY
AND SETTLEMENTS
OF THE YAKÖ AND
THEIR NEIGHBOURS

S-E. NIGERIA

FIG. 9

and within half a mile or less of the village. The occupants of these hamlets continue to participate as fully as they can in the life of the main village. With the increase in size of settlements the areas appropriated for cultivation and the collection of forest products have been extended, but the overall density of population has not so far risen high enough to cause deleterious pressure on land. Even in the territory of Umor, where the density is highest, at about 230 per square mile, there are still some tracts of unfarmed land.

The Yakö are predominantly subsistence cultivators; they collect and prepare oil-palm products for external trade, but take little part in the river traffic with Calabar and the lower Cross river. A wide range of bush products is collected for local use and petty trade, but hunting is now of minor importance. Interests are concentrated on the growing of yams and secondary crops which are cultivated jointly by men and women on household farm plots. These plots are held individually by men as household heads within the framework of the wider collective rights of kin groups to be described later. But a household only cultivates in any one year about a fifth of the plots to which it has established rights. The rest is left in bush fallow and cultivated in rotation over a period of years.[1]

HOUSEHOLD AND FAMILY

The elementary family is the nucleus of the Yakö household, but the majority of the older men have more than one wife. In polygynous households every wife has a right to occupy a separate house provided by her husband and has personal property in food-supplies and domestic equipment (see Fig. 10, Woman's House). She rears her own children and in both productive and recreational activities is in principle free from the interference of any other wife. Although co-wives normally occupy adjacent houses there are, from the point of view of daily food-supply, as many households as there are adult able-bodied women. The single household head has equal rights and obligations in each. Food should be prepared for the husband by each wife in turn, but the length and regularity of the periods appear to be very variable. But in farming, a man with his several wives normally constitutes a single farming unit, although each wife has her specific interests, rights, and duties which do not extend over the entire farm plot, and one wife does not control the farm labour of the others. The close proximity of the houses of plural wives and their common concern with the affairs of one husband involve personal relations between the wives, but these are informal in character. They depend on individual temperament and vary according to the particular circumstances. Attitudes are not determined in advance either

[1] For an account of the settlement pattern, agricultural cycle, and land utilization, see my paper 'Land and Labour in a Cross River Village, Southern Nigeria', *Geogr. J.* xc. 1, July 1937, pp. 24–57.

by rules of domestic co-operation or by the relative status of wives. The first married or the senior existing wife has no formal superiority or prerogative. Yakö say that each wife has an equal claim on the time, attention, and energy of the husband. Similarly each wife has an equal obligation to participate in household duties, including especially farm work and preparing food for the husband, and is responsible for the well-being of her own children. In practice, owing to differences in the aptitudes and inclinations of wives and in the sentiments of the husband towards them, there may be considerable differences among them both in their participation in domestic activities and in their prestige in the compound. But such differences are not subject to the control of the senior wife. On the farm it is the husband who tells each wife what he wishes her to do. Mutual helpfulness between wives in farming and domestic activities is by no means absent, but at the same time it is quite common to find an age-mate of one wife helping her in some task at home or on the farm while the other wife is working independently. The relations between wives of one man may range from real companionship to a minimum of contact punctuated with outbursts of hostility. The failure of a wife to live amicably with another in the compound is a recognized ground for dismissing the aggressor.

The yams of a man and those of his wife or wives are planted and harvested separately. They are tied on distinct groups of uprights in the husband's harvest stack and the separate harvests of each are used in turn to provide household supplies according to well-established rules. The lesser crops are the wives' responsibility. Each owns and controls her own harvests, but she is at the same time under obligation to provide her husband and children with adequate supplies during the year. A wife who, for any reason, is unable to carry out all the farm work that falls to her lot should find and recompense helpers from among her age-mates or her kin. If she lacks sufficient yams to supply her share for the needs of her husband and children she is expected to work on other people's farms at busy times, and especially at planting and harvesting, when she will be given yams for each day's work which will help to remedy her own deficit. But a husband with a large harvest of yams will himself give a wife extra yams in recognition of her farming services to him if her own crop is short.

On the other hand, fruit-trees and oil-palms are not held by women. They are planted or tended individually by men, and rights to them are transmitted to male heirs. A husband is expected to provide his wife with supplies of palm-nuts for the preparation of kernels which she sells, and failure to do so is a very common source of friction between them. This he commonly does in the course of his collection of palm-fruit for the preparation of palm-oil, the marketable surplus of which belongs to him. There is a division of labour between men and women in the successive processes, the wife normally receiving the nuts for cracking and

U

disposal of the kernels as part of her share in the product and her reward for assisting in the production of the oil.[1]

There is no limitation, apart from inclination and the resources he commands, on the number of wives that a man may have at any one time, and demographic conditions, at least in the recent past, have been favourable to a high incidence of polygyny.[2] Plural marriage is an undoubted advantage in maintaining a large farm every year, for weeding the farm, cultivating secondary crops and carrying the yam harvest, and also in the preparation of oil-palm products for sale. Men frequently explain their later marriages by saying that increase in their yam harvests or the death of one wife made it necessary for them to seek another without delay. But plural marriage is also valued as a means of rearing a larger number of children and so of increasing the strength of a man's patrilineage and of his own prestige within it. On the other hand, the increasing adoption of trading pursuits by younger men who, in consequence, can clear only small farms, is rendering polygyny difficult or expensive for them. Such men also tend to be less strongly concerned in the traditionally high value placed on numerous offspring. Moreover, there is little emphasis on the number of wives as a direct expression of an individual's status or prestige. The priest leaders of the clans, both patrilineal and matrilineal, for example, are not distinguished by a markedly higher degree of polygyny than the adult male population in general.

A man takes further wives according to his needs and opportunities throughout his earlier life, but as old age approaches he does not marry again. Elderly widowers, although they maintain their own farms, often do not remarry late in life, but are dependent on the aid of daughters or sons' wives for farm work. There is thus no tendency among the Yakö for old men as a class to secure a disproportionate number of women as wives at the expense of younger men.

Young men usually marry girls of their own age in the first instance. On the other hand, in later marriages men often take women who differ widely from them in age, and the general tendency is to marry younger women. There is a particular inducement to take a second wife very shortly after the first if the latter has borne a child, for a child is normally suckled for two years during which intercourse between the parents is forbidden. In such a situation the second wife is often a previously unmarried girl.

The sex ratios at birth and at marriageable age appear to be normal

---

[1] Wives retain for their personal use any oil left over after filling the 4-gallon tins used as units in oil trading. Any surplus less than half a tinfull the wife claims for domestic use and for disposal in small occasional gifts to kin, affines, and neighbours with whom she is on good terms.

[2] See my *Marriage and the Family among the Yakö in South-Eastern Nigeria*, Monographs on Social Anthropology, No. 5, London, 1941.

among the Yakö. It is therefore likely that the general practice of polygynous marriage has been made possible only through the purchase of foreign children, mainly from Ibo country, west of the Cross river, who are known as *yafoli*, and are adopted into the household and kin groups of the purchaser, and the great majority of whom have been girls. There has recently been increasing governmental check on this trafficking in children, but it has for a considerable period made available a surplus of girls especially for marriages to older men as later wives.

Divorce as well as polygyny is frequent among the Yakö and both produce a situation in which a man's children fairly often consist of several groups which are half-siblings to one another. All will be members of the father's patrilineage, but their matrilineal affiliations and considerable rights and obligations associated with them will be divergent. A man is not usually concerned, for example, in his paternal half-sister's marriage; her children are not among his heirs. But a full sister and a maternal half-sister are equally among his closest matrilineal kin.

The household of an older man will often include not only his wives but also divorced or widowed kinswomen, among whom mother, sisters, daughters, and sisters' daughters are the most frequently encountered. A woman widowed late in life usually joins one of her sons in whose farm she will plant her crops. A younger woman who has been widowed or divorced may temporarily rejoin her parents or go to her mother's brother or to an older brother. Such women are given houses of their own, but, unless they are infirm, they provide their own food-supplies and assist the head of the household. Their rights and obligations are in many respects similar to those of the wives, and any young children with them will be treated like foster-children. Elderly widowers are also to be found as dependants in the households of sons or other patrikin. There are, too, in many Yakö households young children of previous marriages related to only one of the spouses.

The majority of household heads provide themselves with a separate man's house, usually a smaller and simpler dwelling than a woman's, in which they keep their personal belongings, meet their friends, and often sleep. Young men before and after marriage frequently share the house of a father, elder brother, or other male relative living in the same compound. (See Fig. 10, Man's House, and Fig. 11.)

Yakö feel that physiological paternity constitutes a right to social fatherhood which, where they conflict, may be asserted against the rights derived through marriage. Although, as will be seen, social fatherhood may be later attenuated if not extinguished following adoption by a foster-father and his lineage, a man's physiological paternity of his wife's child is generally axiomatic, for there is not usually any knowledge or assumption to the contrary. But rights to social fatherhood based on physiological paternity outside marriage can in another context be successfully asserted over those derived from marriage to the mother. In

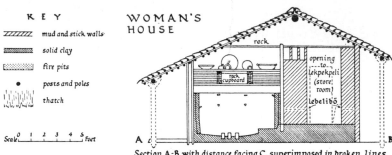

KEY

⧄⧄⧄	mud and stick walls
▨▨▨	solid clay
⬚⬚⬚	fire pits
•	posts and poles
ᵛᵛᵛ	thatch

Scale: 0 1 2 3 4 5 feet

WOMAN'S HOUSE

rack

opening
---to---
Lekpekpeli
(store room)

Lebelibō

rack
cupboard

A L̄   B

Section A-B, with distance, facing C, superimposed in broken lines

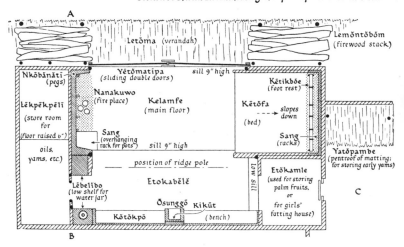

A

Letōma (verandah)

Lemōntōbōm (firewood stack)

Nkōbānāti (pegs)

Yētōmatipa (sliding double doors)   sill 9" high

Kētikbōe (foot rest)

Lēkpēkpēli
(store room
for
(floor raised 6")
oils,
yams, etc.)

Nanakuwo (fire place)

Kelamfe (main floor)

Kētōfa (bed)

slopes down

Sang (racks)

Yatōpambe
(pentroof of matting;
for storing early yams)

Sang (overhanging rack for pots)   sill 9" high

position of ridge pole

low sill

Etōkamle
(used for storing
palm fruits,
or
for girls' fatting house)

C

Lēbelibo
(low shelf for water jar)

Etokabēlĕ

Ōsunggō Kikūt

Kōtōkpō   (bench)

B

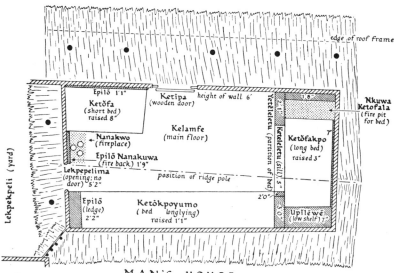

edge of roof frame

Lekpekpeli (yard)

Epilō 1'1"

Ketōfa (short bed) raised 8"

Ketipa (wooden door)   height of wall 6'

Nkuwa Ketofala
(fire pit for bed)

Nanakwo (fireplace)

Kelamfe (main floor)

Ketōfakpo (long bed) raised 3"

Yetēleletu (partition of bed)

Kraeleletu (sill) 5"

Epilō Nanakuwa (fire back) 1'9"

Lekpepelima
(opening; no door) 5'2"

position of ridge pole

2'0"

Epilō (ledge) 2'2"

Ketōkpoyumo
(bed longlying) raised 1'1"

Uplēwē (low shelf) 7"

MAN'S HOUSE
FIG. 10

other words, an adulterer can in some situations successfully claim the social fatherhood of his child. It is said that claims which would give rise to such a conflict are not frequently made, but they are held to be justified where a woman has left her husband and has a liaison with another man, before any divorce has been arranged by repayment of marriage money. The rights of the husband and his patrikin are then confined to compensation for adultery and a return of the marriage money, but do not include fatherhood of the child or its membership of his patriclan. And this has been held to be so even when the woman eventually returns to her husband.[1]

PATRILINEAGE AND CLAN

Yakö dwellings are usually built round small four-sided compounds (*akɔmsunga*, sing. *lekɔmsunga*) on to which face from five to ten separate women's and men's houses. A compound usually contains the houses of several household heads, but the latter, as will be seen, are nearly always close patrilineal kin and despite the crowding of houses in the parts of the villages that have been long occupied, an effort is made to extend the compound and maintain the unity of the related households if they increase in number. Thus a Yakö child brought up in the house of its mother is one of a considerable group of children of various ages. Most of them will be linked in patrilineal kinship both among themselves and to the men of the compound, although, as will appear later, foster-parentage, and the fact that young children usually accompany their mother if she leaves her husband's compound on divorce, introduce some who are connected by other ties. More important at this stage is the fact that a child grows up in the company of age-mates from different households and, as it grows up, takes an increasing part in the activities of the compound as a whole. A boy goes out with his father and with his father's brothers from an early age when they are clearing bush or collecting palm products. Unless relations between his own parents and others happen to be strained he is made to run messages or take food out to the farm during busy seasons for any grown-up of the compound. Later he becomes a regular helper in work on his father's farm and in the

---

[1] In one case, which came for decision to the village head in Umor, a woman left her husband, went to live under the protection of a matrikinsman, and had a liaison with one of the latter's neighbouring patrikin, giving birth to a son. Her husband, wanting her to return, had not brought a charge of adultery or claimed return of marriage money and a year later she did return to him. The lover then claimed the child before the village head, who, with some of the council, held that the child belonged to him and his clan to which it should later return. The lover was told he should compensate the husband for the adultery, but more stress was laid on their living in peace, and no compensation was in fact made. Nevertheless at about 12 years of age the boy was brought back by the lover to his patriclan and has grown up there as his son and a member of his patrilineage.

co-operative working parties of kinsmen and others in which his father joins. A girl accompanies her mother to the farm or looks after younger children in the compound when the older women have to be away farming or at the market. When a young man reaches 17 or 18 years and payments have been made for his first marriage, he is given his first farm plot and help in building a house by his father and other patrilineal kin in the compound (see Fig. 11a).

But the compound in which a man is born and grows up is only one segment of a larger settlement group of patrilineal relatives and their wives. It is this larger group, normally a cluster of several adjacent compounds, which collectively maintains rights to a section of the village site and to tracts of farm-land in the surrounding country. In one house area examined in Umor, nineteen out of a total of thirty-two men, whose fathers were still living, lived in the same compound or house cluster as their fathers. Of the nine adjacent compounds in this dwelling-area, four were almost exclusively occupied by men who were close patrilineal relatives. Each of these sets of close patrikin neighbours, together with a few individuals living elsewhere, constitutes a self-conscious group known as an *eponama* (pl. *yeponama*), a term derived from the Yakö word for the urethra and thus stressing the biological link through males. The *yeponama* are corporate patrilineages whose members trace descent through birth or adoption from a common ancestor three to five generations back, from whom they name themselves as a corporate group, e.g. *Eponama Etung Enamuzo*. They will vary in strength from half a dozen to thirty adult men. If a lineage becomes much larger than this, one or more branches tend to drift apart and their ancestors of three or four generations back become the point of reference for the segmentation.

The patrilineage is thus a small group of kinsmen with, as will be seen, their adopted adherents, the internal coherence of which lasts only so long as the group remains small and intimate; in conditions of increasing population it is likely to persist as a stable and undivided group for only three or four generations. The patrilineage rather than the single compound is the most important corporate group beyond the household of which a Yakö is conscious. Its members claim and distribute among themselves succession to rights in house sites, farm plots, oil-palm clusters, and planted trees that are not made use of by actual sons. A senior man of standing, referred to as *uwo womon* (our father), arbitrates in disputes among them and is their leader in affairs with other groups. And they may also speak of themselves and be referred to as his people, e.g. *Yanen bi Ikpi Esua*.

But the patrilineages are aggregated into larger groups or patriclans which are also territorially compact. These larger groups are known as *yepun* (sing. *kepun*). Each has a recognized and even demarcated dwelling-area (*lekɔm*, pl. *akɔm*), in which live the great majority of its

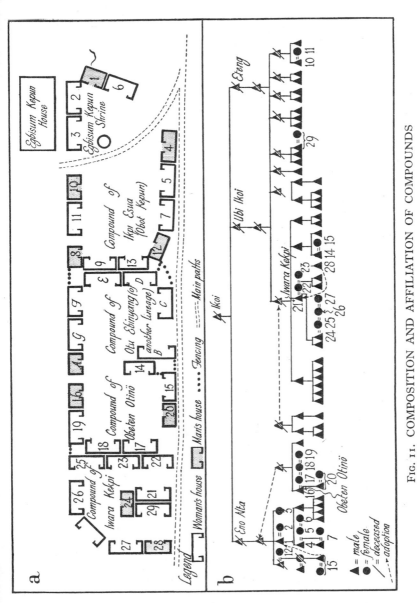

(a) Diagram of four adjacent compounds in Egbisum Kepun, Umor.

(b) Lineage of Ikpi Esua (*Obot Kepun*) to show affiliations of occupants.

Numbers refer to houses in the diagram of compounds. All living adult males of the lineages are shown. Those without numbers live elsewhere.

FIG. 11. COMPOSITION AND AFFILIATION OF COMPOUNDS

men with their wives and children. Each has a name which is used to refer both to the members and to the dwelling-area. These names do not refer to ancestors, actual or mythical. Some refer to natural and other features suggesting that conditions connected with the site led to the naming. *Loseni*, for instance, relates to the name of a tree. But several *yepun* in different wards have the same name.[1]

The boundary between the dwelling-areas of two patriclans is often marked by a narrow gap, a pathway, a shallow ditch, or even a row of posts, and the adjacent houses of the two groups are built back to back on either side of the boundary, emphasizing by their orientation the separateness of the adjacent groups (see Fig. 12).

Within the dwelling-area there is a large open-sided meeting-house (*lepema*) built of massive timbers where *kepun* feasts are held. Here, rather than in their houses, men spend their leisure hours and to it they often bring some task they have in hand. Here, as well as in his own compound, the death of a man is ceremonially recognized when his name is drummed on the *kepun* gong. The patriclan house is not ritually barred to women, but they have no concern with it. Near the meeting-house is the shrine of the *kepun* (*epundet*, pl. *yepundet*), a low mound of small boulders surmounted by some chalk-stained pots, usually set in the shade of a tree. The *epundet*, and the recurrent rites performed there, symbolize for everyone from childhood the corporate group.

But the coherence of the *kepun* is not conceived by the Yakö in terms of contiguity alone. The *kepun* membership of every person is normally established at birth, for a child born in the village is automatically recognized as a member of its father's *kepun*, and continues to be so regarded unless special circumstances result in a *de facto* transfer of membership later in life. Although, as will be seen, individuals may be adopted into the group either as children or even when adult, the majority of the members of a *kepun* at any one time belong to it in virtue of patrilineal descent.

On the other hand, the *kepun* is not a single lineage of wider span than the *eponama* in the sense that all members are held to be descended from a single ancestor to whom genealogical connexion is traced or even ascribed. Yakö may and do say of their *kepun* fellows, 'We are all brothers', and imply common descent in this way, but in other contexts, particularly in disputes over dwelling-sites or prior claims to the use of tracts of farm-land, the separateness of the lineages and their alleged distinct origins are emphasized. Moreover, while, in response to genealogical inquiry, the named ancestors of two lineages are occasionally held to be siblings and their father's name is given, in the majority of cases ignorance or doubt is expressed concerning any patrilineal kinship

---

[1] Many *kepun* names incorporate the Yakö term for dwelling-area, e.g. *letekɔm*, place of smithing; *lekpangkɔm*, place of *kekpan* (= grouping). Others, however, e.g. *ibenda*, *unebu*, &c., omit this combination.

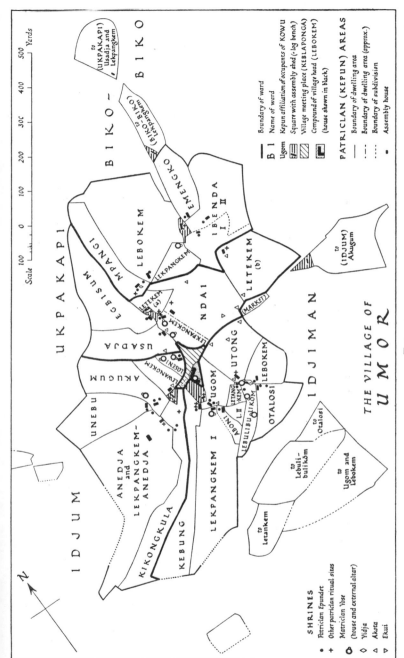

SHRINES

- • Patriclan Epundet
- + Other patriclan ritual sites
- ☉ Matriclan Yose (house and external altar)
- ◇ Yidja
- △ Akata
- ▷ Ekui

Boundary of ward

B 1 Name of ward

Ugom — Kepun affiliation of occupants of KOWU

▨ Square with assembly shed (= log bench)

▩ Village meeting place (KEBLAPONGA)

L Compound of village head (LEBOKEM) (house shown in Black)

PATRICLAN (KEPUN) AREAS

--- Boundary of dwelling area

··· Boundary of dwelling area (approx.)

·-· Boundary of subdivision

■ Assembly house

THE VILLAGE OF UMOR

FIG. 12

between the founders of lineages in a *kepun*, and in some a definite tradition of arrival as a stranger accounts for the ancestor's existence. The sociologically important point is that the separateness of the lineages within the *kepun* is in these ways frequently emphasized.

The patriclans are, nevertheless, strictly exogamous and the rule is enforced with no great difficulty, since post-marital residence is patrilocal. At marriage a woman leaves the compound and *kepun* of her birth to join her husband, usually elsewhere in the same village. Thus, apart from returned widowed or divorced daughters, the women living in a patriclan area (*lekɔm*) are wives and not members of the *kepun* kin. The women who are *kepun* kin are scattered, according to their marriages, all over the village and to a lesser extent in other villages.

The Yakö *kepun* may therefore be summarily described as an exogamous, corporate, and territorially compact patriclan composed of a number of separate lineages with collective rights to a delimited dwelling-area in the village and to tracts of farm-land in the territory, possessing a shrine and an assembly house for group rites and social intercourse. Priority in rights to particular tracts of house and farm-land are claimed by the various component lineages. A Yakö thinks of a *kepun* in terms of all these attributes, but social groups are plastic, liable to departures from the recognized norm and subject to growth, decay, and the impact of other social institutions. Increase in numbers, the development of friction within groups, the concomitant recognition of matrilineal ties, opportunities for house-building on new sites, and for farming in new directions have all operated to complicate the formal plan.

The data summarized for the village of Umor in Table I and on the map (Fig. 12) and diagram (Fig. 13) show how the actual *yepun* often diverge from the ideal pattern. If the groups are defined in terms of the named dwelling-areas alone, we find twenty-six in all. But there are five areas in which there are two shrines (each with its own priest), and two assembly houses are usually maintained in these areas. In each there are two sets of lineages with independent *kepun* rituals forming separate exogamous groups, for there is no bar to marriage between members of the two groups; in some cases they unite in farm activities and recognize a single leader for each of the paths to their farm tracts, others do not. On the other hand, there are eight named dwelling-areas the occupants of which have their own elders, farm-road leaders, and assembly house, but which contain no shrine. The members of such groups belong to a larger ritual group and the shrine with its priest is found elsewhere. In all such cases the two separately named groups form a single exogamous unit and have joint rights to tracts of land.

In Yakö thought and practice patriclanship and exogamy apply to all persons who supplicate at a single shrine (*epundet*), so that there are in Umor, on the one hand, nominally distinct residential groups, which

TABLE I

Patriclans (Yepun) of Umor

Showing linked groups, sites of *yepun* shrines, and number of component lineages (*yeponama*).

IDJIMAN WARD			IDJUM WARD		
1. Lebokem*	. . .	3	17. Anedja-	. . .	1
2. Lekpangkem I	. .	1	18. -Lekpangkem*	. .	7
3. Lekpangkem II	. .	1	19. Lewangkem .	. .	2
4. Ugom I .	. . .	1	20. Loseni*	. . .	6
5. Ugom II*	. . .	2	21. Akugum I† .	. .	2
6. Letangkem	. . .	1	22. Akugum II† .	. .	?
7. Lebulibulikom .	. .	1	23. Kikongkula I	. .	?
8. Aboni .	. . .	1	24. Kikongkula II	. .	1
9. Kebung .	. . .	1	25. Unebu‡	. . .	3
10. Otalosi .	. . .	?			
11. Utong† .	. . .	3			

UKPAKAPI WARD			BIKO-BIKO WARD		
12. Lekpangkem* .	. .	3	26. Emengko*	. . .	4
13. Ndai .	. . .	5	27. Lebokem	. . .	3
14. Egbisum .	. . .	3	28. Mpangi*	. . .	4
15. Letekem	. . .	3	29. Ibenda I	. . .	1
16. Usadja .	. . .	3	30. Ibenda II .	. .	2
			31. Lekpangkem†	. .	

Distinct territorial groups sharing a single shrine bracketed on the left.
Groups with separate shrines but a combined dwelling-area bracketed on the right.
Groups with shrines in their dwelling-areas shown in italics.
Groups of which one or more lineages have migrated to other dwelling-areas indicated by *.
A group composed of, or including in its dwelling-areas, lineages from other clans indicated by †.
Incipient clan composed of discrete migrant lineages indicated by ‡.

constitute a single ritually united exogamous entity, and, on the other hand, single residential groups which in fact consist of two exogamous units each with its independent ritual. The position may be summarized thus:

Patriclan dwelling-area names 26
Exogamous groups each with its own shrine 22
Named groups with separate dwelling-areas but lacking exclusive shrine . 8
Exogamous groups with named sub-groups occupying distinct dwelling-areas 6
Groups with a single named dwelling-area, consisting of two or more exogamous units with separate shrines 5
Exogamous groups, many members of which (all or part of one or more lineages) live in the dwelling-area of another group 7

These divergencies in territorial arrangement and ritual organization result from processes of fission and accretion whereby the structure and composition of many of the patriclans has been modified during a period of marked and doubtless uneven growth of population. Thus the Utong people in Umor consists of three lineages, two of which are recognized

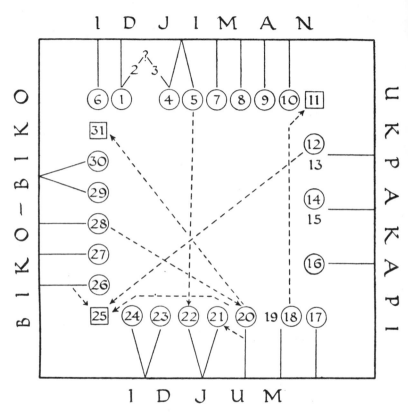

FIG. 13. DIAGRAM TO SHOW THE LOCATION AND RELATIONS
OF PATRICLANS IN UMOR

Groups are arranged by wards on the four sides and are numbered in accordance with Table I. Circles indicate groups with patriclan shrines in their dwelling-area. Squares indicate separately named territorial groups recently formed by migrations of lineages. Broken lines indicate recorded migrations of lineages.

as being descended from migrants from other villages but are now regarded as having combined with one native lineage. The group as a whole recognized the ritual authority of the shrine and priest of the patriclan Anedja-Lekpangkem from which the original lineage itself migrated. The three lineages of Unebu are similarly recognized as descendants of migrants from three different patriclans. Here fusion has not progressed so far. Two of the lineages still consider they belong to their parent *yepun* and resort to the shrines there, while a recent action of the third demonstrates a stage in the process of actual *kepun* fission. After a dispute which came to a head in connexion with a rite at the shrine of the parent clan, they determined to create their own shrine at Unebu. This creation of a new *epundet* with a material nucleus of pots and boulders obtained from an earlier foundation is a recognized if rare procedure, and several are pointed to as having been established in the past generation.[1] If the rift between lineages in a clan is deep the dissident group may, as recently happened in Akugum in Umor, seek the nucleus of pots and boulders with which to establish their new shrine not from that of the clan they are leaving but from one in the Ugom *kepun* known as Elamalama which is held to be the first *epundet* to be established at the foundation of the village. This ritually expresses the complete severance of former clan ties and at the same time the continued adherence of the group to the wider village community.

Fission and fusion in varying degrees imply that the wide range of social activities characteristically grouped within a coherent patriclan may not, in practice, always be so tidily arranged. The customs of exogamy, of economic and ritual co-operation, and the underlying sentiment of kinship maintain a general stability, but all can be weakened by internal strains and can be reforged in a new grouping.[2]

The provision of food-supplies at funeral rites is a special concern of the dead man's lineage, and the inheritance of membership in men's associations falls to a lineage-fellow before it is offered to, or expected by, other members of the *kepun*. Moreover, the offices of *kepun* priest and his assistant are properly filled by members of certain lineages only. The choice is almost always restricted to one or two lineages; when more than one lineage is concerned, these provide the priest in rotation.

The estimate of the numerical strength of the patriclans will of course depend on the criteria adopted to define them, but they may be said to range in size from about 50 to 150 grown men. They are therefore comparatively small groups whose residential unity obviously strengthens their social coherence. Born and growing up in one dwelling-area, playing from childhood with others who will later be his neighbours in the village and his companions in farm work and palm tending, a man

[1] Patriclans which have thus recently come into existence by fission sometimes lack a name of *kepun* type. Members of such groups distinguish themselves by using the name of the priest, that is, by calling themselves 'the *kepun* of So-and-So', or by using the lineage names in addition to a *kepun* name shared with another group, e.g. Ibenda comprises two clans distinguished as 'Ibenda yi Iwara Kekbiyen' and 'Ibenda yi Iwara Edo'.

[2] On the other hand, individuals may for particular reasons live outside their patriclan dwelling-area without dissociating themselves from it. When, for example, a man succeeds to a matrilineal priesthood he should go to live in the *lekɔma* where the shrine is situated.

comes to regard his *kepun* group as a community within the larger village. This corporate sense extends to outlying farm and forest lands, since the patriclan provides the framework within which each family head secures personal rights to the tracts from which he obtains his food-supply and palm-oil. A farm-road elder (*oponotam eta*), often the head of one of the lineages, adjusts the claims of individuals in each tract of land claimed by the patriclan.

In the larger villages the patriclan dwelling-areas are grouped in districts or wards known as *yekpatu* (sing. *kekpatu*). It is necessary here only to emphasize that the grouping together of certain patriclans within a single ward and the organizations based on the ward, of which the age-sets and some men's associations are the most important, are purely territorial and are not based on any assumption of kinship ties between them.

LEADERSHIP IN PATRICLAN AND LINEAGE

The *Obot Kepun*, the priest who officiates at its shrine and is custodian of the sacred tusk trumpets and staves, is the ritual head of a patriclan. He is treated with considerable deference. He receives gifts from the participants in rites and from all men of the clan at the annual New Yam ceremonies. It is also his duty to maintain harmony in the group, to compose disputes and announce decisions. But in this he is much dependent on the balance of opinion among the elders of the clan (*yaponotam*, sing. *oponotam*) and particularly the heads ('fathers') of the component lineages. For he is primarily a priest and a peacemaker, and active leadership and the mobilization of opinion on public affairs are left to the play of personality among the elders. A clan may be dominated at a particular time by a leading man in one of the lineages. If so, the *Obot Kepun* will accept him as his agent and representative in arranging its affairs. At other times there may be serious rivalry between factions among the lineages and his task is more difficult. But the priest himself is expected to listen to all sides, to avoid partisanship and, unless it flagrantly disregards custom, to accept the prevailing opinion on any question at issue. He is not, therefore, the active manager, far less an autocrat, in the clan. On the other hand, no question of substance is considered properly settled until it has been thrashed out before him and his judgement has been given. Disputes between clansmen are heard by him together with the elders concerned and delinquents are ordered to pay small fines and, for ritual offences, to make an offering at the shrine which is shared among them. Each priest has a regular assistant—'the pourer of palm wine' in rituals at the *epundet*—who should succeed to the priestship. His recognition as assistant in fact depends on his being the designated and accepted successor to the priest.

The accepted leader of a lineage, its 'father', who is turned to for advice and who acts as its spokesman, takes the initiative in composing any internal disputes, and is expected to speak on behalf of any individual or group in the lineage accused of an offence or suffering a grievance. Both men and women make him small gifts when they seek his services. Although seniority in patrilineal descent is emphasized, succession depends largely on personality. A leader usually chooses, from among his male relatives a few years junior to himself, an acceptable lieutenant who acts as his messenger and general supporter. This man, if he gets on well with his fellows and shows qualities of moderation, succeeds without discussion or formal appointment. There is, however, a tendency for the leadership to revert to a descendant in the direct line of a former head. Alternate succession may be the rule when a lineage has two branches. But the head of a lineage should not merely be eligible by descent and seniority; he should be notable and prosperous, impressive and conciliatory.

ADOPTION INTO A PATRILINEAGE

When the genealogical structure of Yakö patrilineages is examined in detail, it soon becomes apparent that many and sometimes the majority of the members do not trace actual descent from the founders, but are descendants of men adopted into the group. Thus in the Ndai-Lekpangkem *kepun* in Umor only seven of the sixteen living adult men of Etung Enamuzo lineage are lineal descendants of the founder, while there are four groups of descendants of individual adoptions. Similarly in Itewa lineage, only five of the present twenty-one adult members are lineal descendants, while the rest are members in virtue of four adoptions at various times. These adoptions, usually effected in childhood or youth, may bring into the group men from other *yepun* within a village, men from other villages, and even strangers from other language groups. Adoption is not marked by any rite whereby a man's status is formally and abruptly changed and an earlier kin allegiance annulled in favour of his new status. It may often be a matter for debate whether or not, at a particular moment, a man has become a member of a new kin group by adoption.

Very young children nearly always accompany their mother if she leaves her husband, and if their mother dies they are as often given to the care of her relatives as to those of the father, and so go to live, at least temporarily, in another patriclan. With older children the customary attitude differs as between boys and girls. Although the father may in a particular case agree that a son should go with the mother, this does not imply his consent to adoption by the mother's patrikin, and he is upheld by his own kin and by the village head if he refuses to let the child accompany her. A girl, however, almost always accompanies her mother, and, although her father can claim his customary portion, the matrilineal kin of the mother in such circumstances may take complete responsibility for her marriage and receive all the marriage payment.

This is symptomatic of the weaker attachment of women to their patrilineage.

A father and other patrikin usually maintain contact with an absent son during his childhood, and encourage his return at manhood to the patriclan of his birth, and if a son is with a stepfather he does nearly always return. But when the child, on the death or divorce of his mother, is entrusted to a mother's brother, he is likely to associate himself more closely with the patrikin of his foster-father, and to be offered a house site and farm-land there when he grows up. Acceptance, which would normally imply an intention to attach himself permanently to the patriclan of his foster-parent, will depend on whether his actual father is still living and is sympathetic to him, and on his relations with his brothers and half-brothers in the patriclan of his birth. The crucial issue is often the provision of funds for marriage payments. If these are provided by his foster-parent, the youth will be expected henceforth to behave as a member of that patriclan. On the other hand, provision of the greater part of the marriage payment by his own father or other close patrikin will be dependent on the return of the youth to his patriclan, where he will find a house site and farming lands.

Foster-children or wards, known as *yawunen* (sing. *owonen*), are quite frequently pressed to stay by their foster-fathers, who desire to increase the number of their households and descendants. They undertake the marriage payments for their adopted sons, and sponsor them in all claims to status in the new kin group. Love-affairs or marriage with women of the foster-father's patriclan will then be forbidden as incestuous to the children of an adopted son, who will be free, on the other hand, to mate with any but close relatives within the patriclan in which their father was born. The decision to adhere permanently to the patrikin of a foster-father does not, however, entitle a man to seek a wife for himself in his own father's patriclan. Many associations and obligations connected with his kinship status during infancy still cling to him. It should also be stressed that adoption is never irrevocable. A man is held to be free to return to the kin of his birth at any time, and should he do so the rights, obligations, and ritual restrictions, such as kin exogamy, which operated with regard to the kin into which he had been adopted are regarded as having lapsed.

The adoptions so far considered involve transfer from one patriclan to another within the village, but persons may also be adopted from other settlements. A stranger may have been invited to live with a clan because of his skill in a craft such as wood-carving, but the majority have come as the kinsmen of women who have come from other villages as wives. A widowed or divorced woman from another village, whether it be Yakö or one in the neighbouring territories such as Ekumuru or Adim, may bring with her a young son who, by the time he is adult, will be accepted as a member of his stepfather's *kepun*. An adult kinsman of the foreign wife may also come as a guest, help her husband in the farm-lands for a season or two, and eventually be taken to the patriclan head and farm-road elders to be given a plot of his own. The majority of adopted foreigners whose personal histories could be obtained were found to be such relatives of foreign wives.

A second class of extra-village adoption arises from the recognition of matrilineal kinship. It consists essentially in the adoption in childhood of a boy or, less often, of a girl from among the foster-parent's matrilineal kin in another village. This form of adoption also commonly results from extra-village marriages. The sons and daughters of a woman who has married into another village will normally become members of that community. But a man often seeks to adopt a sister's son, especially if he is without sons of his own, while, on the other hand, such a child may be offered to his care in consequence of some dislocation in the sister's household. In addition to actual sisters' sons, more remote and putative matrilineal kinship may be the occasion for such extra-village adoption.

But a considerable number of children of completely alien origin have also, as has been mentioned earlier (p. 291), been adopted into Yakö households and so into the patriclans. These children, known as *yafoli* (sing. *ofoli*), have been brought to the village by strangers and have been handed over in return for payments, usually made in money. This may have occurred more frequently than the genealogical data reveal, for both the inferior status of the descendants of *yafoli* and the punishment, under slave-dealing ordinances, of the sale and purchase of children have probably led to the concealment of such actions in the past, and to the misrepresentation of *yafoli* as *yawunen*, or actual begotten children. During the period of increasing wealth, with the growth of the palm-oil trade over the past four or five decades, the adoption of *yafoli* has certainly contributed to the rapid growth of the population which is indicated by the expansion of the villages. To purchase an *ofoli* has been a meritorious display of wealth, and an achievement necessary for one who claims to be a man of substance (*osu*, pl. *yasu*) and to partake in the reciprocal funerary feasts of the rich. *Yafoli* have been acquired far more frequently by men than by women, but childless wives often urged their husbands to get a child in this way. Both boys and girls have been obtained, but girls more frequently than boys. The adoption of girls is expressly stated by the people themselves to reflect the desire to increase the numbers and prestige of the matrilineal kin. It is also valued as giving a woman a companion and helper in her farm work. *Yafoli* have not usually been married by their purchasers and the status and signi-ficance of a girl *ofoli* is more often that of a daughter. For a short period she may make possible an increase in the size and productivity of her foster-father's farm, and later he receives a marriage payment for her. After that she is likely to have little significance for the patriclan unless serious matrimonial disputes arise, for her children are matrilineal, not

x

patrilineal kin of her foster-father. The boy *ofoli* likewise ranks as a potential if inferior matrilineal heir, but he also grows up as an adopted member of the patriclan of his purchaser. He can inherit status there from his foster-father, although he ranks below a begotten son, and his origin may be used against him in abuse in moments of anger both by kinsmen and by other villagers.

An adopted youth, whether originally a kinsman (*owunen*) or an *ofoli*, can often be a direct economic asset. A man will farm and build, collect palm products, and engage in petty trading for at least fourteen years before any son of his own is old enough to act as a regular and effective male helper. A young married man, therefore, often welcomes an opportunity to adopt a boy 10 or 12 years of age. But even more influential than these economic benefits is the widespread desire to enlarge the household and increase the number of descendants in lineage and clan.

MATRIKIN AND MATRICLAN

The patrilineal *kepun* is not, however, the only group of kin within which a Yakö has rights and obligations. It has already been seen that ties of matrilineal kinship underlie many of the adoptions of men into *yepun*. These ties not only involve rights and duties between persons closely related in this way; they are also the foundation of matriclans, known as *yajima* (sing. *lejima*), complementary to the patriclans just described. Apart from full siblings, the persons composing the patrikin and the matrikin of each individual are normally distinct, and it is of importance for the understanding of the social relations that are established through matrilineal kinship to bear in mind that, among close relatives, only full brothers and sisters will of necessity belong to both groups. Since residence is patrilocal, the members of a matriclan must be dispersed among the patriclan territories of a village while a minority will be living in other villages.

The rights and obligations which derive from matrilineal kinship do not formally conflict with those derived patrilineally. Over the greater part of the fields of economic activity, ritual observance, and succession to property, a clear distinction between their spheres of application has, until very recently, been maintained. Matrilineal kinship should take precedence over patrilineal in the inheritance of transferable wealth, especially livestock and currency, in the receipt of payments made to a woman's kin at her marriage, in the corresponding responsibility for the return of payments received for women who later unjustifiably leave their husbands, in responsibility for debts incurred by an individual, and also in obligations and rights in respect of recompense for bodily injuries. On the other hand, patrilineal rights and obligations, as has been seen, largely relate to the use of land and houses and to the provision of co-operative labour, especially in the annual farm-clearings at the beginning of the agricultural season. Yakö say that 'a man eats in his *kepun* and inherits in his *lejima*'.

In the present generation, however, matrilineal ties are being undermined, especially in the villages of Ekuri and, to a lesser degree, Umor, by successful claims of sons to their father's personal possessions and by the retention of marriage payments by fathers. Administrative confirmation of decisions in this sense in the Native Authority courts have strengthened this tendency. But in the thirties the majority of the Yakö still adhered to earlier custom, and, although some are now determined to flout them, no Yakö denies that matrilineal rights exist.

Close matrilineal relatives will be in touch with all important events and circumstances in each other's households and will give mutual support within the framework of the accepted kinship obligations. Although in the larger villages many members of one's matriclan may be encountered only occasionally, all are made vividly aware of their fellowship two or three times a year in rituals which are the visible symbols of the unity and social reality of the matrilineal groups.

The matriclans are similar in numerical strength to the patriclans. The largest do not much exceed 100 adult males and some are much smaller. The prefix *ya*, signifying 'the people of . . .', is incorporated in the names of the matrilineal kin groups which are quite distinct in form from those of the patrilineal groups.[1] Some are held to have been independent groups at an indefinitely remote period. Such clans have priesthoods. Others are ritually attached to one or other of these groups and are in some cases held to be offshoots of the clan from which the priest of the spirit (*yose*, pl. *ase*) they recognize is chosen. Other secondary groups are held to have transferred their ritual dependence to another shrine when they separated from a parent group. Fig. 14 and Table II summarize the position in the village of Umor, where it will be seen that although 23 distinct matriclans are recognized, there are only 10 cult groups. Twelve of the former, although they are independent with respect to other rights, depend for their supernatural benefits and for the ritual validation of decisions by their elders on rites carried out by the priests of other clans. All but four of the priests officiate for more than one matriclan and these four are said to be priests of groups which were themselves dependent on others before they established shrines and priesthoods of their own.[2]

In every matriclan there is a group of elders known as *yajimanotam*—old men and women of the *lejima*—from six to a dozen of the more

---

[1] Thus *Yabaye* refers to one matriclan as a corporate entity as well as to a plurality of members. An individual member is an *obaye*. But the name of a *kepun* such as Egbisum is distinct from the term for members, who would be referred to individually as Ogbisum and collectively as Yagbisum.

[2] For details and documentation of these processes see my earlier paper on 'Kinship in Umor'. *Amer. Anthropologist*, xli, 4, Oct.–Dec. 1939, pp. 523–53.

senior and active members and leaders in component lineages who, although they have no ritual functions and no ceremonial duties and maintain their numbers by informal co-option from time to time, do in

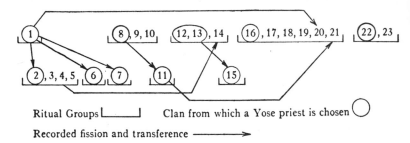

Ritual Groups └────┘   Clan from which a Yose priest is chosen ◯

Recorded fission and transference ─────────▶

FIG. 14. DIAGRAM OF MATRICLAN LINKS IN UMOR

TABLE II

Matriclans (Yajima) of Umor

Lejima	Yose	Lejima	Yose
1. YABOT I	Odjokobi*	12. ⎰YAKUMIKO	Osengawe-
2. ⎰ Yabot II (from	Obolene*	13. ⎥YABUNG	kongkong*
Yabot I)		14. ⎱ Yakpambot of	(Obot Lo-
3. ⎱ Yakpambot	..	Idjiman	kona)
4. ⎥Yawambot	..	15. Yangyɵ (from	Obete Edet
5. ⎱Yadjemi	..	Yakumiko-	
6. Yakoibot (from	Kupatu*	Yabung)	
Yabot I)		16. ⎰YABOLETETE	Esukpa
7. Yosenibot (from	Okarefong*	17. ⎥Yabuna	..
Yabot I)		18. ⎥Yakamafe	..
8. ⎰YAKANG-	Atewa*	19. ⎱ Yatebö	..
KANG		20. ⎥Yakpölö (from	..
9. ⎥Yatioma	..	Yabot I)	
10. ⎱Yayale	..	21. ⎱Yanali (from	..
11. Yabaye (from	Atalikumi	Yabaye)	
Yakangkang)		22. YAPUNI	Otabelusanga
		23. Yadjokpoli	..

Capitals indicate matriclans providing *ase* priests and not known to have separated from another group.

Italics indicate matriclans said to have separated from others as indicated to create their own *ase*.

Ase which may not be moved from the site of their alleged foundation indicated by *.

Nine matriclans have an exclusive right to elect priests; two have rights in alternation; twelve provide no priests; one is in process of fission; eight (seven and a section of an eighth) have transferred their allegiance and five of these have created new *ase*.

fact exert considerable influence both on the members and on village affairs that concern the group. Recompense for offence by one member of the matriclan towards another can be enforced by requesting the priest of the *yose* to declare the offender excommunicated. By appeal to the village council they are able, as will be seen, to protect the interests of particular members of the group in the payments and responsibilities involved in the marriages of their matrilineal kin. On the death of a matriclan priest they nominate his successor.

Within each village one of the matriclan spirits is held to be superior in power and in ritual status. Its cult is maintained, not only for the benefit of members of the matriclan of its priest and of any others secondarily attached to it, but also on behalf of the village as a whole. Its shrine has precedence in all village rituals and the priest, as ritual head of the local community, is known as *Obot Lopon* (Leader of the Village). But this does not confer any formal authority or superior status on the members or elders of the matriclan itself. Indeed, the matriclan organization, like the patrilineal groups already discussed, exhibits a characteristic absence of systematic ranking of groups.

While all members of a matriclan within a village are not only ritually associated but regard one another as kin, they are not an undifferentiated group. The exercise and transmission of rights operate within smaller units of close relatives known as *yajimafat* (sing. *lejimafat*). These matrilineages are comparable in size and span to the patrilineages and it is within these smaller groups that most rights and obligations between matrilineal kin are exercised and transmitted. The collective term for matrilineal kin—*yatamban*—usually refers to the matrilineage, although it may apply also to the clan.

It is only within the matrilineage that exogamy is now strictly enforced. Formerly marriage within the matriclan was strongly disapproved. Old people still hold that such a marriage is likely to be sterile and to weaken the beneficient power of the *yose*. But during the thirties, starting first in Ekuri, both practice and attitude were changing in connexion with the conflict over inheritance rights between sisters' sons and sons. There has been a general tendency in recent years for sons to lay successful claim to at least a share in the movable goods left by their father which, by former custom, passed entirely to matrilineal heirs. Marriage with a girl of another lineage in one's own matriclan has come to be encouraged as a device whereby this conflict can be resolved, the son of such a marriage being regarded as the matrilineal heir of his father. Such sons are successfully claiming sole inheritance of their father's movable goods as members of his matriclan and virtual members of his matrilineage, while young men are being encouraged by elders of their own matrilineage to make their first marriage with a girl of another lineage in the matriclan, so that they will be able to transmit their wealth to their eldest sons.

Unlike the patriclan system, which does not extend beyond the village, the màtriclans in one village are held to correspond with clans in others. There are no common rituals, but there is a considerable parallelism in names of clans and clan spirits, and even a vague belief in ultimate common descent. People coming from another village, including not only individuals bent on trade or visiting a close kinsman who has migrated but also parties of young girls who commonly make stays of several weeks in the rainy season, can expect hospitality from members of the corresponding matriclan. Women marrying into another village are, together with their children, automatically accepted as members of the appropriate matriclan there. Formerly sons of such women lost no rights as matrilineal heirs of their mother's brothers in her village of origin.[1]

MATRILINEAL RIGHTS AND OBLIGATIONS

It has been seen that rights to dwelling-sites, farming land, and the more important forest resources are obtained by virtue of membership of a patrilineal group; but that when attention is transferred from rights in economic resources to the transmission of accumulated wealth, matrilineal kinship comes into prominence. The funeral and the disposal of a dead person's property are supervised by a close matrikinsman, a mother's brother or a sister's son, who in the case of a man is chief heir. All currency, whether it be in brass rods or modern coinage, and all livestock, should by custom pass to matrilineal relatives who also receive the greater share of the implements, weapons, household goods, and any stores of food. The movable property of women, which is usually less considerable, passes mainly to their daughters, but sons should expect very little from their parents. A man may obtain a gun or cutlass that was his father's; the rest will be claimed by his father's brother or sisters' sons.

With these rights of inheritance are associated corresponding obligations, and, in particular, responsibility for debts of matrikinsmen, a readiness to make reasonable loans at need, and the duty of providing a part, although a minor share, of the currency and goods transferred by a sister's son at marriage. If an outside creditor is unable to obtain satisfaction for a debt he will often seize a goat or cow belonging to a close matrilineal kinsman of the debtor who can obtain no recompense through either the Village Council or, in more recent times, the Native Authority court, if the existence of an unduly prolonged debt is satisfactorily established. Considerable payments are involved in membership of men's associations among the Yakö and debts are often contracted in this connexion both with individuals and the clubs themselves. If the debtor is dilatory, his matrilineal kinsmen are summoned and

---

[1] Marriage with women of other villages appears to have been largely confined to Umor.

requested to make arrangements for settlement. If they refuse or fail to carry out their agreement, the Village Council would formerly have approved the seizure of their livestock by one of the associations. Nowadays most disputes over considerable debts are taken to the Native Authority court established by the Nigerian Government, but the responsibility of an offender's matrilineal kin to contribute if necessary has been recognized there. The court likewise summons the matrilineal kinsmen of a bankrupt debtor and orders them to undertake a settlement. Finally, if a man at his death leaves outstanding debts, his matrilineal kinsmen succeed to the obligations.

When a man dies, his household usually continues to function as a productive unit with the aid of brothers and sons until the yam harvest of the farm is gathered in.[1] The dead man's crop, which will be considerably larger than those of his wives, is at the disposal of his matrilineal kin. But since the chief claimant is often a full brother, who is also a patrikinsman and undertakes obligations to the children of the dead man if they remain in the *kepun*, a considerable part may in fact be used for the benefit of these children. The widows will remarry or join either their grown sons or their own parents, and unless they are still caring for young children of their dead husband, when they will be given a portion, they have no right to any share of their dead husband's yams. The rest of the surplus is taken by brothers and adult sisters' sons for planting in their farms or for sale. But the dead man's children will themselves go later to his brothers, as to a 'father', for a supply of yams to make their first farms.

The position of women as wives and as owners of property in their husbands' farms is similarly the concern of their matrilineal kin. When a wife dies, both her rights and duties in her husband's farm pass for the rest of the farming-season to one or more matrikinswomen. If she dies after a harvest, her yams in the household yam store are claimed by her matrilineal kin and are usually taken by a sister or a grown daughter. If, on the other hand, a woman dies during the growing-season, the husband asks to be given the services of one or more of her 'sisters' to care for the farm and carry in the harvest. When the crop is dug, the yams of the deceased wife are carried away by the women who have taken her place, for distribution among themselves and other matrilineal kin.

Apart from the recent open challenging by sons of the inheritance rights of matrikin referred to earlier (p. 309), some evasion by men and their sons is said to be of long standing. Hoards of brass rods and later of Nigerian currency have not infrequently been hidden by secretly burying them in farm-land. Apart from the ease of concealment, the profound suspicion of magical malpractice which is aroused by trespass

[1] For an account of relevant farming practice see my 'Land and Labour in a Cross River Village'.

on another's farm-land and the magical safeguards against it render such a cache in farm-land fairly secure. A man may confide in one or more of his sons the whereabouts of such a hoard while withholding knowledge of it from his matrikin so that the former may quietly take possession after his death.

Matrilineal kinship confers no settled right to economic resources which are exploited within the patriclan, that is, to farm plots as distinct from specific harvests, to oil-palm groves or to planted trees. But the categories are not entirely clear cut since matrikin should supply one another when there is special and occasional need. A man should never refuse a reasonable request from a sister's son or other matrikinsman for some of the produce of his planted trees and will seek approval from the head of his patrilineage for him to collect palm products on their land. Moreover, a considerable number of the valuable clumps of raphia palms, largely confined to swampy ground not used for farming, which provide much valued building material for houses and yam stacks are in fact the property of matrilineages. It is recognized that a man who plants a new clump may share it during his lifetime with his sisters' sons and leave it to one or more of them at his death. The right of control then passes matrilineally, although conversely owners' sons in each generation are then allowed access to the clump for their own needs. This practice runs counter to the general principle of patrilineal succession to farm and forest resources and appears to be related to the very uneven distribution of the scarce raphia-bearing swamps among the lands of the patriclans. Finally each matriclan claims the right to collect palm-wine over a tract of village territory for use in the funeral rites of matriclan elders, at the installation of their priests, and in certain other rituals. This temporarily overrides the rights of those who have prepared the trees in their patriclan lands, and enables a matriclan to act corporately in assembling a large supply of palm-wine.

Membership in most of the men's associations among the Yakö is obtained by succession to a deceased member. This may be either patrilineal or matrilineal, since a man's right, which is also an obligation, to join a society may be inherited from either a matrilineal or a patrilineal kinsman and this right should pass on by the same rule as that whereby the deceased succeeded. The close kin, both matrilineal and patrilineal, are expected to contribute to the fees required, but the more substantial payment is made by the group providing the successor, and in their case the obligation extends beyond the close relatives and concerns all the older members of the lineage and other notables of the clan.

Homicide within a village also initiates a series of customary claims for compensation which are the concern of the kinsfolk of those directly involved. Formally no distinction is made between deliberate and accidental homicide, and while it is admitted that murder of one villager by the deliberate violence of another is a danger to be guarded against, anger is little tempered by evidence, however obvious, that the injury was accidental. If a man is killed, the reactions and claims of the two sets of his kinsfolk, patrilineal and matrilineal, are clearly distinct. In both groups anger is aroused, but the immediate crisis and the danger of retaliation is much greater among the patrikin. When the body is brought into the compound, there is a likelihood that the close patri- lineal relatives will urge the men of the patriclan to attack the offender and his patrikin. Fights arising in this way have fairly frequently occurred. Indeed it is customary for the offender to seek shelter in the compound of the Village Head, and stay there while the Village Speaker is sent to the assembly house of the dead man's patriclan bearing the village elephant-tusk trumpet and drum which, by supernatural sanction, impose restraint and an obligation on the bereaved patriclan to keep the peace. The offender, or one of his close patrikin, has also on occasion been seized as a hostage by the *kepun* of the dead man and held until a pay- ment was made to them for his release.

Nevertheless, if one of their number, man or woman, is killed the patrilineal kin have no customary right to compensation, material or ritual, from the patriclan of the offender. This concerns only the matri- clans of the deceased and the person held responsible. A matriclan which suffers loss by the violent death of a grown member at the hands of an outsider has a recognized right to compensation which is ritually safe- guarded. It is required that the offender and also, where an adult man has been killed by another, one of the former's matrilineal kinswomen be transferred to the dead man's *lejima* in a ceremony at its *yose* shrine. The transfer of the woman has, however, been commonly compounded by a payment sufficient to purchase a female *ofoli*. There is a keen sense of loss over those who have been transferred, but they must attend and contribute conspicuously at the funeral rites of members of their new matriclan and must avoid ostentatious participation in rituals of their former matriclan. The transfer of a woman, which is always permanent, results, if she bears children, in the numerical increase of the matriclan she has entered and also in the transfer, by inheritance, of property from the people of the offending *lejima*. It was fairly clear that restoration of the strength of the injured *lejima* was the most vital aspect of these trans- fers and they reflected a sentiment, more consciously developed in the matrilineal than in the patrilineal groups, which is being continually enhanced by the fertility rituals at the *ase* shrines.

This practice of compensating the matrilineal kinsfolk alone is not intelligible from a material point of view. Any children that a man who is killed might later have begotten would have been no concern of his matrilineal kin and, since his existing property should pass to them in the ordinary way, any loss to the matriclan is confined to wealth he might subsequently have accumulated. The patriclan, on the other hand, suffers the loss of a breadwinner and a progenitor by the death of a grown man, yet it can legally claim no compensation from the offender's patriclan either in services or supplies of food for the household, nor are any males transferred to membership of the bereaved *kepun*. The strong sentiments concerning fertility and peace within the *lejima* as described later appear to be responsible for the maintenance of these practices, but there is nevertheless a lack of symmetry. The matrikin are given the emotional satisfaction of restitution but the patrikin are not, while in economic terms the matrilineal kin are over-compensated and the patrilineal kin remain without recompense. It is held that these obligations to the matrilineal kin of victims of homicide are not affected by close patrilineal kinship between the parties. The murder or killing of a half-brother, a son, or other *kepun* kinsman would involve restitution to the bereaved matrilineal kin in the ordinary way. On the other hand, no claim for compensation could arise from a killing that involved two men of the same matrilineal group.

Rights to inheritance of property, to aid in the accumulation of their marriage payments, and sometimes to succession in associations inevitably strengthen the ties between youths and their senior matrilineal relatives, and there is usually an intimate relation between a man and his sister's son—the classic relationship which cuts across parental ties in societies stressing matrilineal descent. And among the Yakö this relationship is often converted when opportunity arises into foster-fatherhood with subsequent adoption of sisters' sons into the patriclan of the mother's brother.

RITUAL AND POLITICAL AUTHORITY OF MATRICLAN PRIESTS

Every matriclan is associated with a fertility spirit—*yose* (pl. *ase*). This is embodied in a miscellaneous set of cult objects, including decorated skulls, figurines, helices, and penannular rings of brass and copper and various pots, which are kept on an altar in a miniature house in the compound of the priest and arranged on an adjacent open-air altar at public rituals. The successive invocation of the fertility spirits at these shrines constitutes the central act of the village rituals at various stages in the farming year, and the *ase*, not the *yepundet*, spirits of the patriclans, are in native belief the spirits primarily active in maintaining the well-being of the village. Every girl is brought by a close matrilineal kinsman, usually an older brother or a mother's brother, to the shrine of the fertility spirit of her matriclan during her first pregnancy. Gifts and materials for an offering are brought on an appointed day when a rite is performed to safeguard her and her unborn child, a future member of the group. A corresponding ritual, in which the woman is accompanied by her father, is performed at her patriclan shrine, but is regarded as less powerful. The priests of the *ase*, each known as the *ina* (pl. *bi'ina*) of the spirit in question, e.g. *Ina Atalikumi*, have, in consequence of this greater ritual power, a prestige and authority superior to those of the priests of the patrilineal kin groups. This power of the *ase*, to which their priests alone have direct access, is the ritual sanction of authority in the wider field of social control in the village as a whole, which overrides authority within the several patriclans. The *ase* priests are the nucleus and strength of a sacerdotal council in each village which has the power to invoke the destructive or beneficent actions of the spirits themselves, and thus commands the strongest supernatural sanctions in the village.

Each is chosen from a certain matriclan and proposed by its elders but acts on behalf of every clan dependent on the spirit concerned. Although a close matrilineal relative of a former priest is considered most appropriate, succession is not rigidly prescribed. Choice usually falls not on one of the elders but on a man in early middle life and, although he is selected by the clan elders, he must be approved, and then instructed in his ritual duties, by the group of *ase* priests as a whole.

A priest should reflect in his own physical well-being, in the serenity of his temperament, and in his peaceable behaviour the beneficent power of the spirit, and he will usually ask the priest of another spirit to deputize for him if he is ailing or has suffered distress at the time of a ritual. If two or more priests of a single *yose* die in succession after only a few years of office, a notion of restoring life-maintaining power by infusing new blood into the priesthood comes into play. It is believed that a weakness revealed by the chain of misfortune can be overcome by selecting as a successor a son of a man of the matriclan, an *okpan*, that is, by breaking the rule of succession within a group of matrilineal kin. This may be and occasionally is done apart from previous misfortunes, if a man, well fitted by physique and temperament on whom the clan elders and the *ase* priests are agreed, cannot be found within the group. A priest appointed in this way is ritually adopted into the *lejima* at his installation.

Although each priest carries out private rituals at his shrine for all persons of the matriclans concerned, the seasonal rites are conducted jointly by all the priests and for the village as a whole. In each village one of them is, as has been said, recognized as the Leader of the Village (*Obot Lopon*), in virtue of his control of the cult of the premier spirit which is regarded as the fertility spirit of the village and the most powerful supernatural force within it. Selected from a single matrilineal kin group, he is as pre-eminent among the priests as is that spirit among the others and he is recognized as the religious head of the village.

This corporation of priests, known collectively as the Leaders (*Yabot*),[1] does not consist solely of the *Bi'ina* but the other members

---

[1] The term *Obot* (pl. *Yabot*) can best be translated as Leader or Head, but its connotation varies with its context. Used alone in the plural it is understood to refer to the indigenous sacerdotal council of the village, the *kepun* heads are distinguished as *Yabot Yepun*. The same term is also, however, the title of

such as *Okpebri* (the village Speaker and prayer-leader in collective rituals) all belong to it in virtue of their appointment to ritual offices at the instance of the other priests. Its functions are not, however, restricted to ritual performances and the securing of supernatural benefits. It also guides village affairs, reaffirms customary law, and attempts to settle major disputes. In Umor the priest of *Odjokobi* is *Obot Lopon* and head of this council. His compound, known as *Lebokem*, is situated on one side of the village assembly square (*Keblaponga*), near the centre of the village and not in the territory of any patriclan or ward. In his compound at the *Odjokobi* shrine all the public rituals of the village are initiated and reach their climax and in it, too, the council assembles to discuss village affairs and to hear disputes that are brought before them.

The *Yabot* thus form a close-knit corporation whose members are linked to the rest of the village through the matriclan system. They are not representative of the patrilineal groups or of any territorial section. They are responsible for announcing the times at which many seasonal activities should begin, and for refusal to comply with their regulation of such activities they impose fines. They have authority both in civil disputes, where they serve as a court of appeal, and in public offences, for which they can impose fines and order expiation.[1] Disputes between persons and groups which cannot be settled by the arbitration of the elders of the kin groups concerned, or by the ward heads in the larger villages, are taken to them by one or other of the contestants. They would also intervene on their own initiative to deal with public offences both secular and religious.[2] The *Yabot* command powerful sanctions both physical and supernatural to enforce their decisions. The supernatural sanctions lie in their own hands. They can refuse an offender and his close matrikin all access to the shrine of his matriclan spirit. More drastic is a ceremonial declaration of the offence to the *yose* and a request that the beneficence of the spirit be withdrawn from the offender and if need be from his *lejima*. By coming in procession and placing their staffs before the entrance to his compound or his house, they can forbid

two matrilineal groups from one of which the *Obot Lopon* is selected (see Table II, p. 308).

[1] The establishment first of a Warrant Chief's Court and more recently of Native Authority Councils and Courts in the Yakö area have reduced the judicial and executive authority of the *Yabot*, but civil disputes, especially those between kin groups, are brought to them and they still intervene against ritual offences. See my paper, 'Government in Umor', *Africa*, xii. 2, April 1939, pp. 129–61.

[2] Their power of action in the public interest may be exemplified as follows: it is the duty of the Speaker acting on behalf of the *Yabot* to quell serious disorders arising from civil disputes and summon the offenders before them. Anyone alleged to have caused a fire in the village would be tried by the *Yabot* and if guilty pay them a fine of a cow and 10 brass rods. For abortion, as a grave ritual offence believed to impair fertility in the community as a whole through action of the *ase* spirits, they impose a fine of a cow which is sacrificed and eaten in a rite of expiation at the shrine of the offender's matriclan.

a person's entering or leaving the dwelling until the fine imposed for an offence has been paid. If their decisions are flouted one of the men's associations is authorized by them to despoil the offender and his close kin.

YAKPAN

It will be appreciated that, with the tracing of distinct lines of descent and the formation of groups of kin through father and son on the one hand and through mother and daughter on the other, every Yakö will, through parents and children, have kin to whose lineal groups he or she will not themselves belong. Such will be the matrilineal kin of one's father and those of a man's children and the patrilineal kin of one's mother and those of a woman's children. The children's kin of the other group will, of course, be those with whom affinal ties were established for the parent at marriage, but the relation is felt as distinct from, or at least as a special reinforcement of, affinal ties as such. Because they are kin groups of one's own closest kin, mutual consideration and helpfulness second only to that expected between patrikin and matrikin is felt to be meet. A man can, for example, seek assistance from them or from the elders of their clans if he is in need of additional land to farm or of raphia supplies for house-building. More specifically both men and women are under obligation to visit and bring gifts at the funerals of members of these patri- and matriclans, occasions when many of them are assembled and sympathy and support can be expressed at a time of loss and grief. For this relation, as will be seen, the Yakö employ the specific and reciprocal term *okpan* (pl. *yakpan*). It is, it should be emphasized, not a relation within and between groups, but between a person and groups of kin to which he or she is individually linked by the cross-ties arising from patrilineal and matrilineal kinship.

THE TERMINOLOGY OF KINSHIP

The kinship terminology of the Yakö clearly expresses the dichotomy between matrilineal and patrilineal affiliation as well as the unity of the kin groups so formed. But, save on formal (ritual or periodical) occasions and when there is emotional stress, kinsfolk below the grandparental generations are usually addressed by their personal names. The terms discussed here are therefore most frequently used for reference (see Fig. 15).

The terms used for parents (*uwo* = (my) father; *muka* = (my) mother)[1] may also be employed in a classificatory sense when referring

---

[1] The terms for parents in Yakö are as follows:

my, our father,	*uwo,*	—mother,	*muka*
thy, your father,	*awo,*	,,	*aka*
his, their father,	*yate,*	,,	*yaka*
my, our fathers,	*buwo,*	—mothers,	*bamuka*
thy, your fathers,	*bawo,*	,,	*ba'aka*
his, their fathers,	*bǝyate,*	,,	*bǝyaka*

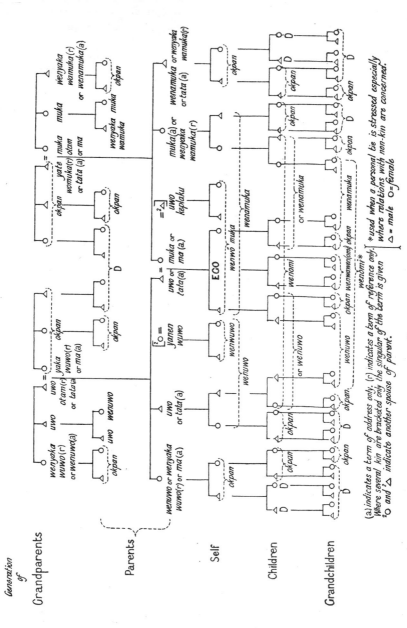

FIG. 15. YAKÖ TERMS FOR KIN

(a) indicates a term of address only. (r) indicates a term of reference only. Where several kin are bracketed only the singular of the term is given ∆o and ²∆ indicate another spouse of parent.

* used when a personal tie is stressed especially where relations with non-kin are concerned. ∆ = male O = female

to collateral kin of their generation if they are of the same sex as well as the same lineage as the parent, i.e. to male patrikin and to female matrikin of this generation. Thus father and father's brother and father's father's brother's son are all referred to and may be addressed as *uwo*, but a mother's brother will not. Similarly, mother's sister and mother's mother's daughter will be called *muka*, but father's sister will not. These terms can also be extended to all men immediately senior in generation in one's patriclan and to all women senior in generation in one's matriclan.

Step-parents are not kin. Another wife of one's father is referred to as such, *yanen wuwo*, and a stepfather is known as *uwo keplaku* (father in daylight), a term which conveys the element of quasi-paternal authority and responsibility he may have as head of the domestic group.

A mother's brother, as are all men immediately senior in generation in one's matriclan, is *wenyaka wamuka* (child of mother of mother). A father's sister, like all women immediately senior in generation in one's patriclan, is *wenyaka wuwo* (child of mother of father).

Among siblings the maternal link has precedence whereby full and maternal half-siblings are designated *wenwömuka* (child of my mother, pl. *benbömuka*), while only paternal half-siblings are called *wenwuwo* (child of my father, pl. *benböwuwo*).

Patrikin and matrikin junior in generation are, however, merged and may all be referred to individually and collectively by the term *wenomi* (pl. *benomi*) which is more specifically used for one's own child.

The paternal grandfather is called *uwo otam* (old father) and the maternal grandmother *muka otam* (old mother). The paternal grandmother may also be called *muka otam* if the grandchild has been much with her, but she is more usually addressed and is always referred to as father's mother (*yaka wuwo*), while the maternal grandfather, of whom a child usually sees little, is never called or referred to as 'old father', but always descriptively as mother's father (*yate womuka*). These terms are now, however, applied to other kin of the grandparents' generation. Those who are male patrikin and female matrikin are merged with the father's and mother's generation as *buwo* and *bamuka* respectively; female patrikin and male patrikin are addressed and referred to by terms which stress lineage membership but ignore generation level, while only descriptive terms or in some cases a reciprocal term (see below) are applied to those belonging to neither of one's own lineages. Here, again, the patrilineal and matrilineal ties are emphasized throughout.

One's own grandchild is called *wenwawen* (*omi*)—child of (my) child— without distinction between children of sons and those of daughters, although they will be members of different patri- and matriclans. But this term is not extended to collaterals of this generation; the latter as kin junior in generation may, as indicated above, be merged with the generation of one's children as *wenomi*. But they may also be referred to according to affiliation by the merging terms for patrikin, for matrikin, or for the members of one's father's matri- or mother's patrikin (see below).

More inclusive classificatory terms which further ignore generation differences are more usually employed in referring to unilineal kin outside the elementary family. They are *wenuwo* (pl. *benuwo*), which refers to all members of the patriclan, and *wenamuka* (pl. *benamuka*), which correspondingly refers to all matrikin. These terms are not, however, applied individually to one's own father, paternal grandfather, or grandchild, or to one's own siblings, children, mother, or maternal grandmother, save when included in a wider group of unilineal kin. They combine the roots for child and father, and child and mother respectively, but are, it should be noted, distinct from those used specifically for siblings—*wenwömuka* and *wenwuwo*—given earlier.

A single reciprocal term (*okpan*, pl. *yakpan*) is used to express the kinship ties between a person and the father's matrikin, the mother's patrikin, the matrikin of a man's children, and the patrikin of a woman's children, i.e. the members of the unilineal groups to which one's parents or children belong but to which one does not belong oneself. Thus, if ego's father is a member of the Yanyö matriclan, ego is an *okpan* of Yanyö, and they are *yakpan* to him. If his mother was born in Anedja patriclan, he is also an *okpan* of Anedja and they are *yakpan* to him.

The patrikin, matrikin, and the two sets of *yakpan* comprise all the persons who are grouped together under broad classificatory terms. There is no single word for kin as such and remote cognates who fall outside these classes can be and are designated when occasion arises only by compound descriptive terms which state the genealogical links (D in Fig. 15). They are, like other persons, addressed by their proper names. The terms applying to wide classes of kin are not customarily used in address, since, as mentioned above, both patrilineal and matrilineal kin other than own parents and grandparents are addressed by personal names usually prefixed, in the case of those senior in generation, by the terms *tata* (for men) and *ma* (for women). These last terms like *wen* (child) are expressive of generation difference rather than of descent itself and may be used in addressing all elders.

In addition to the terms for parents, children, siblings, grandparents, and the classificatory terms for the various groups of unilineal kin with which a Yakö is related, descriptive terms are also employed to designate the kinship links between persons by combining the roots for child (*wen*), the father (*yate*), or the mother (*yaka*). To these may be added where required an indication of the mode of descent: borne by (a female) —*womani*—or begotten by (a male)—*wamponi*—together with the sex of a person: male—*wodo'odam*, or female—*wodoyanen*, compounded from the terms *odam* (male) and *yanen* (female) plus kin. In these fuller descriptive terms, precedence is again given to matrilineal descent in that the maternal link is used where, as among full siblings, there is both a matrilineal and a patrilineal relation. We have seen that children of one mother, whether full or half-siblings, are all *wenwömuka* to one another, while only paternal half-brothers and sisters are *wenwuwo*. Similarly, where a relationship between patrilineal kin is to be more precisely indicated by the use of a descriptive term, the link is traced back to the mother, not to the father of the siblings from whom they are respectively descended. Thus a father's sister is designated *wenyaka wuwo wodoyanen* (child of mother of father: female). Grandchildren can be distinguished as *wenwawenwɔmponi* (child of child I begot) by a grandfather and *wenwawenwomani* (child of child I bore) by a grandmother. They too may be differentiated in sex as *wodo'odɔm* (male) and *wodɔyanen* (female).[1]

MARRIAGE AND AFFINAL RELATIONS

It will already be appreciated that marriage, with the establishment of a new household and family, is the concern of several distinct sets of relatives, of the matrikin and patrikin of the husband and those of the wife. In addition to the direct affinal relations of each spouse with kin of his or her partner, certain of these relatives also undertake obligations to one another. But the roles of the matrilineal and patrilineal kin of the husband and those of the wife are not symmetrical. The domiciliary factor, with patrilineal succession to house sites and land, is dominant on the husband's side and his patrikin are most concerned in the marriage. His children will be members of his patriclan but not of his matriclan. On the woman's side, however, the dominant aspects both of fertility and of the responsibility accepted in receiving marriage payments are felt to be preponderantly a concern of the matrilineal kin. Her children will be members of her matriclan, they will be the matrilineal successors and heirs of her brothers—her own mother's sons. The links of the children with her patriclan will, like their links with their father's matriclan, be limited to occasional acts of kindness and the ceremonial expression of friendship and sympathy due from them as *yakpan*.

During betrothal and the marriage ceremonies, indeed until she actually takes up residence in her husband's dwelling-area, which is generally subsequent to the birth of her first child, a wife has little contact with and no formal obligations to her husband's patrikin. Later, when resident with the patriclan of her husband and children, she is likely to be a close neighbour of her father- and brothers-in-law with whom she will in favourable circumstances be on easy terms, being treated as a daughter and sister. Apart from her mother-in-law, she has much less to do with her husband's matrikin, although these will be *yakpanen* (*yakpan* people) of her children.

For a man, on the other hand, the affinal relation of major significance

[1] Affinal terms are discussed in a later section; see p. 328.

Y

is that with one or more of his wife's senior male matrikin. During the betrothal he is as a suitor dependent on the goodwill of his future wife's parents. But once the marriage payments have been accepted and, more particularly, when his wife has come to live with him, it is her mother's brother, or one of her own elder brothers acting in his place, who, as her closest senior matrikinsman, takes responsibility should serious disputes arise and the marriage be threatened or actually dissolved.[1]

During the period of betrothal (*keplö kesi*) before the first marriage of a girl, which may last from one to two years, the suitor is obliged to perform specific services for his prospective bride and her parents and to make them gifts. He will be asked to help and to bring his age-mates to assist in any considerable tasks that the father-in-law undertakes, such as the lifting and tying of yams at harvest, building, and repairing houses. And it was formerly customary not only to bring the future father-in-law a daily calabash of palm-wine but also to carry water for the mother-in-law, a task which otherwise is woman's work. During the annual *leboku* rites, at the time when parents give special food and ornaments to their children, a suitor should make gifts not only to his betrothed but also to her parents.

In the ceremonials and exchanges of marriage itself there are no direct relations between the kinsfolk of the bride and those of the groom. Indeed, a most remarkable feature of Yakö marriage ceremonial is the emphasis on the relations of the chief participants each to their own friends or age-set mates, who need not be and often are not kin, and the lack of emphasis on their relations to either kinship groups or particular circles of kinsfolk as such.

Apart from later rituals at her matriclan and patriclan shrines, when the bride is pregnant, the clans of the bride and the groom have no corporate relation to the marriage ceremonies. The patriclans of the bride and groom have an interest in maintaining the exogamic rule which would be sustained by the intervention of the *Obot Kepun* if an infraction was threatened, but they otherwise take no corporate action concerning the marriage. Nor does the matrilineage of the bride, although it has, as will be seen, an interest in the maintenance of the marriage once established, participate in its ceremonial recognition. It is only after the last wedding-feasts which the bride's parents severally give to their own personal friends, particularly their age-mates, that her father should go, or send a message to, his wife's brother as the closest senior male among the matrilineal relatives of the bride, informing him that the wedding feasts have been concluded, that the marriage payment has been made, and that he is ready to hand over the customary portion to him.

In considering the provision of the marriage payment (*libeman*, marriage money), which formerly consisted mainly of brass rods, but is

---

[1] For an account and fuller analysis of betrothal and marriage see my *Marriage and the Family among the Yakö in South-Eastern Nigeria*.

now, apart from a few token rods, handed over in Nigerian currency, a distinction must be made between the first marriage of a youth and the later marriages of older men. For the latter the responsibility for payment is usually entirely the husband's, although he may often borrow from matrikin. But for his first marriage, while labour services are made by the youth himself, his father normally takes the main responsibility, although his mother's brothers and often more distant kin on both sides will make contributions varying according to the individual circumstances. If the mother's brother is the foster-father of the groom he replaces the father as the main contributor. The marriage payment should properly be handed over by age-mates, i.e. age-set friends, of the groom to the father or foster-father of the bride when she returns to the village after the clitoridectomy rite which should form part of the marriage ceremonies. Frequently only a portion of the payment is transferred on this occasion and the balance is later handed over informally in a number of instalments. By the wife's father and her mother's brother the marriage money is regarded as provided by the husband. It is he, not his father or any other kinsman, who claims its return and the fact that it is the groom himself who offers it is emphasized in the transfer.

Transfers involved in marriage payments are not directly reciprocal between the households or kinsmen involved. A father receives for his daughter much less than he gives for his son. A mother's brother receiving for a bride does not give correspondingly for her brothers. There is no doubt that it is the transfer of the *libeman* which gives the husband legal rights to his wife's services and to the social fatherhood of the children born to her during the marriage. The retention of a portion of the marriage money by the father, like its initial transfer by the groom to him, is not regarded by the Yakö as an indemnity for any economic value of a daughter. It is to be explained by the fact of paternal authority in the household. A father has the established right to control the domicile of his unmarried children. No daughter may go or be removed from his household and parental authority without his consent. The acceptance of the marriage money and the retention of a portion of it mark the curtailment of the father's parental authority and signify his consent to his daughter's departure from his household. His share of the marriage payment is a consideration for that consent.

But the husband is securing at marriage not merely the curtailment of paternal authority over the bride. He is also placing the bride under a positive obligation to perform certain services. Should she fail, compensation cannot be secured from the bride herself and the obligation to return the marriage money to the husband devolves not on the father but on those who in Yakö law have responsibility for ensuring the fulfilment or compensation of all personal obligations, namely, the matrilineal kin. It is on account of this potential obligation that a matrilineal kinsman is considered entitled to receive from the father the greater part of the payment. It should be observed that the obligation to return what was received relates to the whole of the marriage money, including the portion retained by the father. That the kinsman who undertakes it and in consequence receives the greater part of the marriage money should be the mother's brother is consonant with the Yakö principle of matrilineal transmission. As the closest matrilineal kinsman senior in generation to the wife, compensation would be claimed from him if she should fail in her marital obligations, while her matrilineal brothers are successors both to this obligation and to the property of the mother's brother.[1]

Thus the Yakö marriage payment is variously related to the several interests involved. It expresses the value of a wife to her husband and confirms his intention to maintain a stable union. It rewards the bride's father for the renunciation of his parental authority while establishing his consent and that of the matrilineal kin to the assertion of marital rights by the husband. It reinforces the responsibility of matrilineal kin for ensuring that the wife shall fulfil her marital obligations by giving the closest senior matrilineal kinsman of the bride a pecuniary obligation with regard to her good conduct.[2]

The relations of a widow to her deceased husband's kin depend on whether she has grown sons. There is neither leviratic marriage nor widow inheritance and a widow, if she is young, is free to remarry where she and her own kin wish. Only if she is widowed while suckling a child has she a right to remain for any length of time in her late husband's

---

[1] The customary obligation of the bride's father to hand over the greater part of the marriage payment to her mother's brother or other close matrilineal relative has, as already mentioned, been increasingly disregarded in recent years, and in a third of the cases in a sample studied it was all retained by the father or someone acting in his place. This was particularly common where the father was a rich man (*osu*, pl. *yasu*), and was not a matter of cupidity but rather an assertion of paternal authority and also of wealth and independence. For a mother's brother can rely on his matrilineal kinsmen to assist him in providing the means of returning a marriage payment, but a father cannot, since the marriage is not the concern of the father's matrilineal kin; nor do his daughter's children belong to his patrilineage. Thus a father who retains the marriage payment faces the possibility of having to refund a large part of it, perhaps many years later, entirely from his own resources: a risk a poor man would be more reluctant to assume.

[2] The role of mother's brother in relation to a girl's marriage and other juridical and ritual obligations should properly be assumed by the senior among the brothers (including maternal half-brothers) of the mother, and where there is no true brother the senior matrikinsman in the senior collateral line should act. But, while this is fairly strictly adhered to in ritual contexts, in situations requiring personal initiative and responsibility the rights and duties may be assumed by a younger brother or other matrikinsman who, through personality or possessions, has greater prestige. Thus marriage payments are not infrequently nowadays handed over by the mother's eldest brother to a wealthier junior who is more ready to accept the contingent responsibility for repayment.

compound and to be given farming facilities by one of his patrikin. She may or may not prefer to rejoin her parents or other relatives, but in any case she cannot remarry until she is ready to wean the child; she is therefore dependent on either the late husband's or her own relatives for farming facilities and food-supplies. On the other hand, a widow has no claim to the livestock and personal possessions of her late husband, although she may, at the distribution of his goods during the funeral rites, be given a cloth and a few other small objects by the matrilineal relative of her husband who is the chief heir. A young widow usually remarries within a year or two. She leaves her late husband's compound after the harvest following his death and joins the household of either her parents or a senior matrikinsman. On the other hand, an older widow who has adult sons living in the patriclan area, and usually in the same compound as her late husband, will often remain there and join the household and farming unit of one of her sons, who is, of course, her closest matrilineal kinsman.

It is rare for a Yakö to take the initiative in divorcing a wife, but if he determines to do so he informs her parents and the matrikinsman who received the marriage money that she must go. As a last resort he will refuse to admit her to his farm in the coming year. But, unless the woman's conduct has been outrageous, the husband forgoes all claim to a return of the marriage payments and the woman is free to marry elsewhere. Divorces arise far more frequently from the voluntary departure of the wife from her husband's compound, and the husband then becomes entitled to a return of his marriage payment. If she goes to live with another man, her new mate becomes liable, not only for the payment of damages to the husband on account of the adultery, but also for refunding to her matrilineal kinsman the amount of the marriage payment which the latter is required to restore to the husband. When, and only when, this payment has been made, is the divorce accepted and the adulterer recognized as a second husband. In recent years, however, deserted husbands, finding it difficult to obtain payment from the wives' matrikin, have been successfully making claims before the *Yabot* and the Native Authority courts for direct recompense by the men with whom their wives have gone to live. If several children have been born, the husband is considered entitled to a return of only a portion of the original marriage payment, usually little more than half. A wife is rarely prevented on divorce from taking young children with her, but she is not always allowed to take older boys and the husband often insists that young sons shall return to him when they reach puberty.

Some aspects of the relations between spouses have been indicated earlier. It is also important to emphasize, in connexion with their several relations with affines, that outside the wife's house, and to a lesser extent the farm, a Yakö man and wife are rarely found together as companions. Not only are men and wives separated in their memberships of economic groups such as age-set path-clearing parties and farm-working parties, as well as of esoteric ritual groups including secret societies, but they also tend to remain apart in both ceremonial and recreational activities. The feasts at a Yakö wedding are given by the bride's father to his friends and by her mother to hers. They are not joint feasts given by the parents to common friends of both sexes. A similar alinement is found in Yakö funerary ritual. There is co-operation between men and wives in ceremonial activities, but they do not constitute a couple in relation to others. This separation extends to minor economic activities, even to those of a strictly household character. Thus it is very unusual to see a Yakö man and wife walking together on a bush path to their farm. Wives go alone or in parties of neighbouring women; husbands likewise go independently or with their friends. On the farm itself each is usually engaged in separate tasks, sometimes with the aid of friends of the same sex. In the preparation of oil-palm products husbands and wives each carry out separate customary operations; a husband will get one or more kinsmen, age-mates or youths of his patriclan, but not his wife, to help him pound fruits in the great log mortar. He, on the other hand, does not take part in boiling the fruit or skimming the oil, while cracking nuts to extract kernels is a woman's task and the kernels are the wife's reward for her share in the work.

Old couples, on the other hand, often do much of their work in common and some depend greatly on each other for companionship; they are, for example, found sitting together at funeral and marriage feasts where the sexes are otherwise segregated. By this time the man usually has only one surviving wife and she needs assistance in all stages of the farm work. The age-mates with whom he might otherwise spend his leisure will be few, while his wife after the menopause will not be excluded from groups of men or male secular activities.

A wife can place no legal restriction on the sexual activities of her husband, but he is entitled to claim monetary compensation from a man with whom she has committed adultery, to divorce her, and receive back the marriage money.

Wives in a polygynous household are not formally graded in status according to seniority in marriage or age and there is similarly no fixed opinion concerning the relative desirability of becoming a first or a later wife. It is probable that the majority of young girls prefer to wed youths who are marrying for the first time, but this appears to be associated rather with the pleasures of courtship and the claim at that time on the exclusive attention of the bridegroom than with any conventional or personal attitude to post-marital status. A man's later wives may, since they are often divorcees or widows, be junior only in order of marriage and not in age-set or years. To be a man's first wife by no means implies therefore that a woman will always be the senior in age or the most experienced woman in the compound, nor does it confer any authority over the other wives. The relations among co-wives range widely from companionable equality to hostility or considerable domination, but these depend on differences not of formal status but of personality and prestige.

The pattern of personal relations between affinal relatives does not appear to be specific among the Yakö. Towards their parents-in-law both man and wife behave in general as they would to senior kinsfolk, and the considerable variation in the degree of intimacy and sympathy between affines appears to depend on the temperamental qualities of the persons involved. Sexual relations with an affinal relative are regarded as highly improper, but most informants said that there was no specific penalty for it because it would not occur, and I did not in fact encounter any instance in marital histories, court records, or discussions of sexual irregularities.

During the period of betrothal and in the early months of marriage a man may become an intimate of his wife's parents' household. He may talk freely to and before his mother-in-law, who will give him food and ask him for gifts. There is neither avoidance nor any exceptional intimacy. A man may, if there is need and relations are good, continue to give his father-in-law occasional help in farm-clearing, house-building, and other work after he has taken his wife to live with him in the area of his own *kepun*. But apart from funeral gifts and annual *leboku* gifts, a husband has few personal relations with his parents-in-law after his wife has come to live with him. Although his wife will frequently go there, he rarely visits his father-in-law's compound and then only on a definite errand. If a wife misbehaves or deserts her husband, it is only when the father is known to have a preponderant influence and especially if he has retained the marriage payment, that he, rather than a mother's brother, is approached.

A wife has normally more frequent contact with her parents-in-law than a husband has. The wife–father-in-law relation often becomes one of considerable affection. A man may frequently be seen gossiping in his daughter-in-law's house. A young wife may also be asked by her mother-in-law to help in a farm or compound task and will generally be ready to do so, but such help is an expression of regard not an obligatory service. But a wife's relations with her parents-in-law may range from the warm friendliness of quasi-parentage to open hostility in which a wife will speak vituperatively to and about her mother-in-law. A man is usually benevolent towards his son's wife, but Yakö consider the relation between a wife and her mother-in-law who is also her close neighbour as a difficult one, and if the two are not mutually sympathetic, a man will take care to keep his farming and household activities strictly separate from those of his father. On the other hand, although her own mother can freely visit a wife to assist in household emergencies and should always be present at a birth, the mother-in-law is also expected to advise and assist in the care of her son's children, who are among her closest *yakpanen*, and it is in this situation that friction often develops.

There are no specific terms for affinal relatives who are referred to by descriptive terms; thus a man's father-in-law is *yatewəyanenomi* (father of my wife), a sister's husband is *odəmwawenwamuka* (husband of the child of my mother). Parents-in-law are addressed as *Tata . . .* or *Ma . . .*, and a mother-in-law may even be called *muka* (my mother) where relations are cordial, while a man often speaks of a favoured son-in-law as *wenomi* (my child). The wife's brother who is the matrilineal guardian of a man's children is not verbally distinguished from other members of the wife's matriclan, who are known as *wenyaka wəyanenomi* (mother's child of my wife). The wife's mother's brother who is trustee for the marriage payment is, however, where the wife's father is dead, referred to as wife's father (*yatewəyanenomi*). His status in relation to the marriage is ceremonially emphasized by token presents of a yam and palm-wine made to him at the time when gifts are made to children and between betrothed couples during the annual *leboku* rites.

<h2>CONCLUSION: THE DUAL SENTIMENTS OF KINSHIP</h2>

This account of the patterns of those personal and group relations among the Yakö which are conceived in terms of kinship ties will have made clear the manner and extent to which the individual is led through childhood and adult life to accept very distinct obligations according to the nature of the bonds of kinship and affinity. The ideas of right and wrong concerning attitudes and actions towards various groups and classes of kin, which are inculcated in each generation, constitute established norms by which individual conduct is judged. But these in turn rest on more general sentiments which are not maintained by kinship behaviour itself, or by exhortations to right conduct. These sentiments, the nature and conditions of which the anthropologist slowly and vaguely perceives amid the welter of heterogeneous events, emerge clearly only from an analysis of the forms in which they find expression in various contexts over the whole range of social life. They may find emphatic and verbal expression in rituals and social crises, but they can only be fully defined and assessed in relation to the culture as a whole. It is not possible, within the limits of this essay, to present adequate evidence for these brief remarks concerning the underlying attitudes which have sustained the kinship system of the Yakö and maintained its general structure by providing its axiomatic foundations in thought and feeling. It is only possible to indicate these attitudes in outline and to make some prediction as to the outcome of present trends.

The striking problem presented by the Yakö system lies in the strength of matrilineal bonds despite the virtual absence of continuous association and frequent co-operation among matrilineal kin and in the presence of such close association and co-operation among patrilineal kin. Men who are patrikin live together, jointly control and utilize tracts of land for farming, collecting, and dwellings. A growing son works for several years on his father's farm plots and collects materials for him and the household. Brothers and patrilineal cousins help each other in farm tasks and have first claim to the use of lands formerly held by their fathers and grandfathers. In manhood brothers will often share a man's house in the same compound. Brothers may and do quarrel. There are jealousies and disputes among them and between sections of patrilineages and clans over rights of succession. But these are disputes, within a framework of habitual co-operation and collective rights, among those who should, and have many inducements to, live and work together.

When, however, we turn to the matrilineal relations, we find no such foundation in the routine of daily life, in the organization of essential production for livelihood, in ties of neighbourhood. The rights and obligations of matrilineal kinship are validated on a different plane. Practical assistance to matrilineal kin, the rights of a matrilineal kinsman such as a mother's brother, and above all the authority of a priest of a matrilineal clan, are linked not with the technical and economic advantages of co-operation and organization in practical affairs nor with inevitable and frequent daily contact and need for adjustment. They are associated, as becomes plain in common speech and in rituals, with mystical ideas concerning the perpetuation and tranquillity of the Yakö world. Central among these are the mysteries of fertility, health, and peace. The fertility and well-being of crops and beasts as well as man, peace between persons and in the community at large, are deeply felt to be associated with and passed on through women. It is by a wife that offspring are produced; it is from one's mother that one's life comes. The children of one mother are bound to mutual support and conciliation. The children of one's mother's sisters are part of one's own lifestream and this extends backward and forward through mothers and daughters. Thus the matrilineage is held together by mystical bonds of common fertility and within it anger and violence are gravely sinful. These sentiments are expressed and reinforced in the cult of the matriclan spirits, whose priests are ritually given the qualities of women—by the rite of chipping and blackening the teeth which is normally the mark of adult status, of wifehood and motherhood, for women. They are also the source of concepts of specific obligation which cut across the patrilineal ties and ordain mutual helpfulness and protection among matrikin despite their segregation in scattered and often opposed patriclans.

Matrilineal bonds can, as we have seen, provide a means of compensating and even replacing patrilineal ties which fail to meet particular needs and difficulties. A young man can be adopted into his mother's brother's lineage and clan. His mother's brother and other matrikin will assist him when resources within his own patriclan are lacking. Further, the organization of ultimate authority in the village in terms of the religious sanctions deriving from the matriclan spirits curbs the rivalry and potential conflict of the patriclans or the wards in which they are grouped. All this is not, however, thought out by the Yakö as a reason for, or justification of, a dual reckoning of descent. For them paternity and maternity contain inherently the different qualities from which flow the rights, obligations, and benefits, both practical and spiritual, which have been outlined.

The same sentiments are, as has been seen, operative with less intense expression at a further remove. One owes and expects consideration and helpfulness in relation to those kinsfolk of one's parents and one's children to whom one is thus linked, even though one does not belong to their patri- or matri-lines of descent. The matrikin of the father and those of a man's son are, for example, extensions of his own self. Their mourning is therefore one's own mourning, and where need arises they should help and be helped. For the Yakö they stand in the special position of *yakpanen*.

These sentiments underlying kinship are, however, being variously affected by the impact of Western trade and administration. The growth of trade in palm-oil and kernels and in imported goods has resulted in the emergence of trading as a specialist occupation. The more adventurous young men can obtain cash incomes for a period before their farming responsibilities become heavy. They are often dependent on an older man, but he may be a substantial trader who is not a kinsman, and where a young man works with or for an older kinsman, a father or a paternal or maternal uncle or an elder brother, the ties and obligations are personal. Individual aptitudes, training, and experience for these new activities are coming to the fore. The solidarity of siblings and of the patrilineage, and the ties between a man and his mother's brother have been weakened by this growing financial independence and differentiation among young men.

At the same time wealth in movable goods, which formerly passed matrilineally, has come to loom larger in Yakö economy. The prestige associated with a large yam farm maintaining a large compound household has shrunk in comparison with that of stocks of cloth, new-style furnishings, and above all accumulations of currency. And status in the organization of the farming economy, as a road elder, as a leader in patrilineage and patriclan affairs concerning both internal and external arrangements for the allocation of farming land, has accordingly declined relatively to the possession and display of wealth in imported goods and to holdings of currency with which services and favours can be bought and children sent to school. Sons and other patrikin are challenging with increasing success the rights of sisters' sons to succeed to such wealth. The matrilineal bonds are being sapped from within in the economic sphere of inheritance.

The superposition of the colonial administration on the indigenous political system has, largely unwittingly, weakened matrilineal ties at the opposite end of the social system. The 'warrant chiefs' recognized in the first phase, although they were often at the outset unofficial nominees of the village council in which succession was matrilineal or subject to the matriclan priests, came, in the exercise of their new duties and powers as agents of Government, to act as independent and alternative sources of internal political power. Although the Yakö seem originally to have thought and acted as if the two spheres, that of internal control of their own affairs and that of adjustment to the requirements and instructions of Government, were independent, the latter has progressively encroached. The Native Court and later the Native Authority were not only 'official' but possessed of physical sanctions backed by Government, while the ultimate physical sanctions which the indigenous village council could formerly employ became illegal or subject to challenge and prohibition in the Native Court.

The prestige and powers of the village councils did not, of course, suddenly collapse, for the pressure of westernization and external administrative action has grown but gradually. The sacerdotal council is still significant, but its power has been subjected to frequent piecemeal erosion. There is rather the general sense that in the last resort on any major issue an innovation has a good chance of being upheld by the administration and any customary declaration of the council of being overruled. Custom is an ageing king, and with the weakening of their real power the matrilineal basis of the old village councils is itself losing its binding force.

Christian ideas and injunctions are beginning to undermine the influence of the rituals of the matriclan priests. Again not rapidly or dramatically, for although mission chapels and elementary classes conducted by visiting African pastors have been established in the larger villages, the numbers of seriously professing Christians in the thirties were still few and by no means all who sent their children to the school to learn to read and write showed interest in either the ethics or the dogmatic teaching of the missions. But there are those who hold the rituals to be savage customs and declare that they should be stopped or boycotted. Moreover Western attitudes in the sphere of morals by no means come only directly from the mission church or school for, though visits of Europeans to the Yakö villages are few and usually brief, African residents, including Yakö, who have gone afield, who know and can expatiate impressively on European ways, are a growing force.

Gradually, therefore, but cumulatively in the spheres of economics, politics, and religion the bonds of matrilineal kinship and the role of the matrikin groups are being reduced. The dogmatic principle that children of one mother and the children, notably the sons, of a man's sisters, have a special bond and are entitled to specific rights not shared by sons is being challenged, not only directly and indirectly by the European bias towards patriliny, but also by the economic and political processes of westernization.

Patrilineal ties might appear not to be affected in this way and even to be reinforced, but reinforcement is effective only within a narrow span. The tie between father and son may often be strengthened, but solidarity with collateral patrikin is weakening in the fields of new wealth and political power. Patriclan and patrilineage remain miniature corporations within the wider village community, since residence and the production of food and cash crops are organized in the old way and there is no serious shortage of land. And politically collective action is encouraged, for the patriclans now have their representatives in the Native Authority Council and Court, but the expression of patriclan solidarity is being cast in a more territorial idiom. As occasion prompts men move their dwellings from one place to another far more easily than they did. Locality as such and individual aptitudes are playing a greater part than a generation ago, and the stress on kinship as the ground for duties and rights outside the family is weaker and more uncertain.

DUAL DESCENT IN THE NUBA HILLS

By S. F. NADEL

THIS essay is concerned with a type of kinship organization the social importance of which has not yet been fully assessed. I am referring to systems based on double unilateral descent, in which clan alinement is reckoned both in the father's and mother's line, the two principles existing side by side, so that every individual belongs both to a patrilineal and to a matrilineal exogamous descent group (a *gens* and a *clan*). Instances of such kinship organization in Africa were recorded a considerable time ago, but have only recently been systematically analysed.[1] They still represent, so far as our present knowledge goes, rather unusual phenomena, though it is possible that they have in the past been overlooked or not fully recognized. Double-descent systems have been reported from several parts of West Africa, among the Ashanti, Gã, Fanti, and Yakö.[2] The present account describes this system among two tribes in the Nuba Hills of the Sudan, and so concerns a partly new field. I say partly, since many features in the culture of the Nuba tribes have close parallels in West Africa, and Nuba culture itself appears in some respects to be closely akin to that of the more primitive pagan tribes in West Africa. This is as far as we can at present go in pointing out ethnological parallels: whether they may ultimately be derived from migration or a former ethnic unity is not a question that can at present be decided, if indeed it can ever be decided.[3]

Though a fully fledged double-descent system may be rare, the combination of paternal and maternal affiliation in some form is widespread. Professor Radcliffe-Brown has emphasized the importance and wide validity of such a bilateral orientation in the distribution of descent-bound rights and obligations in primitive societies.[4] The bilateral factor is visible also in the Nuba tribes. There it is, in fact, very pronounced, and in some cases appears to shade over into the double-unilateral descent system. I shall therefore mention the transitional as well as the

---

[1] See D. Forde, 'Double Descent among the Yakö', in this volume.

[2] See M. J. Herskovits, 'The Ashanti Ntoro: A Re-Examination' (*J. Roy. Anthrop. Inst.* lxvii, 1937). Herskovits also reports the same kinship system among the negroes of Dutch Guiana.

[3] It is possible that a similar double unilateral descent system exists among the Kunama in western Eritrea, a negro enclave among the Hamitic Beni Amer, who in many respects resemble the Sudanese Nuba. My knowledge of the group, however, is superficial, and I cannot be certain that the co-existence of group segments defined by paternal and maternal descent amounts to a co-existence of two systems of reckoning descent, and not merely to some transitional form of social organization of the kind referred to in the following pages.

[4] 'Patrilineal and Matrilineal Succession', *Iowa Law Reveiw*, xx, 1935, pp. 290–2.

clear-cut types and attempt, through comparison, to define their social relevance. The term 'transitional' is here understood merely in its morphological sense, as defining a form of social organization standing somewhere between other forms. Whether the term can mean more, namely, a phase in social evolution, will emerge from the discussion.

I. NYARO SOCIETY

I have elsewhere given a full analysis of ten Nuba societies, and may therefore be allowed to refer the reader to that account for more detailed information on the Nuba economic, social, and political organization.[1] The society described here, the tribe known as Nyaro, though not included in my Nuba book, falls within its general description. The main features of Nyaro society may here be briefly outlined.

Settlement

The Nyaro live in the extreme east of the Nuba mountain area, about 10 miles from the Nile near Kaka, at the foot of the last low hills in which this zone of scattered hills and mountains breaks up towards the river valley. The Nyaro Hills are almost completely isolated from the rest of the Nuba Mountains by vast stretches of shrub-covered plain with sparse habitations. The separation is an ethnical one as well; for such population as there is in the area between Nyaro and the nearest Nuba tribe to the west, Tira, is of Arab stock (settled as well as nomadic) or consists of Nuba groups which have become completely assimilated to the Arabs.

The Nyaro live on one of four neighbouring hills, each of which has its own settlements and population. The groups inhabiting the four hills bear the same name as these—Nyaro, Kao, Fungur, and Werni. The Nyaro and Kao share language and social organization and are in fact usually classed together. They also claim common origin and are to-day administratively joined. The people of Fungur are believed to be of different origin, but certain clans and gentes of Nyaro also occur in Fungur; the two languages, Kao-Nyaro and Fungur, are only slightly different, and mutually intelligible. The three groups intermarry freely. Werni language differs radically from the rest, though many of the Werni people are bilingual; nor are there any recognized descent connexions between Werni and the other groups, though here, too, there seems to be intermarriage. I have, however, no knowledge of Werni society, and must therefore disregard it. The population is extremely small, that of Kao-Nyaro-Fungur together numbering perhaps 1,500–2,000.

It is not easy to define the three groups, which have no common ethnic name, in terms of 'tribe' or 'sub-tribe'. Each represents a local

[1] *The Nuba,* 1947.

and political unit, partly leading a separate communal life; yet all three
are also linked by the segments which they have in common: for where
the clans or gentes spread over the different local communities, the clan-
bound rights and obligations spread equally. Moreover, even segments
which occur only in Kao or Fungur belong—from the point of view of
Nyaro—to a common list of clans and gentes, and complete that list.
It is this consciousness of the 'common list' and of the co-ordination of
action it entails which offers the relevant criterion: in accordance with it
we must describe the three communities as local sections of the same
('tribal') society. In the following account the organization of that society
is outlined from the standpoint of Nyaro.

The people are sedentary cultivators but own some livestock (cattle,
goats, and pigs). All three groups have traditional chieftainship as well
as a small priesthood, which is mainly concerned with rituals relating to
hunting, cultivation, and rain. We shall see that the priestly duties are
bound up with descent. The people live in compact villages, each divided
into several wards. This local subdivision is less conspicuous in Nyaro
and Kao than in Fungur. The wards are usually referred to as *tawo*,
which is the name for the community huts which stand in the centre of
the ward. Mostly there are two of them in each ward, one used for ritual
purposes, the other as a place where older men may meet or sit during
the day and the young men foregather during dances. Here also the
dance drums are kept. The *tawo* is a large oval hut, much better built
than any of the ordinary village huts. It has a grass roof resting on
upright posts fixed in a low wall, leaving enough space between the roof
and the wall to permit of the latter being used as a seat; there are also
benches and seats inside. The community house is built by the young
men of the gens (to which, as we shall hear, the house belongs). Women
and girls never enter the house.

Descent, Patrilineal and Matrilineal

As said before, every individual belongs both to a clan and gens.
Neither offers any known ancestor; genealogies, in fact, can only in the
case of chiefs or priests be traced beyond the third generation. But the
conception of common descent is strong and unequivocal. Nor are there
heads of clans or gentes, though in some gentes there is a recognized
elder who is entrusted with priestly functions. Residence is patrilocal;
the gens therefore is bound up with locality, which the clan is not. Yet
even the gens is to some extent irregularly dispersed over the village,
though it has a local focus in the community houses mentioned above. At
least, this is true of Kao and Nyaro; in Fungur the more conspicuous
division of local wards also goes hand in hand with a more marked
(though not complete) local division of the gentes.

The (matrilineal) clan is known as *ŋeneŋé* (pl. *ŋeneŋēna*). There are fourteen clans, named as follows: Kyambo, Tidiyare, Wero, Koli, Teŋen,

Pelel, Botyo, Tuma, Kyeya, Kombolle, Kandiyaŋ, Mogo, Mega, Ballo. A few have two or three subsections. The (patrilineal) gens is known as *leridh* (pl. *melgéridya*), though sometimes the word *tawo* is also used (see above), and there are ten such segments—sixteen, including subsections. The subsections of the gens are much more definitely regarded as separate segments than are those of the clan; only the former bear a distinguishing second name and are differentiated in the group-bound rights and obligations.

The table below shows the names of the gentes and their subsections, their distribution over the three communities, and their association with community houses. Certain names of gens-sections are linguistically identifiable; the meaning of these names, whose import will become clear later, is given in brackets. The table also indicates a certain linkage of the gentes, to be discussed presently, which implies that 'linked' gentes may eat with each other but not with other gentes not so linked. The column on the extreme right, finally, shows the burial directions obligatory for the gentes (see p. 339 below).

Gens	Subsections	Community Houses	Burial Directions
1. ⎰ Lrore	Lrore*	..	West
	Kagyo* (Of the Rain)	..	West
2. ⎱ Lrmdi	Lelalle	A	North
3. ⎰ Lrkuber	Gowna	B	North
	Kabobwa	B	North
4. ⎱ Lkurena	..	C	North
5. ⎰ Lriyor	..	A	North
2. ⎱ Lrmdi	Lbet	B	North
6. ⎰ Lrnyaro	..	A	North
7. ⎱ Lrlam	..	D	West
8. ⎰ Lrkora	..	D	North
9. ⎱ Ltoren	Lakamdr (Of the Lion)	D	North
	Kaŋwa (Of the Grain)	D	North
	Detiŋen (Of God)	D	North
	Lgawdha	D	North
10. ⎱ Lrimi*	..	..	North

The brackets on the left of the gens names indicate 'linked' gentes. Gentes marked with an asterisk are found only in Kao and Fungur; the rest occur in all three communities. The capital letters in the third column indicate different or identical community houses in Nyaro.

It will be seen that certain gentes share their community house. It will also be seen that gentes residing in different communities are yet linked by the rules of eating together. The twofold descent links of each individual are illustrated by the following diagram, which shows the genealogy of the Nyaro chief (clan names are shown in ordinary letters, gens names in italics); for the third generation only one affiliation is given—clan for the woman and gens for the man—since the other affiliation is no longer remembered.

Kyambo = *Lrkuber*   Pelel = *Lrore*
 ○   △   ○   △
 Kyambo/*Lrkuber*   =   Pelel/*Lrore*
 ○   △
        Kyambo/*Lrore*
              △

Clan Rights and Obligations

Let me preface this discussion by a few methodological remarks. We are here considering social relations within and between group segments. All social relations materialize in and are visible through co-ordinated actions which, to the individual in the group, appear as rights and obligations. And in segments these may be of two kinds. They may concern an internal co-ordination of action, the activity, though institutionalized for the community, being actuated only within each segment; the rights and obligations thus define the unity of the segment in terms of internal solidarity. Or the co-ordination of action may be such that different institutionalized actions appear in different segments, or the same action is characteristically modified in the different segments. Here, then, the rights and obligations define the unity of the segment in terms of differentiation from other segments. To the observer orientating himself on the segment these twofold rights and obligations appear as *syncretic* and *diacritical* respectively; an instance of the former is blood feud, of the latter, clan food-taboos. The diacritical rights and obligations may possess—and do possess in the society here considered—a significance beyond that of a formal differentiation. This, on the level of the group at large, takes the form of differentiated social tasks vested in the segments, so conceived that each segment is necessary for the welfare of all the other segments, and thus of the whole community. A segmentary structure of this nature I have elsewhere defined as *symbiotic*, and this terminology will be employed in this paper.[1]

Now, clan membership in Nyaro entails only three sets of rights and obligations, all of a syncretic nature: exogamy, collective responsibility in blood feud, and a certain ritual duty involved in the final funerary feast.[2]

The breach of exogamous rules entails no sanction—it is merely considered 'bad', and has, so far as I could gather from genealogies, not

[1] See 'Social Symbiosis and Tribal Organization', *Man*, 1938, p. 85. It will be noted that when, in the exercise of symbiotic obligations, the members of the segment act in co-operation, the action is syncretic and diacritical at the same time.
[2] Exogamy stands between syncretic and symbiotic rights and duties. Exogamy is essentially a negative definition of group unity—the exclusion of a certain interaction from the segment. Thus it causes the action to occur outside, that is, between segments.

z

recently occurred. Where clans are subdivided, only the section, not the clan at large, is exogamous.

The burial and funeral rites concern only the gens of the deceased, but after one to three years the kinsmen who belong to the clan of the deceased give a big feast to which the whole village is invited, and at which there is dancing and drinking.

The obligation of blood feud refers only to homicide between clans; it takes the form of talion and is imposed primarily upon full brothers, though it may involve a much wider section of the clan. Formerly, the blood feud could be avoided through the intervention of the chief, who would strip the culprit of all he possessed. To-day blood money, amounting to 20 cows, has replaced both blood feud and forcible dispossession, but many men have never seen either a murder committed or revenge exacted. Killing between clan fellows (once more not remembered as having actually happened) is considered a most grievous sin, not punishable by secular means; the retribution is left to the (undefined) judgement of God (*teŋen*).

Gens Rights and Obligations

These are more numerous, both syncretic and diacritical, and in the everyday life of the group more conspicuous than the rights and obligations derived from clan membership. Of patrilocal residence, which results in a fairly strong local concentration of the patrilineal group, we have already spoken.

To begin with the syncretic rights and obligations. The gens, no less than the clan, is exogamous. This double exogamy is extended by the rule forbidding marriage also in the father's clan (though not in the mother's gens). The Nyaro chief, whose genealogy is shown above, is thus debarred from marrying into the following three segments: the clans Kyambo and Pelel, and the gens Lrore. Gens, like clan, exogamy entails no sanction.

The gens further stands under the eating prohibitions described before; but again, offences against the rule entail no sanctions. The gentes which may share meals are also bound together by the prohibition against fighting each other in the favourite tribal game of 'bracelet-fighting'. In this game, in which young men of the age-set of 18–20 engage, the combatants wear heavy brass bracelets on their right wrists with which they must try to hit the opponent on the head. The brass bracelets have sharp edges, and the sport not infrequently leads to serious injuries. This point is important; for, although the risk of killing one's opponent exists, there is no prohibition of this dangerous sport between young men of the same clan, who, if they killed each other, would commit the terrible sin of clan homicide. Admittedly no such cases are remembered. Yet the fights are, at least in some measure, forbidden between gens fellows, between whom homicide would not be a sin, but only a crime calling for blood feud (now blood money).

The two funeral rites which devolve on the gens are called *kedá* and *klu*. The *kedá* is held two days after the burial (which takes place on the day of the death) and one day after a preliminary ritual, called *ɲriny*, which will be discussed later. In the *kedá* ritual two men and two women, specially selected as officiants for all the funerary rites, carry the head of a cow sacrificed at the *ɲriny* to a rock outside the village; they carve the meat, which is then ceremonially eaten by a female congregation. These women are of the gens of the deceased, while the four officiants are chosen from the gentes linked with the deceased person's gens by the rules of eating together. There are two exceptions: in the gens Lkurena and Lrimi the officiants are reduced to two, one man and one woman, who belong to one of the 'linked' gentes and to the gens of the deceased respectively.

On the next day the *klu* ritual takes place. This ceremony concerns only men—all the old men of the community. They go out to the farm of the deceased, where they snuff tobacco, drink beer, and kill a goat. Part of the animal is roasted and eaten by the men—grouped according to gens relationship, the rest of the meat (legs and tail) being afterwards distributed among the five community houses.

The *klu* is performed only at the death of men; when a woman dies only the first, gens-bound, and the final, clan-bound, rituals are performed. We note, then, that for men the ritual duties devolving on patrilineal kin outweigh those devolving on matrilineal kin. In the case of women both are equal. This emphasis on the patrilineal kinship ties of a man and the matrilineal ties of a woman applies also in other contexts. The remembering of genealogies is one such context: thus the gens of a grandmother, or even of a mother, and the clan of a grandfather are often unknown or forgotten. We have also seen that in the rules of plural exogamy the sex-opposed affiliation of the mother (or woman in general) is similarly 'underweighted'.

Of purely diacritical characteristics, such as varying food taboos (which are common in other Nuba tribes), there are only a few inconclusive instances. One gens—Lkurena—has a food taboo of fowl, which is otherwise quite unconnected with the tribal observances. Another formal characteristic (also common elsewhere in the Nuba Hills), the 'ritual direction', appears in Nyaro reduced to two burial directions: thirteen sections bury their dead so that the head of the corpse points north; in the remaining three the corpse is buried pointing west.

The majority of gens-bound diacritical rights and obligations are embodied in a single institution, the funeral ceremonial; for one in its cycle of rites is characteristically modified in accordance with gens membership. Through this rite, the funeral ceremonial is linked with magic and sometimes quasi-totemic conceptions, which bear on the welfare of the community at large. All are concerned with the mastery of nature. The quasi-totemic links imply no belief in descent from the (always predatory) animals; they merely indicate some supernatural association by means of which the group segment can control the animal and its actions. The emphasis is on that control.

The varying observances vested in the individual gens thus represent unalterable duties, designed to secure certain magic benefits for the community or, conversely, endangering the community if neglected or inadequately observed. Each gens, therefore, through its performance of the funeral ceremonial, contributes to the common weal and is vital to it. The survival of the community, in this spiritual interpretation, entails the interdependence of all segments: it is to this kind of segmentary differentiation that the term *symbiotic* is here applied.

The funeral rite in question is the *ŋriny* previously mentioned. It will be sufficient to describe here the observances of five gentes, and it will be understood that different rites, with different magic consequences, characterize the remaining segments. It must be mentioned that one gens, Lkurena, does not observe the *ŋriny* and is without the corresponding magic powers. We remember that this gens is the only one which has a food taboo: it thus has its diacritical characteristic, though this is of a purely formal nature.

The largest gens is Ltoren, whose name, in fact, means 'large' or 'great'.[1] At its *ŋriny* ritual this gens performs a libation which is believed to cause the grain to thrive. The beer is brewed of grain supplied by the whole community, which thus contributes to the magic through which a good harvest is ensured. The gens has also quasi-totemic associations with lions and leopards. When a man of Ltoren has killed a lion or leopard the men of the gens eat the meat ceremonially in their community house and perform a special dance called *kamdr* (i.e. lion) round the head of the animal, in which the hunting and stalking of the animal is imitated. Members of other gentes who happen to kill a lion or leopard must present the head, skin, and right foreleg of the animal to the priest-elder of Ltoren (of whom more later).

The lion appears also in the context of another gens ritual, that of Lrimi. During their funeral rite they perform a special dance (called *wundr*) which is said to stop lions from attacking the herds. If this dance were omitted, lions would kill the sheep and cattle of the tribe.

The leopard reappears in the burial rite of the Lrlam, who sacrifice a cow and hide its intestines in a cave for the leopards to eat: by this act leopards will be prevented from attacking the herds.

The Lrmdi funeral ceremony includes a ceremonial fight with whips, the two sections of the gens opposing one another. No other gens performs this fight, which is said to ensure the health of the whole population.

---

[1] This is one of the few gens or clan names which are linguistically identifiable. See also names of sections, p. 336, above.

For the funeral of Lrkuber-gowna the gens relations of the deceased catch a rat, roast it over the fire, and smear the ashes, which they mix with corn gruel, over their eyes. This ritual keeps rats from the grain stores and is also a protection from blindness.

Other gentes, by similar rituals, secure rain or ample honey, or control locusts and monkeys which might destroy the crops.

The rituals vary greatly in complexity. The magic powers of some are, as we saw, duplicated in different funeral rites. They are also duplicated, apart from the funeral rites, in the sense that the natural phenomena to which they refer are equally the concern of special priests. Thus the tribe has a grain-priest and two rainmakers; these men, however, come of the gentes associated with the magic of grain or rain.

The magic involved in the funeral rite, finally, can be separated from it and applied in its own right whenever the need arises. In the gens which has no special priest any old man can perform the magic at the request of any individual, e.g. to stop a plague of rats, to 'pacify' a leopard, or to secure rich finds of wild honey. The performance of this magic aid is once more conceived of as a gens-bound duty, and these services command no payment. The blindness-magic of Lrkuber is an exception: though it operates for the community at large, it cannot be invoked 'to order'. Of the functions of the gens priests we shall hear more later.

Family and Kindred

We now turn to the narrower kinship unit, based on traceable family ties. Patrilineal and matrilineal affiliation will here appear in the form of paternal and maternal ties.

In the communal activities of this very small group traceable paternal and maternal descent ties do not stand out very sharply from the more abstract patrilineal and matrilineal bonds. Funeral and other rituals always involve the whole descent group, not only close relatives, though the latter may be allotted certain special duties. Thus, in the funeral rite of Lrkuber-gowna the rat is caught and roasted by close relations on the father's side; and in blood feud close relatives on the mother's side may pursue the blood feud before the clan itself is mobilized. In the burial ceremonial, on the other hand, duties are allocated merely on grounds of gens-relation; the grave is dug by two men, and the body washed by two women, selected from the eating-group to which the deceased's gens belongs.

Family as against clan or gens ties are prominent only in the context of family activities proper, that is, marriage, childbirth, and inheritance, which we may briefly outline.

Marriage involves a small, loosely fixed bride-price, consisting of certain repeated gifts in kind and special services for the in-laws. The gifts are contributed by the bridegroom's father and the bridegroom himself, and go to the bride's 'elementary family'; they include a single payment of 2–4 goats and annual payments of 2–3 baskets of grain or sesame, continued for 5–6 years. The services take the form of farm work, for two days annually between the betrothal and the time when the bride moves into the husband's house, and of building a house for the father-in-law. These services are performed by the bridegroom and his age-mates and friends.

The betrothal is concluded before the girl is sexually mature. When she is considered to have reached maturity (when her breasts fill out), consummation takes place in the girl's house. She leaves it for the husband's house when she is pregnant. By then the husband will have left his paternal home and built himself a house of his own. But for the first as well as all subsequent births the wife returns to her parents.

Marriage involves no change in the descent affiliation of the wife: she remains a member of her clan and gens and, until her death, is subject to these group obligations. She is buried, and her funeral is performed, in accordance with the rules governing her own, not her husband's, descent group.

In inheritance the property of men must be distinguished from that of women. Both men and women own livestock and personal belongings, but only men own land, wives working, with their husbands, on the farms. The woman's livestock is either inherited or a present from the husband.

Land is inherited in the first place by sons, and in the second place by full brothers; failing these, the land goes to other male relatives in the same gens. The house, also man's property, goes to sons or sons' sons. The man's livestock is inherited by sisters' sons, who must, however, hand a small share to the sons of the deceased. This form of male property is therefore inherited by males, but matrilineally. If there are no sisters' sons, their place is taken by other relatives of the son generation in the same clan. Personal belongings of the man—spears, hoes, guns, fighting bracelets, or the throwing-knives carried by young men on ceremonial occasions—go to sons or, failing sons, to sisters' sons.

Of the woman's property, personal belongings—beads, ornaments, household utensils—go to her daughter or to another female relative of the daughter generation and the same clan, for example, a sister's daughter. Livestock is distributed between sons and daughters or relatives of that generation in the same clan.

The general rule, then, shows a fair balance between patrilineal and matrilineal privileges; inheritance of the man's property, which is larger than the woman's, includes both; the woman's property is inherited only in the matrilineal line. Inheritance is largely from male to male and from female to female. That part of a woman's property which is also useful to men (livestock) is an exception, being inherited both by males and females.

The importance of the clan for a woman and the gens for a man is visible also in the rules of widowhood. An old man who has lost his wife and does not wish to remarry stays in his house, being assisted by his sons. An old widow leaves the house and goes to live by herself in a small hut outside the village, up on the hill-side. Her daughters will bring her food, and she will never come down to the village. This is the only indication of a change in descent affiliation through marriage; for the old widow does not return to her own people, from whom marriage has separated her. Yet equally she has not been absorbed by her husband's group, and her isolation after her husband's death expresses her position as an individual without fully valid descent alinement. While widows are still of marriageable age this social isolation is exhibited in their freedom to remarry—mostly in (non-compulsory) levirate with the husband's brother or gens-kinsman.

Political and Religious Institutions

It now remains to examine the influence of the descent system upon institutions which point beyond the descent group to affairs of communal concern.

Chieftainship appears to be loosely hereditary. It is impossible to be more precise since the remembered genealogy is short, embracing only three predecessors of the present chief. The chief is called *weleny*. The remembered chiefs in three communities all belong to the same gens, Lrore; in Nyaro the first two chiefs were classificatory brothers; the third was no relation of his predecessors but the father of his successor, the present chief.[1]

The rainmakers, of whom there are two (both in Kao), are called *wurwagyo* (*gyo* meaning rain), and their office is hereditary in the gens Lrore-kagyo. The rainmakers possess a number of round, red and white stones which they bury in a hole in the ground during the dry season and dig up when the rains should begin to fall.[2] This magic rite affects only the regular change of seasons. In the event of an unseasonal drought the procedure differs. Upon an appeal from the people, the rainmakers would sacrifice a goat or pig and eat it with their near patrilineal kinsmen. If this action proved of no avail, the young men of the village might band together, take the two rainmakers prisoner, tie them up, and take them to an ant-heap. Here the two priests would be beaten with twigs, which is considered an infallible, though admittedly extreme, device. Once the whipping is over, the victims are taken back to their houses, and their wounds are washed and dressed. The attack upon the unhappy magicians is conceived of as setting in motion a purely mechanical causality. There

---

[1] Administratively, only Kao and Fungur have full chiefs; the village head of Nyaro, though a descendant of 'chiefs', is merely a 'deputy' of the Kao chief.

[2] The stones are positively described as 'male', but the hole in the ground has no sexual association.

is no thought (as there is in other Nuba tribes) of killing the rainmaker in anger, or of blaming his evil intention for the failure of the rains.

The two rainmakers must apparently function together. They also each have an assistant, from another gens, whose office is equally hereditary in the father's line. If the rainmakers stand under obligation to the community, the latter reciprocates: annually, at the beginning of the rainy season, all the women of the village cultivate the rainmakers' land.

There is, besides, a grain-priest, called *worŋwon* (lit. 'priest of the grain'), whose office is again hereditary in the gens (Lrore). He possesses a small hut which no other person may enter, and where he performs his rites in secrecy. He may not have a fire in this hut lest the crops be destroyed by fire. Once a year, at sowing time, he sacrifices and consumes a he-goat semi-publicly, that is, together with the rest of his gens. Failure of the crops may be averted by the same radical means as failure of the rains.

Two other priestly experts occur only in Fungur, though their services are utilized to some extent by the other villages also. The first of these priests is the lion-and-leopard expert of the Ltoren gens mentioned before. He supervises the lion dance, obligatory if a Ltore man kills a lion or leopard, and he is the recipient of the lion's head and skin offered by any successful hunter of lions. The priest is known as *woraŋa-teŋen*, which means 'priest of God', and the gens section to which he belongs as the 'section of God'. But there is no explanation of why this ambitious title was bestowed on a relatively insignificant office or the group in which it is vested. According to some informants the gens name itself—the Great Gens—reflects the fact that this (nominally) paramount office is vested in it; but other informants see in the name merely a reference to the size of this fourfold group.

The gens Lrlam of Fungur includes a priestly expert in charge of a 'swearing stone' (called *leru*), used in ordeals. Nyaro, too, once possessed this priest and his magic (though here he belonged to the Lriyor gens). But he died childless long ago, and his magic and para-phernalia were lost.

If political and religious institutions are thus bound up with patri-lineal descent, there is one field of supernatural beliefs—witchcraft—which stands apart. Witchcraft is called *kamerge*, and, in its milder form, roughly corresponds to the evil eye. Possession of witchcraft can only be discovered by the results, and though these may recommend caution towards a suspected 'witch', they are not sufficiently serious to warrant counter-action or sanction. The evil eye operates irrespective of sex or descent, and is not hereditary.

The power of *kamerge* becomes more sinister if exercised against an evil-doer. Thus a man who possesses *kamerge* may exercise it, by mere wish, against the paramour of his wife, a relation who has cheated him over inheritance, or any person who has abused or cursed him. If the suspected culprit was really guilty of the offence he will die; if not, the witchcraft will react, with equally deadly effect, against the evil-wisher. *Kamerge* is thus a double-edged sword, to be used cautiously, and conceived of essentially as an agency of just (though perhaps disproportionate) retribution. The power of *kamerge* is, moreover, subject to one at first sight puzzling restriction: it is powerful only within the clan. The fear of witchcraft, absent in the gens, thus disturbs relations in the matrilineal descent group. This may seem illogical even in this socially less important segment: the suspicions and fears which such a belief would cause operate in a group which must be united for the common pursuit of blood feud and the performance of the final funerary rite. Yet if this belief attributes to matrilineal kinsfolk sinister powers, these are sinister only in that they exact fatal retribution for any wrong committed against matrilineal kin. In this sense, then, the belief emphasizes clan cohesion, and probably tends to prevent offences against the clan bond. It represents a bond of mutual interdependence in the segment which, compared with the patrilineal descent group, is less generously endowed with integrative rights and obligations.

In conclusion one related field of activity must be mentioned in which descent plays a subordinate part. The community possesses female healing experts, called *worowallere*, who treat minor forms of illness (headache, ulcers, &c.) by bleeding. This expert knowledge is not conceived of as magic or supernatural, but merely as an empirical craft which can be acquired by training. Though it is widely hereditary, being bequeathed from mother to daughter, it is hereditary only incidentally, in the sense that the close association between parent and child lends itself more easily to the perpetuation of the craft. It represents, among the activities designed to control the unpredictable forces of nature, the only one not conceived of as genealogically determined. Indirectly, however, it bears upon this conception: being restricted to the female sex, the healing craft adds weight to the matrilineal inheritance.

The Dual Principle

The main feature emerging from the foregoing description is the wide effectiveness of the genealogical factor in the social life of the community. That the political system should be organized on descent lines is not in any way remarkable; this is a familiar feature in many primitive societies. The comprehensiveness of the descent factor in religious life appears more striking. Though the Nyaro have priests, these are representatives of segments and exercise their office as a right and obligation derived from their descent. Moreover, the magic powers of the priests represent only one sector of the range of magic powers thought to be available for the community, and this wider range is distributed among the gentes as in an army the various military tasks are distributed among specialized branches and units.

In this distribution of rights and obligations, religious and otherwise, among the descent groups, patrilineal factors are clearly the more heavily weighted. The local continuity of the kin group, through residence and inheritance of land, is determined exclusively by the patrilineal factor; the same is true of the spiritual continuity, as it is expressed in individual access to the varied supernatural possessions of the community. Yet the social identity of the individual retains unequivocally its dual character, and patrilineal and matrilineal affiliation are balanced in many fields. In inheritance, utilitarian considerations cause the paternal link to become more important; but here it is inheritance of males from males that counts rather than the inheritance based on descent in the father's line. Where practical reasons do not favour such complete unilineal inheritance, matrilineal ties equally play a part. In group cohesion, finally, the matrilineal segment, less rich than the patrilineal in collective tasks, possesses the additional integrative bond of *kamerge* magic.

That we can rightly speak of a 'balance' is shown in the largely friction-less life of the community. Serious crime is absent; there is no memory of homicide or blood feud; the ordeal could disappear without leaving a serious gap. Social control seems unobtrusive and smoothly effective; without the fear of sinister sanctions, exogamy is apparently invariably observed. Even in moments of momentary passion, as in the bracelet fights, extremes can always be avoided, and no lasting enmity ever results. That there is momentary passion, that the fighting is fierce and leads to far from negligible injuries, but that tempers can yet finally be controlled, I have witnessed myself.

The dual descent system thus appears as an efficacious mechanism of social control. But whether such a conclusion is justified only wider comparison can show.

II. TULLISHI SOCIETY

On the western fringes of the Nuba Mountains, once more as an outpost of the Nuba tribes and their culture, we find a community which has evolved a kinship system closely resembling that of Nyaro. This community is the small tribe of Tullishi, about 3,500 strong, living in physical isolation on the plateau of a high massif. Let me emphasize that Tullishi and Nyaro are culturally and ethnically completely unrelated.

Settlement

Tullishi is divided into six compact villages, which lie close together and are arranged roughly in two arcs of three villages each, facing one another across an axis running north–south. This dual physical division into an eastern and western half is of extreme importance in the social life of the community. The twice-three villages—Karlenya, Lataro, and Tikepa in the east; Terdi, Tutu, and Lau in the west—play characteristically varying roles in the life of the tribe, much as do the gentes of Nyaro. The same is true, on a higher level, of the dual sections, which appear as strikingly symmetrical and in many ways complementary units. Let me briefly outline the position.

Chieftainship is vested in two dynasties which take the office in turn, and is hereditary in the father's line. The chief must always reside in the western village of Terdi. The paramount religious office of the tribe, that of the Great Grain Priest, is also held by two dynasties in alternate, patrilineal succession; it is vested in two eastern villages, Lataro and Tikepa. Chief and Great Grain Priest are in many respects counterparts: they have the same magic of sacred ear-rings, the sight of which is conceived of as fatal to the other man; thus the chief and grain-priest must never meet, and when they travel one must go eastward, the other westward and neither may trespass upon the other's territory. Another grain-priest resides in Lau, in the west, but he has an assistant who comes from Karlenya in the east. Here it must be noted that the co-operation of all grain-priests is required for the agricultural rituals of the tribe. One village in the east and another in the west practise circumcision of boys, which practice is forbidden in the remaining villages, where, it is believed, it would cause immediate death. The eastern and western sections each possesses a 'king-maker', whose services are enlisted in the appointment and enthronement of new chiefs and whose office is again patrilineally inherited. The eastern section, finally, is believed to control locust magic, the western, rain magic. If there is a drought, the people in the western villages are held collectively responsible and accused of 'stealing' the rain; to combat this magic theft the eastern villages attack the western group in a real, by no means ceremonial, war (as I had occasion to witness).

This potential suspicion and hostility is further strengthened by the belief in witchcraft, which operates only between the dual divisions of the community. It is, however, thought to be effective only in the case of young people, and is also in abeyance on occasions when kinsmen or women have to cross the magic boundary—for weddings, funeral feasts, &c. Yet in spite of suspicion and hostility there is a fundamental interdependence between the two sections and the villages they embrace: for rain and locust magic, for the thriving of crops and political rule (which is conceived of as sacred and magical), they depend upon one another and upon the localized supernatural agencies which each village may dispense. The 'circumcision-villages' fit, though more obscurely, into the same scheme: they observe this usage, again conceived of as magic, as their own specific possession; though no ideas have crystallized formulating some benefit for the community at large, the usage is regarded as a primordial and inescapable obligation (or privilege) of the local segments concerned.

The chart which follows summarizes this complex yet systematic apportionment of social tasks and usages.

East		West	
Village	*Locally vested institution*	*Village*	*Locally vested institution*
Karlenya	Circumcision ⎫	Terdi	Circumcision ⎫
	King-maker ⎪		Chieftainship ⎪ Rain
Lataro ⎱	Assistant grain-priest ⎬ Locust	Tutu	King-maker ⎬ magic
Tikepa ⎰	Great Grain Priest ⎭ magic	Lau	Grain-priest ⎭

Descent, Patrilineal and Matrilineal

The villages are inhabited by patrilineal kin, that is to say, sons and grandsons continue to live in the village of their fathers and grand-fathers, as close as possible to their houses, and marriage is patrilocal. Each village therefore contains massed patrilineal lineages, and its com-munity may even amount to a single, indefinitely extended lineage. No corresponding social formulation, however, exists. With the exception of chief, king-maker, and grain-priest, no one can trace his genealogy beyond three generations, or considers a long pedigree (patrilineal or matrilineal) important. As we have noted, these tribal offices are hereditary in the father's line; so far as they may be regarded as the epitome of the locally apportioned social tasks, the patrilineal constitu-tion of the local sections is socially recognized. In all other respects it is merely a physical, not a social reality; it is absorbed and, as it were, rendered anonymous, by the local identification. For the ordinary individual, patrilineal descent beyond the traceable short lineage offers no definition of social identity. This is solely derived from the matri-lineal clan, and this aspect is emphasized by the habit of calling a person often by his (or her) clan name rather than by the personal name.

Tullishi has ten clans (disregarding subsections), named as follows: Kafunya, Karre, Kawe, Kadibenda, Kame, Kadowa, Kamdu, Kasselo, Keffi, Karore.

Clan membership entails the following privileges and duties: exogamy (sanctioned by severe but ill-defined illness); the performance of funeral rites by the clan collectively; blood feud, which is forbidden in the clan and, in inter-clan homicide, enjoined upon matrilineal relatives; the rule that only members of the same clan may eat certain food together, though this restriction does not apply in the elementary family; within the clan, finally, the threat of witchcraft separating the dual sections does not operate.

In comparing the social rights and obligations involved in patrilineal and matrilineal descent respectively we are forced to move on three different levels. On the first we compare the matrilineal clan with the (institutionally unemphasized) patrilineal descent group. On the second, the maternal affiliation (coinciding with affiliation in the clan line) with paternal affiliation. On the third, links with the mother's clan and links with the father's clan.

Adopting the first approach we discover that all rights and obligations vested in the patrilineal descent groups are symbiotic-diacritical in nature, while all clan-bound rights and obligations are syncretic. There are two exceptions: clan exogamy, in this very nearly endogamous community, shades over into symbiotic interdependence (see above, p. 337, n. 2); and the fights over rain between the dual sections express both the syncretic and symbiotic principle. For in the raids by the eastern upon the western section the individuals in the former act collectively; yet in doing so they merely exercise a prerogative which is vested in the (theoretical) patrilineal lineage, as is also the presumed abuse of rain magic which they attack.

The second viewpoint bears upon the institutions of marriage and the family. Here paternal and maternal influences are set against each other. Newborn children receive a name expressing the order of birth by the same mother, and the mother plays a much greater part in education than the father. The bride-price on behalf of sons, on the other hand, is usually paid by the father, though financial help from the mother's brother is optional. In the event of widowhood a modified levirate with the husband's full brother, sister's son, or some other matrilineal relative is recommended but not strictly enforced. But old widows who cannot remarry return to their father's locality and home. Paternal affiliation, finally, constitutes an exemption from the inter-clan eating avoidances.

In inheritance, maternal and paternal affiliation are combined in a somewhat complicated pattern. Let us consider male property first. The house, house farm-plot, and the farms in the plain are inherited by sons or, in the second place, daughters or grandchildren. All movable property of a man goes to his matrilineal relations—full brothers, sisters' sons, sisters, sisters' daughters, or mother's sisters' sons. The category of matrilineally inherited property also includes livestock, farms on the hill-side, and the crops standing in the fields or stored in the granaries. A woman's property is divided between her sons and daughters.

Inheritance is thus not from male to male and from female to female, and the utilitarian viewpoint that certain property is more suitable for one or the other sex is disregarded. It creeps in, however, in the practice whereby, in the inheritance of land, women (e.g. sisters) may act as trustees for their male offspring. At first sight the division between paternal and maternal inheritance may seem well balanced; in practice, it leads to several incongruities. First, sons lose the title to their father's hill-side farms, which sometimes represent the largest part of the landed property, and inherit instead their mother's brother's land, which may lie on the other side of the hill—on 'forbidden ground'. This difficulty is fully recognized, and overcome in two ways: while still alive, the father may 'sell' one of his hill-side plots (never more) to his son at a nominal price; or the heir to the land will sell it, again for a small, nominal sum, to his dispossessed cousin.

Secondly, the wife and her small children are left without sustenance since all the father's grain goes to his matrilineal relations (e.g. his sister's son). This incongruity is met both by the levirate marriage of the widow and by the duty of the heir to adopt the orphans and bring them up in his house. Here we notice a change of affiliation: the orphans are not looked after by their own patrilineal or matrilineal kinsfolk, but by their father's matrilineal (i.e. clan) relatives—an oblique relationship to which we shall return presently.

Thirdly, every gift or economic benefit which a father during his lifetime grants to his children means a deduction from the future inheritance which his sister's son may expect. Of this fact the people are fully conscious, and the potential consequences are strongly felt. As a result the relationship between a man and his sister, or between their sons and daughters, is embittered by suspicion and jealousy, and often leads to serious quarrels and lasting hostility. Tullishi society has devised no means of overcoming this conflict.

Our final approach concerns the juxtaposition of mother's and father's clan. It is expressed, above all, in the rules forbidding marriage both in one's own and one's father's clan. I have called the link with the father's matrilineal descent group an 'oblique' relationship: by this term I meant to express the break in the straight descent line which this double clan affiliation implies. It can best be illustrated by comparison with the twofold 'straight' descent system as it exists in Nyaro; if this system were true also of Tullishi, the rules of exogamy there would apply to the maternal clan and to the local group. That they do not is due essentially to the absence of a social recognition, i.e. a recognition in descent terms, of the local group. Thus in the Tullishi rules the individual conceives of his (or her) marriage avoidances as being focused, not in mother and father, but in mother and father's mother, in other words, in his clan and his father's clan. This obliqueness can be visualized in the following diagrams:

Tullishi   *Nyaro*

Ego   Ego

Myth of Origin

Now, this obliqueness in the descent conception is rendered conscious, above all, in the tribal myth of origin. As we shall presently understand, it plays an extremely important part in the social life of the community. The myth, in brief, is this. The ancestors of the tribe were a man and a woman who sprang from a gourd.[1] They had numerous offspring, but later quarrelled and separated; the man, with some of the children, occupied the eastern part of the hill, the woman, with her share of the offspring, the western. Hating each other, the man and woman forbade their children to visit each other, lest they should be bewitched by the other spouse. Thus the dual local division arose. The children who stayed with their father grew numerous, strong, and aggressive; the children who went with their mother were less prolific, less robust, and meek and submissive in character. This distinction is still believed to obtain, and that this mythical belief has effectively moulded the outlook of the people is clearly visible in the behaviour of the local groups: the eastern 'male' section behaves in an overbearing, boisterous, and often rebellious manner, and is expected to behave like this, while the 'female' western section is more docile and never spontaneously aggressive. The attacks by the eastern upon the western group in the event of drought represent an institutionalized occasion for the manifestation of this presumed hereditary difference in temperament.

The analysis of the myth reveals a number of socially relevant beliefs —relevant in that they both extend and reinterpret the existing descent alinement. To begin with, the myth of origin gives ideological recognition to a feature in the descent alinement which the social system fails to recognize: the myth admits the coexistence of paternal and maternal affiliation, and the patrilineal foundation of the local grouping. Yet it does so in a way inconsistent with reality. In the myth, association with the father and mother respectively is made the criterion of group identity; in reality, the dual local sections both derive their social identity from the mother and their physical continuity and identity from the father. The result is a fictitious 'oblique' descent alinement of the same kind as we discovered in the marriage rules of the tribe. In the latter, the direct alinement on the mother's side (mother-mother-mother) contrasts with the oblique alinement on the father's side (father-mother-mother). In the myth, the eastern ('male' or father's) section derives its physical continuity in the line father-father . . . father, and the western ('female' or mother's) section in the line father-father . . . mother; conversely the social (i.e. clan) identity of the eastern section appears, in the mythical pedigree, as an oblique line (mother-mother . . . association with the father), and in the western section as a direct line (mother,

---

[1] One of the Tullishi clans is called 'gourd', *kafunya*,—incidentally the only clan name which is linguistically identifiable.

mother . . . association with the mother). This can be clearly seen in the following diagram:

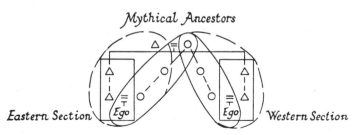

(The ovals drawn in unbroken line show clan affiliation; the ovals drawn in broken lines the dual local division interpreted in terms of the mythical affiliation; the squares show the concrete affiliation underlying the dual local division.)

In speaking of an 'oblique' descent alinement in which unilineal affiliation is broken or deflected, we are defining a purely structural arrangement visible to us, through the analysis of the methods by which the group traces descent. But the descent alinement expressed in the myth also appears as a content in the minds of the people and as a conscious determinant of their behaviour. And here we note that from the alinement in terms of descent a new alinement springs forth, namely, one in terms of sex. The juxtaposition of father-mother turns into one of male-female. A conscious ideology of behaviour ascribes to the mythical descent groups temperamental characteristics conceived of as typical of the sexes; it formulates a contrasting heredity which expresses sex-polarity and antagonism. Think of the traditional hostility and suspicion of witchcraft separating the 'male' and 'female' section; the licensed aggressiveness of the 'male' section; and the expected malevolence of the 'female' section in disputes over rain. This aspect needs further examination.

Sex Antagonism

The sex antagonism expresssed in the myth to some extent merely reflects an antagonism pervading concrete social life: as the 'female' group is credited with depriving the 'male' group of rain, so a man's sister deprives his sons of part of their economic sustenance in inheritance. The hostility and suspicion which can be observed in everyday life between women and their brothers' sons are transferred on to the plane of a mythically vouchsafed sex-rivalry.

Let me emphasize that these conflict motives, whether on tribal or family scale, amount to widely visible maladjustment. Frequent quarrels over inheritance and the periodical feuds over rain are only two of its expressions. The violence licensed there pervades group life in all its aspects: crimes of all kinds are rife; homicide and blood feud are frequent. So is open jealousy of husbands—which is directed as much against the wife as against the paramour. Here it will be seen that the relative position of the male and female in the myth is conceived of as the converse of that position in reality. In the myth the 'male' section is aggressive, overbearing, and domineering, and the 'famale' section weak, submissive, and pliable. Nothing could be farther from the truth. The Tullishi woman is domineering and independent: she takes charge of the education of her children; it is she who has to decide when they are old enough to brave the danger of the magic boundary between east and west; it is she who watches carefully over their claims of inheritance, and in disputes over it she, not the man, is the aggressive party.

This contradiction may be the result of one of two things: either the male-female polarity as represented in the myth is a reflection of a concrete kinship situation which once existed but is no longer true; or it must be a reaction to a contrasting real situation, an ideological compensation for a felt frustration—a 'wish fulfilment'. The first alternative is ruled out; for the matrilineal descent-structure as it exists, and since it has existed in the tribe, already ascribes to the woman a dominant, not a submissive, role in kinship life. The second alternative must therefore be the correct one.

But here we note that the myth does not merely present a wish fulfilment compensating male frustration; it also projects it on to a different, non-sexual, grouping. It transfers the male-female antagonism to two sections both embracing men and women, and both recruited through descent in the male line. One might argue that if the myth had not done so, if it had contrasted the dominant male with the submissive female sex, it would have pictured a situation flatly contradicting reality. Through the transference the myth avoids this absolute conflict with reality; moreover, it places the sex-antagonism in a relationship— between the dual sections—where it is afforded realization and catharsis. It is this twofold psychological motive behind the construction of the myth, of 'wish fulfilment' and 'transference', which produces the incongruity between the myth of descent and the actual descent alinement.

I assume here, first, that the myth is essentially man-made; and secondly, that there has been a genetic process at work operating somewhat on these lines:

> matrilineal kinship structure → male resentment
> male resentment → myth
> myth → hostility between dual sections

The first assumption is supported by the fact that in the religious life of the tribe it is the men who represent the active element. The second assumption is, of course, purely speculative; but the speculation is based on well-established psychological mechanisms. Yet this genetic process leaves unexplained one initial maladjustment—the matrilineal kinship structure which failed to give adequate recognition to the paternal factor. In my interpretation, then, Tullishi erred somewhere in the process of evolving its descent system.

Yet where precisely does the error lie? 'Adequate' is a relative term; if in Tullishi the recognition of the paternal factor is inadequate it is so because certain paternal claims are presupposed. Claims for recognition of paternal descent do not exist *a priori*. They must have been created—by the same social structure which fails to recognize them. Thus matrilineal succession clashes, not with patrilineal alinement *in abstracto*, but with a patrilineal alinement already associated with rigid patrilocality, without the loophole—familiar from many matrilineal societies—of adoption or optional change of residence. Matrilineal inheritance becomes iniquitous when crossing patrilineal inheritance in the same field. Social identity derived in the mother's line is translated into unwelcome maternal dominance in a household or local community otherwise patrilineally orientated.

The term 'inadequate' should thus read 'inconsistent'. The 'error' of the Tullishi descent system lies in its inconsistent evolution—in having fostered patrilineal claims yet failed to satisfy them.

This is not as much of a circle as it might seem. For though patrilineal claims, in the strict descent sense, do not exist *a priori*, paternal claims, viewed as claims of the male against the female sex, do so exist: they arise from the impulses and responses, from the conflict of submission and dominance, inherent in sexual and procreative relations. Sex polarity is, as it were, *a priori*. It is the Archimedean fulcrum in this universe of social interaction. It is under this aspect, I think, that we must approach the problem.

III. CONCLUSIONS

Tullishi society has not evolved an even recognition of both descent factors, so that sex polarity has emerged as an autonomous, ill-regulated force, whose action is visible in the overt maladjustment of the group. The other society which we considered, Nyaro, is without such maladjustment, and equally without pronounced sex-antagonism; but here full and even recognition is granted to both descent factors. The Nyaro social system would thus appear to be a success where the Tullishi system is a failure.

Obviously there are many other social systems—all the unilineal systems of descent—where no such even recognition is admitted yet open sex-antagonism and maladjustment are absent. Now, sex polarity is a *given physical fact*; paternal and maternal alinement represent two of its three possible social elaborations, the dual descent system being the third. In simple unilateral systems sex polarity is, viewed under the aspect of descent, a background factor: such problems as it presents can

DUAL DESCENT IN THE NUBA HILLS 355

be solved outside the field of descent organization. In a fully double-unilateral system, like that of Kao-Nyaro, sex polarity merges with descent alinement. In the incomplete double-unilateral descent system of Tullishi sex polarity stands half-way between these two extremes: it exists in the foreground of descent organization, but does not coincide with it. It may well be that within certain limits (to be described presently) the double descent system offers the most adequate solution of this problem—how to absorb sex polarity and so neutralize a potentially powerful social tension. The initial 'error' of Tullishi appears to lie in having attempted this 'third' solution but having failed in the attempt.

This failure does not by itself account for the maladjustment of Tullishi as compared with the well-balanced society of Kao-Nyaro. A short survey of the main cultural differences separating the two groups will show what I mean.

In Kao-Nyaro the segment-bound rules of conduct function without the threat of supernatural sanctions, while in Tullishi breaches of eating restrictions or exogamous rules are associated with mysterious illness. In Tullishi, too, we find such segment-bound magic as the circumcision of two segments, spelling death to other segments which might trespass on this preserve of usage. In Nyaro witchcraft represents essentially a just retribution, and so merely sanctions internal clan obligations; in Tullishi witchcraft is openly malevolent, but the clan offers a sanctuary. In other words, in Nyaro witchcraft operates within the segment whose unity it emphasizes; in Tullishi it operates against segments other than the one whose unity it emphasizes. Inheritance in Nyaro satisfies the conditions of double affiliation while recognizing the utilitarian aspect of patrimonial inheritance; in Tullishi the two principles clash, affiliation overruling the masculine inheritance. In consequence, men excluded from the line of inheritance suffer serious deprivation and are inevitably placed in the position of frustrated and inconvenient rivals.

These various features show two factors at work. First, the machinery for regulating in-group relations in Kao-Nyaro entails no magic threats and no appeal to mysterious punishment; secondly, it entails no outward hostility against individuals outside the circle of set relations. In Tullishi the opposite is true. The first factor operates so that a greater emotional weight is brought to bear on the observances of in-group conduct. This seems consistent with the more emotionally charged, conflict-fraught atmosphere of Tullishi, of which the social structure with its emphasis on sex-antagonism is another expression. The second factor, the attitude of outward hostility created by in-group unity, is involved, in some measure, in any group-formation. Cohesion within the group or group-segment must always mean some separation from coexisting groups or segments. Concentration of group members upon their unity always means some alienation from, and even antagonism towards, those 'who do not belong'. This negative coefficient of social cohesion varies widely in different societies; in Nyaro it is at a minimum, in Tullishi at a maximum.

In Tullishi it is, once more, consistent with the emotional tension pervading group behaviour. We cannot go much farther than this indication of a psychological and cultural consistency. Whether the emergence of the high emotional tension in Tullishi is derived from the social structure with its initial 'error' and nucleus of conflict, or whether the conflict-fraught structure emerged from an emotionally weighted mentality, is a question which cannot be answered on the grounds of social observation alone—and perhaps cannot be answered at all.

But two final questions may be asked. One is: Are sex-antagonism and the negative coefficient of social cohesion independent variables? The other: Why did only two groups among so many other Nuba tribes evolve, or attempt to evolve, the dual descent system?

1. So far as my Nuba data go, pronounced sex-antagonism and outward hostility as a concomitant of the cohesion of segments are independently variable factors. Ten of the twelve Nuba tribes without dual descent system which I have studied have only one or the other. The presence of either must entail a predisposition towards pervasive sentiments of hostility and suspicion. But only in two tribes, Moro and Korongo (disregarding here Tullishi), does this predisposition crystallize in both behaviour patterns. Thus one factor by itself seems to offer only a potentiality—and nothing more.

2. The second question is much more difficult to answer, if indeed it can be fully answered. In previous studies of dual descent systems their social implications have been assessed mainly in terms of family rights and obligations, such as titles of succession and kinship loyalties. The social structures here studied suggest that a different aspect may be at least as relevant. It concerns the way in which syncretic and diacritical-symbiotic rights and obligations are vested in the descent group. In the unilateral system the two are united; in Tullishi and Nyaro they are divided between patrilineal and matrilineal segments. Let me formulate this structural difference in terms of individual consciousness. The statement 'we are one in that we are different from the rest and have different contributions to make to the common weal' applies only in the patrilineal segment; the statement 'we are one in that we collaborate with each other' applies only in the matrilineal segment.[1]

Now, it has been shown that even strictly unilateral descent groups extend certain kinship rights and obligations 'bilaterally'. These concern invariably forms of co-operation—i.e. syncretic actions—and not diacritical actions as well. The same is true of the Nuba tribes. All the twelve tribes with unilateral descent systems show such bilateral orienta-

---

[1] Exogamy is once more an exception, being valid in both segments. This is consistent with the ambiguous nature of exogamy explained above.

tion. In all matrilineal groups paternal relations too are invested with important kinship rights and duties, and in patrilineal groups this is true of maternal kin. Among the Nuba, moreover, the double kinship orientation goes beyond mere family ties extended to both parents. It is positively expressed in clan (or gens) terms, that is, in terms of the same 'oblique' descent alinement which we discovered in Tullishi. Thus nearly all Nuba tribes have double exogamy.[1] In two groups especially, Otoro and Heiban, the double descent link is strongly emphasized. Among the Otoro, for example, blood feud is a collective duty of the gens; but the duty to substitute a kinsman or woman for the victim— which arrangement may replace blood feud—devolves on the maternal gens of the culprit. In Heiban every man has an 'opposite number' among the women of his mother's gens, with whom he must co-operate on important ritual occasions.

The two tribes, then, and in a lesser degree others as well, seem to have gone some way towards that separation of the diacritical-symbiotic aspect (restricted to the single, paternal descent group) from the syncretic aspect (extended bilaterally) which Nyaro and Tullishi have carried to the extreme.[2]

It may here be noted that the Otoro and to some extent the Heiban share with Kao-Nyaro a few kinship terms.[3] The links are too slender to permit deductions as to a possible common origin of the kinship systems. But even if such deductions could be drawn, we should be unable to decide whether the Nyaro system must be regarded as the prototype from which Otoro-Heiban have deviated, or whether Nyaro represents a special development not attempted by the other tribes. An even more equivocal position characterizes Tullishi; for next door to that tribe a group closely akin in language and general cultural features —the small tribe of Kamdang—has a strictly unilateral, matrilineal descent system.

But perhaps Tullishi and Nyaro possess cultural characteristics not found among the other tribes, which could be conclusively correlated with the divergent social structure? Both are small groups (Nyaro being here considered one group with Kao and Fungur); but there are other

---

[1] The Otoro, where exogamy has altogether disappeared, are an exception. But there is good reason to assume that double exogamy was practised even two generations ago.

[2] In the Ashanti dual system this separation appears to be both less extreme and based on an initially different principle. There syncretic rights and duties seem to be restricted to the matrilineal segments while diacritical-symbiotic actions (e.g. totemic associations and food taboos) are extended over both descent groups. To my knowledge a dual division of syncretic and diacritical features in which each descent alinement involves a share in both has nowhere been attempted. Perhaps such a division must nullify unilateral segmentation altogether.

[3] The term for gens is *eridh* in Kao-Nyaro and *erido* in Otoro; the term for parents-in-law is *ŋwuna* in Kao-Nyaro and *ŋuna* in Otoro and Heiban.

small groups among the Nuba without the crucial trait, and elsewhere in Africa a large tribe like the Ashanti shares it. Both Nyaro and Tullishi have a symbiotic clan system—but so have various Nuba tribes, large and small. Both, finally, are physically isolated and do not practise outside marriage to any considerable extent; but this again is true of Nuba tribes with unilateral descent systems.

Yet combined, these three aspects gain relevance—the relevance of delimiting factors. Indiscriminate outside marriage combined with a patrilocal and dual kinship system must tend to confuse the juxtaposition of patrilineal and matrilineal segments; for while the former would remain unchanged and restricted to one community, the matrilineal segments, with their syncretic connotation, would become haphazardly increased and would extend collaboration over diverse communities. In other words, the people who wear the 'badge' of unity and co-operate for the welfare of their tribe would become increasingly differentiated from those who co-operate in kinship rights and duties.[1] Again, in a group too large for all its members to meet constantly and come into contact in various collective tasks, the segments defined by such divided integration would tend to become ineffective; kinship co-operation, embracing individuals who rarely if ever meet, would not even have the external unity of diacritical characteristics to support it, nor would it be duplicated in the common symbiotic tasks.

Let me support my hypothesis by this evidence: of the fourteen Nuba tribes whose social structure I have recorded (at least in the essential features) only Nyaro and Tullishi show the three 'delimiting' features combined, as is indicated in the chart below.

Tribe				Population	Social isolation	Symbiotic structure
Otoro (p)	.	.	.	40,000	—	—
Heiban (p)	.	.	.	2,000	—	—
Tira (p)	.	.	.	8,000	—	+
Moro (p)	.	.	.	20,000	—	+
Korongo (m)	.	.	.	14,000	—	—
Mesakin (m)	.	.	.	6,000	—	—
Dilling (p)	.	.	.	7,000	—	+
Koalib (p)	.	.	.	20,000	—	—
Kadura (p)	.	.	.	7,000	—	+
Nyima (p)	.	.	.	37,000	—	—
Miri (m)	.	.	.	14,000	—	—
Kamdang (m)	.	.	.	1,500 (?)	—	—
Tullishi (mp)	.	.	.	3,500	+	l
Nyaro (mp)	.	.	.	2,000	+	+

Plus signs indicate the presence, minus signs the absence of the feature in question; (m) matrilineal, (p) patrilineal groups.

[1] From a different point of view, considering kinship rights and obligations, Professor Radcliffe-Brown equally correlates the emergence of unilateral descent

To return to our hypothesis. It will be seen, then, that the adequacy of the dual descent system in absorbing sex polarity is balanced by the separation of the two sets of rights and obligations which seem designed to reinforce one another. Against efficacy in one sphere must be set weakness in another—the danger of disintegration as soon as the group grows too large and ceases to be socially isolated. The size and relative isolation of groups appear to delimit the chances of success of this social experiment.[1]

I suggest it is indeed as an 'experiment' that we have to regard the dual descent system. The 'third solution', as I called it above, is an experiment in the sense of those biological species which emerge in the course of evolution but are later abandoned and discontinued. The motive behind the emergence of the social 'species' is the absorption of sex polarity in the descent structure. To some extent all societies betray the presence of the motive. Whether the tendency to try the experiment is more pronounced in the Nuba Mountains than in other cultural areas we must, for the moment, leave undecided.

systems with the change from local endogamy to exogamy. For where marriage goes beyond one 'corporate group' a fully bilateral succession to kinship rights and duties would become too confused to be workable (*Iowa Law Review*, xx, 1935, pp. 300–1).

[1] The fact that the dual descent system also exists in the large Ashanti tribe does not, in my view, contradict the hypothesis just expressed. The Ashanti kingdom emerged from a fusion of several small communities, where the dual descent system must have arisen. But in the Ashanti kingdom it is vague and ill defined, the matrilineal alinement almost eclipsing the patrilineal. I suggest, then, that this decline is correlated with the expansion of the group within which kinship bonds are valid. Among the Yakö the difficulties involved in the dual descent system are already clearly visible. They are significantly overcome by widely practised adoption from clan into gens, i.e. adoption of sister's sons into their mother's brother's patrilineal descent groups (see D. Forde, op. cit.). This genealogical device may be regarded as indicating a trend towards an eventual reduction of the double to a simple unilateral system.

KINSHIP AND THE LOCAL COMMUNITY AMONG THE NUER

By E. E. EVANS-PRITCHARD

INTRODUCTION

I HAVE already devoted several articles to Nuer marriage[1] and so I will not discuss that topic again in this essay, but will confine myself to discussing some features of Nuer kinship. I have described elsewhere the oecological and political background.[2]

The Nuer are a Nilotic people of some 200,000 souls living in open savannah country near the Nile and its tributaries in the Anglo-Egyptian Sudan. They are primarily a cattle people, the ebb and flow of whose transhumant life follows the alternation of wet and dry seasons. They are divided into a number of tribes, the largest political groups of their society, and these tribes are segmented into sections and sub-sections corresponding structurally to the lineages of the clans dominant in each tribal territory. In *The Nuer* I have described the form of segmentation in political and descent groups and I have attempted to show the principles which underlie it. In that book I omitted all but the briefest references to the kinship system because I believed, and still believe, that political structure presents problems which are better inquired into apart from social relations of a different kind.

In *The Nuer* I have merely stated that the village is the smallest corporate group of a political kind among the Nuer and that, in reading my description of their political structure, the reader would have to take for granted the network of kinship and affinal ties within a village. I must now ask him to remember that, though I here describe relations between persons within local communities without again describing the wider political structure, the local communities within which these relations function and which they serve to maintain are the basic units of that structure. I must also make it plain, in view of the considerable writing about lineages which has since appeared, that in *The Nuer* I was chiefly interested in the relation of clan segmentation to tribal segmentation and therefore in discussing lineages gave chief attention to the syste-

---

[1] 'Some Aspects of Marriage and the Family among the Nuer', *Zeitschrift für Vergleichende Rechtswissenschaft*, 1938 (reprinted as Rhodes–Livingstone Institute Paper, no. 11, 1945); 'Nuer Bridewealth', *Africa*, xvi. 4, Oct. 1946, pp. 247 57; 'Bridewealth among the Nuer', *Afr. Studies*, vi. 4, Dec. 1947, pp. 81–8; 'Nuer Marriage Ceremonies', *Africa*, xviii. 1, Jan. 1947, pp. 29–40; 'A Note on Courtship among the Nuer', *Sudan Notes*, xxviii, 1947, pp. 115–26; 'A Note on Affinity Relationships among the Nuer', *Man*, ii, Jan. 1948, pp. 3–5; 'Nuer Modes of Address', *Uganda Journal*, xii. 2, Sept. 1948, pp. 166–71; 'Nuer Rules of Exogamy and Incest', *Social Structure*, 1949.

[2] *The Nuer*, 1940. A bibliography is given there.

matic form their structure presents when co-ordinated with tribal or political structure. To avoid misunderstanding it is perhaps desirable to emphasize that in Nuerland there are also small lineages which have fewer branches and less depth than the dominant clans to which I gave particular attention in my book. These less systematized descent groups may be associated with local communities smaller than tribes and their larger segments, but they are only associated with them in terms of the tribal structure as a whole through some relationship to its dominant clan, and often they are not associated with local communities at all. This fact will be evident in the account which follows.

<h2 style="text-align:center">VILLAGES AND CAMPS</h2>

A village (*cieng*) is a corporate group with a feeling of solidarity. Though its members have contacts with persons in neighbouring villages, and even in other sections of their tribe and in adjacent tribes, the greater part of their activities are carried out within their own village community and their strongest ties are with other members of it. Nuer have great affection for their homes and, in spite of their wandering habits, men born and bred in a village are likely to return to it even if they live elsewhere for some years. Villagers fight side by side in defence and attack and they support one another in feuds. When their youths attend dances in the district they enter them in a war line (*dep*), singing their special war chant, and they remain together during the dancing lest some incident should lead to fighting, for it sometimes happens that when the dancing parties of different villages duel their play passes into fighting and spears take the place of clubs. Villagers also have close economic relations and common economic interests which make a village a corporation owning in common its cultivations, water-supplies, fishing-pools, and grazing-grounds; the ownership being spoken about in terms of the lineage with which the village is socially identified. There is, especially in the smaller villages, much co-operation in labour and much sharing of food. At the beginning of the drought the villagers may scatter to camp round different pools in the bush and some families, and even large aggregates of relatives, may spend the dry season with kinsmen of different villages; but the scattering is temporary and as a rule families which live in the same village in the rains share the same cattle camp (*wec*) at the height of the drought.

Nevertheless, in spite of their many contacts with one another and of their concerted action in their relations with other villages, there may be rivalries between members of different parts of a single village. This is more noticeable in the larger villages, where groups of kin occupy distinct sections of the village site and have a feeling of exclusiveness towards each other. *Wa pekda*, 'I go to my end (of the village)', often indicates, besides direction, a particular loyalty within the wider village. As an example of this feeling I mention an experience in the village of

Nyueny, which is referred to again later. I gave spears to two youths who often visited me from the other end of the village than that where I had pitched my tent, and a man at our end protested to me in private: 'When you have gone they will think nothing of killing us with your spears.' When I expostulated that they were all members of the same village he replied: 'Have you not noticed that between our end and their end there is a wide gap?'

Nuer villages vary greatly in size and form, both of which depend very largely on local conditions. Some are small communities of not more than a few dozen residents living on riverside mounds, accumulations of debris which have been dwelling-places for long periods. Some of these may more properly be regarded as colonies attached to larger communities. Larger villages, of some hundreds of souls, are generally strung out along the backs of ridges, but where there is a wide stretch of high ground a village may be distributed in all directions over several miles of country.

Indeed, it is a characteristic of all Nuer villages, to which Jules Poncet alludes,[1] that they are spread out as freely as the nature of the ground permits in little groups of habitations, each separated generally from its neighbours by some fifty to several hundred paces. A group of this kind often consists of a single homestead, a cattle byre with its attendant hut or huts, the dwelling of a family. The Nuer speak of a man's homestead as his *gol*, the primary meaning of which word is the heap of smouldering cattle-dung and the hearth around it that is a feature of every byre. It occupies the centre of the byre and a branch serving as a shrine to the ancestral spirits of the lineage is planted near it. In its social use the word means 'family', the occupants of the homestead, and it may also therefore have the further sense of 'household' since there may be other persons living there than members of the owner's family who count nevertheless, as we should say, as members of the family. Frequently the byres and huts of two or three families, the heads of which are commonly brothers or a man and his married sons, are grouped around a common kraal so that we may then speak of a composite homestead; or several homesteads, owned generally by close kin, are adjacent to one another and form distinct clusters which we may call hamlets. Nuer speak of a composite homestead as the *gol* of so-and-so, naming its senior member, although they also refer to each of its component homesteads as the *gol* of its particular owner; they may use the same word to describe what I have called a hamlet, though a cluster of this kind with the land around it is also designated by the word *dhor*, combined with the name either of its senior member, as *dhor* Nyang, the hamlet of Nyang, or of some natural feature, as *dhor ngop*, the hamlet of the fig-tree. One might speak—somewhat loosely it is true—of the occupants of a composite homestead, and sometimes of a hamlet also,

[1] Jules Poncet, *Le Fleuve Blanc*, 1863–4, p. 40.

as a joint family since they have a measure of common residence and, if not a common herd, rights in each other's herds. 'Joint family' in this sense would have a different meaning from that which I have given to the expression 'extended family', as I will explain in the next section.

When the Nuer leave their villages in the dry season they collect, often after temporary dispersal, in large waterside camps. There is then greater solidarity, both spatial and moral, than during the rains. The community is crowded together in grass windscreens and little beehive huts, and the herds, which in the rains are tethered in separate kraals, are now tethered in the same kraal or in adjacent kraals. In the rains, when water is abundant and pasturage near at hand, the cattle are either not herded at all or each family or joint family herds its own; but in the dry season, when conditions are different, the cattle of a camp are watered and pastured together and the different families take it in turn to provide herdsmen. Activities performed of necessity or by preference in parties— hunting, fishing, and collecting—are dry-season activities. Also, milking, cleaning kraals, making up fires, cooking, pounding grain, and other chores, which are performed separately and at different times by each household in the villages, tend to be performed in unison in the camps. The greater density of the community and the rigours of the season impose a common regimen. Another feature of cattle camps which has some social importance is their composition. Neighbouring village communities which, in the rains, occupy different sites, often divided by wide swamps, frequently make common camp or camp near to each other, so that there are more intimate relations between their members in the dry season. The radius of effective kinship is greater in the dry season than in the wet.

Although there is this greater cohesion in camps, the families and joint families and larger clusters of kin, whose social distinction is evident in the distribution of homesteads in the villages, maintain their identity in the distribution of camp windscreens and huts. Each family has its own windscreen, corresponding to its byre in the village, and in the centre of it is the *gol*, its hearth of ashes, and at the entrance its shrine. Attached to the windscreen are the grass beehive huts of the womenfolk, just as in the villages their wattle-and-daub huts are attached to the byre. The windscreens of' those whose homesteads adjoin in the villages are generally adjacent to, almost touching, one another in the camps and form clearly demarcated rows in the circle of camp dwellings. When a large village is clearly segmented the separation observable in the distribution of its homesteads can also be noted in the dispersal of smaller camps within the general camping area. These social alinements are most evident in the early part of the dry season, before the large concentrations of the main season have been formed, for then small groups of kin often make independent camps around isolated pools, sometimes at a considerable distance from each other.

LINEAGE AND KINSHIP

All the members of such a village or camp as I have briefly described are kin to one another. Before giving examples in illustration of this statement I must say again what I have already said in *The Nuer* about the difference between lineage relations and kin relations, because it is a very important difference. In speaking of lineages I refer to unilateral *groups* of kin—among the Nuer groups of agnates—and in speaking of kinship I refer to *categories* of kin. In speaking of lineage relations I therefore refer to relations between groups within a system of such groups, whereas in speaking of kin or kinship relations I refer to relations between persons standing to one another in certain categories of relationship within a system of such categories. It is not always easy for those who have not lived in a society with a lineage structure to appreciate the distinction I have drawn, because the relationship between collateral lineages of the same clan is necessarily also one that can be expressed in terms of a kinship category; and it is possible in certain circumstances even to speak of the relation between lineages of different clans in similar terms, for they may wish on occasions to stress a genealogical nexus between themselves, indicating thereby that, for example, the one stands to the other as *gaatnar*, children of the maternal uncle. But in these cases it is a relationship between groups that is referred to and not a personal relationship between individuals, except in so far as it is derived from the relationship between the groups to which they belong.

As I have explained in *The Nuer* the lineages of Nuerland are dispersed groups, though in a certain sense they may be regarded as corporate groups in the form they take as political segments in fusion with other elements. They provide the conceptual framework of the political system within which they also function as its organizing principle through the expression of political fission and fusion in terms of their segmentary structure. The identification of lineage segments with tribal segments in a political context is brought about by the acknowledgement that certain clans and their lineages have rights in certain tribal areas and by the residence in those areas of a sufficient number of members of these dominant groups to act as nuclei of local and political groups. It probably never happens that all members of a lineage of any order—maximal, major, minor, or minimal—live in the area associated with it and to which it gives its name, though very many of them may do so.

Because the usual reference to a lineage is in a political context it is generally spoken of as the *cieng* of such-and-such a people (the name of the lineage being given), for *cieng* has always a residential, and not an exclusive descent, connotation. When reference is made to a lineage in a context in which it is desired to particularize it as an exclusive descent group, a group of agnatic kin descended from a common ancestor, the Nuer use the expressions *thok dwiel* or *thok mac*, literally the doorway to a hut or the hearth, to denote it; but these expressions are little used because, in the life of the Nuer, abstraction of a lineage from its social and political matrix has only rarely to be made: on certain ritual occasions and in connexion with feuds and rules of exogamy.

The distinction between an agnatic lineage relation and an agnatic kinship relation is clearly made by the Nuer themselves, from whom indeed I learnt it. They use the word *buth* to describe agnatic kinship between collateral lineages, that is to say, kinship between groups and between individuals only in virtue of their membership of these groups. They use the word *mar*, on the other hand, to describe any, and every, relationship of a kinship kind between persons. All persons with whom a man acknowledges any kind of kinship, through however many other persons, are *mar*, kin, to him. People say of him and of any such person *teke mar*, 'they have kinship'; and he speaks of any or all of his relations as *jimarida*, 'my kinsmen'. The term *mar* classes together what we may for convenience distinguish: relatives through the father, whom we may call the paternal kin, and relatives through the mother, whom we may call the maternal kin. We may speak of the paternal and maternal kin of a man together as his kindred, and this is the meaning the word *mar* has when used by Nuer collectively and without restrictive qualification. Nuer also sometimes use *mar* when speaking of affinal relations, especially when they are long established. In a broad sense they also are kin in the eyes of Nuer just as in our own society we include our affines in the category of relatives.

Where there is a *buth* relationship between lineages there must also, in one way of speaking, be *mar* between the members of one and the members of the other, for the relationship between collateral lineages is agnatic and the members of the one must therefore be patrilineal kin to the members of the other. The question therefore arises: at what point in the spread of an agnatic line, conceived of existentially as a number of living patrilineal kinsmen, does inter-personal *mar* relationship become the inter-group relationship the Nuer call *buth*, so that we may speak of these kinsmen as falling into segmentary groups or lineages? The question may be put in another way: how many generations back do Nuer trace patrilineal ascent before they reach the first ancestor from whom bifurcate collateral lines of descent of the kind they collectivize in their representatives as a *thok dwiel*, a lineage?

A Nuer, when asked about this matter, gave an historical explanation: 'In the days when people scattered, brother and son went raiding and they settled where they raided. Then kinship ceased (*ce mar thuk*) and there remained only a lineage relationship (*ce dwoth ni buth*).' This could only have happened, however, as the Nuer themselves also say, after some generations had elapsed. Even to-day, descendants of Nuer who settled to the east of the Nile, after raiding the Dinka in what are now the Jikany and Lou tribal areas, sometimes travel to the homes of their forebears to the west of the Nile to receive cattle which are their due on the marriages of the daughters of kinsmen, from whose fathers and grandfathers their fathers and grandfathers separated. While the privileges of kinship are thus claimed the persons concerned cannot be regarded as *jibuthni*, members of collateral lineages. In my experience Nuer do not generally speak of lineages till four or five generations back in patrilineal ascent, and I think also that there are sound methodological reasons for following Nuer usage in this matter and not speaking of lineages before at least the third generation in ascent is reached.

Although any relative of a man is *mar* to him, the word refers in normal usage to close relatives only and, on the paternal side, generally implies those persons on the marriage of whose daughters a man can claim a portion of the bride-wealth; which means an agnatic relationship deriving from any forebear as far back as, but not beyond, the bride's great-grandfather. The Nuer commonly explain such matters in terms of cattle-rights. In a very general sense therefore all agnates descended from a common great-grandfather have rights, actual or potential, in each other's daughters and, in the same general sense, in each other's herds, for their herds all derive, at least theoretically, from the great-grand-father's herd and the mothers of the daughters were married with these cattle. It is this which gives them a right to a portion of the bride-wealth of their paternal kin. Moreover, it is for descendants of the great-grand-father that specific kinship terms are used in their primary reference. I therefore propose, because it is desirable to give precision to the terms used in this account, even if the relativity of relationships makes any definition seem to some extent arbitrary, to refer to the grouping, in relation to any person, of agnates of three generations in depth as his extended family.

Beyond this point we enter into the structural relations of the lineage system where the Nuer begin to speak of collectivities of agnates. There is always *buth* between collateral lineages of the same clan and there may also be *buth* between clans, as I have explained in *The Nuer*. Also a captured Dinka boy may be *lath buthni*, given *buth*, as the Nuer say, and thereby made a member of his captor's lineage. Groups which have no *buth* between them have *rul* between them; they are 'strangers'. *Buth* means 'to share'. It is a word much used in reference to division of meat, especially on ritual occasions. When clans have a *buth* relationship they share the meat of each other's sacrifices at wedding and mortuary ceremonies. Thus, when the Gaatnaca clan sacrifice, the Thiang clan can claim a hind leg, the Jimem clan a foreleg, and the Gaat dila Buli clan a foreleg. In the same way the Jaalogh clan are said to share meat with the Kwe clan, the Gaawar clan with the Kwook clan, and the Gaat-gankiir clan with the Ngok Dinka (or some of their lineages). This reciprocity must be wholly theoretical in most cases, because there would not be a man of the privileged clan present at the sacrifices. If he were, he would certainly receive meat as the representative of his clan, but presumably only a token piece of the joint said to be his right, since these joints are also the right of kinsmen of certain categories. The joint is a symbolic rather than an actual right, but Nuer are agreed that his representative status would be recognized in the division of the carcass.

Collateral lineages of the same clan also share the meat of sacrifices, though once again, it must be added, in theory at any rate; and if a Dinka boy is adopted into a lineage, which happens very often, he may then share the meat of its sacrifices and may also claim a portion of the meat of any other lineages to which this lineage stands in a *buth* relationship. *Buth* relationship is also stated by the Nuer in terms of elephant tusks, in the division of the tusks or of the cattle exchanged for them in Abyssinia. When hunters kill an elephant the right tusk belongs to the *koc*, the man who first speared it, and the left tusk to the *gam*, the man who next speared it. The kinsmen who share a girl's bride-wealth and a man's blood-wealth share also the tusk or the cattle obtained for it, but those standing in a *buth* relationship to the spearers are also said to have a claim. When discussing these matters with some old men of the eastern Jikany Nuer, I was told that the various branches of the Gaatgankiir clan, the dominant clan of the Jikany tribal areas, share the meat of each other's sacrifices; but I noticed that they preferred to state this *buth* relationship in terms of the division of elephant tusks. Thus they said that when a man of the Gaajok maximal lineage kills an elephant one section of the tusk belongs to the Gaajok maximal lineage and one section to the Gaagwong maximal lineage. They explained that this means that a section goes to the particular *thok mac*, in this context 'minimal lineage', of these maximal lineages with whom the spearer's *thok mac* 'have from olden times exchanged', in other words, to the *gwan buthni* of the spearer's family,[1] a man whose functions will now be described.

Each family has its *gwan buthni* who acts as master of ceremonies at its rites, a son taking his dead father's place in this service. He acts on such occasions as weddings, mortuary rites, composition and atonement for homicide, sacrifices to honour the ghosts, sacrifices to sever kinship and allow marriage or cohabitation, sacrifices at the building of new byres, and in connexion with initiation, raiding, and elephant hunting. It is particularly his function to call out the clan spear-name in rites where this is customary and to slay sacrificial beasts and to cut their scrota. 'He is the cutter of the scrota of cattle.' 'The *jibuthni* are the people who cut the scrota of cattle.' He has a right to some of the meat of sacrifices of the family he serves, to a section of the tusk of any elephant they may kill, and to the first turtles and the skins of the first leopards and genets killed by youths of the family. The same man may

---

[1] See also P. P. Howell, 'A Note on Elephants and Elephant Hunting among the Nuer', *Sudan Notes*, xxvi. 1, 1945, pp. 95–103.

act on behalf of several families of the same extended family, and one of his close agnatic kin may act in his stead, since he carries out his functions not as an individual but as the representative of a lineage. The office is not necessarily reciprocal, for a man may act as *gwan buthni* to a family of one collateral lineage and have as the *gwan buthni* of his own family a man of a different collateral lineage. Also, a family may have more than one *gwan buthni*. There is, perhaps, more to be learnt about this office, but my information, as far as it goes, shows that the master of ceremonies of a family is a member of a lineage collateral to that of the head of the family, a distant agnatic kinsman outside his minimal lineage; though I believe that if one of the persons who usually acts in this capacity is not available his place may be taken by any distant kinsman who can by some fiction be held to represent him.

THE VILLAGE OF KONYE

Having made what preliminary explanations seemed to be necessary, I now record some examples of the network of kinship ties in typical Nuer villages and camps.

As I have said earlier, members of a village are all *mar*, kin, to one another: any villager can trace kinship with every other person in his village, either by a direct kinship tie or through a third person who is in different ways related both to himself and the other person. Furthermore, he can establish kinship of some kind—real, assumed, by analogy, mythological, or just fictitious—with everybody he comes into contact with during his lifetime and throughout the length and breadth of Nuerland; and this is necessary if he has frequent dealings with them, for all social obligation of a personal kind is defined in terms of kinship. But within his local community the links are definite and well known. All members of a village or cattle camp can be placed on a single genealogical chart showing relationship by blood, adoption, and marriage.

The village of Konye, of which I give a sketch-map and genealogical table (Figs. 16 and 17), is on a site on the left bank of the Pibor and a few miles to the south of Akobo Post. It is on the periphery of Nuerland, on their present-day frontier with the Anuak, and has only recently been used by Nuer of the Lou tribe as a permanent wet-season settlement, though they have probably long camped on the site in seasons of severe drought. Nevertheless, the social cluster found in occupation of it in May 1935 is typical of small communities in every part of Nuerland. In that month and year the village consisted of eleven homesteads perched on a high mound some eighty paces in diameter, with four attached homesteads lying between 400 and 600 paces to the south of the mound. On a very rough estimate the population of the village and attached homesteads was eighty to a hundred souls. I spent only a few days in the village and restricted my inquiries there to an effort to discover its genealogical pattern by ascertaining the kinship ties between

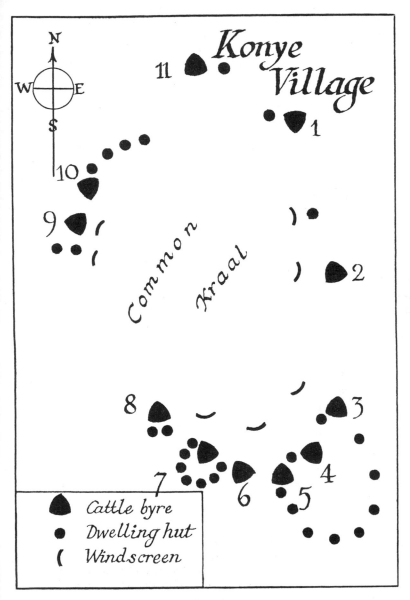

FIG. 16

the men who owned the fifteen cattle byres, that is to say, between the fifteen heads of families of the settlement. This might seem a simple task, but in Nuerland it is by no means so, and the genealogy had to be pieced together by eliciting why each owner of a byre had come to live at Konye, an inquiry which was answered by mentioning his relationship to someone already living in the village. There may be other ties of kinship or affinity between members of the different families which have not been recorded. There may also be a number of domestic unions other than the union of simple legal marriage which are not shown on the chart.[1] Irregular unions are not easily unearthed in a rapid survey which is not directed to that end. The genealogical table, which includes the owners of the outlying homesteads, is not a complete record of all the persons living at Konye.

The chief man of the village is Rue-Wor (homestead 8), and his son Deng-Rue (homestead 12) is the chief man of the outlying hamlet. The community is grouped round Rue who, although he belongs to the Gaanwar clan and therefore counts as a stranger (*rul*) and not as an aristocrat (*dil*) of the Lou tribe in whose territory he resides, is the *tut*, the 'bull', as the Nuer say, of this community. He has among them the leading position of a bull in a herd. There are several Lou tribal aristocrats in the village, but they have only a lineage, and no special personal, status in it. Kinsmen of the villagers from the interior of Lou country spend the dry season in the village.

I wish to direct attention to some features of the genealogy which are typical of many small Nuer communities. The Konye community is not in itself in any sense a lineage group, though it is attached to one of the main Jinaca lineages of the Lou tribe. Its nucleus is the family of Rue-Wor, the 'bull' of the village, and linked to it, some in one way and some in another, are a group of kin related to Rue and to each other. Any relationship of a man with any other member of the community serves to attach him to it and to give him status in it, for any tie to a particular person gives him further ties with all its other members. The tie may be of different categories and of varying degrees of kinship. Within the complex of village kinship ties and the circuit of daily contacts all relationships are given equal weight, for what is significant is less the category or degree of kinship than the fact of living together in a small and highly corporate community.

It will be noted that a considerable proportion of the owners of byres in the village are living there because of affinal relationships, and I must here say again that although *mar* is properly kinship traced through

---

[1] Two are known to me. Nyanthou is living in leviratic marriage with Riek (homestead 5), her husband, Galuak, being dead. Nyanyali was at one time concubine to Cuol and on his death went to live with Nyang, a captured Dinka, by whom she bore Deng (homestead 11). She took her daughter Mandeang with her, so that Mandeang and her uterine brother Deng were brought up together.

father or mother, long-standing affinal relationships count in Nuer eyes as being equal to kinship, being a kind of kinship through the children of marriage unions, especially when the affinal relatives live together, as so many of them do at Konye. As a Nuer at another village, Kurmayom on the Sobat river, put it: 'Well, you have seen my home and the people who live here; are they not the husbands of my sisters? Well, all our cattle are exhausted from giving them to our brothers-in-law. They are our people and form part of our community (*cieng*) Nyabor. Their children are known by the names of their mothers while they remain in our village. If they go to the homes of their fathers they will be known by the names of their fathers.' Affines may therefore be regarded in a general social sense as *mar* and we may speak of Konye community as a cluster of kin (see Fig. 17).

THE VILLAGE OF NYUENY

My second example is the village of Nyueny in the Leek tribal territory of western Nuerland. The village is spread along the arc of a sandy ridge for about a mile and a half. It comprises three hamlets, Nyueny, Dakyil, and Kamthiang, and about a mile to the north of it lies the hamlet of Dhorpan, the occupants of which used to form part of the main village. In 1936 the population of Nyueny was reckoned to be about 130 souls, distributed in 26 homesteads. As I had already recorded the genealogical pattern of other Nuer villages and camps I did not aim at drawing up a complete genealogy for Nyueny but rather at a survey of domestic unions, the results of which I published some years ago, and the genealogy recorded here (Fig. 18) has only now been constructed for the purposes of this paper from the information collected during that survey. Consequently, the kinship links between the owners of four homesteads (numbers 1, 5, 22, and 26) and other persons in the village cannot be stated. This merely means that the relationship did not emerge from an inquiry conducted for other ends than their discovery, for links of some kind may confidently be assumed to exist. It should also be pointed out that there are other connexions between some of the persons whose names are shown on the chart which are not indicated there, though they are recorded elsewhere,[1] and there may be others unknown to me. Only persons significant for the present discussion are tabled and I have simplified the presentation by treating ghost-marriages as though they were simple legal marriages.

The village site belongs to the Riaagh lineage of the Keunyang maximal lineage of the Gaatbol clan, the dominant clan in the Leek tribal area of which Karlual area, where Nyueny is situated, is a section. Members of that lineage with their wives and concubines and their affines account for ten out of the twenty-six homesteads. The people of Nyueny hamlet, the central and northern parts of the village, are known

[1] *Some Aspects of Marriage and the Family among the Nuer*, pp. 29 ff.

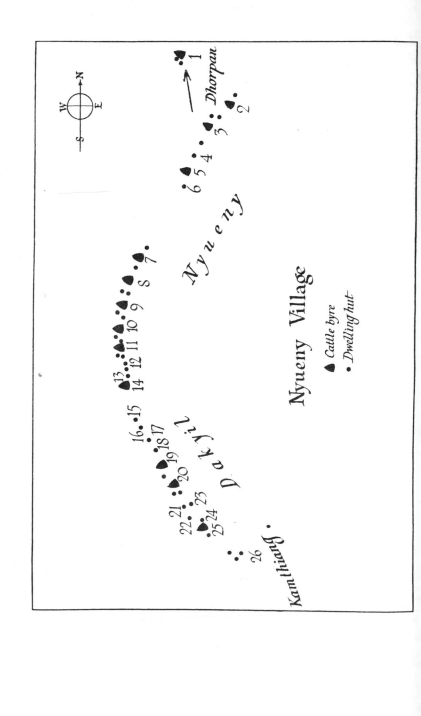

Nyueny Village

◗ Cattle byre
• Dwelling hut

as the children of Jany, and Jany's descendants with their wives and concubines and affines account for another ten homesteads. The children of Jany, whose *tut* is Karlual (homestead 9), count collectively as *gaatwac*, children of the paternal aunt, or as the Nuer often put it, *gaatnyiet*, children of daughters, to the Riaagh lineage, whom they call *gaatnar*, children of the paternal uncle. The senior Riaagh men are the 'bulls' of the village in the general tribal sense of the word *tut*.

It will be observed that the village is not an exclusive lineage group with its wives but is a cluster of kin (including affines). In this case, however, there is a lineage core to the village community and this core, the descendants of Riaagh, is, moreover, that branch of the dominant clan of the tribe which owns the village site. Some members of its collateral minimal lineage, the Gom, also live in the village. I draw attention to further typical features. We saw that at Konye many of the heads of families were living there because of affinal relationships with other members of the village. The counterpart to this is the relationship of sister's son to mother's brother, for when the children of a resident sister or daughter grow up in a village those who stand in an affinal relationship to their father stand in an avuncular relationship to them. This is a very significant feature of Nuer local communities and from it follows another common feature: in course of time a maternal link of this kind may be treated as though it were a paternal link and therefore within the genealogical structure of the principal lineage of the community. Jany's mother Duai is so treated. In this manner cognation comes to be regarded, for ordinary social purposes within community life, as equal to agnation. A sister's son–mother's brother relationship may come about in a village, not by a man going to live with his wife's people, but by widows bringing their children to live with their own people after their husbands have died: a mode of residence which in certain circumstances may continue after the deaths of the mothers. This is illustrated at Nyueny by the daughters of Jany. The widows may take lovers in the village, or they may take them from a different village and their lovers come to live with them. This custom is another feature of interest, for some ties between members of a village may be through widow-concubines, or even through unmarried concubines. Any such ties are *mar*, kinship. I have not indicated in the genealogy those persons who are adopted Dinka. They count as full members of the families and lineages of their adoption. A number of persons in the village have a Dinka origin: some have been adopted and some not.

Allowing for the fact I have mentioned, that when people live together as members of the same small local community female links are often given equivalence to male links in a genealogy, a cluster of kin such as that of Nyueny can be presented as descended from a common ancestor. It might be described as a cognatic lineage, but I think it wise to restrict the term 'lineage' to a group of agnates within a system of such groups and to speak of a cluster like that of Nyueny as being a lineage to which are attached, on account of common residence, other lines of kin through females. For if an attached family or extended family of this kind were to leave the common residence, the link which binds them to the lineage would cease to be significant for them and would lose its importance in favour of some new link more appropriate to their new attachment, whatever that might be, in their new village. Within a cluster of this kind relations between persons are regulated by the values of the kinship system. Seen as a unit from the outside, and in its unitary and corporate relations with other village communities, lineage values are dominant.

A CATTLE CAMP AT YAKWAC

My next example is a cattle camp at which I resided for close on three months in 1931. Yakwac is a small mound on the left bank of the Sobat. Like Nyueny, it is on the periphery of Nuerland where the Lou tribe faces the small Balak Dinka people who at one time occupied both banks of the river. I should explain that it was necessity rather than choice which led me to spend a large part of my time among the Lou Nuer at peripheral points. As I had no land transport and the Lou could not be induced to act as porters I had to rely on transport by canoe, and the larger rivers are in many places the tribal frontiers. Yakwac village consisted of only three byres and a few attached huts. Later I built a fourth byre there for myself and herded my cattle in the common kraal. The chief man of the village is Cam-Carau, who owns one of the byres, the other two being owned by Bithou, his brother, and Kirkir, a distant kinsman of his mother. The real 'bull' of the village is, however, Cam's mother Nyagen, and the village is often spoken of as *cieng* Nyagen. She has what amounts to the honorary status of a man, not only on account of her age but also, and principally, because she is a Lou aristocrat and it is through her that Cam and his family link themselves on to the dominant lineage of the area in which they live, for Cam is a Jikany tribesman and, although an aristocrat in his own tribal territory, is a stranger in the Lou country. He married his first wife to the name of his maternal uncle, Dar, with Dar's cattle, so that his eldest son and the other children born of this wife count as Dar's children and not as his own; and as Dar and Cam are of different clans and tribes the distinction between pater and genitor is emphasized. His eldest son, Wia, belongs to the dominant clan of the Lou territory and he himself does not.

In many years Cam's maternal kinsmen, the minor lineage known as *cieng* Pual, the community (of the descendants) of Puol, come during the dry season to water and pasture their cattle and to fish and bathe at Yakwac from their inland village of Majok in the Nyerol district. This minor lineage has four branches, the minimal lineages of Diel, Malual, Kwoth, and Mar, members of all of which figure in the genealogy of the camp (Fig. 21). The entire population of Majok was not at Yakwac in 1931, for most of the womenfolk had remained inland and some families spent the dry season at other camps on the Sobat. The women who came to Yakwac slept in the huts of the village, so no grass beehive huts were erected. The population of the camp was about eighty souls. I have again simplified the genealogy by showing ghost-marriages as simple legal marriages, but I have indicated, by the use of different type, those members of the camp who are known to be Dinka or of Dinka descent. Those among them who are shown as members of the Pual lineage have been adopted into one of its branches. The names of women and small children are not shown on the genealogical table, which is intended to demonstrate the kinship ties between the fifty-six occupants of the windscreens. I first list them below by windscreens.

Windscreen	Occupants	Total
1	Kirkir-Tutcar and his (natural) sons, Wan, Buth, Mun, and Thoar	5
2	Nhial-Tutcar and his sons Dang and Kong	3
3	Ngwoth-Dak, his paternal half-brother Turuk, his paternal half-sister's sons Pauk and Fajok, his brother's son Thon-Garang, his wife's brother Deng-Pur, and his sister's son Nhial-Deng	7
4	Kwek-Wol, his brother Juet, Wan-Cuol, and Cuol-Deng	4
5	Mut-Bicok and his brother Ruec	2
6	Ghuth-Kong, his brothers Kai and Deng, his father's brother's daughter's son Nyaal, and his distant affines Kun-Kurcam and Turuk-Buth	6
7	Gik-Kol, his brother Gai, and Riek-Garang	3
8	Mut-Mancom, Gwanien-Tiek, and Gwanien's brother Baiyak	3
9	Gai-Catiem and his brother Mun. (This windscreen was previously occupied by Ngony and his sons Duobkir and Rue. Ngony and Duobkir had returned to the interior)	2
10	Thon-Nyal, his paternal uncle Rek-Lath, and his father's father's sister's son Bilieu-Lith	3
11	Nhial-Mitmit and his son Mayan	2
12	Duob-Dhordieng	1
13	Rwot-Nhial and his brother's son Rue	2
14	Roam-Wor and his brother Malual	2
15	Keat-Gut and his brother Reath	2
16	Bithou-Carau and Deng-Nyajal (Deng-Cul)	2
17	Nyagen-Tutnyang (mother of Cam)	1
18	Cam-Carau, his (natural) son Wia, his mother's father's brother's son's son Banyge, his mother's brother's daughter's son Cuol-Mer (Cuol-Rwac), and his wife's brothers Minyaal and Nyok	6
	TOTAL	56

A study of the genealogy of Yakwac cattle camp reveals the features we have already noted as being significant in the genealogy of Nyueny. It is a lineage structure—the lineage being a branch of the dominant clan in the tribal area and that branch which is dominant in the district in which the camp was formed—to which are attached other lines through females, thus giving the genealogy a cognatic form, and affines. In order to graft themselves on to the tree of this dominant clan the linked families trace their descent through females at the points of graft

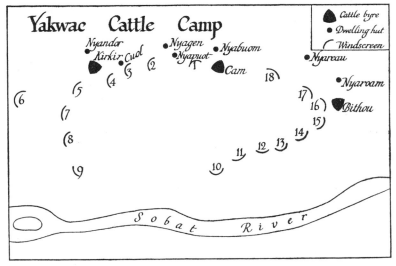

FIG. 20

as though these women had been men. It was a long time before I discovered, for example, that Kirkir's paternal grandfather was Buom and not Kol. A rather unusual example in which this process is strikingly illustrated is the line of ascent of Deng-Nyajal through females in three generations to the point of graft, Gai. The explanation here is that Nyanhial and her daughter Nyajal were captured by the Anuak on a raid into Lou country and for many years lived in Anuakland, where Deng was begotten by an Anuak father. In the camp Deng was always referred to as Deng-Nyajal after his mother and not as Deng-Cul after his father because Nyajal, and not Cul, is genealogically significant in Deng's social milieu. In the same way we referred always to Cuol as Cuol-Mer and not as Cuol-Rwac. In this cluster of kin at Yakwac camp the importance of affinal and maternal ties is evident.

Where I have satisfactory evidence for them, I have indicated Dinka origins in the table, partly in order to show the very considerable absorption of Dinka which has taken place, by adoption into Nuer lineages and through marriage, and partly in order to account for some marriages which might otherwise appear to be breaches of the Nuer rules of exogamy. These Dinka are of varied tribal origin. Among those whose names appear in the genealogy I have recorded Bor, Fadang, Luac, Thoc, and Dunjol origins. The absorption of so many Dinka has affected, through the practice of adoption, the rules regulating marriage, and it has also frequently led to matrilocal conditions, since a Dinka who has not been adopted into a Nuer lineage readily attaches himself to his wife's people or to the people who have married his sister or daughter, as do also his children to their maternal uncle's kin. The absorption of Dinka has led to a further complication in the already very complicated patterns of Nuer genealogies, for it sometimes happens that captured Dinka brothers or other kin are adopted into different lineages or even into different clans.

I would also draw attention to the different tribal origins of those Nuer in the genealogy who are not members of the dominant lineage, because they illustrate the movement of individuals and families which is so characteristic a feature of Nuer society: Yit was a Bul tribesman, he and Pinien being children of sisters or, as the Nuer say, a man and his *gatmanlende*, his mother's sister's son; Carau and Wan-Wang were Jikany tribesmen, Carau being an aristocrat of the Lony section of the Jikany, though begotten by an Anuak; Nhial-Deng is of Thiang tribal origin; Kurcam was a man of the Jimem clan, a clan which is found throughout Nuerland and without a tribal territory of its own; and so forth. Indeed, it is necessary to point out that not all these outsiders attached to the lineage core remain attached to it. Nuer move about their country freely, and reside for some years with one lot of kin and then for some years with another.

The genealogy of Yakwac camp gives us a typical cross-section of a Nuer tribal society. We see how the local community is built up around a lineage, or a section of a lineage, through the attachment to it of extra-lineage persons by the stressing of one or other category of kinship, and we thus see also the relation of the lineage structure to the kinship system within the framework of the tribal society. The collateral, and in a structural sense opposed, lineage to the Pual is the Dumien, who live near Pul Thul and Pul Nyerol in the same Nyerol district in which the Pual have their wet-season home and who, like them, often camp on the Sobat river in the drought. A genealogical analysis of the Dumien community would disclose the same kind of cluster as has been disclosed for the Pual community—a *thok dwiel*, lineage, to which are linked in many different ways through kinship values *rul*, strangers, and *jang*, Dinka, the whole forming a *cieng*, a local community who are kin. Pual and Dumien together form a single major lineage called Leng, the collateral to which is the Nyarkwac lineage whose home is adjacent to the home of the Leng. The Nyarkwac lineage in its community form consists of similar clusters composed of its branches and their accretions. Leng and Nyarkwac lineages form the Gaatbal maximal lineage, occupying the northern part of the Lou tribal territory and one of the three maximal lineages of the Jinaca clan, which is the dominant clan of the Lou tribe.

THE VILLAGE OF YAKWAC

As from the beginning of my study of the Nuer I pieced together the genealogical pattern of each village and camp where I resided, I could furnish further examples of configurations of kin in their local communities. However, rather than merely adding to the number of illustrations of this kind, I propose to examine a few small kin-clusters under a more powerful lens, for Nuer networks of kinship ties within a community are more complex than appears in the simplified genealogies I have so far presented. Not only are there several kinds of domestic union other than that of simple legal marriage, as I have endeavoured to show in my paper on Nuer marriage, but any man's descent when investigated in detail may reveal further complications.

When the rains came and the visitors departed from Yakwac for the interior, the hamlet contained only the households of Cam, Bithou, and Kirkir. Cam's family consisted of a ghost-wife Nyabuom, whom he had married to the name of his maternal uncle when, on his father's death, he came to live permanently with his maternal relatives, and their son and three daughters; his wife Nyareau and their two sons and a daughter; and his unmarried concubines Nyapuot and Nyandor. Bithou's family consisted of his wife Nyaroam and their two daughters. Kirkir's family consisted of his ghost-wife, whom he had married to the name of his dead elder brother, and their four sons. Living in Cam's home were also his mother Nyagen, Minyaal and his brother Nyok, and Cuol-Mer. Living in Bithou's byre was Deng-Nyajal. I have already referred to Cuol and Deng. In a nearby hamlet were living a leopard-skin chief called Jok and his brother Roam and Jok's wife. Jok's presence there is accounted for by his marriage to Nyalam the daughter of Thiep the son of Gun the son of Malual, the founder of the Malual minimal lineage of the genealogy.

I will not attempt to describe the tangled history of Cam and his brother Bithou and will only mention that their two paternal half-brothers were at the time living in the Lak tribe, whence their mother had come. I have in my paper on Nuer marriage given some account of the history of this family and in the same paper I have related the remarkable story of Mer the mother of Cuol, an unmarried concubine who lived with four men in turn, by three of whom she bore children. As an example of the complexities of Nuer kinship relations I will discuss instead the history of Nyok and Minyaal, because their story illustrates at the same time the hardships of Dinka in Nuerland before they have been assimilated into the Nuer kinship system.

Bul-Malou, a Dinka of the Thoc tribe, married a girl of that tribe, called Nyalue, by payment of spears and other objects during a period of Nuer invasion when most of the cattle of the tribe had been lost. Later and under stress of hunger, Bul and his wife took refuge in the Lou Nuer tribe at the home of a man called Kwenwar. Bul there lost his life in some fighting and Nyalue and her two children, her son Minyaal and her daughter Nyareau, went to live at Mwot Dit in the Lou country, where she cohabited with an aristocrat called Tutyil, by whom she bore her third child Baiyak. Tutyil maltreated her and, as she had no kin to protect her against him and the jealousy of his wife, she fled to the home of her sister in eastern Gaajok country, where she cohabited with a man called Bul-Yong, by whom she bore her fourth child Nyok. Tutyil followed her and stole from her her daughter Nyareau. Nyareau quarrelled with Tutyil's wife and ran away to the home of her father's brother's son Ter. Tutyil brought her back to his home, but she ran away a second time to Ter's home and was married from it; Ter took her bride-wealth on both the father's side and the mother's side, an act which involved him in course of time in a long, and still unsettled, dispute with Nyareau's surviving brothers Minyaal and Nyok, who came to live with their sister's husband Cam-Carau at Yakwac since they had no cattle of their own and had to live with someone who possessed a herd. This is a common reason for Nuer attaching themselves to kin or affines. A Nuer cannot live for long without cattle and those who possess only a few beasts sometimes find it a convenience to tether them in the byre of a kinsman rather than build a byre of their own. I must emphasize, however, that some of these events could not have occurred had the family been Nuer and not kinless Dinka living among the Nuer, for Nyalue's husband's kin would then have made themselves responsible for the children she bore to her lovers. In the circumstances they had no strong body of paternal kin to protect them and no lineage attachment.

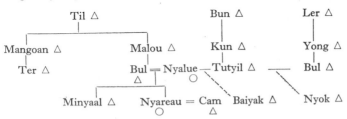

I did not visit Yakwac again till the rainy season of 1935. There had been some changes. Kirkir, the owner of one of the three byres of the 1931 chart, had died and his ghost-widow had gone to live in the interior with her eldest son Wan and two others of her children. Wan had there married a wife to the name of his dead father Kirkir because Kirkir had married Wan's mother to the name of his dead brother Duob and had not been able to marry again a wife in his own right. The two other children, now youths, Mun and Thoar, were still living at Yakwac (homestead 11), but no longer in their old home on the mound itself, which was occupied by Cam, his mother Nyagen, and his brother Bithou. Cuol-Mer had committed incest in the village and had departed to live with his mother in Jikany country. Cam's brother-in-law Minyaal had died. The leopard-skin chief Jok and his brother Roam had also left the neighbourhood. On the other hand, during the four years of my absence the settlement, with its population increased to fifty-three souls, had spread out and now comprised thirteen homes, three perched on the mound itself and ten running on either side of it along the narrow ridge which in the rains divides the Sobat from the waterlogged plain behind it. I give a brief account of the kinship pattern of this small community because it shows how a new settlement comes into being through the operation of the values of the kinship system. Only adults are shown in the genealogical table (Fig. 22).

Badeng-Lok (homestead 4), a man of the Jikul clan of Lak tribal territory, whose wife was living in adultery with a man in Jikany country, came to live near Cam-Carau because of their relationship to one another through a concubine, Car, whose wanderings had given her children by two unrelated men, as shown in the genealogy. Badeng's nephew Nyuot was living with him. Jok-Leau (homestead 5), a man of the Gaanwar clan, had come to Yakwac with Badeng because the two men were what the Nuer call *warumbaini*, men married to sisters. His wife's brother Deng was living with him. The widowed mother-in-law of Badeng and Jok, Thiec, had her own hut (homestead 6). Mun-Liec (homestead 7) was an aristocrat of the Lony section of the Jikany tribe, his father being Cam's paternal cousin. His mother Nyantui (homestead 8) was at the time of my visit concubine to Deng-Nyajal (homestead 9), one of the members of the small 1931 community and at that time sharing Bithou's byre. He had since married and his wife had borne him two children. Nyantui's daughter, Mun's sister Nyaluit, was betrothed to Nyok (homestead 10), another of the 1931 community. He was then sharing Cam's byre. I have just related the history of his family and given the reasons for his joining Cam at Yakwac. His brother Minyaal had died since my previous visit as a consequence, I was told, of incestuous congress with Cam's concubine Nyapuot. Thian-Jok (homestead 12) was by origin a Shilluk and had lived for some time with the Ngok Dinka, with whom Cam had some affinal connexions through one of his concubines. He was living at Yakwac with a concubine, Nyariek, of Lak tribal origin. The occupant of the last homestead was Monythem-Karjok (homestead 13). He was an Anuak in origin and appears to have come to live at Yakwac partly because he was related in

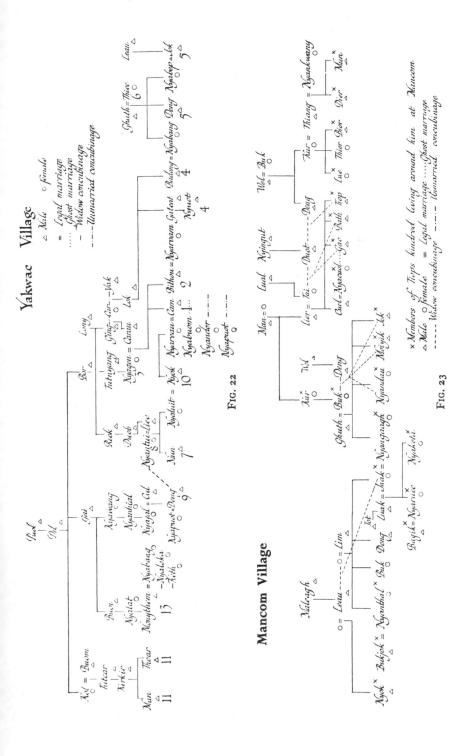

Yakwac Village

FIG. 22

Mancom Village

FIG. 23

some way to Deng-Nyajal, who, it may be remembered, was begotten by an Anuak father in Anuakland; and partly because he was attached through his mother to the dominant Pual lineage, as shown in the genealogical table. He was living at Yakwac with two concubines, both widows, in addition to his wife.

I do not know the reasons why these persons left the villages in which they were previously living; only the reasons given by themselves and others for their coming to live at Yakwac. We see, in the notes I have given and in the genealogy, features to which I have already drawn attention when commenting on other Nuer settlements: the attraction of a prominent personality, in this instance Cam-Carau, the 'bull' round whom the herd gather, the leader round whom his kindred gather; the importance of maternal and affinal ties; the significance of alien elements; and, in general, a stranger's need to establish in one way or another a kinship link with someone in the community which will give him a kinship status towards every other member of it, and lacking which he would not join the community. As at Konye, the first village I described, the lineage structure, in the sense in which I am using the word 'lineage', is neither so evident nor so significant as in the larger communities. This is what we might expect in view of the political functions of Nuer lineages, which are performed in the tribal system through the structural relationships of the 'bulls' to one another. It is true that Cam is only a 'bull' in a general social sense and is not a tribal 'bull'—a member of the dominant clan of the tribe—as well, but, as I have pointed out, the social personality of the 'bull' of the Yakwac 'herd' rests in his mother Nyagen, who is a member of the dominant Jinaca clan. It is through her that the community is brought within the political system of the Lou tribe as a whole by its association with the Pual lineage, to which reference was made in the last section. I do not pursue this theoretical analysis further because in the present context we are more interested in what our lens shows us of the kinship texture of local clusters than in the broader interrelations of local communities within the tribe.

THE VILLAGE OF MANCOM

My next example is from the eastern Jikany village of Mancom, a large settlement at the mouth of the Nyanding river which was found in 1935 to have a population which included a large number of persons of Dinka descent. I visited the village and spent about a month there in that year because it was the home of Tiop-Lier, a boy whom I knew well and who was at the time acting as my cook, whose relatives were certain to make me welcome on his account.

I made an investigation into the kinship structure of the village, but I propose here only to give a brief account of Tiop's own home, the immediate companions of his daily life. Lier, Tiop's pater, was a Luac

Dinka. He married Tai, who bore him a son Cuol, who died from the bite of a snake while still a boy. After her husband's death Tai went to live with a man called Duot. Duot and Lier are known to have been distantly related through their mothers, being *ram kene gatmanlen*, a man and his mother's sister's son (in a classificatory sense), but Tiop and his brothers were unable to trace the relationship between them with genealogical precision. By Duot, Tai bore two sons, Gac and Bath. Between the births, however, Tai had a disagreement with her lover and went to live for a time with a man called Deng-Wel, now living in the interior of Lou country, in the Rumjok division, by whom she bore my friend Tiop. It is interesting to note that Tiop is called either 'son of Lier' after his pater, or 'son of Duot' after the genitor of his brothers, depending on what part of the country he happens to be in, but very seldom 'son of Deng' after his genitor, and he does not use this cognomen himself. Gac, the eldest of the three brothers, had recently married a wife, Nyacuol, to the name of his dead paternal half-brother Cuol. It had been arranged that when Bath married he was to take a wife to the name of his dead genitor Duot.

Tiop, through whose eyes I saw the social world around us at Mancom, had come to live there to be near his natural *wac*, his genitor's sister, Kur (since dead) and her sons, and in 1935 he and his brother Bath were sharing a byre with Dier and Mun, the sons of her co-wife. Tiop and Bath called these youths *gaatwacda*, sons of my paternal aunt, and they called Tiop and Bath *gaatnara*, sons of my maternal uncle, though in the usual Nuer fashion they all addressed each other as *demar*, my mother's son. Later Tiop brought to live at Mancom his legal *wac*, his pater's sister, also called Kur, from Lak tribal country. This Kur had a daughter called Buk who had married a husband, Ghuth, and had borne him a daughter, Nyangaagh, before leaving him on account of ill treatment to go to live in the country of the Luac Dinka from which her mother's people had originally come. There she lived as concubine to Deng-Wol, to whom she bore a daughter and two sons. All efforts by her husband to secure her return failed and, though he seized Nyangaagh and brought her back to his home, she escaped and returned to her mother. Later, in a year of famine, Tiop's brother Gac brought Kur and her daughter Buk and Buk's children to live at Mancom. Ghuth contented himself with taking the cattle on the father's side on the marriages of Buk's daughters.

The eldest of them, Nyangaagh, was married by a woman, Jaak-Lim, to the name of her dead brother. The father of Jaak, Lim, had two daughters at the time of his death, Buk and Nyanthal. His widow became concubine to Leau-Maleagh to whom she bore a third daughter Jaak who, as already stated, married Nyangaagh, Tiop's *nyanyawac*, paternal aunt's daughter's daughter. Jaak had herself been previously married to Luak-Tot and had borne him two children before his death.

She called in Nyok, the son of her genitor, to give her, or rather to give her dead brother, children by Nyangaagh (see Fig. 23).

It will thus be seen that to Tiop and his brothers the immediate and intimate circle of kinsmen among whom they live and share their daily experience are the clusters of kin around their paternal aunt Kur and Tiop's natural paternal aunt of the same name. It is for this reason that in giving me the kinship connexions of his family Tiop always stressed the female links which united him to those around him and neglected the names of the husbands of these women, for they had little interest for him. I would draw attention here to the great importance among the Nuer of natural, as contrasted with what we may call legal, ties of kinship brought about by unions other than the union of simple legal marriage, and to the great number of these ties in Nuer communities, as manifested in the Mancom example I have just given. The recognition of them, in the Nuer system of kinship values, as social ties and not merely as natural relationships further enhances the significance of women as persons through whom descent is traced for the purpose of establishing kinship with those with whom the Nuer have relations in their community life. No doubt these features are particularly striking where, as in the example of Tiop's kinsmen, many of the persons are Dinka immigrants, but this is a very common circumstance in Nuerland and they are to be noted also where immigrants are absent or too few for the features to be explained by this factor alone.

THE VILLAGE OF KURMAYOM

The importance of both maternal and natural descent in Nuer society is brought out especially clearly in my final example. I quoted, at the beginning of this essay, a remark made to me about affinal relations by a Nuer of Kurmayom village, and it is to his village that I now turn. Kurmayom is a village of the Lou tribe to the west of Yakwac and, like it, on the Sobat river. It is near the border between the Lou tribe and the Ngok Dinka. The most prominent person in the village in 1931 was a noted magician called Bul-Kan, and it is his family that I shall now briefly examine. He and the cluster of kin around him then occupied eleven byres. His family belong to a minimal lineage called *cieng* Nyabor after the name of his mother's mother. She was a woman of the Nyarkwac major lineage of the Jinaca clan who bore her children in unmarried concubinage to two men. Their fathers legitimized them by payment of cattle. Lim, Nyawin, and Tonydeang thus became members of the Jidiet clan since their pater, called Kwaclath, was a man of this clan, and Gir, Thakjaak, and Nyanhial became members of the Jimem clan, their pater Bilieu being a man of this clan. One of these children, the girl Nyawin, married Kan-Kwoth of the Kiek clan to whom she bore Yuth, Nyakong, and Nyatony before he died. She continued to live in his home after his death and there took a lover, a man of the Ngok Dinka called Cie, to whom she bore Bul, Nyang, and Mun. These three sons count, of course, as children of Kan-Kwoth. The Dinka Cie then, at the behest of Nyawin and her sons, took a wife to himself with cattle of the herd of Kan-Kwoth and by her begat Yual. Yual was therefore not only a natural paternal half-brother of Bul, Nyang, and Mun but also their brother in a further sense, for he was *gat ghokien*, the child of their cattle. I was told that he had also been formally adopted by Bul into his lineage. Mun had died before 1931 and Bul and Nyang were already elderly men whose sons and daughters had homes and herds and children of their own.

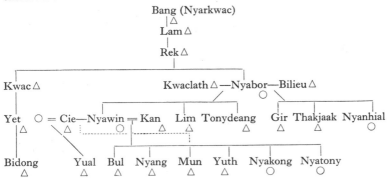

It will be noted that, although Bul is called after his father Kan and is a member of the Kiek clan and his mother was a woman of the Jidiet clan, the lineage now call themselves *cieng* Nyabor and trace their ascent through Nyabor into the stem of the Nyarkwac branch of the dominant Jinaca clan, neglecting for ordinary social purposes the patrilineal lines of both Kan and Kwaclath. They attach themselves in this way to the lineage which owns the village site and with whom the tribal section in which it is situated is identified, its chief 'bull' in the village being Bidong-Yet, whose name I have therefore inserted in the table.

CONCLUSIONS

The purpose of this paper is limited in scope and the conclusions which can be drawn from it are therefore also limited. I have attempted to give an account of the network of kinship and affinal ties which link to one another the members of a Nuer local community, and by so describing their kinship composition to supplement the analysis of these communities as parts of a political system which I made in *The Nuer*; I have also attempted to correct the distortion of the reality of Nuer social life to which the abstractions made in that analysis necessarily, and intentionally, led. With this view in mind I have presented a selection of configurations of kinship ties within a number of villages and in a cattle camp; I conclude by summarizing and discussing further what appear to me to be the chief points established by this survey.

The kinship relations of persons to one another in a Nuer community are, I think it will be agreed, very complex. They are also difficult to discover. They are complex largely on account of the different forms of domestic union obtaining among the Nuer and of their python-like assimilation of vast numbers of Dinka through adoption or intermarriage. Whether linked through the one or the other, the Dinka lack the full range of kinship ties of a true Nuer until assimilation is complete. The nature of kinship ties between persons is difficult to discover because Nuer will not co-operate in a systematic question-and-answer inquiry, which would not only fail but would also jeopardize the friendships so hardly made with them. Indeed, if I had not lived with them for many months in intimate discomfort in village and camp and if I had not learnt their language, in the process of learning which I learnt also what I know of their kinship system, it would not have been possible for me to discover the relationships between persons in the places where I resided, and so laboriously to piece them together in the genealogies I have recorded. It was only when my study was well advanced that I became aware of some of the complications mentioned in this paper, and it is for this reason that I have not reproduced any of the genealogies compiled during my first six months' work among the Nuer. Even the genealogy of Yakwac cattle camp was found to contain some far from negligible errors when it was revised on my return to Yakwac in 1935, although it was written during my second expedition to Nuerland; and it was not till my final visits to Nuerland in 1935 and 1936 that some important features of the kinship system became at all clear to me. As I was still learning something new about it up to the time of my last departure it may be assumed that the study was far from complete.

The first conclusion is a negative one: that a Nuer community, whether small or big, is not composed exclusively of members of a single lineage and their wives or, correspondingly, that not all members of a lineage live in the same community. On the other hand, a further conclusion was reached: that in any large village or camp there is represented an agnatic lineage of one or another order and that into the growth of this lineage are grafted, through the tracing of descent through females, branches which are regarded, in certain situations and in a certain sense, as part of it and, in other situations and in a different sense, as not being part of it. Other lines and persons are grafted on to the tree of lineage descent by adoption, but this can only happen to Dinka and other foreigners, not to men of true Nuer origin; and, although adopted Dinka are in other respects accepted as full members of the lineage into which they are adopted, their fictitious descent may be taken into consideration to permit modification of the Nuer rules of exogamy. Attached to the lineage, directly or indirectly, are also a considerable number of affines of diverse kinds.

In their collective relations with other communities, and as seen collectively by the members of these communities, there is a fusion of the attached elements with the lineage. They are incorporated in it and the resultant whole is spoken of as the *cieng* or *wec* (community) of the lineage, which is both its core and the symbol of its social identity as a unit in the tribal system. But within the community itself there are occasions when a formal distinction between the lineage and its incorporated elements has to be made and the status of its members defined to the exclusion of the *rul*, strangers, the *gaatnyiet*, children of daughters (of the lineage), and the affines.

In daily contacts between persons within the community their relations are expressed, not in the language of lineage structure, but in the language of the kinship system, by reference to categories of kinship within that system. Thus men of the same minimal lineage have only an undifferentiated lineage relationship on occasions when the lineage acts or is thought of as a group. Otherwise, and as persons, their relationship to one another is one of *gwanlen*, father's brother, *gatgwanlen*, father's brother's son, *wac*, father's sister, and so on. Even when two men belong to collateral minimal lineages between which there is a *buth* (agnatic lineage) relationship, each is also *mar*, kin, to the other; that is to say he stands in his personal relationship to him in a kinship category of the kind I have mentioned above. Similarly, persons tracing their descent from the genealogical tree of the lineage through a daughter of the lineage are collectively to the lineage *gaatnyiet*, children of daughters, but each stands to individual members of the lineage in the personal kin relationship of *gatwac* or *nyawac*, father's sister's son or father's sister's daughter, or possibly in some other kin relationship. Likewise, an affine is *conyimar*, husband of sister, *conyal*, husband of daughter, or of some other affinal category, and is addressed as *gwa*, father, *demar*, my brother, or *gatda*, my son, as the case may be. Lineages are articulated as groups of agnatic kin at a different situational, usually ritual, level of the social life and are articulated as conglomerates fused with other elements at yet a different situational, the political, level. Kinship ties belong to another order of social relations, relations between persons and not between groups. The members of a lineage group are socially undifferentiated as such in the interlineage structure because it is a structural relationship between groups. In the kinship system they are socially differentiated—this being an essential characteristic of the system—because the kinship system is a system of relationships between persons.

As we have seen, members of a Nuer community are all *mar*, kin, to one another. Whoever is kith must also be kin. Common membership of a village or camp does not in itself provide a man with a secure basis for his personal relations with its other members. That is provided chiefly by the kinship system by which a kinship tie established with any person in the village or camp gives a man a kinship status of some kind with every other person in the village or camp, with all his neighbours. A village or camp is a community of kin. This means that from the point of view of any of its members the other members are his kindred (including affines in this term) and also that he knows, at any rate more or less, in what way any one of them is related to a third person. It does not, however, mean that together they constitute a specific kinship group. As a group they are a residential unit and in a political context are identified with a lineage (or, in the case of a very small village or outlying hamlet, attached to one).

Each member of the community can place every other member of it in a category of the kinship system in reference to himself and his kindred, and as everyone can do this a local community consists of a great number of cross-strands which create an intricate network of kinship ties. It is the drawing together of these many strands by, and into, the lineage structure that gives the local community its unitary character in the tribal life of the Nuer.

I wish to make it clear that kinship clusters of the kind we have examined in this paper are not structurally differentiated kinship groups, though they may be thought of as lineage groups. The pattern of relationships in such a cluster is variable and in any particular example unpredictable. It is also highly fluid, for its component parts may have only a transitory association; Nuer frequently change their homes, so that the texture of relationships in any particular local cluster may change not only from year to year but from season to season. When a cluster is thought of by the Nuer as a unit, it is not as a kinship group but as a lineage group or as a residential group—a village or camp. Its members are *jicieng* so-and-so, the people of the community of a certain lineage, or *jiciengda*, people of my home or community, a residential collectivity. *Jimarida*, my kindred, has quite a different sphere of reference. It is a set of personal relationships to a given person and includes men and women who do not belong to the cluster at all. Since these residential groups are often spoken of in terms of lineages we may say that in its political connotation the lineage is transformed into a group of cognates, for which I know of no convenient term. The word 'stock' might be used to distinguish it from the true lineage, the unilateral group of agnates.

The part played in this transformation by the absorption of Dinka on so considerable a scale has been significant. The relation between the two peoples and their societies is an ethnological and sociological problem of the first importance, but an entire solution of it cannot be attempted until more is known of the Dinka congeries of tribes and, in particular, of their social structure. Here I wish to consider only the aspect of it which concerns our present discussion. As I have pointed out in *The Nuer*, assimilation of conquered Dinka tribes and tribal sections has not, for various reasons, resulted in a class or caste, or in any other rigid hierarchical structure. It has been brought about by their incorporation into Nuer lineages by adoption and by their assimilation to them through intermarriage.

When Dinka are adopted into a lineage, absorption into Nuer society presents no great difficulty. Their Dinka origin is remembered by members of the lineage of their adoption, at any rate for some generations, but after one or two generations it may not be known to outsiders, and I suppose that in course of time it may be forgotten within the lineage itself. They are part of the lineage, have the same status as its other members, and are points of growth in the branch equal to men born into it. But when Dinka are not adopted into a Nuer lineage, absorption is achieved with greater difficulty and by circuitous means. If we examine closely the history of those persons in the genealogies I have recorded who have attached themselves permanently to an affinal or maternal family and through it to a minimal lineage, and if we trace also the histories of those persons who through such an attachment in the past now trace their descent from the lineage through a female, we shall find that in a very great number, I venture to say in the vast majority, of cases they are Dinka. This is a development which it is easy to understand because captured Dinka or Dinka immigrants into Nuerland have lost their status in their own kinship and lineage systems, and if they are not adopted into Nuer lineages they can only acquire status in Nuer society through affinal relationships; their children, having no kin on the father's side, identify themselves with the mother's kin and, having no lineage on the father's side, seek fictitious affiliation to the mother's lineage. It is true that we find strangers of Nuer clans as members of clusters of kin around a lineage core of the dominant clan of the tribe, but where the attachment is permanent these strangers are, in my experience, generally persons of those Nuer clans which have no tribal territory of their own—no *wec*, local community, as the Nuer say—like the Jimem, Jikul, and Kiek clans which have, moreover, in some cases, mythological beginnings placing them outside the main family of Nuer clans and suggesting foreign origin. Assimilation in these cases can never be so complete as in the case of Dinka, because members of Nuer clans have their own clan symbols and their own *buth* relationships which attach them to the lineages of their birth.

Another factor which has certainly had some influence in bringing about attachments of outsiders to groups of agnatic kin other than their own is the custom of concubinage. I need not describe the different forms of concubinage to be found in Nuerland as I have already given a detailed account of them in my paper on Nuer marriage. Here it is sufficient to point out that it is a very common practice for widows to leave their dead husbands' homes and to take lovers in the villages of their parents, or to go to reside in the villages of their lovers. When they do so they take their young children with them and, though the sons almost invariably return to their paternal homes before initiation, they have grown up in the homes of their maternal kinsmen, or of their foster-father's kin, and may have so strong an affection for them that they later return to reside with them, at any rate for a time, when they are married men and their own masters. The likelihood of this happening is greater when the dead man was the head of a polygynous family, for then friction between co-widows and between paternal half-brothers may easily lead to a widow going back to her paternal home, where her sons may join her and live for many years, even if in the end they go back to their paternal kin.

Widows, whether living in their maternal villages or in their dead husbands' villages, attract lovers, sometimes from the village, sometimes from a neighbouring village. In either case a new social tie is established and the lovers may continue to cohabit with the widows as members of their communities for long periods and nurture the children they beget by them. Also, when women marry other women, as sometimes happens among the Nuer, a man has to be brought into the union to beget children, and this may be a man from a different community. A poor man is only too glad to obtain a housekeeper and mate without expense by means of either widow-concubinage or unmarried concubinage, and if he is an unadopted Dinka he may remain with the concubine and his children by her.

There are in Nuerland a considerable number of unmarried concubines. The sons they bear to lovers become the legal children of these lovers by payment of cattle, but they do not feel so securely attached to the homes of their fathers as do children born of the union of marriage, and there is a strong tendency for sons of the same woman by different fathers to stick together, usually wherever their mother may be, especially if the fathers are dead or if they do not possess large herds.

There are two other facts to be taken into consideration. Among the Nuer it is not uncommon for a man to make his home among his wife's people, though in my experience a true Nuer usually returns to his own people eventually. As I have explained, sons-in-law who live with their wives' people are often Dinka and Dinka are likely to remain with their affines, as they may have no kin of their own to return to; but one also finds Nuer in the same position. These are usually poor men who cannot afford to pay the full bride-wealth, part of which is forgone by the wife's family in view of the fact that the man who has married their daughter has joined their community and is bringing up his children as members of it. They may even give him some of their own cattle to help him build up a herd. The second fact to be taken into consideration is the Nuer custom, for various reasons not always observed, for the eldest

child of a marriage to be brought up by her or his maternal grandparents, if the grandmother is alive, a girl till marriage and a boy till
initiation. It is said that eldest children belong to *cieng mandongni*, the
home of their (maternal) grandmothers, and a child brought up in his
maternal kinsmen's village naturally feels that in some respects it, and
not his paternal kinsmen's village, is his home. The many peculiar
prescriptions which adhere to the status of eldest child may, in part at
any rate, be connected with his pivotal and ambiguous position between
the families of his father and mother.

I have remarked that it is the drawing together by, and into, the
lineage system of the many different strands of kinship (and affinity)
composing the network of social ties in a Nuer community which gives
the community its unitary character. The points at which they are
drawn together are the 'bulls' of the kinship clusters, and especially the
tribal 'bulls', those men who are persons not only of age,[1] wealth, and
character but also members of the dominant clan of the tribe—tribal
aristocrats. These tribal 'bulls' are the centres of clusters of kin, but
they are also agnates and each has in relation to the others a structural
position in the lineage system of the dominant clan. Through them,
therefore, all the tribesmen are attached to the dominant clan of the
tribe and all the local communities are assimilated to the highly consistent structure of its segments, in which they are conceptualized. It
is the ambition of every man, of the dominant clan especially, to become
a 'bull' and the centre of a cluster of kin, and Nuer say that it is for this
reason among others that families and extended families often break
up and cousins and brothers part, each to seek to gather his own 'herd'
around him.

In conclusion, I would hazard the opinion that it is the clear, consistent, and deeply rooted lineage structure of the Nuer which permits
persons and families to move about and attach themselves so freely, for
shorter or longer periods, to whatever community they choose by whatever cognatic or affinal tie they find it convenient to emphasize; and that
it is on account of the firm values of the structure that this flux in the
state of social relationships does not cause confusion or bring about
tribal disintegration. It might well be, in some degree, because the
agnatic principle is unchallenged in Nuer society that the tracing of
descent through women is so prominent and matrilocality so prevalent.
However much the actual configurations of kinship clusters may vary
and change, the lineage structure is invariable and stable.

---

[1] I do not discuss in this article the Nuer age-set system, though it has some
bearing on the kinship system. An account of it will be found in *The Nuer* and
in a paper devoted to the subject in *Sudan Notes*, xix, 1936, pp. 233–71.

INDEX

Adoption, 40, 89.

Adultery, 50, 76, 92, 122–3, 137, 138, 181, 186, 187, 194, 201, 202, 216, 225, 233, 238, 269, 271, 275, 280, 293, 325, 326.

Affines, 107–9, 115, 124, 170–1, 387 *et passim.*

Age-sets, 28–9; regiments, 181, 203, 205; sexual intercourse and, 27.

Age-village organization and age-mates, 111, 115, 128, 129, 130, 323; senior men in, 131.

Agnates and agnatic lineages, 13–14, 18, 20–2, 23, 67–8, 100, 113, 114, 143, 144, 147, 148, 158, 163, 177, 178, 179, 185, 194–5, 366, 386.

Akan, 252, 253 *n.* 2.

Ambundu, 212.

American Indians, 8.

Ancestors, the, 28, 36, 54, 86, 213, 214, 223, 232, 242–3; cult of, and the spirits, 73–4, 76, 80, 93, 97, 105, 109, 130, 137, 143, 207, 214, 224, 228 and *n.* 1, 237, 249, 257, 271, 362.

Anthropology, v, 55, 72, 85.

Arabs, 69, 231.

Ashanti, 29, 65, 66, 79, 80, 81, 84, 85, 252 ff., 357 *n.* 2, 359 *n.* 1.

Australia, 29.

Australian aborigines, 6, 57, 64, 68, 70, 71, 72.

Authority, 323, 324; over children and wife, 77, 79, 207–8, 215–16, 217–18, 226–7, 235, 236, 239, 246, 249, 268.

Avoidances, 55–6, 57 ff., 83, 103, 107, 128, 131, 132, 177, 259–60, 262, 350; mother-in-law, 55, 127, 128; relatives-in-law and, 127 ff., 171.

Avunculate, 217–18, 227, 230–1, 236, 250. *See also* Uncles.

Azande, 191, 192, 203, 205.

Badzing, 218.

Bairu, 178.

Banbata, 216.

Bangweulu, 222, 227.

Bantu, 58, 82, 197, 213, 216, 218, 236, 249; Central, 207 ff., 246 ff.; Southern, 34, 152, 164, 165, 176, 198, 199, 203–4, 205, 213.

Bari, 32.

Barotseland, 166.

Barrenness in women, 51, 149, 152, 185, 188, 239, 262 *n.* 1.

Basutoland, 50.

Bedouin, 206.

Behaviour, customary, and relationships, 9, 10–11, 25, 26, 34, 37, 56,

98, 129–30, 137 ff., 143–4, 145–6, 161, 177, 258, 270, 276; children with parents, 27, 28, 95; *hlonipha*, 93, 105; patterns of, 36, 63, 91 ff., 170, 176; privileged, 36.

Bemba, 5, 42, 65, 80, 167, 218, 221, 222, 223 ff., 233, 234, 238, 242–3, 245, 248, 250–1.

Bena, 202.

Betrothal, 47, 49, 116, 151, 162, 189, 278, 321, 342.

Bisa, 221, 222, 227, 245.

bivumu (matriclans), *see* Clans: matriclans.

Black magic, 70.

Blood feuds, 337, 338, 339, 357.

Bomvana, 204.

Boys, 79, 133, 230, 240–1, 303, 304, 305, 306, 325; circumcision of, 347.

Bracelet-fighting, 338–9.

Bride, 'capture' of the, 49.

Bride-wealth or bride-price (*lobola*), 95, 99, 103, 186, 190, 191, 216–17, 219, 239, 241, 341–2, 349, 379, 390. *See also* Marriage payments.

Brothers, 90, 115, 119–20, 144, 221, 329; eldest, 234; half-, 118–19, 196, 221; linked sister and, 52–3, 98; senior, 215, 235; senior and junior, 31; sisters and, 24, 98, 118, 132, 230, 242, 246, 247, 273–5; -in-law, 108–9, 177.

Bul-Kan, 384–5.

Bwila, 236.

Camps, 363; cattle, 374–8; wind-screens, 363, 375.

Cattle, 82, 83, 92, 93, 98, 117, 120, 125, 135, 170, 192, 231, 234, 236, 238–9, 250, 363, 366, 379, 390; (beast of the fire), 196–7; *bogadi*, 149, 150, 153, 162, 163; *chiko*, 250, 239; *ciwololo*, 233; *emabeka*, 88, 89, 93, 98, 109; exchange of, 121–2; *ilobolo*, 194; *imsulamnyembeti*, 95; *lipakhelo*, 93; marriage-, 47, 50, 52, 53–4, 106, 109, 112, 118, 121–2, 123, 133, 134, 195; milking one another's cows, 117–18; *ubulunga* beast, 80.

Central Africa, 42, 166 ff., 178, 207 ff.

Ceremonies, 74, 82–3, 105, 111, 142, 171, 214, 232, 243, 260, 302; betrothal, 150; burial, *see under* Rituals; girls' puberty, 257, 265; marriage, 74, 76, 90, 99, 322, 323; tying of the *tali*, 74. *See also* Rituals.

Cewa, 223 *n.* 1, 227, 230 ff., 245, 247.

Chaga, 198.

Cherokee, 83.
Chewa, 167.
Chiefs and chiefdoms, 109, 130–1, 163, 171, 172, 213–14, 215, 226–7, 228–9, 232, 238, 241, 252, 259, 260–1, 265, 269, 275, 279, 281, 335, 336–7, 338, 343, 347, 378; Akan stools, 254, 256; genealogies of, 114; marriage and, 184; succession to, 224.
Child-bearing, 262–3.
Children, 80, 201–2, 207–8, 214–15, 222–3, 241 ff., 262; adoption of, 40, 89; Ashanti and, 263 ff.; foster-, 202, 304, 305; illegitimate, 4, 25–6, 170, 184, 187, 189, 201, 384; lobola and, 88; Lozi, 171–2; male, 95; marriage and, 49, 51, 54; Mayombe, 214–15, 217; parents and, 4, 94 ff., 133–5; sexual activities and, 126–7, 133; yafoli, 291, 305; Yakö, 291 ff., 303 ff.; Zulu clans and, 170. See also Authority.
China, 14.
Christianity, 17, 112, 113, 120, 123, 128, 135–6, 138, 150, 154, 271–2, 331.
Clans, 39 ff., 67, 68, 73, 86 ff., 169–70, 213 ff., 223, 232, 254, 335 ff., 348, 371; corporate groups, 41–2; eight Ashanti, 259–60; grading of, 87; lineage distinguished from, 39–40; matriclans, 40, 41, 42, 213, 241–2, 243–4, 306 ff., 314 ff.; mukoa, 237; patriclans, 40, 41, 76, 296, 298, 299, 301–2, 306, 314, 321, 322; royal, 87, 222–3, 227, 228; sub-caste, 237; sub-clans, 18 n. 3, 40, 86; totemic, 242–3.
Cognatic system and cognates, 4, 13, 25, 42, 66–7, 78, 81, 82, 114, 177, 320; unilineal system and, 67.
Colonial government, 1.
Compensation for death of a kinsman, 312–13.
Compounds of priests, 316; Yakö, 293 ff.
Concubinage, 182–3, 184, 389–90.
Congo, the, 38, 41, 212–13, 250; tribes of the, 80.
Consanguinity, 4.
Co-operation, see under Labour.
Councils, 220.
Courts, 136, 325.
Cousins, 18 n. 3, 32, 104, 147–8, 170, 173, 179; cross-, 8, 9, 21, 38, 53, 74, 104, 145, 147–8, 161, 162, 170, 179; parallel, 8, 9, 104, 147, 161. See also Marriage: cousin.
Crops, 111, 116, 193, 194, 197, 222, 288, 289, 311, 344.
Culture contact, 119, 150, 261, 282, 330–2.

Curses, 37, 173, 223.
Customs, 3, 29, 55–6, 58, 60, 80, 82–3, 87, 263; ijabwipwa, 125; marriage, 49–50, 64, 65, 278; mother's brother's curse, 37; twins and, 126, 130; ukulobola, 88; vasu, 36.

Dahomey, 198.
Dances, 340, 344, 361.
Daughters, 97.
Descent groups, 4, 13, 232, 234, 237; dual, 214, 236, 249, 285 ff., 333 ff.; lunungu, 237–9, 244.
dikanda (matriclans), see Clans: matriclans.
Dinka, 199 n. 1, 366, 367, 373, 375, 376–7, 378, 383, 386, 388–9, 390.
Disrespect, custom of permitted, 29. See also Relationships; joking.
Divorce, 12, 45, 48, 50, 65, 74, 75, 76, 92, 114 n. 1, 122, 123, 124, 133, 135, 138, 139, 174, 175, 178, 180, 181, 182, 185, 186, 188, 189, 190–1, 191–2, 193, 194, 202 and n. 2, 203, 204, 206 and n. 2, 215, 217, 220, 226, 233–4, 238, 239, 250, 256, 263, 270, 272, 275, 278, 280, 281, 283, 291, 325, 326.
Dobu, 248 n. 1.

Economy, native, 222; Lower Congo, 212–13; Lozi, 168; Zulu, 169. See also Crops.
Elders, 141, 302, 308–9, 315, 335.
Elephant tusks and buth, 367.
Endogamy, 68.
Etiquette, 11, 25, 31, 56, 59, 60. See also Behaviour.
Exogamy, 40, 60, 67, 88, 129, 241, 242, 246, 257, 259, 298, 305, 337, 338, 346, 348, 349, 350, 357.

Family, the: biological, 4–5; compound, 5, 24, 84, 112, 113, 114, 120, 146, 183, 195, 219; elementary, 4, 5, 6, 24, 27, 88, 91, 112, 116, 288; extended, 5, 141, 210, 211, 219, 227 ff., 228, 239–40, 247, 249; grand, 218, 227, 228, 229, 235; joint, 73, 363; leviratic, 183; Lozi and Zulu, 193 ff.; parental, 5, 75, 79, 84, 210, 218, 227; royal, 155, 156, 158; simple legal, 183, 194; types of structure, 211 ff.
Family Council (lusendvo), 87, 97–8, 110.
Family-group, 141.
Father-right, 51, 65, 76–7, 78, 80, 81, 83, 190, 192, 203.
Fathers, 96, 234–5; and child, 264 ff.; father's sister, 277.

Fathers-in-law and sons-in-law, 108, 136.
Fetishes, 214.
Fines, 89, 92, 93, 107, 108, 122, 123, 137, 187, 194, 257, 265, 271, 302, 361 and n. 2.
Folce, 135, 136.
Funerals, 256. See also Rituals: burial.
Fungur, 334, 335.

Ga, 248 n. 1.
Galla, 39, 55, 56, 59.
Ganda, 29, 55, 192, 205.
Gê, 285 n. 1.
Generations, merging of alternate, 29, 30, 31.
Gens, 40, 336, 338 ff.
Gifts, 46, 47, 52, 74, 75, 76, 97, 120, 125, 135, 137, 142, 189, 225, 260, 266, 268, 269, 272, 278, 280–1, 302, 303, 314, 322, 327, 328, 341; gift-exchange, 51–2, 233; morning-gift, 44, 46.
Girls, 113, 133–4, 229–301, 241, 278, 291, 303, 305; initiation of, 129, 225.
Gold Coast, the, 252.
Grandchildren, 263, 321.
Grandfathers, 228.
Grandmothers, 26, 83, 105, 106, 263, 276.
Grandparents and grandchildren, 28, 29, 30–1, 32, 34, 37–8, 104 ff., 133, 263, 276 and n. 3, 321.
Great-grandparents and great grand-children, 29.
Guardian spirits, see under Spirits.
Gwamile, Mdluli, Queen-mother, 106.

Headmen, 42, 90, 91, 130, 141, 167, 169, 172, 227, 228, 229, 232, 233; abusua panin, 255–6; tut('bull'), 370, 373, 374, 381, 391. See also khazi.
Hehe, 26, 28, 65.
Heiban, 34, 357.
Heir, 94, 95, 100, 113, 119, 120, 172; main, 97, 98, 109, 195. See also Inheritance.
Henga, 29, 30.
Hera, 35, 61.
Herero, 192, 205.
History, 1–2; pseudo-, 1–2, 18, 23, 72.
hlonipha, see under Behaviour.
Hoeing, 116, 121. See also Labour.
Homesteads, 90, 113, 362, 363, 368 ff.
Homicide, 17, 312–13, 314.
Hopi, 209, 211, 247.
Households, Tswana, 141.
Houses, patriclan, 296; Yakö assembly, 293, 298.
Hurons, 8.
Hvana, 25, 59, 212.

Ibo, 198.
Ila, 30, 42, 80, 167, 193, 203, 205, 218, 236–7, 243–4, 246, 249, 250.
Incest, 61, 69, 70, 71–2, 104, 153, 257, 278–9, 380.
Indonesia, 190.
Inhalanti, see under Wives.
Inheritance, 16, 17, 96, 98, 113, 119–20, 125, 131, 133, 194, 195, 196–7, 198–9, 201, 210, 236, 238–9, 257, 261, 271–2, 310–11, 342, 346, 349, 353, land and, 18, 342, 349–50; property and, 196 ff., 199 n. 1, 215, 224. See also Property; Widows: inheritance.
Intermarriage, 86, 173, 334.
Iroquois, 8.
isifunza, 87.
Isobongo (clan-name), see Names: clan.

Jikany, 374, 377, 380.
Joking relationship, see under Relationships.

Kaffirs, 24.
Kavirondo, 198.
Kamba, 60, 198.
Kambi Maseko, 110.
Kamdang, 357.
Kao, 334, 335.
Kaonde, 30, 221, 243 n. 2.
kepun (patriclan), see Clans: patriclans.
Kgatla, 148, 151, 153, 154, 155, 157, 159, 160, 164.
Khasi, 72, 75, 76.
khazi, 215, 216, 217, 219, 220, 221.
Khimba, 214.
Khurutshe, 151, 154, 157, 160, 164.
Kikuyu, 198.
King, Swazi, 86, 87; wives of, 89–90.
King-maker, 347.
Kinship organization, vi, 1 ff., 4 ff., 13 ff., 68, 76, 77, 78, 81–9, 100 ff., 116 ff., 283–4, 364 ff.; buth, 365, 366, 367, 387, 389; Central Bantu, 207 ff.; corporate groups, 43, 201; cousinage and, 16; equilibrium and disequilibrium in, 10–11; generation principle, 25, 31 ff.; gwan buthni, 367–8; kingadi, 214; kitata, 214; lineage and, 364; local kin groups, see Residential units; mar, 365, 366, 373, 387; marriage and, 46; matrilineal, see matrilineality; mystical power of seniors, 131, 136–8; parentelic, 16; patrilineal principle; Roman, 18, 76, 77, 78; social function, 3; social relationships, 4, 6; 'stocks', 16; structural principles, 2, 5, 39 ff., 62, 63 et passim; Teutonic, 15 ff.; theories, 1; terminology of, 6 ff.; types of, 79; uni-

lineal agnatic groups, 200 ff.; *yak-pan*, 317, 320; Zulu, 169 ff. *See also* Relationships; Residential units; Segmentations; Unilineal descent; Wards.
Kipsigis, 18 *n.* 3, 20 *n.* 1.
Kitara, 25, 32–3.
Koalib, 34.
Kololo, 169.
Kongo, 211, 212, 213–14, 241, 242, 245, 248, 249.
Korongo, 356.
Kunama, 333 *n.* 3.
Kwena, 151, 152, 153, 155, 157, 160, 164.

La Ndlela, 103.
Labour, 134, 135, 326; boys and, 293–4; co-operation in, 116–17, 125, 129, 306–7, 361; division of, 91, 289–90; girls and, 294; women and, 94, 263, 289.
Lak, 378, 380.
Lala, 221, 222.
Lamba, 167, 221–2, 225, 229, 243 *n.* 2, 245.
Lamtana Dlamini, 103.
Land, 18, 41, 342, 349–50.
Lango, 40.
Law, Ashanti, 280.
Lendu, 55–6.
Lenge, 26, 35.
Lenje, 237.
Levirate, the, 12, 26, 64, 97, 109, 140, 153, 154, 159, 160, 161, 164, 183, 185, 186, 188, 194, 257, 271, 343, 349, 350.
Lineages and the lineage structure, 14–15, 22, 40, 68–9, 87, 254 ff., 364 ff., 373 ff.; clans distinguished from, 39–40; groups, 15, 169, 388; married women and, 20–1; matrilineages, 14, 23, 41–2, 73, 75, 79, 213, 223 ff., 232, 238, 241 ff., 254 ff., 261–3; maximal, 213, 241, 257 ff.; minimal, 213, 241–2; *mvumu*, 213, 215, 216, 217, 219–21, 241; passage of cattle and, 125; *see also* Cattle: marriage-cattle; patrilineage, 22, 33, 38, 65, 69, 237, 303; principle, 259, 260, 276; royal, 100; stock compared with, 22, 388; unity of, 33–4, 35, 38, 65, 257, 278; *Yeponama*, 294. *See also* Agnates; Clans; Cognatic system; Matrilinearity; Patrilinearity; Relationships.
Lobedu, 53, 66, 164.
Lomawa, Queen-mother, 103.
Lou, 366, 368, 370, 374, 381, 384.
Lozi, 42, 64, 65, 67, 68, 78, 81, 84, 166 ff.
Luba, 207 *n.* 1.

Lunda, 221.
lusendvo, see Family Council.

Magic, 214, 220, 341, 344, 345, 346, 347, 355; rain magic, 347, 348, 349.
Malay Archipelago, 51.
Malete, 151, 154, 160.
manavalan, 160.
Mangu, 212.
Marriage, 1, 3, 5, 43 ff., 74, 114, 115–16, 140, 149 ff., 173 ff., 180 ff., 199 ff., 236, 342–3, 358; African, 46, 179; Ashanti, 278 ff.; Bemba, 225–6; by service, 48, 121, 221; contract of, 208, 215–17, 225–6; cousin, 151–2, 157–8, 162, 163, 173; cross-cousin, 53, 54, 60–1, 65, 74, 104, 114 *n.* 2, 124, 151, 154, 156, 160, 164, 173, 228, 240 and *n.* 2, 248, 279, 281–2, 282 *n.* 3; Cewa, 233–4; early English, 44–5, 48; ghost, 89, 183–4, 189, 371, 375, 378; group-, 23; Ila, 239; legal, 46–7, 50 ff., 88, 112, 121–2, 184, 186, 270, 280; Lozi and Zulu, 180 ff.; maternal grandmother's clan and, 105–6; Mayombe, 215 ff.; parallel cousin, 156; romantic love and, 45; parents and their children's, 269; prohibited relationships, 9–10, 16, 17, 22, 54, 60, 67, 71, 72, 86, 152, 149, 150–1, 152, 159, 161, 164–5, 170, 175, 267, 278–9; preferential, 60, 62, 64; regulation of, 66–7; removal of the bride and place of residence, 208 ff., 212, 215, 225, 226, 228, 229, 233, 236, 239, 249, 250; rights of the husband, 12, 50–1, 75–6, 200, 215–16, 225, 226, 280, 323, 324; Roman, 48, 76, 78; rules of residence at marriage, 221; *sambandham*, 74–5; secondary unions, 149, 152–4, 158–9; *tiri nsa* (head wine) and, 280, 281; Tswana, 145–6, 149 ff.; *ugogo*, 104; uxorilocal, 209, 211, 246, 247–8; virilocal, 209, 229, 235, 247, 248, 250; with deceased wife's sister, 62–3; with first cousins, 140, 156, 160; with half-sisters, 150–1; with materterine cousins, 151; with mother's brother's daughters, 69; with near kin, 155 ff.; with wife's brother's daughter, 124; woman-, 4, 184, 390; Yakö, 321 ff.; Yao, 233. *See also* Cattle: marriage-cattle; Matrilocality; Patrilocality; Polyandry; Polygyny.
Marriage payments, 40, 44, 46, 47, 48, 50, 51 ff., 80, 89, 183, 184, 185, 186, 187, 188, 191, 192, 193–4, 199 ff., 215, 216–17, 225, 227, 233, 236,

244, 249–50, 304, 322 ff.; counter-payments, 47, 52. *See also* Cattle: marriage-cattle.
Masai, 18, 20–2, 23, 25, 27, 31, 32, 34, 37.
Matrilinearity, 1, 4, 40, 41, 84, 167, 192, 200, 207 ff., 211, 215, 219 ff., 232–3, 236, 254 ff., 283, 305 ff., 310 ff., 329–30, 341–3, 354.
Matrilocality, 150, 167, 200, 207, 208–10, 377.
Mayombe, 211 ff., 223 *n.* 1, 241–2, 244, 248, 250.
mbumba (descent groups), *see* Descent groups.
Menangkabau, 72, 75, 81, 209, 247.
Mesakin, 34.
Minang-kabau, 190.
Mmanaana-Kgatla, 153.
Moieties, 39.
Montenegro, 8.
Moro, 356.
Mother, the, 36; and children, 262–4.
Mother-right, 51, 72, 73, 75, 76–7, 78, 79–80, 81, 83, 192, 193.
Mothers-in-law, 58, 107–8, 116, 171, 327–8; and sons-in-law, 107–8, 327.
Mpungu, 216.
mvumu, *see under* Lineages.
Myths, 128; of origin, 351–3.

Names, 14, 58, 60, 93, 266, 282; children and, 266; clan, 86, 87, 91, 169, 232, 348; family, 113; Lozi descent-, 172–3, 174, 177–8; Swazi, 86–7; *Yepun*, 296.
Nandi, 18 *n.* 3, 32, 33, 37.
Nayars, 51, 72, 73 ff., 81, 193, 211, 247.
Ndau, 25, 34, 35.
Ndebele, 197.
Negri Sembilan, 209.
Nephews, 7–8, 270, 271.
Ngonde, 30.
Ngoni, 111, 197, 231, 233.
Nguni, 58, 60, 68, 69, 80, 86, 88, 103–4, 107, 120, 164, 165, 197, 204.
Ngwaketse, 150, 151, 152, 153, 154, 155, 156, 157, 159, 160, 164.
Ngwato, 140, 141, 150, 151, 153, 155.
Nieces, 8.
Nilo-Hamites, 198.
Nilotes, 198.
nkasi, 30.
Nkosi, 86–7; Dlamini, 86, 87.
Nkundo, 38–9, 47, 49, 53, 61, 207 *n.* 1.
North America, 29, 36.
Ntoro, conception of, 264–5, 266–7.
Nuba, 37, 83, 248, 333–4, 356 ff.; fourteen tribes, 358.
Nuba Hills, 34, 59, 333 ff.
Nuer, 40, 64, 77, 84, 183, 184, 185, 186, 190, 192, 200, 201, 202, 360 ff.

Nyakyusa, 82, 111.
Nyamwezi, 51.
Nyaro, 40, 83, 334 ff., 354, 357, 358; Kao-Nyaro, 355, 357.
Nyasaland, 79, 230 ff.
Nyima, 34.
Nzima, 274 *n.* 1.
ŋanda ('house'), 223–4.

Oraons, 29.
Ordeals, 344.
Orphans, 264, 274, 350.
Otoro, 34, 357 and *n.* 1.
Ovambo, 192, 200, 205.
Oyoko, 260.

Parents-in-law, 59–60, 107 ff., 127–8, 170, 233, 283, 327–8.
Patriarchy, 18.
Patrilinearity, 40, 41, 67, 75, 77, 81, 84, 86, 143, 167, 173, 174, 211, 236, 293 ff., 329–30, 332, 341–3, 354.
Patrilocality, 104, 107, 167, 174, 208–10, 262, 298, 348.
Pedi, 164.
Pende, 30.
Polyandry, 5, 64, 75.
Polygyny, 5, 89, 112, 113, 128, 138, 180, 220, 229, 248, 281, 290–1; sororal, 64, 65, 182, 195; *ukusakula*, 124.
Pondo, 204–5.
Pregnancy, premarital, 265–6.
Prestations, 47–8.
Priests and priesthood, 91, 120, 298, 301, 302, 307, 308, 309, 314–17, 329, 335, 340, 341, 344, 345; grain-priests, 341, 344, 347; rainmakers, 341–4; *Yabot*, 315–17.
Primogeniture, 98, 131, 234, 236, 248.
Procreation, theories of, 207, 213, 222.
Property, 73, 96–7, 119–20, 192 ff., 205, 210, 211, 215, 216, 232, 238, 268, 310–11, 342, 349–50.

Quarrels, 119, 136, 137, 257, 352.
Queen Mothers, 256–7, 264, 275; stools of, 257; Swazi, 86, 98, 109.

Rainmakers, *see under* Priests.
Rank, 38, 39, 109–10; differences in, 31–2, 35.
Relationships and relatives, 142; by affinity, 152; cognatic, 4, 6, 15, 20; 'cross', 148; dyadic, 84; elements of, 11; joking, 36, 56, 57, 59, 83, 102, 145, 161, 162–3, 177, 274 *n.* 1; 'linked', 52–3, 142–3, 145; mater-terine, 148; orders of, 6; rights and duties, 11–12; senior and junior, 24; three categories, 143. *See also* Kinship organization; Lineages; Marriage; Terminologies.

Relatives-in-law, 127 ff., 145–6, 148–9, 177, 225, 235, 321–2.
Religion, 43, 76, 86, 91, 93. *See also* Rituals; Shrines; Spirits.
Residential units, 210–11, 218 ff., 227–30, 239–41, 250.
Rhodesia, 34, 79, 221–2, 236–1, 247, 250.
Rights, 12–13.
Rituals, 41, 87, 114, 125–6, 130, 226, 256, 266–7, 277, 296, 298–9, 312, 313, 315–16, 326, 331, 335, 339 ff., 367; burial, 36–7, 125, 126, 130, 260, 268, 271, 301, 337, 338, 339–41, 348, 366; death, 126; *kuingishya*, 225; *leboku*, 322, 328; matriclan, 314; *ntoro*, 265, 266–7; rain, 343–4.
Rolong, 150, 151, 153, 154, 156, 157, 160, 164.
Ronga, 34, 35, 37, 203.

Sacrifices, 26, 28, 36, 54, 105, 257, 316 *n.* 2, 339, 340, 343, 344, 366, 367.
Sakata, 212.
Sala, 237.
Sanctions, 11, 61, 70, 85, 89, 107, 134, 138, 203, 252, 258, 264, 313, 315, 316, 330, 331, 338, 346, 355.
Science, 2.
Segmentations and segments, 40, 169, 255, 257 ff., 335, 336, 337 ff., 360.
Sencaɓapi, 99.
Sex antagonism, 352–3.
Sex polarity, 354–5.
Sexual intercourse, 27, 70–1, 181; extramarital, 61, 71; parents and children and, 126–7, 133; separation from different generations during, 126–7; sexual shame, 59.
Shangana, 198.
Shangana-Tonga, 34, 35, 52–3.
Shona, 34, 35, 198, 204.
Shona-Ndau-Tonga, 38.
Shrines, 41, 90, 256, 296, 298, 299, 301, 302, 309, 314, 315, 363.
Siblings, 83–4, 97 ff., 114, 131–2, 142, 143, 144, 146–7, 149, 170, 174, 175, 176, 273–6, 319, 321; definition of, 4; full, 5, 24, 132; half-siblings, 5, 24, 132, 174, 270, 276, 291, 319; group, and the unity of, 23–4, 25, 26, 27, 64–5, 77, 99.
Sibs and sib-ship, 15 ff., 22, 32, 68.
Sisters, 98, 123, 154, 274; headman's, 229; wifehood and, 180. *See also* Brothers: sisters and.
Sisters-in-law, 63, 108–9, 177.
Slavery and slaves, 212, 213, 217, 218, 220, 224, 226, 234, 239, 248, 249, 254, 255.
Sobhuza, 99, 102.

Social structures, 2, 43, 57, 131 ff.; seniority and, 131.
Songe, 207 *n.* 1.
Songo, 212.
Sons, 113, 134, 268, 269; first-born, 96–7. *See also* Boys.
Sorcery, 144, 179, 180, 217, 220.
Sororate, the, 26, 64, 97, 140, 154, 158–9, 160, 185, 188.
Sotho, 69, 86, 103–4, 144, 164, 165, 197.
Spirits: fertility (*yose*), 314, 315; guardian, 223, 224, 237, 249; matriclan, 329, 330.
Step-parents, 319.
Swazi, 80, 83, 84, 86 ff., 169, 211.

Taboos, 87, 93, 106, 107, 225, 226, 256, 267, 273 *n.* 1, 279, 339, 340.
Tallensi, 40, 61, 189 *n.* 1, 198.
Tawana, 150, 151.
Terminologies, kinship, 6 ff., 18 ff., 23 ff., 31, 33 ff., 40, 71, 97, 100 ff., 161, 164, 170 ff., 261, 357, 387; *aputani*, 33; Ashanti, 253 ff., 258, 259, 270–1, 277–8; asymmetrical and symmetrical, 32; 'brother', 8, 9, 18, 53, 170, 174, 260; 'chief', 37; 'children', 53, 175, 258; 'children of our children', 38; classificatory system, 8 ff.; descriptive, 7, 10; division of generations and, 27–9; dyadic, 39; *eme* or *eam*, 38; equilibrium and disequilibrium, 58; 'fathers', 8, 9, 24, 25–6, 36, 38, 39, 53, 81, 131, 170, 259, 267, 271; 'fathers-in-law', 35; female father (*sewa*), 25–6, 170, 259, 267, 277; generation principle, 25, 31 ff.; 'grandchildren', 35, 38, 57, 258, 319–20; 'grandfather', 34–5, 37, 38; 'grandmother', 33, 35, 83; 'grandparents', 39, 57, 319–20, 258, 259; 'husband', 29–30, 133; *ikikolo*, 114; *isinini*, 86; *isizalo*, 186; jural, 36, 75, 77–8, 274; *kamet*, 32; *kunambitsisa*, 102; Maine, Sir Henry, and, 9; 'male mothers', 25, 33, 34, 36, 38, 100, 102–3, 170; *malume*, 34; *mama*, 34; *mamana*, 34; *mananye*, 32–3; Masai, 18 ff.; *mufubalume*, 175, 176; Morgan, Lewis, and, 8, 10, 23; 'mother', 8–9, 24, 25–6, 32, 33, 34, 36, 38, 81, 95, 131, 170, 258, 264; 'mother's brother', 32, 33, 34, 258; *mupsyana*, 34; *mwhiwha*, 33; *mwinangu*, 30; 'my child', 170, 171, 277; Nyakyusa kinship, 139; *ol-akwi*, 20; *ol-apu*, 20, 21, 33, 34; *omaha*, 33–4; siblings and, 35, 132, 175, 176, 258, 278; 'sister', 8, 9, 18, 174; *sotwa*, 21, 22, 32; Swazi, 100 ff.; Tswana, 146–

9; *ukukamanila*, 118; *umwilima*, 115; 'uncle', 38; *uwo womon* (our father), 294; value of studying, 10; *wamyitu*, 30; 'wife', 29–30, 133, 271, 278; wife's father, 35; 'wife's sisters', 35; Yakö, 317 ff.; Zulu, 170.
Thonga, 96, 198, 203, 205.
Timba Maseko, 104.
Tiop-Lier, 381 ff.
Tira, 34, 334.
Tlingit, 248.
Tlôkwa, 140, 141, 151, 154, 155, 157, 159, 160.
Todas, 5.
Tonga, 167, 237.
Tonga and Fiji, 36, 37.
Tonga Tonga, 99.
Toro, 55.
Tswana, 55, 69, 140 ff., 197; tribes, 140 and *n*. 1.
Tullishi, 83, 346 ff.; clans of, 348.
Twins, 279; customs and, 126, 130.

Umalume, see Terminologies: 'male mothers'.
Uncles, 7–8; maternal, 37, 38, 145, 217, 226–7, 230, 234, 249, 258, 270–1, 272, 273, 281, 328; *wofa*, 270. *See also* Avunculate.
Unga, 222.
Unilineal descent and relationships, 14, 17, 18, 23, 40, 42–3, 67, 68, 81–2, 84, 210, 223, 285.
Unnatural offences, 70.
Ushi, 222.

Va Kongo, 25.
Venda, 144, 197.
Villages, 42, 111, 167 ff., 210, 228–30, 231–2, 235–6, 347–8, 360 ff.; Bemba, 229–30; *cieng*, 361 ff., 371, 374, 377, 387; head of Mayombe section, 215; Konye, 368–9; Kurmayom, 384–5; Lozi, 167 ff., 172, 177–8; Mancom, 381–4; Nyaro, 335; Nueny, 371 ff.; royal, 168; Yakö, 286; Yakwac, 378 ff.

Wa Yao, 24.
Wards, 141, 254–5, 302, 335.
Wergild, payment of, 17.
Werni, 334.
Widows, 64, 76, 97, 113, 119, 120, 174, 183, 184, 185, 189, 194, 195, 197, 229, 238, 248, 256, 271, 291, 311, 324–5, 343, 349, 350, 373, 389–90; inheritance of, 64, 123, 127, 149, 153, 183, 217, 226, 271, 273.
Winnebago, 36.
Witchcraft, 70, 94, 113, 115, 138, 258, 264, 275, 344–5, 347, 348, 355.
Wives, 24, 91 ff., 172, 183, 195, 288–9, 321 ff.; chief, 183; co-wives, 64, 89, 91, 93, 94, 95–6, 98, 99, 112, 113, 116, 133, 146, 174, 180, 281, 288–9, 327; first (or great), 24, 93–4, 113, 183, 326–7; *inhalanti*, 94, 99, 103, 108; main, 89, 184; replacing a dead wife, 123–4, 133, 184–5; relations with husband, 91, 103, 135–6, 179–80, 280, 325–6, 288–90; *seantlo*, 152–4; stool, 279.
Women: authority of, 234; Central Bantu, 208; exchange of, 50–1; *kepun* and, 298; Nyakyusa, 136; property and, 96, 195–6, 197, 215, 216, 311; Tullishi, 353; unmarried, 48–9. *See also* Barrenness.
worowallere (healing experts), 345.

Xhosa, 204, 205 *n*. 2.

Yafrina, see Clans: patriclans.
Yaka, 211.
Yakö, 41, 79, 82, 84, 85, 200, 249, 285 ff., 359 *n*. 1.
Yanzi, 212.
Yao, 25, 30, 167, 209, 230 ff., 243, 245, 247, 248.
Yepun, 294–6.

Zulu, 64–5, 67–8, 77, 78, 80, 81, 84, 166 ff., 210.

REPRINTED LITHOGRAPHICALLY IN GREAT BRITAIN
AT THE UNIVERSITY PRESS, OXFORD
BY VIVIAN RIDLER
PRINTER TO THE UNIVERSITY